Biblical Hermeneutics

AN ADVENTIST APPROACH

Biblical Hermeneutics: An Adventist Approach
Biblical Research Institute Studies in Hermeneutics
Vol. 3

Copy Editor
Schuyler Kline

Inside Layout
Joel Iparraguirre

Cover Design
Philipp Grau

Biblical Hermeneutics

AN ADVENTIST APPROACH

Frank M. Hasel
Editor

Biblical Research Institute
Silver Spring, MD 20904

2020

Biblical Hermeneutics: An Adventist Approach
[edited by] Frank M. Hasel
1. Bible—Hermeneutics 2. Bible—Criticism, Interpretation
BS476.B6

Editorial Safeliz, S.L.
Pradillo 6, Pol. Ind. La Mina, E-28770 Colmenar Viejo, Madrid (España)
admin@safeliz.com, www.safelizbibles.com

Printed in China
ISBN 978-0-925675-37-8

Contents

Contributors

Leonard Brand, Ph.D., is Professor of Biology and Paleontology at Loma Linda University. He received his Ph.D. from Cornell University. He is heavily involved in geology and paleontology research and has published over 40 scientific research papers. He has also published numerous articles in church publications, and seven books, including *Faith, Reason and Earth History* (Andrews University Press, 2009), *The Prophet and her Critics* (Pacific Press, 2005), *Choose You This Day* (Pacific Press, 2013), *God, Science, Friends: and God's Love for You* (Pacific Press, 2019). The most recent is *Genesis and Science: Where is the Evidence Going* (Pacific Press, 2019). He is the recipient of a Zapara Award for Distinguished Teaching, a best student paper award at national meetings, and a Distinguished Service Award from Loma Linda University.

Elias Brasil de Souza, Ph.D., serves as director of the *Biblical Research Institute* of the General Conference of Seventh-day Adventists. Previously he served as church pastor in the Southern Brazil Union, professor of biblical studies, and dean of the Theological Seminary at Northeast Brazil College, in Bahia. He holds a BA and MA in theology from the Latin American Adventist Theological Seminary, and a Ph.D. in Old Testament from Andrews University (Berrien Springs, MI). His main areas of interest are the Sanctuary, Hermeneutics, and the Hebrew language. He has authored, co-authored, and published several academic publications in English and Portuguese, among them *The Heavenly Sanctuary/Temple Motif in the Hebrew Bible* (Adventist Theological Society, 2005), and *The Book of Daniel* (Pacific Press, 2019).

Richard M. Davidson, Ph.D., is professor of Old Testament Interpretation at the Seventh-day Adventist Theological Seminary at Andrews University (Berrien Springs, MI). He has a Ph.D. in religion from Andrews University (Berrien Springs, MI). He is the author of numerous articles in theological journals and other publications. He has authored numerous books, including *Typology in Scripture: A Study of Hermenteutical* τύπος *Structures* (Andrews University Press, 1981), *Love Song for the Sabbath* (Review and Herald, 1981), *Hermeneuticã biblicã* (Editura CARD, 2003), *In the Footsteps of Joshua* (Review and Herald, 1995), and his magisterial work *Flame of Yahweh: Sexuality in the Old Testament* (Baker, 2007).

Kwabena Donkor, Ph.D., serves as associate director of the *Biblical Research Institute* of the General Conference of Seventh-day Adventists. He earned his Ph.D. in systematic theology from Andrews University (Berrien Springs, MI). In 2003 he published his work *Tradition, Method, and Contemporary Protestant Theology* (University Press of America), and edited *The Church, Culture and Spirits: Adventism in Africa* (BRI, Review and Herald, 2011). He has written scholarly articles for various journals and magazines and contributed to *Reclaiming the Center: Confronting Evangelical Accommodation in Postmodern Times*, edited by Millard J. Erickson, Paul Kjoss Helseth, and Justin Taylor (Crossway, 2004).

Frank M. Hasel, Ph.D., serves as associate director of the *Biblical Research Institute* of the General Conference of Seventh-day Adventists. He received his theological training in Germany, England, and the United States, where he received his Ph.D. from Andrews University (Berrien Springs, MI). He has written and edited six books, including *Adventists and Military Service: Biblical, Historical, and Ethical Perspectives* (Safeliz, 2019), *How to Interpret Scripture* (Pacific Press, 2019), and *Living for God: Reclaiming the Joy of Christian Virtue* (Pacific Press, 2020). He has published widely in Adventist and other scholarly journals, Bible Dictionaries, and Encyclopedias, such as *The Encyclopedia of the Bible and its Reception* (de Gruyter), *Eerdmans Dictionary of the Bible, The Lexham Bible Dictionary,* and *The Encyclopedia of Christian Civilization* (Wiley-Blackwell). He is the editor of the "History of Theology and Ethics" section of the *Encyclopedia of Seventh-day Adventism.*

Michael G. Hasel, Ph.D., (University of Arizona) is professor of Religion/Near Eastern Studies and Archaeology and Director of the Institute of Archaeology and Lynn H. Wood Archaeological Museum, Southern Adventist University. He has held Samuel H. Kress (Israel) and Fulbright Fellowships (Cyprus) and has excavated extensively at ten different sites in Israel, Jordan, and Cyprus. Most recently he co-directed projects at Khirbet Qeiyafa, Socoh, and Lachish. He has written and edited more than ten books including *Jerusalem: An Illustrated Archeological Guide and Journal* (Lynn H. Wood Archeological Museum, 2016), *In the Footsteps of King David: Revelations from an Ancient Biblical City* (Thames & Hudson, 2018), and *How to Interpret Scripture* (Pacific Press, 2019). He has written hundreds of articles in journals, encyclopedias and dictionaries published by Abingdon, Thames and Hudson, Lexham, InterVarsity, Israel Exploration Society, and Oxford University Press.

Denis Kaiser, Ph.D., is assistant professor of church history at the Seventh-day Adventist Theological Seminary at Andrews University (Berrien Springs, MI). He earned his Ph.D. in Adventist Studies and Historical Theology from Andrews University (Berrien Springs, MI). He serves as annotation project editor of *The Ellen G. White Letters & Manuscripts with Annotations*, vol. 2 (1860-1863), and subeditor of the "History of Theology and Ethics" section of the *Encyclopedia of Seventh-day Adventism*, and has published widely in numerous journals and books. In 2019 he published his work *Trust and Doubt: Perceptions of Divine Inspiration in Seventh-day Adventist History*, and is a coeditor of the forthcoming *Oxford Handbook of Seventh-day Adventism*.

Wagner Kuhn, Ph.D., is the chair of the Department of World Mission and professor of Mission and Intercultural Studies at the Seventh-day Adventist Theological Seminary, Andrews University (Berrien Springs, MI). He has served as pastor, administrator, and missionary in three continents and as the associate director of the Institute of World Mission for the General Conference of Seventh-day Adventists. He has written several articles for scholarly journals, magazines, and books, which include *Christian Relief and Development* (Andrews University Press, 2005), *The Book and the Student* (as editor, Andrews University, 2012), *Biblical Principles for Missiological Issues in Africa* (as co-editor, Andrews University, 2015), and *Redemption and Transformation* (Andrews University, 2013).

Ekkehardt Mueller, D.Min., Th.D., serves as associate director of the *Biblical Research Institute* of the General Conference of Seventh-day Adventists. His Th.D. degree in Biblical Exegesis and Theology is from Andrews University (Berrien Springs, MI). He has written numerous articles for scholarly books, journals, and magazines as well as several books in English and German, such as *The Letters of John* (Pacific Press, 2009), *Die Lehre von Gott* ("The Doctrine of God," Wegweiser Verlag, 2010), *Der Erste und der Letzte: Studien zum Buch der Offenbarung* ("The First and the Last: Studies on the Book of Revelation," Peter Lang, 2011), and *Marriage: Biblical and Theological Aspects* (as co-editor, BRI, Review and Herald, 2015). A number of these have been translated into various languages.

John C. Peckham, Ph.D., is professor of Theology and Christian Philosophy at the Seventh-day Adventist Theological Seminary at Andrews University (Berrien Springs, MI). He earned his Ph.D. in Systematic Theology from Andrews University (Berrien Springs, MI). He has written numerous articles and is the author of a number of books, including *The Concept of Divine Love in the Context of the God-World Relationship* (Peter Lang, 2014), *The Love of God: A Canonical Model* (IVP Academic, 2015), *Canonical Theology: The Biblical Canon, Sola Scriptura, and Theological Method* (Eerdmans, 2016), *Theodicy of Love: Cosmic Conflict and the Problem of Evil* (Baker Academic, 2018), and *The Doctrine of God: Introducing the Big Questions* (T&T Clark, 2019),

Gerhard Pfandl, Ph.D., is a retired associate director of the *Biblical Research Institute* of the General Conference of Seventh-day Adventists. He is a native of Austria and earned his Ph.D. in Old Testament from Andrews University (Berrien Springs, MI). He has worked as a church pastor in Austria and in the Southern California Conference. From 1977-1989 he was Professor of Religion at Bogenhofen Seminary, in Austria. Prior to joining the *Biblical Research Institute* in 1999 he served for seven years as Field Secretary of the South Pacific Division, in Sydney, Australia. He has published many articles for scholarly and popular journals in German and English and is the author of *Daniel: The Seer of Babylon* (Review and Herald, 2004), and *The Gift of Prophecy* (Pacific Press, 2008).

Clinton Wahlen, Ph.D., serves as associate director of the *Biblical Research Institute* of the General Conference of Seventh-day Adventists. He received his Ph.D. in New Testament from Cambridge University, and spent eleven years teaching New Testament and Greek in Zaoksky Adventist University, Russia, and Adventist International Institute of Advanced Studies (AIIAS), in the Philippines. He is the author of numerous scholarly articles and several books, including *Jesus and the Impurity of Spirits in the Synoptic Gospels* (Mohr Siebeck, 2004), *James* (Adult Bible Study Guide, 2004), editor of *"What Are Human Beings That You Remember Them?"* (BRI, Review and Herald, 2015), and co-author of *Women's Ordination: Does It Matter?* (2015). Most recently, he wrote the commentary on Luke for the *Andrews Bible Commentary* (2020) and is the author of a forthcoming commentary on Matthew for the Seventh-day Adventist International Bible Commentary series.

Abbreviations

General Abbreviations

א	Codex Sinaiticus
A	Codex Alexandrinus
AD	*anno Domini* (in the year of our Lord)
ANE	Ancient Near East
b.	Babylonian Talmud
B	Codex Vaticanus
BC	before Christ
BHK	Biblica Hebraica, ed. R. Kittel
BHQ	Biblica Hebraica Quinta
BHS	Biblia Hebraica Stuttgartensia
C	Codex Ephraemi
ca.	circa (about)
cf.	*confer*, compare
$D^{(*)}$	Codex Bezae
Diss.	Dissertation
ed.	edited, editor
ET	English Translation
f^{13}	*family 13*, a group of Greek gospel manuscripts
Gr.	Greek
Heb.	Hebrew
Lat.	Latin
lit.	literally
Lt	Letter
LW	American Edition of Luther's Works. Jaroslav Pelikan and Helmut Lehmann, eds. (Philadelphia and St. Louis, 1955-)
LXX	Septuagint (the Greek Old Testament)
m.	Mishnah
MT	Masoretic Text (of the Old Testament)
ms, mss	Manuscript(s)
NA^{28}	*Novum Testamentum Graece*, Nestle-Aland, 28th ed.
NT	New Testament
OT	Old Testament
P^{45}	Papyrus 45

P^{46}	Papyrus 46
P^{47}	Papyrus 47
P^{52}	Papyrus 52
P^{64}	Papyrus 64
P^{66}	Papyrus 66
P^{72}	Papyrus 72
P^{75}	Papyrus 75
P^{112}	Papyrus 112
Tg(s).	Targum(s); Targumic
TR	Textus Receptus
UBS^{5}	*The Greek New Testament*, United Bible Society, 5th ed.
vs., vss.	Verse(s)
WA	D. Martin Luthers Werke. Kritische Gesamtausgabe (Weimar: Bohlau, 1883-1983)
WADB	D. Martin Luthers Werke. Deutsche Bibel (Weimar: Bohlau, 1906-)

Bible Versions

AMP	The Amplified Bible
ASV	American Standard Version
CEB	Common English Bible
CSB	Christian Standard Bible
ESV	English Standard Version
GNB	Good News Bible
HCSB	Holman Christian Standard Bible
KJV	King James Version
LB	The Living Bible
MEV	Modern English Version
MSG	The Message: The Bible in Contemporary Language
NAS95	New American Standard Bible
NASB	New American Standard Bible
NEB	New English Bible
NET	New English Translation
NIV	New International Version
NIV11	New International Version
NLT	New Living Translation
NKJV	New King James Version
NRSV	New Revised Standard Version
REB	Revised English Bible
RGT	Revised Geneva Translation
RSV	Revised Standard Version
TCW	The Clear Word

TEV	Today's English Version
TLV	Tree of Life Bible
TNIV	Today's New International Version
WEB	Word English Bible

Books of the Bible

Old Testament

Gen	Genesis
Exod	Exodus
Lev	Leviticus
Num	Numbers
Deut	Deuteronomy
Josh	Joshua
Judg	Judges
Ruth	Ruth
1 Sam	1 Samuel
2 Sam	2 Samuel
1 Kgs	1 Kings
2 Kgs	2 Kings
1 Chr	1 Chronicles
2 Chr	2 Chronicles
Ezra	Ezra
Neh	Nehemiah
Esth	Esther
Job	Job
Ps (Pss)	Psalm (Psalms)
Prov	Proverbs
Eccl	Ecclesiastes
Song	Song of Songs
Isa	Isaiah
Jer	Jeremiah
Lam	Lamentations
Ezek	Ezekiel
Dan	Daniel
Hos	Hosea
Joel	Joel
Amos	Amos
Obad	Obadiah
Jonah	Jonah
Mic	Micah
Nah	Nahum

Hab	Habakkuk
Zeph	Zephaniah
Hag	Haggai
Zech	Zechariah
Mal	Malachi

New Testament

Matt	Matthew
Mark	Mark
Luke	Luke
John	John
Acts	Acts
Rom	Romans
1 Cor	1 Corinthians
2 Cor	2 Corinthians
Gal	Galatians
Eph	Ephesians
Phil	Philippians
Col	Colossians
1 Thess	1 Thessalonians
2 Thess	2 Thessalonians
1 Tim	1 Timothy
2 Tim	2 Timothy
Titus	Titus
Phlm	Philemon
Heb	Hebrews
Jas	James
1 Pet	1 Peter
2 Pet	2 Pet
1 John	1 John
2 John	2 John
3 John	3 John
Jude	Jude
Rev	Revelation

Apocrypha or Apocryphal Books

1 Esd	*1 Esdras*
2 Esd	*2 Esdras*
Tob	*Tobit*
Jdt	*Judith*
Add Esth	*Additions to Esther*

Wis	*Wisdom of Solomon*
Sir	*Sirach (Book of Ecclesiasticus)*
Bar	*Baruch*
Ep Jer	*Epistle of Jeremiah*
Add Dan	*Additions to Daniel*
Pr Azar	*Prayer of Azariah*
Sg Three	*Song of the Three Young Men*
Sus	*Story of Susanna*
Bel	*Bel and the Dragon*
1 Macc	*1 Maccabees*
2 Macc	*2 Maccabees*
3 Macc	*3 Maccabees*
4 Macc	*4 Maccabees*
Pr Man	*Prayer of Manasseh*

Dead Sea Scrolls and Related Texts

1QDeut[b]	1QDeuteronomy[b]
1QIsa[a]	1Qisaiah[a]
1QIsa[b]	1Qisaiah[b]
1Q5	Qumran, cave 1, Scroll 5
7Q4	Qumran, cave 7, Scroll 4
7Q5	Qumran, cave 7, Scroll 5

SBL Transliteration Charts (Modified for SDAIBC Use)

Hebrew Alphabet

א = ʾ	ח = *ḥ*	פּ = *p*
בּ = *b*	ט = *ṭ*	פ = *p̱*
ב = *ḇ*	י = *y*	צ = *ṣ*
גּ = *g*	כּ = *k*	ק = *q*
ג = *g̱*	כ = *ḵ*	ר = *r*
דּ = *d*	ל = *l*	שׂ = *ś*
ד = *ḏ*	מ = *m*	שׁ = *š*
ה = *h*	נ = *n*	תּ = *t*
ו = *w*	ס = *s*	ת = *ṯ*
ז = *z*	ע = ʿ	

Masoretic Vowel Pointings

ַ = *a*	ִי = *î*
ָ = *ā*	ֹ = *ō*
ֲ = *ᵃ*	ֳ = *ᵒ*
ֶ = *e*	וֹ = *ô*
ֵ = *ē*	ֻ = *u*
ֶי ֵי = *ê*	וּ = *û*
ִ = *i*	

Greek Alphabet

α = *a*	ζ = *z*	λ = *l*	π = *p*	φ = *ph*
β = *b*	η = *ē*	μ = *m*	ρ = *r*	χ = *ch*
γ = *g*	θ = *th*	ν = *n*	σ,ς = *s*	ψ = *ps*
δ = *d*	ι = *i*	ξ = *x*	τ = *t*	ω = *ō*
ϵ = *e*	κ = *k*	ο = *o*	υ = *y*	‘ = *h*

Introduction

Frank M. Hasel

For a movement such as the Seventh-day Adventist Church, which has affirmed the great Protestant principle of *sola Scriptura* ("by Scripture alone") from its historic beginnings, the issue of biblical hermeneutics[1] is of crucial significance. Unlike other churches, where church tradition and creeds have become decisive elements that function as hermeneutical keys, or faith communities, where experience or human reason have gained a normative role in the interpretation of Scripture, the Seventh-day Adventist Church is committed to having Scripture alone as its final norm for all we believe.[2] Without allowing other sources to authoritatively determine

---

[1] By the word "hermeneutics" we mean the art and process of interpretation. The origin of the word comes from the Greek *hermeneuein*: "to interpret." In the Greek language the word contains a reference to Hermes, the messenger of the gods who made intelligible to human beings what otherwise could not be grasped (cf. Acts 14:12, where Paul at Lystra is called "Hermes" because he was the chief speaker and bridged the gap between the divine and human realm). In Luke 24:27 Christ at Emmaus interpreted to the disciples: "beginning with Moses and with all the prophets, He explained (*diehermeneusen*) to them all the things concerning Himself in all the Scriptures" (NASB). Biblical hermeneutics explores how we read, understand, and interpret biblical texts that were written in a time, culture, and context different from that of ours. For a helpful overview of different aspects of the hermeneutical task and the need for a biblical hermeneutic that is commensurate with the biblical claims, see Gerhard Maier, *Biblical Hermeneutics* (Wheaton, IL: Crossway, 1994), 15–28.

[2] Fundamental Belief 1, "The Word of God," states, "The Holy Scriptures, Old and New Testaments, are the written Word of God, given by divine inspiration. The inspired authors spoke and wrote as they were moved by the Holy Spirit. In this Word, God has committed to humanity the knowledge necessary for salvation. The Holy Scriptures are the supreme, authoritative, and the infallible revelation of His will. They are the standard of character, the test of experience, the definitive revealer of doctrines, and the trustworthy record of God's acts in history. (Ps 119:105; Prov 30:5–6; Isa 8:20; John 17:17; 1 Thess 2:13; 2 Tim 3:16–17; Heb 4:12; 2 Pet 1:20–21)." See also *Seventh-day Adventists Believe: An Exposition of the Fundamental Beliefs of the Seventh-day Adventist Church*, 3rd ed. (Silver Spring, MD: Review and Herald, 2018), 11–22.

the meaning of the Bible, Seventh-day Adventists are committed to affirming Scripture alone as the final norm for all of our theology and praxis. Thus, for Seventh-day Adventists, the Bible is the *norma normans*—that is, the norming norm from which our theology is derived. This makes the issue of biblical hermeneutics a watershed for any theology, and particularly for Seventh-day Adventist theology. A hermeneutic not in harmony with the self-claims of Scripture produces serious theological problems, leads to wrong conclusions, and, ultimately, even generates heretical teachings. That is why a sound hermeneutic is crucial for the correct understanding of our Bible-based theology, message, and mission.[3] No wonder the issue of biblical hermeneutics is such a controverted issue in the Seventh-day Adventist church. Indeed, much is at stake!

Affirmation of the *sola Scriptura* principle does not, by itself, negate the influence of other sources on our theology; nor does it deny the need for careful interpretation of the biblical text. Nevertheless, *sola Scriptura* includes some basic principles that guide our interpretation of the Bible.

Yet even within the Seventh-day Adventist Church the Scriptures are sometimes looked at differently and interpreted using different hermeneutics, leading to, at times, sharply different conclusions about the meaning of some passages. Hence, at the 2015 General Conference Session in San Antonio, Texas, a request was made from the floor to study what Adventist hermeneutics is all about. It was worded as follows:

> We have a world church looking at the same Scriptures and coming up with very different interpretations. I think that points out that this church has very divided hermeneutics or rules of interpretation. The world church should take time to study and to bring together what our hermeneutic really is, because we're using two very different ones.[4]

On July 9, 2015, representative leaders, theologians, and church members from around the world voted in response to the motion on the

---

[3] See Frank M. Hasel and Michael G. Hasel, *How to Interpret Scripture* (Nampa, ID: Pacific Press, 2019), 8, the official companion book to the Adult Sabbath School Bible Study Guide on *How to Interpret Scripture* that the Seventh-day Adventist Church studied during the second quarter 2020 (April–June).

[4] "Thirteenth Business Meeting: Sixtieth General Conference Session: July 9, 2015, 9:30 a.m.," https://www.adventistreview.org/thirteenth-business-meeting (accessed May 25, 2020). See also the background information in the interview with Frank M. Hasel and Michael G. Hasel, "Hermeneutics: Understanding Scripture Today," *General Conference Executive Committee Newsletter*, April 2020, 4–9, https://executivecommittee.adventist.org/newsletter/ (accessed May 25, 2020).

floor "to refer to the Steering Committee the idea of developing a specific hermeneutic for the world church."[5] The next day, Myron A. Iseminger, then undersecretary of the General Conference of Seventh-day Adventists, reported the result of the Steering Committee's deliberations:

> Yesterday we voted an action with a request to the Steering Committee that the world church take time to study our hermeneutic, or our system of biblical interpretation. The Steering Committee sees value in that request, and they have agreed to work with the Biblical Research Institute to address the issue. In fact, the Biblical Research Institute is already studying the issue and has plans to publish their findings in the form of a revised second edition of the book currently available on biblical interpretation.[6]

The present book, *Biblical Hermeneutics: An Adventist Approach*, is a direct response to this request. It explores biblical hermeneutics from a Seventh-day Adventist perspective. Building on previous publications of the Biblical Research Institute (BRI) that have addressed the issue of biblical hermeneutics,[7] this new volume examines in greater depth current issues of biblical interpretation from a Seventh-day Adventist perspective and addresses some questions that have not received adequate attention in previous publications. The BRI, in deliberating on the Steering Committee's request, presented details of the book project in 2017 to the Biblical Research Institute Committee (BRICOM), comprised of over forty scholars and administrators from around the world, representing a wide range of theological disciplines. A number of Adventist scholars have contributed chapters to the book, dealing with various topics that need to be addressed. These were then presented to BRICOM for discussion and input. The

---

[5] "Thirteenth Business Meeting."

[6] "Fifteenth Business Meeting: Sixtieth General Conference Session, July 10, 2015, 1:59 p.m.," https://www.adventistreview.org/%E2%80%8Bfifteenth-business-meeting (accessed May 25, 2020).

[7] Previous publications by the Biblical Research Institute on hermeneutics include Gordon M. Hyde, ed., *A Symposium on Biblical Hermeneutics*, prepared by the Biblical Research Committee, General Conference of Seventh-day Adventists (Washington DC: Review and Herald, 1974); Gerhard F. Hasel, *Biblical Interpretation Today: An Analysis of Modern Methods of Biblical Interpretation and Proposals for the Interpretation of the Bible as the Word of God* (Washington, DC: Biblical Research Institute, 1985); George W. Reid, ed., *Understanding Scripture: An Adventist Approach*, Biblical Research Institute Studies 1 (Silver Spring, MD: Biblical Research Institute, 2005); and Gerhard Pfandl, ed., *Interpreting Scripture: Bible Questions and Answers*, Biblical Research Institute Studies 2 (Silver Spring, MD: Biblical Research Institute, 2010).

feedback was communicated to the authors, and the revised versions of the chapters were then read and approved by BRI. This book builds on and complements the material published in the first two volumes of the Biblical Research Institute Studies series on biblical hermeneutics.[8]

In chapter 1, "Presuppositions in Hermeneutics," Kwabena Donkor shows how presuppositions influence our thinking in subtle ways. He explores the philosophical underpinnings that impact our interpretation of biblical statements and explains how presuppositions operate on different levels in the task of biblical interpretation. He also reveals how our thinking and the presuppositions with which we approach Scripture can be shaped by the Bible to reflect a biblical worldview.

In chapter 2, Frank M. Hasel deals with important factors that are significant for a biblical hermeneutic that is in harmony with Scripture's self-claims. Learning from Jesus and the biblical writers, this study explores the divine-human nature of Scripture as well as its historical dimension and its literary character. This has important implications for the relationship between faith and reason and other aspects of biblical research.

In chapter 3, Clinton Wahlen investigates issues pertaining to textual variants, versions, and biblical interpretation. Since we do not possess the original documents of the biblical books, and have available only copies of copies that have been carefully transmitted and later translated into numerous languages, this is an area that has important implications for biblical interpretation.

In chapter 4, Michael G. Hasel explores the intricate relationship between history, the Bible, and hermeneutics. He unfolds the biblical view of history and sheds light on the various concepts that theologians describe as *Historie*, *Geschichte*, and salvation history and how modern views of history have impacted our understanding of the Bible and its interpretation. He also unfolds the importance of the historical nature of the biblical material for our faith.

In chapter 5, Clinton Wahlen and Wagner Kuhn investigate the complex and fascinating issue of culture, hermeneutics, and Scripture. They explore biblical principles that can guide us to a text-centered approach of recognizing what in the Bible is universal in scope and what is not.

In chapter 6, Leonard Brand deals with the challenging relationship between faith, science, and the Bible. As an accomplished biologist

---

[8] The first volume in the series, *Understanding Scripture*, deals with foundational principles of interpretation. The second volume, *Interpreting Scripture*, applies those principles to various questions connected with the interpretation of specific biblical passages.

and researcher in the natural sciences, he brings a unique perspective to the discussion of hermeneutics, shedding light on connections between faith and science.

In chapter 7, Ekkehardt Mueller unfolds important steps in the process of interpretation that help in the exegesis of biblical passages and the understanding of biblical themes. He illustrates this with practical biblical case studies and looks at some modern challenges and ethical issues.

In chapter 8, Richard M. Davidson deals with one of the most vexing problems of biblical theology: the inner-biblical interpretation of Scripture. He explores the biblical writers' use of Scripture and provides valuable insights that show they did not use Scripture out of context but were faithful to the meaning of the text in its original historical and literary context.

In chapter 9, Gerhard Pfandl details the biblical principles for the interpretation of apocalyptic prophecy and describes the various approaches for understanding apocalyptic literature. Additionally, and of great significance for Seventh-day Adventists, Pfandl helps readers understand certain special aspects that need to be considered when interpreting prophetic portions of Scripture.

In chapter 10, Elias Brasil de Souza carefully examines the biblical statements that deal with the salvation and restoration of Israel. This chapter deals with some important principles of biblical interpretation that have to do with the nature of Old Testament prophecy, conditional prophecy, and the role of Israel in the Bible.

In chapter 11, Michael G. Hasel examines the Genesis creation account as a test case for biblical hermeneutics. Taking the account in Genesis 1–2 as his starting point, he describes how different hermeneutical approaches to the first book of the Bible result in vastly different interpretations and understandings of the biblical text. He also shows how different hermeneutical approaches result in significantly different perceptions of the Sabbath, marriage, and other foundational biblical teachings.

In chapter 12, Denis Kaiser surveys the presuppositions, perceptions, and methods of biblical interpretation by early Adventist pioneers and Ellen G. White from 1845 to 1910. A knowledge of the dynamics that were at work in their approach to Scripture can be helpful for us today as we seek a text- and history-oriented approach to understanding the Bible.

In chapter 13, John C. Peckham delineates the important relationship between the prophetic gift as witnessed in Scripture and *sola Scriptura.* If we truly want to do our theology based on Scripture alone, how are we to relate the gift of prophecy to the Bible? Peckham explores this important question while dealing with some misconceptions and faulty conclusions and opening our understanding to a biblical perspective.

In chapter 14, Frank M. Hasel deals with some recent trends in methods of biblical interpretation. In the wake of the historical-critical method that has dominated biblical scholarship for two hundred years, some new methods of biblical interpretation have emerged over the past few decades that focus more on the canonical text of Scripture and tend to be more literary-oriented in nature. This chapter looks at the developments that spawned these new methods, at attempts to modify the historical-critical method, as well as at some methods that seem to give greater respect to the canonical text of Scripture by focusing on the literary unity and rhetorical features of the biblical text. The chapter also deals with approaches in which the reader ultimately determines the meaning of the text and with christological approaches to biblical interpretation.

These fourteen chapters tackle many important aspects of biblical hermeneutics from a Seventh-day Adventist perspective that takes seriously the divine-human dimension of the Bible. They provide valuable insights into how Seventh-day Adventists approach the Bible and seek to interpret it. They also provide a theological perspective that illuminates our past history and that can guide our interpretation of the Bible in the future. They elucidate inner-biblical hermeneutics so that we can better grasp and follow the Bible consistently. It is hoped that this book will guide readers toward a deeper exploration of Scripture and sound methods for its proper interpretation. It shows why the text of Scripture remains the highest and final authority for the faith and practice of Seventh-day Adventists.

May we always be known as faithful students of the Bible, diligently searching the Word of God, tenaciously studying its meaning, and joyfully practicing the insights we have gained so that the Bible can be a lamp to our feet and a light to our path (Ps 119:105). For "not unto us, O Lord, not unto us, but to Your name give glory, because of Your mercy, because of Your truth" (Ps 115:1, NKJV).

CHAPTER 1

Presuppositions in Hermeneutics

Kwabena Donkor

The title of this chapter hints at the fact that presuppositions affect hermeneutics. But what do these two terms mean? To simplify matters, we will begin by defining "presuppositions" as "assumptions" and "hermeneutics" as "interpretation." Thus, the idea implied in the title is that our assumptions affect our interpretations. This relationship between assumptions and interpretation has long been generally recognized as a fact of the reflective nature of humans. It has been said that presuppositions or assumptions "constitute the background logic for all thinking and doing."[1]

We may illustrate this relationship with a simple exercise from my particular ethnic community. Consider this sentence: "Woman without her man is a savage." If presented to an audience, older folks will almost invariably say something to the effect that "if a woman does not have a husband, she is a savage." They would feel quite confident about their

[1] David K. Naugle, *Worldview: The History of a Concept* (Grand Rapids, MI: Eerdmans, 2002), 271. Naugle thinks that presuppositions are the work of the mind, which establishes the foundation of all human expression and experience. He remarks, "Though mostly hidden, and often ignored, these most basic intuitions guide and direct most, if not all of life. They are compasslike in effect, a Polaris in the night sky. They are gyroscopic amid many imbalances, a thread in the labyrinth of life. These baseline beliefs are so humanly significant, they are like a nest to a bird or a web to a spider" (ibid., 272). Ted Peters, "The Nature and Role of Presuppositions: An Inquiry Into Contemporary Hermeneutics," *International Philosophical Quarterly* 14 (June 1974): 210, expresses the same view in saying that presuppositions "refer us to our fundamental vision of reality and the self-evident truths which are tacitly acknowledged in everything we comprehend and assert." For a Seventh-day Adventist perspective, see Frank M. Hasel, "Presuppositions in the Interpretation of Scripture," in *Understanding Scripture: An Adventist Approach*, ed. George W. Reid (Silver Spring, MD: Biblical Research Institute, 2005), 27–46; and Winfried Vogel, "Why do Christian Scholars Interpret Scripture in so Many Different Ways?," in *Interpreting Scripture: Bible Questions and Answers*, ed. Gerhard Pfandl, Biblical Research Institute Studies 2 (Silver Spring, MD: Biblical Research Institute, 2010), 97–104, esp. 100–101.

interpretation until an alternative interpretation is suggested by a younger woman who may punctuate the sentence to read, "Woman: without her, man is a savage." One might then suggest that the sentence was read differently because of the different presuppositions or assumptions of the readers, which created different worldviews for them.

Something like this exercise happens in every attempt to comprehend God's will as expressed in the Bible. Interpretation is involved when a person tries to figure out what a text meant to the original recipients and what it means specifically to him or her. Since presuppositions are involved in the process of interpretation, proper interpretation is impossible without proper presuppositions.[2] For this reason, it is important to understand a bit more clearly the nature of both presuppositions and hermeneutics, and to clarify the nature and implications of the connection between them.

What is Hermeneutics?

Christians who take the Bible as their only rule of faith and practice deem it important, when reading it, to ensure that they do not read their own ideas into the biblical text but rather allow the text to have authority over them. The result is that over the course of time in Christian history, rules and procedures for reading the Bible correctly have emerged to guide the reader in the process. "Hermeneutics" is the broad term used to refer to this "rule-governed biblical interpretation."[3] The word "hermeneutics" comes from the Greek verb *hermeneuein*, which basically means "to interpret, translate or explain." This is the basic meaning of the word in Luke's account of Jesus' exposition (*diermeneusen*) to the disciples on the way to Emmaus (Luke 24:27). But among evangelical Christians, the term has commonly come to stand for the *science* of interpretation, which for Bernard Ramm means that hermeneutics "is guided by rules within a system."[4] Consequently, the term often describes "a set of techniques for extricating the meaning from the (sometimes obscure) text. In practice, it even became reduced to a list of rules."[5] Since this understanding of hermeneutics developed in

---

[2] Cf. Frank M. Hasel, "Presuppositions," 27–28.

[3] Iain Provan, "How Can I Understand, Unless Someone Explains It to Me?" (Acts 8:30–31): Evangelicals and Biblical Hermeneutics," *Bulletin for Biblical Research* 17/1 (2007): 2.

[4] Bernard Ramm, *Protestant Biblical Interpretation: A Textbook of Hermeneutics*, 3rd ed. (Grand Rapids, MI: Baker, 1970), 1.

[5] The list of rules may be found in Millard J. Erickson, "Presuppositions of Non-Evangelical Hermeneutics," in *Hermeneutics, Inerrancy, and the Bible*, ed. Earl D. Radmacher and Robert

the scientific context of modern times, it shared in the positivistic spirit of the times. Thus, it is assumed that the proper application of these rules would yield an objective outcome. Often the term was used interchangeably with "exegesis."[6] Stanley Porter and Jason Robinson explain the rationale behind this common understanding of the term:

> In its earliest modern forms, hermeneutics developed primarily as a discipline for the analysis of biblical texts. It represented a body of accepted practices for interpreting an author's intended (and inspired) meaning, as well as providing the proper means of investigating a text's socio-historical context. This form of hermeneutics was focused on the many dynamics that exist between author, text, and reader. It was assumed that in order to achieve a clear and accurate reading of a text one had to employ definitive rules of interpretation to clarify and safeguard the proper untangling of a rather obvious and commonsense relationship; that is, someone (at a specific place, at a specific time, with a specific language) had written something with the intention of having a later reader understand what he or she had in mind.[7]

In recent times, however, hermeneutics has taken on a broader meaning as evinced even in *The Chicago Statement on Biblical Hermeneutics*, where it is affirmed that whereas the term hermeneutics historically signified the rules of exegesis, it "may properly be extended to cover all that is involved in the process of perceiving what the biblical revelation means and how it bears on our lives."[8] Thus, the term is applied in a generalized way to the conditions of thinking that make all human understanding possible.[9] In the course of these developments, an issue that has become front and center in current discussions on hermeneutics is an appreciation of the interpreter's participation in the creation of meaning and understanding. Understanding, according to this view, occurs when a person (subject) actively interacts with an object such as

---

D. Preus (Grand Rapids, MI: Zondervan, 1984), 595–596.

[6] Provan, 2.

[7] Stanley E. Porter and Jason C. Robinson, *Hermeneutics: An Introduction to Interpretive Theory* (Grand Rapids, MI: Eerdmans, 2011), 3.

[8] *The Chicago Statement on Biblical Hermeneutics*, Article IX, quoted in Provan, 3. See also Randy L. Maddox, "Contemporary Hermeneutic Philosophy and Theological Studies," *Religious Studies* 21 (1985): 517.

[9] Porter and Robinson, 5.

a text. In this interaction, the interpreter's role is not limited to just correctly and disinterestedly applying rules to the text, but she actively contributes to the understanding that results because of the assumptions (presuppositions) she brings with her. For this reason, it is necessary to clarify as far as possible the package of assumptions that an interpreter brings to a task of interpretation. Hence, the notion of presuppositions.

What are Presuppositions?

Until now, we have used the terms "assumptions" and "presuppositions" interchangeably. But it is important to define presuppositions more precisely. Generally, when humans think, we take some things for granted. And, when it comes to theoretical thinking, the things we take for granted usually depend on the area of life on which the thought is focused. Thus, scientists assume that it is possible to know nature, that such knowledge can be reliably based on sense experience, and that the laws of the universe are regular. These things are assumed without proof. Similarly, in doing theology, presuppositions are drawn from the Scriptures. Among the things we assume without proof are that God exists (Heb 11:6) and that He has revealed Himself reliably in the Bible. So, when the term "presupposition" is used generally in academic circles, it means more precisely the number of beliefs we accept without support from other beliefs, arguments, or evidence.[10] But in this precise way, presuppositions are not just any assumptions we may hold. Rather, presuppositions appear as principles. Thus, assuming that lunch will be served at noon is not a presupposition in a technical sense. But presuming that eating is necessary for human survival is information about the nature of human beings expressed as a principle. And that may qualify as a presupposition. So, David Naugle speaks of presuppositions as those first principles most people take for granted. "Multifaceted in character, and knit together, they make up the most basic psychic layer of life. . . . They do not rest upon other principles but are rested upon; they are not argued *to* but argued *from*."[11] It is easy to see then, how presuppositions are responsible for how the world appears to us and how life is conducted,[12] and therefore why they are necessary if we are to think at all.

---

[10] See Ronald H. Nash, *Worldviews in Conflict: Choosing Christianity in a World of Ideas* (Grand Rapids, MI: Zondervan, 1992), 21.

[11] Naugle, 271–272.

[12] Ibid.

Still, because we as humans accept a great number of beliefs without support in the course of our lives, it may be necessary to ask whether all these beliefs should be considered presuppositions in a technical sense. The fact is, if all these beliefs were to be considered presuppositions, it would not be very helpful for analytical purposes, simply by virtue of the sheer numbers of them involved. Scholars have, therefore, tried to bring more precision to what principles may qualify as presuppositions in a technical sense. Paul Helm, for example, compares presuppositions to premises that are employed in rational inquiry, and from that perspective, he offers three features that characterize presuppositions when we consider them in a technical sense.[13] First is their broadness to cover an entire field of study or even an entire approach to all data. For this reason, presuppositions are often philosophical in character. For example, they may be metaphysical in nature when they relate to principles concerning God, humans, or the world. They may also concern principles about knowledge (epistemology) when they touch on principles regarding, for example, the nature of truth.[14] Helm identifies the second feature of technical presuppositions as a matter of commitment. He observes that "once they cease to function as presuppositions they can be revised, abandoned, or adopted. . . . But insofar as they maintain their place as presuppositions they are unrevisable."[15] Or as Michael Polanyi describes it, once we accept a set of presuppositions as the framework we use to understand life, "we may be said to dwell in them as we do in our own body."[16] Finally, according to Helm, a principle becomes a presupposition when it exercises *control* over an inquiry.[17] In other words, a presupposition allows nothing to be admitted as the conclusion of an inquiry if that thing is inconsistent with the presupposition.[18]

Clearly, beliefs or principles that meet the three characteristics outlined by Helm qualify as the *technical* or *theoretical* foundation for all thought and inquiry, including biblical interpretation. Nevertheless, it would be naïve to suppose that only beliefs or principles that meet those criteria should be considered in figuring out factors that affect

---

[13] Paul Helm, "Understanding Scholarly Presupposition: A Crucial Tool for Research?," *Tyndale Bulletin* 44/1 (1993): 145–146.

[14] Helm, 146.

[15] Ibid.

[16] Michael Polanyi, *Personal Knowledge: Towards a Post-Critical Philosophy* (Chicago, IL: University of Chicago Press, 1958), 60, quoted in Naugle, 272.

[17] Helm, 146.

[18] Ibid.

interpretation and how a person arrives at meaning and understanding. Ronald Nash makes the case that theoretical thinking in science, philosophy, and even theology is often strongly affected by nontheoretical considerations. He remarks that often "theoretical judgments seem inordinately affected by nontheoretical factors. This is the case, for example, when racial prejudice causes people to hold certain untrue beliefs about those who are the objects of the prejudice."[19] Bill Flat agrees: "Any interpreter's work is influenced by his own attitudes, prejudices, and personality."[20] Here is where a person's culture, upbringing, and life experiences may unduly affect a person's judgments. In a similar vein, the present study contends that positive biblical, spiritual attitudes and values such as faith, piety, reverence, and love for God belong in this category of nontheoretical foundations for biblical interpretation. In the tradition of Western thought, Naugle provides a moving biblical, philosophical, and theological testimony to the importance of spiritual attitudes in religious interpretation.

> Saint Augustine recognized that comprehending the truth of Christianity was no mere intellectual exercise, but rather an act of the heart that must first be reconditioned by faith. John Calvin affirmed Augustine's order of knowing in reissuing the principle that piety, which is "reverence joined with love of God," is a prerequisite for a knowledge of Him. People do not have the eyes to see, he said, "unless they be illuminated by the inner revelation of God through faith." Blaise Pascal believed that the truth is known "not only by means of the reason but also by means of the heart." Jonathan Edwards believed that life, and especially religion, is a function of the "affections" of the heart, which, as one commentator puts it, "express the whole man and give insight into the basic orientation of his life."[21]

---

[19] Nash, 24.

[20] Bill Flat, "The Function of Presuppositions and Attitudes in Biblical Interpretation," in *Biblical Interpretation: Principles and Practice*, ed. F. Furman Kearley, Edward P. Myers, and Timothy D. Hadley (Grand Rapids, MI: Baker, 1986), 60. For a Seventh-day Adventist perspective, see Norman R. Gulley, "The Influence of Philosophical and Scientific World Views on the Development of Method," *Journal of the Adventist Theological Society* 4/2 (1994): 137–160.

[21] Naugle, 272–273.

Role of Particular Presuppositions in Hermeneutics

The discussion so far has focused on the nature of hermeneutics and presuppositions in more or less general theoretical terms. It is time now to explore, in greater detail and with some particularity, the types of presuppositions and the ways in which they influence or affect the process of biblical hermeneutics.

This section will examine the influence of presuppositions that are more theoretical in nature and analyze them from the perspective of three interrelated levels: macro, meso, and micro.[22] Later, under the subheading "Biblical Presuppositions for Biblical Hermeneutics," the discussion will address the significance of the influence of the nontheoretical presuppositions for faithful biblical interpretation. This section introduces the terms "macro," "meso," and "micro" presuppositions/hermeneutics that need to be explained and clarified, but before doing so, returns to the illustration of "Woman without her man is a savage." Why would the elder in my ethnic community understand the sentence to mean "If a woman does not have a husband, she is a savage," with the focus on women? And why would the younger woman see the possibility of the sentence being punctuated differently to produce a different meaning that focuses on men? To help clarify the different levels of presuppositions explained below, this study focuses on the elder in my community. At the level of words, grammar, and syntax, the interpretation "If a woman does not have a husband, she is a savage" is an acceptable possible interpretation of the sentence "Woman without her man is a savage." This is the "micro level," where the meaning of the sentence is determined by presuppositions (assumptions) about the meanings of particular words and word order.

This study asserts, however, that deeper factors were at work that led the elder to his particular interpretation. These factors take the form of concepts or dogmas about women ingrained in men within that particular ethnic community. For example, it is commonly found on the lips of men in this community that *ɛmaa adwene sua* (literally, "Women have small minds"), or that *ɛmaa ɛnwene nkɔ akyiri* (literally, "Women do not think deep or far"). A person who harbors such deeply ingrained concepts about how women think, could very well see them as needy,

---

[22] Among Seventh-day Adventists, Fernando Canale was the first to borrow from the language of Hans Küng and speak of three hermeneutical levels, namely, macro, meso, and micro hermeneutics. See, for example, his "Evangelical Theology and Open Theism: Toward a Biblical Understanding of the Macro Hermeneutical Principles of Theology?" *Journal of the Adventist Theological Society*, 12/2 (2001): 20.

and perhaps even insecure. It should not be surprising that an elderly man who has been socialized in this cultural community would instinctively interpret the sentence the way he did. At this level, the presuppositions affecting the interpretation of the sentence are conceptual or dogmatic in nature. This is the "meso level," where the meaning of the sentence is influenced by presuppositions that take the form of concepts or doctrines.

Still, the elder's interpretation of the sentence could have been influenced by elements even deeper than conceptual ones. This is the "macro level," where the meaning given by the elder to the sentence could have been influenced by presuppositions about the *being* or core nature of a woman (ontology). This level will also include traditionally honed ways or principles of *knowing*, such as what has been *handed down by elders* of the community (epistemology). In many traditional African societies, men are valued higher than women as a result of lingering traditional ideologies. Africans traditionally believe in a hierarchy of beings, much like Aristotle's great chain of being, in which men rank higher than women.[23] For this reason it is not uncommon in my ethnic community for a woman after giving birth to a child to be asked, *wo woo ɔbaa anaa ɛnipa?* (literally, "Did you bring forth a female or a human being?"). My own sister experienced this several times. For this reason, a woman who brought forth many males was honored with the title *owoanini* ("the one who brings forth males").

With the illustration given above, we will now discuss the three levels of presuppositions a little more technically, hoping that the illustration will help clarify them. We will proceed from bottom up.

Macro-Level Presuppositions

Macro-level presuppositions concern principles that are responsible for determining the conceptual framework that every interpreter brings to the interpretive task, and about which many interpreters are often unconscious. Two of these key principles are, *first*, those that we may describe as metaphysical in nature (ontology), when they relate to *principles* concerning subjects such as God, humans, or the world (who/what are these?), and *second*, those about knowledge (epistemology) when,

[23] "In African societies, the traditional gender roles are usually maintained by a system of patriarchy which sees men as pre-eminent human beings and women as secondary whose roles are meant to complement those of men. Men are not generally seen as complementing women and this one sided notion of complementarity is, therefore, problematic: women are perceived as existing for men and not really as human beings in their own right" (Ani Casimir et al., "The Church and Gender Equality in Africa: Questioning Culture and the Theological Paradigm on Women Oppression," *Open Journal of Philosophy* 4 [2014]: 170, https://www.scirp.org/journal/paperinformation.aspx?paperid=46171 [accessed August 03, 2020]).

for example, the focus is on principles regarding issues such as the nature of truth and how it may be known. It is important to realize that when we ask in principle who is God, what are humans, and what is the world, these questions can be answered in many different ways. Thus, among Christian thinkers the interpretations of God include pantheism, panentheism, deism, classical theism (incorporating a view of timelessness that makes God impassible, etc.), open theism, and process theism. An interpreter of the Bible does not come to the text of the Bible with the mind *tabula rasa*—a blank slate devoid of one, or possibly, a confused combination of these understandings of God in his or her conceptual framework. Similarly, the concept of humans attracts different interpretations. On the question of human nature alone, different interpretations within Christian circles include trichotomism, dichotomism, and monism.[24] This is not to mention views on human nature that incorporate scientific and philosophical conceptions. Do humans even have natures? Is the being of humans culturally constituted? Is "the human being . . . an artifact, a natural biological organism, not born as a human person or a human self, but artificially transmuted by the process of socialization into what we know as man?"[25] The latter questions involve contemporary issues on anthropology that are answered differently and incorporated into the conceptual frameworks of interpreters as presuppositions. The principle of the "world" is the last of the ontological presuppositions that are interpreted differently in the conceptual schemes of biblical interpreters. Is our world, the world of nature, real or is ours a transient, illusory world that only mirrors the *real* world of God with timeless principles? Is the universe a closed continuum that only functions with fixed, natural laws or is it open to supernatural causation? Is the universe eternal and was the world

---

[24] See Millard Erickson, *Christian Theology* (Grand Rapids, MI: Baker, 1990), 522–523. Dichotomism holds that man is composed of two elements: the body, which is material, and the soul or spirit, which is immaterial. More recently, dichotomists make a distinction between the Old Testament and New Testament views. It is said that the Old Testament presents a unitary view of man, whereas the New Testament replaces the Old Testament view with a dualistic one. In this view man is composed of a body, which is the physical part that dies, and an immaterial soul, which survives death. Trichotomists postulate that humans are composed of three substantial entities: spirit, soul and body. In this view the body refers to the physical part; the soul, the seat of the personality; and the spirit, the part capable of knowing God. Monism, on the other hand, according to Erickson, "insists that humans are not to be thought of as in any sense composed of parts or separate entities, but rather as a radical unity. In the monistic understanding, the Bible does not view a human as body, soul, and spirit, but simply as a self" (ibid., 524).

[25] See Joseph H. Fichter, "The Concept of Man in Social Science: Freedom, Values and Second Nature," *Journal for the Scientific Study of Religion* 11/2 (1972): 113.

created? These and many more questions like them, which individuals may or may not have consciously thought through, shape and influence the conceptual framework or worldview of biblical interpreters.

The principle of knowledge is also a macro-level presupposition that works in a complementary way with the ontological principle. For example, when a person says human beings *are* (ontology) composed of soul, spirit, and body, they can say so only from a particular perspective of knowledge (epistemology) they have. Or, the presumption that men are higher than women (ontology) may be based on a person's cultural pre-reflective knowledge about women that forms his or her epistemological framework. Among the questions that the principle of knowledge asks and get answered, albeit unreflectively, are the following: What are the roles of reason and sense experience in knowledge? Is there any relationship between religious faith and reason? Is God able to reveal Himself to human beings? Indeed, is knowledge of God possible? If so, in what way/s? And if not, why not? Is there absolute truth or is all truth relative? Is the scientific method the best or the only legitimate way of acquiring knowledge of our world? Persons will ask these knowledge questions from what we may call their "epistemological framework," and they will be answered according to how they think *things are*, based on what we may call their "ontological framework." In this way meaning, understanding, and coherence in a person's conceptual framework is achieved at the *macro* level.

Meso-Level Presuppositions

Meso-level presuppositions take the form of doctrines formulated within the limits set by the interpreter's conceptual framework based on its ontological and epistemological determinations. The hermeneutical role or effect of macro-level presuppositions working at the meso level consists precisely in the fact that, usually, doctrines that are inconsistent with the macro-level principles can hardly be entertained. For example, a person who holds an ontological presupposition of monism[26] regarding human nature cannot consistently maintain the theological doctrine of the immortality of the soul. Similarly, an interpreter who, ontologically, has a panentheistic view of God would be less inclined to accept traditional Christian teachings or doctrines on predictive biblical prophecy.[27]

---

[26] Monism is the view that there is only one kind of ultimate element or substance.

[27] John Polkinghorne, who is sympathetic to panentheism, remarks, "If the universe is one of true becoming, with the future not yet formed and existing, and if God knows that world in its temporality, then that seems to me to imply that God cannot yet know the future. This is no

Micro-Level Presuppositions

Micro-level presuppositions exercise their control at the level of individual texts/pericopes, but not without the impact or influence of both macro- and meso-level presuppositions. Here is where the supposed neutrality of the erstwhile modern positivistic exegesis was clearly inadequate in claiming objectivity in the interpretive task.[28] *First*, it is a fact that micro-exegetical results are routinely affected by macro- and meso-hermeneutical presuppositions. To see this interrelationship, we come back to the example of the panentheist, whose view of God (ontological presupposition) not only detracts, for example, from the traditional eschatological teaching of the literal, personal, visible second coming of Christ based on biblical prophecy (meso-presupposition), but also influences the approach to specific biblical texts on the subject (micro-exegesis). So John Polkinghorne, a panentheist, warns that the language of Christ ascended and sitting at the right hand of the Father (Luke 24:51; Acts 1:6–11; 2:34–36; Heb 8:1) is so heavily symbolic that

> we are not committed to the quaint picture, sometimes found in medieval stained glass, of the Lord's feet projecting from the underside of a cloud, as he sets out on his space-journey to the heavenly realm. In Scripture a cloud is the symbolic presence of God (Exod 19:16; Dan 7:13; Mark 9:7), and its role in the story of the ascension is to emphasize the divine authority of the exalted Christ.[29]

In handling the ascension of Christ in Luke 24:51 and Acts 1:6–11 in such a symbolic manner, Polkinghorne manages to deny the literal,

---

imperfection in the divine nature, for the future is not yet there to be known. Involved in the act of creation, in the letting-be of the truly other, is not only a kenosis of divine power but also a kenosis of divine knowledge." See John Polkinghorne, *Belief in God in an Age of Science* (New Haven, CT: Yale University Press, 1998), 73.

[28] Positivistic exegesis was connected with modern methods of "historical criticism," a phrase that "refers to a family of methods characterized by commitment to the model of a supposed neutral or objective interpreter and its nonnegotiable emphasis on interpreting biblical texts with reference to their historical contexts alone." See Joel B. Green, "Modern and Postmodern Methods of Biblical Interpretation," in *Scripture and Its Interpretation*, ed. Michael J. Gorman (Grand Rapids, MI: Baker Academic, 2017), 189.

[29] John C. Polkinghorne, *The Faith of a Physicist: Reflections of a Bottom-Up Thinker* (Minneapolis, MN: Fortress, 1996), 123. Polkinghorne continues to observe that "a similar [ostensibly symbolic] purpose is served by the mythological language of the heavenly session. The words of Psalm 110:1: 'The Lord says to my Lord: "Sit at my right hand, till I make your enemies your footstool,"' afforded the early Church some clue to how the Lordship of Christ was related to the fundamental Lordship of God" (ibid.).

personal, and visible second coming of Christ that seems to be clearly expressed in that same passage in Acts (Acts 1:10–11).

The point should not be missed that at the micro level, Polkinghorne is forced to adopt a symbolic interpretation because his macro- and meso-hermeneutical presuppositions preclude him from embracing a literal, historical reading of the text. *Second*, it is also a fact that, at the micro-exegetical level, macro-hermeneutical presuppositions affect one's choice of exegetical method for biblical interpretation. Enlightenment-minded interpreters who adopt historical critical approaches toward biblical interpretation do so because the method's principles of criticism, analogy, and correlation (derived from particular macro-hermeneutical principles) fit the modernistic, anti-supernatural, scientific interpretations of reality, the world, and knowledge that they espouse.[30] Among modern critical methods are source criticism, form criticism, tradition criticism, and social-scientific criticism. On the other hand, postmodern interpreters, while retaining the critical sensibilities of modernity, have no burden for an objectively determined truth on which to stand and make judgments. So, for postmodern interpreters, "meaning is not simply a property of the text that the reader must discover or excavate but is somehow the product of the integration of readers with texts."[31] This postmodern approach to biblical texts (micro-level hermeneutics) derives directly from postmodernism's macro-hermeneutical presuppositions on ontology (anti-realist metaphysics)[32] and

[30] For a concise explanation of these principles, see Gerhard F. Hasel, *Biblical Interpretation Today* (Washington D.C.: Biblical Research Institute, 1985), 77. The principle of criticism means that judgments about the past cannot simply be classified as true or false. They should rather be understood as claiming only a greater or lesser degree of probability and thus always are open to revision. This is a macro-epistemological presupposition. In other words, we must always begin with doubt. The next two principles are macro-ontological principles reading the nature of the world and reality. The principle of analogy requires that we proceed on the assumption that the events of the past are analogous to the events of our own present experience. In other words, all historical events are fundamentally homogenous. This means that present reality determines the truth status of the past. It is for this reason that miracles are deemed improbable today. Finally, the principle of correlation requires us to see every historical event as correlated with others in the same series, the essence of which John Macquarrie, *Twentieth-Century Religious Thought* (Philadelphia, PA: Trinity Press, 1988), 142–143, captures well: "There is an integral continuity in history, so that everything which happens has to be considered as immanent in the immensely complex causal nexus. Troeltsch can even say that 'the history of mankind merges in the purely evolutionary history of the earth's surface.' . . . The point of the principle of correlation is, however, that although there may be distinctive events, and even highly distinctive events, all events are of the same order, and are explicable in terms of what is immanent in history itself."

[31] Gorman, 197.

[32] Anti-realism is the view that insofar as there are objects, they are dependent on our

epistemology (holism).[33] Postmodern critical methods include narrative criticism and post-modern literary criticism.[34]

Biblical Presuppositions for Biblical Hermeneutics

The discussion so far has highlighted the fact that first, all interpreters approach a text (micro-hermeneutics), including the biblical text, with a conceptual framework that incorporates ideas (macro-hermeneutics) of a metaphysical and epistemological nature that are derived from macro-hermeneutical presuppositions. Second, biblical interpreters approach their task with doctrinal beliefs (meso-hermeneutics) shaped by their macro-hermeneutical conceptual framework. These points have been illustrated with perspectives from modern and postmodern *critical* approaches to biblical interpretation. This leads us to look more closely at biblical presuppositions and their importance for biblical hermeneutics.

Theoretical Biblical Presuppositions for Biblical Hermeneutics

The previously outlined dynamics between presuppositions and hermeneutics, however, are *not* limited to critical approaches to biblical interpretation. Therefore, it seems that in order to arrive at a true faith-based biblical interpretation, an interpreter's conceptual framework needs to be shaped in a way that is faithful to Scripture. This faith-based approach is possible by developing and adopting presuppositions (macro, meso, and micro) that are faithful to the Bible, and with which one may approach the task of biblical interpretation. How does one begin to formulate this task? It begins with an appreciation of what has been called the "epistemic circle." The concept of the epistemic circle states that "how we know is controlled by the nature of the object and the

---

experience, thought, and language. In other words, we do not encounter a world that is simply given "out there," but one that we actively construct by the use of concepts we bring to it. This view is a rejection of the philosophical concept of essentialism—the idea that there are some ideal meanings. See Keith Yandell, "Modernism, Post-Modernism, and the Minimalist Canons of Common Grace," *Christian Scholars Review* 27 (1997): 18–19.

[33] Epistemologically, postmodernity represents a rejection of the Enlightenment's quest for "objective knowledge" and its attendant foundationalism and referentialism. See Nancey Murphy, "Philosophical Resources for Postmodern Evangelical Theology," *Christian Scholars Review* 26/2 (1996): 185–193. With holism, no beliefs are inherently unrevisable. Thus, the hallmarks of holism are corrigibility, perspectival plurality, and process.

[34] For a comprehensive, up-to-date discussion of methodical approaches to the Bible, see Joel M. Lemon and Kent Harold Richards, eds., *Method Matters* (Atlanta, GA: Society of Biblical Literature, 2009).

nature of the object is revealed through our knowledge of it."[35] Applying the concept to the study of God, we have to admit that God is not physically available for our study, but Bible-believing interpreters acknowledge that God can be known because He has revealed Himself in the Bible. Thus, the Bible takes center stage in providing the necessary presuppositions for the interpretive task as well as shaping the framework of the interpreter. As will be shown later, the formation of biblically faithful presuppositions is a dynamic, ongoing, iterative process between the interpreter and the Bible. But for now, it is important to outline what, from an Adventist perspective, may be reasonably affirmed as basic presuppositions that are faithful to the Bible.

At the macro level, we begin with particular biblical principles that concern the nature of reality. These are technically described as ontological principles, and we will examine those that concern the reality of God, humanity, and the world.

God

From an Adventist perspective, here are some basic principles about the *Being* of God (ontology) that need to shape an Adventist interpreter's conceptual framework. Adventists understand the Bible to present God in His being as a *personal* God whose existence is taken as an *a priori* fact (Gen 1:1; Heb 11:6). By themselves and apart from God's own self-revelation, humans might know that there is a God (cf. Rom 1:19–28) but they do not necessarily know about His personal and loving nature. Humans are incapable of knowing God and His love by themselves apart from His own self-revelation (Job 11:7; Ps 145:3). God as a personal being is eternal as well as supernaturally transcendent (2 Chr 6:18) in ways that do not restrict God from being immanent—namely, interacting with things that are temporal and historical (Exod 40:34–38; 2 Chr 5:13–14). He is love (not without wrath)[36] in a way that defines His essence (1 John 4:8) and surpasses human knowledge and understanding (Eph 3:19), although it has become visible in the life and death of Jesus Christ. God's wrath, which is not in contradiction to His love, is caused by human rejection of His offer of salvation and may be averted by repentance (1 Kgs 8:46–49; 2 Pet 3:9). In His love, God acts with perfect knowledge (Job 37:16) both in the creation of the world and His provision for it (providence). He may even act directly to intervene and guide human history either through the revelation of

---

[35] Polkinghorne, *The Faith of a Physicist*, 32.

[36] On the wrath of God, see Frank M. Hasel, "The Wrath of God" *Ministry*, 64 (1991): 10–12.

His will to persons or by supernatural, miraculous acts. He created by speaking the world into existence (Ps 33:6) and with a direct command He brought the universe into being (Ps 148:5, 6; Heb 3:4). This biblical God is also a holy God who is entirely free of sin and evil and seeks to establish a loving relationship with human beings who are created in His image.

Humans

With regard to what ought to inform an Adventist interpreter's frame of mind concerning humans, the Genesis creation account is foundational. In Genesis, we find a twofold account of the creation of humans: first in Genesis 1:26–27, and then in Genesis 2:7, 21–23. Whereas critical scholars see in these accounts a reflection of the biblical writer's effort to piece together two supposedly independent and contradictory creation narratives (Gen 1:1–2:3 and Gen 2:4–25), many scholars, including Seventh-day Adventists, see it differently and affirm the unity of the two narratives.[37] To the latter group of scholars, the first narrative recounts the creation of all things in the order in which it occurred, while the second narrative groups things in their relation to humans.[38] From these accounts we affirm that humans originated from God. Indeed, humanity (both male and female) is created in the image of God. This particular affirmation entails two significant components with respect to the identity of humans—namely, their *existence* and *essence*. Humans' existence and essence both originate from God. On the one hand, the affirmation of God as the ground of humans' existence involves not only the physical dimension of personal existence, but also the purpose of individual existence. It is to confess God as the one from whom meaning, purpose, and goal are bestowed on the life of the individual.[39] Affirming the nature of humankind as being derived from God lets us realize that God created man with a purpose, which God calls each human being to acknowledge, reflect on, and actualize.[40] Furthermore, the affirmation informs us that God is both the source and determiner of all values, including human values.

With regard to the being of humans, Adventists understand the Bible's perspective on the composition of human life to be schematized as

---

[37] See William H. Shea, "Creation," in *Handbook of Seventh-day Adventist Theology*, ed. Raoul Dederen (Hagerstown, MD: Review and Herald, 2000), esp. 425–427.

[38] See Louis Berkhof, *Systematic Theology* (Grand Rapids, MI: Eerdmans, 1996), 182.

[39] See Stanley J. Grenz, *Theology for the Community of God* (Grand Rapids, MI: Eerdmans, 1994), 140.

[40] Ibid., 142.

follows: dust of the ground + breath of life = living being. Commenting on God's life-animating breath or spirit, which He added to the dust of the ground in creating Adam and Eve, Niels-Erik A. Andreasen writes, "Hereby the Bible indicates that the life-breath does not represent a second entity, added, like an ingredient, to the body, capable of separate existence, but an energizing, spiritual power from God that transformed the earthen body into a living being."[41] Subsequent to the creation of humans, the entrance of sin in God's creation, and the fall of Adam and Eve, sin has had effects on their posterity that linger on to the present—pride, self-deception, doubt, separation between God and humans, disobedience, and ultimately death.[42] Death of humans is the reversal of the schematization of life.[43]

The World

As Adventists understand it, the biblical view of the world is that it does not exist as a brute fact. The Bible declares that "in the beginning God created the heavens and the earth" (Gen 1:1). Genesis 1:1 requires an understanding of origins as an absolute historic/temporal beginning. Hence the phrase "in the beginning God created" in Genesis 1:1, while denoting origination, discourages a notion of origins whose inner structure would be an eternally standing relation with the being of God.[44] "The cosmos is not eternal, self-sufficient, or self-explanatory."[45] God created the world freely and *ex nihilo*. Furthermore, if the world is created, it must not be purposeless. In the creation account in Genesis 1, the divine word repeatedly affirms, "God said," "and it was good," thereby implying a purposeful act of the

---

[41] Niels-Erik A. Andreasen, "Death: Origin, Nature, and Final Eradication," in *Handbook of Seventh-day Adventist Theology*, ed. Raoul Dederen (Hagerstown, MD: Review and Herald, 2000), 316.

[42] For some discussion on the effects of sin on humans after the fall, see Frank M. Hasel, "Presuppositions," 30–32.

[43] Stanley J. Grenz, *Theology for the Community of God* (Grand Rapids, MI: Eerdmans, 1994), 163, observes, regarding death, that "not only does it usher in the end of functioning among the living, death calls into question the meaning of a person's entire life. For this reason much 'Christian' talk about death as merely the door to a higher existence is unfortunate, if not detrimental."

[44] Robert W. Jensen, "Aspects of a Doctrine of Creation," in *The Doctrine of Creation: Essays in Dogmatics, History, and Philosophy*, ed. Colin E. Gunton (Edinburgh: T&T Clark, 1997), 18–23, expresses the notion of creation as the absolute origination of reality with the following theses: 1) There is indeed other reality than God, and that it is really other. 2) That there is other reality than God depends entirely on His will. 3) All the above holds precisely in the present tense. The world at any moment would not be did God not will it. 4) The reality other than God has an absolute beginning.

[45] Nash, 36.

Creator.[46] Creation of the world also means that the world is contingent, which means that creation does not exist as a necessary phenomenon in the sense that it *had* to be or can continue to be by itself. The created order is connected with, conditioned by, subject to, and dependent upon the supernatural, transcendent, immanent, and personal God. The creation is the subject of God's personal, continual support and care (Col 1:25, 28). God's providence means that the world is not a mere mechanistic system; neither is it a self-enclosed system where everything that happens in it must be explained by its immanent causes. God, being transcendent and immanent, can act supernaturally within His contingent creation.

Adventists also understand that the present world is the battleground in a great controversy between good (God) and evil (Satan). In the Bible, the devil or Satan is the one who introduced sin and evil into the universe. He is depicted as an accuser and slanderer (Rev 12:10; 13:6; cf. Job 1–2; Zech 3:1–2; Jude 9), a deceiver and tempter of the whole world from the beginning (Matt 4:3; Rev 12:9; cf. John 8:44; Acts 5:3; 1 Cor 11:3; 1 John 3:8; Rev 2:10), and a usurping ruler of this world (John 12:31; 14:30; 16:11; cf. Matt 12:24–29; Luke 4:5-6; Acts 26:18; 2 Cor 4:4; Eph 2:2; 1 John 5:19). The Bible depicts cosmic or celestial rulers and/or powers with authority and jurisdiction over what occurs on earth (Rev 12:7–9). There is a kingdom of darkness, which Christ has come to conquer and replace with His own everlasting kingdom (cf. Dan 2:44–45).[47]

Continuing at the macro level, some key biblical views on what we know and how we know (epistemology) must be outlined.

Knowledge (Epistemology)

The Bible is not a philosophy textbook. Technically speaking, it does not have a set epistemology, though the Bible speaks of knowledge and truth. The fact that, as Christians, *how* we know is controlled by the nature of the object (the Bible) means that we can use biblical teachings to discern which epistemological positions are correct to adopt as presuppositions for biblical interpretation and which presuppositions are not correct. But before we do so, it is necessary to know how we should think about the Bible itself as the foundational source of knowledge.[48]

---

[46] See Jensen, 22, where he observes that in the Genesis story "the 'and it was good' belongs to the creative act itself: things are good in that they are judged good by God. *Tov* in Hebrew works just like 'good' in English: it says 'good *for*' something. Things are good in that God judges that they are good for his purposes."

[47] Ibid.

[48] See Frank M. Hasel, "Presuppositions," 36-40. Some views we consider to be unfaithful to

Interpreters who come to the Bible uncritically presuppose the principle of Scripture that was captured in the Reformation slogan of *sola Scriptura*.[49] *Sola Scriptura*, in the context of the Reformation, served to focus attention on the Bible as a principle of interpretation against competing principles.[50] Several other necessary principles of hermeneutical importance are derived from the *sola Scriptura* principle: the authority of Scripture,[51] the necessity of Scripture,[52] the perspicuity/clarity of Scripture,[53] the sufficiency of Scripture,[54] and the unity of Scripture.

Scripture are mentioned in Kwabena Donkor, "Contemporary Responses to *Sola Scriptura*: Implications for Adventist Theology," Biblical Research Institute, https://adventistbiblicalresearch.org/sites/default/files/pdf/Contemporary_Responses_to_Sola_Scriptura_0.pdf (accessed July 28, 2020). See also chapter 2 by Frank M. Hasel, "Elements of Biblical Hermeneutics in Harmony With Scripture's Self-Claims," in the present volume; and Frank M. Hasel, "Theology and the Role of Reason," *Journal of the Adventist Theological Society* 4/2 (1993): 172–198, esp. 179–188.

[49] On the meaning of *sola Scriptura*, see the discussion in chapter 13 by John C. Peckham, "The Prophetic Gift and *Sola Scriptura*," in the present volume; and Peckham, *Canonical Theology: The Biblical Canon,* Sola Scriptura *and Theological Method* (Grand Rapids, MI: Eerdmans, 2016).

[50] See G. C. Berkouwer, *Holy Scripture* (Grand Rapids, MI: Eerdmans, 1975), 306. Luther's clarion call, therefore, was not a return to the Bible merely as an original source (humanism and the Renaissance advocated that). It was not even a call to renounce every bit of tradition (both Luther and Calvin had great respect for church tradition). Luther's call was to recover the true tradition of biblical truth through correct interpretation of the Bible, unhampered by an assumed, necessary congruity between the Bible and traditional church teaching.

[51] J. I. Packer, "'Sola Scriptura' In History and Today," in *God's Inerrant Word: An International Symposium on the Trustworthiness of Scripture*, ed. John W. Montgomery (Minneapolis, MN: Bethany Fellowship, 1973), 44, remarks, "What Luther thus voiced at Worms shows the essential motivation and concern, theological and religious, of the entire Reformation movement: namely, that the Word of God alone must rule, and no Christian man dare do other than allow it to enthrone itself in his conscience and heart."

[52] The necessity of Scripture was designed to combat two separate tendencies. On the one hand, there was the self-sufficient, Bible-warranting Roman Catholic Church, which, though needing tradition, did not really need Scripture in spite of professing it to be a norm. On the other hand, there were groups such as some Anabaptists and Cathari for whom the Bible was really superfluous. By exalting the inner word against the external, and regarding the Bible not as the Word of God but as a testimony, these groups considered the real Word of God as that which was spoken by the Holy Spirit in the hearts of God's people. Against both tendencies, the Reformers insisted on the necessity of the written Word of God.

[53] To ascribe sole authority or necessity to a Bible that is unclear would make no sense. Leading up to the time of the Reformers, a climate had built up regarding the obscurity of Scripture, for which reason the laity were not encouraged to read it.

[54] The issue of the sufficiency of Scripture was the background for *sola Scriptura*. Indeed, the *sola* in the formulation *sola Scriptura* was intended to highlight the sufficiency of Scripture. The various doctrines, institutions, and traditions the church had put in place, with no basis in Scripture, were an indication to the Reformers that Rome deemed the Bible to be insufficient.

Granting the foregoing presuppositions about the Bible as the foundational data source for theology, certain determinations can be made about the Bible's own views on knowledge. *First*, against skepticism, the Bible teaches that knowledge is possible and integral to human existence.[55] The creation narrative in Genesis 2:16–17 sets up the primary parameters for knowledge. It seems quite clear that knowledge, represented here by the tree of the knowledge of good and evil, is part of the material world, accessible to humans, but also a prerogative of God (cf. 1 Sam 2:3; Dan 2:27–28).[56] Furthermore, the parameters of knowledge set in the context of Genesis 2 seem to be the most fundamental knowledge of all. It has to do with the origin and relation of the world and humans to the Creator.[57] The tree of the knowledge of good and evil may be seen as symbolizing a boundary marker, which suggests that failure to abide by true knowledge has disastrous consequences on both persons and physical reality (Gen 2:16–17; 3:14). Since humans are placed in the context of knowing, they are considered to be morally responsible for their beliefs and actions with respect to the parameters set in that fundamental knowledge in Genesis 2 (cf. Rom 1:20). Implied in the first point is a *second* one: From the perspective of the Bible, there is such a thing as *the truth* (John 8:32), in contrast to postmodern relativism and pluralism—truth that is bound up with Jesus Christ (cf. John 14:6). Human knowledge, including that gained through biblical interpretation, is partial (1 Cor 13:9). Yet, the possibility of attaining it is upheld in the Bible (Ps 25:5; 43:3; Isa 61:8; John 16:13). The Holy Spirit is a key epistemological agent for Adventist hermeneutics because He is presented in the Bible as the Guide to *all truth*.[58] And the idea that, biblically, the truth may be known with divine help suggests a *third* point. An epistemology such as empiricism that relies totally on materialistic principles is contrary to the Bible. It is true that the fundamental knowledge about the origin and relation of the world and humans to the Creator is provided as special revelation in the Bible. Yet, in the Bible we also find knowledge that is the product of empirical research and human reflection

[55] See Frank M. Hasel, "Theology and the Role of Reason," 179–186.

[56] See Kenneth Ngwa, "Knowledge," in *The Oxford Encyclopedia of the Bible and Theology*, ed. Samuel E. Balentine (Oxford: Oxford University Press, 2015).

[57] See Allan R. Killen, "Know, Knowledge," in *Wycliffe Bible Encyclopedia*, ed. Charles F. Pfeiffer et al. (Chicago, IL: Moody, 1975), 997.

[58] On the role of the Holy Spirit from an Adventist perspective, see Frank M. Hasel, "A Doutrino do Espirito Santo," in *Pneumatologia Pesso e Obrado do Espirito Santo*, ed. Reinaldo W. Siqueira and Alberto R. Timm (Engenheiro Coelho, SP: Unaspress, 2017), 523–541, esp. 529–531.

(Eccl 1:16, 18; 7:12, 25)—even empirical research that may form the basis for special revelation, as in Luke's gospel (Luke 1:1–4). However, the Bible is clear that though knowledge can be taught (Prov 1:4, 23), it is not an autonomous knowledge that exists independently from God, but a fundamentally divine gift that grows out of a right relationship to the creator (Prov 2:6, 10).[59]

The previously mentioned elements on epistemology have implications for micro-hermeneutics (exegesis). Just as historical critical approaches toward biblical interpretation fit the modernistic, anti-supernatural, and naturalistic scientific interpretations of reality, the world, and knowledge, so also macro-presuppositions that are faithful to Scripture influence the preference for a particular method—namely, the historical-grammatical method. Its presuppositions include, among other aspects, the inspiration of the Bible, scriptural perspicuity, authorial intentionality, and objectivity.[60]

A person who holds the set of micro-, meso-, and macro-presuppositions previously discussed may be said to indwell an interpretive system or possess a hermeneutic, a method/theory of interpretation or worldview,[61] even a paradigm, with which they approach the Bible as they seek its meaning. A consistent application of this interpretive system or method by an interpreter to the Bible will yield results, understandings, and ideas that are coherent with the presuppositions of the system. Any ideas that are offered to this interpreter as biblical but found to be incoherent with the presuppositions of the interpreter's system will be judged as unacceptable by such an interpreter. It may be possible that interpreters with different interpretive systems or paradigms may come to what seems to be a similar conclusion on a biblical idea. However, a closer examination of the idea in the context of the respective interpretive systems/paradigms will expose some differences in meaning. Such, for example, is the case with the doctrine of the Trinity. While Seventh-day Adventists and Roman Catholics

---

[59] Cf. Frank M. Hasel, "Theology and the Role of Reason," 180–188.

[60] For a helpful discussion, see Jason S. Sexton, "Emerging Church Hermeneutics and the Historical-Grammatical Method," *Southwestern Journal of Theology* 53/2 (2011), 154–174. On the issue of objectivity, Kevin J. Vanhoozer, "Lost in Interpretation? Truth, Scripture, and Hermeneutics," *Journal of the Evangelical Theological Society* 48/1 (March 2005): 110, remarks helpfully that "to come to Scripture is to be confronted with a truth that is both objective and rational on the one hand and personal and relational on the other."

[61] For an Adventist perspective, see also Gulley, 137–160; and Fernando Canale, "From Vision to System: Finishing the Task of Adventist Biblical and Systematic Theologies," *Journal of the Adventist Theological Society* 16/1 (2005): 114–142.

both agree on the fundamental idea of a triune God, the two communities of faith attach different meanings to the doctrine of the Trinity.[62]

Nontheoretical Biblical Presuppositions for Biblical Hermeneutics

It is of utmost importance to recall that from a noncritical biblical point of view, humans embark on biblical interpretation as sinful persons. The thought mentioned earlier that prejudice may interfere with one's assessment of truth finds its source in human sinfulness. Subjected to enfeeblement, depravity, and enslavement, the human heart tends to be disinclined toward God (Rom 1:18-25) such that theoretical thinking is prone to deception (Jer 17:9). From the point of view of the Bible, pride, self-deception, doubt, and separation from God are some of the characteristics of sinful humanity that may affect a person's interpretational efforts. In his reflections on human inability to contemplate God in His works, the Reformer John Calvin depicts the human mind as a factory in the production of superstitions and falsehoods.

> Hence that immense flood of error with which the whole world is overflowed. Every individual mind being a kind of labyrinth, it is not wonderful, not only that each nation has adopted a variety of fictions, but that almost every man has had his own god. To the darkness of ignorance have been added presumption and wantonness, and hence there is scarcely an individual to be found without some idol or phantom as a substitute for Deity.[63]

On the other hand, openness and honesty (John 7:17), faith (1 Cor 2:14), humility (Jas 4:6), obedience (Ps 119:100), love (Jer 29:13), and prayer are some of the positive attitudes on the part of the interpreter that promote proper understanding of God's Word. These issues have been discussed extensively elsewhere and so will not be further elaborated here.[64]

---

[62] So Merlin Burt observes about some in the Adventist church, "Some think that the Trinity doctrine comes from Catholic theology and therefore must be false. Many have not realized that the Catholic doctrine of the Trinity has differences from the Seventh-day Adventist biblical doctrine of the Trinity. These include eternal generation of the Son and Divine impassibility, which are influenced by Greek philosophy." See Merlin D. Burt, "The Trinity in Seventh-day Adventist History," *Ministry*, February 2009, 5-8; and Burt, "History of Seventh-day Adventist Views on the Trinity," *Journal of the Adventist Theological Society* 17/1 (2006): 125–139.

[63] John Calvin, *Institutes of the Christian Religion*, trans. Henry Beveridge (Grand Rapids, MI: Eerdmans, 1989), I.V.12, p. 59. For a more expansive discussion, see Frank M. Hasel, "Presuppositions," 29–33.

[64] See Frank M. Hasel, "Presuppositions," 33–35.

Presuppositions in the Dynamic Process of Interpretation

So far, we have examined the nature of presuppositions and hermeneutics, showing how particular presuppositions may affect the outcome of biblical interpretation. What needs to be addressed now is the *process* by which an interpreter, based on the foregoing discussion, may interact with the Bible in a way that maximizes the chance of attaining its correct interpretation. It is necessary to introduce at this point the idea of the "*hermeneutical circle/spiral*." As it is understood in contemporary hermeneutics, the concept of the hermeneutical circle relates to the idea that "we can only understand the parts of a text, or any body of meaning, out of a general idea of its whole, yet we can only gain this understanding of the whole by understanding its parts."[65] Underlying the concept is the basic idea that there is no such thing as an understanding without presuppositions. While traditional and more methodically inclined hermeneutics tends to view presuppositions with suspicion and tried to avoid them, contemporary hermeneutics seeks first to acknowledge them as necessary in any understanding, and endeavor to "replace them by more authentic ones which would be assured by the things themselves."[66] The goal is to conceive of a circle that will enable the interpreter to attain an understanding of a work or text that is independent of one's personal prejudices.

Considering the Bible in its entirety as the object of interpretation, the quest for biblical presuppositions that are consistent with biblical hermeneutics involves two interconnected moves that entail two hermeneutical circles: one between the reader and text and the other between the parts and the whole of the canon.[67] Each of these circles involves exegesis at a different level, yet the two levels impact each other. Micro-exegesis (relation of reader and text) concerns the procedures of grammatical-historical exegesis at the level of periscopes, while macro-exegesis (relation of parts and the whole) refers to interpretation that goes beyond a particular pericope toward seeking the conceptual framework (that is, the biblical theological idea) that the text suggests. Yet the interpreter is conscious of a hermeneutical spiral of micro-exegesis and macro-exegesis that continually subjects the interpreter's conceptual

---

[65] Jean Grondin, "What is the Hermeneutical Circle," revised 2017 version of an essay published in N. Keane and C. Lawn, eds., *The Blackwell Companion to Hermeneutics* (Oxford: Blackwell, 2016), 299–305, at https://www.academia.edu/13944229/What_is_the_hermeneutical_circle, 1, (accessed on August 3, 2020).

[66] Ibid, 2.

[67] For a complete discussion of the two hermeneutical circles and the reciprocal relationship between micro- and macro-exegesis, see Peckham, *Canonical Theology*, 212–216.

framework and interpretations to criticism and correction by the text. The metaphor of a "spiral," rather than a circle, is extremely helpful here as it brings to view an ongoing dynamic process by which an interpreter gets closer and closer to the intended meaning of a text faithful to the biblical worldview. So, while micro-exegesis uncovers the intention that may be detected in the text in its immediate context, macro-exegesis uses the data derived micro-exegetically, disclosing the conceptual framework conveyed in the text that in turn undergirds and circumscribes its meaning. Consequently, the canonical text is read to inform and possibly transform one's conceptual framework.[68] Thus, in this hermeneutical spiral, details of a text are examined first, and from them broader macro-hermeneutical presuppositions are drawn to undergird further explorations of particular texts and periscopes.[69] In this way, the interpreter gets closer and closer to preventing nonbiblical presuppositions from being imposed on the text. This dynamic interaction between the reader and the text, as well as the relationship between the parts and the whole of Scripture as outlined, together with the adoption of the biblical understandings of God, man, world, and knowledge, goes a long way toward advancing true, biblical hermeneutics.

Conclusion

While proper hermeneutics is of the utmost importance to the understanding of God's will as expressed in the Bible, the presuppositions that an interpreter brings to the text significantly influence the interpretation. Since interpretation without presuppositions is an impossibility, it becomes extremely important not only to reflect on the nature of an interpreter's presuppositions but also to understand the manner in which they affect interpretation. On the nature of presuppositions, this study has analyzed them into theoretical and nontheoretical types, showing that the former may be investigated

---

[68] See Anthony C. Thiselton, "The New Hermeneutic," in *New Testament Interpretation*, ed. I. H. Marshall, vol. 1 (Grand Rapids, MI: Eerdmans, 1977), 328. "As one interacts with the text, there is a *continuous* dialogue of question and answer until his own continual horizons are creatively enlarged" (as quoted in Flat, 71).

[69] Peckham, *Canonical Theology*, 214, remarks that "methodologically, the text at the microhermeneutical level holds priority and one thus intends to recognize, temporarily suspend, and put on the table for examination one's pertinent and identifiable operative examine pertinent and identifiable operative macro- and meso-hermeneutical presuppositions, toward allowing the text as canon to inform all three levels in an ongoing hermeneutical spiral."

from the perspective of three interrelated levels—macro, meso, and micro. An interpreter's work, however, may also be influenced by attitudes, prejudices, and personality factors that are less theoretical in nature but still of significant importance. Especially in order for biblical interpretation to be faithful to the Bible, faith, piety, reverence, the indwelling of the Holy Spirit, and love for God become indispensable for the correct discernment of God's will expressed in Scripture. These are the spiritual virtues needed to help the interpreter be conscious and submit to the hermeneutical spiral of micro-exegesis and macro-exegesis that continually subjects the interpreter's conceptual framework and interpretations to criticism and correction by the biblical text.

CHAPTER 2

Elements of Biblical Hermeneutics in Harmony with Scripture's Self-Claims

Frank M. Hasel

Any serious student of the Bible faces the challenge of reading and studying the Bible correctly. Doing so means that we engage in biblical interpretation in such a manner that our hermeneutic is in harmony with Scripture and correctly interprets the message of the biblical text. But how can we interpret the Bible in such a way that our interpretation is faithful to Scripture, not distorting it to our own liking or superimposing foreign categories on the text or twisting the meaning of the Bible? We know that no one studies Scripture with a blank mind. We all bring our presuppositions and experiences to the task of biblical interpretation.[1] Presuppositionless exegesis is a self-deception.[2] This realization can be daunting, especially in light of numerous, often conflicting, approaches to biblical interpretation that are in vogue today and in light of the fact that even our best intentions and our presuppositions are shaped and influenced by sin. But this does not need to deter our efforts. For God has promised that we can come to an understanding (of Scripture) that is pleasing to Him (cf. John 6:68–69; 7:38; 8:31–32; 9:31; 14:23, 26). God is willing to make this happen, even if He needs to challenge our

---

[1] On the importance of presuppositions in the process of biblical interpretation, see Frank M. Hasel, "Presuppositions in the Interpretation of Scripture" in *Understanding Scripture: An Adventist Approach*, ed. George W. Reid (Silver Spring, MD: Biblical Research Institute 2005), 27–46. See also the chapter 1 by Kwabena Donkor, "Presuppositions in Hermeneutics," in the present volume.

[2] Gerhard Maier, *Biblical Hermeneutics* (Wheaton, IL: Crossway, 1994), 25, 45.

thinking and correct our distorted presuppositions through His written Word.[3] An Adventist approach to biblical hermeneutics, therefore, is motivated to develop and follow an approach to the interpretation of Scripture that not only respects the text of Scripture, but that deliberately seeks to be open to the divine reality we encounter in its pages. In what follows we describe a number of factors that must be taken into consideration in any approach to biblical hermeneutics that seeks to be in harmony with the Bible itself.

The Method of Biblical Interpretation is Determined by its Object

It is a truism that every method is determined by its object. The structure of the atoms and the DNA of our genotype is not possible to explicate by historical methodology. The time of a one-hundred-meter world record cannot be measured by a yardstick. The literary meaning of a text is not uncovered by a chemical analysis of the ink with which it was written.[4] Every object determines the method with which it is studied. Thus, our study of the Bible is ill-advised if it simply takes over methods from other scientific disciplines. When we read the Bible, we encounter a unique reality that confronts us in various manifestations. Biblical writers repeatedly make reference to the supernatural reality of God and assert God's supernatural existence throughout the pages of the Old and New Testaments. They claim to speak and write on behalf of God and perceive their message to be of divine origin. Thus, in the study of the Bible we seek to learn more about God and His will for us. A responsible Adventist theology, therefore, should adequately reflect the reality of the living God in Scripture, whose will is revealed in the words of Holy Scripture.[5] This raises the crucial question of how the biblical writers and Jesus Himself viewed Scripture.

---

[3] In this chapter we focus on principles of *biblical* hermeneutics because the biblical text is the object that we study and try to interpret. Before God commanded biblical writers to deposit His message in written form, He communicated orally with His people and God's message was transmitted and delivered orally. Even after the biblical message existed in written form, it was often read—that is, performed orally—but even then, the reading is based on the written text of Scripture. Recent studies point out that oral transmission in biblical cultures was remarkably accurate and reliable. See Birger Gerhardson, *Memory and Manuscript With Tradition and Transmission in Early Christianity* (Grand Rapids, MI: Eerdmans, 1998); and Gerhardson, *The Reliability of the Gospel Tradition* (Grand Rapids, MI: Baker Academics, 2001).

[4] See Helge Stadelmann, *Grundlinien eines bibeltreuen Schriftverständnisses* (Wuppertal: R. Brockhaus Verlag, 1985), 88, for other illustrations about the same point.

[5] The term "Holy Scripture" reflects the wording of the apostle Paul in Romans 1:2 and 2 Timothy 3:15.

How did Jesus and the Apostles see Scripture?

Committed Christians ought to ask how Jesus and the apostles saw and treated Scripture.[6] Jesus gave Scripture a very exalted position and clearly affirmed its divine origin and enduring theological authority. "For if you believed Moses, you would believe me; for he wrote of me. But if you do not believe his writings, how will you believe my words?" (John 5:46–47).[7] Here Jesus clearly refers to what Moses had written and what was part of the canonical literature of the Old Testament. Jesus makes clear that if we do not believe what Moses wrote, then we cannot believe His words either. Scripture is the foundation for believing Christ. Jesus did not worship Scripture. He was no bibliolater. But He encouraged people "to search the Scripture" because "it is they that bear witness about me" (John 5:39). Thus, for Jesus correct doctrine and teaching flow from a correct interpretation of Scripture: "Whoever believes in me *as the Scripture has said*" (John 7:38, emphasis supplied). For Jesus Scripture determines our correct belief in Him, which in turn will result in "rivers of living water" (John 7:38). His attitude toward the entire Old Testament was one of reverent assent and voluntary obedient submission. For Jesus Scripture cannot be set aside; it "cannot be broken" (John 10:35). According to Matthew, Jesus taught that "not an iota, not a dot, will pass from the Law until all is accomplished" (Matt 5:18). He accepted the statements of Scripture as true and trustworthy and believed that they would retain their validity and significance as long as this earth exists. The Word as "it stands written" (*gegraptai*,

---

[6] Biblical critics have vocally denied the possibility of formulating a view of Scripture from Scripture itself. James Barr, *Fundamentalism* (London: SCM, 1977), 78, for instance, claims, "There is no such thing as 'the Bible's view of itself' from which a fully authoritative answer to these questions can be obtained. This whole side of traditional conservative apologetic, though loudly vociferated, just does not exist; there is no case to answer." For a sustained response to Barr's sharp criticism and a balanced account of the evidence Scripture provides on this issue, see the discussion in Sinclair B. Ferguson, "How Does the Bible Look at Itself?," in *Inerrancy and Hermeneutic: A Tradition, a Challenge, a Debate*, ed. Harvie M. Conn (Grand Rapids, MI: Baker, 1988), 47–66, reprinted in Peter A. Lillback and Richard B. Gaffin Jr., eds., *Thy Word Is Still Truth: Essential Writings of the Doctrine of Scripture from the Reformation to Today* (Phillipsburg, NJ: P&R, 2013), 1207–1222; John M. Frame, "Scripture Speaks for Itself," in *God's Inerrant Word*, ed. John W. Montgomery (Grand Rapids, MI: Bethany Fellowship, 1974), 178–200, reprinted as Appendix F in John M. Frame, *The Doctrine of the Word of God: A Theology of Lordship* (Phillipsburg, NJ: P&R, 2010), 440–462 and in Lillback and Gaffin, 1224–1241. See also Wayne A. Grudem, "Scripture's Self-Attestation and the Problem of Formulating a Doctrine of Scripture," in *Scripture and Truth*, ed. D. A. Carson and John D. Woodbridge (Grand Rapids, MI: Zondervan, 1983), 19–59.

[7] All biblical quotations are from the ESV, unless otherwise indicated.

Matt 4:4, 7, 10) was enough for Jesus to settle any issue. From early childhood on (cf. Luke 2:49), Jesus understood His mission in the light of the Old Testament prophecy, declaring Himself to be both the Son of Man whom Daniel talked about (Daniel 7:13) and Isaiah's suffering servant of the Lord (Isaiah 42:1) who must suffer many things, be killed, and after three days rise again (Mark 8:31). Thus Jesus will just go "as it is written about him" (Matt 26:24). Jesus lived by the written Word of God, obeyed it, and expected others to follow His example with regard to the authority of Scripture.[8] John Stott points out that for Jesus "this personal submission to Scripture and this recommendation of Scripture to others came down to his belief that what Scripture said, God said."[9] In similar manner the apostles affirmed the full authority of all of Scripture. The apostle Paul states, "For *whatever* was written in former days was written for our instruction, that through the endurance and through the encouragement of Scripture we might have hope" (Rom 15:4, emphasis supplied). Paul affirms that "all Scripture is breathed out by God and profitable for teaching, for reproof, for correction, and for training in righteousness" (2 Tim 3:16), and the apostle Peter also confirms that "no prophecy was ever made but an act of human will, but men moved by the Holy Spirit spoke from God" (2 Pet 1:21, NASB). Thus, everything that was written in Scripture was important to the apostles. Scripture can give encouragement, hope, and theological guidance and correction because it is God who speaks through it to us.

The Old Testament Evidence for Scripture Being Authoritative and Normative

Already in the Old Testament we find some evidence of a canonical, and thus authoritative, self-consciousness in the sense that there is a recognition that what was written is given by God to rule and direct His people.[10] Written documentation accompanies the covenant relationship between God and His people and these written words are intended to guide and rule their lives. In the Old Testament we read

---

[8] For a detailed discussion of the inner-biblical hermeneutics that Jesus and the apostles used, see chapter 8 by Richard M. Davidson, "Inner-Biblical Hermeneutics: The Use of Scripture by Bible Writers," in the present volume.

[9] John Stott, *Christ in Conflict: Lessons from Jesus and His Controversies* (Downers Grove, IL: InterVarsity, 2013), 86; John Wenham, *Christ and the Bible*, 3rd ed. (Grand Rapids, MI: Baker, 1994): 16–44, esp. 17; and Mark D. Thompson, "The Generous Gift of a Gracious Father: Toward a Theological Account of the Clarity of Scripture," in *The Enduring Authority of the Christian Scriptures*, ed. D. A. Carson (Grand Rapids, MI: Eerdmans, 2016), 632.

[10] Here we follow the argument ably set forth in Ferguson, 50–54.

that Moses not only proclaimed the "words of the LORD," but also "wrote all the words of the LORD" (Exod 24:3–4). Similarly, to Jeremiah God said, "Write in a book all the words that I have spoken to you" (Jer 30:2) and to Habakkuk God commanded, "Record the vision and inscribe it on tables" (Hab 2:2–3) so that future readers would have access to it. Thus, Scripture tells us that God's covenantal revelation should be written, preserved, and passed on.[11] The phrase "the word of the Lord came to me" occurs so often that it can be considered to be a foundational element of prophetic self-consciousness in the Old Testament. We can say that the Old Testament grew from this root.[12]

The New Testament Evidence for Scripture Being Authoritative and Normative

The New Testament recognizes the divinely given books that are part of the canon we now know as the Old Testament, and both Jesus and the apostles use Old Testament Scripture in a normative canonical sense. The New Testament use of words like "Scripture" (*graphē*) or such expressions as "the law and the prophets" or "it is written" or "God said" and "scripture says" illustrate the fact that the New Testament writers understood Scripture to be sacred, authoritative, and normative.[13]

---

[11] Cf. Exodus 17:14; 24:4; 31:18; 34:27; Deuteronomy 10:5; 29:29; 31:9–12, 25–26. See also Deuteronomy 4:2; 5:22, 32; 6:4–8; 29:9; 30:9–10, 15–16; Joshua 1:7–8; 8:34; 1 Kings 2:3; Nehemiah 8:8–18; 9:3; Jeremiah 30:2. Cf. John C. Peckham, *Canonical Theology: The Biblical Canon, Sola Scriptura, and Theological Method* (Grand Rapids, MI: Eerdmans, 2016), 31, for more references in support of this fact.

[12] See the discussion in Peckham, *Canonical Theology*, 16–47; and Robert I. Vasholz, *The Old Testament Canon in the Old Testament Church: The Internal Rational for Old Testament Canonicity* (Lewiston, NY: Edwin Mellen Press, 1990). On the issue of the Old Testament canon, see Roger T. Beckwith, *The Old Testament Canon of the New Testament Church and Its Background in Early Judaism* (London: SCPK: 1985); Sid Z. Leiman, *The Canonization of Hebrew Scripture: The Talmudic and Midrashic Evidence* (Hamden, CT: Transactions of the Connecticut Academy of Arts and Sciences, 1976); F. F. Bruce, *The Canon of Scripture* (Downers Grove, IL: InterVarsity, 1988), David G. Dunbar, "The Biblical Canon," in *Hermeneutics, Authority and Canon*, ed. D. A. Carson and John D. Woodbridge (Grand Rapids, MI: Zondervan, 1986), 299–362, esp. 301–315; Graham A. Cole, "Why a Book? Why This Book? Why the Particular Order Within This Book? Some Theological Reflections on the Canon," in *The Enduring Authority of the Christian Scriptures*, ed. D. A. Carson (Grand Rapids, MI: Eerdmans, 2016), 456–476; and more recently Andreas J. Köstenberger and Michael J. Kruger, *The Heresy of Orthodoxy: How Contemporary Culture's Fascination With Diversity Has Reshaped Our Understanding of Early Christianity* (Wheaton, IL: Crossway, 2010); Michael J. Kruger, *Canon Revisited: Establishing the Origins and Authority of the New Testament Books* (Wheaton, IL: Crossway, 2012); and Kruger, *The Question of Canon: Challenging the Status Quo in the New Testament Debate* (Downers Grove, IL: InterVarsity, 2013).

[13] Gottlob Schrenk, "Γράφω, Γραφή, Γράμμα, Ἐγγράφω, Προγράφω, Ὑπογραμμός," in *Theological Dictionary of the New Testament*, ed. Gerhard Kittel, Geoffrey W. Bromiley, and Gerhard Friedrich,

With regard to the Old Testament Jesus believed that Moses taught the Word of God (Mark 7:10–13). David wrote under inspiration (Mark 12:36). For Jesus the inspired writings of the Old Testament were normative (John 10:35; Luke 16:17). In a similar manner, the apostles affirmed that in the Old Testament God spoke through the mouth of His prophets (Acts 3:21). What the holy Scriptures say is inspired by God (Acts 1:16; 2 Tim 3:16; Heb 3:7) and hence, what Scripture says, God says (Rom 9:17; Gal 3:8). Hence Scripture is accepted as truth (Pss 12:6; 19:7–8; 119:160; John 17:17; 5:46–47). The apostolic confession in the New Testament states that the apostle served the God of his fathers, "believing all things which are written in the law and in the prophets" (Acts 24:14, KJV). For the apostle Paul it was clear that "*whatever* was written in earlier times was written for our instruction so that though perseverance and encouragement of the Scriptures we might have hope" (Rom 15:4, NASB, emphasis supplied).[14]

The New Testament Evidence About Its Divine Revelation, Inspiration, and Authority

The New Testament writers affirm that "no prophecy was ever made by an act of human will, but men moved by the Holy Spirit spoke from God" (2 Pet 1:21, NASB). The messages of the apostles were regarded as given by divine authority and the "N[ew] T[estament] evidence suggests the apostles viewed themselves and others as divinely commissioned, often explicitly in virtue of their apostolic connection to the risen Christ."[15] Paul believed that the things he spoke were "not in words taught by human wisdom but by the Spirit" (1 Cor 2:13, NASB). That is why their message was received by the apostolic church "not as the word of men, but for what it really is, the word of God" (1 Thess 2:13, NASB). The apostle Paul followed his divine commission as an apostle who was "not sent from men nor though the agency of man, but through Jesus Christ and God the Father" (Gal 1:1). The gospel he preached was received "through a revelation of Jesus Christ" (Gal 1:12; cf. 1 Cor 2:13; Eph. 3:3–5; 1 Thess 2:13).Therefore, believers are called to uphold the gospel message

---

vol. 1 (Grand Rapids, MI: Eerdmans, 1964), 755, points out that this was the later Judaistic view of Scripture. On the use of the term "Scripture," see Benjamin B. Warfield, "'Scripture,' 'the Scriptures,' in the New Testament," in *The Works of Benjamin B. Warfield: Revelation and Inspiration*, vol. 1. (Bellingham, WA: Logos Bible Software, 2008), 113–168; and his longer article under the same title in *The Princeton Theological Review* 8/1–4 (1910): 560–656.

[14] Cf. the parallelism between Romans 15:4 and 15:5, where the perseverance and encouragement of Scripture is parallel to the perseverance and encouragement of God.

[15] Peckham, *Canonical Theology*, 28–29.

and should not depart from it (Gal 1:8–12; 2 Cor 11:2–4). The apostolic words as recorded in Scripture should be upheld by the believers (cf. 2 Tim 1:13; 2 Thess 2:15; 3:14; 2 John 9–10; Jude 3) and functioned to "exhort in sound doctrine and to refute those who contradict" (Titus 1:9 NASB). For the apostle Paul the Scriptures are "the oracles of God" (Rom 3:1–2).This is why the Bible is called "holy Scriptures" (Rom 1:2). A careful study of the way in which Jesus used the term "the Scriptures," "it is Written," and similar expressions demonstrates that He attributed the Hebrew Scriptures with ultimate and unquestionable authority.[16] For Jesus, Scripture was the Word of God that cannot be broken (John 10:35). He repudiated the temptations of the devil with a decisive "It is Written"(Matt 4:4, 7, 10). He frequently appealed to Scripture as forecasting His messianic ministry (Luke 4:17–21; John 5:39–47), and after His resurrection He explained from all the Scriptures to His disciples the things concerning Himself (Luke 24:27).

We can clearly say that the words of Scripture were "regarded as trustworthy, accurately representing the divine message," and they carried divine authority and had the power to settle controversial issues.[17] Jesus showed us an attitude of reverent assent and voluntary submission to the Scriptures of the Old Testament. While He referred to the human writers of the Old Testament Scriptures, He took it for granted that there was a single divine Author behind them all.[18]

Furthermore, among the New Testament writers there is a consciousness that as a whole the authority of their writings is on par with that of the Old Testament.[19] Paul also acknowledges the inspiration and authority

---

[16] Schrenk, 1:745, points out that "in the OT writing down is an important mark of revelation. . . The authoritative significance of writing in the OT, in so far as it mediates the declaration of the will of God, is fully endorsed in the NT."

[17] Richard M. Davidson, "Who Is the Author of the Bible?" in *Interpreting Scripture: Bible Questions and Answers*, ed. Gerhard Pfandl (Silver Spring, MD: Review and Herald, 2010), 3. When faced with insidious temptations, Jesus referred back to Scripture to refute the temptations of the devil! See also Richard M. Davidson, "The Bible and Hermeneutics: Interpreting Scripture According to the Scriptures," in *Christ in the Classroom: Adventist Approaches to the Integration of Faith and Learning*, ed. Humberto M. Rasi, vol. 31-B (Silver Spring, MD: Education Department, General Conference of Seventh-day Adventists, 2004), 82–131; and Richard M. Davidson, "Interpreting Scripture According to Scripture," *Perspective Digest* 17/2 (2012).

[18] John Stott, 86–87, writes, "He could equally say 'Moses said' or 'God said.' He could quote a comment of the narrator in Genesis 2:24 as an utterance of the Creator himself. Similarly, he said, "Isaiah was right when he prophesied about you" (Matthew 15:7) when what he then went on to quote is the direct speech of the Lord God."

[19] For instance, John introduces quotations from the Old Testament with the words "it is written" (John 6:31; 8:17; 12:14; etc.). It is a phrase that expresses the authority of what is being quoted (see Ferguson, 51). Yet a similar expression, "these are written," marks the end of John's own gospel

of other parts of the New Testament. In 1 Timothy 5:18 he quotes a word of Jesus as Scripture: "For the Scripture says, 'You shall not muzzle an ox while it treads out the grain,' and, 'The labourer is worthy of his wages'" (NKJV). The first part is a quote from Deuteronomy 25:4 and the second from Luke 10:7. Both statements are listed and quoted on equal standing as Scripture. Similarly, Peter refers to the writings of Paul as Scripture (2 Pet 3:16). Thus, it has been pointed out that "the New Testament writings, generally speaking, were intended to be documents with an authority equivalent to that of Scripture."[20] No wonder the New Testament believers are depicted as "continually devoting themselves to the apostle's teaching" (Acts 2:42). When they searched the Scriptures and received the Word readily the believers in Berea were praised (Acts 17:11).

The Divine-Human Dimension of Scripture

Our understanding of the origin and nature of Scripture significantly influences the way we read and treat the Bible. If the Bible is a human book that was written just like any other book and was put together by fallible human beings, we could not fully trust it and it certainly would not carry divine authority. The biblical writers clearly state that through them God speaks in what they write and communicate. If we acknowledge this fact at face value, it means that in the Bible we have a most unusual and unique object that is beyond the limited bounds of immanent reality. The respect for this supernatural reality demands to be taken seriously when we interpret the Bible. To ignore it would amount to an ideological surrender of the divine singularity and particularity of the biblical message.[21]A denial of the supernatural dimension would affect the interpretation of Scripture because it shapes the very methods that are employed to investigate and explain the Bible.[22] Without an acknowledgement of the divine dimension in the

---

(John 20:31). Here the verb *grapho* (write) seems to retain its quasi authoritative sense (cf. Pilate's words in John 19:22: "What I have written, I have written"). Letters of the apostles were read not only by the church but alongside the sacred writings of the Old Testament in and to the church (Col 4:16). In the book of Revelation, the reader is warned not to add anything or take away anything (Rev 22:18–19). This seems to echo the warning in the Old Testament (Deut 4:2). The book of Revelation seems to claim the same authority assumed by the Old Testament itself.

[20] Kruger, *The Question of Canon*, 154.

[21] Cf. Maier, esp. 22.

[22] Murray Rae, "Theological Interpretation and Historical Criticism" in *A Manifesto for Theological Interpretation*, ed. Craig G. Bartholomew and Heath A. Thomas (Grand Rapids, MI: Baker Academic, 2016), 103, says "that if God is involved in history, then any non-theological account of what history is and of its telos will be 'inadequate at best, or simply false.'"

origin of Scripture, the Bible has to be interpreted solely with the nexus of immanent cause and effect.

Adventists, however, believe that the Scriptures come to us as the oracles of God, and therefore the Bible carries divine authority. But what does that mean? The English word "authority" is derived from the Latin *auctoritas* and refers to the reputation of persons and their capacity to exercise influence.[23] It stems from the recognition of someone's superior excellence in a given sphere.[24] Thus, when we speak of the authority of Scripture we express the idea that the Bible has the superior right to command us what to do, to exact obedience, and to determine and judge the validity and rightness of our faith and practice.[25] As such, Scripture has the right to guide us and does have the final word in our theology. Its message is filled with the aroma of truth.

The Christological Analogy of Scripture

Just as Christ's authority originates out of divine love and is defined by truth, so the Scriptures speak to us with that same authority. It has long been recognized that there exists a profound parallel between Christ, the Word made flesh, and Scripture, the Word of God expressed in human language. Ellen G. White draws attention to this parallel between Christ and the Bible when she writes,

> The union of the divine and the human, manifest in Christ, exists also in the Bible. The truths revealed are all "given by inspiration of God;" yet they are expressed in the words of men and are adapted to human needs. Thus it may be said of the Book of God, as it was of Christ, that "the Word was made flesh and dwelt among us." And this fact, so far from being an argument against the Bible, should strengthen faith in it as the word of God.[26]

---

[23] Rolf Schieder, "Authority. II. History and Theology," in *Religion Past & Present: Encyclopedia of Theology and Religion*, ed. Hans Dieter Betz et al., vol. 1 (Leiden: Brill, 2007), 519. See also Waldemar Molinski, "Authority," in *Encyclopedia of Theology: The Concise Sacramentum Mundi*, ed. Karl Rahner (New York: Seabury Press, 1975), 61.

[24] Molinski, 61.

[25] Cf. H. D. McDonald, "Authority," in *Evangelical Dictionary of Theology*, ed. Walter A. Elwell, 2nd ed. (Grand Rapids, MI: Baker Academic, 2001), 153. N. T. Wright, *Scripture and the Authority of God* (New York: Harper Collins, 2013), 21, points out that "'the Authority of Scripture' Is a Shorthand for 'God's Authority Exercised *through* Scripture.'"

[26] Ellen G. White, *Testimonies for the Church*, vol. 5 (Nampa, ID: Pacific Press, 1948), 747.

The parallel often has been expressed in terms of the servant form of both Christ and the Bible. Bernard Ramm notes, "Both the divine Savior and the divine Scriptures bear *the form of a servant* even though both contain within themselves the divine glory."[27] While limitations to the christological analogy exist,[28] it is appropriate to apply to the Scriptures what was said of the words of Jesus: "No man ever spoke like this Man!" (John 7:46, NKJV), and also, "He taught as one having authority" (Matt 7:29, NKJV). While Christ "made himself nothing, taking the very nature of a servant, being made in human likeness" (Phil 2:7, NIV), yet He spoke with divine authority. Likewise, while the Scriptures are given in the weakness and imperfection of human language,[29] nevertheless, "every word of God is pure" (Prov 30:5, NKJV), "is truth" (John 17:17), "is living and powerful" (Heb 4:12, NKJV), "cannot be broken" (John 10:35), and "stands forever" (Isa 40:8, NKJV). Just as Jesus was a true human being, yet wanted to be acknowledged not just as a human being but for what He truly was—the Son of God—so Scripture is given in true human words, but wants to be accepted for what it also is: the Word of the Living God. As such, the words of Scripture address us with the divine authority of the one true God and invite an obedient response.

Apart from God's highest and most explicit revelation, that we can see in the incarnation of His Son Jesus Christ, the most efficient and widely used form of divine revelation can be found in the words of inspired Scripture. Interestingly, for Jesus, and the apostles as well as the Old Testament biblical writers, human language was never a barrier to effective communication by God.[30] In the Bible we find repeated references to the God who speaks.[31] His Word is given to His spokespersons the prophets. The numerous references to phrases like the "word

---

[27] Bernard Ramm, *Special Revelation and the Word of God* (Grand Rapids, MI: Eerdmans, 1961), 34.

[28] The Bible is the written Word of God but it is not the incarnation of the Word! Only Christ Jesus became flesh and blood, a truly human being. We are saved by faith in Christ alone; we are not saved by a book, even though we would not know about Christ's salvation without the Bible.

[29] Ellen G. White, *Selected Messages*, vol. 1 (Washington, DC: Review and Herald, 1958), 20, makes this comparison: "The Bible is not given to us in grand superhuman language. Jesus, in order to reach man where he is, took humanity. The Bible must be given in the language of men. Everything that is human is imperfect."

[30] Cf. Frank M. Hasel and Michael G. Hasel, *How to Interpret Scripture* (Nampa, ID: Pacific Press, 2019), 21–27. See also Grudem, 20; and Peter F. Jensen, "God and the Bible," in Carson, *Enduring Authority*, 477–496.

[31] This is pointed out in critical conversation with philosophical concepts that challenge the idea that God speaks and communicates effectively with human beings, in the set by Carl F. H. Henry, *God, Revelation, and Authority*, 6 vols. (Wheaton, IL: Crossway, 1999).

of the Lord," or "thus says the Lord," or the "word that the Lord spoke" testify to this fact. This divine speaking is the Word of the Lord and eventually leads to the embodiment in a written document. The writing down of God's Word also is the result of God's initiative (Exod 17:14; 24:4; Josh 24:26; etc.).

What is the purpose for God's written revelation? God could have taught His people without Scripture.[32] But God saw it fit to make His Word accessible in written form. As such it is a constant reference point for His people. It enables God's people to continually hear it and be careful to do what it says (cf. Deut 30:9–10). A written document can be preserved better and more reliably than an oral message. There is greater permanency with a written text than an orally spoken word. A written document protects against the infirmities of memory and can be defended more easily against deceits and corruptions. A written document can be copied and multiplied, and thus made available to many more people in many different locations than any oral message could ever be. And it is available across time and can be a blessing to readers and listeners many generations later. As a written record, it remains a norm for the veracity of the biblical message throughout the ages.

The Self-Testimony of Scripture and Implications for its Interpretation

Any thoughtful student of Holy Scripture will take the self-testimonial passages (cf. the classic texts in 2 Pet 1:19–21; 2 Tim 3:16; etc.) seriously and will not ignore them.[33] While the divine origin of Scripture is clearly attested in the Bible, the writers of the biblical books were not simply God's mechanical pens but His penmen—that is, they wrote in their own characteristic style, language, and thought form under the guidance of the Holy Spirit. Some biblical books—like

---

[32] This has been pointed out by Cole, "Why a Book?," 468–470.

[33] Peter Maarten van Bemmelen, *Issues in Biblical Inspiration: Sanday and Warfield* (Berrien Springs, MI: Andrews University Press, 1987), 377, raises the point that "once Scripture is accepted as the only legitimate starting-point and source of reference in our quest, we must face up to the question whether the effort to establish the doctrine of inspiration by letting the Bible speak for itself should proceed primarily from the multifarious phenomena of the content and structure of Scripture or whether it should start from the explicit assertions of the biblical writers or whether both should receive equal standing." Van Bemmelen concludes, "The inherent logic of the principle to let Scripture speak for itself requires that the teachings (or assertions, claims, or whatever other terms may be used) should be given priority over the phenomena. We use advisedly the word priority, for the phenomena cannot and should not be ignored" (ibid., 378).

Kings, Chronicles, and the Gospel of Luke—provide evidence of careful historical research (1 Kgs 22:39, 45; 1 Chr 29:29; Luke 1:1–4). In all this, "the Holy Spirit's guidance did not overrule the thinking and the writing process of biblical writers but supervised the process of writing in order to maximize clarity of the ideas and to prevent, if necessary, the distortion of revelation, or changing divine truth into a lie."[34] If we believe that the claims the biblical writers make about God in the text of Scripture are divine revelation, then our hermeneutical method to interpret Scripture cannot proceed on the basis of metaphysical naturalism.[35] A Seventh-day Adventist student of the Bible, therefore, will carefully avoid any interpretive methods that are in conflict with the explicit claims of the Bible.[36] Methods that read and interpret Holy Scripture "as if God would not exist" (*etsi Deus non daretur*) do not do justice to the worldview that we encounter in the biblical text and therefore are not appropriate for a Seventh-day Adventist biblical hermeneutic.[37]

---

[34] Fernando Luis Canale, "Revelation and Inspiration," in Reid, 65.

[35] Metaphysical naturalism is the view that "for science to be science, by definition it can pursue, identify, and entertain only natural causes as plausible explanations of natural phenomena with the universe as a whole regarded as it were a closed system of natural causes" (Brad Gregory, "No Room for God? History, Science, Metaphysics, and the Study of Religion," *History and Theory* 47 [December 2008]: 506, as quoted in Rae, 97–98). Cf. Alvin Plantinga "Two (or More) Kinds of Scripture Scholarship," in *"Behind" the Text: History and Biblical Interpretation*, ed. Craig Bartholomew et al., (Grand Rapids, MI: Zondervan, 2003), 19–57. See also the discussion in chapter 6 by Leonard Brand, "Faith, Science, and Biblical Interpretation," in the present volume.

[36] While nobody will deny that all theologians and historians approach the text with some presuppositions, V. Philips Long, "'Competing Histories, Competing Theologies?' Reflections on the Unity and Diversity of the Old Testament's (Readers)," in Carson, *Enduring Authority*, 372, points out that careful "reflection reveals that it is not just historians but historical methods themselves that assume a 'philosophical or theological base.' Methods are neither neutral nor self-evident. Rather than assuming, therefore, that 'method' provides a value-free zone, where bias is quashed and background beliefs can be safely ignored, interpreters must instead recognize that scholarly methods themselves, no less than those employing them, are undergirded by 'control beliefs.' Indeed, control beliefs, or worldviews, are involved at every level of scholarly engagement." According to Long this also means that as an interpreter I have to "seek to gain a more conscious awareness of my own worldview, but I must also seek to discover the worldview embodied in the text I am studying, the worldview undergirding the method I am applying, and the worldviews held by other interpreters whose writings I may consult. . . . If the interpreter's model of reality is distinctly different from that embodied in the text, there will be tension. If a method is applied to a text whose fundamental assumptions about the world and reality run counter to the assumptions underlying the method, there will be tensions. If interpreters approaching a given text disagree fundamentally on how they view reality, they will likely also disagree on how to interpret the text, or at least on whether the text, once interpreted, is to be believed and obeyed" (V. Philips Long, *The Art of Biblical History* [Grand Rapids, MI: Zondervan, 1994], 172, as quoted in Long, "Competing Histories," 372).

[37] The well-known New Testament scholar Adolf Schlatter, who taught at the University of Tübin-

On the other hand, any responsible interpretation of Scripture will take seriously the historical character of God's revelation and the biblical text that tells us about it.

The Historical Character of Scripture and Hermeneutical Implications

The biblical message has the double characteristic of being written in truly human words and at the same time claiming to be truly God's Word. The God of Scripture is not timeless,[38] but reveals Himself in time and space.[39] In other words, God's message in Scripture is historically constituted.[40] The biblical writers wrote in specific historical circumstances and in specific cultural contexts that can shed light on the meaning of some biblical passages.[41] They used existing human languages (that is, Hebrew, Aramaic, and Koine Greek). Hebrew and Greek have their own linguistic and grammatical peculiarities and the understanding of them is relevant for our interpretation of Scripture. Thus, we must take into account the typical features of the language in which it was written as well as the history and culture in which it originated and was first transmitted. At the same time, a careful interpretation of Scripture will not be limited to a methodological naturalism where everything is explained by purely immanent cause and effect relationships. An Adventist hermeneutic will take seriously the historical character of Scripture and yet will not categorically negate the supernatural dimension that is attested in many

---

gen, points out the problematic nature of such an atheistic approach in biblical interpretation in *Atheistische Methoden in der Theologie* (Wuppertal: R. Brockhaus, 1985).

[38] On the problem of God's eternal timelessness, see Fernando Luis Canale, *A Criticism of Theological Reason: Time and Timelessness as Primordial Presuppositions*, Andrews University Seminary Doctoral Dissertation Series, vol. X (Berrien Springs, MI: Andrews University Press, 1983).

[39] "A striking feature of the biblical witness is that God is identified again and again through reference to historical events. . . . The Bible does not present us with a set of timeless or universal truths that can be abstracted from history but directs our attention to the God who makes himself known precisely through the particularities of history. On the face of it, therefore, attention to what goes on in history is an imperative of biblical faith" (Rae, 96).

[40] Rather than being historically conditioned by purely immanent cause and effect relations, and thereby rendering Scripture relative and not universally binding, God's written Word is divinely conditioned and historically constituted. Thus, it remains binding upon all men at all ages and in all places (Frank M. Hasel, "Reflections on the Authority and Trustworthiness of Scripture," in *Issues in Revelation and Inspiration*, ed. Frank Holbrook and Leo Van Dolson [Berrien Springs, MI: Adventist Theological Society, 1992], 208–209).

[41] For some illustrations of how biblical customs differ from our modern Western situation and culture, see Gerhard F. Hasel, *Understanding the Living Word of God* (Mountain View, CA: Pacific Press, 1980), 44–46.

places in the Bible. Instead it requires an openness on the side of the interpreter to the supernatural element of God's reality in history.[42] Such openness to the divine dimension of Scripture includes a willingness to be obedient to the Word and a readiness in humility to subject even our reason to the Word of God. Prayer in the work with the word of Scripture expresses our need for guidance through the Holy Spirit.[43]

The Literary Character of Scripture and Hermeneutical Implications

Since Scripture is composed of human words and these words are grouped together in meaningful sentences, a biblical hermeneutic will be knowledgeable of the biblical languages and their translation, grammar, and rhetoric.[44] Familiarity with the biblical languages will greatly help the interpreter to better understand the biblical meaning and usage of certain terms and concepts. As a literary work, the interpretation of Scripture requires sound philological methods for its proper understanding.

It is part of the foundational conviction of Protestant and Seventh-day Adventist hermeneutics that the literary[45] meaning of holy Scripture

---

[42] "If God exists and is involved in history, however, as the biblical writers attest, then a naturalistic historiography will severely inhibit our capacity to understand what is going on in the world. Furthermore, the imposition of naturalistic constraints that preclude the inquirer from discerning what is really going on can hardly be counted as good scholarship. Only with a radically different, nonnaturalistic account of what history is will it be possible for readers of Scripture to apprehend what has gone on in the past in sympathy with, rather than in direct opposition to, the biblical writers themselves" (Rae, 103). Gerhard F. Hasel, "Biblical Theology: Then, Now, and Tomorrow," *Horizons in Biblical Theology* 4 (1982): 75–76, argues for an approach to biblical theology that "seeks to do justice to all dimensions of reality to which the biblical texts testify." On the historical character of the Bible and the different connotations of what history involves, see chapter 4 by Michael G. Hasel, "History, the Bible, and Hermeneutics," in the present volume.

[43] On the presuppositions of openness, faith, humility, obedience, love, and prayer in the hermeneutical task, see the brief discussion in Frank M. Hasel, "Presuppositions in the Interpretation of Scripture," 33–35. On the role of reason in theology, see Frank M. Hasel, "Theology and the Role of Reason," *Journal of the Adventist Theological Society* 4/2 (1993): 171–198, and for the role of reason in the task of Biblical hermeneutics see Ángel Manuel Rodríguez, "Human Reason and Biblical Hermeneutics: An Introduction," *Journal of the Adventist Theological Society*, 27/1–2 (2016): 85–97.

[44] This is one reason why the Protestant Reformers were keen to emphasize the need for a good knowledge of the biblical languages and this is why the study of Hebrew and Greek has been a hallmark of every solid theological education. On rhetorical criticism, see chapter 14 by Frank M. Hasel, "Some Recent Trends in Methods of Biblical Interpretation," in the present volume.

[45] We use the phrase "literary" meaning, rather than "literal" meaning. The literary meaning certainly includes the literal meaning of the Bible, but we also find many figures of speech and

can be understood through a careful study of the historical-grammatical meaning of the biblical text.[46] When Jesus and the apostles refer their conversation partners back to Scripture and raise the questions "What is written in the law? How do you read it?" (Luke 10:26) and "What is written?" (Luke 22:37; cf. 1 Cor 4:6; Rev 1:3), they implicitly assume that Scripture has a definite meaning and that this meaning can be discovered and clearly determined.[47] Otherwise such questions would not make sense. If God wanted to communicate His thoughts in Hebrew, Aramaic, or Greek, He was able to do this successfully in a way that could be understood because human language has the potential and carries the ability to express meaning distinctly and unambiguously.[48]

---

symbolic language in Scripture. Such figures of speech and symbols reflect a rather nonliteral usage of biblical language. When we talk about the literary meaning of Scripture, we refer to the meaning the writers of the Bible have placed in the text (see J. Scott Duvall and J. Daniel Hays, *Grasping God's Word: A Hands-On Approach to Reading, Interpreting, and Applying the Bible* [Grand Rapids, MI: Zondervan, 2012], 206–207).

[46] Martin Luther has insisted against his Roman Catholic opponents and against the fourfold allegorical interpretation of the biblical text that only the literal meaning can be accepted as expressed in the grammar and normal use of language. Cf. *D. Martin Luthers Werke. Kritische Gesamtausgabe* (Weimar: Bohlau, 1883–1983), [hereinafter *WA*] *WA* 7,650,20–21; *WA* 18,700,33ff. This has been pointed out by Armin Buchholz, *Schrift Gottes im Lehrstreit: Luthers Schriftverständnis und Schriftauslegung in seinen drei großen Lehrstreitigkeiten der Jahre 1521–28* (Frankfurt: Peter Lang, 1993), esp. 76–77. This does not deny the fact that some passages of Scripture are more difficult to understand, as the apostle Peter readily acknowledges about some things Paul has written (2 Pet 3:15–16). It is useful to remember that Peter did not say that everything Paul wrote in his letters is difficult to understand. Our confidence that even difficult texts can be understood is anchored in God's desire to communicate effectively with us and the fact that human language ultimately is not a human invention, but rather God's gift, and as such is reflective of His own capacities as the Giver (Thompson, "Generous Gift of a Gracious Father," 634). D. A. Carson, "Is the Doctrine of 'Claritas Scripturae' Still Relevant Today?," in *Dein Wort ist die Wahrheit: Festschrift für Gerhard Maier*, ed. Eberhard Hahn, Rolf Hille, and Hans-Werner Neudorfer (Wuppertal: R. Brockhaus, 1997), 97, points out that the question of the clarity of Scripture is of enormous importance because "one can talk endlessly about the centrality of Scripture, the authority of Scripture, the truthfulness of Scripture, and so forth, but none of this has more than theoretical interest unless some form of responsible doctrine of claritas scripturae—what the English-speaking world often refers to as the perspicuity of Scripture—can be sustained."

[47] See the detailed discussion in Thompson, "Generous Gift of a Gracious Father," 624–632.

[48] While words have the capacity to miscommunicate when they are abused—deliberately or otherwise—we should also not lose sight of the fact that "most of our human communication succeeds most of the time and God is certainly not subject to our propensity to confuse or deceive" (Thompson, "Generous Gift of a Gracious Father," 634). Furthermore, "often the difficulty of such texts is magnified because they are treated in isolation from their context in the whole of Scripture" (ibid., 639). Hence the hermeneutical principle of letting Scripture be its own interpreter, where one text is compared with other canonical passages, can help overcome many difficulties. The biblical canon thus becomes an important

This does not mean that there are no passages in Scripture that are difficult to understand (2 Pet 3:16) or that words and sentences can be used to deceive and mislead others. But the fact that we can detect such a deception shows that a correct reading and understanding must be possible. We can expect that God, who delights in truthfulness and has called us not to bear false witness (Exod 20:16), would abide by the same truthfulness and not deceive us or mislead us in the things He communicates.

While the meaning of words and the structure of grammar and syntax can be complex, they are not arbitrary. It is possible to find out what the author meant by carefully studying the usage of words within a specific literary, historical, and cultural context. An allegorical interpretation of Scripture, in contrast, while not denying divine inspiration, does not limit the meaning of the text to its literal sense and has a surplus of meaning that is no longer determined by the biblical text itself.[49] In an allegorical interpretation there is a second, third, and fourth meaning of the text that goes beyond the literal, grammatical-historical meaning of the words.[50] A grammatical-historical interpretation of the biblical text, on the other hand, looks "for the key to the text's sense in the text itself."[51] Thus, the exclusive criterion for an adequate theological understanding of Christian doctrine comes from the text of Scripture as perceived through a careful historical-grammatical analysis.[52] Martin Luther made clear that "the Holy Spirit is the most ingenious writer and speaker who is in heaven and earth. Therefore, his words cannot have more than the simple meaning, which we call the written

---

resource for reading Scripture rightly. This obviously involves a commitment to the unity of Scripture (Thompson, "Generous Gift of a Gracious Father," 639).

[49] On the problem of *sensus plenior*, or the "fuller sense," see Raymond E. Brown, *The 'Sensus Plenior' of Sacred Scripture* (Baltimore, MD: St. Mary's University, 1955) and for a critical interaction from a Protestant perspective, see Douglas J. Moo, "The Problem of Sensus Plenior," in Carson and Woodbridge, *Hermeneutics, Authority, and Canon* (Grand Rapids, MI: Zondervan, 1986), 179–211, esp. 201–204; and Douglas J. Moo and Andrews David Naselli, "The Problem of the New Testament's Use of the Old Testament," in Carson, *Enduring Authority*, 730–734.

[50] The "*allegorical interpretation* looks for the hidden sense of a text with the aid of an interpretative key from outside it" (Werner G. Jeanrond, *Theological Hermeneutics: Development and Significance* [New York: Crossroad, 1991], 14). "*Allegorical Interpretation* of Scripture attempted to understand the spiritual meaning of a text with the help of perspectives not derived from the text and usually not even informed by it. Rather the text is understood symbolically: it points beyond itself to a deeper realty" (ibid., 17). The problem with this kind of interpretation is "the arbitrariness with which it tended to ignore many of the demands of the texts themselves" (ibid., 19). See also William W. Klein, Craig L. Blomberg, and Robert L. Hubbard Jr., *Introduction to Biblical Interpretation*, 3rd ed. (Grand Rapids, MI: Zondervan, 2017), 82–91.

[51] Jeanrond, 14.

[52] Ibid., 31.

or literal meaning."[53] In his dispute with Erasmus, Luther states, "In short, if Scripture is obscure or ambiguous, what point was there in God's giving it to us? . . . Those who deny that the Scriptures are quite clear and plain leave us nothing but darkness. . . . In opposition to you [Erasmus], I say with respect to the whole Scripture, I will not have any part of it called obscure."[54] Such a literary, historical-grammatical interpretation of the biblical text is very different from a literalistic reading of Scripture, where the context, grammar, and genre of the text is ignored and the interpretation of Scripture is distorted. A careful literary interpretation takes into consideration with as much ancient literary competence as possible the context of the passage, the biblical usage of words, the grammar, and syntax of the sentences. The literary, historical-grammatical interpretation of the biblical text takes into consideration that prose is interpreted as prose, that poetry is treated as poetry, that a parable is a parable, that a figure of speech is a figure of speech, or typology is interpreted accordingly. In the final analysis, the entirety of the biblical text is accepted as authoritative and remains the norm for its own understanding. Thus, the text of Scripture provides the clues that determine the meaning of a biblical statement. The meaning of the biblical text is accessible through a thoughtful and careful study of these literary parameters. In other words, it is Scripture in its totality that provides the context to help determine the use of its own words and how thoughts are expressed through them. This has been called the external clarity of Scripture.[55]

---

[53] *WA*, 7,650,21f (author's translation of the following statement: "Der heylig geyst ist der aller eynfeltigst schreyber und rether, der ynn hymell und erden ist, drumb auch seyne wortt nit mehr denn eynen einfeltigsten synn haben kunden, wilchen wir den schrifftlichen odder buchsablischen tzungen synn nennen"). See also Luther's statement "that Scripture has a simple and pure natural meaning of the words; it has a grammar and use of language that God created in humanity" ("ubique inhaerendum est simplici puraeque et naturali significationi verborum, quam grammatica et usus loquendi habet, quem Deus creavit in hominibus" (*WA*, 18,700,33ff, author's translation). John Calvin, *The Epistles of Paul to Galatians, Ephesians, Philippians and Colossians* (Edinburgh: Oliver and Boyd, 1965), 85, comments that the exegete must grasp the true sense of Scripture that is genuine and simple (*qui germanus est et simplex*).

[54] Martin Luther, *Luther's Works*, vol. 33: *Career of the Reformer III*, ed. Jaroslav Jan Pelikan, Hilton C. Oswald, and Helmut T. Lehmann (Philadelphia, PA: Fortress, 1999), 93–94.

[55] The clarity of Scripture does not mean that every part of the Bible is equally easy to understand or equally and uniformly clear and that every opinion of what the biblical text means is equally valuable. It means, however, that human language itself is a gift from God and God has chosen to communicate His redemptive purposes in language He gave to His image-bearers (so Thompson, "Generous Gift of a Gracious Father," 615–643). The clarity of Scripture is that quality of the Bible that arises from the fact that God ensures that the meaning of the text is accessible to all who come to it in faith. We don't need a teaching

Ellen G. White and the pioneers also support and affirm the need of a careful reading and interpretation of Scripture that takes into consideration all that Scripture says on a given subject and also takes into consideration the historical and literary context.[56] Ellen G. White affirms a literal interpretation of Scripture that is cognizant of the historical and literary contexts and the meaning of words,[57] and in this sense supports that we should take Scripture "just as it reads."[58]

---

magisterium to teach us what is clearly being said in Scripture. The clarity of Scripture does not mean that there are no disputes in interpretation, but that the resolution of such disputes is found in a careful study of Scripture itself, not in any other authority. Cf. D. A. Carson, "Summarizing FAQs," in *Enduring Authority*, 1170. On the clarity of Scripture, see Friedrich Beisser, *Claritas Scripturae bei Martin Luther* (Göttingen: Vandenhoeck & Ruprecht, 1966); Rudolf Hermann, *Von der Klarheit der Heiligen Schrift: Untersuchungen und Erörterungen über Luthers Lehre von der Schrift* (Berlin: Evangelische Verlagsanstalt, 1958); Bernhard Rothen, *Die Klarheit der Schrift: Teil 1 Martin Luther: die wiederentdeckten Grundlagen* (Göttingen: Vandenhoeck & Ruprecht, 1990); Mark D. Thompson, *A Clear and Present Word: The Clarity of Scripture*, ed. D. A. Carson, New Studies in Biblical Theology 21 (Downers Grove, IL: InterVarsity, 2006); and D. A. Carson, "Claritas Scripturae," 97–111; Moisés Silva, "Clear or Obscure? Reformation Doctrine and the Contemporary Challenge," in Lillback and Gaffin, 1095–1107; Frame, *Doctrine of the Word of God*, 201–209; Larry D. Pettegrew, "The Perspicuity of Scripture," *Master's Seminary Journal* 15, no. 2 (2004): 207–225; and from a Seventh-day Adventist perspective, Norman R. Gulley, *Systematic Theology*, vol. 1, *Prolegomena* (Berrien Springs, MI: Andrews University Press, 2003), 665–667.

[56] Gerhard Pfandl, "Ellen G. White and Hermeneutics," in Reid, 309–328, esp. 312–313. While Ellen G. White, *Selected Messages*, 1:16–17, acknowledges that some parts of Scripture are difficult to understand and that some passages have been obscured in the process of transmission, she affirms the basic clarity of Scripture—especially in matters of salvation, so that nobody needs to be lost (ibid., 1:18). She states, "Men of ability have devoted a lifetime of study and prayer to the searching of the Scriptures, and yet there are many portions of the Bible that have not been fully explored. Some passages of Scripture will never be perfectly comprehended until in the future life Christ shall explain them. There are mysteries to be unraveled, statements that human minds cannot harmonize. And the enemy will seek to arouse argument upon these points, which might better remain undiscussed." (*Gospel Worker*, [Hagerstown, MD: Review and Herald, 1943], 312). With regard to the interpretation of unfulfilled prophecy, Gerhard F. Hasel, "Foreword," in *Chariots of Salvation: The Biblical Drama of Armageddon*, ed. Hans K. LaRondelle (Hagerstown, MD: Review and Herald, 1987), 7, cautions against speculative interpretation, stating, "In regard to unfulfilled prophecy, there is always the danger for the interpreter to speculate or to subtly become a prophet himself."

[57] Pfandl, "Ellen G. White and Hermeneutics," 312–313.

[58] Cf. Ellen G. White, *Selected Messages*, 1:18; Ellen G. White, *Counsels on Stewardship* (Washington, DC: Review and Herald, 1940), 92; Ellen G. White, *Darkness Before Dawn* (Nampa, ID: Pacific Press, 1997), 7; Ellen G. White, *Evangelism* (Washington, DC: Review and Herald, 1947), 434; Ellen G. White, *The Great Controversy* (Mountain View, CA: Pacific Press, 1911), 521; and Ellen G. White, *Mind, Character and Personality*, vol. 1 (Nashville, TN: Southern Publishing, 1977), 93.

Other Important Factors in the Process of Interpretation

Beyond a biblical-historical-grammatical interpretation of Scripture that benefits from a good knowledge of the biblical languages, there are a few other factors that enhance or inhibit our ability to interpret Scripture correctly. We will briefly look at some of them.

Intellectual Openness and Carefulness

When we come to Scripture, we should approach it with an open mind, willing to learn from Scripture. This requires an openness to actually carefully listen to the biblical text. Such openness grants the biblical text the determinative role in its own interpretation, rather than superimposing one's own ideas on the text. Such openness will lead the interpreter to read and study the biblical text patiently, thoroughly, and carefully, again and again with open and alert eyes and a willingness to learn. Adolf Schlatter expresses this attitude of carefully observing Scripture by stating that the science of biblical interpretation "is first: seeing, and second: seeing; and third: seeing, and time and again seeing."[59] It is perhaps more from carelessness about biblical truth than from intentional deception that there is so much falsehood about biblical teachings. Carefulness in our interpretation of the Bible means that we refuse to rush to hasty conclusions based on limited knowledge and data. Instead we make sure that in our study of the Bible we are thorough and diligent, cautious not to overlook important details of the biblical text.[60] We should be committed to thinking and working carefully, in an even-handed and openminded way, listening to all the evidence at hand and even viewing issues of interpretation from the perspective of those with whom we disagree because we are aware that we might not have the most complete or accurate perspective on a given topic. Such carefulness also implies an intellectual honesty[61] of being committed not to distort the biblical truth by taking information out of context, exaggerating facts, or using loaded language. Nor will we use statistics or other supporting evidence that might have a deceptive effect on our interpretation. If we don't have a solution to a particular problem, it is

---

[59] Adolf Schlatter, "Atheistische Methoden in der Theologie?," in *Zur Theologie des Neuen Testaments und zur Dogmatik: Kleine Schriften*, ed. U. Luck (1969), 142, quoted in Helge Stadelmann, *Evangelikales Schriftverständnis: Die Bibel verstehen – der Bibel vertrauen* (Hammerbrücke: Jota, 2005), 116.

[60] On the virtue of intellectual carefulness, see Philip E. Dow, *Virtuous Minds: Intellectual Character Development* (Downers Grove, IL: InterVarsity, 2013), 32–38.

[61] On the importance of honesty in the pursuit of knowledge, see ibid., 61–69.

better to honestly acknowledge our tentative and incomplete knowledge rather than be dogmatic about our ignorance.

The Storyline of Scripture

Interpretation of the Bible requires not just a careful linguistic-grammatical analysis and exegesis of the biblical text. The Bible is not just a collection of short, disconnected words and sentences or unrelated paragraphs. The Bible tells many stories that are embedded in a large metanarrative. In Adventist parlance, the Bible tells us about the great controversy between good and evil. Themes of this grand story or metanarrative "are intertwined throughout the text from paragraph to paragraph. Numerous markers and connections tie these paragraphs together."[62] The message of Scripture is not restricted to small units of text, but is embedded within the larger flow of its story. While it is important to start with the small details at the sentence level, we also need to understand the larger units of the biblical material and see how different parts are connected to and fit into this larger storyline of Scripture.

Deficient and Wrong Approaches in Biblical Interpretation

The literary meaning of the biblical text is jeopardized on many fronts. On the one hand, there are pious and even devout readers of Scripture who come to the biblical text expecting mainly some personal edification. Here the Bible is sometimes used like a divine oracle and the decisive question often is: "What does the text say *to me*?" Whatever then comes to mind is interpreted as being God speaking subjectively to the individual person, no matter whether it is in harmony with the original context of the text or not.[63] Such spiritualizing of the biblical text often leads to quite arbitrary interpretations. When we attempt to find a deeper spiritual meaning for ourselves, we easily move into the area of reader response hermeneutics, as if *we* were the ones determining the meaning of the text instead of the text itself.[64] Rather than focusing on our personal situation, it would be better to first find out what the text actually does say and then accept this meaning and implement it into one's life and practice it.

---

[62] J. Scott Duvall and J. Daniel Hays, *Grasping God's Word: A Hands-On Approach to Reading, Interpreting, and Applying the Bible* (Grand Rapids, MI: Zondervan, 2012), 91.

[63] This has been aptly pointed out by Stadelmann, *Evangelikales Schriftverständnis*, 116.

[64] On reader-response criticism, see the discussions in chapter 14 by Frank M. Hasel, "Some Recent Trends in Hermeneutics," in the present volume.

Others ignore the historical context of Scripture and interpret the text by a loose association of certain aspects and words that are strung together, without allowing the Bible to actually define its meaning in its original, historical, and literary context.

Others ignore the literal meaning of the biblical text by critically reconstructing hypothetical literary stages behind the text in an assumed early genesis of the written text.[65] These pre-literary stages often gain an interpretative priority over the actual text.

Others deny the supernatural dimension of the biblical text because it does not match their closed naturalistic, immanent worldview. While they deny the facticity of the biblical text, they may admit an existential interpretation that nevertheless is divested from the literal meaning of the text.

Still others do not listen to what the text literally says, but rather let the text only respond to current questions that are posed by the modern reader. As attractive as this might sound, there is the danger that the Bible is allowed to answer only to those questions that the modern person poses. In the final analysis modern man is left with himself and his questions, without the guiding and correcting norm of Scripture. Similarly, in many modern hermeneutical approaches the meaning of the biblical text is reconstructed in the interaction between the text and the reader. The biblical text is at best a dialogue partner in an interpretative process in which the final determinative meaning is left with the interpreter. This leads us to look more closely at what it means to read the Bible obediently.

Following Scripture Obediently

If we take the biblical record seriously, we have to acknowledge that the process of biblical interpretation involves more than merely reading and interpreting Scripture correctly. The aim of reading the Bible goes far beyond gaining a merely intellectual knowledge. Biblically speaking, "knowing the Word of God" implies a relationship between the reader and God as the ultimate subject matter of the Bible. This

---

[65] Brevard S. Childs criticizes this historical-critical approach and has pointed out even a certain similarity to an allegorical reading of the text. In a historical-critical reading of Scripture the literal meaning of the text is exchanged with a speculative layer under and beneath the existing text, just as in an allegorical interpretation a deeper meaning is sought beyond the existing text. See Brevard S. Childs, "The Sensus Literalis of Scripture: An Ancient and Modern Problem," in *Beiträge zur alttestamentlichen Theologie*, ed. Herbert Donner, Festschrift für Walther Zimmerli zum 70. Geburtstag (Göttingen: Vandenhoeck & Ruprecht, 1977), 80–93, esp. 90–92. See also James Barr, "Allegory and Historicism," *Journal for the Study of the Old Testament* 69 (1996): 105–120.

relationship is characterized by love, fidelity, and obedience. These spiritual qualities guide our Christian living and should also guide our hermeneutical endeavors. The apostle Paul expresses the intricate unity between knowing and doing, or doctrine and living, when he admonishes his young coworker Timothy with these words that are applicable to us as well: "Keep a close watch on yourself and on the teaching. Persist in this, for by so doing you will save both yourself and your hearers" (1 Tim 4:16). In 1 Timothy 3:9 Paul calls the elders of the church to hold "to the mysteries of the faith with a clear conscience" (NASB). As believers we are called not only to intellectually affirm the biblical faith, but to abide in it and practice it faithfully. Otherwise there is the danger of not handling the word of truth accurately, which will lead to ungodliness (2 Tim 2:15–16).

Spiritual things go beyond an abstract intellectual grasp of the biblical material and a theoretical knowledge of Scripture. Spiritual things require a spiritual response: joyful obedience. A mere neutral and skeptically distant analysis and explanation of Scripture does not unfold the spiritual thrust of God's Word. God's Word was given with the intention to transform the reader.[66] This calls for an appropriate reaction on the part of the interpreter. To understand the biblical statements only with an academically distant mentality without realizing their practical and life changing implications does not do them justice. To illustrate, suppose that a man discovers his house is burning and wants to warn the other inhabitants. He quickly decides to use a verbal communication in the language the people are familiar with—English. He shouts, "The house is burning!" Would it be enough for the people who hear him to simply analyze his words on the syntactical level and come to the conclusion "He says the house is burning!" only to take no further action? Would it be enough to analyze the man's social, historical, and cultural background to determine the meaning of his message? Have they actually understood what is important to him and what is crucial for them? His words are intended to be acted upon. They should hear his words and get up and leave the burning house in order to be safe. In similar manner, the mere syntactical analysis of biblical passages (that is, the biblical writer says this or says that) will not reach the intended goal if we stop the process of understanding at this level. The biblical concept

---

[66] See the promise in Isaiah 55:10–11, where God states that "as the rain and the snow come down from heaven, and to not return there without watering the earth and making it bear and sprout, and furnishing seed to the sower and bread to the eater, so will My word be which goes from My mouth; it will not return to Me empty, Without accomplishing what I desire, and without succeeding in the matter for which I sent it" (NASB).

of understanding goes beyond a mere distant analysis of the semantic range of biblical words. It seeks to establish an obedient encounter with the one who addresses us in His Word. In the words of Kevin Vanhoozer, "neither standing nor understanding . . . is the final word in interpretation. The final word belongs to following."[67]

Following God's Word obediently raises some important questions with regard to the relationship between faith and thinking in the act of interpretation, to which we will now turn.

Does a Hermeneutic of Faith Require a Sacrifice of Our Thinking?

Human beings do not like to be told by an external authority what to do. Modern people tend to think autonomously, and their highest norm is often their own reasoning power. In such a context, the question is sometimes raised whether a hermeneutic of faith requires a sacrifice of our intellect and thinking. The straightforward answer to this is: no, this is not required. In the words of a leading Evangelical scholar, our engagement in the process of interpretation and understanding "requires the sanctification of the intellect, not the sacrifice of the intellect. One is not required to get a frontal lobotomy to believe the Bible is God's written Word. It is not the brain that is required to be sacrificed, it is the self."[68] As Christians we are not asked to give up our thinking. Our ability to think is given to us by God as a talent to be used. But the decisive issue is that as believers we are called to do our thinking properly, *coram deo*—that is, as someone who stands responsibly before God. Biblically speaking, we are called to think in relationship with God and in harmony with His Word. Any thinking that aims at a fundamental autonomy from our creator denies our creaturely existence and is self-centered, and thus in danger of being misleading. The apostle Paul, who certainly was not idle in his thinking, therefore encouraged us to take captive every thought to make it obedient to Christ (2 Cor 10:5).

Sometimes people are hesitant to affirm the full trustworthiness of Scripture. They begin to question some passages of Scripture. But there is a disastrous consequence of such an approach. In the words of Ellen G. White,

---

[67] See Kevin J. Vanhoozer, *Is There a Meaning in This Text?: The Bible, the Reader, and the Morality of Literary Knowledge* (Grand Rapids, MI: Zondervan, 1998), 467.

[68] Ben Witherington III, *The Living Word of God: Rethinking the Theology of the Bible* (Waco, TX: Baylor University Press, 2009), 195.

> they begin to question some parts of revelation, and pick flaws in the apparent inconsistencies of this statement and that statement. Beginning at Genesis, they give up that which they deem questionable, and their minds lead on, for Satan will lead to any length they may follow in their criticism and they see something to doubt in the whole Scriptures[69]

It is interesting to read how Ellen G. White describes the slippery slope they have chosen to enter:

> Their faculties of criticism become sharpened by exercise, and they can rest on nothing with certainty. You try to reason with these men, but your time is lost. They will exercise their power of ridicule even upon the Bible. They even become mockers, and they would be astonished if you put it to them in that light.[70]

In our attempt to find problematic passages, our critical faculties are sharpened and soon we are left with a Bible that is effectively robbed of its trustworthiness and reliability and stripped of its infallibility in significant ways. Should we close our eyes to problematic passages of Scripture? No, this is not the solution to the problem.[71] The question, however, is whether those who attempt to first solve all problems before they are willing to accept in faith Scripture's claim of truth are not overestimating themselves. We will probably never be able to solve all questions we might have about Scripture. And even if one were able to find answers to all known problems, one still could not be certain that no new problem could be discovered.

The Virtue of Humility as Prerequisite for Understanding

This calls for an attitude of humility, being aware of our own deficiencies and remembering that our own experience might be too limited, and our circle of logic might be too narrow.[72] Humility is also appropriate and "a prime interpretive virtue" because we recognize "that

---

[69] Ellen G. White, *Selected Messages*, 1:17–18.

[70] Ibid., 18.

[71] Cf. Frank M. Hasel, "Living With Confidence Despite Some Open Questions: Upholding the Biblical Truth of Creation Amidst Theological Pluralism," *Journal of the Adventist Theological Society* 14/1 (2003): 229–253.

[72] Witherington, 197.

the interpreters are not the makers but receivers of meaning."[73] Thus "humility enables the reader to wait upon the text, to participate in the covenant of discourse, and, if need be, to empty oneself for the sake of the text."[74] It has been pointed out that such an attitude of humility in the interpretative process needs to be balanced by conviction.[75] Convictions grow when we realize that we do not possess absolute knowledge but we nevertheless can have adequate knowledge.[76] While there is more new light to be discovered in our study of the Bible we can "have a firm enough grasp of the overall story line as to encourage boldness in our witness."[77]

Humility also helps us remember that in our attempt to understand God and His written Word our inductive approach is stretched to its limits where the greatness of the divine object surpasses the cognitive faculty of the finite individual.[78] We are not called to reject our thinking, but to think obediently with a renewed mind. Romans 12:1–2 is reasonably clear. As Christians we are to present ourselves to God as living sacrifices, holy and acceptable to God by *the renewing of the mind*. When we commit ourselves to God wholeheartedly, "one of the intended outcomes is the renewal of the mind—its stimulation, invigoration, inspiration."[79]

Anselm of Canterbury suggested the right relationship between divine revelation and thinking when he wrote, "I do not seek to understand in order to believe, but I believe so that I may understand [*neque enim quaero intelligere ut credam, sed credo ut intelligam*]."[80] Faith does not stand at the end of a long, inductive thinking process that

---

[73] Vanhoozer, 464. On the positive aspects of humility, see also Dow, 70–75.

[74] Vanhoozer, 464. On the virtue of humility, see Frank M. Hasel, *Living for God: Reclaiming the Joy of Christian Virtue* (Nampa, ID: Pacific Press, 2020), 53–59. On the importance of humility in the scientific search for truth, see Peter C. Hill, "It Is Good to Be Humble: An Empirical Account," in *Virtue and Voice: Habits of Mind for a Return to Civil Discourse*, ed. Gregg Ten Elshof and Evan Rosa (Abilene, TX: Abilene Christian University Press, 2019), 33–42; and Jason Baehr, "Intellectual Virtues, Civility, and Public Discourse" in Elshof and Rosa, 9–31.

[75] See Vanhoozer, 465–466 on this important aspect.

[76] Alvin Plantinga, *Knowledge and Christian Belief* (Grand Rapids, MI: Eerdmans, 2015), 30–44, calls it "warranted belief."

[77] Vanhoozer, 465.

[78] Stadelmann, *Grundlinien eines bibeltreuen Schriftverständnisses*, 71.

[79] Witherington, 195.

[80] Anselm of Canterbury, *Proslogion*, 1, https://sourcebooks.fordham.edu/basis/anselm-proslogium.asp#CHAPTER%20I (accessed: June 23, 2020).

has solved every question.[81] Faith is the starting point of our proper thinking about God: *credo ut intelligam*! Faith is not an enemy of our thinking. Faith is the foundation of genuine insight and understanding, where the believer is invited to explore God's revelation in a thinking manner in order to gain a better and deeper understanding. This leads us to some concluding thoughts about some significant biblical ideas that are important for a proper biblical hermeneutic.

Important Biblical Ideas for a Biblical Hermeneutic

To take the biblical claims of its divine origin seriously leads us to propose a special *biblical* hermeneutic.[82] Beyond the above-mentioned aspects, such a biblical hermeneutic will include at least the following ideas that will impact our interpretation of Scripture:

God Exists

The biblical writers do not attempt to prove the existence of God. They simply assume God's existence as a given fact from the very beginning. If we want to take the text of Scripture seriously, we have to employ a method that is open to the fact that God exists. Any method that explains the text of Scripture as if God does not exist does not do justice to the biblical material.[83]

God is Supernatural

The biblical writers not only affirm that God exists; they also affirm God as a supernatural being who is beyond the limits of creaturely existence. This transcendent reality cannot be understood adequately by a methodology that is based on purely immanent cause and effect and is limited by pure analogy to immanent facts and acts. An appropriate method to interpret the biblical message will employ a methodology that is deliberately open to God's supernatural and transcendent reality.

God is Active in Time and Space

While God is supernatural, He has also chosen to reveal Himself

---

[81] On this important relationship, see the helpful discussion in Helge Stadelmann, *Grundlinien eines bibeltreuen Schriftverständnisses*, 71–72.

[82] On the important issue of pursuing a biblical hermeneutic, see Maier, 21–38.

[83] "The real problem with historical-critical inquiry, subject as it is to the demands of methodological naturalism, is that it imposes limits on the reading of Scripture that are simply not suited to Scripture's own nature as an instrument of God's communicative presence in the world" (Rae, 109).

in time and space and has acted in time and space. In doing so, God is sovereign and capable of intervening in history. He is also sovereign to perform miracles. God is also knowledgeable of the future and hence can reveal future events. This is the reason why there is predictive prophecy in Scripture. The ability to know the future is one of the hallmarks of the living God (Isa 44:6–7, 26; 45:21; 46:9–10; 48:3, 16).

When God reveals Himself in history, His new revelation is consistent with past revelation.[84] As such, any new light would not contradict any old light or previous revelation.[85] One corollary of this biblical revelatory consistency is that there is unity among the biblical writings and a progression in the biblical history of God's salvation. The prophets after Moses could be tested by the standard of the law and the New Testament could be tested in light of the Old Testament as the fulfillment thereof. Here the passage in Isaiah 8:20 is important: "To the law and to the testimony! If they do not speak according to this word, it is because they have no dawn" (NKJV). This unity of Scripture also means that all of Scripture (*tota Scriptura*) is taken into consideration in the process of interpretation.

The Triune God is Personal

The biblical writers not only affirm God as a supernatural being who exists, but also describe God as a deeply personal being. In the biblical worldview, the triune God is one in love.[86] He is not a plurality of deities like in polytheism. This one God is a personal being who is characterized by the following aspects: God is able to communicate in a highly personal manner. God is affirmed as someone who speaks, who hears, who acts in history, and who is sovereign in His acting. As a God who speaks He is the originator of language. He has created human beings in His image and therefore is able to use words effectively to communicate His will to humanity. Human beings are capable of understanding God and can respond to Him, and therefore are responsible for their response. This means that God uses propositional revelation to communicate with human beings. Such propositional content goes beyond a vague revelatory encounter.[87] Therefore, the interpretation of words, which are the substance of any language, and are at the heart of His revelation with humankind, and meaningful

---

[84] This has been pointed out by Peckham, *Canonical Theology*, 37.

[85] Num 23:19; 1 Sam 15:29; Deut 4:1–2; Mal 3:6; Matt 5:17–18; 24:35; Titus 1:2–3; Heb 6:17–18; 13:7–9.

[86] Cf. John C. Peckham, *The Love of God: A Canonical Model* (Downers Grove, IL: InterVarsity, 2015).

[87] Jensen, 487–489.

sentences that are constructed out of them, will play an important role in biblical hermeneutics. A biblical hermeneutic that takes responsibly the significance of words and sentences will strive to understand the literal, historical-grammatical meaning of Scripture. A personal God who hears implies that God is willing to react to our prayers and is capable of intervening. In biblical parlance hearing includes doing. In all this God is sovereign in His actions and is not restricted to immanent causes and effects.

Noetic Effect of Sin and the Work of the Holy Spirit

The Bible also makes clear that there is a noetic[88] effect of sin on our understanding.[89] Because of sin, our thinking is not neutral. It is self-centered. Because of sin our thinking has a propensity to disobedience rather than to obedience. We are inclined to distort truth and often have an unwillingness to follow it. Sin overshadows our thinking and clouds it with blindness. Therefore, we need the help of the Holy Spirit to enlighten our understanding and create a new willingness in us to follow the Word of God (John 7:17). To understand the revealed Word of God is not enough; it also needs to be embraced and calls for our obedience to it. Not all who hear or read the Word of God follow its message. Embracing the scriptural Word of God is the work of the Holy Spirit.[90] Revelation, inspiration, proper understanding, *and* obedience to the revealed Word—*all* come from the Holy Spirit. Without the Holy Spirit there is no appreciation of the divine message and no desire to obey it. "There is no faith, hope, and love in response. The existential significance of the scriptural word is not seen, only its linguistic meaning."[91] The Holy Spirit enables us to understand what He has inspired (1 Cor 2:12; 14–15; Eph 1:17–19; Ps 119:8). Traditionally this enabling of understanding through the Holy Spirit has been described with the

---

[88] According to Merriam-Webster, "*Noetic* derives from the Greek adjective *noētikos*, meaning 'intellectual,' from the verb *noein* ('to think') and ultimately from the noun *nous*, meaning 'mind.' (*Nous* also gave English the word *paranoia* by joining with a prefix meaning 'faulty' or 'abnormal.') *Noetic* . . . refers to the action of perceiving or thinking" (*Merriam-Webster*, s.v. "noetic," https://www.merriam-webster.com/dictionary/noetic [accessed June 23, 2020]).

[89] There is a noetic effect of sin that is often overlooked. See Frank M. Hasel, "Presuppositions in the Interpretation of Scripture," 30–33. This is also recognized by others such as Maier, 25; and John M. Frame, *Systematic Theology: An Introduction to Christian Belief* (Phillipsburg, NJ: P&R, 2013), 1138; see also Stephen K. Moroney, "How Sin Affects Scholarship: A New Model," *Christian Scholar's Review* 28/3 (1999): 432–451.

[90] Graham A. Cole, *He Who Gives Life* (Wheaton, IL: Crossway, 2007), 264.

[91] Ibid., 264–265.

word "illumination."[92] The Holy Spirit's work with Scripture did not end in the distant past.[93] He continues to speak to people through the Bible today, making the written Word of God come alive, as He helps us understand the significance and relevance of the biblical text for our life in the present.[94] The Holy Spirit bridges, so to speak, the ugly historical ditch that Gotthold Lessing bemoaned.[95] According to Ellen G. White, "the Holy Spirit has been given as an aid in the study of God's word."[96] Thus, the Holy Spirit will lead us to a willing and loving obedience of the written Word of God. Through His Spirit God will not lead us away from the words of Scripture, but has committed Himself to the sure words of the Bible. In the famous words of Ellen G. White: "the Spirit was not given—nor can it ever be bestowed—to supersede the Bible; for the Scriptures explicitly state that the Word of God is the standard by which all teaching and experience must be tested."[97]

Calvin points out another important aspect of the work of the Holy Spirit in countering the disturbing effects of sin on our thinking, showing in a most convincing manner that it is the Holy Spirit who establishes the authority of Holy Scripture as certain. This is what Calvin calls the internal witness of the Spirit (*testimonium Spiritus sancti internum*).[98]

---

[92] See the insightful discussion of the biblical material in support for illumination in Cole, *He Who Gives Life*, 265–266.

[93] Stanley J. Grenz, *Theology for the Community of God* (Nashville, TN: Broadman and Holman, 1994), 499; and Thompson, "Generous Gift of a Gracious Father," 637.

[94] Grenz, 500. The Holy Spirit does not provide a semi-Gnostic secret knowledge that is restricted to the enlightened insider and is not available to others. The Holy Spirit does not add something to Scripture before it is intelligible. "At the level of cognitive understanding, the Spirit appears to play a minimal role" (Duvall and Hays, 227). Anyone can read the words of Scripture in the way other human words are read. They are not jumbled nonsense. But although people may understand the words of Scripture, without the Holy Spirit "the significance of what is said will be lost on them" (Thompson, "Generous Gift of a Gracious Father," 637). In other words, "they will not be persuaded of its truth and will not live it out. They may grasp the meaning of the biblical text, but they refuse to allow the text to grasp them. We cannot apply the Word of God without the help of the Spirit of God" (Duvall and Hays, 228).

[95] For Lessing the "accidental truths of history can never become the proof of necessary truths of reason" (*Lessing's Theological Writings*, ed. Henry Chadwick [Stanford, CA: Stanford University Press, 1957], 53). This, for Lessing, is "the ugly, broad ditch which I cannot get across, however often and however earnestly I have tried to make the leap" (ibid., 55). See also Cole, *He Who Gives Life*, 268.

[96] Ellen G. White, "The Holy Spirit an Aid to Bible Study," *Atlantic Union Gleaner*, June 9, 1909, para. 1.

[97] Ellen G. White, *The Great Controversy*, vii.

[98] "Let this point therefore stand: that those whom the Holy Spirit has inwardly taught truly rest upon Scripture, and that Scripture indeed is self-authenticated; hence it is not right to subject

This witness is stronger than any human reasoning. Scripture is self-authenticated.[99] This assurance is not accomplished by skeptical reason. Rather, it is received in faith. This is just as much a faith experience as our justification and sanctification is achieved by faith alone.[100] It enables us to proclaim the message of Scripture with conviction. This is no bibliolatry.[101] We do not worship the Bible. By embracing the scriptural Word as trustworthy and true, we are led by the Spirit to accept the living Word of God, Jesus Christ, as our Savior and Lord, as proclaimed in Scripture. Thus, faithfulness to Scripture is an expression of our love

---

it to proofs and reasoning. And the certainty it deserves with us, it attains by the testimony of the Spirit. For even if it wins reverence for itself by its own majesty, it seriously affects us only when it is sealed upon our hearts through the Spirit. Therefore, illumined by his power, we believe neither by our own nor by anyone else's judgment that Scripture is from God; but above human judgment we affirm with utter certainty (just as we were saying upon the majesty of God himself) that it has flowed to us from the very mouth of God by the ministry of men. We seek no proofs, no marks of genuineness upon which our judgment may lean; but we subject our judgment and wit to it as to a thing far beyond any guesswork! This we do, not as persons accustomed to seize upon some unknown thing, which, under closer scrutiny, displeases then, but fully conscious that we hold the unassailable truth! Nor do we do this as those miserable men who habitually bind over their minds to the thralldom of superstition; but we feel that the undoubted power of his divine majesty lives and breathes there. But this power we are drawn an inflamed, knowingly, and willingly, to obey him, yet also more vitally and more effectively than by mere human willing or knowing!" (John Calvin, *Institutes of the Christian Religion*, vol. 1 [Philadelphia, PA: Westminster John Knox], I.vii.5). Similarly: "Unless this certainty, higher and stronger than any human judgment, be present, it will be vain to fortify the authority of Scripture by arguments, to establish it by common agreement of the church, or to confirm it with other helps. For unless this foundation is laid, its authority will always remain in doubt. Conversely, once we have embraced it devoutly as its dignity deserves, and have recognized it to be above the common sort of things, those arguments – not strong enough before to engraft and fix the certainty of Scripture in our minds – become very useful aids" (ibid., I.viii.1)

[99] "As to their question: 'How can we be assured that this has sprung from God unless we have recourse to the degree of the church'—it is as if someone asked: Whence will we learn to distinguish light from darkness, white from black, sweet from bitter? Indeed, Scripture exhibits fully as clear evidence of its own truth as white and black things do of their color, or sweet and bitter things do of their taste" (ibid., I.vii.2).

[100] On the relationship of faith and reason, see Frank H. Hasel, "Theology and the Role of Reason," 172–198.

[101] It has been pointed out that "critics sometimes accuse conservatives of biblicism, which makes sense to them since they separate God from the Bible. But if the Bible is God's word, the charge falls away. To submit to Scripture is to submit to the Lord who reveals Himself in it. Notice Romans 9:17, which begins, 'For the Scripture says to Pharaoh, "I raised you up for this very purpose. . ."' This is from Exodus 9:16, where *God* speaks to Pharaoh. Thus, for Paul 'Scripture says' = 'God says.' Believers respond to the Author through his word. Yet it would be a deadly error if someone related to Scripture in itself and missed God himself" (Daniel M. Doriani, "Take, Read," in Carson, *Enduring Authority*, 1142 n. 74).

for Jesus and the triune God. As we read in 1 John 5:3, "for this is the love of God, that we keep his commandments. And his commandments are not burdensome".

CHAPTER 3

Variants, Versions, and the Trustworthiness of Scripture

Clinton Wahlen

The foundation of all biblical study is the text of Scripture itself. The Bible is, by far, the best attested ancient book. The Old Testament is well-attested in several medieval Hebrew manuscripts and over two hundred fragmentary copies of biblical books from among the Dead Sea Scrolls, pushing back our understanding of the Hebrew text by over one thousand years.[1] The earliest Old Testament text discovered so far (from Num 6:24–26) is preserved on silver amulets that date to the mid-seventh century BC.[2] The New Testament has even stronger attestation with over six thousand catalogued manuscripts,[3] a few of

---

[1] Emanuel Tov, *Textual Criticism of the Hebrew Bible*, 2nd ed. (Minneapolis, MN: Fortress, 2001), 103, noting also (104–105) that the largest number of copies found were of the books of Psalms (36), Deuteronomy (30), and Isaiah (21).

[2] Paul D. Wegner, *The Journey From Texts to Translations: The Origin and Development of the Bible* (Grand Rapids, MI: Baker, 1999), 185; Gabriel Barkay et al., "The Challenges of Ketef Hinnom: Using Advanced Technologies to Recover the Earliest Biblical Texts and their Context," *Near Eastern Archaeology* 66/4 (2003): 162–171; and Gabriel Barkay et al., "The Amulets from Ketef Hinnom: A New Edition and Evaluation," *Bulletin of the American Schools of Oriental Research* 334 (2004): 41–71.

[3] Carl P. Cosaert, "Erasmus, the Reformation, and the Text of the New Testament" (paper presented at the Adventist Theological Society annual banquet, Boston, MA, November 17, 2017), 6. Cf. Justin Taylor, "An Interview With Daniel B. Wallace on the New Testament Manuscripts," The Gospel Coalition, March 22, 2012, https://www.thegospelcoalition.org/blogs/justin-taylor/an-interview-with-daniel-b-wallace-on-the-new-testament-manuscripts/ (accessed December 12, 2019), indicating that there are "certainly . . . tens of thousands" of ancient versional witnesses in languages such as Latin, Coptic, Syriac, Slavic, Armenian, Georgian, and Gothic. See also Bruce M. Metzger and Bart D. Ehrman, *The Text of the New Testament: Its Transmission, Corruption, and Restoration*, 4th ed. (Oxford: Oxford University Press, 2005), 50.

which may date to within decades of the work's composition.[4] The next best attested ancient work is Homer's *Iliad*, with 647 copies,[5] the earliest complete copy of which dates from the tenth to eleventh century AD (about 1,700 years after its composition).[6] Compared to this and other works from antiquity, copies of Biblical books were produced much closer to the time of their original composition,[7] and the written accounts of the Gospels seem to be faithful renderings of the oral content of Jesus' teachings.[8]

Yet, despite the Bible's solid textual attestation, the manuscripts are not identical in every respect. All we have are copies of the original manuscripts (the "autographs") that date to a later period—some several centuries after they were originally written. As the biblical manuscripts were used and copied, the autographs themselves did not survive:

> Wear and tear, frequent use, and imperial edicts demanding the destruction of the Christian sacred books account for their early disappearance. However, the early believers did not wait

---

[4] Philip Comfort, *Encountering the Manuscripts: An Introduction to New Testament Paleography & Textual Criticism* (Nashville, TN: Broadman and Holman, 2005) dates P^{52} (which preserves a few verses of John 18) to the early second century, "only about twenty years away from the original" (143) and P^{66} to the mid-second century (147); cf. 126–127 on the questionable identification of 7Q4 and 7Q5 as New Testament fragments. More skeptical of the dating accuracy of early manuscripts is Brent Nongbri, *God's Library: The Archaeology of the Earliest Christian Manuscripts* (New Haven, CT: Yale University Press, 2018), 47–82.

[5] D. A. Carson, *The King James Version Debate: A Plea for Realism* (Grand Rapids, MI: Baker, 1979), 18 (457 papyri, two uncials, and 188 minuscules).

[6] Stanley E. Porter and Andrew W. Pitts, *Fundamentals of New Testament Textual Criticism* (Grand Rapids, MI: Eerdmans, 2015), 50; F. W. Hall, *Companion to Classical Texts* (Oxford: Clarendon Press, 1913), 241; cf. F. F. Bruce, *The New Testament Documents: Are They Reliable?* 6th ed. (Grand Rapids, MI: Eerdmans, 1981), 11. Homer's *Iliad* and *Odyssey* were originally "published" orally and written down only after his time, as was the case with the teachings of Socrates (Comfort, 1).

[7] Some of the information detailed in Hall, 199–285, is conveniently summarized in Josh McDowell, comp., *Evidence That Demands a Verdict: Historical Evidences for the Christian Faith* (San Bernardino, CA: Campus Crusade for Christ, 1972), 48, who lists the works of sixteen writers (ranging from the sixth century BC to AD 160). Most of these survive in fewer than ten copies; except for Demosthenes (two hundred manuscripts stemming from a single copy) and Sophocles (one hundred copies), none survive in more than twenty copies.

[8] Note the conclusion of Robert K. McIver, *Memory, Jesus, and the Synoptic Gospels* (Atlanta, GA: Society of Biblical Literature, 2011), 180: "What is known of the characteristics of human memory, the teaching methodology almost certainly adopted by Jesus and his disciples, and the evidence of the Synoptic parallels all support the contention that aphorisms and parables were likely to have been transmitted with great reliability in earliest Christianity." While variations in Jesus' teachings are found in the Synoptic Gospels, their overall consistency is remarkable.

long before they made handwritten copies of the autographs and distributed them among the communities of faith (cf. Col 4:16).[9]

Of the earliest manuscripts of the New Testament, a few were copied by individuals with very limited ability in Greek, while others are in a "bookhand" script characteristic of professional scribes; most, however, were produced by Christians "trained in writing documents," but who were not professional scribes.[10] The older manuscripts, written in capital letters (called "uncial" or "majuscule" script), only rarely exhibit punctuation marks, and even lack spaces between words (until about the sixth century).[11] Cursive script came into use in the third century and, by the ninth century, copies were made using very small letters ("minuscules").[12] Extant New Testament manuscripts presently include 140 papyri, 323 uncials, 2,956 minuscules, and over 2,400 lectionaries.[13]

Of the thousands of copies of surviving New Testament manuscripts, it is estimated that there are hundreds of thousands of variations among them.[14] Nevertheless, modern critical editions of the Greek New Testament[15] on which most recent Bible translations are based exhibit a ninety-eight percent agreement with the traditional text.[16] In view of the differences that exist between manuscripts (called variants), choices

---

[9] Arthur Ferch, "Which Version Can We Trust?" 1, https://adventistbiblicalresearch.org/sites/default/files/pdf/Which%20Version%20Can%20We%20Trust_0.pdf (accessed March 2, 2020).

[10] Comfort, 20–22; similarly, Kim Haines-Eitzen, *Guardians of Letters: Literacy, Power, and the Transmitters of Early Christian Literature* (Oxford: Oxford University Press, 2000), 75.

[11] Paul D. Wegner, *A Student's Guide to Textual Criticism of the Bible: Its History, Methods and Results* (Downers Grove, IL: InterVarsity, 2006), 80.

[12] Ibid., 46, 80–81.

[13] Carl Cosaert, personal communication, May 10, 2020; these numbers continue to increase as cataloging proceeds.

[14] On the number of variants, see Peter J. Gurry, "The Number of Variants in the Greek New Testament: A Proposed Estimate" (Cambridge: University of Cambridge, 2014), https://core.ac.uk/download/pdf/77409535.pdf (accessed February 27, 2020). Typical is the estimate of three hundred thousand in Daniel B. Wallace, "The Majority Text and the Original Text: Are They Identical?" *Bibliotheca Sacra* (1991): 157.

[15] *Novum Testamentum Graece*, ed. Barbara Aland, Kurt Aland, et al., 28th ed. (Stuttgart: German Bible Society, 2012) and *The Greek New Testament*, ed. Barbara Aland, Kurt Aland, et al., 5th ed. (Stuttgart: German Bible Society, 2014) are "eclectic" texts of the New Testament, based on a careful assessment of which manuscripts best preserve the original text, presenting the major differences in an apparatus at the bottom of each page. The text of these two editions is identical, except for minor differences in punctuation and capitalization.

[16] Wallace, 157–158. The traditional text of the New Testament is based on the Byzantine text type, which is represented by the vast majority of extant Greek manuscripts (discussed below) and this was used as the basis for the widely used King James and New King James versions.

must necessarily be made regarding whether a specific word, word order, or even a whole verse or more was part of the original manuscript composed by the biblical writer(s),[17] or whether it came in later through the process of transmission. Some of these differences in the ancient manuscripts are reflected in modern translations of the Bible. The task of identifying as far as possible the original wording of the text of Scripture is known as "textual criticism"[18] or, better, "textual analysis."[19] Determining the original form of the Old Testament is challenging since fewer complete manuscripts and versions have survived and there is no clear consensus on its transmission history.[20] Until the discovery of the Dead Sea Scrolls, the manuscripts preserved by the Masoretes (attested in the Aleppo Codex, ca. AD 920, and the Leningrad Codex, ca. AD 1008, and used for modern editions of the Hebrew Bible) were the oldest complete manuscripts of the Old Testament in Hebrew.[21] The biblical manuscripts of the Dead Sea Scrolls that were found in caves near Khirbet Qumran beginning in 1947 reflect a text that is one thousand years earlier than the Masoretic Text.[22]

---

[17] Some of Paul's epistles mention additional authors or amanuenses in the salutation (e.g., Timothy in Phil 1:1 and Col 1:1; Silvanus and Timothy in 1 Thess 1:1 and 2 Thess 1:1).

[18] See the similar definitions and new directions in textual criticism in Eldon Jay Epp, "Issues in New Testament Textual Criticism: Moving from the Nineteenth Century to the Twenty-First Century," in *Rethinking New Testament Textual Criticism*, ed. David Alan Black (Grand Rapids, MI: Baker Academic, 2002), 71–75; cf. Wegner, *From Texts to Translations*, 177 (in connection with Old Testament textual criticism): "The science and art that seeks to determine the most reliable wording of the biblical text." For a more detailed explanation, see Porter and Pitts, 1–6, who point to a secondary, sociohistorical task: study of a text's transmission history may shed light on the social history of early Christianity. This secondary task requires a starting point, but "what can that starting point be if not the original text?" (Comfort, 291).

[19] In this chapter, the term "analysis" is preferred to "criticism" in order to exclude presuppositions that undermine the authority of Scripture. See Richard M. Davidson, "Biblical Interpretation," in *Handbook of Seventh-day Adventist Theology*, ed. Raoul Dederen, Commentary Reference Series 12 (Hagerstown, MD: Review and Herald, 2000), 69.

[20] An overview of the various proposals is given in Wegner, *From Texts to Translations*, 169–171. For detailed discussion of the manuscript evidence for the Old Testament and other aspects of textual criticism of the Hebrew Bible, see Tov.

[21] The Leningrad Codex, currently held in the National Library of Russia in St. Petersburg, is the base text used in all editions of the Biblia Hebraica (BHK, BHS, and BHQ).

[22] While textual variety is attested in some of Qumran's biblical manuscripts, "the MT had a privileged position as reflected in the number of proto-Masoretic manuscripts found at Qumran, which showed evidence of careful scribal work (Stephen Dempster, "Canons on the Right and Canons on the Left: Finding a Resolution in the Canon Debate," *Journal of the Evangelical Theological Society* 52 (2009): 67). See also Tov, 114–117, who describes the vast majority of differences among the proto-Masoretic-Text manuscripts as "small" and that "the consonantal framework" of the text "changed very little, if at all, in the course of more than one thousand years" (30).

Comparing these with the other available Old Testament manuscripts, it has been estimated that "90% of the text is without significant variation."[23] Recent discoveries have heightened an appreciation for the overall accuracy of the transmission of both the Hebrew Bible and the New Testament, but questions remain that are important for us to consider: What is the history of textual transmission? Do the principles of textual analysis adequately explain the process of transmission or are some methodological refinements necessary? How can we know which text is more original?

Besides these questions, recent developments in the fields of linguistics (the study of how language functions) and hermeneutics have significantly impacted the methods employed in Bible translation and interpretation, which has led to a proliferation of Bible versions. Is every edition and version of the Bible trustworthy despite their differences? Which translation is the best? Are some translations more reliable than others? In this chapter we will explore these questions and consider some important guidelines to assist an in-depth study of Scripture.

The Importance of Textual Analysis for Biblical Interpretation

We turn our attention first to the process of textual analysis, illustrating with some examples from both the Old and New Testaments why it is important and how it has impacted the most recent translations of the Bible.[24] The most noticeable variants to the common reader of the Bible are those in which a sizeable portion of text is added

---

[23] Wegner, *From Texts to Translations*, 178, citing Bruce Waltke's assessment of the variants listed in BHS. For a more recent appraisal, which details some of the most significant variations between the Masoretic texts and 1QIsa[a], see Eugene Ulrich, *The Dead Sea Scrolls and the Developmental Composition of the Bible* (Leiden: Brill, 2015), who mentions over 2,600 variants of the Masoretic Text with 1QIsa[a] (Ulrich, 113). In view of the comments of Tov (see previous footnote), few would be of exegetical significance. Even more remarkable, 1QIsa[b] (containing most of Isa 38–66) has only one significant variant (53:11, on which see ibid., 138). The remaining variants are described as "minutiae" by Tov, 31.

[24] This brief introduction to the technical subject of textual analysis is intended to make more understandable the discussions of the topic in commentaries. For a more detailed discussion, see Wegner, *Textual Criticism of the Bible*; Metzger and Ehrman; and Kurt Aland and Barbara Aland, *Der Text des Neuen Testaments: Einführung in die wissenschaftlichen Ausgaben sowie in Theorie und Praxis der modernen Textkritik* (Stuttgart: Deutsche Bibelgesellschaft, 1982). For more recent approaches to the topic, see Black, *Rethinking New Testament Textual Criticism*.

or omitted, which sometimes includes whole verses.[25] But, by far, the vast majority of significant variants involve only a word or phrase. Since Hebrew is a consonantal language, some variants seem to have arisen as a result of differing vocalization.[26] Another issue that has arisen from vocalization appears in the way a few versions translate God's name. Since the Jews considered it blasphemous to pronounce God's name, when vowel points began to be added to the Hebrew text by the Masoretes (ca. AD 500–800) the vowels for the word *Adonai* ("Lord") were used with the Hebrew consonants for God's name YHWH, resulting in the hybrid pronunciation "Jehovah." The pronunciation of this tetragrammaton as "Yahweh" is essentially an educated guess because the actual pronunciation has not been preserved.[27]

Textual analysis of the Old Testament is aided by a small number of Hebrew and Aramaic manuscripts and fragments, including those found among the Dead Sea Scrolls. Also considered as possible sources, under the assumption that they may reflect an earlier form of the Hebrew text, are the Samaritan Pentateuch and ancient Greek translations of the Old Testament (the Septuagint, Old Greek versions, and those by Aquila, Symmachus, and Theodotian), as well as the Syriac Peshitta, Aramaic Targums, Origen's Hexapla, and the Latin Vulgate,[28] but not all are agreed on this approach.[29] To do textual analysis, whether of the Old or New Testament, it can be helpful to display the range of textual variants in a table, together with the source or sources that support each one.[30] For those unfamiliar with Greek and Hebrew, Bible

---

[25] Some examples are: Jeremiah 25:14 (an addition compared to the LXX); Mark 9:44, 46; Acts 8:37; Romans 16:24 (omitted from the texts of NA[28] and UBS[5]).

[26] Wegner, *From Texts to Translations*, 178, refers to Jeremiah 9:21 (ET 9:22), in which the word *dbr* in Hebrew can be vocalized as 1) *dibbēr* ("say"), 2) *dābār* ("word"), or 3) *deber*, ("plague, pestilence"). Context usually makes clear what meaning is intended, as it does here; "say" is regarded as the intended meaning judging from the context.

[27] Ibid., 173–175, citing Jerome, *Epistulae*, 25, who indicates that, to the Jews, this name is ineffable, not to be uttered (Gk. *anekphōnēton*, "unpronounced letters"). With the passage of time, the real vowel sounds of the tetragrammaton were lost.

[28] Wegner, *From Texts to Translations*, 178, 185–204; Amy Anderson and Wendy Widder, *Textual Criticism of the Bible*, rev. ed. (Bellingham, WA: Lexham, 2018), 70–90; cf. Ralph W. Klein, *Textual Criticism of the Old Testament: From the Septuagint to Qumran* (Philadelphia, PA: Fortress, 1974), 1–26.

[29] See Stephen Pisano, *Additions and Omissions in the Books of Samuel: The Significant Pluses and Minuses in the Massoretic, LXX and Qumran Texts* (Göttingen: Vandenhoeck & Rupprecht, 1984), 3–17; cf. Wegner, *Textual Criticism of the Bible*, 103–104.

[30] See, e.g., Anderson and Widder, 97–98 (on Isa 40:7–8); and Wegner, *Textual Criticism of the Bible*, 250 (on Eph 1:1).

translations often include textual notes showing the major variant readings. Before looking at some of these cases, however, it will be helpful to describe the texts on which modern translations are based, followed by an explanation of some of the most common types of copying errors.

Texts and Translations

Modern translations of the Hebrew text of the Old Testament are based on what is known as a diplomatic edition, taking the Leningrad Codex as the base text because not only is it considered quite accurate, but it is also the oldest complete manuscript of the Old Testament in Hebrew.[31] Modern translations of the New Testament rely on an eclectic text, which is based on the text's presumed transmission history and a selection of the "best" variants compiled from extant manuscripts, ancient versions, and patristic quotations in order to "reconstruct a hypothetical original text."[32] Two basic approaches to textual analysis have dominated the study of New Testament manuscripts: the Alexandrian-priority hypothesis and the Byzantine-priority hypothesis.[33]

---

[31] Wegner, *From Texts to Translations*, 177; Anderson and Widder, 63–64.

[32] Ibid., 52; Wegner, *Textual Criticism of the Bible*, 224. Many now prefer to speak of the "initial" text (*Ausgangstext*), underscoring their skepticism about ascertaining the text of the "original." See Michael W. Holmes, "From 'Original Text' to 'Initial Text': The Traditional Goal of New Testament Textual Criticism in Contemporary Discussion," in *The Text of the New Testament in Contemporary Research: Essays on the Status Quaestionis*, ed. Bart D. Ehrman and Michael W. Holmes, rev. ed. (Leiden: Brill, 2013), 637–688. Variations in eclectic method exist: the "documentary approach," based principally on external evidence; "thoroughgoing eclecticism," based principally on internal evidence; and "reasoned eclecticism," emphasizing a balanced use of both internal and external evidence (ibid., 239). Nevertheless, despite attempts at objectivity, these text-critical practices have not arrived at any measure of consensus. A quite different approach, labelled "reasoned transmissionalism" by its adherents, "evaluates internal and external evidence in the light of transmissional probabilities" (see Maurice A. Robinson, "The Case for Byzantine Priority," in Black, *Rethinking New Testament Textual Criticism*, 125–139, abbreviated from its much more substantial form found now in the appendix to *The New Testament in the Original Greek: Byzantine Textform*, comp. Maurice A. Robinson and William G. Pierpont (Southborough, MA: Chilton Book, 2005), 567–620, https://ia801303.us.archive.org/9/items/RP-2005KoineGreekNTinByzantineTextform/The_New_Testament_In_The_Original_Greek.pdf (accessed April 15, 2020). The quotation is from the latter, more complete essay (544). On the Robinson-Pierpont text, see P. J. Williams, "Review of *The New Testament in the Original Greek: Byzantine Textform*," January 24, 2006, http://evangelicaltextualcriticism.blogspot.com/2006/01/review-of-robinson-and-pierpont.html (accessed April 16, 2020).

[33] For a concise overview of the history of text-critical studies in the New Testament, see J. H. Petzer, "The History of the New Testament Text—Its Reconstruction, Significance and Use in New Testament Textual Criticism," in *New Testament Textual Criticism, Exegesis, and Early Church History: A Discussion of Methods*, ed. B. Aland and J. Delobel (Kampen: Kok Pharos, 1994), 18–25. See also Epp, 17–76. A more recent and much more detailed history may be found in Robert F. Hull Jr., *The Story of the New Testament Text: Movers, Materials, Motives, Methods,*

These two hypotheses differ in how they view the history of transmission of the New Testament, which in turn affects which manuscripts are considered to reflect most closely the original autographs.

Those who accept the Alexandrian-priority hypothesis believe that, during the early period of transmission, the text of the New Testament was freely modified and augmented by various scribes.[34] This expansionist and paraphrastic form of the text is represented in the "Western" grouping of manuscripts. A second grouping, seen as a more accurate form of the text, are the "Alexandrian" manuscripts, which were copied by those whose scribal practices were much more careful and similar to methods used in Alexandria.[35] A third cluster of manuscripts, referred to as "Byzantine," are characterized by "fuller readings" that combine elements of the other two groups of manuscripts. According to this view, the Byzantine text type is later and cannot reflect the original form of the New Testament text.[36]

By contrast, the Byzantine-priority hypothesis assumes that the books of the New Testament were widely copied and disseminated from the beginning, thus establishing a "consensus text" that would be difficult, if not impossible, to displace on a wide scale by a rival text

---

and Models (Atlanta, GA: Society of Biblical Literature, 2010).

[34] See, e.g., Gordon D. Fee, "Textual Criticism of the New Testament," in *Studies in the Theory and Method of New Testament Textual Criticism*, ed. Eldon J. Epp and Gordon D. Fee (Grand Rapids, MI: Eerdmans, 1993), 9; and Metzger and Ehrman, 276–277. Brooke Foss Westcott and Fenton John Anthony Hort, *The New Testament in the Original Greek*, rev. ed. (London: Macmillan, 1907), 7, describe it as "early textual laxity." For a concise summary of this reconstructed history, see Aland and Aland, 74–81; Anderson and Widder, 116–117; and Wegner, *From Texts to Translations*, 207. The modern critical consensus stems largely from work done by Johann Salomo Semler (1725–1791), Johann Jakob Griesbach (1745–1812), Karl Lachmann (1793–1851), Friedrich Constantin von Tischendorf (1815–1874), Samuel Prideaux Tragelles (1813–1875), and, above all, Brooke Foss Westcott (1825–1901) and Fenton John Anthony Hort (1828–1892). See Metzger and Ehrman, 161–162, 165–183, who conclude, after detailing the text-critical principles of Westcott and Hort, that "the general validity of their critical principles and procedures is widely acknowledged by textual scholars today" (183). However, current trends reflect a shifting sentiment, as noted by Comfort, 293. The prioritization of the text of Codex Vaticanus by Westcott and Hort, who considered it "neutral"—meaning, as Comfort puts it, "almost a perfectly transmitted text from the original" and "void of corruption"—has been deemed overly subjective and resulted in a growing skepticism toward external evidence based on a genealogical reconstruction of the text's transmission history. Thus, the tendency has been to place more weight on internal evidence and the variant that best explains the rise of all the others. Nevertheless, Metzger's assessment accurately reflects the continuing influence of these two critical scholars.

[35] See, e.g., Hull, esp. 148; and Westcott and Hort, 113–146.

[36] Westcott and Hort, 117, 119, based on their earlier discussion of manuscript transmission (112–118), prioritize texts characterized as Alexandrian (129).

type, which would explain why the vast majority of New Testament manuscripts are Byzantine. According to this view, the Alexandrian manuscripts represent a local recension of the consensus text characterized by shorter readings reflecting attempts to "purify" the text.[37] This approach is to be distinguished from the more popular "King James Only" movement that favors the Textus Receptus as the base text.[38]

The strengths of the Alexandrian-priority position include the following: this text is reflected in nearly all the earliest papyri and manuscripts of the Greek New Testament, its methods have been refined over several centuries of manuscript scrutinization, and it is held by the vast majority of modern textual critics. However, the resulting eclectic text is hypothetical—although based on a careful analysis of actual variants, the reconstructed text *as a whole* differs significantly from any actual New Testament manuscript. The appeal to the earliest manuscripts sounds persuasive until it is recognized that these derive from a single textual stream produced by Alexandrian-influenced scribal practices. The strengths of the Byzantine-priority position include the fact that, although this text is also reconstructed, it is largely reflected in nearly all the extant witnesses from the mid-fourth century until printing was invented in the sixteenth century. However, while there are Byzantine readings found among the early New Testament papyri, no papyrus has yet been found that is characteristically Byzantine and citations of such witnesses from church fathers do not appear until the late fourth century.[39] The tendency of the Byzantine text to harmonize Gospel accounts and retain elements that lent themselves to liturgical reading also suggest that it often (though not

---

[37] See Robinson, "Appendix: The Case for Byzantine Priority," in Robinson and Pierpont, iii.

[38] Ibid., 533; and Hull, 149. On this movement see Carson, *The King James Version Debate*. Regarding the Textus Receptus and its differences with the Majority (or Byzantine) Text, see W. Edward Glenny, "The New Testament Text and the Version Debate," in *One Bible Only? Examining Exclusive Claims for the King James Bible*, ed. Roy E. Beacham and Kevin T. Bauder (Grand Rapids, MI: Kregel, 2001), 76–101. On views within the Adventist Church regarding the Textus Receptus underlying the KJV and NKJV, which is similar but not identical to the Byzantine text type, see "Modern Versions and the King James Version" (1997), https://adventistbiblicalresearch.org/sites/default/files/pdf/kjversion.pdf (accessed April 21, 2020).

[39] Dirk Jongkind, *An Introduction to the Greek New Testament, Produced at Tyndale House, Cambridge* (Wheaton, IL: Crossway, 2019), 98. For a more detailed discussion, see T. David Andersen, "Arguments For and Against the Byzantine and Alexandrian Text Types," in *Digging for the Truth: Collected Essays Regarding the Byzantine Text of the Greek New Testament. A Festschrift in Honor of Maurice A. Robinson*, ed. Mark Billington and Peter Streitberger (Norden: FocusYourMission, 2014), 154–188.

always) reflects a later form of the text.[40] Unfortunately, both positions also suffer from the fact that only a very small fraction of the total evidence for the New Testament text has been collated, let alone analyzed, and both rely heavily on theoretical reconstructions of the history of textual transmission. Nevertheless, both approaches recognize the existence of scribal changes to the text, both accidental and intentional, and utilize internal and/or external evidence in assessing the likelihood that a given variant reflects the original text.

Before looking in greater detail at variants and how they are analyzed, it is important to mention a third approach to textual analysis that has emerged more recently. This approach, known as the Coherence-Based Genealogical Method (CBGM), utilizes computer technology to analyze the relationships between various texts of the New Testament or "witnesses."[41] This process proceeds in several steps, beginning with an analysis of variation at all points in the textual tradition in order to determine the degree of coherence between witnesses prior to assessing likely genealogical relationships (thus it is referred to as "pre-genealogical coherence"). A second step attempts to determine the direction of the relationship—that is, which witness represents an earlier form of the text (referred to as "genealogical coherence"). From this process predominant textual flow diagrams may be constructed to show the most likely path of textual development. The CBGM offers a totally new way to analyze variants that bypasses the debate over text types.[42] So far, its results have only impacted the eclectic texts of the General Epistles but the analysis of other New Testament books is ongoing, with Acts, John, and Revelation currently being studied. Interestingly, the results so far have led to "a renewed appreciation for the so-called Byzantine text."[43] It also represents one of the most significant developments in the study of the transmission of the New Testament.

---

[40] Jongkind, 99–100.

[41] See Peter J. Gurry, "How Your Greek New Testament Is Changing: A Simple Introduction to the Coherence-Based Genealogical Method (CBGM)," *Journal of the Evangelical Theological Society* 59/4 (2016): 675–689 (the CBGM definition of "witness" is given on 679). The description of this method is summarized from Gurry. See also Tommy Wasserman and Peter J. Gurry, *A New Approach to Textual Criticism: An Introduction to the Coherence-Based Genealogical Method* (Atlanta, GA: SBL Press, 2017).

[42] Wasserman and Gurry, 8–10. See also the caution in Stephen C. Carlson, "A Bias at the Heart of the Coherence-Based Genealogical Method (CBGM)," *Journal of Biblical Literature* 139/2 (2020): 319–340, suggesting that a "common-error criterion" could be incorporated to provide "a more accurate calculation of genealogical coherence" (339).

[43] Gurry, "How Your Greek New Testament Is Changing," 685.

Unintentional Scribal Errors

We now turn our attention to a more detailed consideration of variants in the Biblical texts. From the numerous manuscripts of the New Testament, it becomes apparent that a large percentage of scribal mistakes are unintentional. These are mostly obvious errors such as misspellings and the transposition of words. While it is not the purpose of this chapter to explain in detail all of the different kinds of variants found in biblical manuscripts, it will be helpful to illustrate some of the more common differences that appear and the terms used to identify them.

One error occurred when the scribe's eye returned to a later instance in the exemplar (that is, the manuscript from which he was copying) of the last word or phrase copied (referred to as haplography or a "scribal leap"). Almost the same occurred when the scribe skipped forward to a line with a word that begins or ends in a similar way (referred to as "homoioarchton" and "homoioteleuton" respectively).[44] An example of a scribal leap is found at Isaiah 4:5–6 in the Isaiah[a] scroll from Qumran Cave 1. The text omits about a dozen words found in the Masoretic Text (given here in brackets): "Then the LORD will create over the whole site of Mount Zion and over her assemblies a cloud by day, [and smoke and the shining of a flaming fire by night; for over all the glory there will be a canopy. There will be a booth for shade by day] from the heat, and for a refuge and a shelter from the storm and rain."[45] It appears that the Qumran scribe resumed copying after the second occurrence of "by day" (Heb. *yomam*), unintentionally omitting the intervening words.[46] Another example of this mistake is the reading in Codex Vaticanus (B) of John 17:15, which omits the words in brackets (bracketed by *ek tou*, "of/from the"): "I do not pray that you should take them out of the [world, but that you should keep them from the] evil one." The omission suggests almost the opposite meaning—that Jesus does not want His followers to be kept from the devil! Codex Sinaiticus (א) omits the whole of Luke 10:32 because both verse 31 and verse 32 end with the same word (*antiparēlthen*, "passed by on the other side"). All three of these instances of haplography can easily be recognized. Therefore, we have little doubt as to the original wording of the text.

---

[44] Many of these as well as other examples may be found in Wegner, *From Texts to Translations*, 178–182; Anderson and Widder, 17–40, 94–109; and Metzger and Ehrman, 250–271.

[45] All biblical quotations are from the NKJV, unless otherwise indicated.

[46] This example with the given translation is from John F. Brug, *Textual Criticism of the Old Testament: Principles and Practice* (self-pub., Lulu, 2015), 21.

At other times, similar-looking letters were confused. One of the most famous examples of mistaken letters is 1 Timothy 3:16, in which some manuscripts have ΟΣ ("he who") and others have $\overline{\Theta\Sigma}$ using the overline to indicate the abbreviation of divine names or titles, "God" (ΘΕΟΣ) in this case.[47] The similarity of the initial letter, particularly when the script was faint and hard to distinguish, seems to have led to the interchange of these two words. An example of this in the Old Testament is the confusion of the Hebrew letters *dalet* (ד, *d*) and *resh* (ר, *r*), leading to "Dodanim" as a son of Javan in Genesis 10:4, but "Rodanim" in 1 Chronicles 1:7.[48] Admittedly, in this case, it is more difficult to decide which name was originally in the text, but there are good reasons to prefer "Dodanim."[49]

Words that have the same pronunciation but different spellings (homophony) could also be easily exchanged for one another (in English, think of words like "there," "their," and "they're"). An Old Testament example is the incorrect substitution in Isaiah 9:2 (ET 3) of *lo'* ("not," in the KJV) for *lô* ("to him/it," translated "its" in the NKJV).[50] Especially common in New Testament manuscripts is the interchange of similar sounding vowels such as the Greek letters *o* (omicron) and *ō* (omega) that we find in Romans 5:1, with some manuscripts having *echomen* ("we have") while others have *echōmen* ("let us have").[51] Many differences in the manuscripts can be accounted for by such interchanges because seven Greek vowels and diphthongs came to have the same pronunciation.[52] This scribal error, known as itacism, led to some striking differences. In 1 Corinthians 15:54–55, for instance, rather than "Death is swallowed up in victory [*nikos*]," several ancient manuscripts—designated Papyrus 46 (P^{46}), Vaticanus (B), and Bezae (D^{*})—have "Death is swallowed

---

[47] Wegner, *Textual Criticism of the Bible*, 45; Aland and Aland, 285; and James R. White, *The King James Only Controversy: Can You Trust the Modern Translations?* (Minneapolis, MN: Bethany, 1995), 207–209. Significantly, *nomina sacra* are also used for "Jesus" ($\overline{\text{I}\Sigma}$), "Christ" ($\overline{\text{X}\Sigma}$), "Son" ($\overline{\Upsilon\Sigma}$), "Lord" ($\overline{\text{K}\Sigma}$), "Savior" ($\overline{\Sigma\text{HP}}$), and also for the Spirit ($\overline{\Pi\text{NA}}$). Further on the significance of *nomina sacra* (among other evidences) for early Christian Christology, see Larry W. Hurtado, *Lord Jesus Christ: Devotion to Jesus in Earliest Christianity* (Grand Rapids, MI: Eerdmans, 2003).

[48] Wegner, *Textual Criticism of the Bible*, 45.

[49] See Gordon J. Wenham, *Genesis 1–15*, Word Biblical Commentary 1 (Nashville, TN: Thomas Nelson, 1987), 219.

[50] Cf. Wegner, *Textual Criticism of the Bible*, 45.

[51] Ibid, 46; and Aland and Aland, 288.

[52] That is, three vowels (*ē*, *i*, *y*), three diphthongs (*ei*, *oi*, *ui*), and one irregular diphthong (*ēi*); cf. Aland and Aland, 287, citing also the interchange of *erchesthai* and *erchesthe*. See Anderson and Widder, 32.

up in conflict [*neikos*]."[53] Context, along with a careful consideration of the weight of evidence, makes clear which word Paul had in mind. Less dramatic scribal errors include substitution of one synonym for another, variation of word order, and the transposition of letters (metathesis) that results in different words. The biblical Qumran text 1Q5 provides an example of metathesis in Deuteronomy 31:1, reversing the last two consonants of the initial verb: "Moses finished [*wykl*] and spoke," rather than "Moses went [*wylk*] and spoke."[54] Another example of metathesis occurs in Mark 14:65, in which manuscripts used by the KJV/NKJV have the Greek word *ebalon* ("struck"), whereas in those used by most modern versions it is *elabon* ("received").[55] Such unintentional changes (summarized in the table below) are almost always quite obvious and usually leave little doubt as to what was originally intended.[56]

Unintentional Scribal Errors			
Error	**Definition**	**Possible Examples**	
		OT	**NT**
Haplography	Omission of a letter or word, usually due to a similar letter or word in context	1QIsa^{a} omits words in Isaiah 4:5, 6 between repetition of "by day"	Vaticanus omits words in John 17:15 between "from/of the" (Gk. *ek tou*)
Mistaken letters	Confusion of similar letters	Dodanim (Gen 10:4); Rodanim (1 Chr 1:7)	Confusion of OΣ and $\overline{\Theta\Sigma}$ (1 Tim 3:16)
Homophony	Substitution of similar sounding words	Substitution of *lo'* for *lô* (Isa 9:2 [ET 3])	Interchange of *o* and *ō* in *ech-* (Rom 5:1)

---

[53] Anderson and Widder, 32. The superscripted asterisk indicates the original reading prior to its subsequent correction by a later scribe.

[54] Anderson and Widder, 29; and Wegner, *Textual Criticism of the Bible*, 48 (who, however, mistakenly cites 4QDtn as the source). According to Martin Abegg Jr., Peter Flint, and Eugene Ulrich, *The Dead Sea Scrolls Bible: The Oldest Known Bible Translated for the First Time into English* (New York: HarperCollins, 1999), n. 147 (on Deut 31:1), OakTree Software (DSSB-E Notes, Version 1.2), the reading *wykl* is supported also by some Masoretic Text manuscripts and the LXX, while the Masoretic Text reading in BHS is supported also by the Samaritan Pentateuch.

[55] Anderson and Widder, 29.

[56] A similar table, from which some of these definitions and examples are taken, is given in Wegner, *From Texts to Translations*, 180, 225.

Unintentional Scribal Errors			
Error	**Definition**	**Possible Examples** OT	NT
Itacism (Greek NT)	Confusion of similar sounding vowels or diphthongs	———	Confusion of *neikos* for *nikos* (1 Cor 15:54, 55)
Metathesis	Reversal in order of two letters or words	1Q5 reverses last two consonants in first word (Deut 31:1)	Transposition of letters (*elabon* to *ebalon*) in Mark 14:65

Sometimes, whether intentionally or unintentionally, it appears that material was added by scribes. In the Synoptic Gospels, for example, we find the harmonizing of texts with similar accounts elsewhere.[57] A conspicuous example is the apparent conforming in many manuscripts of the Lord's Prayer in Luke 11:2–4 to the longer and more familiar form found in Matthew 6:9–13.[58] Another way this scribal tendency appears is in the alteration of New Testament quotations to match their form in the Septuagint more closely (for example, Matthew 15:8, which quotes Isaiah 29:13, may not have included the words "draw near to Me with their mouth, And…"). The expansion of the name of Jesus is also frequent, as in Galatians 6:17, with various manuscripts having "Jesus Christ," "the Lord Jesus," "the Lord Jesus Christ," or "our Lord Jesus Christ."[59] None of these additions affect the truth of the Bible, nor are they difficult to recognize.

---

[57] See, e.g., Matthew 18:11 (cf. Luke 19:10); Matthew 19:17 (cf. Mark 10:17; Luke 18:18); Matthew 23:14 (cf. Mark 12:40; Luke 20:47); Mark 15:28 (Luke 22:37); and Luke 17:36 (Matt 24:40). In NA[28]/UBS[5], only Matthew 19:17 is retained (in a substantially different form; see Bruce M. Metzger, *A Textual Commentary on the Greek New Testament*, 2nd ed. [New York: American Bible Society, 1994], 39–40), while in Robinson and Pierpont, 170, only the last reference (Luke 17:36, found in D and *f*[13]) is omitted as a harmonization.

[58] Cf. Robinson and Pierpont, 152, retaining the longer form, defended in Andrew J. Bandstra, "The Lord's Prayer and Textual Criticism: A Response," *Calvin Theological Journal* 17 (1982): 80–84. For an explanation of these differences from the Alexandrian-priority perspective, see Metzger, *Textual Commentary*, 130–132.

[59] Cf. Robinson, "Appendix," 550, who asserts that "such cases remain sporadic, localized, and shared among only a small minority of scribes. Most New Testament scribes did *not* engage in wholesale pious expansion" (emphasis original). He suggests that the shorter reading "may be due to accidental omission triggered by common endings (*homoioteleuta*) among the various *nomina sacra* within a phrase" (ibid.).

Rules of Textual Analysis

These examples should make obvious the importance of the work of textual analysis, which evaluates the various readings of the extant manuscripts in an effort to ascertain the earliest form of the text. So, how should a given variant be assessed and how can it be determined which one is the earliest? There are several canons (or rules) that have proved useful for determining which reading is likely to be authentic, classified under two headings: internal evidence (derived from the text itself) and external evidence (derived from the antiquity, quality, and geographic distribution of manuscript support).[60]

Internal Evidence

In connection with internal evidence, the "genealogical principle" is very important, namely, that the reading from which the other readings could most easily have developed is most likely the original.

Put differently we can say that the simplest explanation, that requires the fewest assumptions and that satisfies all the data, is to be preferred. For example, in Luke 11:4, the majority of manuscripts add the words "but deliver us from the evil one." If this were the earlier reading, it is hard to understand why a scribe would delete that phrase. However, if it were not in the text being copied it is easy to see how the scribe could have added it in order to harmonize it with Matthew 6:13. From this basic principle, two other rules of textual analysis based on internal evidence follow:

1) The more difficult reading is likely to be the original. We can see how this principle (sometimes referred to as *lectio difficilior*) explains the change in Luke 11:4. But it is also important to exclude from this rule obvious errors in transcription, such as those that lead to nonsense readings (as distinct from difficult readings), such as the replacement of *linon* ("linen") by *lithon* ("stone") in Revelation 15:6 so that the seven angels are described as "robed in pure bright stone."[61] Such a reading is patently wrong. Another example can be found in Acts 20:28, where we find three related variants: 1) "the church of God"; 2) "the church of the Lord"; and 3) "the church of the Lord and God." The third variant obviously conflates the first and the second. But which is the more difficult? "The church of the Lord" occurs nowhere else in the New

---

[60] The rules as they are presented here are adapted from J. Harold Greenlee, *The Text of the New Testament: From Manuscript to Modern Edition* (Peabody, MA: Hendrickson, 2008), 59–68. The application of these rules leads to different results depending on whether the Alexandrian-priority or the Byzantine-priority hypothesis is favored.

[61] This nonsense reading is found in A (Alexandrinus), C (Ephraemi), and other manuscripts.

Testament and "the church of God" appears nowhere else in Luke's writings but eleven times in Paul, and Paul is speaking in this passage. However, the second is actually the more difficult reading because of what immediately follows: ". . . which He purchased with His own blood." It appears that a scribe, who was perplexed at the thought of God having blood, changed "God" to "Lord."

2) The shorter reading is generally preferable if the longer reading seems to have resulted from an intentional change by a scribe. Accidental omissions (such as a scribal leap that shortens the text) are excluded for obvious reasons. The rationale for this rule is that it would seem to be easier for scribes to add words to the Scriptures (especially to clarify or soften something) than to delete inspired material.[62] An example of this is in Matthew 5:22: "Whoever is angry with his brother [without a cause (Gk. *eikē*)] shall be in danger of the judgment." Although the words in brackets appear in most manuscripts, including some important uncials, the shorter reading is judged by most to have better support: an early papyrus (P^{64}) as well as א and B.[63] The word *eike* would seem to have been added to soften Jesus' statement and harmonize it with expressions in the Psalms (35:19; 69:4; cf. 109:3; 119:78, 161).

External Evidence

The category of external evidence is based on the classification of manuscripts into the three basic families or text-types described earlier (Alexandrian, Byzantine, Western).[64] Manuscripts classified as Alexandrian (e.g., P^{46}, P^{66}, P^{75}, א, B) stem from scribes schooled in Alexandrian scriptoral practices, which emphasized the accurate transmission of manuscripts. That is why this text type is considered by most scholars to best reflect the earliest form of the text and, therefore,

---

[62] Note, however, James R. Royse, *Scribal Habits in Early Greek New Testament Papyri* (Leiden: Brill, 2007), 608, that, for early papyri (P^{45}, P^{46}, P^{47}, P^{66}, P^{72}, and P^{75}), the longer reading is better unless it can be shown otherwise on genealogical (that is, history of manuscript transmission), harmonistic, or grammatical grounds.

[63] The support is considered better because the early papyri and these two uncials are generally held to be more reliable. Nevertheless, the documented tendency of early scribes toward omission (see previous note), which all three of these manuscripts would tend to follow, may suggest that the longer reading is better.

[64] See Metzger and Ehrman, 276–280; cf. 305–313 for more detailed description of these three types, as well as their acknowledgement of a fourth type, the Caesarean family of manuscripts, a mixed text type at best that has found far less acceptance. Cf. Aland and Aland, 180–181, who prefer (as described on 116–117) to classify manuscripts based on their faithfulness to what they consider to be the "original" (*ursprüngliche*) text, as indicated through a selection of "test passages" (*Teststellen*)—a procedure criticized by Metzger and Ehrman, 238, as essentially circular.

to be more reliable.[65] The Western text-type (e.g., P[112], D, 0171, Old Latin versions) tends to be longer and is more paraphrastic, but may occasionally preserve the more original text.[66] The Byzantine text-type (e.g., A [in the Gospels], 049 [in Acts and the Epistles], and most later manuscripts), is generally considered less reliable because these manuscripts tend to be smoother, clearer, and theologically preferable. That is, most textual critics contend that, in the process of transmission, it is more likely that scribes would "improve" the text rather than make it less clear and theologically less attractive.[67] The basic rule for external evidence is: the reading supported by the most reliable text-type or combination of text-types and having wide geographic distribution is likely to be earlier.

In other words, manuscript support should be weighed, not counted. But which manuscripts are considered more reliable? The vast majority of scholars think that if a variant is supported by several Alexandrian manuscripts as well as witnesses from one or both of the other text types it has strong support. In addition, a variant with widespread independent attestation (especially as indicated by ancient versions and quotations in the Greek and Latin church fathers) has more weight.[68]

Most who have studied the history of the New Testament text believe that analyzing a given reading based on both internal and external evidence will generally yield secure decisions in determining the reading that most likely reflects the earliest form of the text.[69] This approach is used both by those who favor the Alexandrian-priority hypothesis and those who support the Byzantine-priority hypothesis. However, the results derived from the application of these methods can vary considerably in the hands of the practitioner, as even a cursory reading of Bruce Metzger's *Textual Commentary*[70] and Maurice Robinson's

---

[65] E.g., Barbara Aland, Kurt Aland, Phillip W. Comfort, J. K. Elliott, Eldon Jay Epp, Michael J. Holmes, Bruce M. Metzger, and Daniel B. Wallace, some of whose works are cited in this chapter.

[66] See Metzger and Ehrman, 70–74, for a description of some important witnesses.

[67] See, however, the reply to this contention in Robinson, "Appendix," 578–580.

[68] For a detailed description of this evidence, see Metzger and Ehrman, 94–134; cf. Wegner, *Textual Criticism of the Bible*, 235–238.

[69] This reflects the "reasoned eclecticism" school of textual criticism (cf. n. 32 above). See Michael J. Holmes, "The Case for Reasoned Eclecticism," in Black, *Rethinking New Testament Textual Criticism*, 77–100.

[70] See especially Metzger, *Textual Commentary*, 14*, for a description of the committee process and an explanation of the letters "A" (certain), "B" (almost certain), "C" (difficulty deciding), and "D" (great difficulty deciding), which suggest the disagreements among committee members in particular cases.

defense of Byzantine-priority[71] demonstrate. Despite this reality, it is helpful to keep in mind that the vast majority of variants are inconsequential scribal errors such as obvious misspellings, transpositions, or substitution of synonyms, which in no way change the meaning of the text. Even in the rare case that a given variant does significantly change the meaning, no major doctrine is negatively impacted because such teachings are based on the broad testimony of clear Bible passages.[72] The same can be said of Old Testament variants.[73] This fact can be illustrated by means of several examples.

Intentional Scribal Changes

Intentional changes made to the text, while extremely rare, do occasionally occur. Generally, such changes arose as attempts to solve perceived "problems" in the text. In Mark 1:2, for example, the quotation from Malachi 3:1 and Isaiah 40:3 is attributed only to Isaiah in earlier manuscripts, while later manuscripts attribute it to "the prophets." What may have seemed problematic to the scribe, that the first quotation is from Malachi, poses no real problem. Only Isaiah is mentioned because he is the major prophet and the source of John's message (Isa 40:3). Mark begins by quoting Malachi simply to introduce John as the Lord's "messenger" (Mal 3:1).

Another example is a perceived geographical "problem" that appears to have been "corrected" by Origen's altering *Bēthania* to *Bēthabara* in John 1:28, resulting in some uncertainty as to the reading of the original text. The Madeba Map places Bethabara on the west side of the Jordan and yet John 1:28 locates John's place of baptizing on the east side. But if *Bēthania* refers to the region of Batanaea (as seems to be the case), the problem disappears and fits quite well with John's other geographical references.[74] In another case, the scribe of Codex B (Vaticanus) found the association in Hebrews 9:4 of the altar of

[71] See Robinson, "Appendix," 544–566.

[72] See Andreas J. Köstenberger and Michael J. Kruger, *The Heresy of Orthodoxy: How Contemporary Culture's Fascination with Diversity Has Reshaped our Understanding of Early Christianity* (Wheaton, IL: Crossway, 2010), 203–231, esp. 228: "It [the manuscript tradition] is so very close to the originals that there is no material difference between what, say, Paul or John wrote and what we possess today." Cf. J. R. White, *King James Only Controversy*, 40, who notes that "no textual variants in either the Old or New Testaments in any way, shape, or form materially disrupt or destroy any essential doctrine of the Christian faith."

[73] Brug, 1: "Only a small percentage of textual variants change the meaning of a passage, and none raise doubts about any biblical doctrine. The great majority are simply spelling variants."

[74] See Rainer Riesner, "Bethany Beyond the Jordan (John 1:28): Topography, Theology and History in the Fourth Gospel," *Tyndale Bulletin* 38 (1987): 29–63.

incense with the Most Holy Place to be problematic, resulting in the reference being moved to verse 2, which describes the other Holy Place furniture. However, Hebrews is describing not the geographical location, but the theological significance of the altar of incense in connection with the divine presence in the Most Holy Place.[75] The problem is not with the text. Such intentional changes by scribes can be problematic but, in this instance, because the change did not filter through into a wider body of manuscripts, there is little doubt as to what was initially written.[76]

We may also find intentional conflation in the manuscripts. Some scribes, it seems, when confronted with two different readings as in Luke 24:53 ("praising God" or "blessing God"), rather than leaving out an inspired sentiment, may have chosen to conflate the two into "praising and blessing God." It is challenging to determine which of the two words Luke had in mind. Because the external manuscript evidence is divided and the same is true of the internal evidence, it is difficult to be certain. The most likely solution in this case is that which is best able to explain how the variant readings arose. Since early and diverse manuscripts and versions support "blessing [*eulogountes*] God" and since this word in Christian writings also came to be used of "praising" God, the former possibility is the best solution.[77] Others, however, argue that this is not an instance of conflation and that omission of one or the other of the two readings is more likely (as reflected for instance in the AMP, MEV, NKJV, and WEB).[78]

---

[75] Harold S. Camacho, "The Altar of Incense in Hebrews 9:3–4," *Andrews University Seminary Studies* 24/1 (1986): 5–12.

[76] There is also some discussion of what the word *thymiatērion* means. Camacho, 7, mentions the translation "censer" in the KJV, Weymouth, Wuest, and the *Concordant Version*, but considers it doubtful. The normal word for "altar" (whether for burnt offerings or for burning incense) is *thysiastērion* (e.g., Lev 4:7), whereas the *thymiatērion* would seem to be used exclusively in the LXX (2 Chr 26:19; Ezek 8:11; cf. *4 Maccabees* 7:11) for the censer used to burn *thymiama* ("incense"). While it would seem odd for the altar of incense to be left out in Hebrews 9:4, it may be a synecdoche in order to stress the function of the altar.

[77] As in the ASV, ESV, NET, and NRSV. See the discussion in Metzger, *Textual Commentary*, 163–164. However, deciding in this case is not as easy as suggested by the number of English translations on biblegateway.com that have "praising" (23) or both "praising and blessing" (20) as opposed to "blessing" (15) or their equivalents.

[78] See James A. Borland, "The Textual Criticism of Luke 24:53 and Its Implications," in Billington and Streitberger, 114–122, who concludes that "praising and blessing" is the original reading based on the following: "It has the early witness of the Diatessaron, the most breadth among the uncials, and is the only reading with practically any continued support past the 5th century. This reading best explains the rise of the other variants, has the greatest geographical support, and is the sole reading to be seen in the Alexandrian, Western, Caesarean, and Byzantine text types. In addition, it best explains the most common error

In another case, Jesus' statement to His brothers that He would not go up to the Jewish feast in John 7:8, and the later acknowledgment that Jesus "also went up . . . not openly, but as it were in secret" (John 7:10), apparently led an early scribe to change *ouk* (not) to *oupō* (not yet). If the original reading had been "I am not yet going up to this feast" (as in the NKJV), why would it be changed from "not yet" to "not" and thus create a problem where none existed? Although this papyrus is very early (mid-second century), the scribe exhibits a tendency to add material to smooth out the text and harmonize it with other passages.[79] These two verses in John are not contradictory. "The issue is not that he [Jesus] will not go, but that he will only go 'secretly' at first, so as not to hasten the appropriate time of his execution (cf. 7:6 with 2:4)."[80] Another issue that periodically surfaces is the tendency of some pious scribes to augment "prayer" with "fasting" in several places (Mark 9:29; Acts 10:30; 1 Cor 7:5).[81] It should also be mentioned that the sometimes idiosyncratic syntax in the book of Revelation seems to have resulted in various "corrections" to the syntax in this book's transmission history.[82] All of these examples are quite exceptional. Intentional changes are by no means common in the manuscripts, and in most of these instances there is little doubt about the wording of the earliest text.

There are only a very few instances of longer variants (Mark 16:9–20; John 5:3–4; 7:53–8:11), suggesting a special history of transmission. These cases deserve to be examined individually in more detail, but such a task is beyond the scope of this brief chapter.[83] Nevertheless, even intentional changes to the text in the course of the Bible's transmission in no way

---

scribes make when copying MSS" (Billington and Streitberger, 122).

[79] Metzger, *Textual Commentary*, 185; and Metzger and Ehrman, 267.

[80] Craig S. Keener, *The IVP Bible Background Commentary: New Testament* (Downers Grove, IL: InterVarsity, 1993), 281.

[81] Ibid., 268.

[82] See esp. Laurentiu Mot, *Morphological and Syntactical Irregularities in the Book of Revelation: A Greek Hypothesis* (Leiden: Brill, 2015), 221, 246, who argues that the unusual Greek of the Apocalypse "is always intentional."

[83] For a discussion of each of these from the standpoint of Alexandrian priority, see Greenlee, 99–103; see also Wegner, *Textual Criticism of the Bible*, 247–248; Metzger and Ehrman, 258, 319–327; Aland and Aland, 236, 293–294, 305; and Metzger, *Textual Commentary*, 102–106, 179, 187–189. For a discussion from the standpoint of Byzantine priority, defending the place of each of these passages in Scripture, see Maurice A. Robinson, "The Long Ending of Mark as Canonical Verity," in *Perspectives on the Ending of Mark*, ed. David Alan Black (Nashville, TN: Broadman and Holman, 2008), 40–79; Andrew Wilson, "The Adulteress and Her Accusers: An Examination of the Internal Arguments relating to the *Pericope Adulterae*," in Billington and Streitberger, 123–141; and Robinson, "Appendix" 580–582.

undermine its inspiration.[84] Notice these comments by Ellen G. White regarding the transmission process:

> Some look to us gravely and say, "Don't you think there might have been some mistake in the copyist or in the translators?" This is all probable, and the mind that is so narrow that it will hesitate and stumble over this possibility or probability would be just as ready to stumble over the mysteries of the Inspired Word, because their feeble minds cannot see through the purposes of God. . . . All the mistakes will not cause trouble to one soul, or cause any feet to stumble, that would not manufacture difficulties from the plainest revealed truth.[85]

> The Lord has preserved this Holy Book by His own miraculous power in its present shape.[86]

> The manuscripts of the Hebrew and Greek Scriptures have been preserved through the ages by a miracle of God.[87]

A far more consequential matter is the shift in translation method that has occurred over the past thirty years, to which we now turn our attention.

Bible Versions and Hermeneutics

All Bible translations must make specific choices with regard to the underlying Hebrew and Greek texts. They choose the base texts in the original languages and must decide on what grounds, if any, they would deviate from that text by selecting a different variant. As explained earlier, nearly all modern translations utilize the Leningrad Codex for translating the Hebrew Old Testament and an eclectic text for translating the Greek New Testament. As a result, while some translation differences in the Old Testament stem from different readings in the underlying manuscripts, many more decisions of this kind must be

---

[84] On apparent discrepancies in the text itself, see Frank M. Hasel, "Are There Mistakes in the Bible?" in *Interpreting Scripture: Bible Questions and Answers*, ed. Gerhard Pfandl (Silver Spring, MD: Biblical Research Institute, 2010), 33–41.

[85] Ellen G. White, *Selected Messages* (Washington, DC: Review and Herald, 1958), 1:16.

[86] Ibid., 15.

[87] Ellen G. White to Brother and Sister Muckersey, February 14, 1899, Lt 32, 1899, para. 8.

made in connection with the translation of the New Testament due to thousands of textual witnesses. Below are some examples of differences between Bible versions due to different choices made as to which variant is more likely to reflect the original text of Scripture.

Some Variant-Caused Translation Differences		
Matt 27:16	"Barabbas" (ESV, NAS95, NKJV, NIV)	"Jesus Barabbas" (NET, NIV11, NRSV)
Mark 1:2	"in the prophets" (NKJV, WEB)	"in the prophet Isaiah" (ESV, NAS95, NIV11)
Mark 2:4	"could not get to/near Him" (ESV, NAS95, RSV)	"could not bring him to Jesus" (CSB, NIV11, NRSV)
John 1:18	"only (begotten) Son" (NKJV, RSV, WEB)	"only (begotten) God" (ESV, NAS95, NET, NIV)[88]
1 Cor 13:3	"give my body to be burned" (ESV, NAS95, NIV, NKJV)	"give my body that I may boast" (NET, NIV11, NRSV)
Phil 1:14	"speak the word of God" (NAS95, NIV, NKJV)	"speak the word" (CSB, ESV, NIV11,[89] NRSV)
Rev 22:14	"those who do His commandments" (NKJV, WEB)	"those who wash their robes" (CSB, ESV, NIV)

Interestingly, not all of the differences are attributable to the choice by a given version of a modern eclectic text over the Textus Receptus (that is, the traditional Greek text reflected in the King James Version). Otherwise we would expect that the left column would not include such a proliferation of modern versions. Differences even appear between different editions of the same version (NIV/NIV11 in Matt 27:16; 1 Cor 13:3; Phil 1:14; and RSV/NRSV in Mark 2:4). Such shifts illustrate a certain subjectivity that is often involved in making judgments as to the most likely wording of the original text.

The element of subjectivity is also manifested in the process of Bible translation. Consider the biblical teaching on the deity of Christ. In an examination of key passages used to support this doctrine, some versions are quite clear while in others ambiguity exists or the teaching is absent altogether. Notice the relative strength or weakness on this point of several translations as given in the table below.[90]

---

[88] Some versions use paraphrase to retain both ideas: "the one and only Son, who is himself God" (CSB, NIV11); "God the only Son" (NRSV).

[89] NIV11 paraphrases the idea: "proclaim the gospel."

[90] The table is adapted and expanded from J. R. White, *King James Only Controversy*, 197.

Comparison of Versions on the Deity of Christ					
Reference	**KJV/NKJV**	**NASB/ NAS95**	**ESV**	**NIV11**	**RSV/NRSV**
John 1:1	Clear	Clear	Clear	Clear	Clear
John 1:18*	**Absent**	Clear	Clear	Clear	**Absent/** Clear
John 20:28	Clear	Clear	Clear	Clear	Clear
Acts 20:28*	Clear	Clear	Clear	Clear	**Absent**
Rom 9:5	Ambiguous/ Clear	Ambiguous	Clearest	Clearest	**Absent/** Ambiguous
Phil 2:5–6	Clear	Clearer	Clearer	Clearest	Clearer
Col 1:15–17	Clearer	Clearer/ Clear	Clearer	Clear	Clear
Col 2:9	Ambiguous	Clear	Ambig-uous	Clear	Ambiguous
1 Tim 3:16*	Clear	**Absent**	**Absent**	**Absent**	**Absent**
Titus 2:13	Ambiguous/ Clear	Clear	Clear	Clear	Clear
Heb 1:8	Clear	Clear	Clear	Clear	Clear
2 Pet 1:1*	Ambiguous/ Clear	Clear	Clear	Clear	Clear

* Indicates significant differences appear in the underlying Greek manuscripts.

As is evident from the above table, some translations are clearer than others on the doctrine of Christ's deity. This may result from a decision to eliminate the ambiguity present in the Greek (e.g., Rom 9:5; Col 2:9). At other times, variations stem from the choice of different variants or the preference of one text type over another (as with the textual variant in 1 Timothy 3:16, which has been discussed above). Another example involving different variants is Acts 20:28 (". . . shepherd the church of God which He purchased with His own blood"). A scribe may have wondered, "Does God have blood?" and proceeded to "clarify" the text.[91] The RSV/NRSV, in harmony with a particular interpretation of the Greek wording in Alexandrian manuscripts, interprets the phrase

---

[91] See Metzger, *Textual Commentary*, 425–427.

"his own" to be a reference to God's own Son.[92] While not necessarily a deliberate attempt to diminish the deity of Christ, this decision does have the effect of eliminating this passage's support of that teaching.

Sometimes translations resort to paraphrase. John 1:18 is a good example of this in attempting to clarify the relationship of the Father and the Son. The NIV11 reads: "No one has ever seen God, but the one and only Son, who is himself God and is in closest relationship with the Father, has made him known" (cf. ESV). Interestingly, attempts at clarifying the meaning of this verse appear already in the history of textual transmission. Most manuscripts read "only begotten Son" (a uniquely Johannine title for Christ: John 3:16, 18; 1 John 4:9), but two early papyri (P^{66} and P^{75}) and the earliest uncials (א, B, C*) have "only begotten God."[93] The table illustrates two important points: 1) In none of these versions does there appear to be a deliberate attempt to diminish the deity of Christ; otherwise we would expect it to be more consistently evident as it is, for example, in the *New World Translation of the Holy Scriptures* produced by the Jehovah's Witnesses.[94] Notably, both the NKJV and the NRSV constitute an improvement over their predecessors in terms of this biblical teaching. 2) The deity of Christ (as with every major Bible doctrine) is so pervasive, clear and indisputable throughout the New Testament that no variants in the manuscripts, no differences in versions, and not even deliberate theological bias can obscure it completely.[95]

---

[92] See the discussion in Charles F. DeVine, "The 'Blood of God' in Acts 20:28," *Catholic Biblical Quarterly* 9 (1947): 381–408, who argues that the passage supports the deity of Christ.

[93] Comfort, 336, pointing out on the same page: "This is a masterful way of concluding the prologue, for 1:18 then mirrors 1:1. Both verses have the following three corresponding phrases: 1) Christ as God's expression (the 'Word' and 'he has explained him'), 2) Christ as God ('the Word was God' and 'an only One, God'), and 3) as the one close to God ('the Word was face to face with God' [Williams translation] and 'in the bosom of the Father')."

[94] Note its tendential translation of several key passages: "the Word was a god" (John 1:1); "and from them the Christ descended according to the flesh. God who is over all, be praised forever. Amen" (Rom 9:5); "Christ Jesus, who, although he was existing in God's form, gave no consideration to a seizure, namely, that he should be equal to God" (Phil 2:5–6); "He is the image of the invisible God, the firstborn of all creation; because by means of him all other things were created in the heavens and on the earth, the things visible and the things invisible, whether they are thrones or lordships or governments or authorities. All other things have been created through him and for him. Also, he is before all other things, and by means of him all other things were made to exist" (Col 1:15–17; the word "other" is inserted by the translators four times and is not found in the New Testament text); "But about the Son, he says: 'God is your throne forever and ever'" (Heb 1:8).

[95] E.g., the New World Translation of John 1:3: "All things came into existence through him [the Word], and apart from him not even one thing came into existence" (brackets supplied).

This discussion raises another important issue. In addition to adjudicating manuscript differences, Bible translations must also decide how much freedom to permit in the translation process. The range of translation approaches may be mapped along a continuum ranging from a formal translation like the English Standard Version (ESV), which aspires to be "essentially literal," at one end to a culturally sensitive translation and paraphrase at the other:[96]

Formal	Functional	Dynamic		Cultural
ESV, NASB, NKJV, RSV	CSB, NRSV	NIV11, NLT	NEB, TEV	LB, MSG, TCW

Versions of the Bible generally explain their methodology in the preface, which should be read carefully before choosing a translation for reading or study. Functional translations aim at faithfulness to the original language but are not strictly literal. The New Revised Standard Version (NRSV) describes it this way: "As literal as possible, as free as necessary." Reading further, the desire to avoid what it calls "linguistic sexism" has led to the elimination of "masculine-oriented language . . . as far as this can be done without altering passages that reflect the historical situation of the ancient patriarchal culture."[97] The Christian Standard Bible (CSB), successor to the Holman Christian Standard Bible (HCSB), has taken smaller steps in a similar direction as the NRSV.[98] The translators of the New International Version (NIV), which aims at "dynamic equivalence," were given even more latitude with the text. Still farther down the road toward cultural equivalence are more paraphrastic translations such as the New English Bible (NEB) and Today's English Version (TEV). Unlike translations such as these, which are done by a committee, paraphrases of the Bible are the work of a single individual who has complete freedom to express the meaning of the text in a culturally clear way, regardless of the original language's underlying words and syntax.

Friedrich Schleiermacher's well know assertion that there are only

---

[96] Glenn J. Kerr, "Dynamic Equivalence and Its Daughters: Placing Bible Translation Theories in Their Historical Context," *Journal of Translation* 7/1 (2011): 16 (mapping of English versions supplied).

[97] Bruce M. Metzger, "To the Reader," The Holy Bible. New Revised Standard Version. 1989, x.

[98] Favoring "optimal equivalence" over "formal equivalence," the CSB approach is explained thus: "When a word-for-word rendering might obscure the meaning for a modern audience, a more dynamic translation is used" (*The Holy Bible*, Christian Standard Bible [Nashville, TN: Holman Bible Publishers, 2017], viii).

two methods of translation vividly represents the two possible extremes of a literal translation on the conservative end and a more paraphrastic translation on the other: "Either the translator leaves the author in peace, as much as possible, and moves the reader towards him; or he leaves the reader in peace, as much as possible, and moves the author towards him."[99] The formal (word-for-word) translation method strives to translate, as far as possible, a given word in the Hebrew or Greek text with the same word in the target language (moving the reader toward the Bible writer). However, recent studies in linguistics have so strongly influenced the field of translation that Bible versions are moving ever closer to the reader and further from the text of Scripture. This newer approach is based on the theory of dynamic equivalence, which

> aims at complete naturalness of expression, and tries to relate the receptor to modes of behavior relevant within the context of his own culture; it does not insist that he understand the cultural patterns of the source-language context in order to comprehend the message.[100]

This shift in translation theory is reflected in the dynamic (meaning-for-meaning) translation method. A third approach, known as optimal equivalence, aims at a translation that accurately reflects all levels of a text's meaning (word, phrase, clause, sentence, paragraph, chapter, book, and canon).[101] The two main approaches (formal and dynamic) follow a similar process up to a point and then diverge. These two different approaches to translation may be diagrammed as shown on the next page:

---

[99] Friedrich Schleiermacher, "On the Different Methods of Translating" [1813], in *Translating Literature: The German Tradition from Luther to Rosensweig*, ed. and trans. André Lefevere (Assen: Van Gorcum, 1977), 67–89, cited in Lawrence Venuti, "Translation as Cultural Politics Regimes of Domestication in English," *Textual Practice* 7/2 (1993): 208–223 (repr., New York: Routledge, 2005), 36.

[100] Eugene A. Nida, *Toward a Science of Translating, With Special Reference to Principles and Procedures Involved in Bible Translating* (Leiden: Brill, 1964), 159. Because this expression had been misunderstood, Nida began to use "functional equivalence" for essentially the same idea.

[101] Lane Keister, "Too Many to Choose from? The English Bible Translation Controversy," *Unio Cum Christo*, 5/1 (April 2019): 63; cf. 61–66 for brief discussions of the four most important factors affecting Bible translations (text-critical approach, translation philosophy, literary quality, and gender inclusivity). Evaluating twelve English versions, Keister, 76, considers those "most highly recommended for use in church" to be the KJV (67: "one of the very best translations of the Bible ever made in any language"), NASB (71: "remarkably free from bias"), NKJV (72: "one of the best translations available for personal and public, liturgical use"), ESV (74: despite faulting its "literary style," judged "one of the very best translations available"), and the CSB (75: "the single best translation available in balancing accuracy and readability, good English style with as much transference from source to target language").

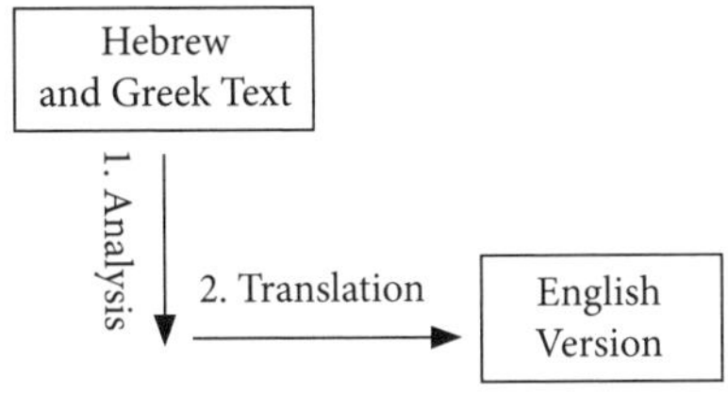

Formal (Word-for-Word) Translation

Procedure

- Analyze the text in the source language
- Translate the text into the target language

Hebrew and Greek Text
English Version
1. Analysis
2. Translation
3. Restructuring

Dynamic (Meaning-for-Meaning) Translation

Procedure

- Analyze the text in the source language
- Translate the text into the target language
- Restructure the material to convey meaning

A formal translation involves a two-step process that 1) analyzes the text in the original (source) language in order to 2) convey the literal meaning of the text in the target language. A dynamic translation adds a third step: restructuring the material in the target language in order to convey the meaning of the text "more clearly."[102] The different translations that result from the use of these two different methods may be illustrated by comparing how several English versions have addressed a perceived ambiguity or lack of clarity in the original language text as listed in the table below.

Meaning-Caused Translation Differences			
#	**Scripture**	**Formal (Word-for-Word) Translation**	**Dynamic (Meaning-for-Meaning) Translation**
1	Josh 10:6	"do not relax your hand from your servants" (ESV)	"do not forsake your servants" (NKJV)
2	Ps 51:5	"I was brought forth in iniquity" (NAS95)	"I was born guilty" (NRSV)
3	Prov 24:26	"He who gives a right answer kisses the lips" (NKJV)	"An honest answer is like a kiss on the lips" (NIV11)

[102] This process is summarized from Gerhard F. Hasel, *Understanding the Living Word of God* (Mountain View, CA: Pacific Press, 1980), 101–103 (apparently, in the layout process for the book, the associated diagrams were inadvertently swapped).

Meaning-Caused Translation Differences			
#	Scripture	Formal (Word-for-Word) Translation	Dynamic (Meaning-for-Meaning) Translation
4	Dan 9:25	"Until Messiah the Prince, There shall be seven weeks and sixty-two weeks" (NKJV)	"to the coming of an anointed one, a prince, there shall be seven weeks. Then for sixty-two weeks . . ." (ESV)
5	Amos 4:6	"I gave you cleanness of teeth" (NRSV)	"I gave you no food to eat" (NET)
6	Matt 2:16	"Herod . . . sent and slew all the male children" (NAS95)	"Herod . . . sent and killed all the children" (NRSV)
7	Luke 9:44	"Let these words sink into your ears" (WEB)	"Let these words sink in" (CSB)
8	Heb 11:11	"Abraham . . . was enabled to become a father" (NIV)	"Sarah . . . was enabled to bear children" (NIV11)

In the above examples, it will be observed that greater clarity appears in the right column, reflecting a dynamic translation, when compared with the left column, reflecting a formal translation. It is also evident that, as with variant-caused translation differences, there is not complete consistency in how a given translation approaches the text. Versions that claim to follow a formal translation method (NKJV, ESV, CSB) sometimes translate the text dynamically and versions that employ a dynamic translation method (NIV, NRSV) sometimes translate the text quite literally. Another important observation is that a dynamic translation definitely clarifies the meaning of some these verses (see the odd-numbered examples).

In other cases, however, the attempt at clarification has significantly changed the biblical teaching conveyed (see the even-numbered examples). Psalm 51:5, as translated by the RSV, appears to teach the Augustinian doctrine of original sin (all humans inherit the guilt of Adam's sin at birth), whereas the words of David may simply refer to being born with a sinful nature without inheriting guilt. Daniel 9:25, as translated by the ESV (based on Masoretic punctuation), predicts the coming of the Messiah in just seven weeks (of years), whereas the Hebrew text is more naturally understood, as in most English versions, to place it after the sixty-nine weeks (7 + 62). Matthew 2:16 is translated as "children" by the NRSV, apparently in an attempt to maintain its practice of gender neutrality, whereas the Greek text uses the masculine form of the article to specify male children. Hebrews 11:11 is translated by the 2011 edition of the NIV as referring to Sarah's faith, despite her barrenness, even though the Old Testament account underscores Sarah's doubt of the promise (Gen 18:10–15) and Paul's interpretation of it elsewhere (Rom 4:19–22) highlights the role of Abraham's faith, not Sarah's. In short, while there are some advantages to the dynamic translation approach, there are serious drawbacks that render it of questionable value and, at least in certain instances, may obscure the meaning of the text.[103] This is an important fact to keep in mind and underscores the need to consult the original languages and/or compare translations in any serious, in-depth Bible study. Dynamic translations may be useful when the meaning of a text in a more literal translation is obscure, but, generally, it is better to rely on a formal translation such as the NKJV, NAS95, or ESV, for an accurate understanding of Scripture.

Interestingly, the theory of dynamic translation, designed to help missionaries translate the Bible, is being increasingly resisted. One researcher even describes it as "an imperialist appropriation of a foreign text."[104] Another researcher indicates that "the general translation community has essentially rejected equivalence as not possible."[105] In any case, regardless of how one may view this debate over dynamic approaches to the text, it is important to evaluate a given Bible translation in light of its purpose. It is also helpful to be aware of the increasing tendency in both Bible translations and paraphrases to take liberties with the text of Scripture.

To illustrate this last point, it will be helpful to see how three recent paraphrases insert theological biases into their rendering of Scripture: the *Living Bible* (LB) by Kenneth Taylor, *The Message* (MSG) by Eugene Peterson, and *The Clear Word* (TCW) by Jack Blanco, a Seventh-day Adventist. It should be noted in passing that, while we will look at single verses, the elimination of versification in MSG gives Peterson even more freedom to rearrange thoughts and focus on the portions of text he considers most important. Notice how differently Daniel 8:14 and Jude 7 are paraphrased by these three men:

---

[103] G. F. Hasel, Understanding the Living Word of God, 103: "To seek thought-for-thought or meaning-for-meaning equivalence, the translator must interpret—and it is here where problems lie."

[104] Venuti, 41. Applying poststructuralism to translation theory, Venuti speaks of "the ethnocentric violence of translation" (45).

[105] Kerr, 16; cf. 18: "Bible translators, while trying to be sound in principle and practice, also have a commitment to loyalty to the human and divine authors of the Bible as well as the intended recipients of the Bible translations."

Daniel 8:14		
LB	MSG	TCW
"The other replied, 'Twenty-three hundred days must first go by.'"	"The other answered, 'Over the course of 2,300 sacrifices, evening and morning. Then the Sanctuary will be set right again.'"	"He answered, 'After two thousand, three hundred prophetic days (which represent actual years), God will restore the truth about the heavenly Sanctuary to its rightful place. Then the process of judgment will begin of which the yearly cleansing of the earthly Sanctuary was a type, and God will vindicate His people.'"

In paraphrasing Daniel 8:14, LB leaves out the last half of the verse altogether, while MSG changes the 2,300 days into 2,300 sacrifices. Making the number refer to sacrifices (contrary to the wording of the Hebrew text) results in a time period of only 1,150 actual days in an attempt to "fit" Daniel 8:14 to the activities of Antiochus Epiphanes in the mid-second century BC; even then, however, it does not fit the historical events. By contrast, TCW reads like a mini Adventist commentary on this important verse.

Jude 7		
LB	MSG	TCW
"And don't forget the cities of Sodom and Gomorrah and their neighboring towns, all full of lust of every kind, including the lust of men for other men. Those cities were destroyed by fire and continue to be a warning to us that there is a hell in which sinners are punished."	"Sodom and Gomorrah, which went to sexual rack and ruin along with the surrounding cities that acted just like them, are another example. Burning and burning and never burning up, they serve still as a stock warning."	"Look at what happened to Sodom and Gomorrah and the surrounding cities. They were so filled with immorality, sodomy, and other sexual perversions that their destruction by fire is an example of what will happen to those who insist on living that way."

In paraphrasing Jude 7, LB clarifies the reference to homosexuality but inserts the doctrine of an eternally burning hell in the last half of the verse; MSG completely obscures the reference to homosexuality but, like LB, inserts language to fit the popular notion of hell, even implying that the cities are still burning; and TCW refers to the cities' sexual sins in more detail and hints at the final, total destruction of sinners by fire.

This same movement away from translation and toward commentary can be seen in many Bible versions, only to a lesser degree. Study Bibles with their extensive notes on the text are also a kind of commentary. Even versions that purport to be literal may, at times, resort to explaining the meaning of the original rather than employing a word-for-word correspondence,[106] as is evident from the following examples:

Text	"Literal" Translation	"Equivalent" Translation
Gen 4:1	"And Adam knew Eve his wife" (ESV, NKJV)	"Now the man had relations with his wife Eve" (NAS95)
Gen 30:27	"If I have found favor in your eyes" (NKJV, NIV11)	"If now it pleases you" (NAS95)
Job 27:3	"as long as my breath is still in me" (CSB, ESV)	"as long as life is in me" (NAS95)
Ps 146:3	"a son of man" (CSB, ESV)	"mortal man" (NAS95)
Luke 14:2	"before Him" (ESV, NKJV)	"in front of Him" (NAS95)
John 1:15	"preferred before me" (NKJV)	"has a higher rank than I" (NAS95)[107]
Acts 2:30	"of the fruit of his body" (NKJV)	"one of his descendants" (ESV, NAS95)

This trend in translation method has some advantages and should not be entirely rejected. What is important is to be aware of it and compare versions. Such a comparison can be useful even for those who are familiar with the original languages, because it may suggest possible translations that had not initially come to mind (e.g., unusual but possible word meanings or alternative ways to understand the syntax). Significantly, Ellen G. White quotes from a variety of versions, sometimes utilizing alternative renderings given by the translators, when

---

[106] See Dave Brunn, *One Bible, Many Versions: Are All Translations Created Equal?* (Downers Grove, IL: InterVarsity, 2013).

[107] With this translation, the contrast between "before" and "after" is lost.

these conveyed the meaning of the text more clearly or accurately.[108] In fact, she emphasizes that the Bible was "not given to us in grand, superhuman language," that "different meanings are expressed by the same word; there is not one word for each distinct idea," and that "the Bible was given for practical purposes."[109]

But the shift in Bible translation method away from strict renderings of the text also presents clear dangers, some of which have long been recognized.[110] Problems occur when ambiguity present in the Greek or Hebrew text is "clarified" by a translator who gets the meaning wrong. For example, some versions translate "the testimony of Jesus" in Revelation 12:17 as referring to our testimony about Jesus (NIV11, NLT, RSV) even though, as the first verses of the book make clear, this phrase refers to Jesus' inspired "testimony" or message through His prophets (see Rev 1:1–2; cf. Isa 8:16, 20).[111]

Movement away from a more literal, word-for-word translation paradigm appears also to have accelerated the trend of conforming Scripture to culture. For example, the NIV's 2011 update, while continuing that version's tradition of dynamic equivalence, attempts in places to be more culturally sensitive than its predecessor. An example of this is Romans 1:27; the 1984 edition translates Paul's evaluation of male same-sex relations as a "perversion" (Gk. *planē*), while in the 2011 edition it is called merely an "error." The newer NIV also appears to soften references to homosexuality in other places, while MSG removes altogether the clear condemnations of homosexuality found in two separate passages, inserting in one a condemnation about abusing the earth. Notice how the underlined portions of these two versions in their translations of 1 Corinthians 6:9b–10 and 1 Timothy 1:9–10 compare with the 1995 edition of the New American Standard Bible (NAS95):

---

[108] For more details, see Arthur L. White, "The E. G. White Counsel on Versions of the Bible" (December 9, 1953, rev. January 1990), 8, White Estate Document File 391b.

[109] Ellen G. White, *Selected Messages*, 1:20.

[110] See D. A. Carson, "The Limits of Dynamic Equivalence in Bible Translation," *Evangelical Review of Theology* 9/3 (1985): 201–211.

[111] The Greek syntax allows for either translation depending on whether the word in the genitive case (*Iēsou*, "Jesus") that follows the noun of action (*martyrian*, "testimony") is understood as the subject or object of the action. In Revelation 12:17, TCW leaves the phrase ambiguous: ". . . and hold to the testimony of Jesus."

1 Corinthians 6:9b–10		
NAS95	**NIV11**	**MSG**
"Neither fornicators, nor idolaters, nor adulterers, nor effeminate, nor homosexuals, nor thieves, nor the covetous, nor drunkards, nor revilers, nor swindlers, will inherit the kingdom of God."	"Neither the sexually immoral nor idolaters nor adulterers nor men who have sex with men nor thieves nor the greedy nor drunkards nor slanderers nor swindlers will inherit the kingdom of God."	"Unjust people who don't care about God will not be joining his kingdom. Those who use and abuse each other, use and abuse sex, use and abuse the earth and everything in it, don't qualify as citizens in God's kingdom."
1 Timothy 1:9–10		
NKJV	**NIV11**	**MSG**
"Knowing this: that the law is not made for a righteous person, but for the lawless and insubordinate, for the ungodly and for sinners, for the unholy and profane, for murderers of fathers and murderers of mothers, for manslayers, for fornicators, for sodomites, for kidnappers, for liars, for perjurers."	"We also know that the law is made not for the righteous but for lawbreakers and rebels, the ungodly and sinful, the unholy and irreligious, for those who kill their fathers or mothers, for murderers, for the sexually immoral, for those practicing homosexuality, for slave traders and liars and perjurers."	"It's obvious, isn't it, that the law code isn't primarily for people who live responsibly, but for the irresponsible, who defy all authority, riding roughshod over God, life, sex, truth, whatever!"

The first passage (1 Cor 6:9b–10) is interesting because Paul employs two different words for homosexual men, referring in turn to those taking more submissive (*malakoi*, "effeminate") and dominant (*arsenokoitai*, "homosexuals") positions in same-sex intercourse.[112] This distinction,

[112] Regarding the Greek words, *malakos* refers to the one "passive in a same-sex relationship, *effeminate* esp. of *catamites*, of men and boys who are sodomized by other males in such a relationship" (W. Bauer, F. W. Danker, W. F. Arndt, and F. W. Gingrich, *A Greek-English Lexicon of the New Testament and Other Early Christian Literature*, 3rd ed. [Chicago, IL: University of Chicago Press, 2000], 613, emphasis original); *arsenokoitēs* refers to "one who assumes the dominant role in same-sex activity, opp[osite]. μαλακός" (ibid., 135).

maintained in NAS95 (and also in NKJV and NRSV), is lost in some English versions.

The gradual but noticeable shift in translation method toward cultural accommodation has influenced even versions that claim to be formal, word-for-word translations. Consider, for example, the frequency of the word "doctrine"[113] in the following versions:

Year	**English version**	**Type**	**Frequency "Doctrine"**
1769	King James Version	Formal	56
1982	New King James Version	Formal	42
1995	New American Standard Bible	Formal	14
2001	English Standard Version	Formal	13

While the semantic range of this word has narrowed since the late eighteenth century, there is still an appreciable difference in word frequencies between the NKJV and other formal translations that is likely due to recent changes in translation methodology. This would seem to fit well with the recent shift toward more culturally sensitive approaches in Bible translation. Further support for this conclusion is the diminishing frequency of "doctrine" even in updates of the same version:

Year	**English version**	**Type**	**Frequency "Doctrine"**
1971	Revised Standard Version	Formal	17
1989	New Revised Standard Version	Functional	8
1984	New International Version	Dynamic	7
2011	New International Version (revised)	Dynamic	6

[113] Several Hebrew words (usually *leqakh*, but also *shemu'ah* and *musar* once each) and Greek words (usually *didachē* or *didaskalia*, but also *heterodidaskaleō* and *logos* once each) are translated this way in the KJV. Carl F. H. Henry, *God, Revelation and Authority*, vol. 4, *God Who Speaks and Shows: Fifteen Theses, Part Three* (Waco, TX: Word, 1979), 129–130, observes a similar phenomenon regarding "inspire" and "inspiration" in connection with divine activity in English versions. Note the frequency of this terminology in formal translations: KJV (twice: Job 32:8; 2 Tim 3:16), NKJV (once: 2 Tim 3:16), ESV (once: Exod 35:34); NAS95 (once: 2 Tim 3:16). Cf. RSV (six times: Exod 35:34; Prov 16:10; Matt 22:43; Mark 12:36; Luke 2:27; 2 Tim 3:16); NRSV (three: Exod 35:34; Prov 16:10; 2 Tim 3:16); NIV (none); but NIV11 (four times: 2 Sam 23:1; Prov 30:1; 31:1; Rev 22:6).

This shift places the NRSV much closer to the dynamic equivalence approach of the NIV, which the 2011 edition has continued and strengthened in places. Another example of apparent cultural accommodation is the tendency in recent times to render the sixth commandment (Exod 20:13) as "You shall not murder" (ESV, NASB, NIV, NKJV, NRSV, HCSB), rather than "You shall not kill" or its equivalent (ASV, KJV, NAB, NJB, RSV).[114] While the Hebrew word for "kill" includes murder within its purview, the command is broader, prohibiting "all killing or taking of human life."[115]

Of course, no translation is inspired or perfect. At best, any version of the Bible only approximates the meaning of the original text, because each language is uniquely built to describe reality through the eyes and culture of its people.[116] Translators are also human and, despite taking precautions to prevent their theological bias from affecting the translation, it is difficult if not impossible to eliminate bias altogether. Therefore, one must be especially cautious when reading a Bible produced by just one person (e.g., LB, MSG, TCW). The selection of a Bible version should be done with a view to the purpose for which it is being used (e.g., deep study, public reading, easy English). Some helpful selection criteria and guidance for the proper use of Bible versions and variants are given in the guidelines "Methods of Bible Study":

> Select a Bible version for study that is faithful to the meaning contained in languages in which the Bible originally was written, giving preference to translations done by a broad group of scholars and published by a general publisher above translations sponsored by a particular denomination or narrowly focused group.
>
> Exercise care not to build major doctrinal points on one Bible translation or version. Trained biblical scholars will use the Greek

[114] See Wilma Ann Bailey, *"You Shall Not Kill" or "You Shall Not Murder"? The Assault on a Biblical Text* (Collegeville, MN: Liturgical Press, 2005), 1–25, 84–85; Ekkehardt Mueller, "The Power of Culture," *Reflections: The BRI Newsletter* 19 (July 2007): 8–10, https://adventistbiblicalresearch.org/sites/default/files/pdf/Power%20of%20Culture.pdf (accessed March 11, 2020).

[115] Jiří Moskala, "'You Shall Not Kill' or 'You Shall Not Murder'? The Meaning of *Ratsakh* in the Sixth Commandment," *Reflections: The BRI Newsletter* 67 (July 2019): 1–7.

[116] Even the LXX exhibits efforts to accommodate Old Testament wisdom material to Greek sensibilities. See Clinton Wahlen, "Wisdom, Greek," in *Dictionary of the Old Testament: Wisdom, Poetry & Writings*, ed. Tremper Longman III and Peter Enns (Downers Grove, IL: InterVarsity, 2008), 842–847.

and Hebrew texts, enabling them to examine variant readings of ancient Bible manuscripts as well.[117]

Generally, the versions that are "most faithful to the meaning" of the text in the original languages are those that employ a formal, word-for-word method of translation (e.g., NKJV, NAS95). This is an especially important criterion for those who are not able to read the Bible in the original languages, since word studies and perceived intertextual relationships in these versions will be more transparent and in keeping with the way the underlying Greek and Hebrew words are used.

Other purposes, such as Bible memorization or writing for publication, may influence the choice of a particular version. Those who do not speak English as a first language may want to use one of the easier dynamic translations (e.g., NLT, TEV).[118] Also, apart from a handful of instances, the differences between an eclectic text used in many modern versions and the Textus Receptus used by the KJV/NKJV are mostly minor.[119] They are certainly not as significant as is sometimes suggested. It should also be remembered that the sale of Bibles is lucrative and that in order to copyright a book the product must be different enough to justify a separate publication. Undoubtedly pragmatic considerations such as these have also contributed to the proliferation of versions. A table listing the strengths and weaknesses of various versions appears at the end of this chapter.[120]

---

[117] See the appendix "Methods of Bible Study," section 2.4.1, in the present volume.

[118] Others may choose to use the King James Version because it is the predominant (though by no means the only) version Ellen G. White used and quoted from in the course of her writing. Note A. L. White, "E. G. White Counsel," 1: "In her writings Ellen White made use of the various English translations of the Holy Scriptures that were available in her day. She does not, however, comment directly on the relative merits of these versions, but it is clear from her practice that she recognized the desirability of making use of the best in all versions of the Bible. What she has written lays a broad foundation for an open-minded approach to the many renderings of the Sacred Text."

[119] According to Wallace, 157, TR and M exhibit 99% agreement, differing in less than two thousand places, while M and "the modern critical text [differ] in only about 6,500 places."

[120] The table has been adapted and expanded from Donald L. Brake, *A Visual History of the English Bible: The Tumultuous Tale of the World's Bestselling Book* (Grand Rapids, MI: Baker, 2008), 293–295. For reading levels of most of these as well as other versions, see Jonathan Petersen, "Bible Translation Reading Levels," June 21, 2016, https://www.biblegateway.com/blog/2016/06/bible-translation-reading-levels/ (accessed April 28, 2020). The age level refers to years of age of the reader; so, for example, "17+" means the Bible translation should be understandable to someone seventeen years of age and older, whereas "12+" indicates that readers who are twelve years of age and older should be able to understand it.

Conclusion: Faith and the Trustworthiness of Scripture

In considering the topics covered in this chapter, several points not only bear repeating but may also deserve further reflection:

1. The Bible is by far the most carefully transmitted and preserved book in history.

The thousands of original language manuscripts and even more numerous copies of ancient versions show the Bible's widespread influence and importance over the centuries, beginning with its earliest writings. No other ancient work even comes close to the Bible in terms of the extent and faithfulness of its preservation. The variations in the manuscripts are mostly insignificant copyist errors that leave little doubt as to the earliest wording of the text. Significant differences between manuscripts are relatively few and do not materially alter the overall teaching of the author or of Scripture as a whole.

2. None of the errors stemming from the process of transcription that have appeared over the centuries in the various extant manuscripts of the Bible threaten a single Bible doctrine.

The vast majority of differences seen in biblical manuscripts stem from inadvertent mistakes made during the copying process; only a few change the meaning significantly, and none affect any major teaching of Scripture.[121] This is true not only of the Greek New Testament but also of the Hebrew Bible, as evidenced by a comparison of the Masoretic text with the Isaiah Scroll found at Qumran, which is one thousand years older. There is some evidence that a few scribes attempted to improve the wording of the text (often through harmonization), but, fortunately, this appears to be the exception rather than the rule.[122] Notice this helpful observation regarding the Scriptures' preservation through history despite some scribal attempts to "improve" the text:

> I saw that God had especially guarded the Bible; yet when copies of it were few, learned men had in some instances changed the words, thinking that they were making it more plain, when in reality they were mystifying that which was plain, by causing it to lean to their established views, which were governed by tradition.

---

[121] See nn. 72 and 73 in this study.

[122] Royse, 488, found only three singular variants (in one papyrus) out of more than a thousand that *may* be theologically motivated; cf. ibid., 376, noting harmonizations of P^{47} in Revelation 10:4a, c; 14:2a; and 16:19a.

> But I saw that the Word of God, as a whole, is a perfect chain, one portion linking into and explaining another. True seekers for truth need not err; for not only is the Word of God plain and simple in declaring the way of life, but the Holy Spirit is given as a guide in understanding the way to life therein revealed.[123]

3. Modern readers of the Bible would be better served if translators, like the ancient scribes before them who preserved the text, did not try to improve upon the message of the text.

As God's Word, the Bible cannot be improved upon. Unfortunately, as we have seen, both scribes and modern versions have sometimes attempted to do this. The efforts of translators to clarify the meaning of the text can be very helpful. At the same time, the wide latitude that is sometimes permitted in the translation process has increased the chances for the misconstrual and mistranslation of some key Bible passages, which may at times have a serious doctrinal impact. For this reason, in any serious study of the Bible it is important to examine, if possible, the original languages, noting any variants that may exist in the manuscripts, and to consult formal, word-for-word translations before reaching conclusions as to the meaning of a particular passage or the teaching of Scripture on a given topic.

4. Modern versions are generally quite reliable in attempting to convey the meaning of Scripture correctly.

Bible translation teams conscientiously incorporate the latest advancements in translation method and the best results from studies of textual transmission in accordance with their best judgments. Even though errors in judgment in connection with textual analysis or translation may occasionally be noticed in any or all versions of the Bible, nevertheless, the overall teaching of God's Word as represented through the various Bible writers comes through clearly. Regardless of the translation, believers who compare Scripture with Scripture and version with version will find that the teachings and doctrines of the Bible remain intact despite the differences in the manuscripts and translation techniques that we have observed.

5. Attentive reading of the biblical text, close study of the context, comparison of different versions, and faith in its divine origin are important keys to understanding.

---

[123] Ellen G. White, *Early Writings* (Washington, DC: Review and Herald, 1882), 220.

It is important not to read the Bible too hastily. This is particularly important for portions of the Bible in which its instruction is highly compressed, as in the book of Proverbs, or symbolic, as in the parables or the apocalyptic books of Daniel and Revelation. Ellen G. White aptly writes:

> There is but little benefit derived from a hasty reading of the Scriptures. One may read the whole Bible through and yet fail to see its beauty or comprehend its deep and hidden meaning. One passage studied until its significance is clear to the mind and its relation to the plan of salvation is evident, is of more value than the perusal of many chapters with no definite purpose in view and no positive instruction gained.[124]
>
> The language of the Bible should be explained according to its obvious meaning, unless a symbol or figure is employed.[125]

Finally, though it is sometimes given less attention than it deserves, the Bible is a book of faith. That is, the Scriptures were penned by those who not only believed in God and the trustworthiness of His Word, but who also acted on their faith. The faithfulness of the Bible's transmission, both in the original languages and in numerous ancient versions, also witnesses to how this book has been revered through the centuries by people of faith. In the same way, we cannot expect to gain a clear understanding of what a given biblical text means apart from faith that it contains God's message to us and a willingness to put its principles into practice:

> The student of the Bible should be taught to approach it in the spirit of a learner. We are to search its pages, not for proof to sustain our opinions, but in order to know what God says.
>
> A true knowledge of the Bible can be gained only through the aid of that Spirit by whom the word was given. And in order to gain this knowledge we must live by it.[126]

---

[124] Ellen G. White, *Steps to Christ* (Mountain View, CA: Pacific Press, 1892), 90.

[125] Ellen G. White, *The Great Controversy* (Mountain View, CA: Pacific Press, 1911), 598.

[126] Ellen G. White, *Education* (Mountain View, CA: Pacific Press, 1903), 189.

Comparison and Evaluation of English Versions			
Version (Date)	**Translation type**	**Text**	**Accuracy**
KJV 1611 Revised 1769	Literal "Formal"	MT/ Textus Receptus	Excellent
ASV 1901	Literal "Formal" Revised ERV	MT/ Westcott-Hort	Excellent
RSV 1952	Formal	BHK/NA^{17}	Good
NASB 1971	Literal "Formal" Revised ASV	BHK/NA^{23}	Excellent
GNB 1976	Free style "Dynamic"	BHK/UBS^{3}	Fair
NIV 1978	Free style "Functional" New translation	BHS/Eclectic	Good
NKJV 1982	Literal "Formal" Revised KJV	BHS/Textus Receptus	Excellent
REB 1989	Free	BHS /NA^{26}	Fair
NRSV 1990	Free "Formal" Revision of the RSV	BHS/UBS^{3}	Fair
The Message 1993 (2002)	Free Paraphrase	"Original languages"	Does not attempt to be true to Hebrew and Greek
NAS95 1995	Literal "Formal" Revised NASB	BHS/NA^{26}	Excellent
NLT 1996 (2004)	Free style "Functional" Revision of Living Bible	BHS/NA^{27}	Good
ESV 2001	"Essentially literal" "Formal" Revision of RSV	BHS/NA^{27}	Excellent
HCSB 2004	"Optimal equivalence"	BHS/NA^{27}	Excellent
TNIV 2005	Free style "Functional" Revision of NIV	BHS/Eclectic	Fair
NET 2005	Functional Dynamic Equivalence	BHS/Eclectic	Good
NIV11 2011	Revision of TNIV	BHS/Eclectic	Fair/Good
CSB 2017	"Optimal equivalence" Revision of HCSB	BHS/NA^{28}-UBS^{5}	Good/ Excellent

Comparison and Evaluation of English Versions			
Beauty of Style	**Clarity/ Age Level**	**Weakness**	**Strength**
Excellent	Good/17+	Archaic language	Beauty; close to the original-language text
Poor	Good/17+	Readability, style	Close to the original-language text
Fair	Good/17+	Considered liberal, often wooden	Close to the original-language text
Fair	Good/16+	Literary style	Close to the original-language text
Fair	Good/12+	Free at expense of accuracy	Ease of reading style
Good	Excellent/ 12+	Sometimes inaccurate	Modern linguistic style
Good	Good/12+	Revision of KJV	Improved KJV revision
Fair	Fair/14+	Excess liberty with text	Attempts to clarify Greek/Hebrew idioms
Fair	Good/16+	Theology; liberal bias	Can be faithful to the original-language text
Good	Excellent/9+	Often quite loose with translation	Response-oriented; seeks to be more relevant than accurate
Good	Good/16+	Literary style	Faithful to the original-language text
Good	Excellent/ 11+	Leads to some inconsistency	Reading ease omits vulgarities of Living Bible
Good	Good/15+	Some inconsistencies	More literal than the NIV, more idiomatic than the NASB
Good	Good-Excellent/ 12+	Occasional inaccuracies	Modern style; accurate
Good	Excellent/ 12+	Work in progress; liberties with text	Modern language; more exegetical than NIV
Good	Excellent/ 12+	Artificial in places	Notes explain choices; accurate
Good	Excellent/ 12+	More liberties with text than NIV	Modern style
Good	Excellent/ 12+	Occasional inaccuracies	Modern style; accurate

CHAPTER 4

History, the Bible, and Hermeneutics

Michael G. Hasel

History is important because all life is rooted in history. History is the ground of all human existence. There is no human existence outside of our historical experience. History is the fabric of life and, therefore, important to our identity. We exist and live in time and space. Our experiences and choices through history shape us, mold us, and create the people we become. Our decisions impact the course of history and historical events. History is also intimately connected to patience, which is one of the characteristics of faithful believers during the end time (Rev 13:10; 14:12). There would be no patience outside the flow of history or the progress of time. The waiting we do, as we remember the events of the past, is in anticipation for a future. History, then, does not just concern itself with the past. History is also shaped in the present and it forms our existential human identity for the future.

The Biblical View of History

According to the biblical worldview our existence and God's existence are intertwined and related. God's acts in our human history are traced and recorded in the Bible as occurring in specific settings over time and place. That is why geography—cities, countries, bodies of water, rivers, mountains, nations—is significant to the biblical narrative.[1] These places

---

[1] By comparison, the number of places mentioned in the entire Qur'an is the same number already accounted for by the time one reaches Genesis 10 in the Bible. On Genesis 10, see Michael G. Hasel, "The Table of Nations: Geography, History and Archaeology," in Jacques B. Doukhan, *Seventh-day Adventist International Bible Commentary: Genesis* (Nampa, ID: Pacific Press, 2016), 168–83.

point to the specific instances where God directed, intervened, and delivered His people.

The biblical understanding of God's work is also linear and forward moving—not cyclical as in the mythical thinking so prominent among the other conceptions of the ancient religious world.[2] God is revealed as one who is the beginning, center, end, and eternal future of human history. He inaugurates time "in the beginning" (Gen 1–2)[3] and creates the sun and the moon "for signs and for seasons, and for days, and years" (Gen 1:14). God sets out the demarcation of His sovereignty as Creator in the perpetual weekly cycle that ends in the seventh-day Sabbath, which He sanctifies and makes holy (Gen 2:1–2). After the fall, the divine-human bond is broken, and the plan of redemption is enacted, pointing forward to the promised Messiah who offers restoration (Gen 3:15). In this way, history and prophecy are inextricably linked as God continues to work to accomplish His plan to save humanity within the theme of the great controversy that has since occupied the intense interest of the universe. Through His covenant promise, God works directly with His agents, Adam, Noah, Abraham, Moses, David, and the prophets to see that history's prophetic destiny of the promise of the Messiah is fulfilled.[4] In the "fullness of time" God sends His Son (Gal 4:4), the ultimate divine act in human history, to pay the penalty and price of humanity's rebellion against the divine law of God's government. All of creation has anticipated the moment when Christ proclaims from the cross, "It is finished" (John 19:30). As prophesied, after three days, He comes forth from the tomb victorious, and after appearing to hundreds of people, He ascends to begin his heavenly ministry in the Holy Place as High Priest, until entering the Most Holy Place in 1844 to begin His pre-advent judgment of the living and the dead, before returning in triumphant glory to claim His ransomed people for the place He is preparing for us, saying, "Surely I come quickly. Amen" (Rev 22:20). The scope of Scripture thus spans from the beginning of human history to the final end of human suffering in the

---

[2] On a comparison between biblical and mythical thinking, see John T. Oswalt, *The Bible Among the Myths: Unique Revelation or Just Ancient Literature* (Grand Rapids, MI: Zondervan, 2009); on the linear nature of biblical historiography, see John Marsh, *The Fulness of Time* (London: Harper, 1952); Thorleif Boman, *Das hebräische Denken im Vergleich mit dem griechischen* (Göttingen: Vandenhoeck & Ruprecht, 1954); English translation, *Hebrew Thought Compared with Greek* (London: W. W. Norton, 1960).

[3] All biblical quotations are from the NKJV, unless otherwise indicated.

[4] On the covenant theme in Scripture, see Gerhard F. Hasel and Michael G. Hasel, *The Promise: God's Everlasting Covenant* (Nampa, ID: Pacific Press, 2020), 1–68.

prophetic restoration of the eternal kingdom of God. No other religious sacred text provides this perspective of totality in time and place nor contains the prophetic messages that indicate God's omniscient foreknowledge of human history and His intervention in human affairs.[5]

The biblical writers universally accepted the historical accounts of previous authors within the canon of Scripture as recording historical, factual events upon which to base their thinking and their theology. Thus, Genesis 1–11 is referred to as a historical event throughout the Old Testament and by every single New Testament writer of the Bible—including Jesus Himself.[6] Concerning the exodus, the repeated phrase in the Old Testament is found: "I am the LORD God who brought you out of the land of Egypt" (cf. Exod 6:7; 20:2; Lev 11:25; 22:33; 25:55; 26:13). His sovereignty over His people is again and again tied specifically to the historical event of their deliverance and salvation from Egypt.[7] As James K. Hoffmeier states, "the Old Testament Scriptures do not treat

---

[5] Bertil Albrektson in his book *History and the Gods: An Essay on the Idea of Historical Events as Divine Manifestations in the Ancient Near East and in Israel* (Lund: Gleerup, 1967) challenges the idea that only Israel's God acts in history. He cites other Mesopotamian texts like the Weidner Chronicle which documents the centrality of Marduk in history. However, there are several important distinctions. First, Marduk, as one of the many created gods, is simply part of a creation in mythical thinking which is continuous. He is not transcendent like Yahweh who stands outside creation as the Creator of all things Himself. Second, Marduk's only concern is to ensure an endless supply of fish for the Esagil temple—that is, to maintain the *status quo*. In contrast, Yahweh is interested in a covenant relationship with His people so that a final restoration of His covenant promise can be fulfilled. Finally, in Mesopotamia, the cosmos was an all-encompassing machine, of which gods and people were only parts. In Scripture, Yahweh is beyond nature; He created the world and gave it to humanity. He breaks into history to establish covenant relationships (see Bill T. Arnold, "The Weidner Chronicle and the Idea of History," in *Faith, Tradition and* History, ed. Alan R. Millard, James K. Hoffmeier, and David W. Baker [Winona Lake, IN: Eisenbrauns, 1994], 145–7). As A. Leo Oppenheim *Ancient Mesopotamia: Portrait of a Dead Civilization* (Chicago, IL: University of Chicago Press, 1977), 19, indicates, "there is a noticeable absence of historical literature; that is, texts are lacking that would attest to an awareness of the scribes of an existence of a historical continuum in the Mesopotamian civilization of which they themselves and their tradition were only a part."

[6] Exodus 20:9–11; Psalms. 33:6, 9; 89:11–12; 104; Isaiah 40:28; Matthew 19:4–5; 24:37–39; Mark 10:6–9; 13:19; Luke 1:70; 3:34–38; 11:50–51; 17:26–27; John 1:1-3, 10; Acts 3:21; 14:15; 17:24, 26; Romans 1:20; 5:12, 14–19; 8:20–22; 16:20; 1 Corinthians 6:16; 11:3, 7–9, 12; 15:21–22, 38–39, 45, 47; 2 Corinthians 4:6; 11:3; Ephesians 3:9; 5:30–31; Colossians 1:16; 3:10; 1 Timothy 2:13–15; Hebrews 1:10; 2:7–8; 4:3, 4, 10; 11:3–5, 7; 12:24; James 3:9; 1 Peter 3:20; 2 Peter 2:4–5; 3:4–6; 1 John 3:8, 12; Jude 11, 14–15; Revelation 3:14; 4:11; 10:6; 12:1–4; 14:7; see articles in Gerald A. Klingbeil, ed., *The Genesis Creation Account and Its Reverberations in the Old Testament* (Berrien Springs, MI: Andrews University Press, 2015); see chapter 11 by Michael G. Hasel, "The Genesis Account as a Test Case for Biblical Hermeneutics," in the present volume.

[7] Walter C. Kaiser, Jr., *Toward Rediscovering the Old Testament* (Grand Rapids, MI: Zondervan, 1990), 67.

the sojourn-exodus-wilderness events as trivial matters. Rather these events stand at the heart of Israel's religious life, as evidenced by the fact that these themes are ubiquitous throughout the Old Testament itself."[8] Otto Piper pointed out years ago, "Of the 2688 references of the OT in the NT . . . Exodus occupies the third place with c. 220 quotations."[9] What would occur to biblical theology if either the creation or the exodus events never took place, or took place without God's divine intervention? These events of the Bible would cease to have meaning in reality and the rest of the Bible, which is founded on those events, would come into serious question.

For these reasons history is essential to the interpretation of the Bible. Because the Bible is historically constituted, history—and by extension geography—is the "place," if you will, where God gives humanity an opportunity to test and confirm the truthfulness of His Word. That is why history and historical details are where the trustworthiness of the Bible and of God's Word are often challenged the most and where criticism begins. This can also be traced through the history of critical scholarship, which began to superimpose external norms onto Scripture.

The Problem of History

Since the Enlightenment, the subject of history has become one of the most difficult problems in biblical studies.[10] This is largely due to the presuppositions of the historical-critical method, which is founded essentially on three guiding principles.[11] First, *the principle of correlation*

---

[8] James K. Hoffmeier, "Why a Historical Exodus is Essential for Theology," in *Do Historical Matters Matter to Faith? A Critical Appraisal of Modern and Postmodern Approaches to Scripture* (ed. James K. Hoffmeier and Denis R. Magary (Wheaton, IL: Crossway, 2012), 111.

[9] Otto Piper, "Unchanging Promises: Exodus in the New Testament," *Interpretation* 11 (1957): 3.

[10] Gerhard F. Hasel, "The Problem of History in Old Testament Theology," *Andrews University Seminary Studies* 8 (1970): 32–35, 41–46; cf. Gerhard F. Hasel, *Old Testament Theology: Basic Issues in the Current Debate* 4th ed. rev. and enl. (Grand Rapids, MI: Eerdmans, 1991), 115–38; see more recently Michael C. Legaspi, *The Death of Scripture and the Rise of Biblical Studies* (New York: Oxford University Press, 2010), 3–26.

[11] "Ernst Troeltsch's essay 'On Historical and Dogmatic Method in Theology' (1898) formulated the principles of historical criticism. The essay still haunts theology" according to Edgar Krentz, *The Historical-Critical Method* (Philadelphia, PA: Fortress, 1975), 55; see Ernst Troeltsch, "Über historische und dogmatische Methode in der Theologie," in *Gesammelte Schriften 2* (Tübingen: Mohr, 1913): 729-53; On the history of the historical-critical method, see Hans-Joachim Kraus, *Geschichte der historisch-kritischen Erforschung des Alten Testaments* (Neukirchen-Vluyn: Neukirchener, 1959); on Troeltsch specifically, see Roy A. Harrisville and Walter Sundberg, *The Bible in Modern Culture: Theology and Historical-Critical Method from Spinoza to Käsemann* (Grand Rapids, MI: Eerdmans, 1995), 155–69; on presuppositions, see Gerhard

denies the possibility of divine action in human history, which is foundational to the biblical worldview. As Walter Dietrich writes, "in the modern age, history must be understood and described *esti deus non deratur* ('as though God did not exist')." But he admits that this makes it difficult when assessing biblical history. In the Bible "God plays an active role . . . God gets personally involved . . . he sends prophets . . . he moves events." Dietrich concludes, "What enlightened person can accept all these things as historical accounts?"[12] This "principle rules out miracle"[13] or as Rudolf Bultmann writes,

> the historical [critical] method includes the presupposition that history is a unity in the sense of a closed continuum of effects in which individual events are connected by the succession of cause and effect . . . and thus to understand the whole historical process as a closed unity. This closedness means that the continuum of historical happenings cannot be rent by the interference of supernatural, transcendent powers and that therefore there is no "miracle" in this sense of the word. Such a miracle would be an event whose cause did not lie within history.[14]

Second, *the principle of analogy* assumes the homogeneity of all events. "Present experience and occurrence become the criteria of probability in the past. This 'almighty power' of analogy implies that all events are in principle similar."[15] This means that unique events in history, such as creation and a worldwide flood, or the miraculous establishment of the nation of Israel following the exodus, are deemed improbable and even impossible because of the lack of evidence for such an event in the present, modern experience.

Finally, the third principle of *methodological doubt or criticism* "implies that history only achieves probability. Religious tradition must be subject to criticism."[16] It recognizes inconsistencies and even

---

F. Hasel, *Biblical Interpretation Today* (Washington, DC: Biblical Research Institute, 1985), 73–8; see chapter 1 by Kwabena Donkor, "Presuppositions in Hermeneutics," in the present volume.

[12] Walter Dietrich, *The Early Monarchy of Israel: The Tenth Century B.C.E.*, trans. Joachim Vette (Atlanta, GA: Society of Biblical Literature, 2007), 102–103.

[13] Krentz, Historical-Critical Method, 55.

[14] Rudolf Bultmann, *Existence and Faith: Shorter Writings of Rudolf Bultmann* (New York, Meridian Books, 1960), 291–292.

[15] Krentz, *Historical-Critical Method*, 55.

[16] Ibid. This principle of criticism was based on the rationalist school and philosophy of René Descartes.

anachronisms within the text.[17] More recently, the Bible's history is approached with "a fundamental skepticism toward textual evidence and a positivistic quest for verification of information before it can be trusted and included in the pool of reliable data used for historical reconstruction."[18] This "hermeneutic of suspicion"[19] approaches the Bible as guilty until proven innocent by the corroboration of external evidence. Even then, such evidence often remains partial and inconclusive.[20] The aim of historical criticism is to analyze carefully the language and text of the Bible and apply the presuppositions of correlation, analogy, and criticism with their resultant methods of source, form, redaction, and tradition criticism and the like, in order to determine what actually happened. The result was that "as scholars focused on textual disorder, the authority of the Bible as an obligatory touchstone for contemporary life also weakened."[21]

Historie, *Geschichte*, and Salvation History

It is important to point out that two terms for what we in English refer to as history have been developed in German scholarship: *Historie* and *Geschichte*. *Historie* determines the facts of events and how they actually took place in the past. *Geschichte* is the way in which history is reported and historians determine what those events mean.[22] If in the

---

[17] John Barton, *The Nature of Biblical Criticism* (Philadelphia, PA: Westminster John Knox, 2007), 9-30.

[18] Jens Bruun Kofoed, *Text and History: Historiography and the Study of the Biblical Text* (Winona Lake, IN: Eisenbrauns, 2005), 3.

[19] James K. Hoffmeier, "The Evangelical Contribution to Understanding the (Early) History of Ancient Israel in Recent Scholarship," *Bulletin of Biblical Research* 7 (1997): 80.

[20] On critiques of the method, see Eta Linneman, *Historical Criticism of the Bible: Methodology or Ideology?* trans. Robert W. Yarbrough (Grand Rapids, MI: Baker, 1990); and Gerhard Maier, *The End of the Historical-Critical Method* (St. Louis, MO: Concordia 1977).

[21] Legaspi, *The Death of Scripture*, 26.

[22] See J. Alberto Soggin, "Alttestamentliche Glaubenszeugnisse und geschichtliche Wirklichkeit," *Theologische Zeitschrift* 17 (1960): 385–98; Soggin, "Geschichte, Historie und Heilsgeschichte im Alten Testament," *Theologische Literaturzeitung* 89 (1964): 721–36; and Magne Saebo, "Offenbarung in der Geschichte und als Geschichte (Revelation in History and as History)," *Studia Theologica* 35/1 (1981): 55–71. Rolf Rendtorff, "Hermeneutik des Alten Testaments als Frage nach der Geschichte (Old Testament Hermeneutics as a Question About History)" *Zeitschrift für Theologie und Kirche* 57 (1960): 27–40; and more recently Mark A. Noll, "History," in *Dictionary for Theological Interpretation of the Bible*, ed. Kevin J. Vanhoozer (Grand Rapids, MI: Baker Academic, 2005), 295–299; P. W. Hasbrouck and J. J. Scott, Jr., "Historie and Geschichte" in *Evangelical Dictionary of Theology*, ed. Daniel I. Treier, and Walter A. Elwell (Grand Rapids, MI: Baker Academic, 2017), 387; and the article "Historie/Geschichte; historisch/geschichtlich"

historical investigation of the text the supernatural was part of the event that took place, it ought not to be accepted as *Historie* or actual fact, but it still might be considered *Geschichte* in the sense of how the later writers of the Bible interpreted the past. For example, the crossing of the Red Sea by the Israelites is described as an event in which God intervened by parting the Red Sea. Critics "tend to emphasize the natural rather than the supernatural aspects of the phenomenon."[23] This result is often an undermining of the event itself. In order to overcome the crisis that this causes to the believer, a third dimension was introduced by theologians, called *Heilsgeschichte* or salvation history. It takes the metanarrative described above, from creation to consummation, as salvation history, which is not understood to be the same thing as *Historie.* For Gerhard von Rad, "Israel's faith is grounded in a theology of history."[24] But this history is not *Historie* in the sense of actual events. Rather, von Rad differentiated between the historical kernel of history (*Historie*) and the kerygmatic picture of Israel's history as perceived by the biblical writers through the work of Yahweh. For von Rad "there are no *bruta facta* at all; we have history only in the form of interpretation, only in reflection."[25] It is the theology behind the event that is important. The message of the story itself is what matters, not necessarily how or if it actually occurred.

The separation between *Historie* and salvation history introduces a dichotomy between actual historical events and theology—between what actually took place in the past and the theology of faith. This dichotomy was also articulated by Krister Stendahl in his well-known differentiation between "what the text meant" and "what it means."[26] For Stendahl, the "what it meant" was the task of biblical theology operating in descriptive mode. "What it meant" is historical reconstruction of the past world of the Old Testament or New Testament based on the sociocultural environment or social setting of the text. Historical reconstruction "understands the Bible as conditioned by its time and

---

in *Handbook of Biblical Criticism*, ed. Richard N. Soulen and R. Kendall Soulen, 3rd rev. and exp. ed. (Louisville, KY: Westminster John Knox Press, 2001), 80.

[23] J. Maxwell Miller, *The Old Testament and the Historian* (Philadelphia, PA: Fortress Press, 1976), 17.

[24] Gerhard von Rad, *Old Testament Theology* (2 vols.; trans. D.M.G. Stalker, vol. 1; New York: Harper and Row, 1962–65), 106.

[25] Gerhard von Rad, "Antwort auf Conzelmann's Fragen," *Evangelische Theologie* 24 (1964): 393; cf. Von Rad, *Old Testament Theology*, vol. 1 (New York: Harper & Row, 1962), 106–111.

[26] Krister Stendahl, "Biblical Theology, Contemporary," *Interpreter's Dictionary of the Bible* vol. 1 (Nashville, TN: Abingdon 1962), 418–432; Krister Stendahl, "Method in the Study of Biblical Theology," in *The Bible in Modern Scholarship*, ed. J. P. Hyatt (Nashville, TN: Abingdon, 1965), 196–209.

surroundings. The Bible's time and place, the Bible's socio-cultural environment among the other nations and religions, become the virtually exclusive key to its meaning. In this sense the Bible is interpreted in the same way as any other ancient document."[27] The "what the text meant" is determined by the principles of historical criticism, but "what the text means" is the task of theological interpretation, which is "the translation of the historically reconstituted text into the situation of the modern world."[28] A number of scholars, both Catholic and Protestant, have critiqued that pure scientific objectivity is possible or desirable in the endeavor of such historical reconstruction.[29] Several issues remain unresolved with such an approach.

Is there truly a distinction between "what the text meant" and "what it means" today? Are biblical faith and history really separable? Is the Bible culturally conditioned in order that it must be reinterpreted in a modern context? Or, put another way, do historical matters matter to faith? Some theologians answer this question unequivocally, with a resounding "Yes, it does matter!" In his critique of von Rad's double-tracking secular history and the kerygmatic history that is theologically meaningful, Franz Hesse insisted that faith must rest upon "that which has actually happened and not that which is confessed to have happened but about which we have to admit that it did not happen in that way."[30] Hesse was not abandoning the historical-critical method, but insisted that only that which can be determined to have actually happened matters theologically.[31] More recently Robin

---

[27] Gerhard F. Hasel, "The Relationship Between Biblical Theology and Systematic Theology," *Trinity Journal* 5 (1984): 117.

[28] Ibid., 118.

[29] Among Catholic scholars, see R. A. F. MacKenzie, "The Concept of Biblical Theology," *Theology Today* 4 (1956): 131–135; Roland de Vaux, "Method in the Study of Early Hebrew History," in Hyatt, *The Bible in Modern Scholarship*, 15–17; de Vaux, "Peut-on écrire une théologie de l'AT?" in *Bible et Orient* (Paris: Cerf, 1967), 59–71; and C. Spicq as quoted in J. Harvey "The New Diachronic Biblical Theology of the OT (1960–1970)," *Biblical Theology Bulletin* 1 (1971): 18–19. Protestants include Brevard S. Childs, "Interpretation in Faith," *Interpretation* 18 (1964): 432–449; Ben C. Ollenburger, "What Krister Stendahl 'Meant' – A Normative Critique of 'Descriptive Biblical Theology," *Horizons in Biblical Theology* 8 (1986): 61–98; and D. H. Kelsey, *The Uses of Scripture in Recent Theology* (Philadelphia, PA: Fortress, 1975), 203.

[30] Franz Hesse, "Kerygma oder geschichtliche Wirklichkeit?" *Zeitschrift für Theologie und Kirche* 57 (1960): 26.

[31] In maintaining the historical-critical method as the means to determine what was historical, Hesse "apparently does not recognize that the historical-critical version of Israel's history is also already interpreted on the basis of historico-philosophical premises" (Gerhard F. Hasel, *Old Testament Theology*, 119).

Routledge, points out that von Rad's "view of history was ambiguous. He acknowledged a gap between actual history (as uncovered by critical scholarship) and the story of faith (history as it was reconstructed in the faith of Israel)." He focuses primarily on the latter in his *Old Testament Theology,* "on the retelling of Israel's history [*Geschichte*], not on the history itself [*Historie*], thus undermining his insistence that history and event are crucial for OT faith."[32] By the end of the nineteenth century historical criticism reigned supreme in Protestant Europe. The historical-critical method, in its attempt to dissect *Historie* from salvation history, or that which Israel construed as the work of Yahweh, brought about a crisis in theology.

The biblical theology movement of William F. Albright, G. Ernest Wright, John Bright and their students in the United States took the importance of history to a new level by insisting that "in biblical faith, everything depends on whether the central events actually occurred."[33] The movement sought to establish the patriarchal period, the exodus and conquest, and the monarchy firmly in the realm of *Historie* based on the *realia* found through archaeological research.[34] However, the movement did not extricate itself entirely from the assumptions of historical criticism. "Biblical theology spoke of the *mighty acts of God* when, in reality, it meant the facts of critical history."[35] The dichotomy between critical history (*Geschichte*) and divine intervention was never overcome. The problem remained that from this perspective, history itself (*Historie*) could not function to be the authenticating factor of revelation. But Scripture claims that biblical revelation, as it interprets that history, is self-authenticating. Canonical Scripture should be used to interpret Scripture and must remain captive to its own internal basis for understanding.[36] This does not deny the importance of history

---

[32] Robin Routledge, *Old Testament Theology: A Thematic Approach* (Nottingham: APOLLOS, 2008), 37.

[33] G. Ernest Wright, *God Who Acts: Biblical Theology as Recital*, Studies in Biblical Theology 8 (London: SCM, 1952), 126–127; cf. Wright, *The Old Testament Against its Environment*, Studies in Biblical Theology, 2 (London: SCM, 1950); and G. Ernest Wright and Reginald H. Fuller, *The Book of the Acts of God: Contemporary Scholarship Interprets the Bible* (New York: Doubleday, 1957).

[34] Thomas W. Davies, *Shifting Sands: The Rise and Fall of Biblical Archaeology* (New York: Oxford University Press, 2004), 47–144.

[35] Christoph O. Schroeder, *History, Justice, and the Agency of God: A Hermeneutical and Exegetical Investigation on Isaiah & the Psalms* (Leiden: Brill, 2001), 38.

[36] This is the Protestant principle of *sola Scriptura* which allows the Bible to interpret itself. It does not rely on external sources to confirm its validity or authenticity. Rather, its authority is based on it being the revelation of God as revealed in the formal statements in Scripture about Scripture itself.

(*Historie*) but elevates the meaning of a transcendent God who truly intervenes in the historical nexus of time and space.[37] The biblical theological movement failed in part because these fundamental issues were never really resolved, and the death of Albright and Wright within a few short years of each other, left their agenda unfinished.

In the mid-1970s Thomas Thompson and John Van Seters wrote two massive volumes independently rejecting the historicity of Abraham, and by implication, Isaac and Jacob—the patriarchal period.[38] Thompson argued, "Not only has archaeology not proven a single event of the patriarchal traditions to be historical, it has not shown any of the traditions to be likely."[39] This was a direct challenge to the Albright-Wright-Bright school. Van Seters likewise cited the lack of evidence for the patriarchal stories in Genesis so that "consequently, without any such effective historical controls on the tradition one cannot use any part of it in an attempt to reconstruct the primitive period of Israelite history."[40] Most followed the new trend both in Europe and in America.[41] The history of Moses and the exodus—already long brought into question in European scholarship, after receiving some support in America—was challenged in the late 1970s and 1980s and subsequently drowned in dozens of articles and books denying the essential historicity of an exodus from Egypt, based on the lack of evidence for such an event found in the Egyptian records.[42] For example, Kenton Sparks states, "The silence from the Egyptian evidence is therefore an important

---

[37] Gerhard F. Hasel, "Biblical Theology Movement," in *Evangelical Dictionary of Theology*, ed. Walter A. Elwell (Grand Rapids, MI: Baker, 1984), 149–152; cf. Brevard S. Childs, *Biblical Theology in Crisis* (Philadelphia, PA: Westminster, 1970).

[38] Thomas L. Thompson, *The Historicity of the Patriarchal Narratives: The Quest for the Historical Abraham* (Beihefte zur Zeitschrift für die alttestamentliche Wissenschaft 133 (Berlin: Walter de Gruyter, 1974) and John van Seters, *Abraham in History and Tradition* (New Haven, CT: Yale University Press, 1975).

[39] Thompson, *Historicity of the Patriarchal Narratives*, 328.

[40] Van Seters, *Abraham in History and Tradition*, 309.

[41] William G. Dever, "What Remains of the House that Albright Built?" *Near Eastern Archaeologist* 56 (1993): 25-35; cf. the response essays in Alan R. Millard and David J. Wiseman, eds., *Essays on the Patriarchal Narratives* (Leicester: IVP, 1980).

[42] J. Maxwell Miller, "Archaeology and the Israelite Conquest of Canaan: Some Methodological Observations," *Palestine Exploration Quarterly* 109 (1977): 87–93; for bibliography and extensive discussions, see Michael G. Hasel, "Merenptah's Reference to Israel: Critical Issues for the Origin of Israel," in *Critical Issues in Early Israelite History*, ed. Richard S. Hess, Gerald A. Klingbeil, and Paul J. Ray, Jr., Bulletin for Biblical Research Supplement, vol. 3 (Winona Lake, IN: Eisenbrauns, 2008), 47–59; and Paul J. Ray, Jr., "Classical Models for the Appearance of Israel in Palestine," in *Critical Issues in Early Israelite History*, 79–93. For a critique, see James K. Hoffmeier, *Israel in Egypt* (New York: Oxford University Press, 1997), 1–60.

argument against the historicity of these miracle reports."[43] In the case of both the patriarchal and exodus narratives, the primary argument became that there is no extrabiblical evidence in support of the events described in the Bible.

Recent postmodern, revisionist attempts to redate the entire Old Testament history to the third and second centuries BC deny the existence of David and Solomon altogether,[44] following the ultimate, logical conclusion in a trajectory that earlier dismissed the patriarchs and the exodus/conquest accounts.[45] In the end, both historical-critics and their postmodern successors have struggled to provide an assured *Sitz im Leben* in the ancient world. This has led biblical scholars to turn increasingly to the archaeology of Israel for answers, but this too has led to varying opinions and interpretations.

In *The Bible Unearthed* (2001) and *David and Solomon* (2006),[46] Israel Finkelstein and Neil Asher Silberman contend that the history of the United Monarchy must be revised, because in their assessment there is "not the slightest evidence of any change in the landscape of Judah until the following century. The population remained low and the villages modest and few."[47] There is "no evidence for David's conquests,"[48] "no sign of monumental architecture or important city in Jerusalem,"[49]

---

[43] Kenton L. Sparks, *God's Word in Human Words* (Grand Rapids, MI: Baker, 2008), 157.

[44] Philip R. Davies, *In Search of "Ancient Israel,"* Journal for the Study of the Old Testament: Supplement Series 148 (Sheffield: Journal of the Study of the Old Testament Press, 1992), 131, writes, "I doubt whether the term 'Deuteronomistic History' should continue to be used by scholars as if it were a fact instead of a theory"; see also Niels-Peter Lemche, "The Old Testament—A Hellenistic Book?" *Scandinavian Journal of the Old Testament* vol. 7 (1993): 163–193; Thomas L. Thompson, *Early History of the Israelite People: From the Written and Archaeological Sources,* Studies in the History of the Ancient Near East, vol. 4 (Leiden: Brill, 1992); and most recently their student Emanuel Pfoh, *The Emergence of Israel in Ancient Palestine* (London: Equinox, 2009), 90–107. See the critique by William G. Dever, *What Did the Biblical Writers Know and When Did They Know It?* (Grand Rapids, MI: Eerdmans, 2001).

[45] Both Thompson and van Seters who earlier rejected the patriarchal period, but once accepted the United Monarchy, have now come to largely dismiss this history as well; see the observations of this trend by Edwin Yamauchi, "The Current State of Old Testament Historiography," in *Faith, Tradition and History,* ed. Alan R. Millard, James K. Hoffmeier, and David W. Baker (Winona Lake, IN: Eisenbrauns, 1994), 21–26.

[46] Israel Finkelstein and Neil Asher Silberman, *David and Solomon: In Search of the Bible's Sacred Kings and the Roots of the Western Tradition* (New York: Free Press, 2006); and Finkelstein and Silverman, *The Bible Unearthed: Archaeology's New Vision of Ancient Israel and the Origin of Its Sacred Texts* (New York: Free Press, 2001).

[47] Finkelstein and Silberman, *David and Solomon,* 96.

[48] Finkelstein and Silberman, *Bible Unearthed,* 131; idem., *David and Solomon,* 96–97.

[49] Finkelstein and Silberman, *Bible Unearthed,* 131.

"no sign of grand scale building at Megiddo, Hazor, and Gezer,"[50] and "no trace of written documents, inscriptions, or even signs of the kind of widespread literacy that would be necessary for a widespread monarchy."[51] In fact, "there is no sign of extensive literacy or writing in Judah until the end of the eighth century."[52] For Solomon the alleged copper mines at Tell el-Kheleifah "proved to be fantasy," for there was "no evidence for smelting activity at the site."[53] There is "no archaeological evidence whatsoever that the situation of north and south [the divided kingdom] grew out of earlier political unity—particularly one centered in the south."[54] The list goes on.[55]

This raises important questions: If the Bible is historically constituted, and that history is not corroborated by external evidence, what recourse is there for the reader of the Bible? Is extrabiblical evidence necessary to accept the historical claims of the Bible? "Should verification be a prerequisite for our acceptance of a tradition as valuable in respect to historical reality?"[56] Or to put it differently, does the lack of evidence determine the lack of historicity? If this is the criterion then where does the methodological doubt end? How far should one go? It is this slippery slope that has led to what has been called the "collapse of history."[57]

History and the "Absence of Evidence"

Archaeologist and attorney Jane M. Cahill states, "Theories based on negative evidence should never be preferred to theories based on positive evidence. Stated another way, absence of evidence is not evidence of absence."[58] Historian David Hackett Fischer maintains that such arguments

---

[50] Finkelstein and Silberman, *Bible Unearthed*, 131.

[51] Idid., 142.

[52] Finkelstein and Silberman, *David and Solomon*, 86.

[53] Ibid., 284.

[54] Finkelstein and Silberman, *Bible Unearthed*, 158.

[55] For further assertions and arguments, see Daniel A. Frese and Thomas E. Levy, "The Four Pillars of the Iron Age Low Chronology," in *Historical Biblical Archaeology and the Future: The New Pragmatism,* ed. Thomas E. Levy (London: Equinox, 2010), 198–99.

[56] Iain Provan, V. Philips Long, and Tremper Longman III, *A Biblical History of Israel* (Louisville, KY see Jens Bruun Kofoed, "Epistemology, Historiographical Method, and the Westminster/ John Knox, 2003), 55.

[57] Leo G. Perdue, *The Collapse of History* (Minneapolis, MN: Fortress, 1994); and Perdue, *Reconstructing Old Testament Theology After the Collapse of History* (Minneapolis, MN: Fortress, 2005).

[58] Jane M. Cahill, "Jerusalem at the Time of the United Monarchy: The Archaeological Evidence," in *Jerusalem in Bible and Archaeology: The First Temple Period* (ed. Andrew G. Vaughn and Ann

are historical fallacies. "Evidence must always be affirmative. Negative evidence is a contradiction in terms—it is no evidence at all."[59] What happens when we do not find extrabiblical evidence for an event or person in history? Is this a reason to doubt that event or the existence of the person? There are perhaps five reasons why evidence of this nature is often elusive in assessing the early kingdom of Judah.

First, it must be recognized that the heartland of David and Solomon's kingdom, as described in Samuel and Kings, has been inaccessible to archaeologists for the past half century. The West Bank/Palestine, with hundreds of sites, remains largely unexcavated, and the results of surveys only provide limited data.[60] Those sites that have been excavated have only been excavated to a limited extent. Jerusalem remains an inhabited city with minimal access due to buildings, roads, and other structures.[61] It is estimated that nearly half of the ancient city is under the Temple Mount and is archaeologically unknown.[62] One might compare similar situations at other ancient cities occupied in modern times, including Damascus, Tyre, and Sidon.[63] After multiple seasons at Gezer in the 1960s and 70s, and more recent renewed excavations in this decade, only about two percent of the site

---

E. Killebrew; Atlanta, GA: Society of the Biblical Literature, 2003), 73. For similar arguments, see Jens Bruun Kofoed, "Epistemology, Historiographical Method, and the 'Copenhagen School,'" in *Windows into Old Testament History: Evidence, Argument, and the Crisis of "Biblical Israel,"* ed. V. Philips Long, David W. Baker, and Gordon J. Wenham (Grand Rapids, MI: Eerdmans, 2002), 32–35; cf. already Kenneth A. Kitchen, *Ancient Orient and Old Testament* (Chicago, IL: InterVarsity, 1966), 30–32.

[59] David Hackett Fischer, *Historians' Fallacies: Toward a Logic of Historical Thought* (New York: Harper and Row, 1970), 62.

[60] The results of surveys in this territory are now published by Adam Zertal, *The Manasseh Hill Country Survey. Volume 1: The Shechem Syncline* (Culture and History of the Ancient Near East, 21/1 (Leiden: Brill, 2004); and Zertal, *The Manasseh Hill Country Survey. Volume 2: The Eastern Valleys and the Fringes of the Desert* (Culture and History of the Ancient Near East, 21/2 (Leiden: Brill, 2007). Earlier surveys from the territory of Ephraim were published by Israel Finkelstein, *The Archaeology of the Israelite Settlement* (Jerusalem: Israel Exploration Society, 1988).

[61] For similar arguments, see Alan R. Millard, "David and Solomon's Jerusalem: Do the Bible and Archaeology Disagree?" in *Israel: Ancient Kingdom or Late Invention?* ed. Daniel I. Block (Nashville, TN: Broadman and Holman, 2008), 194–198.

[62] Amahai Mazar, "Remarks on Biblical Traditions and Archaeological Evidence Concerning Early Israel," in *Symbiosis, Symbolism, and the Power of the Past: Canaan, Ancient Israel, and Their Neighbors from the Late Bronze Age Through Roman Palaestina. Proceedings of the Centennial Symposium W. F. Albright Institute of Archaeological Research and American Schools of Oriental Research, Jerusalem, May 29–May 31, 2000,* ed. William G. Dever and Seymour Gitin (Winona Lake, IN: Eisenbrauns, 2003), 91.

[63] Millard, "David and Solomon's Jerusalem," 196–198.

has been investigated for Iron IIA material.[64] At Megiddo, more of the site was exposed by the early Chicago excavations, but less than five percent of the Iron Age site has been reexcavated by Tel Aviv University.[65]

Second, of those sites that have been excavated, few are fully published. The final Chicago report of the Megiddo excavations pertaining to this crucial period was published only after a period of seventy years, and the interpretation of the data seriously undermines the conclusions and recent publications of the Tel Aviv excavations and the Low Chronology.[66] The conclusions that Jerusalem was wholly unoccupied, or at best an impoverished village, ignores the fact that *all* the major excavators of Jerusalem—Kathleen Kenyon, Yigal Shiloh, and now Eilat Mazar—concluded otherwise.[67] Shiloh insisted that the stone-stepped structure found by Kenyon in the City of David represented monumental architecture and was constructed in the early Iron Age or earlier.[68] In fact, "virtually every archaeologist to have excavated in the City of David claims to have found architecture and artifacts dating to these periods."[69] Mazar has also claimed to have found in her

---

[64] Steven M. Ortiz, personal communication, January 12, 2011; now Steven M. Ortiz and Samuel R. Wolff, "Tel Gezer Excavations 2006–2015: The Transformation of a Border City," in *Recent Archaeological Research in the Shephelah of Judah: The Iron Age*, ed. Oded Lipschits and Aren M. Maeir (Winona Lake, IN: Eisenbrauns, 2017), 61-102; and Ortiz and Wolff, "Guarding the Border to Jerusalem: The Iron Age City of Gezer," *Near Eastern Archaeologist* 75 (2012): 4–19. For the Hebrew Union College excavations at Gezer, see the final publications, William G. Dever, H. Darrell Lance, and G. Earnest Wright, *Gezer I: Preliminary Report of the 1964–66 Seasons* (Jerusalem: Hebrew Union College Biblical and Archaeological School, 1970); William G. Dever, et.al. *Gezer II: Report of the 1967-70 Seasons in Fields I and II*, ed. William G. Dever (Jerusalem: Hebrew Union College/Nelson Glueck School of Biblical Archaeology, 1974); Seymour Gitin, *Gezer III: A Ceramic Typology of the Late Iron II, Persian, and Hellenistic Periods at Tell Gezer* (Jerusalem: Hebrew Union College/Nelson Glueck School of Biblical Archaeology, 1990); *Gezer IV: The 1969-71 Seasons in Field VI, the "Acropolis"*, ed. William G. Dever (Jerusalem: Hebrew Union College/Nelson Glueck School of Biblical Archaeology, 1986).

[65] Israel Finkelstein, David Ussishkin, and Baruch Halpern, eds., *Megiddo III: The 1992-1996 Seasons* (Tel Aviv: Tel Aviv University, Sonia and Marco Nadler Institute of Archaeology, 2000); and Finkelstein, Ussishkin, and Halpern, *Megiddo IV: The 1998–2004 Seasons* (Tel Aviv: Sonia and Marco Nadler Institute of Archaeology, Tel Aviv University, 2006).

[66] Timothy P. Harrison, *Megiddo 3: Final Report on the Stratum VI Excavations* (Chicago, IL: Oriental Institute Publications, 2004).

[67] Kathleen Kenyon, *Jerusalem: Excavation 3000 Years of History* (New York: McGraw-Hill, 1967), 31–62; Kenyon, *Digging Up Jerusalem* (London & Tonbridge: Ernest Benn, 1974), 98-106; and Yigal Shiloh, "The City of David, 1978-1983," in *Biblical Archaeology Today: Proceedings of the International Congress on Biblical Archaeology, Jerusalem April 1984*, ed. Avraham Biran, et al.; (Jerusalem: Israel Exploration Society, 1985), 453–454.

[68] Cahill, "Jerusalem at the Time of the United Monarchy," 76.

[69] Ibid.; Jane M. Cahill and David Tarler, "Response to Margreet Steiner—The Jebusite Ramp

excavations of Jerusalem a monumental building that may have been the palace of David, but this too is contested.[70]

Third, the reason that some data elude the modern investigator is that there has been massive destruction of archaeological remains and structures over the centuries. We find what survives and what the ancients did not need and left behind. What evidence of literacy should one expect when parchment and papyrus do not survive in the climate of the central hill-country? Alan Millard points out that "of about 120 kings known from a dozen Iron Age states of the Levant, including Israel and Judah, at the most only 20 have left inscriptions that are known today."[71] In some cases, materials were carried away by invading armies, destroyed, or reused; there are several ways that cultural and natural formation processes affect material remains.[72] Erosion is also a major factor on hill-country sites.[73] Then the question might also be asked, would one really expect monumental inscriptions when Egypt was in decline at this time and Assyria had not even risen to domination in the east?[74]

---

from Jerusalem: The Evidence from the Macalister, Kenyon, and Shiloh Excavations," in *Biblical Archaeology Today 1990: Proceedings of the Second International Congress on Biblical Archaeology*, ed. Avraham Biran and Joseph Aviram (Jerusalem: Israel Exploration Society, 1993), 625–626; Jane Cahill, "David's Jerusalem: Fiction or Reality, It is There, The Archaeological Evidence Proves It," *Biblical Archaeology Review* 24/4 (1998): 34–41; and Cahill, "Jerusalem in David and Solomon's Time: There Really Was a Major City in the Tenth Century BCE," *Biblical Archaeology Review* 30/6 (2004): 20–31, 62–63.

[70] Eilat Mazar, "Did I Find King David's Palace?" *Biblical Archaeology Review* 32/1 (2006): 16–27, 70; E. Mazar, "The Undiscovered Palace of King David in Jerusalem: A Study in Biblical Archaeology" [Hebrew], in *New Studies in Jerusalem: Proceedings of the Second Conference*, ed. Avi Faust (Ramat Gan: Bar-Ilan University, 1996), 9–20; E. Mazar, *The Summit of the City of David, Excavations 2005—2008, Final Reports, Volume I* (Jerusalem: Shoham Academic Research, 2015); and see now the comments by William G. Dever, *Beyond the Texts: An Archaeological Portrait of Ancient Israel and Judah* (Atlanta, GA: Society of Biblical Literature, 2017), 276–283.

[71] Millard, "David and Solomon's Jerusalem," 198.

[72] See Michael B. Schiffer, *Formation Processes of the Archaeological Record* (Tucson, AZ: University of Arizona, 1987).

[73] Cahill, "Jerusalem at the Time of the United Monarchy," 77.

[74] This argument has been made by Amihai Mazar, "Search for David and Solomon," 134–135; and A. Mazar, "Remarks on Biblical Traditions and Archaeological Evidence Concerning Early Israel," in *Symbiosis, Symbolism, and the Power of the Past*, 90. One major inscription that we do have at Megiddo is the fragment of a stela left by Shishak, king of Egypt, commemorating his campaign, which is also recorded in detail at Karnak. Shishak's Karnak inscription mentions entities in both the north and seventy entities in the Negev of Israel. As Mazar points out, "the only plausible explanation for this, must be the existence of a political power in the central hill country that was significant enough in the eyes of the Egyptians to justify such an exceptional route for a campaign" (Amihai Mazar, "Search for David and Solomon," 124; and A.

Fourth, the ancients left us with texts dealing with what *they* were interested in. What external records are we to expect of major campaigns, especially when they experienced defeats? These kinds of admissions are exceedingly rare and in most cases not existent at all among ancient sources.[75] In terms of the archaeological record itself, what kind of evidence for ancient military activity, be they David's or another king's, would exist today? How often do we actually find textual records that can pinpoint the cause of a given archaeological destruction or discontinuity conclusively? What the adherents of the Low Chronology paradigm do is take one destruction, such as that traditionally attributed to Shishak/Sheshonq I, and simply redate it to Hazael, in this way shifting the entire sequence.[76] But by what internal (textual) and external (archaeological) criteria are these decisions made? Are destructions systematically analyzed (in order to ascertain what the specific correlates of destruction are in the archaeological record) to justify this reassignment?[77] Or is the shift simply based on the *a priori* assumption that the architecture could not date to Solomon?

Mazar, "Remarks on Biblical Traditions," 92–93). On the campaign of Shishak/Sheshonq I, see Kenneth A. Kitchen, *The Third Intermediate Period in Egypt (1100-650 BC)*, 2nd ed. (Warminster: Aris and Phillips, 1996); Kitchen, "The Sheshonqs of Egypt and Palestine," *Journal for the Study of the Old Testament* 93 (2001): 3–12; Kitchen, "Egyptian Interventions in the Levant in Iron Age II," in Dever and Gitin, *Symbiosis, Symbolism, and the Power of the Past*, 121-127; and Michael G. Hasel, "A Sociospatial Analysis of the Campaign of Pharaoh Shishak (Shoshenq I)," in *Lexham Geographic Commentary on the Old Testament Historical Books*, ed. Barry J. Beitzel (Bellingham, WA: Lexham, 2021), forthcoming.

[75] Kenneth A. Kitchen, *On the Reliability of the Old Testament* (Grand Rapids, MI: Eerdmans, 2003), 246. The assertion by Kenton L. Sparks, 156-157, that modern scholars do not demand such evidence is altogether false (*God's Word in Human Words* [Grand Rapids, MI: Baker, 2008], 156–7). It is precisely because the external evidence is lacking for an event that it is summarily dismissed. Sparks himself states, "The silence from the Egyptian evidence is therefore an important argument against the historicity of these miracle reports" (157). If anything, the Old Testament account, which includes the defeats as well as the victories of ancient Israel, presents a more balanced history than the nuanced propaganda found in the ancient Near East.

[76] This shift to another biblical king's reign, whether Ahab or Hazael, still employs the Bible as the primary reference for the historical synchronism; see Michael G. Hasel, "The Archaeology of Destruction: Methodological Desiderata," in *From Sha'ar Hagolan to Shaariam: Essays in Honor of Prof. Yosef Garfinkel*, ed. Saar Ganor, et al. (Jerusalem: Israel Exploration Society, 2016), 205–228.

[77] On the archaeological correlates of destruction in warfare, see Michael G. Hasel, *Domination and Resistance: Egyptian Military Activity in the Southern Levant, 1300-1185 BC* (Probleme der Ägyptologie, 11; Leiden: Brill, 1998), 9–11, 240–256; Michael G. Hasel, *Military Practice and Polemic: Israel's Laws of Warfare in Near Eastern Perspective* (Berrien Springs, MI: Andrews University Press, 2005) and Michael G. Hasel, "Assyrian Military Practices and Deuteronomy's Laws of Warfare," in *Writing and Reading War: Rhetoric, Gender, and Ethics in Biblical and Modern Contexts*, eds. Brad Kelle and Frank Ames, SBL Symposium Series, 42. (Atlanta, GA: Society of Biblical Literature, 2008), 67–81.

Fifth, reports and interpretations of specific sites and their contribution to understanding the history of the region remain tentative and may change with the next season of excavation. For example, the triumphant tone of Philip R. Davies and others[78] who declared in 1992 that David and his kingdom were mythical, based on the absence of evidence for his name in the archaeological record, must now be modified by the discovery in 1993–1994 at the site of Tel Dan of an inscription mentioning the "house of David."[79] The phrase "house of David" was subsequently identified in 1994 by André Lemaire in line 31 on the Moabite Inscription found in Dibon, in Jordan.[80] Later Anson Rainey identified the name David in line 12 of the same text.[81] The "house of David" is the clause that the Bible consistently uses to refer to the southern kingdom of Judah (cf. 2 Sam 2:11; 5:5; 1 Kgs 12:20–26; 2 Chr 8:11). More significantly, in both of these inscriptions the phrase "house of David" identifies the founder of the Judean line of kings over a century after David's existence. Finally, Kenneth Kitchen suggests that "the heights of David" is a toponym listed among the Negev sites mentioned in the Shishak reliefs at the Temple of Amun at Karnak.[82] It is remarkable that in a matter of two years not one, but four separate references to David were identified by scholars in Egyptian, Aramean, and Moabite inscriptions testifying to the foundational influence of this early Israelite king. Today few scholars argue that David did not exist. In terms of Judahite settlement, cities, and fortifications, new surveys and excavations at Khirbet Qeiyafa, Socoh, Khirbet el-Rai, Tel Burna, Khirbet Summeily and Lachish (2007–2020) have shown

---

[78] Philip R. Davies, 69, declares that "the biblical 'empire' of David and Solomon has not the faintest echo in the archaeological record–as yet;" see Michael G. Hasel, review of *In Search of "Ancient Israel"*, by Philip R. Davies, *Andrews University Seminary Studies* 32 (1994): 260–262.

[79] Avraham Biran and Joseph Naveh, "An Aramaic Stele Fragment from Tel Dan," *Israel Exploration Journal* 43 (1993): 81–98; and Biran and Naveh, "The Tel Dan Inscription: A New Fragment," *Israel Exploration Journal* 45 (1995): 1–18. For an overview of the interpretations of the Dan inscription, see Hallvard Hagelia, *The Tel Dan Inscription: A Critical Investigation of Recent Research on Its Palaeography and Philology*, Acta Universitates Upsaliensis; Studia Semitica Upsaliensia, 22 (Uppsala: Uppsala Universitet, 2006).

[80] André Lemaire, "'House of David' Restored in Moabite Inscription," *Biblical Archaeology Review* 20/3 (May/June 1994): 30–37.

[81] Anson F. Rainey, "Mesha' and Syntax," in *The Land That I Will Show You: Essays on the History and Archaeology of the Ancient Near East in Honor of J. Maxwell Miller*, ed. J. Andrew Dearman and M. Patrick Graham, Journal for the Study of the Old Testament Supplement Series, 343 (Sheffield: Sheffield Academic, 2001), 287–307.

[82] Kenneth A. Kitchen, "A Possible Mention of David in the Late Tenth Century B.C.E., and Deity *Dod as Dead as the Dodo?" *Journal for the Study of the Old Testament* 76 (1997): 39–41.

increasing evidence for major settlement and growth of the early kingdom of Judah.[83] Evidence for literacy is now found at Tel Zayit, Jerusalem, Khirbet Qeiyafa, and Gezer.[84] For these reasons, conclusions based on both the presence and lack of evidence must be tentative and provisional, avoiding sweeping generalizations.

Reestablishing the Relationship Between History and Theology

It may seem a daunting task to reestablish a relationship between history and theology when there has been such an utter collapse of history in our modern and postmodern age.[85] Today any sense of certainty concerning the events of the Bible or even secular history is questioned on every level. The secular path of Enlightenment thinking has not brought us clarity of understanding. Instead, "methodological doubt" and philosophical naturalism, with its closed continuum, have led us further into uncertainty and we are left less able than ever

---

[83] On Khirbet Qeiyafa, see Yosef Garfinkel, Saar Ganor, and Michael G. Hasel, *In the Footsteps of David: Revelations from an Ancient Biblical City* (New York: Thames and Hudson, 2018); and Garfinkel, Ganor, and Hasel, *Khirbet Qeiyafa Vol. 4 Excavation Report 2007–2013: Art, Cult, and Epigraphy* (Jerusalem: Israel Exploration Society, 2018). On Socoh, see Michael G. Hasel, Yosef Garfinkel, and Shifra Weiss, *Socoh of the Judean Shephelah: The 2010 Survey* (Winona Lake, IN: Eisenbrauns, 2017). On Khirbet el-Rai: Yosef Garfinkel, et al. "Lachish Fortifications and State Formation in the Biblical Kingdom of Judah in Light of Radiometric Datings," *Radiocarbon* 61/3 (2019): 695–714; Yosef Garfinkel, Kyle H. Keimer, Saar Ganor, Christopher Rollston and David Ben-Schlomo, "Khirbet el-Ra'i in the Judean Shephelah: The 2015-2019 Excavation Seasons," *Strata* 17 (2019): 13–50. On Khirbet Summeily, James W. Hardin, Christopher A. Rollston, and Jeffrey A. Blakely, "Iron Age Bullae from Officialdom's Periphery: Khirbet Summeily in Broder Context," *Near Eastern Archaeology* 77 (2014): 299–301; and most recently, Michael G. Hasel, "The Geographical Extent of the Kingdom of Judah (Shephelah and Negev) in the Tenth Century BC," in *Lexham Geographic Commentary on the Old Testament Historical Books*, ed. Barry J. Beitzel (Bellingham, WA: Lexham, 2021), forthcoming.

[84] On the Tel Zayit inscription see Ron E. Tappy, et al., "An Abecedary of the Mid-Tenth Century from the Judaean Shephelah," *Bulletin of the American Schools of Oriental Research* 344 (2006): 5–46; and Ron E. Tappy and P. Kyle McCarter, *Literate Culture and Tenth-Century Canaan: The Tel Zayit Abecedary in Context* (Winona Lake, IN: Eisenbrauns, 2008). On the Ophel inscription from Jerusalem see Eilat Mazar, David Ben-Shlomo, and Shmuel Ahituv, "An Inscribed Pithos from the Ophel, Jerusalem," *Israel Exploration Journal* 63 (2013): 39–49. On the inscriptions from Khirbet Qeiyafa see Haggai Misgav, Yosef Garfinkel, and Saar Ganor, "The Ostracon," in *Khirbet Qeiyafa, Vol. 1: Excavation Report 2007–2008*, Yosef Garfinkel and Saar Ganor (Jerusalem: Israel Exploration Society, 2009), 243–257; and Yosef Garfinkel, et al., "The ʾIšbaʿal Inscription from Khirbet Qeiyafa," *Bulletin of the American Schools of Oriental Research* 373 (2015): 217–233.

[85] On postmodern approaches to biblical history, see William G. Dever, *What Did the Biblical Writers Know and When Did They Know It?*; John J. Collins, *The Bible After Babel: Historical Criticism in a Postmodern Age* (Grand Rapids, MI: Eerdmans, 2005); and Dever, *Beyond the Texts*, 332–341.

before to articulate what actually happened than ever before. Some have entered into the realm of nihilism, stating that "if historical (verifiable) truth should be our only concern, the history of ancient Israel should not only be very short (written on ten pages or so), but it would also be utterly boring."[86] So how can one even begin to approach the Bible and history?

First, we approach Scripture humbly recognizing that it is the inspired Word of God with an authority unlike any other source (1 Tim 3:16; 2 Pet 1:16–21). We see that this was the attitude with which Jesus repeatedly used Scripture. When tempted after His baptism, His defense came from Scripture alone on all three occasions (Luke 4:1–13). At the cross, in His final moments, Jesus again quoted from Scripture, pointing His listeners back to the authoritative and prophetic Word (Pss 22:1; 31:5). Relying on Scripture does not place us in the limited position of a closed continuum as we find it in philosophical naturalism. Instead, it expands our vision beyond this world and its natural laws to the God who set those elements and its history in motion and continues to work in sustaining His creation. This greater reality allows us to ask different questions and accept biblical answers. Because of its divine inspiration, Scripture sits in judgment over us; we do not sit in judgment over the Bible.

Second, the primary evidence for the biblical view and understanding of history must derive from the Bible itself, not from a superimposed series of presuppositions that essentially deny the Bible's foundational premises. The Bible must be the source upon which to base and establish the meaning of history, for it intrinsically claims to give us the inspired account of God's acts in history among His people and for His people. It also recounts how the people responded to that invitation throughout history. One of the elements that creates trust in the authenticity of Scripture for the historian is that the Bible provides for us not only the victories and triumphs of God's people, but also their lowest struggles and defeats. This adds credibility to the biblical account and is in singular contrast to the literature of major civilizations that glossed over their defeats to present a consistently victorious nation.

Third, we approach Scripture from a perspective of trust and faith that results in obedience, not mistrust and doubt. "The 'starting point' of our exegetical work is, therefore, emphatically not 'scientific skepticism' for skepticism is rooted, after all, in Cartesian thinking. . . .

[86] Hans M. Barstad, "History and the Hebrew Bible," in *Can a "History of Israel" Be Written?*, ed. Lester L. Grabbe, Journal of the Study of the Old Testament: Supplement Series, 245; (Sheffield: Sheffield Academic Press, 1997), 64.

this relates most closely to the notion of autonomous reason as this made its victorious march during the Enlightenment. The starting point is rather obedience, the obedience of the person whose communion with God is one of fervor."[87] Nowhere in Scripture do the biblical writers cast doubt on the reliability or authority of the biblical account of history and events. In no single case does Ellen G. White take such an approach either. The Bible is not approached by other biblical writers as "guilty until proven innocent." Instead we find a consistent pattern of taking the text at its simple word. In fact, from the biblical account we learn that external evidence apart from the Word of God is not a prerequisite for knowledge and understanding or an acceptance of God's Word as authoritative. It is not necessary for faith that every instruction be corroborated by evidence outside of God's Word itself. Before the flood, Noah received no external confirmation for the flood event. By faith He relied on God's Word alone "concerning events as yet unseen" (Heb 11:7). The antediluvian empiricists would have argued for the "absence of evidence" as it had never rained upon the earth.[88] Noah continued preaching for 120 years, and "in reverent fear constructed an ark for the saving of his household. By this he condemned the world and became an heir of the righteousness that comes by faith" (Heb 11:7). In the end, it was not his preaching that saved the human race; it was his obedience in building the ark. Likewise, Abram left Ur and then Haran without any prior evidence or direction. His faith in God's instruction was acted upon and he went, trusting and obedient to go where God would lead (Heb 11:8–10).

Fourth, *Historie*—those events that actually took place in the past—in and of itself is not revelatory. History needs to be revealed and explained. This is not a subjective enterprise; it requires divine revelation to interpret and explain history. The cross does not, in and of itself, tell us anything about the meaning of the historical event. Thousands of people died futile deaths on crosses during the Roman era. After the revolt by Spartacus, the Romans under Crassus lined the Appian Way from Rome to Capua with six thousand crucified individuals.[89] So what was one more crucifixion in Jerusalem? And what separated this Jesus of

---

[87] Gerhard Maier, *Biblical Hermeneutics* (Wheaton, IL: Crossway, 1994), 57–58. On the role of reason in theology see Frank M. Hasel, "Theology and the Role of Reason," *Journal of the Adventist Theological Society* 4/2 (1993): 172–198.

[88] On the nature of the dew watering the earth before the flood, see Gerhard F. Hasel and Michael G. Hasel, "The Hebrew Term *'ed* in Gen 2,6 and Its Connection in Ancient Near Eastern Literature," *Zeitschrift für die alttestamentliche Wissenschaft* 112 (2000): 321–340.

[89] Appian, *Civil Wars*, 1.120.

Nazareth from the other two thieves who were crucified with Him? It is only through the revelation of the Bible that the meaning of the cross becomes certain and that certainty is based solely on the historical reality of the Old Testament prophecies and their fulfillment in Jesus Christ. That is why the New Testament writers emphasize not only the reality of the cross and the resurrection, but its connection to the typology of the lamb sacrificed for generations by the Israelites and fulfilled on that Passover Friday in AD 31.[90]

The gospels painstakingly connect the historical events of the life of Christ with the statements made concerning Him throughout the law and the prophets. They connect history, prophecy and the historical event, which they witnessed themselves. They recount the study of the Magi that led to their following the star that had been prophesied by Balaam (Num 24:17; Matt 2:1–2). Jesus Himself points back from the cross to the Messianic prophecies that testify of the manner of His death (Pss 22:1; 31:5).[91] They relay the testimonies of the women and Mary Magdalene who first came to the tomb on Sunday morning and saw her risen Savior (Mark 9–11; John 20:11–18). They tell their experience with Jesus on the road to Emmaus and how He expounded to them the Scriptures (Luke 24:13–27). He appears to them in the upper room. The doubts of Thomas are removed by Jesus speaking to him directly and eating with them (John 20:24–29). Hundreds of eyewitnesses saw Him after his resurrection. John says, "This is the disciple who testifies to these things and wrote these things; and we know that his testimony is true" (John 21:24).

Paul's writings reaffirm the centrality of the historical event when he writes to the Corinthian church, "For I delivered to you first of all that which I also received: that Christ died for our sins according to the Scriptures, and that He was buried, and that He rose again the third day according to the Scriptures, and that He was seen by Cephas, then by the twelve. After that He was seen by over five hundred brethren at once, of whom the greater part remains to the present, but some have fallen asleep. After that He was seen by James, then by all the apostles. Then last of all He was seen by me also, as by one born out of due time" (1 Cor 15:2–8). Paul emphasizes and reaffirms what the gospel writers have given testimony to, providing the very scriptural evidences for Christ's death and the certainty of his bodily resurrection. Then he says, "Now

---

[90] For arguments supporting the date AD 31 for the crucifixion, see Grace Amadon, "Ancient Jewish Calendation," *Journal of Biblical Literature* 61 (1942): 227–280; and Amadon, "The Crucifixion Calendar," *Journal of Biblical Literature* 63 (1944): 177–190.

[91] On the Messianic prophecies and a hermeneutic to understand their significance, see Walter C. Kaiser, Jr., *The Messiah in the Old Testament* (Grand Rapids, MI: Zondervan, 1995).

if Christ is preached that He has been raised from the dead, how do some among you say that there is no resurrection of the dead? But if there is no resurrection of the dead, then Christ is not risen. And if Christ is not risen, then our preaching is empty, and your faith is also empty" (1 Cor 15:12–14). For Paul the historical reality of the resurrection was the basis for the faith of Christianity. History, theology, and faith were inextricably linked. It was the connection to history and prophecy that made the claims of the Messiah true.

Fifth, the details of history matter. It is not enough to say that an exodus took place, but then redefine the event in rationalistic or naturalistic terms. To explain and relegate the ten plagues as mere natural events based on weather, red algae, or the like is to remove the divine agency and thereby their meaning as divine judgments against the ideology of ancient Egypt.[92] Likewise, to use rationalistic explanations for the numbers of Israelites because we cannot conceive of that number surviving in the desert is to remove the divine element of sustenance through manna and water and God's direct guidance in the pillar of fire and protective cloud. Without doubt we may face unresolved questions regarding the Bible's history, but that should drive us to study deeper and ask new questions that might result in satisfactory answers.[93] Edwin Thiele, when faced with the seemingly impossible task of reconciling the numbers of the kings of Israel and Judah, researched carefully on the basis of the text itself and found a solution using the Bible and the internal evidence it contained. His work is still widely cited as the defining study of this subject today.[94]

The minutiae of detail found in the Bible matter and provide the very level of authenticity one might expect. Often the names of individuals mentioned in passing have been confirmed through archaeological

---

[92] Michael G. Hasel, "Exodus, Book of," in *Andrews Bible Commentary: Old Testament*, ed. Ángel Manuel Rodríguez; (Berrien Springs, MI: Andrews University Press, 2020), 196–236.

[93] On resolving difficult passages in the Bible, see Gleason F. Archer, Jr., *New International Encyclopedia of Bible Difficulties*, 2nd ed. (Grand Rapids, MI: Zondervan, 2001); Walter C. Kaiser, Jr., et al., *Hard Sayings of the Bible* (Downer's Grove, IL: InterVarsity, 1996); Gerhard F. Pfandl, ed., *Interpreting Scripture: Bible Questions and Answers*, Biblical Research Institute Studies 2 (Silver Spring, MD: Biblical Research Institute, 2010); and Frank M. Hasel and Michael G. Hasel, *How to Interpret Scripture* (Nampa, ID: Pacific Press, 2019), 113–120.

[94] Edwin R. Thiele, *The Mysterious Numbers of the Kings of Judah and Israel* (Chicago, IL: University of Chicago Press, 1944) and subsequent editions. Assyriologist Donald J. Wiseman of the British Museum writes, "The chronology most widely accepted today is one based on the meticulous study by Thiele," (Donald J. Wiseman, *1 and 2 Kings*, Tyndale Old Testament Commentaries [Leicester: InterVarsity, 1993], 27).

research, such as the Babylonian official Nebu-sarsakim in Jeremiah 39:3,[95] or the Judean head of Hezekiah's palace, Eliakim, the scribe Shebna, King Hezekiah himself; and now possibly Isaiah the prophet—all mentioned in Isaiah 37:1–2.[96] Then there are some details that are rather unexpected, such as the Hebrew word *pîm*, which is only used once in the Bible in reference to the Israelites getting their iron tools sharpened by the Philistines: "The price for sharpening proved to be a *pîm* for the plowshares" (1 Sam. 13:21). We know today that this was the name of a specific weight unit measuring 7.82 grams or two-thirds of a shekel, thanks to the discovery of these weights by archaeologists.[97] Responding to minimalists who claim that the biblical text was written only in the Hellenistic period, William G. Dever writes,

> [It] cannot possibly have been "invented" by writers living in the Hellenistic-Roman period several centuries after these weights had disappeared and had been forgotten. In fact, this bit of biblical text . . . would not be understood until the early 20th century A.D., when the first actual archaeological examples turned up, reading *pîm* in Hebrew. . . . If the biblical stories are all 'literary inventions' of the Hellenistic-Roman era, how did this particular story come to be in the Hebrew Bible? One may object, of course, that the *pîm* incident is "only a detail." To be sure; but as is well known, "history is in the details."[98]

The Bible's historical accuracy is, likewise, demonstrated in the details.

History, Meaning and Identity

When we remove history, we remove meaning and identity. Without David in history who would defeat the Philistines, bringing under control

---

[95] The tablet confirming his existence is in the British Museum, BM 114789; Michael Jursa, "Nabu-šarrūssu-ukīn, *rab ša-rēši*, und 'Nebusarsekim' (Jer. 39:3)," *Nouvelles Assyriologiques Breves et Utilitaires* 1 (2008): 9–10.

[96] On Eliakim, see Martin G. Klingbeil et al., "Four Judean Bullae from the 2014 Season at Tel Lachish," *Bulletin of the American Schools of Oriental Research* 381 (2019): 41–56. On Shebna, see, Robert Deutsch, "Tracking Down Shebnayahu, Servant of the King," *Biblical Archaeology Review* 35/3 (2009): 45–49, 67. On Hezekiah and Isaiah, see Eilat Mazar, *The Ophel Excavations to the South of the Temple Mount 2009–2013: Final Reports Volume II* (Jerusalem: Shoham Academic Research, 2018), 253–256.

[97] Raz Kletter, *Economic Keystones: The Weight System of the Kingdom of Judah,* Journal of the Study of the Old Testament: Supplement Series 276 (Sheffield: Sheffield Academic, 1998), 85.

[98] Dever, *What Did the Biblical Writers Know*, 227.

decades of antagonism and conflict (1 Sam 17, 19, 23; 2 Sam 5; 1 Chr 18:1)?[99] Without David the Jebusite city of Jerusalem would not have been conquered and established as a capital that still survives today after three thousand years (2 Sam 5). Without David, the seventy-three Psalms attributed to him would not have been written and could not be part of the liturgy of worship then or today in synagogues and churches around the globe. Without David, Solomon would not have succeeded to the throne and built the temple that lasted for nearly four hundred years. Finally, it is through the line of Jesse and David that the Messiah is promised to Israel (Isa 11:1–10; Rev 22:16).[100] For these reasons no other person is mentioned more frequently throughout the Old and New Testaments than David—from the earliest references in Ruth to the final chapter of Revelation.[101] His son Solomon builds the temple in Jerusalem; refortifies the cities of Megiddo, Hazor, Gezer, and Jerusalem (1 Kgs 9:15); and establishes an extensive trade network, exponentially increasing the wealth of Israel. Without David, the Bible would not be trustworthy, and its history would have to be completely rewritten.

The power of the study of history is that it seeks truth. It seeks to discover those things that really took place in order to find purpose, meaning, and a future hope. A God who is reduced to timelessness and removed from space and place as an abstract idea or philosophy cannot act in history, and so history and our existence become meaningless. If God did not accomplish what He said He did, then why should we believe He can accomplish it in our lives today, or for that matter, why should we believe His promises for the future? The Greco-Roman culture after millennia of pagan superstition and mythical thinking was bankrupt and resorted to the escapism of the circus and the coliseum.

---

[99] On the extended life and final demise of the Philistines in the archaeological record, see Seymour Gitin, "Philistia in Transition: The Tenth Century and Beyond," in *Mediterranean Peoples in Transition, in Honor of Trude Dothan*, ed. Seymour Gitin, Amahai Mazar, and E. Stern (Jerusalem: Israel Exploration Society, 1998), 162–183; and Gitin, "Philistines in the Books of Kings," in *The Books of Kings: Sources, Composition, Historiography and Reception*, ed. André Lemaire and Baruch Halpern (Leiden: Brill, 2010), 308–309.

[100] On the messianic descriptions pertaining to David, see Philip E. Satterwaite, "David in the Books of Samuel: A Messianic Hope?" in *The Lord's Anointed: Interpretation of Old Testament Messianic Texts*, ed. Philip E. Satterthwaite, Richard S. Hess, and Gordon J. Wenham (Grand Rapids, MI: Baker, 1995), 41–65; Daniel I. Block, "Bringing Back David: Ezekiel's Messianic Hope," in Satterthwaite, Hess, and Wenham, 167–188; and Block, "My Servant David: Ancient Israel's Vision of the Messiah," in *Israel's Messiah in the Bible and the Dead Sea Scrolls*, ed. Richard S. Hess and M. Daniel Carroll (Grand Rapids, MI: Baker: 2003), 17–56.

[101] The name David is mentioned 1,087 times: 976 times in the Old Testament and 111 times in the New Testament.

We are repeating that history today. But fiction does not engender hope; it only provides a fleeting feeling of excitement and emotion. Fiction is not reality, but an escape from reality. A movie based on a fictional story of spaceships and invading creatures from another galaxy (think *Star Wars* or *The Avengers*),[102] will not have the same impact as witnessing the real life experience of Desmond Doss, who miraculously and courageously rescued fellow American and enemy Japanese soldiers from Hacksaw Ridge.[103] What makes the Bible so powerful is not only that it testifies that there is a God who acts in history,

> but that this is the *only* place he acted that had significance for human beings, that those actions were according to a consistent, long-term purpose [of love], and that he was using the details of the human-historical behavior to reveal that purpose, and that he was just as capable of using enemies as he was friends to accomplish his good purpose.[104]

This interlinking of history and prophecy is not found anywhere else in the religious writings of the ancient or modern world. This combination as exposed through sound historical-grammatical hermeneutics, is what demonstrates the uniqueness of the Bible in human history.

---

[102] The idea of an impersonal "force" that is found throughout the universe is not a progression but rather a regression to the paganism of the ancient mythic world of Egypt that sought to counterfeit the personal design of an all-loving God who intercedes for His people (e.g. the exodus).

[103] Booton Herndon, *Redemption at Hacksaw Ridge* (Coldwater, MI: Remnant, 2016), now a feature film entitled *Hacksaw Ridge*.

[104] Oswalt, 142.

CHAPTER 5

Culture, Hermeneutics, and Scripture: Discerning What is Universal

Clinton Wahlen and Wagner Kuhn

In examining the topic of culture in relation to Scripture, it may be helpful at the outset to share from which cultural perspectives we as authors approach the topic. Clinton Wahlen grew up in the United States but has worked outside his homeland for more than fifteen years—a year in New Zealand, where he first discovered he had an "American accent"; six years in Russia (attaining fluency); three years in Cambridge, United Kingdom, where he received his PhD in New Testament; six months in Germany; and five years in the Philippines. Wagner Kuhn, professor and chair of the Department of World Mission at the Seventh-day Adventist Theological Seminary, Andrews University, with his PhD in Missiology and Intercultural Studies from Fuller Theological Seminary, is from Brazil (where he began his ministry) but has worked for many years in Central Asia and the United States. This broad cross-cultural mission experience has informed and enriched our study of the Bible by enabling us to hear how its message resonates and finds application within diverse cultural contexts. It has also helped us appreciate our own limitations in understanding ancient texts, considering that no single perspective can capture the fullness of meaning resident in Scripture.[1]

One's view of the Bible significantly influences how one interprets it.

---

[1] Still helpful in this regard is the discussion on the globalization of hermeneutics by Craig L. Blomberg, "Critical Issues in New Testament Studies for Evangelicals Today," in *A Pathway into the Holy Scripture*, ed. P. E. Satterthwaite and D. F. Wright (Grand Rapids, MI: Eerdmans, 1994), 65–69.

Some consider the Bible almost as a "book from heaven," untouched and untainted by cultural influences and human frailties. Others, influenced by critical approaches to it, may question the uniqueness of the Bible altogether. Seventh-day Adventists consider the Bible unique because it is divinely inspired.[2] But it is also a human book, since the inspired content is expressed in human language.[3] This fact encourages its exploration in relation to culture. Various definitions of culture have been offered, reflecting diverse settings and purposes, with each contributing a meaningful perspective.[4] For our purposes it will be useful to define culture as "the complex of values, customs, beliefs, and practices which constitute the way of life of a specific group."[5] These cultural components find expression in many and diverse ways, including in art, music, food choices, eating habits, clothing, and more.

Before proceeding further, it may be helpful to consider some questions relevant to this topic: What role did culture have in relation to the writing of the Bible? How does culture impact the interpretation of Scripture? And how do our answers to these questions affect our hermeneutical methods and the resulting interpretation? Did cultural influences affect the way the Bible writers themselves interpreted Scripture? If so, does that relativize certain Bible passages or limit their application? Does the Bible reveal principles of interpretation that can assist us in understanding how a specific passage relates to the cultural milieu within which it was written? Can we identify cultural

---

[2] Seventh-day Adventist Church, "1. The Holy Scriptures," in *28 Fundamental Beliefs* (2015), 3, https://www.adventist.org/fileadmin/adventist.org/files/articles/official-statements/28Beliefs-Web.pdf (accessed October 21, 2019). The fact that this doctrine is listed first among the 28 Fundamental Beliefs indicates its foundational importance for the Church and its authoritative role in determining Adventist faith and practice. See also, "The Word of God," in *Seventh-day Adventists Believe: A Biblical Exposition of Fundamental Doctrine[s]*, 3rd ed. (Silver Spring, MD: Review and Herald Publishing Association and the General Conference of Seventh-day Adventists, 2018), 11–22.

[3] On the issue of Bible transmission and translation, see chapter 3 by Clinton Wahlen, "Versions, Variants, and the Trustworthiness of Scripture," in the present volume.

[4] See four separate definitions in Joshua D. Chatraw and Karen Swallow Prior, eds., *Cultural Engagement: A Crash Course in Contemporary Issues* (Grand Rapids, MI: Zondervan Academic, 2019), 23–24; cf. Donald Moorman, *Harvest Waiting* (St. Louis, MO: Concordia, 1999), quoted in William W. Schumacher, "Theology for Culture: Confrontation, Context, and Creation," *Concordia Journal* 42/3 (2016): 214: "An interrelated system of thought, belief, morality, ethical principles, social and family structures, and physical products developed by a group in order to organize life in ways which are understandable and workable so that they can survive, attain their valued goals, and successfully adapt to change in their environment."

[5] Chatraw and Prior, 24, citing Terry Eagleton, *The Idea of Culture* (Oxford: Oxford University Press, 2000), 34.

concerns expressed in the text and, if so, are they still relevant? Can we identify principles that transcend culture and that can be applied in multicultural settings globally within the Seventh-day Adventist Church?[6]

In this chapter we will explore these questions, keeping in mind that the Bible is a divine-human composition written from various perspectives at specific times, in specific places and social contexts. Therefore, we must look closely at the historical and cultural elements in Scripture and how they can be understood in relation to contemporary cultural concerns.

Relationship Between the Bible and Culture

In examining this topic, we need to recognize that influences flow in both directions. That is, culture influenced how the Bible writers conveyed their God-given message, but God's Word, from the beginning, has also had a significant influence on people, their thinking, and their culture. The Bible has had a profound impact on virtually every area of human inquiry and expression—art, literature, government, history, music, film, fashion, science, education, medical care, and more. Many of the positive values that have enabled modern civilization to thrive have been derived from the Bible. While it is also true that many of the worst atrocities in history have been committed by people who tried to justify their actions based on the Bible, it should be recognized that persecution, violence, war, slavery, and even genocide are neither intrinsically nor necessarily connected to biblical faith, and therefore cannot be considered as valid expressions of a biblical faith. Rather, they are the result of selective and twisted readings of the Bible. Thus it is crucial for us to understand how critically important is a responsible use of Scripture. We want to be wise in how we read and interpret the Bible, and should be cognizant of the impact our views of the Bible have on those within our sphere of influence.

All human communication operates within a specific historical, cultural, social, and philosophical context, and the Bible is no exception. But since it is a divine-human product, to what extent does the biblical revelation originate within culture, and to what extent does it

---

[6] For a discussion on some of these questions as they relate to culture, biblical hermeneutics, theology, and mission, see Wagner Kuhn and Andrew Tompkins, "Theology on the Way: Hermeneutics from and for the Frontline," *Journal of Adventist Mission Studies* 12/1 (2016): 5–22. See also Andrew Tompkins, "Constructing a Theology of Relational Life Through the Themes of Creation, Incarnation, and Re-Creation as an Alternative to Current Categories of Religions" (PhD diss., Andrews University, 2019).

transcend culture? In harmony with our understanding of the Bible's divine inspiration, the biblical writings did not spring from human imagination and intention, but from the direct agency of the Holy Spirit upon the mind of the writers (2 Pet 1:21), imbuing them with thoughts (revelation) so that the ideas expressed (through inspiration/inscripturization) become the Word of God.[7] Inspired or "God-breathed" thoughts (2 Tim 3:16) are expressed in both speech and writing so that God's direction of the process of thought inspiration covers both.[8]

The mind of the inspired writers is also deeply involved in this process, so that inspired ideas are expressed in a way unique to them.[9] We see this operating clearly in the four Gospels, especially when something is described by more than one of them. The Gospel of Mark, apparently written from a Roman context, is normally brief and concise regarding Jesus' teachings but more expansive in describing the miracles than other Gospel accounts.[10] The Gospel of Matthew, however, focuses more on the teachings of Jesus and displays more sensitivity to Jewish

---

[7] Ellen G. White, *Selected Messages*, (Washington, DC: Review and Herald, 1958), 1:21: "The divine mind and will is combined with the human mind and will; thus the utterances of the man are the word of God." On the meaning of the terms "revelation," "inspiration," "inscripturization," and "illumination," see Fernando Canale, *Back to Revelation-Inspiration: Searching for the Cognitive Foundation of Christian Theology in a Postmodern World* (Lanham, MD: University Press of America, 2001), 57–59.

[8] See Fernando Canale, "Revelation and Inspiration," in *Understanding Scripture: An Adventist Approach*, ed. George W. Reid, Biblical Research Institute Studies 1 (Silver Spring, MD: Biblical Research Institute, 2006), 49, who distinguishes this view from "thought inerrancy" by which "infallible truth [is] presented in fallible language," "but stops short of reaching their [the biblical writers'] words" (ibid., 56; cf. 58); cf. ibid., 66–67 for a biblical model of revelation-inspiration. Similarly, Peter M. van Bemmelen, "Revelation and Inspiration," in *Handbook of Seventh-day Adventist Theology*, ed. Raoul Dederen (Hagerstown, MD: Review and Herald, 2000), 22–57. This conception of how inspiration operates is to be distinguished from what is commonly called "verbal inspiration," "which generally emphasizes God as the author and works from a strong Calvinistic predestinarian worldview. Such a notion of inspiration conceives of the Bible as originating in a timeless, nonhistorical realm and requires its inerrancy—thus transforming its every statement into 'absolute truth'" (Canale, "Revelation and Inspiration," 53). Cf. Ellen G. White's statement that "the writers of the Bible were God's penmen, not His pen" (*Selected Messages*, 1:21). See also Alberto R. Timm, "Divine Accommodation and Cultural Conditioning of the Inspired Writings," *Journal of the Adventist Theological Society* 19/1–2 (2008): 164–165. The preservation of the very words of the divine message occurs only rarely by way of exception (e.g., Deut 10:4; 2 Sam 7:5–16; Isa 38:4–6; Rev 2:1–3:22).

[9] Cf. Ellen G. White, *Selected Messages*, 1:20, that "the Bible was given for practical purposes" and "God, as a writer, is not represented" (ibid., 1:21).

[10] Clinton Wahlen, *Jesus and the Impurity of Spirits in the Synoptic Gospels*, Wissenschaftliche Untersuchungen zum Neuen Testament, 2nd ser., vol. 185 (Tübingen: Mohr Siebeck, 2004), 83. Miracle stories represent about a third of the Gospel and half of the material up to Mark 11:1 (ibid., n. 72).

concerns. Luke highlights Jesus' ministry to the poor, the sick, and other marginalized groups, while John reveals Jesus as the Incarnate Word and underscores the "cosmic conflict between light and darkness embodied in Jesus and his human adversaries."[11] At the same time, "the Holy Spirit guided the prophets in the writing process, ensuring that the prophets' own words expressed the message they received in a trustworthy and reliable form."[12]

The gift of the Holy Spirit at Pentecost enabled Peter and the other apostles to speak to people from many different nations and cultures in their native languages (Acts 2:5). Paul, being bicultural, deftly addresses both Jewish and Gentile concerns, though not necessarily at the same time or in the same epistle. These differences among the various Bible writers affect their individual emphases, but not the truth of what is written.[13] On the contrary, a more complete picture is given than would otherwise be the case.[14]

In thinking biblically about culture, the book of Genesis is foundational because it describes the origin and development of the original human culture on this planet prior to its being derailed and distorted by sin. Although the biblical account of creation was written within a Hebrew context, partially, it seems, as a polemic against polytheistic ideas,[15] its message is not bound or limited by the cultural standpoint from which it was written. As a product of the human writer, it speaks to culture, but because it is an *inspired* account of creation it also

---

[11] Wahlen, *Jesus and the Impurity of Spirits in the Synoptic Gospels*, 20.

[12] Canale, "Revelation and Inspiration," 59; cf. Carl F. H. Henry, *God, Revelation and Authority*, vol. 4, *God Who Speaks and Shows: Fifteen Theses, Part Three* (Waco, TX: Word, 1979), 148–149: "The Spirit of God made full use of the human capacities of the chosen writers so that their writings reflect psychological, biographical, and even sociohistorical differences." Rightly understood, there is no dichotomy between the writer of the text and the text itself.

[13] Ellen G. White, *Selected Messages*, 1:22: "The Creator of all ideas may impress different minds with the same thought, but each may express it in a different way, yet without contradiction. . . . Each dwells on particular points which his constitution and education have fitted him to appreciate. The sunlight falling upon the different objects gives those objects a different hue."

[14] Ellen G. White, *Manuscript Releases*, vol. 6 (Silver Spring, MD: Ellen G. White Estate, 1990), 328: "The gospels differ, yet in them the record blends in one harmonious whole. One writer brings in points that another does not bring in. . . . Some speakers dwell at considerable lengths on points that others would pass by quickly or would not mention at all. Thus the truth is presented more clearly by several than by one."

[15] Gerhard F. Hasel, "Polemic Nature of the Genesis Cosmology," *Evangelical Quarterly* 46 (1974): 81–102; and Gerhard F. Hasel and Michael G. Hasel, "The Unique Cosmology of Genesis 1 Against Ancient Near Eastern and Egyptian Parallels," in *The Genesis Creation Account and Its Reverberations in the Old Testament*, ed. Gerald A. Klingbeil (Berrien Springs, MI: Andrews University Press and the General Conference of Seventh-day Adventists, 2015), 9–29.

transcends culture because it is written in a way that speaks authoritatively to our time about creation. Assuming the account's historical accuracy, God is not only presented as the Creator of all things and Lord of heaven and earth (Gen 1:1; cf. Exod 20:11), but His voice also speaks the world into existence. He becomes intimately involved in the creation of human beings, including human culture (Gen 1:26-2:25). The Bible concludes, in a similar way, with God creating "a new heaven and a new earth" (Rev 21:1)[16] and saying, "Behold, I make all things new" (Rev 21:5). We would be remiss in our study of the Bible and culture if we did not take into account the implications of this wider canonical context. This cosmic, transcultural frame of the canon within which the content of the Bible is revealed can assist our interpretation of the more "earthy" elements in Scripture. Before addressing these elements, however, it is important to notice what constituted the Edenic world described in Genesis.

God did not create a colorless, cultureless world. To the contrary, it was filled with life and diversity and guided by divine law, including the Sabbath (Gen 2:1–3), which reflects the ideal God-human relationship, and marriage (Gen 2:24), which reflects the ideal husband-wife relationship. At the same time God gave human beings, who are created in His image (Gen 1:26; 2:15), the ability and freedom to express their love to Him and to one another through these two divinely established institutions and in other creative ways that reflect their cultural diversity, as long as they stay within the limits of His law. As part of the divine blessing, the man and the woman were instructed to "be fruitful and multiply; fill the earth and subdue it" (Gen 1:28). Having children would eventually enable the human family to extend their benevolent rule over the entire animal kingdom. Food was provided for all in the form of a vegetarian diet (Gen 1:29; Ps 104:14).

God also interacts personally with human beings. He "planted a garden eastward in Eden" (Gen 2:8) as their home. Adam is given moral legislation and entrusted with naming the animals (Gen 2:16–20). He also calls Eve "woman." In the Hebrew there is no trace of domination in the relation between husband and wife; rather, it expresses the close relation Adam and Eve share as the first humans and the first couple, as well as the differentiation between the sexes that God designed into them (Gen 2:21–23).[17] Human beings are given dominion over "every

[16] All biblical quotations are from the NKJV unless otherwise indicated.

[17] The verb "call" (Heb. *qara'*) is a neutral word, used for God naming "day" and "night," "heaven," "earth," "seas," as well as Adam naming the animals (Gen 2:19–20). Upon seeing Eve for the first time, Adam breaks into poetry (Gen 2:23). In Hebrew, "man" is *ish* and "woman" is *isha*.

living thing" as a sign of their unique status above the animal creation (Gen 1:26, 28). The benevolent nature of their rule is suggested by the use of the same verb in connection with the Messiah's rule "from sea to sea, and . . . to the ends of the earth" (Ps 72:8).[18] The absence of shame in this idyllic, Edenic culture (Gen 2:25) is highly significant. Since shame in Scripture is associated with sin and impurity (e.g., Isa 1:27–29; 45:16–17; Jer 6:15; Zeph 3:11–13), the absence of shame underscores the holiness and purity that existed before the fall.[19] It is an indication of the reverence of human beings for God, His laws, and His system of government as well as their respect and love for each other and care for the created world. Although from a modern (or postmodern), phenomenological perspective culture is considered a purely human creation, from a biblical perspective it is far richer and more complex.[20] First, Genesis describes God working together with the human beings He made to create the parameters for a vibrant, Edenic, "heavenlike" culture for human beings.[21] Second, every element of this culture has a vertical, God-oriented dimension, as

---

[18] Only in two verses (Gen 1:26; Ps 72:8) does the Hebrew verb *radah* ("rule, have dominion") appear as a jussive.

[19] The fact that God clothes Himself "with light as with a garment" (Ps 104:2) may suggest that human beings, who are made in His image, also had garments of light before the fall. Cf. Ellen G. White, *The Story of Patriarchs and Prophets* (Mountain View, CA: Pacific Press, 1958), 45: "The sinless pair wore no artificial garments; they were clothed with a covering of light and glory, such as the angels wear. So long as they lived in obedience to God, this robe of light continued to enshroud them."

[20] According to Helen Spencer-Oatey, "What Is Culture? A Compilation of Quotations," *GlobalPAD Core Concepts* (2012), https://warwick.ac.uk/fac/soc/al/globalpad/openhouse/interculturalskills/global_pad_-_what_is_culture.pdf (accessed April 29, 2020), the concept of "culture" has been "notoriously difficult" to define. It was first defined in an anthropological sense by Edward B. Tylor, *Primitive Culture: Researches into the Development of Mythology, Philosophy, Religion, Language, Art and Custom* (London: J. Murray, 1871), 1: "that complex whole which includes knowledge, belief, art, morals, law, custom, and any other capabilities and habits acquired by man as a member of society."

[21] Although Ellen G. White does not use the term "culture" in a technical, anthropological sense, insight into the nature of this original, God-oriented culture designed for human beings may be found in Ellen G. White, *Patriarchs and Prophets*, 44–51; Ellen G. White, *The Story of Prophets and Kings* (Mountain View, CA: Pacific Press, 1917), 730-733. That the heavenly principles underlying the original culture of Eden is to be instilled in God's people now is also made clear by Jesus Himself (Matt 6:10). Note Ellen G. White's comments on this verse: "The will of God is expressed in the precepts of His holy law, and the priciples of this law are the principles of heaven" (*Thoughts From the Mount of Blessing* [Mountain View, CA: Pacific Press, 1956], 109; cf. Ellen G. White, *God's Amazing Grace* (Washington, DC: Review and Herald, 1973), 362: "The life on earth is the beginning of the life in heaven; education on earth is an initiation into the principles of heaven"; Ellen G. White, *Prophets and Kings*, 609: "Ezra became a mouthpiece for God, educating those about him in the principles that govern heaven." See also n. 130 below.

well as a human-oriented dimension. The "work" of tending the garden was assigned by God, and the results of that work, though a product of human creativity and design, would be exercised within the boundaries established by God.

This perfect world was damaged as a result of God's Word being questioned and His laws being broken (Gen 3–4). This cause-effect relationship should be remembered in our further exploration of culture in Scripture. Interestingly, the line of Cain and the line of Seth seem to be set up in contrast to each other (Gen 4:16–5:32). In connection with the line of Cain, various societal and cultural developments are mentioned, but there is no indication that their otherwise useful skills in music or metalworking, for example, were used to honor and glorify God (Gen 4:21–22).[22] Cain's building of a city (Gen 4:17) at this early stage of human expansion and development seems to be in direct defiance of the divine command for human beings to "fill the earth" (cf. Gen 11:4, 8),[23] and Lamech's introduction of polygamy by taking "for himself two wives" marks another major departure from the Edenic culture for which human beings were designed (Gen 2:24). Like Cain himself (Gen 4:3–8, 16; cf. Heb 11:4),[24] his descendants apparently had little regard for God's instructions regarding worship, including the Sabbath, as no mention is made of their observing them and none of the cultural elements created by them are described as having any religious significance (Gen 4:20–22).[25] Their disregard of these two institutions established in Eden (marriage and the Sabbath) exhibits also a disregard for God's holiness and for the inviolability of His laws, which were designed to strengthen the relation of husband

[22] Cain's descendants distinguished themselves by "mere earthly and material progress" (Ellen G. White, *Patriarchs and Prophets*, 81).

[23] The irony has been observed that the first murderer built the first city, but this should not lead us to see all references to cities in the Bible in negative terms. "People of antiquity understood far better than we that civilization and the existence of the city are coterminous. We who can live in comfort in rural areas do not easily understand the brutish nature of village life in early times. Of course the concentration of power in the city made possible new forms of suffering, so the biblical picture is ambiguous. . . . Still, we must not forget that in both Testaments the new heaven and new earth are depicted in the form of a city, the New Jerusalem (Isa. 65:17–25; Rev. 21:1–22:5). But that will be a city without the violence of the one who killed his brother or of his descendant who threatened vengeance seventy-seven fold" (Donald E. Gowan, *From Eden to Babel: A Commentary on the Book of Genesis 1–11*, International Theological Commentary [Grand Rapids, MI: Eerdmans, 1988], 74).

[24] *Nod* in Hebrew means "wandering," which suggests travel away from God and His presence and from Eden where that presence had been centered.

[25] Cf. Ellen G. White, *Patriarchs and Prophets*, 81: "They [Cain and his descendants] chose their own time for labor and for rest," ignoring the "express command" of God regarding the Sabbath.

and wife to each other and the relation of human beings to God.

The line of Seth is described quite differently. First, it is linked both to the "seed" of the woman as carrier of the messianic promise (Gen 4:25) and to the genealogy of "Adam"—not merely as the fountainhead of humanity, but as the father of a godly line.[26] Adam begets Seth "in his own likeness, after his image" (Gen 5:3; cf. 1:26–27), which suggests, on the one hand, resemblance to Adam physically (including the inheritance of a fallen nature), and, on the other hand, resemblance spiritually in terms of receiving instruction in the ways of God (cf. Gen 2:16–17). In view of the wholistic definition that the Bible provides for the image of God, marred though it is now by sin,[27] we should likely understand restoration into God's image to embrace, as far as possible, an understanding and practice of the elements of the culture exemplified in Eden.[28]

The godly culture nourished through the line of Seth ("the sons of God") becomes intertwined and eventually overshadowed by the culture of evil thoughts that descend through the line of Cain ("the daughters of men"), leading to the destruction of the world by a global flood (Gen 6:1–7).[29] Noah's finding "grace" (or favor) in the eyes of the Lord enables the godly line to continue—but how? Through Noah's faith in God's Word that a flood was coming and his obedience to the instructions given him by God (Heb 11:7). Evidence of Noah's passing

---

[26] Ellen G. White, *Patriarchs and Prophets*, 125: "God has ever preserved a remnant to serve Him. Adam, Seth, Enoch, Methuselah, Noah, Shem, in unbroken line, had preserved from age to age the precious revealing of His will." Interestingly, Cain's genealogy is linked with begettal by Eve, distancing it from Adam's line (Gen 4:1, 17). The significance of both the man and woman being called by the name of the man prepares the way for the begettal of the line of Seth through a succession of fathers beginning with Adam.

[27] Cf. Ellen G. White, *Christ's Object Lessons* (Washington, DC: Review and Herald, 1941), 194: "As the coin bears the image and superscription of the reigning power, so man at his creation bore the image and superscription of God; and though now marred and dim through the influence of sin, the traces of this inscription remain upon every soul. God desires to recover that soul and to retrace upon it His own image in righteousness and holiness."

[28] On a wholistic definition of the image of God, denoted by "image" (*tselem*) and "likeness" (*demut*), including both physical/bodily and spiritual/mental qualities, see Richard M. Davidson, "The Nature of the Human Being From the Beginning: Genesis 1–11," in *"What Are Human Beings That You Remember Them?" Proceedings of the Third International Bible Conference, Nof Ginosar and Jerusalem, June 11–21, 2012*, ed. Clinton Wahlen (Silver Spring, MD: Biblical Research Institute, 2015), 18–19.

[29] Mention of the role of "daughters" recalls the female begetting of the line of Cain. On the interpretation of Genesis 6:4, see Donn W. Leatherman, "Who were 'the sons of God' and 'the daughters of men'?" in *Interpreting Scripture: Bible Questions and Answers*, ed. Gerhard Pfandl (Silver Spring, MD: Biblical Research Institute, 2010), 135–137.

on to his sons aspects of this God-oriented culture is seen in the fact that all three sons were monogamous, they believed God's revelation through Noah, and they were obedient to God's commands by entering the ark (with their wives). Although Noah is not a stellar example in everything (Gen 9:21) and sin continued to infiltrate the human family, the destruction of the entire human race, except for these eight people, vividly demonstrates how crucial to God's plan for the salvation of humanity is the passing on of spiritual instruction through the preservation of a godly line in whom God's image is being restored.

The universality of the divine intention, that this godly line is not exclusive but open to all, is underscored by this pattern of godly instruction being given by God "to Noah and to his sons with him" and God's making of the covenant with all four of them as well as with their descendants (Gen 9:1–11). Unfortunately, but also unsurprisingly, sinful choices continue to be made by the human family, as seen in the violation of God's law, first by Noah utilizing the vineyards he cultivated for winemaking and becoming drunk, and then by Ham showing disrespect to his father (Gen 9:20–27; cf. Exod 20:12), which eventuates in the cursing, not of Ham but of the Canaanite people descended from him. "Presumably Canaan already walked in the sins of his father, and those sins became such a strong feature in the national character of Canaan's descendants that God later ordered their destruction."[30] From the three sons of Noah emerge the peoples, nations, languages, and cultures that have inhabited the earth up to the present (Gen 10:32–11:9; cf. 10:5). More importantly, in order for God's intention for humanity to eventually come to fruition, the godly line through whom God's Word is conveyed and His covenant promises fulfilled must be preserved.

Since this line descends through Abraham, the father of the Hebrews (Gen 14:13), we will now turn our attention to various aspects in the Bible of Hebrew life and thought, including influences from the surrounding nations, especially the Canaanite, Egyptian, and Babylonian cultures. Not to be underestimated, however, is the influence of biblical thought on the Hebrew culture. Despite questions raised in recent years about the antiquity of Israel, archeological data continue to confirm biblical accounts of a very early literary culture, with the temple and the Davidic monarchy being among its most prominent

---

[30] Francis D. Nichol, ed., *The Seventh-day Adventist Bible Commentary*, vol. 1 (Washington, DC: Review and Herald, 1978), 267. Accordingly, "there are no grounds . . . for an ethnic reading of the 'curse' as some have done, supposing that some peoples are inferior to others" (Kenneth A. Matthews, *Genesis 1:1–11:26*, New American Commentary 1A [Nashville, TN: Broadman and Holman, 1996], 423).

institutional elements.[31] Also significant in this regard is the godly determination to perpetuate the principles of wisdom underlying the God-oriented culture found throughout Scripture. Two examples of this continued concern are: Solomon's description of David's instruction to him and of his conveyance of that instruction to his son (Prov 4:1–4),[32] and Paul's instruction to Timothy to continue in "the things that you have heard from me" and to "commit these to faithful men who will be able to teach others also" (2 Tim 2:2). In addition, the role of the Psalms should not be overlooked as another highly significant influence in cultivating and perpetuating the worship and religious consciousness of God's people down through history.

Elements of Culture in Scripture

Due to its language (Hebrew, Aramaic, and Greek) the Bible itself is a cultural document. The attentive reader of Scripture will frequently encounter further cultural elements in various Bible stories. Many of these reflect practices that the Hebrews had in common with other peoples of the ancient world. For example, similar food practices (baking of bread, treading of grapes, production of oil, etc.) pertained within Israel as elsewhere, and tools, textiles, and other commercial products were traded widely throughout the ancient world. Certain legal materials show commonality with law codes of the ancient Near East, though biblical laws permitting impoverished individuals to gather food in small quantities are "without any known Mesopotamian precedent."[33]

Hebrew Idioms

Another important factor related to culture in studying the Bible

---

[31] See Yosef Garfinkel, Saar Ganor, and Michael G. Hasel, *In the Footsteps of King David: Revelations From an Ancient Biblical City* (New York: Thames and Hudson, 2018).

[32] Three generations are linked in these verses (Derek Kidner, *Proverbs: An Introduction and Commentary*, Tyndale Old Testament Commentaries 17 [Downers Grove, IL: InterVarsity, 1964], 63); cf. Roland E. Murphy, *Proverbs*, Word Biblical Commentary 22 (Nashville, TN: Thomas Nelson, 1998), 27: "The implication of this verse may be that after the early training received from the mother, the father assumed responsibility. So the speaker is ostensibly describing the training that he received and is now going to pass on."

[33] Robert C. Ellickson and Charles DiA. Thorland, "Ancient Land Law: Mesopotamia, Egypt, Israel," *Faculty Scholarship Series* 410 (Yale Law School, 1995), 344, https://digitalcommons.law.yale.edu/fss_papers/410 (accessed December 16, 2019); see also 341–345 here 344, https://digitalcommons.law.yale.edu/fss_papers/410 (accessed December 16, 2019). It should be noted that the authors date biblical materials in accordance with critical presuppositions rather than accepting the traditional dating derived from Scripture.

is the idiomatic way in which God is described as actively doing or causing things. "He permits or does not prevent from happening, for example, the hardening of Pharaoh's heart" (e.g., Exod 4:21; 7:3).[34] It should be noted, however, that other passages clearly indicate how Pharaoh hardened his own heart (e.g., Exod 8:15, 32). This same phenomenon is reflected in the statement that God "moved David" to number Israel (2 Sam 24:1), later clarified that, in fact, "Satan . . . moved David to number Israel" (1 Chr 21:1).[35] Both of these examples underscore two vital hermeneutical principles: 1) *all* of what the Bible says on a given topic should be considered before drawing any conclusions, and 2) seemingly problematic passages may be illuminated by other parts of Scripture, especially if they are parallel accounts. Especially significant for our purposes, these examples also show that, within the Bible record, the divine intention is made clear, despite the use of expressions reflecting a Hebrew mentality that may differ substantially from our own.[36]

Reckoning of Time

Another cultural element in the Bible is the reckoning of time, which can be confusing because ancient peoples generally followed an agricultural calendar so important to various rural occupations such as that of farmers and shepherds (either spring to spring or fall to fall). Some Bible texts seem to suggest that the Hebrew calendar began in the spring (Lev 23:5), while other passages suggest that it began in the fall (Exod 34:22).The simplest solution is to consider the Passover beginning in "the first month" as marking the start of the civil and religious calendar (Num 28:16) and "the Feast of Ingathering at the end of the year" in the fall as indicating the end of the agricultural calendar (Exod 23:16).

The chronology of the kings seemed hopelessly irreconcilable until it was discovered that the differences stem from the use of inclusive and

---

[34] See the appendix "Methods of Bible Study," section 2.4.16, in the present volume.

[35] Paving the way for David's misstep was a tendency not limited to ancient Israel: "Intercourse with heathen peoples led to a desire to follow their national customs and kindled ambition for worldly greatness" (Ellen G. White, *Patriarchs and Prophets*, 746).

[36] It is important "not to go beyond what is written," 1 Cor 4:6, (ESV). In an otherwise outstanding contribution that uses the paradigm of "progressive moral wisdom" to understand the application of the OT laws to the Christian faith, Roy E. Gane, *Old Testament Law for Christians: Original Context and Enduring Application* (Grand Rapids, MI: Baker Academic, 2017), 213–218, extrapolates from moral values seen in the Bible in order to construct a "trajectory" that reaches beyond what is written so as to find what are, in his view, "appropriate" applications to contemporary issues. But such applications are sometimes speculative and may not accurately reflect the scriptural intention.

non-inclusive systems of reckoning and that the Northern Kingdom began its year in the spring while the Southern Kingdom began its year in the fall.[37] The Israelite year was 360 days, consisting of twelve thirty-day months.[38] But since the actual lunar year is only 354.5 days, an extra month had to be added seven out of every nineteen years to resynchronize the calendar with the seasons. Thus certain elements in Scripture, such as the reckoning of time, reflect the cultural peculiarities of the Hebrew people.

Negative Cultural Influences

Practices out of harmony with biblical principles are frequently mentioned without being endorsed, including "the use of alcohol, polygamy, divorce, and slavery."[39] These negative cultural influences to which Israel succumbed were widespread, and so it is not surprising to find these practices mentioned in Scripture. As we have seen, the first mention of polygamy is in connection with Cain's evil descendants, which is hardly an endorsement. In fact the Bible never describes polygamy in a positive light; instead, it candidly reveals the baleful impact on the people touched by it, and Mosaic law discourages the practice (Lev 18:18; Deut 17:17).[40] Significantly, polygamy is never mentioned in the New Testament, perhaps due in part not only to its rarity in the Roman era but also to Jesus' affirmation of monogamy and rejection of divorce on demand (Matt 19:3–6) based on Eden's God-oriented culture (Gen 2:24; cf. Mal 2:14–16).[41]

Biblical Wisdom

Of course not all outside cultural influences or practices are necessarily bad. Wisdom sayings in Scripture bear some resemblance to the wisdom literature of other nations.[42] Sayings possibly written by

---

[37] Edwin R. Thiele, *The Mysterious Numbers of the Hebrew Kings* (New York: Macmillan, 1951).

[38] The number of days in a month is implicit in the chronology of the flood (Gen 7:11 and 8:3–4 describe a period of five months totaling 150 days) and a twelve-month year is explicit (1 Kgs 4:7; 1 Chr 27:1–15).

[39] Appendix "Methods of Bible Study," section 2.4.16, in the present volume.

[40] See Ronald A. G. du Preez, "Polygamy in the Bible with Implications for Seventh-day Adventist Missiology" (DMin diss., Andrews University, 1993).

[41] Cf. Gane, *Old Testament Law*, 303–306.

[42] John H. Walton, *Ancient Near Eastern Thought and the Old Testament: Introducing the Conceptual World of the Hebrew Bible* (Downers Grove, IL: Baker Academic, 2006), 309: "Relatively few sayings could be found in ancient Near Eastern literature that would be contrary or unacceptable to Biblical wisdom, and vice versa."

non-Israelites and compatible with biblical principles were, under inspiration, incorporated into the canon (e.g., Prov 30:1–33; Acts 17:28; Titus 1:12). In fact, biblical wisdom generally exhibits a universal outlook, a feature not always present in non-Israelite wisdom literature, which again suggests the Bible's transcultural purpose.[43]

Head Coverings

A cultural practice related to marriage is Rebecca's veiling of herself just before meeting Isaac. While this was appropriate attire for a bride meeting her bridegroom (Gen 24:65), it would be a mistake to generalize from this that women in Israel normally veiled themselves in public or even wore head coverings.[44] Such a practice in both Judaism and in Christianity seems to have developed only much later, after the biblical period. The notion that Christian women should wear a head covering of some kind in church seems to be based on a misinterpretation of 1 Corinthians 11. In this passage, Paul indicates that a woman's "head covering" [Gk. *peribolaion*] is her "long hair" (1 Cor 11:15).[45] Even if, as some contend, a literal head covering is in view, the larger issue transcends the customs of first-century Corinth.[46] The specific wording chosen underscores the underlying principle that both men and women are to preserve the male-female gender distinction by their outward appearance and decorum in worship (cf. Deut 22:5).

Levirate Marriage

Another cultural practice, one sometimes misunderstood, is that of levirate marriage. Not confined to Israel, this was a system whereby the

---

[43] E.g., Hellenistic wisdom tended to be more ethnocentric (Clinton Wahlen, "Wisdom, Greek," in *Dictionary of the Old Testament: Wisdom, Poetry & Writings*, ed. Tremper Longman III and Peter Enns [Downers Grove, IL: IVP Academic, 2008], 843).

[44] Douglas R. Edwards, "Dress and Ornamentation," in *Anchor Bible Dictionary*, ed. David Noel Freedman, 6 vols. (New York: Doubleday, 1992), 2:237: "No clear evidence . . . exists for 1st century Jewish or Christian women wearing a separate veil. It was acceptable for women to go unveiled in public." See also Roland de Vaux, *Ancient Israel: Its Life and Institutions*, trans. John McHugh (Grand Rapids, MI: Eerdmans, 1997), 30; and Samuel Krauss, "The Jewish Rite of Covering the Head," *Hebrew Union College Annual* 19 (1945–1946): 127: "The [Israelite] women wore veils only on certain occasions (Gen 24.65; 38.14)"; cf. 159–160.

[45] Literally, "the hair is given her instead of [Gk. *anti*] a [head] covering." While the issue of what hair length may be considered "long" varies through time and from culture to culture, these variations are not significant unless they blur the distinction between male and female—including in outward appearance.

[46] See James B. Hurley, *Man and Woman in Biblical Perspective* (Grand Rapids, MI: Zondervan, 1981), 168–171.

relative of a man who dies without sons would marry his widow so that the firstborn son from this union could inherit the man's property and perpetuate his name. Similar to God's temporary provision for divorce (Deut 24:1; cf. Matt 19:7–10), levirate marriage was advisable in certain circumstances. Cultural pressures based on shame and honor encouraged the performance of this duty and incentivized the best possible outcome for the widow (Deut 25:5–10).[47] Jesus responded to a question about the resurrection that was based on this practice by affirming that heavenly relationships, like that of the angels, will transcend earthly ones (Matt 22:23–30).

God related in different ways to the practices of pagan nations of the ancient Near East that, at a minimum, needed some correction:[48]

1. Sometimes the Bible indicates a complete rejection and condemnation of pagan practices as incompatible with God's character (e.g., communion with the dead, Deut 18:10–11; child sacrifice, Lev 20:1).
2. In other cases, through the writers of the Bible, God interacts with pagan peoples, challenging their beliefs and practices. While condemning idol worship, the Bible frequently reminds its readers of the absurdity of the practice: idols have mouths but cannot speak and eyes but cannot see (Ps 115:5). They have to be made by human hands, carried about, and set in place, and though one cries to an idol for help, "yet it cannot answer nor save him out of his trouble" (Isa 46:6–7). Hosea condemns Canaanite fertility rituals by pointing out that God, not Baal, sends the rain enabling crops to grow, cares for the animals, and blesses His people with prosperity (Hos 2:5, 8).
3. God occasionally adapts practices found among the nations while correcting their erroneous pagan notions, as in the case of kingship. In Scripture, kingship is ultimately a divine concept: God is King over all the earth (Pss 47:7; 68:32) and especially over His people (1 Sam 12:12). While in Egypt the king was divinized, in Israel the king was subservient to God and, as His son, was to be instructed by His Word in accordance with "the law of the king" (Deut 17:14–20).

---

[47] See also Gane, 212–213.

[48] The ensuing classification with examples has been adapted from Ángel Manuel Rodríguez, "Culture's Role in Writing Scripture," Biblical Research Institute, http://adventistbiblicalresearch.org/materials/cultures-role-writing-scripture (accessed December 4, 2019).

4. Some harmful cultural practices, such as polygamy and slavery, were tolerated for a time, but were eventually corrected through a further exposition of Eden's God-given principles within the biblical record (Matt 19:4–6; Gal 3:28; Col 3:11).[49]

Up to this point, the cultural elements we have examined are fairly straightforward. However, when certain passages or teachings in the Bible conflict with one's own cultural understanding it becomes more difficult to assess and interpret them objectively. In recent years, cultural approaches to biblical interpretation have become increasingly popular because they highlight issues that are socially, economically, and/or politically relevant and often controversial.[50] Before examining specific cases, it will be helpful first to introduce these newer hermeneutical approaches.

Reader-Centered Methods of Interpretation

Within biblical scholarship, the more familiar historical methods of interpretation, such as the grammatical-historical method generally used by Seventh-day Adventists, have been supplemented with reader-centered methods that focus on the Bible as story. The advantage of this latter category of methods is that they interpret the text as it has come down to us (its "final form"),[51] rather than conjecturing about the historical process that created the text.[52] But this comes at a price. Reader-centered methods may derive meaning more through the process of reading the text than in and from the text itself, which has led to a bewildering variety and multiplicity of *reader-determined* interpretations.

Reader-centered approaches grew out of the philosophical hermeneutics of Hans-Georg Gadamer, who emphasized that interpretation of a text, as with its writing, is a process inevitably affected by one's own culture

[49] See also Ronald A. G. du Preez, "Epics & Ethics: Vital Biblical Principles for Interpreting Scripture Stories," *Journal of the Adventist Theological Society* 10/1–2 (1999): 107–140.

[50] For an overview, see Gerald A. Klingbeil, "Cultural Criticism and Biblical Hermeneutics: Definition, Origins, Benefits, and Challenges," *Bulletin for Biblical Research* 15/2 (2005): 261–277.

[51] It should be remembered that reference to the text's *final* form generally assumes the results of historical-critical approaches that perceive a lengthy process for a text's composition, development, and redaction.

[52] Note the caution of I. Howard Marshall, *Beyond the Bible: Moving From Scripture to Theology*, Acadia Studies in Bible and Theology (Grand Rapids, MI: Baker Academic, 2004), 22, regarding the tendency of Evangelicals to sidestep historical questions in favor of the "final form of the text": "If the text does not witness to a genuine saving and judging intervention of God in human history, then 'we are of all men most miserable.'"

and language. It involves an experience *with* the text and with its historical continuum of interpretation (*Wirkungsgeschichte*), not unlike how significant works of art are understood by observation and experience. Accordingly, meaning grows out of and transcends the text as historical communication and resides in the reader in the present moment.[53] Gadamer speaks of two horizons: that of the past (the author) and of the present (the reader). He argues that the use of a scientific method to extract some putative historical meaning *from* the text is a chimera because the author's horizon (which includes everything the author could know and experience) is not fully accessible to the contemporary interpreter. Consequently, readers only have access to the text through their own questions, concerns, and filter of ideas—that is, their horizon (which remains an inseparable part of the historical continuum from which the text sprung and in which it was preserved). This means, for Gadamer, that the meaning of a text always goes beyond its author.[54] While, according to Gadamer, the horizons of the ancient author and modern reader are separated by widely different cultures and concerns, some degree of understanding is nevertheless possible through a "fusion of horizons" (*Horizontverschmelzung*) whereby the text is understood by the reader because it not only has (a historical) meaning but also has become meaning*ful*.[55] Therefore, he argues, it is not only impossible but pointless to search for *the* meaning of the text because its "meaning" is mediated, understood, and appropriated differently by different readers and is thus never final. One difficulty is that Gadamer does not adequately distinguish between the *meaning* of a text and the *significance* of that meaning to a present situation. The meaning of a text is that which the author meant by the particular linguistic symbols he uses. It is the same whenever and wherever it is understood

---

[53] Hans Georg Gadamer, *Truth and Method*, 2nd ed. (London: Sheed and Ward, 1989), esp. 144–147, 159–165. E.g., ibid., 164: "Just as we were able to show that the being of the work of art is play and that it must be perceived by the spectator in order to be actualized (*vollendet*), so also it is universally true of texts that only in the process of understanding them is the dead trace of meaning transformed back into living meaning." Cf. ibid., 300–301 on the important role of *Wirkungsgeschichte* in connection with a "historically effected consciousness (*wirkungsgeschichtliches Bewußtsein*)."

[54] See the discussion in E. D. Hirsch Jr., *Validity in Interpretation* (New Haven, MA: Yale University Press, 1967), 245–264.

[55] Gadamer, 304–307. Also influential in this regard has been the conception of revelation as encounter introduced by Martin Buber, *I and Thou*, trans. Ronald Gregor Smith (Edinburgh: T&T Clark, 1937). Further on Gadamer's hermeneutic, see Anthony C. Thiselton, *New Horizons in Hermeneutics: The Theory and Practice of Transforming Biblical Reading* (Grand Rapids, MI: Zondervan, 1992), 313–330.

by another and does not change. However, to the reader the significance of this meaning is different, since his situation is different.[56] Not surprisingly, reader-centered methods based on this concept of the text may actually invite and welcome multiple meanings because every reader appropriates and interprets the text in a unique way.[57]

Reader-determined interpretations of the Bible have had at least as devastating an impact on the study of Scripture as the historical-critical method, if not more so. While a reader-centered approach often starts with the biblical text in its final form and thus ostensibly affirms the unity and coherence of various biblical books, it may also privilege the reader's present context and concerns over the text. Consequently, even contradictory interpretations may be accepted as equally valid, as long as they are based on a close and coherent reading of the biblical text. Changing the focus from the text itself to the reader of the text has opened the door to a variety of agenda-driven interpretations including Marxist, feminist, ethnic, and other postmodern readings of Scripture.[58] The reader, by using a particular reading strategy, is enabled to adjust the meaning she or he perceives in the text by putting on a different set of interpretative glasses,[59] which determine how the text is understood. So, for example, if a passage clashes with a reader's views on homosexuality, a "gay" lens can be utilized to find an alternative interpretation more in keeping with his/her personal-cultural construct and perspective on human sexuality.

---

[56] Hirsch, 255. See also Clinton Wahlen, "Hermeneutics and Scripture in the Twenty-First Century," *Reflections: The BRI Newsletter* 50 (2015): 10–11.

[57] An outgrowth of these methods is cultural criticism, which "emphasizes dialogue, because no absolutes exist," allows for "partial readings or solutions," and aims to challenge "existing power structures" (Klingbeil, "Cultural Criticism," 274–275).

[58] Further, see Thiselton, 411–470. The sheer variety of hermeneutical "lenses" employed within the various units associated with the Society of Biblical Literature is "bewildering," as the listing in Keith D. Stanglin, *The Letter and Spirit of Biblical Interpretation: From the Early Church to Modern Practice* (Grand Rapids, MI: Baker Academic, 2018), 187, illustrates: "African, African American, animal, Asian and Asian American, Eastern Orthodox, ecological, ethnic Chinese, feminist, gender, ideological, Islanders, Jewish, Korean, Latino/a and Latin American, Latter-Day Saints, LGBTI/Queer, metaphor, minoritized, performance, postcolonial, psychological, social-scientific, and trauma." Stanglin adds, "Identity hermeneutics, not unlike identity politics, results in endless division" (ibid.).

[59] Pushing back, without denying the basic contention that Marxist, feminist, and other interpretative strategies "are like glasses—lenses through which an interpreter reads a text," is Michal Beth Dinkler, *Literary Theory and the New Testament* (New Haven, CT: Yale University Press, 2019), 34, who declares that "we can't always put on and take off critical glasses at will; certain lenses are welded to our faces." One may accept that there is no such thing as presuppositionless interpretation *and* that interpreters can and do vary their presuppositions and reading strategies to further their respective religious agendas.

Similarly, transgender readers by using a "trans" lens can find passages in Scripture to validate their experience. A reader-centered approach has also been likened, with some justification, to "a picnic to which the author brings the words and the reader the meaning."[60]

Reader-determined interpretations, rather than pursuing truth based on the evidence of what the text is actually saying, focus on what is found "truthful," thereby depending primarily on what is understood and defined by the individual reader as true.[61] It would be well for all of us, as readers of the Bible, to ask ourselves to what extent we allow the text itself to speak or whether, on some issues at least, we succumb to reading the Bible through one or more of our own preferred lenses. As we shall see, by employing such an interpretative reading strategy, meaning comes to derive less from the text itself than from the reader and his or her interaction with the text: "meaning [is] uncovered in an experience of the reader."[62] Thus, like other critical methods, a reader-centered approach tends to place the interpreter above the text as the preferred determiner of meaning.

To read the text in order to discover a meaning that differs from the seemingly obvious one is referred to as a "hermeneutic of suspicion," or "reading against the grain."[63] Such an approach may be carried out in three steps:

1. Analyze the natural (or "dominant") reading of the text.
2. Examine the underlying beliefs embedded in the text.
3. Challenge the natural reading with a "resistant" reading.

---

[60] John Barton, "Thinking About Reader-Response Criticism," *Expository Times* 113 (2002): 147–151, calling this form "hard," in which "the reader has the leading role ('is privileged') over the author and indeed over the text, and uses the text as a vehicle for meaning which ultimately derives from elsewhere." Instead, Barton advocates a "soft" form of reader-response criticism that does not deny that there is a meaning resident in the text, but asks, "I have seen this in the text; can you not see it too?" (ibid., 151).

[61] Edgar V. McKnight, *Postmodern Use of the Bible: The Emergence of Reader-Oriented Criticism* (Nashville, TN: Abingdon, 1988), 265; cf. Gerhard F. Hasel, *Biblical Interpretation Today* (Washington, DC: Biblical Research Institute, 1985), 81.

[62] McKnight, 267.

[63] See David Penchansky, "Deconstruction," in *The Oxford Encyclopedia of Biblical Interpretation*, ed. Steven L. McKenzie, vol. 1 (Oxford: Oxford University Press, 2013), 202, who describes the process in terms of four "interpretive strategies": 1) read suspiciously, 2) look for the cracks and fault lines in the master narrative, 3) note the binaries and overturn them, and 4) look for the marginal.

As one curriculum describes this process, "when students read against the grain, they learn to push back against the foregrounding and privileging of a dominant point of view (often heterosexual, non-disabled, Christian, white, or male)."[64]

In order to understand how this method of reading against the grain works, some examples are helpful. We will begin with Paul's reference to homosexuality in Romans 1:24–27.[65] The natural reading of this passage understands it to be saying that people should know of God's existence by observing nature, and that those who choose idolatry should know better. Similarly, people should recognize right sexual practice from the complementary way that male and female bodies are made. It follows that homosexuality is wrong and that God's wrath is against those who violate nature's moral order. However, from a reader-centered standpoint there are many different ways to read a given text. Following the three-step process outlined above, a reader-determined interpretation would note that the dominant reading privileges Judeo-Christian and heterosexual viewpoints and that these need to be challenged. Consideration of this passage using a "gay" lens provides several possible resistant readings:

- *Gay Reading 1*: Homosexual practice is only condemned in connection with idolatry and the sexual prostitution associated with it (see Rom 1:23, 25).
- *Gay Reading 2*: Paul is condemning pederasty (which was not forbidden by Roman law) rather than homosexual practice.

---

[64] "Reading Against the Grain," Teaching Tolerance, https://www.tolerance.org/classroom-resources/teaching-strategies/close-and-critical-reading/reading-against-the-grain (accessed October 22, 2019), a resource intended for grade levels 6–8 and 9–12. The reading is part of the K–12 curriculum "Perspectives for a Diverse America: A K–12 Literacy-Based Anti-Bias Curriculum." See also the criticism of postmodernism's anti-Christian hermeneutic in Jonathan Chaves, "Soul and Reason in Literary Criticism: Deconstructing the Deconstructionists," *Journal of the American Oriental Society* 122 (2002): 828–835, esp. 830 (on the anti-Christian orientation of postmodern literary criticism), 833 (on its relegation of the individual to being merely a representative of the "class, sex, and race" to which they belong so that a man represents "maleness" and "a white person represents the entire white race"), and 834 (on Michael Foucault, who, based on his homosexual perspective, "sees any attempt to define heterosexuality as normal, and homosexuality as perverted, as being oppressive"). Chaves further observes that gay, feminist, and Marxist readings have in common an attack on various categories of "normalcy," considering them as oppressive, "arbitrary expressions of power" (p. 834).

[65] Further, see Robert A. J. Gagnon, *The Bible and Homosexual Practice: Texts and Hermeneutics* (Nashville, TN: Abingdon, 2001), 229–277. For an Old Testament perspective, discussing Leviticus 18:22 and 20:13, on which similar reading strategies are employed to avoid the natural interpretation of these verses, see Gane, 361–365.

- *Gay Reading 3*: Homosexual practice is only wrong if it is done "unnaturally"—that is, by heterosexuals.
- *Gay Reading 4*: The passage condemns homosexual practice if coercion is employed.

Such attempts to reread the text in harmony with contemporary mores are made possible by screening out key elements of the text. The first reading ignores the connection made between homosexuality in Romans 1:26–27 and the ensuing list of sins that are also condemned (Rom 1:29–31) and are always wrong, whether idolatrous worship is present or not. The suggestion that Paul speaks against pederasty fails on account of no children being mentioned, only "men" and "women." The third resistant reading overlooks the fact that alongside this passage's condemnation of sex that is "unnatural" is the affirmation of sex that is "natural" (Rom 1:26–27). That is, Paul argues for a "right" sexual practice from the complementarity of male and female that, from nature, is *phaneros* (Rom 1:19, "evident," CSB; "plain," ESV; "clear," MEV; "visible," RGT); it is male-male and female-female sex that Paul calls unnatural or, more literally, "contrary to nature" (*para physin*), because male and female biologically fit together for a sexual purpose while same-sex couples do not. Finally, there is no indication that the homosexual relations referred to are coerced; to the contrary, both women and men seem to choose same-sex activity quite willingly. Each of these resistant readings subvert the dominant and clear message of the text by excluding one or more elements of the passage from consideration. Notice that sometimes not only what a text says but also what it does not say may be significant to interpretation, as here with its silence in regard to children.[66]

It may be helpful to consider another example of reading against the grain of the text, this time using a "trans" lens. An article entitled "Permeable savior," published in a widely read Christian journal, offers a resistant reading of Mark 5:25–34 to support transgenderism.[67] The dominant reading of this passage is straightforward: A woman who was hemorrhaging blood, and therefore categorized as unclean by Levitical purity laws, touches the hem of Jesus' garment and is healed.

---

[66] Cf. Paul's recognition of the significance of Scripture's silence in connection with his interpretation and exposition of Old Testament passages related to Christ's Melchizadekian priesthood (Heb 7:14).

[67] Julie Morris, "Permeable savior," *The Christian Century*, January 18, 2017, 12–13; the online version carries a different title: "A Story of Two Leaky Bodies," *The Christian Century*, https://www.christiancentury.org/article/first-person/story-two-leaky-bodies (accessed October 22, 2019).

Jesus, recognizing that "power" had gone out from Him to heal, asks, "Who touched Me?" Eventually, the woman confesses that she was the one who touched Him and Jesus tells her, "Your faith has made you well. Go in peace, and be healed of your affliction" (Mark 5:34).

The resistant reading offered in support of transgenderism finds embedded in the text the belief that the woman who approaches Jesus fits the category of "feminine"—that is, she is weak and inferior, with a "leaking, porous body." To counter this disagreeable notion, the author finds a way to describe Jesus, the dominant male, in feminine (i.e., weak) terms: power "leaked out" from Him as a result of the woman's touch. "For Jesus' body to begin leaking when a leaky woman touches him is a blatantly feminizing act. Furthermore, it is a *female* who exerts power over a male body, extracting healing from him." Jesus' body aligns with hers.[68] This reading creates a role reversal that blurs the line between male and female in order to make room for transgenderism.

In view of these resistant readings of Bible passages, which employ a hermeneutic of suspicion in order to question the dominant message of the text, we may wonder with Alice in Wonderland "whether you *can* make words mean so many different things."[69] A text-centered approach, on the other hand, is not suspicious of the text. To the contrary, it encourages a "tactful" reading of "textual intention"[70] because, although the reader is capable of understanding the text correctly, he or she may also distort its meaning.[71] Without ignoring the importance of understanding the historical and cultural contexts in which the Bible writers wrote, it is important also to recognize that our own cultural biases can easily blind us to what the text is actually saying.[72] This was, in fact, the reason that many Jews, including the leading Bible experts of the time, rejected Jesus and His teaching.[73] Therefore, as readers of

---

[68] Morris, "Permeable savior."

[69] Lewis Carroll, *Through the Looking Glass, and What Alice Found There* (New York: Rand McNally, 1917), 99.

[70] Such an approach is "now urged by a number of professional literary critics" (Markus Bockmuehl, *Seeing the Word: Refocusing New Testament Study* [Grand Rapids, MI: Baker Academic, 2006], 49).

[71] Ibid., 55: "Many of this past century's gravest injustices were the consequence of ahistorical and unhistorical misappropriations of texts for ideological purposes."

[72] Ibid., 52: "In its fixated concern to hear what the scriptural texts are *not* saying, the hermeneutic of suspicion often loses the ability to hear attentively what in fact they *are* saying."

[73] Note Jesus' gentle but frequent rebuke ("Have you not read . . .") of those who were not as familiar with the Scriptures as they purported to be (Matt 12:3, 5; 19:4; 21:16, 42; 22:31, etc.), suggesting that they screened out certain passages from their interpretative grid used for constructing their

the text, rather than seeking to construct our own meaning for the Bible's cultural elements, we should humbly ask whether clues for understanding these elements may be found in the text itself and/or within the larger context of Scripture. As we turn now to analyzing carefully a number of cultural elements in Scripture that are frequently considered problematic, we should seek an approach that can be applied consistently on widely different topics while yielding interpretations that fit well in light of the context and message of the whole Bible.

A Bible-Centered Approach for Interpreting Cultural Elements

As we have seen, the biblical text exhibits a variety of cultural elements. Most of these are readily recognizable, uncontroversial, and pose little problem for interpretation. However, when the message of the text seems to conflict with one's preunderstanding (whether from religious, educational, and/or cultural upbringing), the interpreter's task is clearly more challenging and the temptation may exist to look for evidence in the text as well as outside of the text, often historically and/or culturally based, that would bend its meaning to our liking or even relegate its message completely to the past. This raises a crucial question: when historical and cultural elements are recognized in the text, how are they to be treated? Can biblical forms or rituals be separated from the *meaning* conveyed by them? If so, how might that impact interpretation?

The Bible teaches truths through a variety of forms, some of which are universal in scope and others which are not. If the form's scope, meaning, and function are all universal, then there is a *direct* application across time and cultures.[74] If, on the other hand, a universal meaning is clothed in a biblical form whose scope is limited (e.g., temporally or geographically), then interpretation of the text must take this into account and the application will be *indirect*. Sometimes the meaning or function of a form is limited, and not intended for universal application. We can summarize the differences in the following table:

---

understanding of God and His will.

[74] Cf. the definition of "universal law" in Gerhard F. Hasel, "The Distinction Between Clean and Unclean Animals in Lev 11: Is It Still Relevant?" *Journal of the Adventist Theological Society* 2/2 (1991): 92, as "law that is not restricted in time to a specific people, ancient Israel, but is universally valid for God's people for all times and in all places." Gane, *Old Testament Law*, 210, gives a somewhat different formulation: "If the modern situation falls within the scope of direct application of the law, *and* if modern direct application would accomplish the same goal as in the ancient setting to which the law was originally addressed, the law should be literally observed today," emphasis original.

Scope	Meaning/Function	Intercultural application
Universal	Universal	Direct
Limited	Universal-symbolic	Indirect
Limited	Limited or Unbiblical	None

Forms (both culturally and divinely instituted, described more fully below), are frequent in Scripture. In order to understand which are universally valid and which are not, it is helpful to look at several specific examples: the Sabbath and marriage, circumcision, ritual washings and baptism, table fellowship, food offered to idols, and slavery. Different conclusions have been reached by Christian interpreters regarding how to relate to these and other forms found in the Bible. We will analyze each of these examples from a biblical perspective in order to understand how Scripture hermeneutically applies them to new circumstances.

The Sabbath and Marriage

The Seventh-day Sabbath and marriage between a man and a woman first appear as part of the creation narrative (Gen 2:1–3, 24), before the entrance of sin and before the later diversification of languages and cultures. These elements are, therefore, part of the God-oriented culture instituted in Eden.[75] God reaffirms the universal validity of these two institutions in the Decalogue (Exod 20:8–11; 20:12, 14), which reflects God's fundamental moral nature. "Because God does not change, the universal moral norms, grounded in His nature, will transcend time and culture."[76] Also, as Jesus makes clear, the Sabbath was created specifically *for* human beings and, Jesus, as "Lord of the Sabbath," explains by precept and example how it is to be kept (Mark 2:27–28).[77]

---

[75] Much is made of the fact that only the verbal form *sabat* occurs in Genesis 2:2–3 and that the noun *sabbat* does not occur until the provision of manna to Israel in the wilderness, but the Exodus narrative implies that prior to this the Israelites were already familiar with the Ten Commandments, including the Sabbath (Exod 16:27–28; cf. 5:5), and the book of Genesis has scattered references to other of the Ten Commandments (e.g., idolatry, murder, adultery, theft).

[76] Ron du Preez, "Interpreting and Applying Biblical Ethics," in Reid, *Understanding Scripture*, 291.

[77] See Tom Shepherd, "Creation in the Gospel of Mark," *The Genesis Creation Account and Its Reverberations in the New Testament*, ed. Tom Shepherd (Berrien Springs, MI: Andrews University Press and the General Conference of Seventh-day Adventists, forthcoming). Further, on the biblical, theological, and historical significance of the Sabbath, see Daniel Bediako and Ekkehardt Mueller, eds., *The Sabbath in the Old Testament and the Intertestamental Period: Implications for Christians in the Twenty-First Century* (Silver Spring, MD:

As with marriage (Matt 19:4–6; cf. Gen 2:24), it was a gift God gave to man and woman "from the beginning" immediately after their creation. The fact that Jesus and the apostles, as well as other followers of Jesus, kept the seventh-day Sabbath (Luke 4:16; 23:55–56; Acts 17:2) also confirms its universal nature in form and meaning.[78] In fact, the Sabbath appears to be an institution of eternal significance since its observance is also mentioned in an eschatological context (Isa 66:23). By contrast, the "ceremonial" sabbath days, such as those connected with the Passover (Exod 12:14–16), were instituted only at Sinai in connection with the temple and its rituals (Lev 23)[79] and met their fulfillment at the death of Christ (Col 2:16–17). The monogamous heterosexual form of marriage as a union of two believers that was established by God "from the beginning" between one man and one woman is also universal in form and meaning, as Jesus and the rest of the New Testament make clear (Matt 19:4–9; 1 Cor 7:2; 2 Cor 6:14).[80] A variety of cultural questions may be raised pertaining to the correct observance of the Sabbath and the proper way in which the marriage ceremony should be conducted. For example: Are some clothes and some leisure activities more appropriate than others on Sabbath? Who is qualified to conduct a Christian wedding? Such specific questions are not directly answered in Scripture, and so we must look for biblical principles rather than to our culture to guide us as believers and as a church in answering these questions.[81]

Form	**Scope**	**Meaning/ Function**	**Intercultural application**
Seventh-day Sabbath	Universal	Universal	Direct → Seventh-day Sabbath

Biblical Research Institute, 2020), and Ekkehardt Mueller and Eike Mueller, eds., *The Sabbath in the New Testament and in Theology: Implications for Christians in the Twenty-First Century* (Silver Spring, MD: Biblical Research Institute, 2020).

[78] Timm, 172; Gane, *Old Testament Law*, 250 (including n. 28).

[79] See Roy Gane, *Leviticus, Numbers*, NIV Application Commentary (Grand Rapids, MI: Zondervan, 2004), 391–395.

[80] Further, see Ekkehardt Mueller and Elias Brasil de Souza, eds., *Marriage: Biblical and Theological Aspects* (Silver Spring, MD: Biblical Research Institute, 2015).

[81] Esther Happuck [pseud.] and Wagner Kuhn, "Seventh-day Adventist Biblical Hermeneutics for Mission in Islamic Context: Five Foundational Principles," *Andrews University Seminary Studies* 56/2 (2018): 277–300, refer to "the Principle of Relational Life," not as an "interpretative tool," but as a presuppositional guide to "find answers in Scripture" as to how the "abundant life" promised by Jesus (John 10:10) can "bring us back" to the Edenic experience (or "culture") and the connectedness with God and one another (292–293).

Form	Scope	Meaning/ Function	Intercultural application
Monogamous heterosexual marriage	Universal	Universal	Direct → Marriage

Circumcision

The cultural nature of circumcision is suggested by the fact that it first originated with Abraham, the first-named "Hebrew" in the Bible (Gen 14:13) and the "father" of Israel (Isa 51:1–2; Luke 1:73; Rom 4:1). He was given instructions that he, all his male descendants, and even the servants he might purchase were to be circumcised as a sign of the "everlasting covenant" that God made with him (Gen 17:10–14). This sign was later codified as a requirement for all male Israelites and any non-Israelite male who wished to eat the Passover (Lev 12:3; Exod 12:43–49). This connection with the Passover shows that circumcision was an integral part of Jewish identity but also closely related to salvation, which the Jewish feast symbolized (cf. 1 Cor 5:7). In fact, the phrase "everlasting covenant" is used regularly in reference to God's covenant of grace and salvation (2 Sam 23:5; Ps 111:9; Isa 61:9; Heb 13:20), showing that, at some level at least, circumcision has ongoing significance. Looking more closely at the meaning of circumcision, several passages refer to "circumcision" of the heart, suggesting that it signifies one's openness to a covenant relationship with God characterized by love and obedience to His commandments (Deut 10:12–16). This openness of heart toward God could also describe uncircumcised foreigners who chose to sojourn in the land of Israel (Deut 10:17–19; cf. Ezek 44:7–9). This inward circumcision enables a person to love God with all their heart and soul (Deut 30:6; cf. Rom 2:28–29).

As Paul points out, Abraham was justified by faith while still physically uncircumcised and received "the sign of circumcision," which pointed inwardly to the "seal of the righteousness of the faith which he had" (Rom 4:11). As with the presence of the temple, having the literal sign of circumcision was no guarantee of God's favor without the right relationship that circumcision symbolized (Jer 4:4; 22:3–5; Acts 7:51). In fact, the time would come when God would treat the circumcised rebels of Israel just like uncircumcised pagans (Jer 9:23–26; cf. 1 Cor 7:18–19), implying that the underlying meaning of the form is what mattered most and calling into question the value of circumcision alone as a sign of covenant faithfulness.[82] Despite circumcision having been given to Abraham as a sign of the "everlasting covenant" between God and His people (Gen 17:7), this prophecy of Jeremiah hints that it would not always function as such and that, while it would continue to function as a sign of Jewish identity, its usefulness as a sign of salvation would come to an end. That such was the divine intention is confirmed by the vision given to Peter and God's pouring out of the Holy Spirit on uncircumcised Gentiles, showing that everyone—Jew and Gentile alike—are cleansed on the basis of faith (Acts 10–11). Thus Christian believers receive a new identity that is now symbolized by baptism.

Problems, however, quickly arose in the church when some Jewish believers tried to insist that circumcision be continued as a universal sign not only of Jewish identity, but also of Christian identity (Acts 15:1–5). But as Peter himself makes clear, Christian faith is evidenced by the gift of the Holy Spirit (Acts 15:7–11; cf. 1 Pet 1:5), which is the New Testament equivalent to the "circumcision of the heart" (Col 2:11).[83] It is this inward circumcision of the heart that God's everlasting covenant of salvation requires. Thus Paul can assert that "in Christ Jesus neither circumcision nor uncircumcision avails anything, but a new creation" (Gal 6:15; cf. 5:6; 1 Cor 7:19). He even contrasts believers who were "once Gentiles in the flesh" with those whose circumcision is merely "made in the flesh by hands" (Eph 2:11). Apparently, by coming to Christ, non-Jewish believers leave behind their old identity as Gentiles. They are "no longer strangers and aliens, but . . . fellow citizens with the saints and members of the household of God" (Eph 2:19), just as fully a part of "God's Israel" (Gal 6:16, WEB) as believing Jews.[84] Thus, Paul refused to circumcise Titus as a sign of *Christian* identity (Gal 2:3) because baptism into Christ has this purpose, but had no problem circumcising Timothy as a sign of *Jewish* identity to facilitate evangelizing among Jews (Acts 16:1–3).

---

[82] Both Jeremiah (Jer 7:1–15) and Jesus (Matt 21:12–13; 23:16–22; John 4:21–24) make a similar point about the temple.

[83] See Clinton Wahlen, "Peter's Vision and Conflicting Definitions of Purity," *New Testament Studies* 51 (2005): 517.

[84] Further, see Clinton Wahlen, "Israel in Prophecy from a New Testament Perspective," in *Eschatology From an Adventist Perspective: Proceedings of the Fourth International Bible Conference, Rome, June 11–20, 2018*, ed. Elias Brasil de Souza, et al. (Silver Spring, MD: Biblical Research Institute, 2020).

Form	Scope	Meaning/Function	Intercultural application
Circumcision	Limited	Universal-symbolic	Indirect → circumcision of the heart

Ritual Washings and Baptism

Under Levitical law, in order to be purified from ritual defilement, washing oneself with water, including full immersion, was sometimes required (e.g., Exod 30:20; Lev 15:11, 16). These regulations, which were connected with the temple, were greatly expanded after the exile by the Pharisees, who taught that even ordinary meals should be eaten in a state of ritual purity (Mark 7:1–5).[85] Thus ritual washings before meals became an important part of Jewish religious life and culture. Dramatic physical evidence of the ubiquity of this practice throughout Israel has appeared from the hundreds of ritual baths that archeologists have discovered.[86] Significantly, Jesus refuses to conform to this religious practice even when dining at the home of a Pharisee (Luke 11:38). In another context, when asked why He and His disciples "transgress the tradition of the elders," Jesus explains the reasons for His rejection of the practice. First, since it was not a biblical requirement, disobeying it would not constitute a moral violation or transgression as the Pharisees had implied (Matt 15:2).[87] Second, the numerous Pharisaic traditions, of which this was but one example (cf. Mark 7:4, 13), tended to make of "no effect" or nullify (Gk. *akyroō*) the commandments of God (Matt 15:3–6). Third, the practice communicated a false religious concept because moral defilement comes from within, not from without (Matt 15:10–20). While such a practice would also be a barrier for the gospel witness "to the end of the earth" (Acts 1:8; cf. Zech 9:10), Jesus does not reject it for reasons of mission but for solely theological reasons. The divine instruction given in Scripture is to guide church practice because theology and religious practice are really inseparable, so that

---

[85] Cf. Josephus, *Ant.* 13.297: "the Pharisees have delivered to the people a great many observances by succession from their fathers, which are not written in the law of Moses." Use of the middle form in Mark 7:4 (*baptisōntai*, "immersing themselves," CEB) shows that some insisted upon total immersion after returning from the market in order to ensure ritual purity when eating.

[86] See Ronny Reich, "The Great Miqveh Debate," *Biblical Archeology Review* 19/2 (1993): 52–53.

[87] The LXX uses the verb "transgress" (*katabainō*) in connection with violation of God's covenant and/or commandments (e.g., Exod 32:8; Num 14:41; Josh 7:11; Hos 6:7; Dan 9:5). The wording of their question in Mark 7:5 is more nuanced: "Why do Your disciples not walk according to the tradition of the elders?"

what might seem justified for missional reasons may lead us "backward and not forward" (see Jer 7:22–26).[88]

By contrast, Christian baptism (Gk. *baptizō*), of which John's baptism of repentance was the precursor, is a unique practice and teaching of Jesus Christ and the New Testament. Through the watery "burial" of baptism, Christ's substitutionary death and resurrection are accepted by the believer (Rom 6:1–4) and by faith the person's heart is cleansed from sin through the Holy Spirit (Acts 15:8–9).[89] Christian baptism (applicable to both males and females) replaces circumcision (which was only for males) as the sign of faith and belonging among God's covenant people.[90] In view of these observations, together with the fact that the command to baptize is given in a universal setting ("all nations," Matt 28:19), we can conclude that, unlike circumcision, which it replaces, and unlike the ritual washings for purification commanded by Moses, which was a temporally limited old covenant form that ceased with the inauguration of Christ's new covenant ministry (Heb 9:10–14), baptism is universal in both scope and meaning and therefore unchanging. Foot washing, although a cultural practice of the time, is given religious significance by Jesus at the Last Supper and linked with baptism (John 13:10), which, as we have seen, is a universal religious form. Jesus' statement to Peter not only connects foot washing with purification from sin, but also indicates that He did not consider it to be optional: should Peter refuse it, He said, "you have no part with Me" (John 13:8–11). Furthermore, Christ's command to follow His example in this (John 13:13–17) shows that He is instituting foot washing as a religious practice for all His followers and that, like baptism with which it is theologically connected, foot washing is universal.[91] Supporting this conclusion is Paul's instruction to Timothy, which indicates not

---

[88] On New Testament principles for mission, see Clinton Wahlen, "Mission in the New Testament," in *Message, Mission, and Unity of the Church*, ed. Ángel Manuel Rodríguez, Studies in Adventist Ecclesiology 2 (Silver Spring, MD: Biblical Research Institute, 2013), 81–104.

[89] Further, see Clinton Wahlen, "Conversion, the Gift of the Holy Spirit, and New Testament Religious Practices," *Reflections: The BRI Newsletter* 62 (April 2018): 1–6.

[90] See, e.g., G. Vermes, "Baptism and Jewish Exegesis: New Light From Ancient Sources," *New Testament Studies* 4/4 (1958): 308: "By circumcision the new-born child enters the Covenant and becomes a son of the Covenant. By baptism, the Christian, as a new-born creature, enters the Church, the Community of the New Covenant. Circumcision is the external sign of membership of the Covenant, the 'seal' of faith [Rom 4:11]. So also is baptism. Circumcision of the flesh is the symbol of the circumcised heart [Rom 2:28–29; Philo, *Spec. Laws*, 1.6], of inner purification. So also is baptism—a 'circumcision made without hands [Col 2:11]'" (bracketed material supplies documentation given by Vermes in the footnotes).

[91] So also Timm, 173.

only that foot washing continued as a religious practice in the Christian church but that it was required for widows to receive the support of the church (1 Tim 5:10).[92]

It should be kept in mind that different forms of religious expression can lead to serious conflict because they carry different meanings and functions. Both the baptism of John and its Christian form practiced by Jesus and His disciples led to some conflicts within a Jewish setting (John 3:25–26; 4:1–3), as did their refusal to keep the religious traditions of the Pharisees. Since various ritual washings for purification were pervasive in Israel at that time (not only those commanded by Moses, but also those taught by the Pharisees and other Jewish groups), the practice of Christian baptism was apparently seen as infringing on the contemporary Jewish culture. But important biblical principles were also at stake. The line between biblical commandment and religio-cultural practice had become blurred in the minds of many, which is why Jesus' teaching and practice reaffirms a clear line of distinction between them. Interestingly, in some parts of the world, because Christian baptism is culturally offensive to Muslims it causes conflict. This reality has led some missiologists to suggest that an alternate form of baptism, such as pouring sand over the head of the candidate, could be used in Islamic settings.[93] In this case, though, the conflict represents not just a clash of cultures but a clash of *convictions* between two religious cultures, Judeo-Christian and Islamic.[94] Muslims reject not only the form but the underlying religious convictions that the form symbolizes.

Form	**Scope**	**Meaning/ Function**	**Intercultural application**
Ritual washings	Limited	Limited	None → ceased with inauguration of Christ's new covenant ministry

[92] Further on the biblical, theological, and practical significance of foot washing and the Lord's Supper, see *Seventh-day Adventists Believe*, 231–242; and Ekkehardt Mueller, "Seventh-day Adventists and the Lord's Supper," *Ministry*, April 2004, 10–13.

[93] Cf. Phil Parshall, *Muslim Evangelism: Contemporary Approaches to Contextualization*, 2nd ed. (Waynesboro, GA: Gabriel Publishing, 2003), 203–208.

[94] Instructive on evangelism to Muslims is Borge Schantz, "'Political Correctness' in Muslim Evangelism?" *Ministry*, June 2004, 12–13. Cf. Happuck and Kuhn, who, observing the importance of macro-hermeneutical issues (297), emphasize the enrichment potential of global perspectives without allowing for relativism or theological pluralism (296).

Form	Scope	Meaning/ Function	Intercultural application
Christian baptism	Universal (since the time of Jesus)	Universal	Direct → Christian baptism
Foot washing	Universal (since the time of Jesus)	Universal	Direct → foot washing

Table Fellowship

Jewish scruples about eating with Gentiles were well known in the Roman world (and generally misconstrued and misrepresented).[95] Peter even mentions to those gathered at the house of Cornelius to hear his message "that it is unlawful for a Jew to associate with or to visit a Gentile" (Acts 10:28, NRSV). This barrier between Jews and Gentiles, erected by Pharisaic tradition, was systematically dismantled, beginning with the teaching and practice of Jesus (Mark 7:1–23).[96] Its dismantling was continued through a vision given to Peter, in which he saw clean and unclean animals mixed together (Acts 10:9–16) and was commanded to kill and eat. Peter's initial resistance ("I have never eaten anything . . . unclean," Acts 10:14) reflects the universal distinction between clean and unclean animals (Gen 7:2, 8; 8:20),[97] his fidelity to the Levitical food regulations (Lev 11; Deut 14), and the continuing validity of these laws. However, his refusal also to eat what was considered "common" (Gk. *koinon*) shows a regard for an unbiblical Pharisaic tradition—refusing to eat biblically "clean" food[98] because it was of

[95] E.g., Diodorus, *Bibliotheca Historica*, XXXIV–XXXV, 1:2 (Menachem Stern, *Greek and Latin Authors on Jews and Judaism: Edited with Introductions, Translations, and Commentary*, 3 vols. [Jerusalem: The Israel Academy of Sciences and Humanities, 1974], 1:183): "The nation of the Jews had made their hatred of mankind into a tradition, and on this account had introduced utterly outlandish laws: not to break bread with any other race . . ."; Tacitus, *Historiae*, V, 5:1–2: "The Jews are extremely loyal toward one another, and always ready to show compassion, but toward every other people they feel only hate and enmity. They sit apart at meals . . ." (Stern, 2:27).

[96] See Wahlen, *Jesus and the Impurity of Spirits in the Synoptic Gospels*, 72–79.

[97] The scope and meaning of this distinction is universal because, by giving it to Noah and his descendants, God was giving it to all humanity because, according to the biblical portrayal, the flood was global, destroying all life on earth (Gen 6:17; 7:18–23; cf. 9:11).

[98] According to Friedrich Hauck, "καθαρός, καθαρίζω κτλ," in *Theological Dictionary of the New Testament*, ed. Gerhard Kittel, trans. Geoffrey W. Bromiley, vol. 3 (Grand Rapids, MI: Eerdmans, 1965), 809, the sense of the Greek verb *ekatharisen* ("cleansed") in Acts 10:15 and 11:9 is declarative—that is, "What God has declared clean [in Lev 11 and Deut 14] you must not call common"

doubtful purity due to its contact with Gentiles.[99] While Peter's motivation may have been to further Christian evangelism among Jews, similar to Paul's expedient circumcision of Timothy (Acts 16:1–3), outreach to the Gentile world would be hindered until this Jewish religio-cultural practice was discarded. Through the providential circumstances arranged by God, Peter grasps the underlying meaning of the vision: "just as the animals were to be reckoned as clean [not common] despite being mixed with the unclean, so Cornelius should be considered 'clean' despite his remaining uncircumcised."[100]

Significantly, the Levitical laws regarding clean and unclean foods were not annulled, despite their constituting a potential hinderance to the Gentile mission. Somewhat later, the Jerusalem Council, in its deliberation on Gentiles and food regulations, sought a biblical basis for the church's evangelistic practice rather than considering the issue solely from a pragmatic missional standpoint.[101] Through a Spirit-guided study of Scripture, the apostles and elders concluded that the Mosaic laws pertaining to Gentiles living in the land of Israel (Acts 15:29; cf. Lev 17–18) should be applied to this new situation, because Old Testament prophecy had foretold that Gentiles were to be included in a new, restored Israel (Acts 15:15–17, quoting Amos 9:11–12).[102] Clearly, then, the food laws prohibiting the eating of unclean animals were also required of Gentiles.[103] Several scriptural indicators show that these laws

(cf. Wahlen, "Peter's Vision," 515).

[99] In the intertestamental period, *koinon* became a Jewish technical term referring to clean animals of doubtful purity (see use of the term in Mark 7:2, 5; Rom 14:14). In the vision, the clean animals were of questionable purity because they were mixed together with the unclean. See Clinton Wahlen, "Did Jesus Make All Foods Clean?" in Pfandl, *Interpreting Scripture*, 301–304; cf. Ellen G. White, *The Acts of the Apostles* (Mountain View, CA: Pacific Press, 1911), 138: "Peter spoke first of the custom of the Jews, saying that it was looked upon as unlawful for Jews to mingle socially with the Gentiles, that to do this involved ceremonial defilement."

[100] Wahlen, "Peter's Vision," 515; see also Gane, *Leviticus, Numbers*, 214–215. On the food laws distinguishing between clean and unclean animals, see Gerhard F. Hasel, "The Distinction Between Clean and Unclean Animals," 91–125; Jiří Moskala, *The Laws of Clean and Unclean Animals of Leviticus 11: Their Nature, Theology, and Rationale (an Intertextual Study)*, Adventist Theological Society Dissertation Series 4 (Berrien Springs, MI: Adventist Theological Society, 2000), esp. 170–173; and Gane, *Leviticus, Numbers*, 204–208.

[101] See Wagner Kuhn, "Adventist Theological-Missiology: Contextualization in Mission and Ministry," *Journal of the Adventist Theological Society* 27/1–2 (2016): 175–208. When the cultural and religious context required some adaptation in mission practice (as with the Jerusalem Council and Paul's mission to the Gentiles), it was carried out in harmony with God's prior revelation in Scripture.

[102] Wahlen, "Peter's Vision," 517–518.

[103] See Davidson Razafiarivony, *The New Testament and Distinction Between Clean and Unclean*

had continuing validity: 1) the distinction between clean and unclean animals was explained to Noah, long before Israel existed (Gen 7:1–3); 2) this type of uncleanness is defined in Leviticus as inherent and permanent (Lev 11:2–23; 41–45; cf. Deut 14:3–20); 3) the terminological categories of "detestable" and "abomination" indicate that these laws are universally applicable; 4) the laws exhibit conceptual connections with the Genesis creation account; and 5) holiness as the rationale for keeping these laws is a universally valid standard of conduct for God's people in every age (Exod 19:6; Lev 11:44–45; Isa 4:3; 6:13; Dan 7:18; 1 Pet 1:15; 2:9). As such, their setting is "universal in outlook."[104] However, since the original diet for human beings was vegetarian (Gen 1:29; 2:9, 16; 3:17–19, 23) and there will be no death in the new earth (Isa 25:8; Rev 21:4), the scope of this practice extends only until the second coming of Jesus.[105]

Form	Scope	Meaning/ Function	Intercultural application
Unclean food laws	Universal (until the second coming of Jesus)	Universal	Direct → unclean food laws
"Common" food	Limited	Unbiblical	None → Jew-Gentile table fellowship allowed

Food Offered to Idols

If believing Jews could eat biblically clean food with believing Gentiles, what about food offered to idols (Gk. *eidōlothuton*)? The apostolic decree had resolved this issue by instructing believing Gentiles not to eat such food (Acts 15:29). But within the Roman culture of the time idolatrous worship was not only pervasive; it was also expected as a sign of loyalty to the empire. Leading cities sought to distinguish themselves by building temples dedicated to Roman emperors, who were worshipped as divine.[106] Public festivals to various

Animals: An Exegetical and Theological Investigation (Atlanta, GA: Scholars Press, 2015).

[104] Gerhard F. Hasel, "The Distinction Between Clean and Unclean Animals," esp. 105.

[105] Cf. Gane, *Old Testament Law*, 122.

[106] Further, see, e.g., Bruce W. Longenecker, "Rome, Provincial Cities and the Seven Churches of Revelation 2–3," in *The New Testament in Its First Century Setting: Essays on Context and Background in Honour of B. W. Winter on His 65th Birthday*, ed. P. J. Williams et al. (Grand Rapids, MI: Eerdmans, 2004), 281–291, esp. 282–287, illuminating this historical context even if the preterist application of it to these chapters of Revelation may be questioned.

deities included meat offered to idols, as did some of the food sold in the marketplace. Thus, Jewish and Christian scruples against eating food offered to idols collided with the prevailing Greco-Roman culture.[107] But what if it was not known whether or not the food had been offered to idols? This is another category of food that some Christians ("the weak") refused to eat because it was of doubtful purity.[108] Paul, in affirming the apostolic decree, clarifies how to apply the decree to this new situation based on whether or not there was an idolatrous intention (1 Cor 8–10). The overarching principle is that Christians must not wound the conscience of a weak brother or sister (1 Cor 8:4, 9–13; cf. Rom 14:13–15). In addition, Paul provides two specific guidelines, depending on the social context, regarding food offered to idols: "(1) Jesus-believers were not to eat food in a pagan cultic context; and (2) Outside of a pagan cultic context, indeterminate food was permitted while known idol food was forbidden. Paul's approach to idol food was consistent with the apostolic decree, but it was a more contextualized application of the principle."[109] In other words, the apostolic decree, based on Mosaic laws applicable to Gentiles,[110] was applied in a new setting to address issues not clearly answered by the decree. This new, indirect application takes into account the person's intention: was idol worship involved? Among believers the answer is clearly no; even among unbelievers (who are potential believers) no questions should be asked (1 Cor 10:25–26). But if an unbeliever indicates that the food has been offered to idols, such an intention makes the meal an act of idol worship, which, since it is prohibited by one of the Ten Commandments, remains a universal prohibition (Exod 20:4–6; cf. Matt 4:10), and the food should therefore not be eaten. Although the scope of this prohibition is limited and not generally applicable today (except in deeply animistic cultural contexts), such a stance, at odds with prevailing cultural practice, is nevertheless instructive in

---

[107] See Craig S. Keener, *1–2 Corinthians* (Cambridge: Cambridge University Press, 2005), 75–76.

[108] Cf. n. 95 in the present study.

[109] David J. Rudolph, *A Jew to the Jews: Jewish Contours of Pauline Flexibility in 1 Corinthians 9:19–23*, Wissenschaftliche Untersuchungen zum Neuen Testament, 2nd ser., vol. 304 (Tübingen: Mohr Siebeck, 2011), 108, cf. 206. See also Wagner Kuhn, "O Dom de Línguas na Missão: Implicações para a Igreja Adventista," in *Pneumatologia: Pessoa e Obra do Espirito Santo*, ed. Reinaldo W. Siqueira and Alberto Timm (Engenheiro Coelho: UNASPRESS, 2017), 609–630, esp. 621–623. In light of 1 Corinthians 9:19–23, it is revealing how Paul deals with difficult practices while applying scriptural principles as demonstrated by 1 Corinthians 8:1–13; 10:14–33; 11:1. Similarly, a parallel can be observed in Paul's confrontation of how the gifts of prophesying and speaking in tongues were being practiced in Corinth and his establishment of procedures to regulate how this practice was to be carried out (1 Cor 14:26–33).

[110] See the section titled "Table Fellowship" in the present study.

that it illustrates early Christian determination to remain faithful to scriptural principles even at the cost of distancing oneself from the surrounding culture.

Form	Scope	Meaning/Function	Intercultural application
Food offered to idols	Limited	Universal	Indirect → intention determines

Slavery

Human beings, created in God's image, were made to be free, not to domineer over each other. They were to care for and rule benevolently over the lower orders of creation (Gen 1:26–28). Thus it is surprising that slavery is nowhere condemned in Scripture, but neither is there any clear commendation of the practice,[111] only its regulation.[112] After Israel's deliverance from slavery in Egypt, God provided that no Israelite would ever be sold into perpetual servitude (Deut 15:12).[113] Slavery in Israel was essentially indentured service, lasting up to six years and available to an Israelite who had no other way to pay off financial indebtedness (Exod 21:2–6; Lev 25:39–43, 47–55). Being a slave in Israel "was not so irksome, since this status involved rights and often positions of trust."[114] Indentured servants had legal protections: they were to be treated fairly, given rest from their labors on Sabbath (Exod 20:10), and had to be set free after fulfilling their term of service. "The Hebrew law was relatively mild toward the slaves and recognized them as human beings subject to defense from intolerable acts, although not to the same extent as free persons."[115]

---

[111] Benjamin Reaoch, *Women, Slaves, and the Gender Debate: A Complementarian Response to the Redemptive-Movement Hermeneutic* (Phillipsburg, NJ: P&R Publishing, 2012), 43.

[112] For detailed discussions of references to slavery in the Bible, see Muhammad A. Dandamayev, "Slavery: Old Testament," in *Anchor Bible Dictionary*, 6:62–65; S. Scott Bartchy, "Slavery: New Testament," in *Anchor Bible Dictionary*, 6:65–73.

[113] However, the same protections were not applied to foreigners (Lev 25:44–46), such as the Gibeonites who, because of their subterfuge, were "made woodcutters and water carriers" in Israel (Josh 9:27). See the insightful discussion on the permanent servitude of foreigners and the biblical ideal of freedom for all based on their creation in the image of God in Gane, *Old Testament Law*, 315–320.

[114] Walter C. Kaiser, "עָבַד. Slave, servant," *Theological Wordbook of the Old Testament*, 2 vols. (Chicago: Moody Bible Institute, 1980), 2:639.

[115] Dandamayev, 65.

References to slaves in the New Testament are dependent upon the circumstances that existed under Roman law; the civil laws of the Old Testament were not in force. The practice of slavery was endemic in the Roman culture and vital to its economy. Both Jews and Christians had to put up with this reality despite the harsh conditions under which a slave sometimes had to work. But, unlike modern forms of slavery, Roman law afforded slaves considerable rights and opportunities,[116] and attempting to overturn the practice could have threatened the advancement of the gospel. Instead, within "the Israel of God," slavery, as with other Mosaic legislation related to Israel as a theocracy, is transcended (Gal 6:15–16),[117] and the principles of the gospel—love, mercy, justice, freedom, forgiveness, grace, and many others—intentionally undermine the practice of slavery, which Paul's letter to Philemon illustrates. While recognizing the legal necessity of returning Onesimus to his owner, Paul also appeals to Philemon as a fellow believer not to treat Onesimus any longer as a slave (Phlm 16). Practical guidelines are also set forth in the New Testament as to how believers living in a culture where slavery was fully accepted were to relate to each other. Slaves are to consider themselves as "the servants of Christ, doing the will of God from the heart" (Eph 6:6). Christian masters, who themselves have been recipients of God's love and grace, are instructed to treat their slaves, in the home and in the church, with compassion as fellow servants of Christ (1 Cor 7:22–23) because, as believers, we are all slaves of God (1 Pet 2:16; Rev 7:3), eternally indebted to Him for our salvation, with Christ as our one Master (Eph 6:5–9; Col 3:22–4:1). Interestingly, the Old Testament describes individual believers in a similar way, as slaves/servants (*'eved*) of God (e.g., Deut 9:27; Ps 34:22; Isa 54:17).

The New Testament perspective advances the notion further.[118] Israel's deliverance from slavery in Egypt is seen as foreshadowing Christ's work of saving people from sin (Matt 1:21; John 8:34–36).[119]

---

[116] See Bartchy, 66, who also notes the significant privileges open to slaves within the Roman empire (e.g., education was encouraged, slaves were given "highly responsible social functions" and could own property, and most would normally be emancipated by the time they were thirty years old), in contrast to the more familiar modern forms of the practice.

[117] See Wahlen, "Israel in Prophecy From a New Testament Perspective"; cf. appendix "Methods of Bible Study," section 2.4.16: "Israel originally was organized as a theocracy, a civil government through which God ruled directly (Gen 18:25). Such a theocratic state was unique. It no longer exists and cannot be regarded as a direct model for Christian practice."

[118] For a more in-depth discussion of the New Testament position on slavery, see Reaoch, 27–46.

[119] This is an example of inner-biblical interpretation, on which see Ganoune Diop, "Innerbiblical Interpretation: Reading the Scriptures Contextually," in Reid, *Understanding Scripture*, 135–151, esp. 143–144.

Within the New Testament church as "the household of God" (Eph 2:19), believers become sisters and brothers in the Lord (Phlm 16) and friends of God (John 15:15; cf. Jas 2:23).[120] In fact, Christians are exhorted:

> He who is called in the Lord while a slave is the Lord's freedman. Likewise he who is called while free is Christ's slave. You were bought at a price; do not become slaves of men (1 Cor 7:22–23).

The terminology for servants and slaves is even used as a messianic appellation.[121] While the practice of slavery had a limited scope within the economy of Israel, as also under Roman law, the symbolic notion that we are all to serve one another as slaves of God and of Christ is universal and of ongoing significance.

In modern times, there is a justified and overwhelming abhorrence of slavery. As one considers the race-based enslavement of men, women, and children in more recent times from the seventeenth to mid-nineteenth century—their forced servitude, inhumane treatment, denial of education, and sale as property—such treatment of fellow human beings is shocking, repugnant, and totally incompatible with biblical principles. But, as we have observed, the practice of slavery in biblical times differs substantially from this modern practice and should never be confused with it.

Historically, whatever form it takes and wherever it has existed, slavery is intimately connected with the prevailing economic system under which it operates. This is largely why it has persisted, been so difficult to eradicate, and still exists in some forms. There are even some places today where it is considered normal.[122] But, a biblically-based faith rejects these notions, insisting that all people are of equal value because we are created in the image of God and Christ died for all.[123] As Paul makes clear, His sacrifice on the cross has opened the door of

---

[120] The writers of the New Testament call themselves "slaves" of God or Christ (e.g., Rom 1:1; Titus 1:1; Jas 1:1; 2 Pet 1:1; Jude 1; Rev 1:1).

[121] This is true both of *'eved* in the Old Testament (Isa 42:1; 49:5–7; 50:10; 52:13; 53:11; Zech 3:8) and *diakoneō* (Luke 22:27; Rom 15:8) and *pais* (Matt 12:18; Acts 3:13, 26; 4:27, 30) in the New Testament.

[122] See Max Fisher, "The Country Where Slavery Is Still Normal," *The Atlantic*, June 28, 2011, https://www.theatlantic.com/international/archive/2011/06/the-country-where-slavery-is-still-normal/241148/ (accessed January 8, 2020), noting the existence of laws prohibiting the practice as well as the various factors that perpetuate it.

[123] Cf. Dandamayev, 65, who affirms that "the early Christian ideology undermined the institution of slavery, declaring an equality of all people in Christ."

salvation to everyone—Jew and Gentile, slave and free, male and female (Gal 3:28).

Form	Scope	Meaning/ Function	Intercultural application
Slavery	Limited	Universal-symbolic	Indirect → free in Christ/slaves of God

In summary, the Bible describes certain biblical forms whose scope and meaning were limited (e.g., ritual washings); in other cases, while the literal form ceased to function, Scripture reveals a symbolic significance that continues (circumcision of the heart, slaves of God/Christ). Other forms are universal in both scope and meaning, whether instituted from the beginning as part of Eden's culture (e.g., the Sabbath and marriage), or later in the history of salvation (Christian baptism). In connection with the biblical categorization of animals that are intrinsically clean or unclean, it may be inferred, based on the dietary instructions given to human beings before and after the fall (Gen 1:29; 3:18), that divine permission to eat clean animals did not exist before the flood (cf. Gen 7:2–3; 8:20) and that it will not exist with the restoration of Edenic culture in the new earth (Rev 21:4).

Form	Scope	Meaning/ Function	Intercultural application
Seventh-day Sabbath	Universal	Universal	Direct → the Sabbath
Monogamous heterosexual marriage	Universal	Universal	Direct → Marriage
Circumcision	Limited	Universal-symbolic	Indirect → circumcision of the heart
Ritual washings	Limited	Limited	None → ceased with inauguration of Christ's new covenant ministry
Christian baptism	Universal (since the time of Jesus)	Universal	Direct → Christian baptism

Form	Scope	Meaning/ Function	Intercultural application
Foot washing	Universal (since the time of Jesus)	Universal	Direct → foot washing
Unclean food laws	Universal (until the second coming of Jesus)	Universal	Direct → unclean food laws
"Common" food	Limited	Unbiblical	None → Jew-Gentile table fellowship allowed
Food offered to idols	Limited	Universal	Indirect → intention determines
Slavery	Limited	Universal-symbolic	Indirect → free in Christ/slaves of God

Is the Bible Culturally Relative?

In addressing the question of whether the Bible is culturally relative, it is important to return to a point we made earlier regarding the cosmic scope of the Bible as indicated by its canonical frame, beginning with the creation of the heavens and the earth and ending with a new heaven and a new earth. This frame places God above culture and prior to human culture. More than that, God is the originator of culture and has created human beings so as to be capable of creating cultural things and traditions, thus making culture not bad in itself, but something intrinsically good and beautiful to the extent that it reflects the intention of God for human beings.

The timeline of Scripture begins thousands of years before the nation of Israel came into existence and concludes thousands of years after its biblical history ended. Many nations and cultures are referenced in the Bible because God is not just the God of Israel—He is the God of all nations and of the whole earth, including all life, not just human life. But, as a result of the fall, every culture has been impacted by sin and evil and, therefore, cultural practices may stand in need of some correction or even abandonment altogether based on biblical principles. The judgment oracles of the Old Testament prophets indict not just Israel but many other nations also (see, e.g., Isa 11–23; Jer 46–51; Ezek 25–32), and the entire book of Jonah illustrates God's love for the peoples and nations of the world as well as His implied sovereignty over them. Even more emphatic is the book of Revelation's seven references (with slight variations) to tribes, tongues, peoples, and nations in need of salvation (Rev 5:9; 7:9; 10:11; 11:9; 13:7; 14:6; 17:15). History has shown that the Bible has the power to speak to widely different cultures. Why? Because the fundamental human condition as sinful is the same across all cultures—the need for forgiveness, the experience of love and grace, and the longing for character virtues are present in all human beings. Some of these things can be expressed differently in different cultures without compromising any biblical truth. In fact, different cultural expressions of the same fundamental biblical truths often add further richness to these truths. For example, parental love and discipline, table manners, courteous behavior, and a worshipful environment may look different in different places, while still according fully with biblical principles.

The stories of Abraham's origin in Ur and journey to Haran en route to Canaan, Israel's sojourn in both Egypt and Babylon, Paul's Hellenistic background, and Jesus' interaction with people of other nations contribute to the Bible's message of salvation for all and its multicultural appeal. With this in mind, we should not be surprised that certain aspects of the Bible actually seem transcultural by design.

Furthermore, the God of the Bible, as the Creator, is also the God of time. He is "from everlasting to everlasting" (Ps 90:2) and declares "the end from the beginning" (Isa 46:10). Although God, through the incarnation, has entered into our world and experienced human culture, He also transcends culture. So it should not be surprising that Scripture, though written by men, also exhibits this transcendent quality by virtue of its divine inspiration. The apocalyptic prophecies of the Bible especially illustrate this aspect. They contain timelines that span hundreds and even thousands of years and many different cultures. They provide instructive descriptions of events that took place before the time of the prophet, including things that transpired in heaven before the foundation of the world and that stretch to the end of the world and beyond, to the new heavens and the new earth.[124] The prophets themselves were not able to understand everything they wrote (e.g., Dan 8:27; 12:8; 1 Pet 1:10–11), because they were inspired to write some things not for their own time but for the distant future (see, e.g., Dan 8:14, 26; 12:4; 1 Pet 1:12). Such apocalyptic and eschatological portions of the Bible are,

[124] On the nature and interpretation of apocalyptic prophecy, see Jon K. Paulien, "The Hermeneutics of Biblical Apocalyptic," in Reid, *Understanding Scripture*, 245–270.

almost by definition, transcultural in application even if the language and symbols employed reflect the cultural milieu in which they were written.

In short, although the Bible contains cultural elements that need to be carefully interpreted in order to be correctly understood, it is not itself culturally limited. "Rather than being historically conditioned by immanent cause and effect relations, and thereby being rendered relative and not universally binding, God's written Word is divinely conditioned **and historically constituted**. Thus it remains binding upon all men at all ages and in all places."[125] This makes perfect sense if the main reason for which the Bible was given is the redemption of human beings, including the inculcation in them of heavenly principles and culture through their restoration into the image of God. Why would a book given by God for such a purpose be culturally relative? In that case it would be difficult to understand clearly which parts of the Bible, if any, are meant to prepare people for heaven and which parts are mere earthly trappings from a remote time and place with little or no ongoing relevance.

At the same time, while the Bible is designed for every culture, God still chose to package His revelations according to the intended audience's social location. As Glenn Rogers observes,

> God interacted with Abraham, Israel, and the Prophets, with Jesus, with the apostles, and with every one of us (including you and me) not in some otherworldly or heavenly context, but in the context of this material world, a world of human culture. . . . God uses human culture as a vehicle for interaction and communication with humans because human culture is the only context in which humans can communicate. This is not because God is limited. It is because humans are limited. Human culture is the only frame of reference humans have.

---

[125] Frank M. Hasel, "Reflections on the Authority and Trustworthiness of Scripture," in *Issues in Revelation and Inspiration*, ed. Frank Holbrook and Leo Van Dolson (Berrien Springs, MI: Adventist Theological Society, 1992), 208–209, emphasis original. The phrase "historically constituted" recognizes the human dimension in which Scripture originated without compromising the divine side of the process of inspiration. See Fernando Canale, "Revelation and Inspiration: The Ground for a New Approach," *Andrews University Seminary Studies* 31/2 (1993): 98; cf. appendix "Methods of Bible Study," section 2.1.4: "Although it was given to those who lived in an ancient Near Eastern/Mediterranean context, the Bible transcends its cultural backgrounds to serve as God's Word for all cultural, racial, and situational contexts in all ages"; section 4.17: "although many Biblical passages had local significance, nonetheless they contain timeless principles applicable to every age and culture."

> If God wants to communicate with humans it must be within the framework of human culture.[126]

The narratives of the Bible are just as relevant to our topic as the principles of the Bible and, in some ways, more relevant because they illustrate how biblical principles operate in real-life situations. A narrative sometimes conveys truth more clearly than if it were only stated as a propositional truth. For example, the gift of manna in the course of six days, with the gathering of a double portion possible only on the preparation day, since no manna would fall on the seventh day, communicated regularly and unambiguously to the Israelites when and how the Sabbath was to be kept (Exod 16:4–30).

The Bible also communicates truth through situations that are unpredictable, messy, and downright dangerous. The early chapters of Daniel are an especially rich source for exploring the interaction between culture and biblical interpretation—a point that is illustrated by the book having been written in two languages. The portions of Daniel that especially concern God's people and their future are in Hebrew (Dan 1:1–2:4a; 8–12). The intervening material was written in Aramaic, the language that united the Babylonian empire and enabled it to flourish just as Greek united the Roman empire. The Aramaic portions reveal through symbols and stories the rise and fall of world empires and how God's people exercise faithfulness in the face of persecution. Recognizing this linguistic difference aids in the understanding and interpretation of the book, including its cultural elements.

From the beginning of the book, God makes clear that He controls world events but sometimes allows other nations to punish His people as a consequence of their intransigence, disobedience, and rebellion.[127] When the Southern Kingdom of Judah was exiled to Babylon, Daniel tells us that "the Lord gave Jehoiakim king of Judah into his hand, with some of the articles of the house of God, which he carried into the land of Shinar to the house of his god" (Dan 1:2; cf. 2 Chr 36:15–21), and the chapter closes with the amazing comment that "Daniel continued until the first year of King Cyrus" of Persia (Dan 1:21); that is, he outlived the kingdom of Babylon—a reminder of the ephemeral nature of nation- and ethnic-based cultures in contrast to that of God's kingdom as well as of the church which is to reflect that kingdom.

---

[126] Glenn Rogers, *The Bible Culturally Speaking: The Role of Culture in the Production, Presentation and Interpretation of God's Word* (Bedford, TX: Mission and Ministry Resources, 2004), 27–28.

[127] Gerhard Pfandl, *Daniel: The Seer of Babylon* (Hagerstown, MD: Review and Herald, 2004), 18.

The story of Nebuchadnezzar's dream in Daniel 2, with its idol imagery, shows that God speaks in language that is understandable and familiar, without endorsing false pagan conceptions.[128] It also reveals the vital role of prayer in the face of cultural challenges, because culture never has the last word. Nebuchadnezzar, clearly dissatisfied with the idea that his empire would be overturned, as would each succeeding one, makes "an image of gold" (apparently symbolizing that his kingdom would last forever, in direct contradiction to the divinely given dream of Daniel 2); then he commands everyone to worship it or be burned alive (Dan 3:1–6). When the three Hebrews refuse to compromise their faith and are challenged by the king, they insist that God is able to deliver them from the flames. Significantly, though, they also add, "Yet even if He does not, let it be known to you, O king, that we will not serve your gods, nor worship the golden image that you set up" (Dan 3:18, TLV). Ultimately, the decision to remain faithful to God rather than succumbing to cultural and religious pressures to conform (cf. Acts 5:29) leaves open the possibility of suffering persecution and even death, as many Christians throughout history up to the present time have experienced.

Revelation 13:15 alludes to the story in Daniel 3 by utilizing similar imagery to depict the final end-time test that separates those who are saved from those who are lost. An image is set up, which all are commanded to worship, and "as many as would not worship the image of the beast" were to be killed. Here, just as in Daniel 3, choices are made in response to cultural pressures to compromise principle and conform on pain of death. While the issues are religious, not just cultural, the path of biblical faithfulness may require a person to make choices that are contrary to the surrounding social context, perhaps even offensive to it.[129] The seal of God and the mark of the beast (Rev 7:1–4; 13:16–17), reflecting contrasting decisions with respect to God's commandments, present another example in which a biblically educated conscience on the one hand and the culture, religion, and customs of end-time Babylon on the other will eventually collide. The fact that Babylon in this context symbolizes a global religio-political union suggests the importance for Christians living just prior to the second advent of prioritizing harmony with God's kingdom and its heavenlike culture over the kingdoms of

---

[128] Cf. Happuck and Kuhn, 283.

[129] Christians who are living today in non-Christian cultures (and sometimes even in "Christian" countries) regularly confront this challenge. See John L. Allen Jr., *The Global War on Christians: Dispatches From the Front Lines of Anti-Christian Persecution* (New York: Penguin Random House, 2016).

this world with their plethora of cultures and unbiblical religions and practices.[130]

The apocalyptic books of Daniel and Revelation are mutually interpretative, using similar and closely related symbols to describe some of the same historical events, even though they were written in different languages, to different cultural contexts, at widely separated points in history.[131] Their message cuts across time and culture to speak powerfully to our present context in which religious freedom is increasingly threatened. The Bible concludes with God's judgment of the wicked in the lake of fire (Rev 20:7–15), "a new heaven and a new earth" (Rev 21:1–2) with the New Jerusalem illuminated by the glory of God and the Lamb (Rev 21:23), whose "nations will walk in its light" (Rev 21:24, WEB), and no longer any mention of tribes or languages. This transcultural dynamic and perspective of the Bible, reflective of its divine Author, should caution interpreters against over-relativizing or over-localizing the message of specific passages as if culture and context were the controlling factors for the inspired people who wrote them. While we should never ignore cultural influences that are present in the Bible, we should always bear in mind, in the process of reading and interpreting Scripture, that God is ultimately the one speaking and that He speaks to every culture and through culture. Interpretations that privilege cultural elements in the text, in order to limit its scope and meaning, without the support of inspired indicators that call for such limitations, risk altering, muting, or even silencing the inspired message of God to His people and to the world.

Conclusion

The Bible's ultimate purpose, the redemption of people "from every nation, tribe, tongue, and people" and their restoration into the image of God, is a transcultural purpose. It aims to instill in us the principles of God's kingdom, which are the principles of heaven.[132] That is why it begins in Eden and ends in the new earth. The record of God's interaction with earthly elements of culture, of human triumphs and failures, the

---

[130] Cf. Ellen G. White, *Education* (Mountain View, CA: Pacific Press, 1903), 74: "He [Christ] came to show how men are to be trained as befits the sons of God; how on earth they are to practice the principles and to live the life of heaven."

[131] See chapter 9 by Gerhard Pfandl, "Understanding Biblical Apocalyptic," in the present volume.

[132] Ellen G. White, *Education*, 125: "The central theme of the Bible, the theme about which every other in the whole book clusters, is the redemption plan, the restoration in the human soul of the image of God."

good and the bad, are all recorded within the pages of the Bible—to warn, to correct, to educate, and, through the plan of redemption, ultimately to uplift. But Scripture can only accomplish its grand purpose if we allow ourselves to be faithful listeners and obedient learners, rather than shapers and molders, of its message.

What hermeneutical principles may be drawn from this brief survey to aid in the interpretation of cultural elements found in Scripture that seem problematic? Based on our survey of some of these elements and our analysis of various teachings that appear in the Bible, the following principles of interpretation may be suggested:

1) Cultural elements found in the Bible need to be understood within the context of the time and place in which they are described as well as within the larger canonical and transcultural frame provided by the Bible's opening and closing chapters and the larger purpose of restoring human beings into the image of God and to the God-oriented culture for which they were created.

2) The recognition that certain Bible passages are more difficult to interpret objectively when elements of its God-oriented culture conflict with one's own religious or cultural understanding should caution us against too readily muting their inspired message or relegating to an irrelevant past the uncomfortable ideas they contain. Careful attention to every element of the immediate context and its connection to all other passages that bear on the same subject can help prevent misreading of the text.

3) Forms or elements of human life that were part of Eden's God-oriented culture, by definition, are universal in scope and meaning—for example, the seventh-day Sabbath and monogamous marriage between a man and a woman.[133] The fact that both these institutions are reaffirmed in the Decalogue, as well as by New Testament practice and teaching, is additional confirmation of their universal scope and meaning. We also noticed that the Sabbath seems to continue into eternity as part of the culture of the new earth. Marriage also, which was instituted by God in Eden, is intended to be a perpetual and universal institution for the human family.[134] As a corollary, any cultural practice that challenges the

---

[133] Du Preez, "Interpreting and Applying Biblical Ethics," 291: "Universal moral norms are identifiable by their basis in the Creation order." Du Preez goes on to point out that some elements in Eden that were dependent on circumstances, such as farming, are temporary rather than universal.

[134] Whether Matthew 22:30 indicates that there will be no levirate marriage, no initiating of new marriages ("they neither are marrying nor are being given in marriage"), or no marriage at all is not completely clear.

biblical creation model, such as Sunday sacredness or same-sex marriage, should be rejected as out of harmony with Scripture and inimical to God's plan for the human family.[135]

4) Biblical laws that are found in universal contexts or linked theologically with universal concepts, such as baptism and foot washing, are also universal in scope and meaning. Another example is the distinction made between clean and unclean animals after the flood. Since, according to the biblical narrative, it is given to all humanity, the scope of the unclean food laws detailed later is also universally applicable until death shall be no more at the second coming of Jesus. Their meaning is also universal because their practice, as indicated by Peter's vision, continues into the New Testament period and they are nowhere repealed in Scripture. However, the Pharisaic teaching that clean foods associated with Gentiles should be regarded as "common" because they were of doubtful purity never received divine sanction—a point underscored in Peter's vision (Acts 15:15). Jesus rejected this teaching, based as it was solely on human tradition and contrary to the biblical teaching that moral defilement is caused by choices that originate in the human heart (Matt 15:8–10, 17–20).

5) Old Testament laws that apply to both Israelites and the Gentiles who sojourned among them, such as the Mosaic requirements in Leviticus 11 and those of Leviticus 17–18 that were explicitly applied to Christian converts by the Jerusalem Council in the apostolic decree, are universal in scope and meaning.[136]

6) Forms that are temporary in scope and meaning should be so indicated in Scripture; otherwise, we could not know that the form is temporary. In each case, inspired indicators must be present to show either that the practice was not to be continued in New Testament times or that the form has fulfilled its purpose. For example, the ritual washings connected with the temple and its services fulfilled their purpose in pointing to the new covenant reality. Forms or practices based exclusively on culture or human traditions and having no divine sanction, such as the food classified by many first-century Jews as "common," have relevance only for that time and may change or disappear altogether with a change in the culture or tradition. Similarly, "practices that are mentioned only in a certain context, without being

---

[135] Cf. Timm, 172: "The interaction within the Biblical canon itself places the prophetic messages as evaluators of culture, instead of mere cultural products."

[136] Similarly, du Preez, "Interpreting and Applying Biblical Ethics," 291.

kept in other ones, are more likely cultural in nature" and not of universal applicability.[137]

A text-centered approach that takes the Bible seriously as divinely sent communication, and a willingness to utilize the principles that the Bible itself suggests for understanding its cultural aspects, will safeguard us from attempting to modify or even neutralize the message of Scripture, which is ever relevant and ever needful because it is God-inspired.

---

[137] Timm, 172.

CHAPTER 6

Faith, Science, and the Bible

Leonard Brand

In its study of the natural world, modern science gains understanding by interpreting data from observations and experiments.[1] While the development of modern science was facilitated within a Christian context, today many see a conflict between science and religion, between science and faith, and between science and the Bible[2]—particularly when the Bible is interpreted as a true history of life and of the earth. Why is this so? The issues behind this conflict have a history that needs to be understood. Therefore, we will briefly look at this development.

A few centuries ago, most of the Western world believed what the Bible said: that God was the Creator of life. However, advances of modern

---

[1] See Leonard Brand with David C. Jarnes, *Beginnings* (Nampa, ID: Pacific Press, 2006), 13–16; Leonard Brand and Arthur Chadwick, *Faith, Reason, and Earth History: A Paradigm of Earth and Biological Origins by Intelligent Design*, 3rd ed. (Berrien Springs, MI: Andrews University Press, 2016), 1–14; Ariel A. Roth, *Origins: Linking Science and Scripture* (Hagerstown, MD: Review and Herald, 1998), 277–297; John F. Ashton, "Can a Christian Be a Good Scientist?," in *Understanding Creation: Answers to Questions on Faith and Science*, ed. L. James Gibson and Humberto M. Rasi (Nampa, ID: Pacific Press, 2011), 208–214; and Martin F. Hanna, "Science and Theology: Focusing the Complementary Lights of Jesus, Scripture, and Nature," in *Creation, Catastrophe, and Calvary*, ed. John T. Baldwin (Hagerstown, MD: Review and Herald, 2000), 172–208. According to Brand and Chadwick, 4, "scientists, in the process of discovery, formulate hypotheses or theories, collect data, conduct experiments to test theories, and develop generalizations called scientific laws".

[2] See Andrew D. White, *A History of the Warfare of Science With Theology in Christendom* (New York: George Braziller, 1955), which points out such conflict. For a more recent critical interaction with this perspective, see William A. Dembski, "Does the Bible Conflict With Science?," in *In Defense of the Bible: A Comprehensive Apologetic for the Authority of Scripture*, ed. Steven B. Cowan and Terry L. Wilder (Nashville, TN: B&H Publishing, 2013), 349–374. From a Seventh-day Adventist perspective, see the brief overview in Hanna, 172–180; and the article "Science and Religion" in *The Seventh-Day Adventist Encyclopedia*, ed. Don F. Neufeld, Commentary Reference Series, vol. 11, 2nd ed. (Hagerstown, MD: Review and Herald, 1996), 559–562.

science and changes in scholarly thought over the last couple of centuries have changed that perspective significantly. Today the majority of scholars are convinced that life is the result of billions of years of evolution. Even most Christian scholars accept this interpretation, although most try to combine it with a few key biblical concepts in the form of theistic evolution or evolutionary creation.[3] If we have a correct understanding of science, does modern science require us to reinterpret the Bible to match current scientific theories of origins? Or does science overstep its legitimate boundaries when it tries to do so? We will explore this topic in our search for answers to this question.

But first let us return to the question of why there has been such a broad shift in thinking about origins. Some three or four centuries ago, Western scientists were seeking to learn how our bodies work, how the heavenly bodies move, and much more. Their knowledge was limited, and some questions seemed beyond explanation by the known processes of nature. It seemed that even scientists at times relied on mystical forces to explain what they could not understand. The idea that God made the laws of chemistry and physics and uses them to operate the universe on a daily basis was not adequately developed. To these scientists it seemed that there must be situations in which God tinkers with chemistry, physiology, or the movements of planets to make them work properly.

It was important for science to move beyond this concept of a God who fiddles with His creation in order to make it work correctly. Scientists gradually learned that research reveals insights into the laws of nature and explains how hearts work and planets move. These things work through understandable mechanisms that are governed by the laws of chemistry and physics.[4] The recognition that God does not tinker with mystical forces to operate the universe was a very significant insight that helped advance rapid scientific progress.

That recognition of the uniformity of natural laws came while another area of thought was changing modern thinking. Since the eighteenth century, scholars were deliberately moving away from the

---

[3] On the incompatibility of evolutionary thought with the biblical concept of creation, see the discussion in the monumental work by J. P. Moreland et al., eds., *Theistic Evolution: A Scientific, Philosophical and Theological Critique* (Wheaton, IL: Crossway, 2017); and Reinhard Junker, *Leben durch Sterben? Schöpfung, Heilsgeschichte und Evolution* (Neuhausen-Stuttgart: Hänssler Verlag, 1994). For a Seventh-day Adventist perspective, see Marco F. Terreros, *Death Before the Sin of Adam: A Fundamental Concept in Theistic Evolution and Its Implications for Evangelical Theology* (PhD diss., Andrews University, 1994); and E. Edward Zinke, "Theistic Evolution: Implications for the Role of Creation in Seventh-day Adventist Theology," in *Creation, Catastrophe, and Calvary*, ed. John Templeton Baldwin (Hagerstown, MD: Review and Herald, 2000), 159–171.

[4] From a believer's perspective, the laws of nature are actually God's laws.

acceptance of authority. For some centuries authority had been in the hands of government and the church, and in the Middle Ages and beyond both institutions were guilty of serious abuse of their authority. The people, weary of being dominated by the established order, were happy to move away from the authorities that were making their lives difficult.[5] As a result, the authority of the Bible was put into question and scholars were ready to jettison it. This development meshed well with a tendency to carry forward the reaction against some old mystical scientific concepts, and finally resulted in pushing God out of our explanations of nature altogether.[6]

This very brief explanation of complex historical movements brings us to where we are today. We live in a culture that has removed God from what science has to say about the origin of the universe, of the earth, and of life, and instead deals with such questions from a perspective of philosophical and methodological naturalism.[7] Before we can decide how to respond to this modern naturalistic, anti-creation culture, we first need to address a series of questions about science and faith. The questions are in regard to the following issues in science: 1) Why is science so successful, with such an aura of authority? 2) What is the relationship between scientific success and its ability to correct its knowledge? 3) How objective and unbiased are scientists? 4) Can we be equally confident of scientific conclusions in all fields of study? 5) What shall we do when

---

[5] See Alister McGrath, *The Twilight of Atheism: The Rise and Fall of Disbelief in the Modern World* (New York: Doubleday, 2004).

[6] On this development, see Paul Tillich, *Perspectives on 19th and 20th Century Protestant Theology*, ed. Carl E. Braaten (New York: Harper and Row, 1967), 24–53; James C. Livingston, *Modern Christian Thought: From the Enlightenment to Vatican II* (New York: Macmillan, 1971), esp. 1–244; and Henning Graf Reventlow, *The Authority of the Bible and the Modern World* (London: SCM Press, 1984), esp. 289–383.

[7] Leonard Brand, "Naturalism: Its Role in Science," *Origins* 64 (2015): 21–37; Keith B. Miller, "The Misguided Attack on Methodological Naturalism," in *For the Rock Record: Geologists on Intelligent Design*, ed. Jill S. Schneiderman and Warren D. Allmon (Berkeley, CA: University of California Press, 2009), 117–140; Robert T. Pennock, *Tower of Babel: The Evidence Against the New Creationism* (Cambridge, MA: MIT Press, 1999); Robert T. Pennock, "Can't Pholosophers Tell the Difference Between Science and Religion? Demarcation Revisited," in *But Is It Science?*, ed. Robert T. Pennock and Michael Ruse (Amherst, NY: Prometheus Books, 2008); Alvin Plantinga, "Methodological Naturalism?," *Origins & Design* 18/1 (1997 a): 18–27; Alvin Plantinga, "Methodological Naturalism? Part 2," *Origins & Design* 18/2 (1997 b): 22–34; Alvin Plantinga, "Two (or More) Kinds of Scripture Scholarship," in *"Behind" the Text: History and Biblical Interpretation*, ed. Craig Bartholomew et al., (Grand Rapids, MI: Zondervan, 2003), 19–57, originally published in *Modern Theology* 14/2 (1998): 243–277; Alvin Plantinga, *Knowledge and Christian Belief* (Grand Rapids, MI: Eerdmans, 2015); and Robert B. Stewart, "The Insufficiency of Naturalism: A Worldview Critique," in *Come Let us Reason: New Essays in Christian Apologetics*, ed. Paul Copan and William Lane Craig, (Nashville, TN: B&H Publishing, 2012), 81–96.

Scripture and science clash? 6)What is the role of science in discovering the truth about our origin and destiny? After examining these questions, we will then turn to questions of how the Bible can be an asset in scientific work, especially in the study of ancient history.[8]

Questions that Underlie Our Understanding of Science and its Relation to Faith

Why is Science so Successful, With Such an Aura of Authority?

Can you think of any scientific discoveries that improve your life or make this world an easier place in which to live? Of course, there is a very long list: Scientific discoveries are the basis of improved healthcare and treatments for diseases that were lethal in past centuries. Many mothers who once would have died in childbirth now have hope. The invention of computers and similar technology has transformed our culture. These inventions support so much research, including health research, and also provide awesome ways to spread the gospel.[9] The many impressive scientific discoveries are so obvious, so why are we raising this question? There is a purpose: to set the stage for what is to come and to emphasize that this study does not downplay the importance or power of science as a search for knowledge.

It is impossible to deny that science does much that could not have been imagined a century ago. In the experiential realm, science has accomplished much good; a general rejection of science, as urged by some, is not warranted. Scientific research helped us discover the laws of chemistry and physics, and helped us gain a better understanding of how things work. This, in many respects, has made our lives better. This success in scientific inquiry is amazing, and the advance in knowledge has given science not just significant influence in our modern thinking and culture, but also an aura of authority. Science's authority today seems to be greater than the power of kings and religious leaders some six hundred years ago.

This study does not downplay the incredible advances in science nor the power science has in its search of knowledge. Yet even science's amazing advances have created some things that we now realize are not blessings. While science has been so successful, "we may forget that it has limits" as well.[10]

---

[8] On the relationship between the Bible and history, see chapter 4 by Michael G. Hasel, "History, the Bible, and Hermeneutics," in the present volume.

[9] Roth, 283.

[10] Ibid., 283, 285.

Science is marvelous, but if we misunderstand and misuse it, it can bring confusion and the power of science is likely to be misapplied. This becomes the source of conflicts between faith and science. The following story illustrates the point under discussion.

Years ago my brother, a pastor, regularly attended the meetings of a local Protestant ministerial fellowship. The chair of the science department at a university was also a regular attendee at the same meetings. Whenever the topic of evolution came up, this scientist quickly and authoritatively said, "Everybody knows that evolution is a proven fact," which ended the conversation. Since my doctoral studies were in evolutionary biology, my brother invited me to attend these meetings and give a talk on the subject of creation and evolution. At the end of the talk, the leaders of the group turned to their resident scientist to respond to my arguments in favor of creation. His answer immediately revealed that his understanding of the theory of evolution was very limited and even naive. This left me feeling uncomfortable because my purpose was to bring improved knowledge of the subject—not to make someone look foolish. But even my most polite response to his arguments revealed to everyone his ignorance about evolution. This scientist had a powerful influence because, as uninformed as he was in the area of evolution, he nevertheless was a scientist and thus was seen as the expert who certainly must know much more than anyone else. How could others try to argue with him? This illustrates the power of science and the power scientists often have in discussions. He no doubt knew a lot about his own field of expertise. Legitimate and awe-inspiring discoveries in medicine or space science give an aura of invincibility even to scientists who are not knowledgeable in other areas of research, such as evolution. No matter how much we know, we are often not in a position to evaluate many other areas of scientific claims. Yet those claims *need* careful evaluation.

The genuine advances of science invest the scientist with power. But it has been pointed out that "scientists, like other professionals, tend to look at reality through their specialized outlook. Such confined viewpoints can be a problem when we are looking for the whole truth."[11]

What is the Relationship Between Scientific Success and its Ability to Correct its Knowledge?

There was a time, not so long ago, when molecular biologists confidently declared that each gene makes one protein. While science does not

---

[11] Roth., 285.

like dogma, many experts were so sure of this idea that they called it the central dogma of molecular biology. But today no one believes that idea anymore. It is known to be false.

Here is another example from a different area of science: During the first half of the twentieth century, any geologist who believed the theory of continents moving around on the earth was not taken seriously. But from about 1960 onwards, continental drift and plate tectonics were confidently accepted as a central part of geological theory, supported by increasing levels of evidence.[12]

These two incidents were not strange anomalies in the history of science. In fact, they tell us something significant about science. There is a very long list of conclusions that were once firmly held by scientists but now known to be wrong. Students are often told, "Half of what we teach you is wrong. We just have to wait for more discoveries to know which half is wrong." Science keeps moving on, finding new evidence that was not expected. It might be tempting to think, "But that was in the past; we now know better than to make such mistakes." But that is actually a very unrealistic hope. Science is moving faster than ever, and new discoveries are changing scientific thinking faster than before. The very success of science is that it keeps making new discoveries—showing that what seemed like good explanations are actually inadequate to explain all the evidence, or sometimes even are wrong. Our confidence in science is only realistic if we recognize this concept of its self-correcting process, which leads us to the third question: how unbiased are scientists?

How Objective and Unbiased are Scientists?

This is another odd question. Aren't scientists trained to be unbiased scholars? Some years ago a news article recommended that the government be operated by scientists because they are unbiased. While being unbiased should be a goal of scientific research, there are examples of this not always being the case. In the early decades of the 1900s, J Harlen Bretz, a geologist, argued that his evidence indicated that the huge system of canyons in eastern Washington state, the Channeled Scablands, was catastrophically carved by a very large volume of water moving at high speed. All the other great geologists of the day ridiculed him—almost abusively. Geologists, because of their worldview based on methodological naturalism, knew there could not have been any large-scale geological catastrophes. But eventually it became

[12] Edward J. Tarbuck and Frederick K. Lutgens, *Earth: An Introduction to Physical Geology*, 12th ed. (Essex: Pearson, 2017).

clear that Bretz was right and the others were wrong.[13] During those several decades of conflict, who was biased and who was unbiased? Perhaps bias is not the most helpful concept for understanding this episode. Accepted geological theory at that time said catastrophes should never be used as an explanation in geology. For a century, the concept of a catastrophe had not been allowed in geological interpretations.[14] Bretz's accumulating data said the Channeled Scablands had to be shaped by catastrophic events, and he was finally, reluctantly, recognized to be correct. As it often happens, the rejection of geological catastrophes had been based on philosophical opinions, not on evidence. If Bretz had been less determined, growth in geological understanding may have been prevented. If the others had been less persistent in their perspective, the independent-thinking Bretz may not have been challenged to keep gathering more data.

This conflict had nothing to do with whether the Genesis flood story was right. They were not asking that question. This is simply an example illustrating that even scientific work is influenced by factors that sometimes go beyond objectivity, necessitating correction.

Philosophers have pointed out how important humility, fairmindedness, and other intellectual virtues are in the scientific search for truth.[15] It is only as science advances, with the discovery of new evidence, that we can recognize which of our scientific ideas are solid and which should be revised or even rejected as disproven, or at least recognized as being on a weak foundation. Current scientific concepts should not be viewed as settled knowledge. The most meaningful description of our accepted body of scientific conclusions is to call it a "progress report"—a description of where we currently are in the search for accurate knowledge. Much, or maybe most, of that knowledge, in many fields, will change with more evidence. Those who study this process of scientific searching recognize that individual scientists are not more unbiased than other people. The objectivity that science achieves results largely from the

---

[13] John Soennichsen, *Bretz's Flood: The Remarkable Story of a Rebel Geologist and the World's Greatest Flood* (Seattle, WA: Sasquatch Books, 2008).

[14] Stephen Jay Gould, *Toward the Vindication of Punctuational Change, Catastrophes and Earth History* (Princeton, NJ: Princeton University Press, 1984).

[15] See Philip E. Dow, *Virtuous Minds: Intellectual Character Development* (Downers Grove, IL: InterVarsity, 2013); Peter C. Hill, "It Is Good to Be Humble: An Empirical Account," in *Virtue and Voice: Habits of Mind for a Return to Civil Discourse*, ed. Gregg Ten Elshof and Evan Rosa (Abilene, TX: Abilene Christian University Press, 2019), 33–42; and Jason Baehr, "Intellectual Virtues, Civility, and Public Discourse," in Elshof and Rosa, 9–31.

discussions and arguments between scientists with differing opinions.[16] The ongoing debate between Bretz and his colleagues, each trying to defend their position, was what finally brought all of them to recognize the explanation that was the strongest. This episode illustrates that the objectivity that science achieves is also dependent on the result of group discussion and debate—not necessarily from individuals who are unbiased. It may not be easy for individuals uninvolved in such debates to understand this part of the scientific process. This is not questioning the legitimacy of the process; it is just facing the reality of human limitations, including scientists and other scholars. Philosophers of science in the past century have increasingly recognized the human element in science. Scientists are not neutral truth-finding machines. Scientific work is influenced by deeply held scientific opinions, social influences, and other very human factors.[17] Our next question will examine a crucial aspect of this human limitation.

Can we bc Equally Confident of Scientific Conclusions in All Fields of Study?

Why should scientists need God to tell them about the origin of life on this earth or the universe? Chemists have learned an awesome amount about what happens when we mix certain chemicals together, and they keep learning more; it does not seem to matter whether they believe the Bible or not. Could this show how science can keep leading us forward in our search for knowledge? It can, but with definite qualifications.

Chemists in their laboratories have one distinct advantage. They do not need to know the history of hydrochloric acid to figure out how it works. It just does what its characteristics cause it to do, as it has always done. The laws of chemistry are, as far as we can tell, the same as they always have been. Whatever you think of the biblical story of Noah, think of the experience of a person in his position. If he had some hydrochloric acid, we presume it would have acted the same then

---

[16] Karl R. Popper, "Science: Problems, Aims, Responsibilities," *Federation Proceedings* 22 (1963): 961–962.

[17] Thomas S. Kuhn, *The Structure of Scientific Revolutions*, 2nd ed. (Chicago, IL: University of Chicago Press, 1970); Imre Lakatos, *The Methodology of Scientific Research Programmes* (New York: Cambridge University Press, 1978); Karl R. Popper, *The Logic of Scientific Discovery* (New York: Harper and Row, 1959); Popper, "Science: Problems, Aims, Responsibilities," 961–962; and Del L. Ratzsch, *Science and Its Limits: The Natural Sciences in Christian Perspective* (Downers Grove, IL: InterVarsity, 2000). For a Seventh-day Adventist perspective, see Roth, 288–295; and Brand and Chadwick, 29–30, 66–68.

as it does now. The discussions and conflicts over scientific theory have not challenged this. The hydrochloric acid that was the digestive juice in his stomach was the same as the hydrochloric acid in all of our stomachs today, and it broke down bread, carrots, and peaches into a useable form the same for him as it still does for us.

Are there other things in nature that Noah would have experienced differently? What about geology, for example? Were there any geological processes that he experienced that differ from our experiences today? Many things were no doubt the same in his time. The laws of physics were, we believe, the same. Water flowed downhill, not uphill. Moving water no doubt carried pebbles and sand the same way it does today. Water flowing very fast could carry huge boulders and ships, as we sometimes see happening today in tsunamis.

But for those who accept the truthfulness of history as recorded in the Bible, it is evident that while Noah was in the ark some geological processes must have happened very differently from what we know today. The differences were not in the laws of physics, but in the circumstances within which those laws were operating. Something disrupted the earth's crust, and flood processes that we occasionally still see today on a local scale occurred at that time on an unprecedented global scale.[18] It apparently had not happened that way before Noah, and it does not happen on that global scale now. We watch rivers, flash floods, and tsunamis carry and deposit sediment in ways that may seem huge to us, but what we observe today is not even slightly comparable to what geological evidence tells us that Noah must have dealt with.

What is the difference between the geological experience of Noah and that of a chemist today in a laboratory? The difference has to do with the role of history. For the chemist, history does not change what happens in the beakers of the laboratory. We do not need to know the history of the earth to understand hydrochloric acid. But in a field like geology, history has a crucial role in our attempt to understand the rocks. Geologists are trying to understand events from the ancient past. Was there a global flood, or was there not? We cannot hope to understand the geological record unless we know the answer to this question. The Bible may have little effect on the work of a chemist who does not believe it. However, whether or not a *geologist* believes that the Bible offers a true history changes everything: it changes whether a given rock formation formed over months or over millions of years, and of course it can radically change our understanding of the processes that deposited

---

[18] See Brand and Chadwick, 359–467.

that rock formation. Geologists, paleontologists, and evolutionary biologists—in contrast to most chemists—seek to understand history, and that is where they face a serious challenge. We cannot go back in time and observe how the sediments forming ancient formations were deposited. We can only use limited circumstantial evidence to try to understand the rocks.

There are some things about history that we cannot know unless a reliable eyewitness tells us—like the crossing of the Delaware River by George Washington and his troops. Someone has to tell us about those events. How did the first living organisms come to exist? Some biochemists try to figure this out, but even if they could produce life in the laboratory (which they emphatically cannot), it would not tell us how life actually began.[19] We can only know how life began if an eyewitness tells us. This leads us to the fifth question: what shall we do when Scripture and science clash?

What Shall we Do When Scripture and Science Clash?

This very crucial question is at the center of huge controversies among Christians. Is it realistic for some who trust the Bible to claim that most of the scientific community, and now many Christian scholars, are wrong, and that only a few scholars are right about geological history and about life? This study submits that the best solution to the conflict between Scripture and science is to allow the Bible to inspire and guide all our scholarly studies—including science. Trustworthy wisdom and guidance comes from the God who has always been here, was the origin of everything, and told us about it. But modern science, with its naturalistic scientific theories and worldview, denying any input from the Bible as relevant for scholarly thinking and explanations, rejects that divine guidance. While it is appropriate for scientists to rely on the known or knowable laws of physics and chemistry, most scientists go beyond that and choose to accept only explanations about the events of ancient history that are based on known natural law. They deny any role for God in history and claim that rational human wisdom is all there is.

But if we accept that the history as given in Genesis is true, why do geologists see so much evidence that seems to flatly contradict biblical history? We can ask the same question about biology and evolution, and many other disciplines. The answers to these questions will have to

---

[19] Stephen C. Meyer, *Signature in the Cell: DNA and the Evidence for Intelligent Design* (New York, NY: HarperOne, 2009).

begin with some human ideas about history and philosophy. If we can answer these basic questions, we can build a basis for understanding the relationship between science and Scripture.

A well-respected evolutionary biologist[20] contrasts what he considers secure scientific facts about evolution with vague, fanciful ideas from religion—ideas, he claims, that could never stand up to scientific investigation. He claims that a dialogue about science between a scientist and a religious person would in fact be a monologue; religion would have nothing to say. And yet, there are other very successful scientists, who are neither Bible believers nor creationists, who in recent years have boldly claimed that according to the latest science, Darwinian theory cannot be true.[21] This indicates that something is at work here that goes beyond a simple understanding of the evidence.

What is going on has to do with philosophical positions or worldviews. A worldview[22] is what orients a person when trying to answer the most important questions in life—questions such as where we came from, why we are here, and where, if anywhere, we are going. Bible-based Christianity is one worldview; Darwinism, which is based on naturalism, is another. A worldview not only gives us answers to these big questions, but also influences the things we accept as true without support from other evidence and thus influences whether we

---

[20] Jerry A. Coyne, *Faith vs. Fact: Why Science and Religion Are Incompatible* (New York: Viking, 2015).

[21] Nelson R. Cabej, *Epigenetic Principles of Evolution* (London: Elsevier, 2012); Jerry Fodor and Massimo Piattelli-Palmarini, *What Darwin Got Wrong* (New York: Farrar, Straus and Giroux, 2010); Eva Jablonka and Marion J. Lamb, *Evolution in Four Dimensions: Genetic, Epigenetic, Behavioral, and Symbolic Variation in the History of Life* (Cambridge, MA: MIT Press, 2005); and James A. Shapiro, *Evolution: A View From the 21st Century* (Upper Saddle River, NJ: FT Press Science, 2011).

[22] A worldview describes the structure of understanding that we use to make sense of our world. Our worldview is what we presuppose. It is our way of looking at life, our interpretation of the universe, and our orientation to reality. It refers to a cluster of beliefs a person holds about the most important issues in life, such as God, the cosmos, knowledge, values, humanity, and history. See Kenneth Richard Samples, "Worldview," in *Dictionary of Christianity and Science: The Definitive Reference for the Intersection of Christian Faith and Contemporary Science*, ed. Paul Copan et al., (Grand Rapids, MI: Zondervan, 2017), 688; see also the discussion in Philip Graham Ryken, *Christian Worldview: A Student's Guide* (Wheaton, IL: Crossway, 2013), esp. 19–32. On the impact of different worldviews on our thinking, see James P. Eckman, *The Truth About Worldviews: A Biblical Understanding of Worldview Alternatives* (Wheaton, IL: Crossway, 2004); and Mark L. Ward Jr. and Dennis Cone, eds., *Biblical Worldview: Creation, Fall, Redemption* (Greenville, SC: BJU Press, 2016). On the meaning of different worldviews from a Seventh-day Adventist perspective, see E. Edward Zinke, "Faith-Science Issues: An Epistemological Perspective," in *A Christian Worldview & Mental Health: A Seventh-Day Adventist Perspective*, ed. Barbara Couden Hernandez et al. (Berrien Springs, MI: Andrews University Press, 2011), 75–96.

notice many smaller things and how we explain them.[23]

Modern science has settled in on a worldview that includes several concepts. One is methodological naturalism, which requires that miracles, or the supernatural, never be used as an explanation in science.[24] Methodological naturalism eliminates any suggestion that God has created anything. The origin of life and of all the variation we see in living organisms and the origin of our human behavior, according to methodological naturalism, must be explained by evolution—by random mutations and natural selection. Correlated with this is the geological position that can be called "conventional geology." This includes a modern version of uniformitarianism, which asserts that the ancient geological record must be explained by processes that can be observed, or are feasible, in the modern world (e.g., rivers deposit sand and gravel, and erode the landscape).[25] While some geological catastrophes do occur, as Bretz and others diligently show us, most scientists categorically deny the concept of a worldwide catastrophe.

Many modern scientists say that we should never invoke catastrophes that could challenge acceptance of deep time (millions and billions of years in earth history). Likewise, we should not accept Bible stories about catastrophes, such as the one Noah supposedly experienced. During the last couple of centuries this worldview, which we will call "conventional science," has come to dominate science and control its conclusions. As previously mentioned, we cannot hope to understand the geological record unless we know the answer to the question of whether or not there was a global flood. Conventional geology gives a philosophical answer, before even looking at any evidence, because methodological naturalism and uniformitarianism tell us that there was not a global flood and that no such thing could be true.

In such an approach scientific research and interpretations are guided, *or even controlled*, by the worldview of the researchers.[26] This is

---

[23] Nancy Pearcey, *Total Truth: Liberating Christianity From Its Cultural Captivity* (Wheaton, IL: Crossway, 2005).

[24] Brand, "Naturalism: Its Role in Science," 21–37; Miller, 117–140; Pennock, *Tower of Babel*; Plantinga, "Methodological Naturalism?," 18–27; and Plantinga, "Methodological Naturalism? Part 2," 22–34. It should be pointed out that methodological naturalism does not openly deny the possible existence of God, as philosophical naturalism does.

[25] Claude Albritton, *Catastrophic Episodes in Earth History* (New York: Chapman and Hall, 1989); William A. Berggren and John A. Van Couvering, *Catastrophes and Earth History: The New Uniformitarianism* (Princeton, NJ: Princeton University Press, 1984); Gould; and Richard Huggett, *Catastrophism: Systems of Earth History* (New York, NY: Routledge, Chapman and Hall, 1990).

[26] Jerry A. Coyne, *Why Evolution Is True* (New York: Viking, 2009); and Pennock and Ruse.

the most seriously misunderstood aspect of science, which is rarely adequately comprehended.[27] Often the confidence in evolution results from a commitment to a naturalistic worldview, rather than from any genuine knowledge about evolution.

The pervasiveness of worldview-dependent thinking is often not adequately realized. For many, their education and experience has never led them to consider alternative models of interpretation; few people proactively seek out and examine other worldviews besides their own.

Christians are often unaware of this concept when they read scientific literature or listen to scientists. As a result, they may accept the conclusions and opinions presented there as if they were facts. This can reduce their confidence in Scripture—or at least cause a lot of confusion about what to believe.

One illustration is the study of fossil hominids (fossil ape-like human relatives) and the resulting theory of the evolution of humans from ape-like ancestors such as *Australopithecus*. That story of human evolution is generally portrayed in very confident terms by paleoanthropologists. They are the experts, so why should their conclusions be questioned? It is wise to remember that most of the scientists who do this research are firm believers in the conventional scientific worldview and, because of this, they "know" there was no creation and that humans had to originate by evolution. As they study the fossils, they are not cogitating over whether the evidence best fits the creation of humans or the evolution of humans. Creation is not on the table for discussion, even though the experts recognize difficulties in interpreting the evidence.[28] It is wise in such instances, when we cannot see how to harmonize the Bible and science, to be patient and wait to see what new research will reveal.[29]

It often seems, when there is a conflict between Scripture and science, that we are dealing with different worldviews[30] influencing the

---

[27] See Cornelius Hunter, *Science's Blind Spot: The Unseen Religion of Scientific Naturalism* (Grand Rapids, MI: Brazos Press, 2007).

[28] See Christopher Rupe and John Sanaford, *Contested Bones* (Waterloo: FMS Publications, 2017).

[29] See Frank M. Hasel, "Living With Confidence Despite Some Open Questions: Upholding the Biblical Truth of Creation Amidst Theological Pluralism," *Journal of the Adventist Theological Society* 14/1 (2003): 229–254.

[30] On various aspects of worldviews and their impact on our thinking, see the discussions in Douglas S. Huffman, ed., *Christian Contours: How a Biblical Worldview Shapes the Mind and Heart* (Grand Rapids, MI: Kregel Academic and Professional, 2011). For a concise comparison of different worldviews, including the biblical worldview and naturalism, see Douglas S. Huffman, "Appendix A: A Comparison of Worldviews," in Huffman, 147–155.

interpretation of the available data. The *Seventh-day Adventist Encyclopedia* states that "there is no reason for conflicts between science and religion. Truth, whether scientific or spiritual, whether measurable or beyond the scope of direct human observation and testing, is consistent with itself in all its manifestations."[31] In other words, Adventists believe that "the natural world, rightly understood, is in complete harmony with the revelation of the divine character, mind, and will set forth in Scripture."[32] Thus, from a Seventh-day Adventist perspective, "the revelation contained in the Word of God is necessary for meaning and perspective in science."[33]

Wolfhart Pannenberg's remarkable words deserve to be taken seriously:

> The theologian must not be too quick to adapt theological ideas and language to the latest outlook in the sciences, especially where such adaptation requires substantial readjustment of traditional doctrine. The theological vision of the world can also function as a challenge to science and as a source of inspiration in developing new strategies of research.[34]

If we thoughtfully weigh the evidence—from science and from the Bible, including all we are told about God, our relationship to Him, and His personal love for us—and if we grasp all we can know of God and His character, we get the impression that the mechanism of evolution is hardly compatible with God's character and the information we have from the Bible.[35] This is not a closed-minded, arbitrary choice. If we put

---

[31] "Science and Religion," 2:559.

[32] Ibid., 2:559. Thus, "the unfortunate conflict that has arisen in recent times between the study of science and religion is not the result of inherent irreconcilability between revealed truth and scientific truth" (ibid., 2:560). Instead, "Seventh-day Adventists have taught that there is a positive relationship between science and religion" (ibid., 2:561). See also Frank M. Hasel, "Living With Confidence," 239.

[33] "Science and Religion," 2:562.

[34] Wolfhart Pannenberg, "Theology and Philosophy in Interaction With Science: A Response to the Message of Pope John Paul II on the Occasion of the Newton Tricentennial in 1987," in *John Paul II on Science and Religion: Reflections on the New View From Rome*, ed. Robert J. Russell et al., (Notre Dame, IN: University of Notre Dame Press, 1990), 78. Unfortunately, Pannenberg himself does not follow his own advice and seems to advocate the readjustment of theological vision and the reassessment of doctrinal affirmations of the past in the light of modern scientific developments as presented by the theory of evolution of life (ibid., 78–79).

[35] Holmes Rolston III, "Does Nature Need to Be Redeemed?," *Zygon* 29/2 (1994): 212, points out that the process of evolution is extraordinarily wasteful and cruel, filled with "predation parasitism, selfishness, randomness, blindness, disaster, indifference, waste, struggle, suffering, death."

the options out on the table for open discussion and allow evidence to speak, the creation of life and of humans is the clear choice from a biblical perspective. If people choose a different option, perhaps it is because they do not really know God or they have arbitrarily allowed distractions to close off what God has told us.[36]

We do not have the answers to all our questions. There are areas of scientific evidence that Bible believers will continue to have difficulty explaining, but we do not have to be afraid of evidence.[37] What we do need to fear is forgetting what firmly held philosophies can do to a person's understanding of evidence.

The finely layered sediment (clay and mud) in the Green River Formation in Wyoming, Colorado, and Utah is considered by geologists to have accumulated over millions of years in a large lake.[38] These thin laminations are often interpreted as varves, which are layers that formed one layer per year. Current evidence contradicts that varve interpretation,[39] but a few laminations per year is still the maximum in many minds. That would be the accumulation of less than a millimeter of sediment per year. Can many millions of fish be buried that slowly and be exquisitely preserved? Can large crocodiles and turtles? The evidence of how animal bodies decay after death is not compatible with anything close to that slow burial. It would be nice to see both contrasting interpretations—rapid, catastrophic burial and slow burial—on the table for candid evaluation, but we do not see that among typical scientists, even though *either* theory raises issues for which there are no adequate scientific answers at this time. Something besides the evidence is determining which theories are given consideration.

Many of the biggest unanswered questions are in geology, but naturalistic science also chooses to explain human nature, our behavior and sociology, and everything else by evolution. Thus, these areas are

---

Philip Clayton, "Metaphysics Can Be a Harsh Mistress," *CTNS Bulletin* 18/1 (1998): 18, pinpoints the problem with interpreting God as directly creating through evolution: "A God who allows countless billions of organisms to suffer and die, and entire species to be wiped out, either does not share the sort of values we do, or works in the world in a much more limited and indirect way that theologians usually imagined."

[36] Leonard Brand and Richard M. Davidson, *Choose You This Day: Why It Matters What You Believe About Creation* (Nampa, ID: Pacific Press, 2013).

[37] See Frank M. Hasel, "Living With Confidence," 229–254.

[38] H. Paul Buchheim, "Paleoenvironments, Lithofacies and Varves of the Fossil Butte Member of the Eocene Green River Formation, Southwestern Wyoming," *Contributions to Geology, University of Wyoming* 30/1 (1994): 3–14.

[39] Ibid.

also affected by our worldviews, and consequently can pose challenges to Christian explanations.

In summary, we would do well to remember how worldviews have a dominating role in determining what answers scientists are willing to accept as they seek to explain nature. Conventional science that works on naturalistic premises *requires* that all explanations be naturalistic explanations, and it does not allow open comparison with other explanations to see which fits the evidence best. Consequently, in such a setting a conflict with Scripture is unavoidable because the supernatural dimension is categorically excluded in the explanation of data. This leads us to our last question.

What is the Role of Science in Discovering the Truth About Our Origin and Destiny?

We have partly answered this question, but will probe a little deeper. We cannot go back in time and see what happened as life began, or how it has varied through time, or how the sediments were deposited and became rock. And yet science is not helpless in its research on these topics. We should not draw arbitrary, absolute lines between what is valid science and what is not. Any general rejection of science is not warranted.[40] But a worldview where natural science adopts an approach of methodological naturalism in support of evolution, where biblical faith in any distinctive sense is precluded from the outset, creates a problem because any Bible-influenced explanation or evaluation of ideas will be rejected on principle. Furthermore, science does not work well in explaining unique events. If an event occurs only once, such as is the case in creation, science is unable to provide much analysis.[41] Last but not least, we have to acknowledge that scientists are only human, and none of us is an expert in all areas of science and none of us has everything right.

What is needed instead is what leading philosopher of science Alvin Plantinga calls "theistic science,"[42] where the possibility of catastrophic events and God's supernatural intervention is taken into consideration. To view nature without God as ultimate elevates it to the place of God. The key point to remember is that serious comparison of conventional scientific explanations and Bible-influenced explanations and the

---

[40] Roth, 283.

[41] Ibid., 288.

[42] Alvin Plantinga, "When Faith and Reason Clash: Evolution and the Bible," *Christian Scholar's Review* 21/1 (1991): 30.

evaluation of these ideas are only done by persons willing to actually consider nonnaturalistic explanations as a possibility. Unfortunately, the bulk of the scientific community seems uninterested in looking at nature this way. However, there has been quite a bit of research by qualified Bible-believing scientists who do this type of comparison with original scientific research. This leads us to the question of biblical interpretation.

Biblical Interpretation

While other chapters in this volume deal with the details of biblical hermeneutics, this study addresses the relationship of science and faith and how it influences biblical interpretation. The traditional Judeo-Christian interpretation understands the Bible as a divinely inspired book, which means, among other things, that God revealed information to the Bible writers.[43] It is not just another human book. The Bible repeatedly states that the authors were spoken to.[44] We have to decide whether this is a legitimate or false—and thus fraudulent—claim. Scripture contains historical records, first-person accounts of events, etc., but the Holy Spirit maintained quality control over the biblical text. Those who read the Bible this way understand that events such as the seven-day creation week and the global flood were literal events that

---

[43] In liberal theology no supernatural divine revelation with any specific information is granted any authority. According to liberal theologian Gordon D. Kaufman, "Doing Theology From a Liberal Christian Point of View," in *Doing Theology in Today's World: Essays in Honor of Kenneth S. Kantzer*, ed. John D. Woodbridge and Thomas Edward McComiskey (Grand Rapids, MI: Zondervan, 1991), 408, it is "*we* who decide that we will do theology: we decide what methods we will pursue in our work; we decide what sources we will use as we try to come to grips with our theological subject-matter and what criteria will govern our judgments; it is we who finally reach the theological conclusions to which we come and who then decide what will be written on the page before us. Theology is in every respect a human work, and we must take full responsibility for everything we do or say theologically. Liberal Christian theologians have recognized this clearly; and they have often, therefore, denounced the claims of traditional theologians to be speaking with divine authorization (that is, on the basis of what they were certain was 'divine revelation') as a presumptuous and insidious form of self-idolatry, a failure to acknowledge that 'God is in heaven, and we are on earth'" (emphasis original). In neoorthodoxy divine revelation is granted, but for Karl Barth this revelation is decisive only in Jesus Christ. And for Emil Brunner this revelation is understood as an I-Thou encounter without any propositional statements. Seventh-day Adventists, in contrast, affirm the propositional character of divine revelation in Scripture. See Peter M. van Bemmelen, "Revelation and Inspiration," in *Handbook of Seventh-Day Adventist Theology*, ed. R. Dederen (Hagerstown, MD: Review and Herald, 2001), 30, 45–46, 50–57.

[44] See chapter 2 by Frank M. Hasel, "Elements of Biblical Hermeneutics in Harmony with Scripture's Self-Claims," in the present volume.

occurred as they are described.[45] To many Adventist scholars, this seems to be the most natural way to read the biblical text. Those who understand it a different way do so for reasons that come from outside of the Bible—primarily from the direct or indirect influence of natural science.[46]

The conventional scientific worldview does not accept the Bible as an authoritative book with correct statements about ancient history. According to that worldview, life was not created, but rather developed from nonliving chemicals by chance chemical interactions, with early life evolving into the myriad life-forms living today. Even if we did not have radiometric dating, this process would, if even possible, take billions of years. The conventional geological worldview, irrespective of the evolutionary process, also requires those millions of years for the Cambrian to recent geological sequence of events.

For many Christians, this dominant view of conventional science rules the interpretation of Scripture. Christian authors advocating long geological ages and theistic evolution generally do not reveal an understanding of the controlling power of the conventional scientific worldview, and how it influences interpretations of the evidence. Unfortunately there is little evidence of a critical evaluation of the evidence for evolution or for conventional geological interpretations.[47] Conventional scientific concepts are accepted as facts, and it seems as if their theology is wrapped around what current science has to say.

In this context, Plantinga raises the question of whether methodological naturalism is the most adequate way to interpret the Bible.[48] It is often claimed that to question methodological naturalism flies in the

---

[45] On the historical reliability and historicity of the Bible, see chapter 4 by Michael G. Hasel, "History, the Bible, and Hermeneutics," in the present volume. On the implications of the biblical seven-day creation account, see chapter 11 by Michael G. Hasel, "The Genesis Account as a Test Case for Biblical Hermeneutics," in the present volume.

[46] Some biblical interpreters argue that the biblical text implies a nonliteral reading, which makes it, in their opinion, compatible with conventional science. See Ian G. Barbour, *When Science Meets Religion* (San Francisco, CA: Harper and Row, 2000); Francis S. Collins, *The Language of God* (New York: Free Press, 2006); Denis O. Lamoureux, *Evolutionary Creation: A Christian Approach to Evolution* (Eugene, OR: Wipf and Stock, 2008); Nancey C. Murphey, *Religion and Science* (Scottdale, PA: Herald Press, 2002); Arthur Peacocke, *Theology for a Scientific Age* (Philadelphia, PA: Fortress, 1993); and John Polkinghorne, *Science and Theology* (Philadelphia, PA: Fortress, 1998).

[47] Jonathan Kane, Emely Willoughby, and T. Michael Keesey, *God's Word or Human Reason? An Insider Perspective on Creationism* (Portland, OR: Inkwater Press, 2016); David R. Montgomery, *The Rocks Don't Lie: A Geologist Investigates Noah's Flood* (New York: W. W. Norton, 2012); Schneiderman and Allmon; and Davis A. Young and Ralph F. Stearley, *The Bible, Rocks and Time: Geological Evidence for the Age of the Earth* (Downers Grove, IL: InterVarsity, 2008).

[48] Plantinga, "Two (or More) Kinds," 19–57.

face of an enormous body of scientific evidence and theory. The following objections are often brought forth against the biblical view on the origin of life: 1) it uses an inappropriate philosophy and 2) creationists cannot be good scientists. We will look at these objections in the following section.

Objection 1: Inappropriate Philosophy is Being Used

Commitment to the conventional scientific worldview, as previously described, controls the interpretation of evidence, especially in the study of ancient history. Christian works recommending that we interpret the Bible in line with theistic evolution are often deficient in their evaluation and understanding of the controlling influence of the conventional scientific worldview. The content of that worldview seems to be accepted and taken for granted. Perhaps that is understandable in light of the unified front that modern science presents in our society, implying that there is no intelligent alternative to its synthesis of the evidence. Actually, the worldview of methodological naturalism excludes many areas of reality, offering only a partial view of reality.[49] Thus a biblical worldview that allows for the divine reality and its activity in the creation of this world exhibits a much broader horizon and is thus able to interpret various evidence differently. Interestingly, accumulating evidence is raising doubts about an unquestioning adherence to methodological naturalism.[50] While we may not have all the answers to every question,[51] we can see more and more evidence that challenges the conventional worldview.[52] There is also what has been called "warranted belief" in God[53] and in the trustworthiness of Scripture.

Objection 2: Creationists Cannot be Good Scientists

Most scientists believe that the conventional worldview is the only one that works in a practical sense. A survey of anti-creationist publications reveals that authors who support methodological naturalism often express that those who accept religious concepts such as creation are out of touch with reality and could never be successful scientists.[54]

---

[49] See Roth, 285–288.

[50] Plantinga, "Methodological Naturalism?"; and Plantinga, "Methodological Naturalism? Part 2. "

[51] On the challenge of living confidently despite some open questions, see Frank M. Hasel, "Living With Confidence," 229–254.

[52] Leonard Brand, *Genesis and Science: Where Is the Evidence Going?* (Nampa, ID: Pacific Press, 2020).

[53] Plantinga, *Knowledge and Christian Belief*, 30–44.

[54] Coyne, *Faith vs. Fact*; Niles Eldredge, *The Triumph of Evolution and the Failure of Creationism*

But these authors clearly show that they do not understand how educated creationists think. It does not have to be this way. It is possible to have very meaningful conversations with secular scientists whose minds are open to recognizing that even someone with a different view of origins may be intelligent and capable in science. The conventional worldview does not explain all the available data in satisfactory ways. Quite often a theological and biblical vision of the world can provide alternative strategies for scientific inquiry and research that lead to new insights and explanations.[55] We will explore that possibility further in the next section.

Can a Bible Believer be an Effective Scientist?

As we seek to reach a skeptical scholarly world with new insights, underlain by a different worldview that is quite unpopular in the scientific community, we realize that arguments and talk alone are insufficient. A few scientists will need to show that our unconventional approach works. Even then, the bulk of the scientific community or liberal Christian scholars may not be convinced. But our goal is to reach those who are open enough to listen.

Historian and philosopher of science Thomas Kuhn recognizes that many of the most significant advances in science happen through what he calls "scientific revolutions":[56] One paradigm (a broad, explanatory theory) is troubled by some anomalies, and a few creative scientists devise what they think is a better paradigm, seeking to develop it and find supportive evidence. Their new paradigm, or theory, will only succeed if a few persons believe in it enough to successfully develop it.[57] The most famous example is the replacement of the geocentric theory by the heliocentric theory. Something similar is needed if the biblical worldview is to make significant progress with its message about origins.

Some scientists who will not accept the biblical worldview will still learn to respect the scientific work we do if they see that we practice good science. A few believing scientists can demonstrate that their

---

(New York: Henry Holt, 2001); and Matt Young and Taner Edis, eds., *Why Intelligent Design Fails: A Scientific Critique of the New Creationism* (Brunswick, NJ: Rutgers University Press, 2004).

[55] See Pannenberg, 78.

[56] Kuhn.

[57] Frank M. Hasel, "Scientific Revolution: An Analysis and Evaluation of Thomas Kuhn's Concept of Paradigm and Paradigm Change for Theology," *Journal of the Adventist Theological Society* 2/2 (1991): 160–177.

approach to scientific research works, and that they are very well capable of doing solid research that results in publishable papers in standard research journals.

This work has already been underway for several decades. There are many in the medical sciences and other scientific fields who believe the biblical creation account as reported in Genesis and are successful in research and publishing. These fields do not normally deal with controversial topics like evolution and geology, and so the conflicts with conventional science usually are not evident in that work. Their success does show, however, that belief in a Creator does not need to introduce obstacles to scientific success.

But it does not stop there. Even in the most controversial fields, such as evolutionary biology and geology, there are scientists whose research and success benefit directly from their biblical worldview. One example is Arthur Chadwick, who in the 1960s began a study of the Tapeats Sandstone, the lowest Paleozoic formation in the Grand Canyon. This formation had always been explained as sand accumulating very slowly, just offshore in a shallow ocean. Chadwick's biblical beliefs about history led him to ask questions that others had not asked and think of hypotheses that would never be considered by conventional geologists. He wondered if the Tapeats Sandstone could have been deposited much faster, and he noticed some convincing evidence indicating it must have been deposited in water hundreds of feet deep, not in shallow water.[58] After several years of research, he presented a paper at a geological symposium, which included the geologists who had developed the existing theory. They concluded that the facts he described made best sense in his model of explanation, rather than in the existing theory. Out in the hallway later, a geologist asked him, "Why did you see this evidence, that the rest of us did not see?" The answer was probably, "Because my worldview leads me to ask different questions, and see things that others may have considered unimportant." Chadwick's research answered some questions, but not all. His data does not say how fast the sand was deposited. But his explanation is consistent with rapid deposition, whereas the old theory was not compatible with rapid deposition.

Chadwick's biblical worldview opened his eyes to see new things and ask new questions. After asking new questions, he had to use the same research methods other geologists use to answer those questions.

---

[58] Elaine G. Kennedy, R. Kablanow, and Arthur V. Chadwick, *Evidence for Deep Water Deposition of the Tapeats Sandstone, Grand Canyon, Arizona, Proceedings of the 3rd Biannual Conference of Research on the Colorado Plateau* (1997).

The Bible tells about the flood but it does not say anything about the Tapeats Sandstone. Chadwick collected his rock samples the same way any other scientist would, and used the same instruments to analyze those samples. The difference was in the questions, not in the methods for answering the questions. A person's worldview has a powerful influence on what features they consider important and what range of explanations they will consider, as they form hypotheses to explain the evidence. The questions he asked were key to his success in this research; after thinking of the new questions, he had to "do" research in the same way anyone else would.

In the last five or six decades there have been a number of research projects such as this, where a biblical worldview suggested new questions and new hypotheses and was followed up by field and laboratory research. Each case that diligently followed this approach has been successful. Each one discovered that the evidence fits a biblical worldview as well as or better than it fits previous explanations. These projects have also led to successful publication in peer-reviewed research journals.[59]

Another example illustrates this point. Several Adventist scientists and I spent about a decade studying fossil whales in the Miocene/Pliocene Pisco Formation in western Peru. When we were introduced to these very numerous fossil whales, we examined the published geological papers from the previous twenty years of research. It was believed that the sand and diatomaceous silt that buried the whales accumulated on the ocean floor a few centimeters thick every thousand years, and this continued for several million years. Our research dealt with the sediments and the taphonomy of the whales. Taphonomy is the study of how and why organisms become fossilized. We were immediately struck with a conflict between the excellent preservation of these articulated whale skeletons and the idea that they were buried so slowly. Whales that die in modern oceans are scavenged and destroyed within a few years. There is no possibility that each whale lay there for thousands of years yet was still preserved. They must have been buried rapidly. This was our hypothesis, and the evidence gave strong support to this hypothesis.

As in the previous example, this success resulted because our worldview opened our eyes to see what we might not have noticed otherwise. Previous researchers had not realized the severe conflict between excellent whale preservation and slow burial over such long time periods. They were not asking the right questions; they were sure they knew how long it took, and this did not provide the incentive to

---

[59] See Brand and Chadwick, 469-477.

question the accepted time scale. Our eyes were opened by our biblical understanding of geological history. Any worldview, even ours, can introduce blinders that keep us from seeing the whole picture. Our advantage was in being very aware of *two* contrasting worldviews, and this contrast is very helpful in suggesting new questions and seeking ways to test between the two perspectives. Our research used methods that others recognized as valid geology and paleontology research, and our findings were published in respected scholarly journals.[60]

Our papers did not discuss the biblical flood, as this would not have been appropriate. Our worldview includes rapid geological processes and a global flood. Our research data could address rapid deposition of at least part of the Pisco Formation, but could not address such a broad concept as a global flood. Such a big topic would require lifetimes of research, not just one project.

These and other similar research projects demonstrate that a biblical worldview merits consideration as a valid possibility to replace the conventional geological worldview. It should not be ignored because of the firmly entrenched conventional worldview.

A Summary of Geological and Biological Evidence

The focus of the previous section and this section is geology, for that is where the biggest questions are. The discovery of biological evidence that supports belief in a biblical explanation of origins is way ahead of the search in geology, and part of that biological evidence comes from scientists who do not even believe in creation.

Recall the contrast between chemistry and geology. Chemists study things like hydrochloric acid that they can observe and investigate right in their laboratories. Biologists have the same advantage in much of their study. Although they cannot observe evolution through the eons, they can study how animals and plants work. They study living things that they can observe repeatedly, right in front of them. They can study

---

[60] Leonard Brand et al., "A High Resolution Stratigraphic Framework for the Remarkable Fossil Cetacean Assemblage of the Miocene/Pliocene Pisco Formation, Peru," *Journal of South American Earth Sciences* 31 (2011): 414–425; Leonard R. Brand et al., "Fossil Whale Preservation Implies High Diatom Accumulation Rate in the Miocene-Pliocene Pisco Formation of Peru," *Geology* 32 (2004): 165–168; Raul Esperante et al., "Exceptional Occurrence of Fossil Baleen in Shallow Marine Sediments of the Neogene Pisco Formation, Southern Peru," *Palaeogeography, Palaeoclimatology, Palaeoecology* 257 (2008): 344–360; and Raul Esperante et al., "Taphonomy and Paleoenvironmental Conditions of Deposition of Fossil Whales in the Diatomaceous Sediments of the Miocene/Pliocene Pisco Formation, Southern Peru—a New Fossil-Lagerstatte," *Palaeogeography, Palaeoclimatology, Palaeoecology* 417 (2015): 337–370.

whole animals, or just living cells and molecules, and the awesome, seemingly impossible complexity of the processes within cells.

Darwin developed his theory of evolution in the mid-1800s. The structure of DNA was determined almost a century after Darwin. The field of genetics first emerged decades after Darwin wrote his book in 1859,[61] and did not get seriously started until the early 1900s. Darwin and his colleagues knew precious little about the complexity of life. Numerous books by creationists and noncreationists alike point out significant weaknesses in Darwinian theory.[62] In recent decades the naiveté of Darwin's theory is becoming painfully evident, especially in recent years with new techniques like the ability to sequence DNA. Most books by evolutionary biologists do not discuss these problems. In the scientific community there is developing a dichotomy between traditional evolutionary biologists and another group—especially molecular biologists—who are aware of what is truly happening inside those awesome living cells. Because of new discoveries that DNA sequencing and other advances are giving us, some of these molecular biologists are boldly stating that the Darwinian theory of biological change by random mutation and natural selection cannot work, except to influence minor variations. The cell is just too incredibly complex and sophisticated for random mutations to be a realistic process for change and evolutionary advance. And yet for the Darwinian theory all change *must* begin with random mutations. If those genetic changes are not random, if genetic changes occur that are beneficial to the organism, that implies that someone knows what the organism needs. It would imply that intelligence was involved in setting up the genetic process. Yet to a certain extent, findings of molecular biologists and others indicate that this is what is happening.[63] These molecular biologists are not necessarily creationists, although some are. They just realize that Darwin's theory is deficient in explaining significant aspects. This is leading to an intriguing conflict within the scientific community,

---

[61] Charles R. Darwin, *On the Origin of Species* (London: John Murray, 1859).

[62] Michael J. Behe, *Darwin's Black Box: The Biochemical Challenge to Evolution* (New York: Free Press, 1996); Michael J. Behe, *The Edge of Evolution: The Search for the Limits of Darwinism* (New York: Free Press, 2007); Brand and Chadwick; Stephen C. Meyer; *Darwin's Doubt* (New York: HarperCollins, 2013); John C. Sanford, *Genetic Entropy & the Mystery of the Genome* (Waterloo, NY: FMS Publications, 2008); and Jonathan Wells, *The Myth of Junk DNA* (Seattle, WA: Discovery Institute Press, 2011).

[63] Cabej, V. Hughes, "Epigenetics: The Sins of the Father," *Nature* 507/7490 (2014): 22–24; Jablonka and Lamb; Massimo Pigliucci and Gerd B. Müller, eds., *Evolution: The Extended Synthesis* (Cambridge, MA: MIT Press, 2010); and Shapiro.

with many evolutionary biologists rejecting the new evidence or trying to downplay its significance. A few evolutionary biologists, on the other hand, recognize that the new evidence is not going away, and are trying to develop a new evolutionary synthesis, called the "extended synthesis."[64] Traditional-thinking evolutionists do not appreciate this group any more than they appreciate the troublesome molecular biologists.

One of these molecular biologists is especially candid and bold.[65] He is not a creationist, but he acknowledges that how evolution happened remains a mystery. His thinking illustrates how scientific prestige can have its influence. He concludes that Darwin's theory of evolution cannot work, but he accepts the general theory that life resulted from some kind of evolution over long ages. He states, "The one issue that has effectively been settled in a convincing way is the evidence for a process of evolutionary change over the past three billion years."[66] He is convinced, but does not present evidence to support that conclusion. Thus, we can see that while significant aspects of the evolutionary process remain a mystery and cannot work, the general process of evolutionary change is still maintained as valid.

We can summarize this section with the conclusion that the theories of the naturalistic origin of life and of Darwinian evolution are in heavy scientific trouble with the potential to seriously question the standard frame of thinking. This opens up new opportunities for believers in creation.[67]

Now let us turn back to geology. Admittedly, those who accept Genesis as factual history have more unanswered questions in geology than in other scientific fields, like biology. Should this worry us? Not necessarily, because continued study is revealing that geological evidence for long ages and against the global flood is also encountering troubled waters.

The strongest case for deep time (millions of years) comes from radiometric dating, and its support for the uniformitarian approach to

---

[64] Cabej; Jablonka and Lamb; and Pigliucci and Müller.

[65] Shapiro.

[66] Ibid., 128

[67] For more detailed study of this topic, see Douglas Axe, *Undeniable: How Biology Confirms Our Intuition That Life Was Designed* (New York: HarperCollins, 2016); Brand, *Genesis and Science*; Brand and Chadwick; Robert Carter, *Evolution's Achilles Heels* (Powder Springs, GA: Creation Book, 2014); and Meyer, *Darwin's Doubt.*

geology.[68] While there is some helpful new information by creationists,[69] we do not have the answer for how to understand everything connected to radiometric dating. This may seem discouraging, and we will probably not have the answers we wish any time soon. This really does not tell us anything about the Bible; it only reminds us that expecting to have quick scientific answers to all the questions about ancient history is not realistic. But it can be helpful to look at a broader range of evidence to see what it tells us. When we do that, we find that there are other areas of geology in which the evidence is not compatible with those long ages of time and with uniformitarian explanations for the ancient rocks. Consequently, this evidence seems to indicate there is something wrong with our interpretation of the radiometric evidence. We will discuss several examples of this geological evidence.

Conventional geology works on the premise that the present is the key to the past. In other words, to understand the origin of the ancient rocks, it is assumed they were formed by the same processes we see in action today, or processes feasible in the modern world. So to understand how an ancient sandstone was formed, we need to study how sand is deposited in rivers, deserts, and by ocean currents (modern analogues), and then apply that comparison to the sandstone, within the accepted timeframe of millions of years. If we trust human wisdom to understand the rocks, this is all we have to go on.

If, however, we are willing to apply a biblical worldview, we look at the same evidence and do not stop there. We do not assume that the conventional time scale is necessarily correct, and we do not assume that modern analogues are always adequate to explain the origin of the ancient rocks. The biblical worldview with its global flood opens up a wider range of possibilities. The processes that formed the rocks could have been on a very different scale of size and time than those we can observe today. If we are studying a sandstone, for example, we can consider that perhaps this body of sand was deposited rapidly, over a very large area in a short period of time. If we wish to know what science says about this, we then proceed with extensive, careful research that can help us understand which of our hypotheses about this process are supported by the evidence.

---

[68] Teresa Mensing and Gunter Faure, *Isotopes: Principles and Applications*, 3rd ed. (Hoboken, NJ: John Wiley and Sons, 2006); and Felix M. Gradstein et al., eds., *The Geologic Time Scale 2012* (Boston, MA: Elsevier, 2012).

[69] Donald de Young, *Thousands . . . Not Billions* (Green Forest, AR: Master Books, 2005); and Larry Vardiman, Andrew Snelling, and Eugene F. Chaffin, eds., *Radioisotopes and the Age of the Earth: A Young-Earth Creationist Research Initiative* (El Cajon, CA: Institute for Creation Research, 2005).

As described in a previous section, we allow our worldview to help us by suggesting hypotheses and new questions to ask. In this process, we are not testing the idea of the flood, but are proceeding with confidence that the flood was a reality, and allowing this to lead us to better explanations. This is how conventional scientists apply their worldview in their research, and we can do the same.[70]

When we use this approach it becomes evident that many ancient rock formations do not seem to be explainable within the conventional deep time theory. The Triassic Shinarump Conglomerate in the western United States is one such example. The term conglomerate tells us it is formed of sand and pebbles. The millions of rounded pebbles in the sand indicate it was deposited by flowing water, like in a braided stream. However, it is less than one hundred feet thick, and it quite uniformly covers over one hundred thousand square miles. Have you ever seen a stream, or even a big river, that flowed over one hundred thousand square miles? Some rivers and streams erode their way from side to side through time, but they do so within a belt, constrained by features of the landscape. The evidence in the Shinarump Conglomerate requires an extensive flow of water and sediment, probably catastrophic, over this very large area.

The Shinarump Conglomerate is not a rare anomaly. Most of the Paleozoic and Mesozoic rock formations (roughly the lower two-thirds of the fossil-bearing geological column) are very widespread deposits of sediments, covering many thousands—even hundreds of thousands—of square miles. Conventional geology theory must try to explain these by the processes seen in those modern analogues, but the modern analogues are not nearly capable of depositing those gigantic ancient rock formations.[71] Why don't conventional geologists see this? A few of them see the problem and make comments about it.[72] However, their worldview does not allow them to take this evidence at face value and recognize the need for major geological catastrophe to adequately explain the evidence.

This is only one of the problems faced by conventional geological explanations. This does not mean that the biblical model is free from challenges; in fact, for some problems we do not yet have satisfactory

---

[70] Brand and Chadwick.

[71] Ibid., 444-447.

[72] Derek V. Ager, *The Nature of the Stratigraphic Record*, 2nd ed. (Hoboken, NJ: John Wiley and Sons, 1981); and C. E. Brett, "A Slice of the 'Layer Cake': The Paradox of 'Frosting Continuity,'" *Palaios* 15 (2000): 495–498.

explanations. But there are also examples of geological evidence that are a serious challenge to conventional theories, which the present study cannot cover. This leads us to some concluding thoughts.

Conclusion

Over the last couple of centuries, science has adopted a philosophy of "conventional science" or "naturalistic science." It includes methodological naturalism (no supernatural explanations are to be given for anything), a time scale for earth and biological history of millions or billions of years, and the geological principle of uniformitarianism in its modern state (ancient geological processes occurred by processes seen or feasible in the modern world). This constitutes a worldview that firmly excludes the biblical account in Genesis of creation and a global flood a few thousand years ago.[73]

Science is a successful enterprise, and has been responsible for a long list of amazing discoveries. This success is laudable, but it has resulted in a sense of invincible prestige for science. It is often the case that a specialist in some field of science says things that almost no other person can begin to understand or challenge. The question is whether the extension of such prestige is justified when science deals with its interpretations of ancient geological history, which no human being has observed.

One concern about such scientific prestige is that scientific conclusions change over time, as new evidence becomes known. Many scientific conclusions are not permanent, but rather may be best described as a progress report along the journey to understanding. Much of what we think is true will change with the finding of new evidence in the future. Individual scientists are not more unbiased than other people. The objectivity that science achieves results primarily from discussion and debate as new ideas are considered and individuals with differing opinions seek to support their preferred theories. Scientific conclusions are not absolute: they change with new data and ongoing debates about how to interpret the data.

It is also true that our ability to decode nature is not equal in all fields. A chemist or physiologist studies processes that can be observed in their laboratory. These processes occur right in front of them, over and over, allowing them to directly collect data on what is happening. Geologists

---

[73] Roth, 334, points out that the Bible gives us a broader approach to reality than naturalistic science.

seeking to understand ancient rocks cannot do that. They are attempting to determine what events occurred in the past. They also hope to understand the processes involved in those events. But they cannot go back in time to see what happened. They are restricted to observing geological processes in the modern world, and interpreting whether these processes occurred in the same way in the ancient past. Global catastrophes are not happening now, and consequently modern analogues introduce a bias toward slow, more local geological processes. This inability to go back in time and see what happened is the most important limitation in geology.

The powerful influence of science's naturalistic worldview is almost never adequately understood, and is not often subject to review. In conventional science, creationist opinions are not open for discussion and comparison with the conventional interpretations, no matter what the evidence may be. To be accepted by science, the origin of the first life-forms must be explained by chance chemical reactions through the ages, even though all the evidence is against that theory.[74] This worldview dominates scientific interpretations of geological and biological history to an extent that is seldom appreciated.

Those who see abundant evidence for confidence in the Bible as an inspired, factual book think that those who reinterpret the Bible message into theistic evolution over deep time are making a big mistake.[75] There are also scientific reasons to object to this reinterpretation. New evidence in areas like molecular biology are presenting serious challenges to Darwinian theory, and even accumulating evidence in geology is more favorable to a biblical worldview than had been previously thought. Also, scientists who accept the Genesis record of creation and the reality of a global flood are being successful in allowing their worldview to guide them in successful research and publication, raising doubts about the adequacy of the conventional approach to science. It seems that scientific inquiry and research can benefit from the biblical perspective and that human wisdom alone is not enough.

What, then, is the appropriate relationship between science and faith? Biblical faith is not necessarily incompatible with science. Those who accept the Bible as a factual, reliable account of origins can accept much of science just as other persons do. This includes the recognition that scientific conclusions are tentative and subject to change, but this does

---

[74] Meyer, *Signature in the Cell.*

[75] Moreland, et al.

not need to disrupt our commonsense application of science in our daily lives.

There are, however, places where there is a clash between science and a faith that accepts the Bible as a factual and reliable account of life, creation, and geological history. If the Bible and science give different answers to questions of how to live our lives, how to treat other persons, or where we came from and when, then we must determine the appropriate relationship between the two sources. Our interpretation of scientific conclusions or of the Bible may both need correction. When they seem to clash, this requires careful study and thought. Seeking to understand the clash can improve our understanding of both science and the Bible.[76] But ultimately, "all true science is but an interpretation of the handwriting of God in the material world. Science brings from her research only fresh evidences of the wisdom and power of God."[77] According to Ellen G. White, "the deepest students of science are constrained to recognize in nature the working of an infinite power. But to man's unaided reason, nature's teaching cannot but be contradictory and disappointing. Only in the light of revelation [Scripture] can it be read aright."[78] This means that an authentic Adventist approach to science and the Bible will acknowledge that we must not test Scripture by our ideas of nature, but we are to test our ideas of nature by Scripture.[79] Thus, "both the revelations of science and the experiences of life are in harmony with the testimony of Scripture."[80] The book of nature and the written Word of God, rightly understood, each shed light on the other.[81]

While some accept science as the more reliable source, and consequently interpret the biblical creation story as a mythical, untrue account —an account of origins that was not divinely communicated to the Bible writers—an Adventist approach places the emphasis differently. Seventh-day Adventists recognize the Bible as a collection of books inspired by God, who knows more about origins and human nature than any of us. This conclusion is based on the truthfulness of Scripture and a careful and in-depth study of the Bible and how the contributions of different biblical authors help us understand the whole. Through a

---

[76] Brand and Chadwick, 120-124.

[77] Ellen G. White, *Patriarchs and Prophets* (Washington, DC: Review and Herald, 1890), 599.

[78] Ellen G. White, *Education* (Mountain View, CA: Pacific Press, 1903), 134.

[79] Cf. Ellen G. White, "Science and Revelation," *Signs of the Times*, March 13, 1884. See also Hanna, 188–190.

[80] Ellen G. White, *Education*, 130

[81] Ellen G. White, "Science and the Bible in Education," *Signs of the Times*, March 20, 1884.

careful interpretation of Scripture, the Holy Spirit has given us a reliable, factual account of God's actions in history and of our origins. If this is true, then the biblical account provides us with the correct understanding of our history, and it is wise to take Genesis as the reliable account of our beginnings. We are not putting down science, but rather humbly recognizing the limits to scientific knowledge. We are able to recognize these limits because God has given us the necessary information to do so.

Thus, ultimately our faith is based on the Word of God, not on science. However, it is interesting that scientific progress gives us new information that increasingly supports our faith in the Bible. And when we put our faith in God's revelation, it even facilitates research by Bible-believing scientists who find better explanations for things that formerly seemed challenging.

Rightly understood, the conclusions of science and Scripture are not in conflict with each other because they each have God as the author.[82]

[82] "When the Bible makes statements of facts in nature, science may be compared with the written word, and *a correct understanding of both will always prove them to be in harmony*. One does not contradict the other" (Ellen G. White, "Science and Revelation," emphasis added).

CHAPTER 7

Principles of Biblical Interpretation

Ekkehardt Mueller

This chapter attempts to show that Scripture must be intentionally interpreted, that it must be correctly interpreted, and how this can be done. The purpose of interpreting Scripture in this study is not just to understand in a better way some type of ancient literature, but to know God and whom He has sent—Jesus Christ, our Savior and Lord. Knowing the triune God leads to eternal life (John 17:3). Since we know God primarily through Scripture, knowing God and accepting the Bible as God's Word, inspired by the Holy Spirit, are related (2 Pet 1:19–21; 2 Tim 3:16–17).

The Importance of Interpreting Scripture Correctly

With the beginning of Jesus' public ministry, people had to determine whether He was the long-expected Messiah or an impostor. The question of who Jesus is has been and still is a crucial one for people worldwide. However, the question can only sufficiently be answered in the light of the biblical data—that is, Old Testament prophecies and New Testament records. In addition, the issue was and is how to interpret this data. From this perspective, the enquiry of whether or not Jesus is the Messiah is largely a question about how to understand Scripture.[1] Given the same piece of literature—a letter, email, or text—and asked about the message's content, people will display different nuances in

---

[1] That interpretation of Scripture is of utmost importance is evident in the incident when Jesus explains to the Emmaus disciples the Old Testament regarding Himself (Luke 24:25–27).

their responses. Some reader may even miss an important point[2] or come up with contradictory explanations.

When trying to understand a document that is several hundred or thousand years old, there are barriers to overcome: 1) The document may have been written in a language different from ours. 2) Even if it were written in our language, meanings of terms may be different because languages are dynamic and change over time. 3) Circumstances and ancient cultural conventions prevalent when a document was composed may have changed over time. 4) People are influenced by their own history and experiences, transmitted values, nationality, position in society, race, etc.[3]—in other words, their worldview.

There is no way to avoid interpreting Scripture. Normally, people unknowingly interpret what they read and hear. All content is evaluated and interpreted by us—even simple conversations. We interpret not only messages to try to understand the author's intentions, but we also interpret tone of voice, facial expressions, and other non-verbal communication. Thus, correct interpretation must be a deliberate approach, following biblical parameters and common sense.[4] Interpretation is necessary not only to understand Jesus, but also to understand God who is revealing Himself—to understand His will, and to understand humanity and God's plan for humanity. Interpretation of Scripture helps us see the big picture and make sense of our lives and the evil we encounter. So, let us begin with Jesus.

As John indicates at the end of the seventh chapter of his Gospel, the authorities tried to have Jesus arrested and killed. Their attempt failed. The officers did not seize Jesus. So, Jesus got away for this time. John 7:45–52 explains:

> The officers then came to the chief priests and Pharisees, who said to them, "Why did you not bring him?" The officers answered, "No one ever spoke like this man!" The Pharisees answered them, "Have you also been deceived? Have any of the authorities

---

[2] See Bruce L. Bauer, "Social Location and Its Impact on Hermeneutics," *Journal of Adventist Mission Studies* 12/1 (2016): 76–77, who reports of an experiment conducted by M. A. Powell. He gives the parable of the prodigal son to both an American audience and a Russian audience. A significant number of people in the United States, who had never experienced a famine, missed completely the famine in the parable. Similarly, a significant number of Russians missed the squandering of money.

[3] See ibid., 75–76.

[4] E.g., taking a sentence of a letter or other document out of its context may completely distort the author's intended meaning.

> or the Pharisees believed in him? But this crowd that does not know the law is accursed." Nicodemus, who had gone to him before, and who was one of them, said to them, "Does our law judge a man without first giving him a hearing and learning what he does?" They replied, "Are you from Galilee too? Search and see that no prophet arises from Galilee."[5]

Pharisees were known for being students of the Bible. The scribes among them in particular were somewhat professional scholars/theologians. The imperatives "search and see" in John 7:54 certainly refer to Scripture. The Pharisees told Nicodemus, a member of their own group, who protested against their illegal procedure in the case of Jesus, "Study the Bible when dealing with Jesus!" This is good advice, but it is very ironic in light of what they themselves did. While consulting the Scriptures, obviously the Pharisees did not come to the right conclusions. The five fallacies found in John 7:45–52 and discussed in this study are just examples of other fallacies that exist when we approach Scripture. But they show how important appropriate and correct interpretation of the Bible is. What are these fallacies in John 7 that need to be avoided?

Fallacies in Biblical Interpretation

First, the Pharisees approached the Bible with biases and preconceived ideas. Although they believed in messianic prophecies, they must have made an a priori decision that Jesus could not be the Messiah no matter what He did, taught, or how He behaved. Political and other reasons may have played a role in their opposition of Him. So, they were not able to see the overwhelming testimony of Scripture confirming Jesus as the Christ. They neglected biblical passages and did not consider the whole picture. At this time, both those who accepted Jesus as the Christ and those who rejected Him had the same Scripture and agreed that Scripture was the Word of God, and yet they came to different results. The effect of the Pharisees' wrong interpretation was a tragedy, leading to the death of the Messiah. Therefore, when approaching Scripture, we have to set aside predetermined ideas and traditions and listen openly and honestly to what God wants to tell us through His Word. Also, we must have a willingness to learn continually.

---

[5] All biblical quotations are from the ESV, unless otherwise indicated.

A second problem with the Pharisees was their appeal to human authority. They brushed off the explanation of the officers who had failed to arrest Jesus, and claimed that they were deceived. Now, deception can happen. But then the leaders should have shown from Scripture that Jesus could not be the Messiah. However, this is not what they did; they appealed to human authority—"No one of the rulers or Pharisees has believed in him, has he?" (John 7:48, NASB). And even with this statement they were wrong. Obviously, Nicodemus believed in Him. By the sheer power of their office they attempted to decide the case. Ellen G. White writes:

> There are today thousands . . . who can give no other reason for points of faith which they hold than they were so instructed by their religious leaders. . . . God has given us His word that we may become acquainted with its teachings and know for ourselves what He requires of us. . . . It is not enough to have good intentions; it is not enough to do what a man thinks is right or what the minister tells him is right. His soul's salvation is at stake, and he should search Scriptures for himself.[6]

Again she explains, "I have been shown that no man's judgment should be surrendered to the judgment of any one man."[7] While we need to consult with others (Prov 11:14; 12:15), we cannot make ourselves dependent on them. We have to study, pray, and choose by ourselves.[8]

Third, the Pharisees exerted pressure on their colleague Nicodemus and used fear to make him subscribe to the majority position. Majority views as well as minority views on theological matters are not necessarily correct, as church history shows. The Pharisees were not only biased against Jesus but they also disdained Galileans and threatened Nicodemus to consider him as one of them.[9] What happens here is an ad hominem argument—an argument directed against a

---

[6] Ellen G. White, *The Great Controversy* (Mountain View, CA: Pacific Press, 1911), 596, 598.

[7] Ellen G. White, *Testimonies for the Church* (Mountain View, CA: Pacific Press, 1875), 3:492.

[8] Protestants have made it clear that popes and councils can err and that each believer is responsible for what he or she holds to be true.

[9] Jo-Ann A. Brant, *John*, Paideia Commentaries on the New Testament (Grand Rapids, MI: Baker Academic, 2011), 141, notes, "Their invitation to search Scripture [verse 52] . . . is a piece of irony, for they circumvent the task of inquiry by providing Nicodemus with the conclusion he must reach in order to be one of them. . . In this quick exchange, John captures the Pharisee's sacrifice of their own reputation as accurate interpreters of the law as well as Nicodemus' struggle to be both constant and loyal to his associates."

person, not dealing directly with the issue on the table. If arguments on the real issue fail, people attack the opponent's integrity, expertise, and/or reputation (John 7:48–49) in order to discredit, threaten or pressure him or her. The worst-case scenario of an ad hominem approach was the killing of Jesus and, later through the centuries, His followers.

The fourth fallacy is the argument from silence. Arguments from silence are arguments that are not derived from what the Bible says but from what the Bible does *not* say. So, they tend to be speculative. The Pharisees claim, "No prophet arises from Galilee." Does the Bible state anywhere that no prophet would come from Galilee? There is no such statement. Actually, Jonah and possibly Nahum came from Galilee. And Jonah was a type of Jesus, who was the antitype.[10] "Indeed, Rabbi Eliezer (c. AD 90) said there was no tribe of Israel that failed to produce a prophet (B. *Sukkah* 27b)."[11] It is true that according to Micah's prophecy the Messiah would come forth from Bethlehem (Micah 5:2). People in the crowd had already pointed that out (John 7:42). But there is nothing in the Bible that says the Messiah could not also come from Galilee. This passage tells us that we must be extremely careful with arguments from silence. It is easy to twist Scripture, if we look for what it does not say instead of listening to what it actually teaches.

The fifth fallacy has to do with the fact that the truth may be more complex than it appears to be at first sight. The Pharisees failed to notice that Jesus was not only a Galilean. He was born in Judea, and He came from Galilee. In addition, He was not only the Son of David but also the Lord of David (Matt 22:42–45), the Son of the Most High. His was the throne of His father David (Luke 1:32). He was fully human and fully God, which is completely out-of-the-box thinking for humans. Even believers in the messianic prophecies were surprised when they had to deal with the phenomenon of who Jesus is. God is always good for surprises, even when He fulfills His promises. So, when we study Scripture, we have to keep in mind that there may be much more than what first meets the eye. We have to submit ourselves to the Word of God and allow it to reveal the beauty of its simplicity as well as the beauty of its complexity. This makes study exciting. We

---

[10] As Jonah was in the belly of a fish for three days and nights so Jesus would be in the tomb from Friday to Sunday (Matt 12:39–41).

[11] Quoted by D. A. Carson, *The Gospel According to John*, The Pillar New Testament Commentary (Grand Rapids, MI: Eerdmans Publishing, 1991), 332.

constantly learn more about God and Jesus, and our love for Him is rekindled and sustained.

The tragic effect of the Pharisees' wrong approach to biblical interpretation led to the rejection and death of the Messiah, the destruction of Jerusalem, and the further dispersion of the Jewish nation around the globe. Correct interpretation of Scripture matters! It is serious business.

An Approach to Biblical Interpretation

So how do we get it right? First, step back and acknowledge that we all have a personal perspective.

Second, try to overcome these biases by using the biblical text: read Scripture alone as well as with others, correcting one another.[12] Attempt to study the Bible—an ancient document that speaks with relevance to the current generation—with the eyes of the original audience, applying it to situations today as much as possible.[13] As previously discussed, fallacies should be avoided by being self-conscious and questioning what we do, why we are doing it, or what we are thinking of while we do it.

Third, acknowledge that Scripture has a divine dimension and that humans, being limited in our understanding of a transcendent God, are not only influenced by sin but also corrupted by it. This means we need God's help to comprehend His Word, and this is given us through the assistance of the Holy Spirit. However, even if it were not for sin that separates us from the Lord, God is not man. God is God, and His thoughts are much higher than ours (Isa 55:8–9). We have to admit that sometimes we might not fully grasp the meaning of a biblical text or might grasp it only partially. Nevertheless, as we engage in the sacred task of interpreting and understanding Scripture, we need to remain humble.

Fourth, and on a positive note, follow certain principles as described in this chapter. As God speaks to us in human terms and in different ways (different biblical authors and different kinds of biblical

---

[12] See Bauer, 81.

[13] If the biblical text is a divine revelation that has come to us through human instrumentalities—as we believe—it is not only given to the original audience but also to later generations (e.g., Deut 5:1–3; 1 Cor 10:6; Rev 1:3). Therefore, in most cases we do not need to distinguish sharply between what the text meant and what the text means. See Ekkehardt Mueller, "Guidelines for the Interpretation of Scripture," in *Understanding Scripture: An Adventist Approach*, Biblical Research Institute Studies 1, ed. George W. Reid (Silver Spring, MD: Biblical Research Institute, 2006), 111–134.

literature or genres), interpreting Scripture may at times be easier and at other times very complex. This chapter suggests a reasonably "simple" approach to interpretation without denying that there is much more that can and often needs to be done.

There are three different issues that relate to the interpretation of Scripture, and this chapter attempts to address all three, though briefly.

1. We may read and study passages of Scripture and need to understand/interpret it. The in-depth study of biblical texts and passages is called "exegesis."
2. We may not study biblical texts but may look for biblical topics and Scripture's big themes. This study is referred as to as doing biblical theology.
3. We may encounter modern challenges or problems to which we have to react as Christians. Such a study deals with biblical principles that help us formulate a biblical-theological response, which some associate with systematic theology and/or ethics.

Interpreting Biblical Texts and Passages: Exegesis

Exegetical Steps

I suggest the following ten steps to the interpretation of biblical passages:[14]

Step One

Take time. Reading Scripture can be a quick exercise and done mechanically. On the other hand, studying Scripture requires time. But the time spent is worth it because treasures can be unearthed that a quick reading cannot discover. Reading, understanding, and practicing receive a divine blessing (Rev 1:3).

Step Two

Turn to God in prayer for help to enlighten and understand His Word.

Step Three

Read the text/passage under consideration, as well as its context, repeatedly and diligently. Just the constant reading or even memorization of the passage may reveal much of its message.

---

[14] See Mueller. See also the important article by Richard M. Davidson, "Biblical Interpretation," in *Handbook of Seventh-day Adventist Theology*, ed. Raoul Dederen (Hagerstown, MD: Review and Herald, 2000), 58–104.

Step Four

Establish the text with the best possible reading. This is a step for biblical scholars because the multitude of biblical manuscripts may contain different readings that must be evaluated.[15]

Step Five

Translate the text. This is again a task for the biblical scholar. One should not be content with existing translations, but provide one's own rendition. This forces the researcher to see dimensions of the text that are naturally lost in the translation process because terms in the original languages may be wider or narrower than in the target language. Also, grammar and syntax may provide options lost in the translation process. However, for the average reader it is useful to read different serious translations to notice that there may be issues with the text.

Step Six

Investigate the context. This is the most important step. First, distinguish the historical context from the literary context. The historical context consists of the political, cultural, religious, and social situation when a biblical book was written and to which the text was addressed. The Bible itself, as well as archeology, geography, and history throw light on the historical context. The literary context is more easily accessible because it consists of the passages preceding and following a text, biblical books, and the entire Bible. The literary context determines to a large extent the meaning of words and the message of the passage. To isolate texts and disregard the context may lead to a distorted meaning. When biblical texts are used out of context they are easily misapplied and often serve as false prooftexts for a certain dogmatic understanding of things, rather than being used properly to prove what Scripture actually states.

The literary context includes the immediate context that surrounds a text or passage. Biblical passages are not randomly put together but are connected to each other, even if the connection is not always immediately evident. The interpreter may want to find such connections.

Beyond the immediate literary context is the context of the entire biblical book from which a passage is taken. It also includes literature

---

[15] Various criteria can help find the best possible reading. The discussion of such criteria, however, would require a paper by itself and cannot be described here. On the issue of textual variants, see chapter 3 by Clinton Wahlen, "Versions, Variants, and the Trustworthiness of Scripture," in the present volume.

of the same author—for example, Pauline or Johannine writings. This larger context must also be considered and is important to the interpretation of the passage.

The largest context is all of Scripture. Biblical texts oftentimes relate to other texts, either in the Old Testament or the New Testament,[16] and may reveal important themes of the Bible.

Studying the context may include providing a structure/outline of the context. It has also to do with the delimitation of biblical passages. Since the extant manuscripts do not contain chapters and verses, an outline may help set boundaries for passages, even though these still relate to the surrounding material. This is especially important in apocalyptic prophecy such as Daniel and Revelation, where the beginning and the end of a passage may be crucial to its interpretation. The study of the context may also need to consider different literary genres (kinds of material) and forms. These genres and forms comprise, among others, narratives including the Gospels, legal texts, Wisdom literature, prophetic literature (classical prophecy and apocalyptic literature), letters, genealogies, and parables. Although the general principles of interpretation apply more or less to all genres, there are yet differences that need to be taken into account.[17]

(Steps six to nine will be briefly illustrated with a New Testament case study.)

Step Seven

Analyze the text/passage. As considerable effort needs to be devoted to the study of the context, so also to the study of the passage itself. Analyzing a biblical text or passage includes the investigation of the structure of the text, its literary genre and form, and its larger units—sentences, phrases, and individual words. Consequently, grammar and syntax must be studied. Words and phrases need to be traced through the entire biblical book in which the text/passage is found—

---

[16] The study of these relations is referred to as "intertextuality." However, one must be careful not to read too much into a text. If the passage under consideration contains a full quotation from another biblical book, the relation is most obvious. If, however, only a part of a source text, a phrase, is use in the target text, we may call this *allusion*. An *echo* to a text in another text is the weakest connection. It occurs if only a word is used or the same concept. See chapter 8 by Richard M. Davidson, "Inner-Biblical Hermeneutics: The Use of Scripture by Bible Writers," in the present volume.

[17] For a more detailed description of approaches to different types of biblical literature, see George W. Reid, ed., *Understanding Scripture: An Adventist Approach*, Biblical Research Institute Studies 1 (Silver Spring, MD: Biblical Research Institute, 2006). This volume is highly recommended.

and sometimes even through the rest of Scripture. However, when this is done one needs to keep in mind that words may have different meanings in different contexts, may change over time, and that root meanings are not always useful. Still, the tracing of words and phrases may help determine the main message of the passage and its interconnectedness to other parts of Scripture. Biblical terms must be understood literally, unless the verse or immediate context indicate a figurative meaning.[18] Furthermore, words must be defined by the biblical context, not by modern usage.[19]

Literary and rhetorical features should be observed—for example, rhetorical questions, irony, sarcasm, and comparisons. Questions such as these must be asked: What is the time frame of the passage? What is its geographic location? Who are the important figures and how do they act and speak? What is the main message? An allegorical approach must be avoided.[20] However, biblical typology should be recognized.[21]

In the case of studying apocalyptic prophecy, an additional step must be taken. After all the previously mentioned exegetical steps have been employed, then and only then are students of the Word ready to carefully identify the symbols of the text with historical realities and developments.

Step Eight

Perform theological analysis. While exegesis can be compared to looking at the trees of a forest, theology looks at the larger picture, the forest itself. Theological analysis is interested in the theological motifs and themes found in a given passage: how they are developed, how they relate to the larger frame of the biblical book in which they appear, and how they contribute to the overall message of Scripture. Theological motifs can be larger categories or subjects that are used in the Bible such as the Godhead, Christ, the Holy Spirit, humankind, sin,

---

[18] Revelation is an exception because here the symbolic meaning is predominant. This is indicated with the word *semainō* in Revelation 1:1, which suggests that the content was symbolized to John.

[19] E.g., biblical judges do not directly correspond to judges in modern democracies. Scripture must be interpreted by Scripture, even on the level of vocabulary.

[20] In this case, an artificial meaning is given to a word or concept.

[21] Hans LaRondelle, *The Israel of God in Prophecy: Principles of Prophetic Interpretation* (Berrien Springs, MI: Andrews University Press, 1983), 36, provides the following definition of typology: "A type is an institution, a historical event or a historical person instituted by God to prefigure in an effective way a truth which in some way or another has to do with Christianity." Therefore, Jesus is, for instance, the second Adam (Rom 5:14), the second Moses (John 6:14; Deut 18:15), and the high priest according to the order of Melchizedek (Heb 7:11, 15, 17).

salvation, sanctuary, sanctification, the covenant, the Sabbath, the law of God, the state of the dead, and eschatology. But theology may also refer to other theological themes such as God's sovereignty, His love, prayer, patience, assurance, and obedience. A careful study of context and text begins to unfold these overarching theological themes. They can be more easily kept in mind than the details of exegesis, although the latter are important to ensure that our theological house is not being built on sand.

Step Nine

Apply the text to life today. This step must be based on the preceding steps. The application does not give us the liberty to do as we please. It has to be based on our study up to point 8. Here the type of literature has to come into consideration. Some texts are of a permanent nature (for example, those based on moral law and wisdom passages) while others are not (for example, those dealing with theocratic laws). In the first case, the application can be direct. In the second case, it has to be based on a permanent principle derived from the passage under consideration.

An application is necessary for personal devotion and for sermons. In the case of an application in a sermon, it is normally better to focus on the most important aspect of the text/passage rather than confuse the audience with many different points of application that people would probably struggle to remember. One major point, however, is easy for the audience to take home and ponder over.

One aspect of application is personalization. Because humans share so much with each other, the text can be personalized on an individual level and on a group level. The following questions are in order: What does God/Jesus want to tell me personally with this passage? How does it affect my devotion and commitment to Him, my spiritual life, my insights into His character and His plan for us, my actions, and my obedience? How can I respond to His message? How does the respective biblical text affect us as a church? In which areas of our church life does Jesus challenge us? How does the text educate and teach us? How does God use the biblical passage to comfort and encourage us? Our response to these questions can, for instance, be praise and thanksgiving, petitions and intercession, and/or changing our lives and value system.[22]

---

[22] See Davidson, "Biblical Interpretation," 86–87.

Step Ten

Use resources. Throughout the process of following these guidelines, the Bible as well as concordances, lexicons, and grammars are to be used. Other resources should not be utilized early on because they could easily serve as a shortcut. In a certain sense, wrestling with the biblical text until we have a deeper understanding makes the text our own. Using other resources too early limits our thinking to what others say, which may only be one aspect of reality. Therefore, bringing resources into our study is the last step. These resources include Ellen G. White writings, commentaries, theological books, articles, and other material. Reading widely can sharpen our work and point to neglected areas in our study.

What follows next is a short, non-exhaustive exegesis of a biblical passage that uses some of the exegetical steps suggested above. It is not exhaustive because otherwise it would fill a complete book.

Case Study

In 1 Corinthians 9:5 an interesting text is found. ESV provides the following translation: "Do we not have the right to take along a believing wife, as do the other apostles and the brothers of the Lord and Cephas?" NASB, NIV, and NJKV translate the text very similarly.

Context

The Larger Context

Paul's first letter to the Corinthians deals with the issue of liberty. Believers in Corinth understood that the gospel of Christ had set them free. They were liberated, saved, with all the privileges that belong to salvation—a wonderful and new situation. In his second letter to the Corinthians, Paul stresses that those who are in Christ are a new creation (2 Cor 5:17).

But the believers in Corinth had taken Christian liberty too far. They made themselves dependent on various teachers and allowed for division in the church (1 Cor 1–4). A process of alienation had taken place. In addition, they allowed for sexual immorality in the church (1 Cor 5–6) and had to be reminded about Christian marriage and a life dedicated to the service of God by remaining single (1 Cor 7). On top of this, believers in Corinth had created a class distinction between the strong and the weak, and between the rich and the poor (1 Cor 4:10; 8–11). The rich had their meals before the Lord's Supper, and the poor went hungry. Spiritual gifts that were given to church members were creating problems instead of uniting the church

(1 Cor 12–14). So, Paul felt he had to address the issue and explain what it means for Christians to be free. He wanted to bring about healing and genuine spiritual growth.

The Immediate Context

In 1 Corinthians 9:1 Paul begins by saying, "Am I not free? Am I not an apostle?" In verses 4 and 5 he continues, "Do we not have the right to eat and drink? Do we not have the right to take along a believing wife, as do the other apostles and the brothers of the Lord and Cephas?" The questions demand a positive answer. But Paul has not made use of all these rights. He has a higher goal which does not make him dependent on the pursuit of these rights. He is truly free.

Finally, he explains that Christian freedom has limitations in spite of all the privileges (1 Cor 9:19–22). True Christian freedom means not being enslaved by one's own ego. Paul is willing to relate to different kinds of people in order to save them or help them mature spiritually, without abandoning his convictions. So his Christian freedom allows him to serve, live under difficult circumstances, and love others whomay not be lovable at first glance (see also 1 Cor 13).

In this connection, Paul talks about the freedom to have a believing wife, one of the privileges that he did not claim for himself. While under certain circumstances it is good to be single, Paul also makes it clear that it is good to be married "in the Lord" (1 Cor 7:39).

Analysis of the Text

Christians and Marriage

It is very clear that the early apostles were married. The text indicates that Peter was married, as were the brothers of Jesus, James and Jude. Marriage is one of the remainders of the paradise that is still with us, designed to be a paradise on earth; so it was also for the believers in Corinth. It is God's wish for the majority of humanity to be married. Paul was an exception; he had the gift of celibacy. The freedom of being married also has limitations. Translations talk about a believing wife, not just any wife. However, this limitation can also be a great blessing, as God's commandments always are. By stressing marriage "in the Lord," Paul may refer back to Deuteronomy 7:3 and similar texts that warn of intermarriage with unbelievers.[23]

[23] Joshua 23:12–13 and Nehemiah 13:23–25.

Translation of 1 Corinthians 9:5

While the above translations of verse 5 reflect the intention of the original text, they have not translated the text literally. A literal translation reads: "Do we not have the right to take along *a sister*, a wife . . . ?" That means that Paul as well as all Christians have the privilege to live with a sister as wife. Yet Paul is not talking about incest or related issues.[24] He does not mean a biological sister but a spiritual sister.

The Term "Sister"

The term "sister" appears a number of times in the New Testament (twenty-six times). It usually describes literal sisters—that is, biological sisters (about sixteen times). For example, Lazarus was ill, and his sisters Mary and Martha sent a message to Jesus, their friend, to come and heal their brother (John 11:1, 3, 5, 28, 39).

However, the noun "sister" is also used metaphorically. In this case it describes a female follower of Christ. Those who do Jesus' will are His brothers and sisters (Matt 12:50). In some cases, Jesus' disciples may have to leave father and mother because after becoming Christians they are sometimes rejected by their own relatives. But Jesus promises that instead they will "receive a hundredfold now in this time, houses and brothers and sisters and mothers and children and lands, with persecutions, and in the age to come eternal life" (Mark 10:30). Phoebe and Apphia were sisters of the believers (Rom 16:1; Phlm 1:2). Younger female church members should not be rebuked when something goes wrong but should be encouraged as *sisters* (1 Tim 2:5). "If a brother or sister is poorly clothed and lacking in daily food" (Jas 2:15), he or she needs to be taken care of. They are family members.

So, followers of Christs are indeed rich and blessed. They have hundreds and thousands of sisters in Christ. These are as real as biological sisters, and sometimes even more so.

The Term "Brother"

The term "brother" (1 Cor 9:5) is found much more frequently than "sisters" in the New Testament (343 times), but as stated, "sisters" are also mentioned and not merely subsumed under the inclusive term "brother." While brothers in the New Testament can be biological

[24] In 1 Corinthians 5 Paul deals with a case of incest and urges the Corinthians to do something about it. One should also keep in mind that the Old Testament incest laws (Lev 18 and 20) are broader than incest as defined by some state laws today. They go beyond the bloodline and include people who have been added to a family by marriage.

brothers, mostly they are believers. The plural does not distinguish between males and females, but covers "all the children of a family, both male and female."[25] "Thus modern Eng. Versions often render it 'brothers and sisters,'" unless the context requires it to be limited to males.[26]

The term "brother" in a spiritual sense appears about 260 times in the New Testament,[27] the term "resurrection" (*anastasis*) about forty times, and the term *agapē* (love) about 120 times. To the noun *agapē* one would have to add the verb "to love" (*agapaō*) and the adjective "beloved" (*agapētos*) to surpass "brother," "sister," and "brotherhood."[28] In other words, the New Testament strongly emphasizes the brotherly and sisterly relationship of the believers. The term "brother" appears in all New Testament books with the exception of 2 John, where one finds "sister."

"But you are not to be called rabbi, for you have one teacher, and you are all brothers" (Matt 23:8). After the Jerusalem Council the delegates sent out a letter: "The brothers, both the apostles and the elders, to the brothers who are of the Gentiles in Antioch and Syria and Cilicia, greetings" (Acts 15:23). Onesimus is no longer to be regarded as a slave but as a "beloved brother" (Phlm 1:16). The brotherhood and sisterhood of Christ's followers is not just a present reality, but it extends back to the apostles: "I, John, your brother and partner in the tribulation and the kingdom and the patient endurance" (Rev 1:9). The New Testament seems to be less interested in an ecclesiastical hierarchy than a big family where believers consider each other as siblings and have a common Father.

Brotherhood reaches its climax in Jesus, whose brothers and sisters we are honored to become: Jesus is "the firstborn among many brothers" (Rom 8:29). He states, "For whoever does the will of God, he is my brother and sister and mother" (Mark 3:35).

> He [Jesus] is not ashamed to call them brothers, saying, "I will tell of your name to my brothers; in the midst of the congregation I will sing your praise." . . . Since therefore the children share in flesh and blood, he himself likewise

---

[25] Moisés Silva, ed., *New International Dictionary of New Testament Theology and Exegesis*, 2nd ed. (Grand Rapids, MI: Zondervan, 2014), 1:149.

[26] Ibid., 151.

[27] "Brother," "sister," and "brotherhood for believers" are found about 270 times.

[28] The instances of all three "love" terms taken together add up to about 320.

> partook of the same things, that through death he might destroy the one who has the power of death, that is, the devil, and deliver all those who through fear of death were subject to lifelong slavery. For surely it is not angels that he helps, but he helps the offspring of Abraham. Therefore, he had to be made like his brothers in every respect, so that he might become a merciful and faithful high priest in the service of God, to make propitiation for the sins of the people (Heb 2:11–17).

"Because Jesus became our brother, we are brothers and sisters of one another. The ruling principle in this relationship is love."[29]

Theological Analysis: The Family of God

With Jesus something very important happened—namely, the foundation of His church is established, which actually is His family, a brotherhood and sisterhood. It is truc that thc Israelites occasionally called themselves brothers. But with His church Jesus went way beyond this concept. His family is no longer a nation. It surpasses all boundaries of race, class, sex, social ranking, and whatever boundaries exist in this world. Jewish Christians are now brothers and sisters of Gentile Christians and vice versa. Christian men and women are brothers and sisters, as are slaves and their owners. This is the miracle and mystery of Christ's church.

But today this concept has to be recovered. As time goes by and the church grows, believers tend to forget that they are brothers and sisters. For instance, to call each other Mister and Missis, Pastor and Elder, professor and doctor in church may desensitize us to the fact that in reality we are siblings Fortunately, one can still experience brotherly and sisterly kindness, thoughtfulness, and love in Christ's church. Marcus Minucius Felix, who died around AD 250 in Rome, defends Christianity in his apology *Octavius*, in which a dialogue on Christianity takes place between the pagan Caecilius Natalis and the Christian Octavius Januarius. He writes, "They [the Christians] love one another almost before they know one another."[30]

Application: What the Term "Sister" Expresses

The terms "brother" and "sister" express closeness and intimacy.

---

[29] Silva, *New International Dictionary*, 151.

[30] Minucius Felix, "Octavius," translated by R. E. Wallis, *ANF* 4.177–178.

These terms picture a loving family as God intended it to be when He created Adam and Eve. My wife is my sister. Your wife is your sister. Your husband is your brother.

Typically, biological brothers do not need to be told to protect their biological sisters and care for them. Normally, brothers care for their sisters. Sisters also take care of their brothers, especially if they are younger brothers.

This is also the case in the church, which is called "the household of faith" (Gal 6:10) and "the household of God" (Eph 2:19; 1 Tim 3:15; 1 Pet 4:17). Therefore, one cannot easily get rid of brothers and sisters, whether biological or spiritual, unless we separate ourselves from the Father and our Lord Jesus Christ.

So, indifference to one's spouse is not an option; neither is divorce. But there is to be respect, attention, a compliment here and there, time for conversation, a little gift—in short, love. Christian couples need to cultivate their human union and their spiritual union. Husband and wife are spiritual siblings, members of the family of Christ, as are the entire community of believers.

Summary

In the enterprise of trying to better understand Scripture, God, and His will, a knowledge of biblical languages are helpful. For those who do not have such access, a look at different translations can be very helpful. The "believing wife" (ESV, CSB, NASB, NET, NIV, NKJV, NRSV), or "a wife who believes" (CEB), or "a Christian wife" (NAB, NJB, NLT) is the husband's "sister" (KJV, MIT, The Voice, TNT, WEB, YLT) in Christ. While the phrase "believing wife" and its variants express what the text in 1 Corinthians 9:5 states, it may miss, to some extent, the aspect of affection and fondness, and the bond of love, that is expressed through the term "sister" and which is so important for marriages and also for the relationships in the church. However, this study does not suggest that the above translations should be dismissed; it only argues that by being mindful of the fact that the Greek text uses the term "sister," the understanding of a Christian wife may be broadened by revealing a closeness, intimacy, and aspects of multilevel relations that followers of Christ today may need to hear again. At the same time, marriage is not only an individualistic covenant between husband and wife but also has a larger dimension as it is incorporated into the community of believers, the family of God.

Interpreting Biblical Themes: Theology

General Discussion

Apart from studies of biblical texts, as just exemplified, there are also thematic studies that deal with biblical topics. These can be subdivided, first into thematic/topical studies in a biblical book—for instance, the sanctuary in Hebrews or a theology of worship in Revelation. Second, they can be expanded to include the entire New Testament or Old Testament. In this case we would not be dealing, for instance, with the theology of Isaiah or the theology of Matthew only, but with a theology of the entire Old Testament or the entire New Testament. As Adventists we have no problem with such an approach because we believe that the entire Scripture is the Word of God, although some critical scholars would be more hesitant to pursue such a study.

The problem is aggravated with the third subdivision: namely, when we are trying to establish a biblical theology comprising the entire canon of Scripture—for instance, a biblical theology of eschatology (the last things) in which both Old Testament and New Testament are represented. Again, we believe this is possible. But it is no secret that theological emphases in different biblical books differ, that biblical vocabulary is used by different authors slightly differently, and that in some cases a development of understanding can be seen in Scripture. For example, Old Testament eschatology expected largely that the current evil age (old age) would be supplanted by the future messianic kingdom (new age). However, New Testament eschatology differentiates: the current evil age (old age) is shaken by the coming of the kingdom of God in the incarnation of Jesus Christ, but the current evil age and the messianic kingdom (new age) overlap for a while, until the evil age comes to an end and God's kingdom of grace becomes God's kingdom of glory exclusively. Therefore, we see in New Testament authors the tension between the "already" and the "not yet." We are already saved here and now and belong to the kingdom of heaven, but we are not yet there completely and are waiting for the second coming and the glorification.

Now, what we describe here looks at the big picture of biblical theology. A consistent biblical theology must attempt to embrace harmoniously all phenomena on a given subject described in the Old Testament and the New Testament and integrate them into a theological whole.[31] In some cases, a few questions may still remain open, but nevertheless a big picture emerges that gives us enough information to believe and hold on to.[32]

This chapter proposes approaching a theological study by gathering biblical data and concepts. They are enshrined in biblical passages. For instance, a study of biblical themes such as the Sabbath or the resurrection of the dead in Scripture would include a search in Scripture for related terms —"Sabbath," "rest," "complete rest," and "to rest," for example. Also included would be an investigation of these texts in their contexts, applying briefly the above mentioned exegetical steps to these texts, and trying to formulate a theology of the topic by looking at all references to the respective topic.

Case Study

The case study mentioned here is not fully spelled out. To do so would go beyond the scope of this paper. It consists of an outline that may give an impression of how a theological topic may be approached. The reader is encouraged to look at a piece dealing with biblical theology in order to get a better grasp of the difference between an exegetical and a theological approach.

The topic chosen is the Christology of Revelation. Christology has been approached differently. Our definition would be the study of Jesus in John's Apocalypse by way of the names, titles, and concepts associated with Him, the revelation of His nature and character, the description of His work, and His influence on people with implications for His followers.

---

[31] There is no room here to explore biblical theology and systematic theology more deeply. So we need to turn to the practical approach. However, the reader may want to consult some Adventist authors such as Gerhard F. Hasel, *Old Testament Theology: Basic Issues in the Current Debate* (Grand Rapids, MI: Eerdmans, 1978), Gerhard F. Hasel, *New Testament Theology: Basic Issues in the Current Debate* (Grand Rapids, MI: Eerdmans, 1978); Gerhard F. Hasel, *Old Testament Theology: Basic Issues in the Current Debate,* 4th ed. (Grand Rapids, MI: Eerdmans, 1991); Ángel Rodríguez, "Doing Theology in the Adventist Church: Role of the Theologian" (unpublished manuscript, February 2003); Ekkehardt Mueller, "The Divisiveness of Theology," https://adventistbiblicalresearch.org/sites/default/files/pdf/Divisiveness%20of%20Theology.pdf (accessed October 21, 2019); and John C. Peckham, *Canonical Theology: The Biblical Canon, Sola Scriptura, and Theological Method* (Grand Rapids, MI: Eerdmans, 2016).

[32] For instance, the New Testament teaches that Jesus was human and divine. What happened to Christ's divinity with His death on the cross is difficult to determine. We need to remember we are dealing with God and not a human being. Additionally, even if such a question is not completely clear, it does not hinder us from accepting the clear teaching on the Godhead and living our lives with Christ. We need to exhibit humility and, sometimes, the ability to suspend our judgment.

The Christology of Revelation

I. Designations and Symbols Used for Jesus in Revelation
   1. The Different Names and Depictions of Jesus
   2. Disputed Images of Jesus
   3. General Observations
      a. Standard Designations for Jesus in the New Testament
      b. Designations that Occur Seldomly in the New Testament
      c. Unique Designations of Jesus in Revelation
II. Overview of Jesus in Revelation
   1. Jesus in the Prologue (Rev 1:1–8)
   2. Jesus and the Message to the Seven Churches (Rev 1:9–3:22)
   3. Jesus and the Seven Seals
   4. Jesus and the Seven Trumpets (Rev 8:2–11:18)
   5. Jesus and the Satanic Trinity (Rev 11:19–14:20)
   6. Jesus and the Seven Plagues (Rev 15–16)
   7. Jesus and the Judgment on Babylon (Rev 17–18)
   8. Jesus, His Marriage Supper, Armageddon, and the Millennium (Rev 19–20)
   9. Jesus and the New Earth and the New Jerusalem (Rev 21:1–22:5)
   10. Jesus in the Epilogue (Rev 22:6–21)
III. Christ's Divinity
   1. Humanity and Divinity
   2. Designation and Titles that Jesus Shares with God the Father
   3. Descriptions and Titles Pointing to Jesus' Divinity
   4. Jesus in the Hymns of the Seal Vision
   5. What Father and Son Share
   6. The Trinity
   7. The Imitation of Jesus
   8. Implications
IV. Jesus as the Lamb
   1. The Nature and Character of the Lamb
      a. The Lamb as a Sacrificial Animal
      b. The Lion and the Lamb
   2. Jesus' Actions and His Ministry
      a. Gaining the Victory
      b. The Theology of the Cross
      c. Effects on His People
      d. The Lamb and Salvation History
      e. The Lamb and Judgment
      f. The Lamb and the Consummation

3. The People of the Lamb
   a. Designations of the People of the Lamb
   b. Discipleship
   c. Service

V. Summary and Conclusion[33]

Interpreting Modern Challenges and Ethical Issues: Theology

This last section about interpretation deals with issues that are not directly mentioned in Scripture. These are relevant issues to which Christians need to respond, such as: How should we relate to embryonic stem cell research, human cloning, and artificial intelligence? Is it morally responsible to use public media, with all the damage they may cause? May Christians today have some kind of slaves because the Bible does not clearly prohibit slavery? What about global warming, ecology, and our responsibility to care for planet earth? In the absence of a clear-cut biblical prohibition, "You shall not smoke," should we be free to gamble, take narcotic drugs, drink alcohol, and smoke tobacco?

These and similar questions cannot be answered by just referring to one or more Bible texts, as some Adventists desire. Some Christians would argue, "Give me a Bible text, and I am fine." But there may be no Bible text at all that directly deals with these issues. God requires more from us than memorizing and applying biblical references. We must learn to think through issues that confront us. We must have the mind of Christ to deal with questions that humanity never had to deal with in the past. Undoubtedly, many of these matters are important and a number of them directly influence daily life. They cannot be ignored.

Christians respond to these challenges differently.[34] One group argues that what Scripture does not mention is prohibited. Such an approach would be difficult to maintain. We would not be allowed to have electricity, travel with a car or plane, have indoor plumbing, use

---

[33] For the actual three-part article, see Ekkehardt Mueller, "Christological Concepts in the Book of Revelation–Part 1: Jesus in the Apocalypse," *Journal of the Adventist Theological Society* 22/1–2 (2010): 276–305; Ekkehardt Mueller, "Christological Concepts in the Book of Revelation–Part 2: Christ's Divinity," *Journal of the Adventist Theological Society* 21/1 (2011): 66–83; and Ekkehardt Mueller, "Christological Concepts in the Book of Revelation–Part 3: The Lamb Christology," *Journal of the Adventist Theological Society* 21/2 (2011): 42–66.

[34] See Ekkehardt Mueller, "Hermeneutical Guidelines for Dealing with Theological Questions," *Reflections: The BRI Newsletter* (October 2012): 1–7.

telephones, computers, etc. Advances in sciences and medicine would be prohibited, as would be the Adventist church structure and all Adventist institutions. Another group takes the opposite approach, in that what is not explicitly prohibited in Scripture is permitted. This would possibly allow for human trafficking, different forms of abuse, taking of narcotic drugs, a congregationalist approach to church structure, and many other issues. A third group mixes the two approaches and takes whichever one is more convenient and pragmatic in a given situation, even though this may be logically inconsistent. But it is never wise to decide issues just on pragmatic grounds, no matter how widely spread situational ethics is these days. All three approaches use in some way or another arguments from silence, as mentioned at the beginning of this chapter.

The fourth group believes that even in such cases where clear biblical references are not available, believers should still seek God's guidance. They believe that such guidance is indeed provided by Scripture—not in the form of individual biblical texts, but in the form of biblical principles. This is the position that Adventists take in many cases. Following biblical principles, they refrain from smoking although there is no single text spelling this out. To a large extent the Adventist health message is based on biblical principles, as are Adventist education, Sabbath School, etc. Jesus Himself argued with a biblical principle when confronted with the question of divorce. He went to the creation account, which does not mention divorce but describes the nature of marriage (Matt 19:4–6, 8) and provides divine principles that help frame marriage according to God's original design.

Recently the Adventist Church voted a statement on abortion. The statement is based on the following biblical principles: 1) the value and sacredness of human life as portrayed throughout Scripture, 2) God's consideration of the unborn child as human life, 3) the unrestricted applicability of the commandment "You shall not kill," 4) God's ownership of all things—including our lives—and our responsibility to serve Him as stewards, 5) God's care for the weak and vulnerable, and 6) God's grace.[35]

How should we proceed in practice?

First, how do we find biblical principles and apply them to the issues we face? Answer: We read Scripture widely and on a

---

[35] To read the statement and see how the issue is handled, see https://www.adventist.org/articles/statement-on-the-biblical-view-of-unborn-life-and-its-implications-for-abortion/ (accessed June 1, 2020).

> regular basis. We ask the Holy Spirit to guide us to the right principles. Also the community of believers is important because generally the church as a whole is able to point us to biblical principles that are applicable to specific situations. Second, which additional criteria should be utilized? (a) When looking for biblical principles, those principles have priority that share the same or similar concerns with the question under investigation. . . . (b) The solution to a specific case must be in harmony with other biblical teachings on the same subject as well as with the entire biblical message. . . . (c) Some issues/principles should be traced throughout the Bible in order to see whether or not changes in practice have taken place. If changes can be observed, the direction of change may be further pursued, as was done, for example, by Christians in the case of the abolition of slavery.[36]

Let us backtrack. In the case of an issue not covered directly by Scripture, we must still go to the Bible and look for biblical principles. These principles are found in groups of related biblical texts and passages. These passages are to be investigated exegetically in order not to misuse them. Then we "extract" from them as a group their theological principles, which may form the guidelines that can help us to make biblical-theological decisions. We aim at following our Lord, understanding His will, and practicing it.

Summary and Conclusion

This chapter has dealt with how to practically go about interpreting Scripture and has addressed three different scenarios. The first was a study of a biblical text or passage, establishing some guidelines of how to do exegesis in order to be faithful to Scripture.

The second scenario was a study of a biblical topic or a theological concept that is fully or partially found in Scripture. In this case, an exegetical approach is not sufficient, and a theological approach is demanded. However, a theological approach does not do away with exegetical checking of biblical data.

With the third type of scenario, the direct biblical data in form of texts or topics may be absent. Still, Scripture speaks to us through its inherent principles. This study has suggested looking for biblical

---

[36] Mueller, "Hermeneutical Guidelines," 6.

principles for each given case. From these principles, found in various places in Scripture, we return to checking exegetically to determine if the texts really say what we think they do. If they do, we are safe to use their theological meaning in the form of biblical principles. The result should lead to decisions and actions in everyday life. Below is an attempt to outline these approaches:

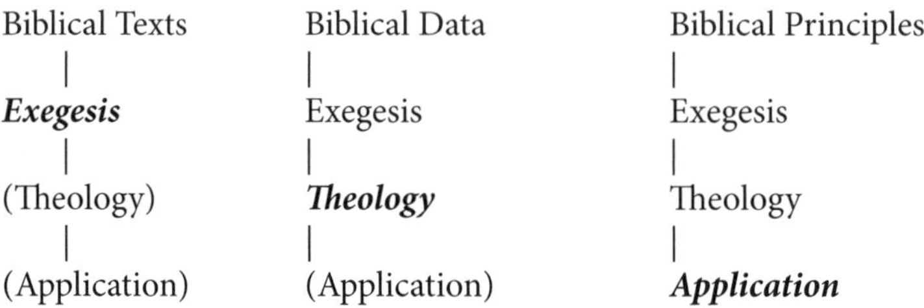

The approaches to scriptural interpretation and doing theology presented in this chapter are aimed at gaining a better understanding of God and His plan of salvation in the context of the great controversy. They aim at being true to Scripture and open to new growth in the knowledge of God and divine correction (2 Tim 3:16). Adventist theological thinking is Christ-centered, and practice-oriented in the positive sense. It takes into account contemporary questions and challenges and tries to respond to them. At the end what counts is a deeper relationship with Jesus Christ, our Savior and Lord, by knowing Him more and more through His Word.

CHAPTER 8

Inner-Biblical Hermeneutics: The Use of Scripture by Bible Writers

Richard M. Davidson

> "The relationship between Old and New Testaments: that is just about the whole story; the whole of theology is involved in that".—N. H. Ridderbos[1]

One of the major issues in biblical hermeneutics is inner-biblical hermeneutics—that is, the use of earlier Scripture by later Bible writers.[2] Scholars have focused mainly upon the relationship between the Old Testament and the New Testament. Walter Kaiser states what is still as true for the twenty-first century as for the previous one: "The relationship between the Old Testament and the New Testament stands as one of the foremost, if not the leading, problems in biblical research of this century."[3]

A prominent biblical scholar who brought this issue to the forefront of modern discussion was Gerhard F. Hasel, whose books on Old Testament and New Testament theology were for many years standard textbooks for some ninety seminaries across North America and beyond.[4] His

---

[1] N. H. Ridderbos, "De verhouding van het Oude en het Nieuwe Testament," *Gereformeerd theologisch Tijdschrift* 68 (1968): 97, cited by Henning Graf Reventlow, *Problems of Biblical Theology in the Twentieth Century*, trans. John Bowden (Philadelphia, PA: Fortress, 1986), 11.

[2] For a very helpful earlier study on inner-biblical interpretation and intertextuality, see Ganoune Diop, "Innerbiblical Interpretation: Reading the Scriptures Intertextually," in *Understanding Scripture: An Adventist Approach*, ed. George W. Reid (Silver Spring, MD: Biblical Research Institute, 2005), 135–151. The present study is in full harmony with Diop's position, but takes a complementary approach in the way the issues are addressed.

[3] Walter C. Kaiser, Jr., *The Uses of the Old Testament in the New* (Chicago, IL: Moody, 1985), 2.

[4] Gerhard F. Hasel, *Old Testament Theology: Basic Issues in the Current Debate*, 4th ed. (Grand

chapters dealing with the relationship between the Testaments trace the history of the debate over this subject[5] and suggest seven patterns of historical and theological relationships that characterize the connection between the Old Testament and the New Testament: 1) the continuous history of God's people, 2) quotations (and allusions), 3) key theological terms, 4) unity of major themes, 5) typology, 6) promise/prediction and fulfillment, and 7) the "big picture" of salvation history. Unfortunately, Gerhard F. Hasel's untimely death prevented him from exploring further this multiplex relationship between the Testaments.

Even though Hasel focused primarily on describing the relationship between the Testaments, his multiplex approach also accurately describes the basic ways the New Testament writers used the Old Testament. Since the publication of Hasel's book, increased attention has been extended beyond the New Testament use of the Old Testament, to include the inner-biblical hermeneutic within the Old Testament—how the later Old Testament writers used earlier Old Testament Scriture.[6] This study organizes a discussion of inner-biblical hermeneutics following Hasel's multiplex synthesis of approaches,[7] examining for each approach the use of earlier Old Testament Scripture by later Old Testament writers, and the use of Old Testament Scripture by New Testament Bible writers.

A fundamental question to be raised in this chapter is whether or not the later Bible writers remain faithful to the original contexts in their

---

Rapids, MI: Eerdmans, 1991); Gerhard F. Hasel, *New Testament Theology: Basic Issues in the Current Debate* (Grand Rapids, MI: Eerdmans, 1978).

[5] Gerhard F. Hasel, *Old Testament Theology*, 172–193, describes how some scholars (e.g., Rudolph Bultmann and Friedrich Baumgärtel), following in the footsteps of the second-century heretic Marcion, see a radical discontinuity between the Old Testament and the New Testament, even regarding the Old Testament as a book of a non-Christian religion. Others (e.g., Wilhelm Vischer and A. A. van Ruler) have gone to the opposite extreme, suggesting that the Old Testament is the only true Scripture, and the New Testament is only its "explanatory glossary" (A. A. van Ruler, *The Christian Church and the Old Testament* [Grand Rapids, MI: Eerdmans, 1971], 74). This chapter affirms that the Old Testament and New Testament are equally inspired and equally important, with a basic continuity between the Testaments.

[6] See Michael Fishbane, *Biblical Interpretation in Ancient Israel* (Oxford: Clarendon, 1985). For a survey of interpretation of inner-biblical hermeneutics within the Old Testament since Fishbane, see esp. Kenneth Bergland, "Reading as a Disclosure of the Thoughts of the Heart: Proto-Halakhic Reuse and Appropriation between Torah and the Prophets" (PhD diss., Andrews University, 2018), 19–160.

[7] As far as the author of the present study is aware, no one has attempted to organize the material concerning the relationship between the Testaments and inner-biblical hermeneutics around these seven approaches, and he offers this attempt in memory of his *Doktorvater*, Gerhard F. Hasel.

use of earlier biblical material. Many modern biblical scholars claim that the New Testament writers often do not incorporate sound exegesis, but rather "twist the Scriptures"[8] by utilizing Christological reapplication based upon first-century interpretational techniques such as rabbinic midrash, Hellenistic allegory, and/or Qumran-style *raz pesher* ("mystery interpretation").[9] It is further suggested by some of these scholars that since the New Testament writers (and Jesus) were inspired, they had the right and authority under the Holy Spirit's guidance to reinterpret and reapply to Jesus what originally in the Old Testament did not refer to Him,[10] or to see a "fuller" meaning in the Old Testament that was intended by God but transcends the human author's intent (*sensus plenior*) and normally "cannot be demonstrated by means of traditional grammatical-historical exegesis."[11]

However, in recent decades studies are challenging the hypothesis that later biblical writers misinterpreted earlier biblical writings, taking them out of context and using interpretational techniques common to their culture that are today considered "eisegesis" (reading into the text a meaning that is not there). For example, against those who assert that the New Testament writers interpreted the Old Testament using rabbinic midrash, David Instone-Brewer examines all the relevant data of rabbinic interpretation, separating the hermeneutical strategies of rabbis before the destruction of the temple in AD 70 from the rabbinic strategies after AD 70, and comes to the startling conclusion that "the predecessors of the rabbis before 70 CE [AD] did not interpret Scripture out of context, did not look for any meaning in Scripture

---

[8] Note the title of the article by S. Vernon McCasland's, "Matthew Twists the Scriptures," *Journal of Biblical Literature* 80 (1961): 143–148.

[9] For a discussion of these methods and the claim that the New Testament writers utilized these approaches, see, e.g., Richard N. Longenecker, *Biblical Exegesis in the Apostolic Period* (Grand Rapids, MI: Eerdmans, 1975), 218 and Peter Enns, *Inspiration and Incarnation: Evangelicals and the Problem of the Old Testament* (Grand Rapids, MI: Baker, 2015), 133–134, 142–143.

[10] See, e.g., Longenecker, *Biblical Exegesis*, 207.

[11] Douglas J. Moo, "The Problem of Sensius Plenior," in *Hermeneutics, Authority, and Canon*, ed. D. A. Carson and J. D. Woodbridge (Grand Rapids, MI: Zondervan, 1986), 201. The dominant voice in the *sensus plenior* discussion, especially among Catholic scholars, is Raymond E. Brown. See esp. his *The* Sensus Plenior *of Sacred Scripture* (Baltimore, MD: St. Mary's University, 1955). Ibid., 92, describes *sensus plenior* as "that additional deeper meaning, intended by God but not clearly intended by the human author, which is seen to exist in the words of a biblical text (or group of texts, or even a whole book) when they are studied in the light of further revelation or development in the understanding of revelation." Moo, "Sensus Plenior," 202, points out that in the definition provided by Brown, "a valid *sensus plenior* can be adduced only on the basis of 'revelation' or 'further development in revelation.' For Brown and other Roman Catholics, this authority includes the church (the 'magesterium') and the New Testament."

other than the plain sense, and did not change the text to fit their interpretation, though the later rabbis did all these things."[12] Since most of the New Testament writers wrote before AD 70, the implication is that they also did not interpret Scripture out of context or impose a meaning upon the text beyond the plain sense. A growing number of biblical scholars forcefully demonstrate (with illustrative biblical evidence) that the New Testament writers use the Old Testament contextually, in continuity and harmony with the meaning found in the Old Testament passages they cite.[13] It is the thesis of this chapter that although the later Bible writers used earlier Scripture in a variety of ways, they were faithful exegetes and theologians in their inner-biblical hermeneutics, remaining true to the meaning of those earlier biblical passages seen in their larger original context, even as they—under inspiration—unfolded by various means the further significance of those passages for their own times and ours.[14] We turn now to the major ways that later biblical writers used earlier Scripture.[15]

---

[12] David Instone-Brewer, *Techniques and Assumptions in Jewish Exegesis before 70 CE* (Tübingen: J. C. B. Mohr, 1992), 1.

[13] Ordered chronologically, see esp. the following: Kaiser, *Uses of the Old Testament*; Richard M. Davidson, "Interpreting Scripture: An Hermeneutical 'Decalogue,'" *Journal of the Adventist Theological Society* 4/2 (1993): 95–114; idem, "New Testament Use of the Old Testament," *Journal of the Adventist Theological Society* 5/1 (1994): 14–39; G. K. Beale, "Did Jesus and His Followers Preach the Right Doctrine from the Wrong Texts? An Examination of the Presuppositions of Jesus's and the Apostles' Exegetical Method," in *The Right Doctrine from the Wrong Texts? Essays on the Use of the Old Testament in the New*, ed. G. K. Beale (Grand Rapids, MI: Baker, 1994), 387–390; James M. Hamilton, Jr., "The Skull Crushing Seed of the Woman: Inner-Biblical Interpretation of Genesis 3:15," *Southern Baptist Journal of Theology* 10 (2006): 30–32; Darrell Bock, "Single Meaning, Multiple Contexts and Referents: The New Testament's Legitimate, Accurate, and Multifaceted Use of the Old," in *Three Views on the New Testament Use of the Old Testament*, ed. Kenneth Berding and Jonathan Lunde, Counterpoints: Bible and Theology (Grand Rapids, MI: Zondervan, 2008), 105–151; Walter Kaiser, Jr., "Single Meaning, Unified Referents: Accurate and Authoritative Citations of the Old Testament by the New Testament," in *Three View on the New Testament Use of the Old Testament*, ed. Kenneth Berding and Jonathan Lunde, Counterpoints: Bible and Theology (Grand Rapids, MI: Zondervan, 2008), 45–89; Michael Rydelnik, *The Messianic Hope: Is the Hebrew Bible Really Messianic?*, New American Commentary Studies in Bible and Theology (Nashville, TN: Broadman and Holman, 2010), 95–111; and Abner Chou, *The Hermeneutics of the Biblical Writers: Learning to Interpret Scripture from the Prophets and Apostles* (Grand Rapids, MI: Kregel, 2018).

[14] In establishing and illustrating this thesis, the author adopts, adapts, and/or updates some parts of his previous articles on the subject: Richard M. Davidson, "New Testament Use of the Old Testament," *Journal of the Adventist Theological Society* 5/1 (1994): 14–39 and idem, "Interpreting Scripture: An Hermeneutical 'Decalogue,'" *Andrews University Seminary Studies* 4/2 (1993): 95–114.

[15] Some examples of inner-biblical hermeneutics could be placed in one of several of these categories because they contain features common to more than one category, but these will be discussed under the category in which the primary issue best fits.

Continuous History of God's People

Later biblical writers consistently remain faithful to the writings of earlier Scripture in their references to the history of God's people. With regard to the early history of God's people in Genesis 1–11, the chrono-genealogies (Gen 5–11) covering the complete line of descendants from Adam to Abraham[16] are repeated accurately by the writer of Chronicles toward the end of the Old Testament period (1 Chr 1), and again by Luke at the beginning of his gospel (Luke 3).[17] The main stories of this period are alluded to by the Old Testament writings and the Prophets.[18] Jesus and *all* New Testament writers refer to Genesis 1–11, with the underlying assumption that it is literal, reliable history, and every chapter of Genesis 1–11 is referred to somewhere in the New Testament.[19]

Moving to the history of Israel, later Old Testament writers summarize this history with careful attention to detail and accuracy, paying attention to the theological dimensions of this history. For example, Psalms 78 and 105–106 provide succinct overviews of the history of Israel, highlighting God's covenant faithfulness and mighty power, and the underlying causes of Israel's success and failure depending upon their faithfulness or unfaithfulness to God.[20] The Old Testament Prophets are replete with allusions to Old Testament history, with the book of Hosea containing the most allusions to Israel's history of any Old Testament prophet.[21] The story of the exodus is a special focus of attention: virtually every book of the Bible after the book of

---

[16] See esp. Gerhard F. Hasel, "Genesis 5 and 11: Chronogenealogy in the Biblical History of Beginnings," *Origins* 7 (1980): 23–37; Travis R. Freeman, "A New Look at the Genesis 5 and 11 Fluidity Problem," *Andrews University Seminary Studies* 42 (2004): 259–286; and Bernard White, "Revisiting Genesis 5 and 11: A Close Look at the Chronogenealogies," *Andrews University Seminary Studies* 53 (2015): 253–277.

[17] The apparent inconsistencies between the genealogies of Luke 3 and Matthew 1 are discussed in Francis D. Nichol, ed., *Seventh-day Adventist Bible Commentary* (Hagerstown, MD: Review and Herald, 1980), 5:720–723 (in the comments on Luke 3:23, 27, and 36).

[18] See, e.g., the reference to the fall of Adam in Hosea 6:7 and to Noah and the flood in Isaiah 54:9 and Ezekiel 14:14, 20. For allusions to the sons of Adam and Eve, see aso Radiša Antić, "Cain, Abel, Seth, and the Meaning of Human Life as Portrayed in the Books of Genesis and Ecclesiastes," *Andrews University Seminary Studies* 44 (2006): 203–211.

[19] See Henry Morris, *The Remarkable Birth of Planet Earth* (Minneapolis, MN: Bethany Fellowship, 1972), Appendix B: "New Testament References to Genesis 1–11" (99–101).

[20] Ellen G. White, *Testimonies to Ministers and Gospel Workers* (Mountain View, CA: Pacific Press, 1923), 98 regards Psalm 105–106 of such importance that she urges they be read every week.

[21] See Richard M. Davidson, "Hosea," in *Andrews Bible Commentary: Old Testament*, ed. Ángel Manuel Rodríguez (Berrien Springs, MI: Andrews University Press, 2020), 1062-1078.

Exodus contains reverberations of the exodus account.[22] The sweep of Israel's history is also accurately portrayed in the prayers of the later Old Testament prophets who lived at the end of Old Testament times (see esp. Dan 9:1–19; Neh 9:1–38), as well as the prayers of the New Testament apostles and prophets (Stephen in Acts 7:1–53 and Paul in Acts 13:13–41).

Jesus and the New Testament writers frequently allude to various events in the Old Testament history of Israel (God's people), remaining accurate to the facts of that history, and building upon that history to draw lessons and implications for the people of God in their time and ours. Examples of this are found in the copious references to Old Testament history by Paul in his discussions of the law, the gospel, Christ, and the church in Romans 1–3, Galatians 3–4, and Ephesians 1.[23] The New Testament church is regarded by the New Testament writers as in basic continuity with the Old Testament Israel, the church being the eschatological remnant of faithful Israel (see esp. Rom 9–11).[24] In short, later biblical writers, and Jesus Himself, use Old Testament history accurately and responsibly, and their theological insights and lessons drawn from that history are true to the earlier writers' portrayal of the history.

The one major passage which scholars have often regarded as a New Testament misuse of Old Testament history is Paul's alleged "allegory" of the two covenants in Galatians 4. Hence this study looks more closely at this verse.

Case Study—Paul's References to Old Testament History in Galatians 4:21–31: Allegory?

Paul has been frequently charged with allegorizing in his discussion of the two covenants in Galatians 4. However, several classic studies of this passage have concluded that despite Paul's use of the verb *allēgoreō* in Galatians 4:24, he does not engage in what the modern term "allegory" implies. Instead, Paul rather recognizes the salvation-historical framework

---

[22] See esp. Bryan D. Estelle, *Echoes of Exodus: Tracing a Biblical Motif* (Downers Grove, IL: InterVarsity, 2018) and Alastair J. Roberts and Andrew Wilson, *Echoes of Exodus: Tracing Themes of Redemption through Scripture* (Wheaton, IL: Crossway, 2018).

[23] See, e.g., Richard P. Choi, "Abraham Our Father: Paul's Voice in the Covenantal Debate of the Second Temple Period" (PhD diss., Fuller Theological Seminary, 1997).

[24] See Richard M. Davidson, "Israel and the Church: Continuity and Discontinuity—I and II," in *Message, Mission, and the Unity of the Church,* Biblical Research Institute Studies in Adventist Ecclesiology 2, ed. Ángel Manuel Rodríguez (Silver Spring, MD: Biblical Research Institute, 2013), 375–428. As these articles show, there are also discontinuities because of Israel's withdrawal from the theocracy by the decisions of its leaders, but God's original ultimate plan for Israel will ultimately be fulfilled to the faithful "Israel" of all ages in the new earth.

of the Old Testament accounts to which he refers in this passage.[25]

One should remember that the Greek verb *allēgoreō* that Paul employs can merely mean "to use analogy or likeness to express something,"[26] and not involve the Platonic-Philonic mode of allegorism. Paul does not assign arbitrary, fanciful meanings to the participants in his "allegory," as was the case in the Jewish allegorism of Philo (and the later Christian allegorical method of the Alexandrian school).[27] In this passage, Paul grasps the heart of parallel historical experiences that centered around salvation by works. Israel at Sinai entered into a covenant with God that (at least initially) they thought they could fulfill by their own efforts. Abraham's union with Hagar was an attempt to fulfill God's promise by human means. These two historical occurrences illustrate the experience of "Jerusalem and her children," contemporary with Paul, who were seeking a righteousness by works.

By contrast, Paul presents the account of the birth of Isaac, accomplished not by the prowess of man, but by the miracle of God in faithfulness to His promise. The birth of Isaac, the promised "seed," embodies the principle of righteousness by faith, and illustrates the experience of Abraham's future spiritual "seed" of true, heavenly Jerusalem and its children. All believers in Christ are the children of promise, Abraham's seed (Gal 3:29). Paul points to rich salvation-historical correspondences illustrating the principles of righteousness by works versus righteousness by faith, and in so doing provides a clear designation of the Christian church as the seed of Abraham, the children of promise.

In Galatians 4:21–31, Paul says, in effect, that the experiences of Sarah and Hagar have a deeper meaning than just telling a story. The two women's experiences represent two rival systems for attaining righteousness—righteousness by faith and righteousness by works. Paul recognizes that in Genesis, Moses presents Hagar's experience with Abraham as an attempt to fulfill the divine promise of a son by taking

---

[25] See, e.g., Leon Morris, *Galatians: Paul's Charter of Christian Freedom* (Downers Grove, IL: InterVarsity, 1996), 143–150; Skip MacCarty, *In Granite or Ingrained? What the Old and New Covenants Reveal about the Gospel, the Law, and the Sabbath* (Berrien Springs, MI: Andrews University Press, 2009), 92–99; and Peter Balla, "Paul's Use of Slavery Imagery in the Hagar Allegory," *In die Skriflig* 43 (2009): 119–134.

[26] W. Bauer, F.W. Danker, W.F. Arndt, and F. W. Gingrich, *Greek-English Lexicon of the New Testament and Other Early Christian Literature*, 3rd ed. (Chicago: University of Chicago Press, 1999), 46 (s.v. ἀλληγορέω).

[27] For an analysis of early Jewish and Christian allegory borrowed from Hellenistic allegorical methods, in contradistinction to biblical typology, see, e.g., Richard M. Davidson, *Typology in Scripture: A Study of Hermeneutical* Τύπος *Structures*, Andrews University Seminary Doctoral Dissertation Series 2 (Berrien Springs, MI: Andrews University Press, 1981), 17–27.

things into one's own hands instead of trusting God; and in Exodus, Moses presents a parallel (initial) experience of the children of Israel at Mount Sinai with their legalistic response to God; and both find a correspondence in contemporary (first-century) Judaism. It is the way of bondage—of righteousness by works. The experience of Sarah, on the other hand (trusting God to fulfill the promise of a son even when it seems humanly impossible, [Rom 4:13–25]), corresponds to the way of "heavenly Jerusalem," of freedom—the way of righteousness by faith.[28]

Thus Paul does not take the Old Testament accounts out of context, but rather points to their inherent deeper significance within salvation history.

Quotations and Allusions

Michael Fishbane is credited for calling special attention to the inner-biblical hermeneutic that was already transpiring in ancient Israel.[29] Abner Chou has collected hundreds of examples of later Old Testament writers' quotations of or allusions to antecedent Scripture, and acknowledges that his list is far from complete.[30] He shows how "every Old Testament book connects with prior revelation, often times in multiple ways."[31] From his examination of the evidence for the prophetic inner-biblical hermeneutic, Chou concludes that "the prophets were scholars of Scripture."[32] He then elaborates:

---

[28] For discussion of the two spiritual destinies of Isaac and Ishmael, based upon the way of righteousness by faith or righteousness by works, already implicit in Genesis, see, e.g., Jacques Doukhan, *Genesis*, Seventh-day Adventist International Bible Commentary (Nampa, ID: Pacific Press, 2016), 229–238, 267–270. For a discussion of this same pattern in regard to the covenant made at Sinai, see Richard M. Davidson, *Exodus*, Seventh-day Adventist International Bible Commentary (Nampa, ID: Pacific Press, forthcoming), commentary on Exodus 19, 24, and 34; and Richard M. Davidson, "Gracia ardiente: La misericordia de Dios en el pacto sinaítico," in "*'La palabra que Yo te diga, esa hablarás': Estudios Selectos en el Pentateuco*", Investigaciones Bíblico-Teológicas UPeuenses 2, ed. Merling Alomia, trans. Joel Iparraguirre (Lima, Peru: Ediciones Theologika – Universidad Peruana Unión, 2017), 85-110.

[29] Fishbane, *Biblical Interpretation in Ancient Israel*; cf. idem, "Types of Biblical Intertextuality," in *Congress Volume*, ed. A. Lemaire and M. Saebo (Leiden: Brill, 1998).

[30] Chou, *Hermeneutics of the Biblical Writers*, 47–120.

[31] Ibid., 53.

[32] Ibid., 47. By "prophets" Chou does not mean to limit his discussion to those who are explicitly called prophets in the Old Testament, but also to the other inspired authors (of the psalms, Wisdom literature, and historical books that form part of the Old Testament canon) who make use of antecedent Scripture. This study follows this usage of terminology.

> These people were united in how they thought about God's Word. They knew what God had revealed and showed care in handling the scriptural texts. They were good exegetes. Furthermore, they were aware of the theological implications of past revelation and developed those concepts via new revelation in ways consistent with the original intent. The Old Testament writers were also therefore theologians. Thus, the prophets were not simplistic in their thinking and writing. Rather, being guided by the Holy Spirit, they were precise and sophisticated.[33]

The inner-biblical hermeneutic of later Old Testament writers and New Testament writers makes use of both quotations and allusions. A quotation may be defined as "a direct citation of an Old Testament passage that is easily recognizable by its clear and unique verbal parallelism."[34] An allusion is "a brief expression consciously intended by an author to be dependent on an Old Testament passage."[35] In other words, "in contrast to a quotation of the Old Testament, which is a direct reference, allusions are indirect references (the Old Testament wording is not reproduced directly as in a quotation)."[36] Helpful criteria have been established for recognizing allusions (sometimes distinguished from "echoes")[37] to the Old Testament by New Testament writers; these criteria also apply to allusions by later Old Testament writers to earlier ones.[38] G. K. Beale summarizes: "The telltale key to discerning an allusion

---

[33] Chou, *Hermeneutics of Biblical Writers*, 48.

[34] G. K. Beale, *Handbook on the New Testament Use of the Old Testament: Exegesis and Interpretation* (Grand Rapids, MI: Baker, 2012), 29. Some scholars distinguish between a citation and a quotation, while others use the terms synonymously. For those making a distinction between the two, a citation is the indication of the specific source from which certain information was gleaned. Citing a source may or may not use the exact language from the original source. A quotation is the direct use of specific language that comes from another source, using the exact same wording as the original source. Generally, in formal writing, one would "cite the source" of the quotation. This study does not make a strong distinction between the two terms.

[35] Ibid., 31.

[36] Ibid.

[37] Those who distinguish between "allusion" and "echo" usually consider the "echo" to be a more subtle reference to the Old Testament than an allusion, with less volume from or verbal coherence with the Old Testament. See ibid., 32.

[38] See Jon Paulien, *Decoding Revelation's Trumpets: Literary Allusions and the Interpretation of Revelation 8:7–12*, Andrews University Seminary Doctoral Dissertation Series 11 (Berrien Springs, MI: Andrews University Press, 1988), 155–186, who suggests three main criteria of verbal, thematic, and structural parallels (the latter being strongest) and Richard B. Hays, *Echoes of Scripture in the Letters of Paul* (New Haven, CT: Yale University Press, 1989), 29–32. Beale, *Handbook*, 32–34, builds largely on Hays' criteria, and he summarizes them under

is that of recognizing an *incomparable or unique parallel in wording, syntax, concept, or cluster of motifs in the same order or structure*."[39]

The Old Testament prophets occasionally quote a substantial amount of earlier Scripture or provide introductory formulae (e.g., Jer 26:18; Joel 2:32), but most often their inner-biblical hermeneutic involved allusions. One example of an elaborate and extended allusion is found in Psalm 104. Here the inspired poet moves systematically through the seven days of creation week depicted in the Genesis creation account, in the same order, filling in explicit details only implied in the Genesis account, such as God Himself as the light source during the first three days of creation (Ps 104:1–2, in parallel with Gen 1:3), and the purpose of the Sabbath as a time for worship, praise, and meditation (Ps 104:33–35, in parallel with Gen 2:1–3).[40]

Kenneth Bergland examines the (re)use of key Pentateuchal legal texts by the prophets,[41] and shows that the prophets' reading of the Pentateuch is "rooted in the source text through an apparent close reading," even though they "do not appear to have been bound by a standard of literalistic repetition."[42] The prophets remain faithful to the meaning of the Pentateuchal legislation, but provide new significance to the text in their contemporary context.

The allusions sometimes refer not only to individual verses, phrases, or words, but to larger sections of biblical text. For example, God's covenant promises to Abraham, Isaac, and Jacob (Gen 12:1–3, 7; 13:14–18; 18:18; 22:16–18; 26:2–5; 28:3–4, 13–15) are alluded to throughout the rest of the Old Testament.[43] The prophets who allude to these Abrahamic promises "do not depart from the original ideas of those guarantees but only give further description to what they will look like when they are fulfilled."[44]

---

seven headings: 1) availability, 2) volume, 3) recurrence, 4) thematic coherence, 5) historical plausibility, 6) history of inter-pretation, and 7) satisfaction.

[39] Beale, *Handbook*, 31. Emphasis original.

[40] For further discussion, see Richard M. Davidson, "The Creation Theme in Psalm 104," in *The Genesis Creation Account and Its Reverberations in the Old Testament*, ed. Gerald A. Klingbeil (Berrien Springs, MI: Andrews University Press, 2015), 149–188.

[41] Bergland, "Reading as a Disclosure," 162–388.

[42] Ibid., 433. In other words, the prophet's reading of the Pentateuchal text engages in "a close reading that reads its source(s) expansionistically. There is a response interwoven into the reading, with trajectories the borrowing author might have seen indicated in the very source(s)" (ibid., abstract).

[43] See allusions in Joshua (24:1–14), the writers of Samuel and Kings (e.g., 1 Kgs 4:20; cf. Gen 22:17), Isaiah (2:2–4), Micah (4:1–6), Jeremiah (32:41), and Amos (9:14), among others.

[44] Chou, *Hermeneutics of the Biblical Writers*, 56.

Another example of this kind of allusion is the reference to the covenant blessings and curses of Leviticus 26 and Deutonomy 27–28, which are foundational for the message of hope and rebuke among the Prophets.[45]

As a sample of Old Testament prophetic passages that scholars claim have misused earlier passages, this study examines Jeremiah 31:28–29 and Ezekiel 18:2–3, and the alleged misuse of Exodus 20:5 and Deuteronomy 5:9.

Case Study—Do Jeremiah 31:28–29 and Ezekiel 18:2–3 Contradict Exodus 20:5 and Deuteronomy 5:9?

The prophetic passages quote a maxim popular in Israel at the time—"The fathers have eaten sour grapes and the children's teeth are set on edge"—and pronounce the word of the Lord that "you shall no longer use this proverb in Israel" (Ezek 18:2–3; cf. Jer 31:28–29 for similar wording).[46] Some scholars claim that God is contradicting or changing a previous revelation through Moses in the Decalogue of Exodus 20 and Deuteronomy 5 (as well as Exodus 34:7). However, upon a closer look at the passages in Exodus and Deuteronomy, God is not stating that children would receive the punishment deserved by the parents, but rather that the *consequences* of punishment would tend to spill over to subsequent generations (as we better understand today, due to genetic and environmental factors).[47] Furthermore, the context of the Pentateuchal passages clarify that these consequences are visited upon "those who hate me" (Exod 20:5; Deut 5:9)—that is, those subsequent generations who continue to disobey God, as did their fathers and forefathers. The Pentateuch never teaches that the children are punished for their father's deeds; in fact, it teaches just the opposite: "The fathers shall not be put to death for their children, nor shall the children be put to death for their fathers; a person shall be put to death for his own sin" (Deut 24:16). Jeremiah and Ezekiel are actually correcting a faulty theology of their day by giving an accurate interpretation of another passage of the Torah that explains the others!

Moving to the New Testament, the number of separate Old Testament quotations has been calculated to be about 295, occupying some 352 verses, or more than 4.4% of the New Testament, and averaging one verse

---

[45] Chou, *Hermeneutics of Biblical Writers*, 56–57. Note how most of the book of Hosea is built upon the covenant lawsuit and its covenant curses, which Israel faces, and the future hope of the covenant blessings for an eschatological repentant Israel. See Davidson, "Hosea," passim."

[46] All biblical quotations are from the NKJV, unless otherwise indicated.

[47] For further discussion of this supposed but illusory contradiction, see Chou, *Hermeneutics of the Biblical Writers*, 64–66.

in every 22.5 verses as quotations.[48] The number of allusions is much higher, ranging from various estimates of about six hundred to over four thousand.[49]

Regarding the *form* of the New Testament quotations of Old Testament passages, they are sometimes word-for-word the same as the Old Testament passage in Hebrew, while at other times they differ slightly, probably due to one or more of several factors: 1) The New Testament writers had to translate their quotations from Hebrew to Greek, or use the LXX, or a combination of both. However, most New Testament quotations seem to be from the LXX—probably because the Bible used by the majority of the readers, who did not know Hebrew, would be the LXX. 2) They were no doubt often quoting from memory, without the same rules for verbal precision as in today's conventions for quotations. 3) They were sometimes paraphrasing their quotations. 4) They were sometimes alluding to Old Testament passages without intending to quote them.[50]

Regarding the *meaning* of the New Testament quotations of (or allusions to) the Old Testament, Chou and others argue that the New Testament writers "used the Old Testament contextually"—that is, in harmony with the original meaning in light of its larger context.[51] Multiple case studies have been provided to document the contextual

---

[48] Roger Nicole, "The New Testament Use of the Old Testament," in *The Right Doctrine from the Wrong Texts? Essays on the Use of the Old Testament in the New*, ed. G. K. Beale (Grand Rapids, MI: Baker, 1994), 13. Of these 295 Old Testament quotations, Nicole counts about eighty-five percent (250) of these that utilize an introductory formula explicitly indicating the author's intent to cite the Old Testament. Chou, *Hermeneutics of the Biblical Writers*, 123, counts nearly two hundred.

[49] Nicole, "New Testament Use," 14, citing C. H. Toy who counts 613 allusions, Wilhelm Dittmar who counts 1,640 allusions, and Eugen Hühn, *Die altestamentlichen Citate und Reminiscenzen im Neuen Testament* (Tübingen: Mohr Siebeck, 1900), whose allusions (*Reminiscenzen*) add up to 4,105.

[50] See Nicole, "New Testament Use," 18–25, for examples and discussion of all of these approaches. Cf. Gleason Archer and Gregory Chirichigno, *Old Testament Quotations in the New Testament* (Chicago, IL: Moody, 1983), who categorize all the New Testament quotations as to whether the source of the citation was the Hebrew Bible, the LXX, or some combination of both. Out of the 410 entries, only thirteen on the surface "give the impression that unwarranted liberties were taken with the Old Testament text in the light of its context. But when due consideration is given to the basic message of the Hebrew passage and the particular purpose that the New Testament author had in mind (under the guidance of God's Spirit), in each case it will be seen that, far from wresting or perverting the original verse, the inspired servant of Jesus brings out in a profound and meaningful way its implications and connotations" (ibid., xxviii).

[51] Chou, *Hermeneutics of the Biblical Writers*, 121; cf. Beale, "Jesus and His Followers," 387–390; Davidson, "New Testament Use," 34–35; Hamilton, "Skull Crushing Seed," 30–32; and Kaiser, "Single Meaning," 88–89.

use of the Old Testament by New Testament writers.[52] This is in contrast to those who claim that the New Testament writers are misinterpreting the Old Testament quotations using faulty (from our modern perspective) first-century hermeneutical methods such as rabbinic midrash (which, as noted above, according to Instone-Brewer's analysis did not even exist until after the destruction of the temple in AD 70, and thus after Paul wrote his epistles). A large portion of these examples, where it is claimed that the New Testament writers have "twisted the Scriptures" in their citation of Old Testament passages, involve the issue of typology or predictive prophecy, with the fulfillment in Jesus Christ, and will be discussed laterin this study. What follows here is one case study not related to typology and predictive prophecy.

Case Study—"You shall not muzzle an ox": 1 Corinthians 9:8–10, Citing Deuteronomy 25:4

It is often claimed that Paul twists Scripture when he cites Deuteronomy 25:4: "You shall not muzzle an ox while it treads out the grain." This is seen as a prime example of biblical writers "interpreting a text in a sense which completely ignores its original meaning, or in a sense whose connection with its original meaning is purely arbitrary."[53] But a careful study of this Pauline passage[54] reveals quite the contrary. Here is a model approach showing Christians how to recognize the underlying principles in the Israelite civil law and apply them in a modern situation. The approach is in harmony with Paul's assertion in Romans 15:4 that "whatever things were written before [Old Testament Scripture] were written for our learning, that we through the patience and comfort of the Scriptures might have hope."

Paul does not depart from the literal sense of Deuteronomy 25:4 by means of allegory, rabbinic midrashic argument, or Hellenistic Jewish exegesis, as some have suggested. Rather, he engages in what Kaiser calls "literal theological exegesis,"[55] drawing what constitutes a "responsible analogy."[56] Paul captures the broader context of Deuteronomy 24–25—a fact that escapes many critical scholars. The laws in these chapters all

---

[52] See esp. Davidson, "New Testament Use," 16–35; cf. Chou, *Hermeneutics of the Biblical Writers*, 131–154, 160–198; Hamilton, "Skull Crushing Seed," 30–54; and Kaiser, *Uses of the Old Testament*, passim.

[53] A. T. Hanson, *Studies in Paul's Technique and Theology* (Grand Rapids, MI: Eerdmans, 1974), 159.

[54] See Kaiser, *Uses of the Old Testament*, 212–220; cf. Roy E. Gane, *Old Testament Law for Christians: Original Context and Enduring Application* (Grand Rapids, MI: Baker, 2017), 144–146.

[55] Kaiser, *Uses of the Old Testament*, 215.

[56] Gane, *Old Testament Law*, 146.

concern the basic principles of mercy and equity. Paul takes the basic principle with regard to the treatment of oxen, and applies the same principle to the Christian minister.

In the case of the oxen, even they deserved to eat from the object of their labor. How much more is it true of the Christian laborers, the ministers, as they deserve to eat from the object of their labors, namely, the Christian churches in which they minister. As F. Godet puts it,

> Paul does not, therefore, in the least suppress the historical and natural meaning of the precept. . . . Far from arbitrarily allegorizing, he applies, by a well-founded *a fortiori*, to a higher relation what God had prescribed with reference to a lower relation. . . . From the literal and natural meaning of the precept he disentangles a profound truth, a law of humanity and equity.[57]

We could look at other similar case studies, such as the quotation of Habakkuk 2:14 in Romans 1:17, where some allege that "Paul stretched, misunderstood, reused Habakkuk," but further study has produced strong evidence of Paul's faithfulness to the context of the Habakkuk passage he cites.[58] As another sample, George Caird analyzes citations of Old Testament passages in Hebrews, in view of alleged faulty exegesis, with the conclusion that "so far from being an example of fantastic exegesis which can be totally disregarded by modern Christians, Hebrews is one of the earliest and most successful attempts to define the relation between the Old and New Testaments, and that a large part of the value of the book is to be found in the method of exegesis which was formerly dismissed with contempt."[59] Walter Kaiser reaffirms this conclusion in his analysis of crucial Old Testament passages cited in Hebrews.[60]

---

[57] F. Godet, *A Commentary on the First Epistle to the Corinthians*, trans. J. W. Leitch (Philadelphia, PA: Fortress, 1975), 155, n. 38, cited in Kaiser, *Uses of the Old Testament*, 215.

[58] R. M. Moody, "The Habakkuk Quotation in Romans 1:17," *Expository Times* 92 (1981): 205–208; cf. A. Rahel Wells, "Did the Reformers Misunderstand Righteousness by Faith? New Perspectives on Habakkuk 2:4b" (paper presented at the National Adventist Theological Society meeting, Boston, MA, November 18, 2017).

[59] George B. Caird, "The Exegetical Method of the Epistle to the Hebrews," *Canadian Journal of Theology* 5 (1959): 49–51. Regarding Hebrews' use of Jeremiah 31, e.g., Caird, ibid., 47, describes this as "a perfectly sound piece of exegesis."

[60] For the exegesis of Psalm 95:7–11 in Hebrews 3–4, see Kaiser, *Uses of the Old Testament*, 153–175. For the exegesis of Psalm 40:6–8 in Hebrews 10:5–7, see ibid., 122–141. Regarding the latter passage, Kaiser, ibid., 138, points out crucial internal clues within Psalm 40—just before and just after the central messianic section—"catchwords that signaled that more was

We can conclude with Chou regarding the New Testament writers' inner-biblical hermeneutic involving quotations (and allusions), that they "did not read and write about the Old Testament atomistically but rather intertextually, a practice done by the prophets."[61]

Key Theological Terms

The inner-biblical hermeneutic of Bible writers also includes the use of key theological terms. Studies on the use of various theological terms in Scripture demonstrate the underlying continuity between the Old Testament and New Testament in the fleshing out of the meaning and implications of these terms, "implications often defined and refined by previous scriptural writers."[62] Samples of these studies include the examination of theological terms for "creation,"[63] "remnant,"[64] covenant,"[65]

underfoot in this public praise than a testimony to God for a rather private and personal escape. Instead it had communal, indeed, world-wide implications; it was another link in God's promise-plan." Kaiser, ibid., further argues that the writer to the Hebrews was not "guilty of using homiletical midrash in Psalm 40 where the original setting was either forgotten or considered irrelevant and thus was blithely applied to Jesus," nor was he using a "*pesher* type of exegesis, according to which the psalmist delivered a mystery (a *raz*) for which he had no explanation, but which only a much later *pesher* could unlock." Although he allows that "Psalm 40:6–8 contains fewer messianic clues and less promise phraseology than other messianic passages," yet "patient attendance on the text will reveal that the writer to the Hebrews was on strong exegetical grounds" (ibid., 141).

[61] Chou, *Hermeneutics of the Biblical Writers*, 129.

[62] Ibid., 153. This section of the present study includes studies that have a major emphasis on key theological terms, even though the study may also include a wider study of a theme or motif, which are dealt within the next section.

[63] See esp. Klingbeil, *Genesis Creation Account,* passim, and the companion volume examining the reverberations of creation in the New Testament by Thomas R. Shepherd, ed., *The Genesis Creation Account and Its Reverberations in the New Testament* (Berrien Springs, MI: Andrews University Press, 2020).

[64] See esp. Gerhard F. Hasel, *The Remnant: The History and Theology of the Remnant Idea from Genesis to Isaiah*, 2nd ed. (Berrien Springs, MI: Andrews University Press, 1972); Gerhard F. Hasel, "Remnant," in *The Interpreter's Dictionary of the Bible: Supplementary Volume*, ed. Keith Crim (Nashville, TN: Abingdon, 1976), 735–736; Kenneth D. Mulzac, "The Remnant Motif in the Context of Judgment and Salvation in the Book of Jeremiah" (PhD diss., Andrews University, 1995); Leslie N. Pollard, "The Function of *Loipos* [remnant] in Contexts of Judgment and Salvation in the Book of Revelation" (PhD diss., Andrews University, 2007) and the discussion in Ángel Manuel Rodríguez, ed., *Toward a Theology of the Remnant*, Biblical Research Institute Studies in Adventist Ecclesiology, vol. 1 (Silver Spring, MD: Biblical Research Institute, 2009).

[65] See O. Palmer Robertson, *The Christ of the Covenants* (Phillipsburg, NJ: Presbyterian and Reformed, 1980); Gerhard F. Hasel, *Covenant in Blood*, rev. ed. (Mountain View, CA and Nampa, ID: Pacific Press, 2012); Thomas E. McComiskey, *The Covenants of Promise: A Theology of the Old Testament Covenants* (Grand Rapids, MI: Baker, 1985); and MacCarty, *In Granite*, passim.

"temple,"[66] "righteousness/justification,"[67] "Holy Spirit,"[68] *sheol* (the grave),[69] and "love,"[70] to name a few. As a case study of a key theological term over which controversy has raged concerning its inner-biblical hermeneutics, we look at the term "seed" (Heb. *zeraʿ*; Gk. *sperma*) throughout Scripture in its Messianic contexts.

Case Study—The Messianic Seed of Genesis 3:15 and Its Inner-Biblical Interpretation by Later Biblical Writers

Genesis 3:15 has been widely regarded as "the *locus classicus* of Old Testament intertextuality."[71] In his exegetical and intertextual study of Genesis 3:15, Afolarin Ojewole categorizes the many different kinds of interpretation of this verse.[72] The traditional interpretation, until the rise of the historical-critical method, was that the text pointed toward the coming of the Messianic Seed who would crush the head of the serpent, representing Satan, but liberal-critical scholars tend to see in this verse "an aetiological myth which attempts to explain the natural hostility between mankind and the serpent world."[73] Even some evangelical scholars

---

[66] See, e.g., Elias Brasil de Souza, *The Heavenly Sanctuary/Temple Motif in the Hebrew Bible: Function and Relationship to the Earthly Counterparts*, Adventist Theological Society Dissertation Series, vol. 7 (Berrien Springs, MI: Adventist Theological Society, 2005); and G. K. Beale, *The Temple and the Church's Mission: A Biblical Theology of the Dwelling Place of God*, New Studies in Biblical Theology (Downers Grove, IL: InterVarsity, 2004).

[67] See, e.g., Richard M. Davidson, "How Shall a Person Stand before God? What is the Meaning of Justification?," in *God's Character and the Last Generation*, ed. Jiří Moskala and John C. Peckham (Nampa, ID: Pacific Press, 2018), 58–102; idem, "The Meaning of *Nitsdaq* in Daniel 8:14," *Journal of the Adventist Theological Society* 7/1 (1996): 107–119.

[68] See, e.g., Jiří Moskala, "The Holy Spirit in the Hebrew Scriptures," *Journal of the Adventist Theological Society* 24/2 (2103): 18–58; cf. Richard M. Davidson, "O Espírito Santo no Pentateuco," in *Pneumatologia: Pessoa e Obra do Espírito Santo*, ed. Reinaldo W. Siqueria and Alberto R. Timm (Engenheiro Coelho: UNASPRESS, 2017), 51–94.

[69] See Eriks Galenieks, *The Nature, Function, and Purpose of the Term Sheol in the Torah, Prophets, and Writings: An Exegetical-Intertextual Study*, Adventist Theological Society Dissertation Series, vol. 6 (Berrien Springs, MI: Adventist Theological Society, 2005).

[70] John C. Peckham, *The Love of God: A Canonical Model* (Downers Grove, IL: InterVarsity, 2015).

[71] Chou, *Hermeneutics of the Biblical Writers*, 83. Cf. Walter C. Kaiser, Jr., *The Messiah in the Old Testament* (Grand Rapids, MI: Zondervan, 1995), 37–38 and James M. Hamilton, Jr., *God's Glory in Salvation through Judgment: A Biblical Theology* (Wheaton, IL: Crossway, 2010), 76–77.

[72] See Afolarin O. Ojewole, *The Seed in Genesis 3:15: An Exegetical and Intertextual Study* (BerrienSprings, MI: Adventist Theological Society, 2002), 12–49. These interpretations include "Literal, Symbolic, Figurative, Naturalistic, Allegorical, Aetiological, Messianic, Mariological, Historical, Political, Christological, Eschatological, Collective, Singular, Representative, Rationalistic, and Form-Critical Interpretations," 12.

[73] Walter R. Wifall, "Genesis 3:15: A Protoevangelium?" *Catholic Biblical Quarterly* 36 (1972): 361.

have begun to question the messianic interpretation of this passage, suggesting that it simply speaks generally of good eventually triumphing over evil,[74] or that the Messianic meaning is only based on later New Testament revelation via *sensus plenior.*[75]

However, recent scholarship provides solid exegetical evidence for the messianic interpretation of Genesis 3:15, as the *protoevangelium* or "first gospel promise."[76] Ojewole shows how in this verse the conflict narrows from many descendants (a collective "seed") in the first part of the verse to a masculine singular pronoun in the last part of the verse—"He"—fighting against the serpent. Elsewhere in Scripture whenever the term "seed" (Heb. *zera*ʿ) is modified by a singular pronoun, it is a single individual that is in view.[77] Thus here God promises victory centered in a person. "He"—the ultimate representative seed of the woman, later to be revealed as the Messiah, shall bruise your head, Satan, and you shall bruise His heel.[78]

Ojewole traces the intra-textual use and referent of the word "seed" (*zera*ʿ) and related pronouns throughout the rest of the Pentateuch, showing how Moses carries forward the messianic interpretation of the term "seed." This is especially evident in Genesis 22:17, where the word *zera*ʿ ("seed") clearly has a plural (collective singular) idea in the context of "the stars of heaven" and "the sand which is on the seashore," but in Genesis 22:17b the *zera*ʿ narrows to a singular Messianic "Seed" who would "possess the gate of *His* [singular] enemies." This is in parallel to Genesis 3:15, where we find the same narrowing of the referent of the word "seed" from collective to messianic singular.[79] The allusion to Genesis 3:15 is also apparent in the Balaam oracle, prophesying a star rising from Jacob who will crush the forehead of Moab (Num 24:17), in parallel

---

[74] See, e.g., John H. Walton, *Genesis*, NIV Application Commentary (Grand Rapids, MI: Zondervan, 2001), 234.

[75] See, e.g., Gordon J. Wenham, *Genesis 1–15*, Word Biblical Commentary (Waco, TX: Word, 1987), 80.

[76] Ojewole, *Seed in Genesis*, 50–220. Cf. O. Palmer Robertson, *Christ of the Covenants* (Grand Rapids, MI: Baker, 1980), 93–100; Chou, *Hermeneutics of the Biblical Writers,* 83–89; and Rydelnik, *Messianic Hope*, 129–145

[77] In support of this point, see esp. Jack Collins, "A Syntactical Note (Genesis 3:15): Is the Woman's Seed Singular or Plural?" *Tyndale Bulletin* 48 (1997): 139–148.

[78] Ojewole, *Seed in Genesis*, 190–207.

[79] For further discussion of Genesis 22:17 and its context, see Ojewole, *Seed in Genesis*, 271–285 and T. Desmond Alexander, "Further Observations on the Term 'Seed' in Genesis," *Tyndale Bulletin* 48 (1997): 363–367.

to the Messianic Seed of Genesis 3:15 crushing the head of the serpent.[80]

The intertextual allusions to the "seed" of Genesis 3:15 are found elsewhere in the Old Testament, including the book of Ruth (4:10–22), 2 Samuel (7:4–19), Psalms (2, 18, 68, 72, 89, 110), and Micah (7:17),[81] giving evidence that Old Testament prophets recognize in Genesis 3:15 the passage that "established God's agenda for the battle of good and evil, culminating in a seed/champion who would vanquish the evil one. Later prophets do not change those ideas but flesh out the ramifications of those ideas on redemptive history."[82] These later prophets catch and further develop the messianic import of the *protoevangelium*.

Allusions to the Seed of Genesis 3:15 (and its parallel passages in the divine promises to Abraham's seed in Genesis 12 and 22) continue in the New Testament, in Romans 16:20 and Revelation 12,[83] as well as Galatians 3. Regarding this latter passage, some New Testament scholars claim that Paul's citation of the Abrahamic "seed" passages in Galatians 3:16 is a good example of his "twisting the Scriptures" by means of some kind of midrashic or rabbinic principle of interpretation.[84] In Galatians 3:16 Paul writes, "Now to Abraham and his seed were the promises made. He does not say, 'And to seeds,' as of many, but as of one, 'And to your Seed,' who is Christ." A surface reading of this verse may suggest that Paul is indeed citing the Abrahamic promises in a way that is not faithful to the Hebrew, since in Hebrew the word *zera'* ("seed") always appears in the singular form, never the plural, just as in English the word "seed" (singular in form) can refer to either one or many seeds. However, a close reading reveals that Paul is citing Genesis 12:7 in light of Genesis 22:17–18, since this latter verse is the one cited in Galatians 3:8,[85] and he does so in a way showing he understands that the use of the Hebrew word *zera'* ("seed") in Genesis 22:17 moves from a collective (plural) idea to a single "Seed," the Messiah, as noted earlier. Then a few

---

[80] See Hamilton, "Skull Crushing Seed," 34.

[81] Ojewole, *Seed in Genesis,* 296–351 and Chou, *Hermeneutics of the Biblical Writers*, 87–89.

[82] Chou, *Hermeneutics of the Biblical Writers*, 89.

[83] See discussion in Ojewole, *Seed in Genesis,* 342–344, 348–349.

[84] See, e.g., David Daube, *The New Testament and Rabbinic Judaism* (London: Athlone, 1965), 440; and E. Earl Ellis, *Paul's Use of the Old Testament* (Grand Rapids, MI: Eerdmans, 1981), 70–73.

[85] Of all the promises of seed made to Abraham, only in Genesis 22:17–18 is reference made to "nations," and Paul's citation, "In you all the nations shall be blessed," clearly refers to this passage. For the summary of evidence that Paul in Galatians 3 is not simply citing Genesis 12, but in particular had Genesis 22:17–18 in mind, see the discussion of Galatians 3:8 in Max Wilcox, "'Upon the Tree'—Deuteronomy 21:22–23 in the New Testament," *Journal of Biblical Literature* 96 (1977): 94–97.

verses later (Gal 3:29) Paul correctly points to the collective plural aspect of this same term, referring to those who are in Christ as "Abraham's seed," also in the wider context of Genesis 22:18.[86]

I conclude with Dale Wheeler, who wrote his doctoral dissertation on the issue of Paul's citation of the Old Testament in Galatians 3:16: "Rather than twisting the Old Testament to prove a point Paul is using the passage in exactly the way it was intended, following its original sense and understanding the nature of who might be its referents."[87]

Unity of Major Themes

This approach of biblical writers in their inner-biblical hermeneutic somewhat overlaps with the previous one, inasmuch as key theological terms are often part of a larger biblical theme or motif. Here we point out that various themes are developed in the Old Testament and the New Testament, focusing on the broader theme or motif[88] beyond a specific biblical term. This section points to numerous studies where Old Testament themes are developed by later Old Testament writers and New Testament writers, demonstrating a basic continuity between the Torah and the Prophets and between the Testaments, in contrast with those scholars who argue for major discontinuity.[89]

Case Studies

With regard to the theme of human sexuality, detailed study reveals that the basic contours of the divine design for human sexuality are set forth in Genesis 1–3, and later biblical writers in both the Old Testament and the New Testament unequivocally remain faithful to upholding that creation design, condemning the distortions of the divine plan, and ever calling humans back to God's original plan.[90] Studies on the Sabbath

---

[86] For further discussion, see Davidson, "New Testament Use," 30–31.

[87] Dale M. Wheeler, "Paul's Use of the Old Testament in Galatians 3:16" (ThD diss., Dallas Theological Seminary, 1987), 332–333.

[88] A "motif" is usually more narrowly focused than a theme; a motif is a recurring image, symbol, or idea in a literary work that explains or develops a central idea or message called a theme. William Freedman, "The Literary Motif: A Definition and Evaluation," *Novel* 4/2 (1971): 127, defines a motif more broadly: a "recurrent theme, character, or verbal pattern, but it may also be a family or associational cluster of literal or figurative references to a given class of concepts or objects."

[89] For a classic overview of the major themes of the Old Testament, see William Dyrness, *Themes in Old Testament Theology* (Downers Grove, IL: InterVarsity, 1979). For a classic overview of the New Testament development of Old Testament themes, see F. F. Bruce, *New Testament Development of Old Testament Themes* (Grand Rapids, MI: Eerdmans, 1969).

[90] See, e.g., Richard M. Davidson, *Flame of Yahweh: Sexuality in the Old Testament* (Grand

throughout Scripture likewise show how the later biblical writers build upon the foundational Sabbath passages in the Old Testament, and remain in continuity with these passages as they expand on the significance of the Sabbath in their time and ours.[91] A recent study on Old Testament law presents a biblically-based method for a modern application of Old Testament laws confirming a basic continuity between the Testaments while acknowledging certain elements of discontinuity.[92] More specialized studies—dealing, for example, with laws relating to clean and unclean foods—expand on the continuity of the two Testaments, documenting how the later Old Testament and the New Testament writers upheld the laws of the Torah.[93] The grand multiplex theme of Scripture, centered in Jesus Christ, will be discussed in the last section of this study.

More examples could be cited, but these are sufficient to show the basic continuity between the Torah and the Prophets and between the Testaments, recognizing the expansion of Torah themes and motifs and their application by later Old Testament writers and the New Testament writers according to sound hermeneutical principles.

Typology

Based upon an examination of the passages in Scripture where the object of a biblical writer's hermeneutical endeavor is specifically labeled

---

Rapids, MI: Baker Academics, 2007). An afterword presents implications for a New Testament theology of sexuality, and shows how the New Testament is in continuity with the Old Testament.

[91] See esp. Kenneth A. Strand, ed., *The Sabbath in Scripture and History* (Washington, DC: Review and Herald, 1982). See also the two volumes on the Sabbath published by the Biblical Research Institute: Daniel Bediako and Ekkehardt Mueller, eds., *The Sabbath in Old Testament and the Intertestamental Period: Implications for Christians in the Twenty-First Century* Biblical Research Institute Studies on the Biblical Sabbath, vol. 1 (Silver Spring, MD: Biblical Research Institute, 2020) and Ekkehardt Mueller and Eike Mueller, eds., *The Sabbath in the New Testament and in Theology: Implications for Christians in the Twenty-First Century* Biblical Research Institute Studies on the Biblical Sabbath, vol. 2 (Silver Spring, MD: Biblical Research Institute, 2020).

[92] Gane, *Old Testament Law for Christians.* Regarding the covenant lawsuit motif throughout Scripture, see Richard M. Davidson, "The Divine Covenant Lawsuit Motif in Canonical Perspective," *Journal of the Adventist Theological Society* 21/1–2 (2010): 45–84.

[93] See Jiří Moskala, *Laws of Clean and Unclean Animals in Leviticus 11*, Adventist Theological Society Dissertation Series, vol. 4 (Berrien Springs, MI: Adventist Theological Society, 2002); Alexandru Breja, "Law and Creation: A Study of Some Biblical Laws Related to Creation—the Sexual, Dietary, and Sabbath Laws of the Pentateuch—and their Interrelatedness" (PhD diss., Andrews University, 2011); and Eike Mueller, "Cleansing the Common: A Narrative-Intertextual Study of Mark 7:1–23" (ThD diss., Andrews University, 2015).

a "type" (Gk. *typos*) or "antitype,"[94] the following definition summarizes the nature of biblical typology: typology is the study of salvation-historical realities or "types" (persons, events, institutions, usually in the Old Testament[95]) that God has specifically designed to correspond to, and predictively prefigure, their intensified eschatological fulfillment aspects (inaugurated, appropriated, consummated) in connection with Christ and/or the gospel realities brought about by Him.[96] According to the hermeneutical principles that emerge from the Bible's use of typology, the Old Testament identifies which persons, events, or institutions are typological, and the New Testament announces the fulfillment of what the Old Testament had indicated. Studies have been conducted on various strands of biblical typology, including the typology of Adam, the flood, the exodus, the sanctuary, Moses, Joshua, David, and Jonah,[97] among many others.[98] It is important to recognize that the principles of typology unlock many seemingly problematic applications of the Old Testament by New Testament writers. This will be illustrated by a case

---

[94] These New Testament passages are: Romans 5:14; 1 Corinthians 10:6, 11; 1 Peter 3:21; Hebrews 8:5; 9:23; cf. the LXX of Exodus 25:40.

[95] There are some examples of New Testament types pointing forward to later events in salvation history. See, e.g., the typology of the destruction of Jerusalem in AD 70 (Matt 24), discussed in Richard M. Davidson, "'This Generation Shall Not Pass' (Matt 24:34): Failed Or Fulfilled Prophecy?," in *The Cosmic Battle for Planet Earth: Essays in Honor of Norman R. Gulley*, ed. Ronald A. G. Du Preez and Jiří Moskala, (Berrien Springs, MI: Old Testament Department, Seventh-day Adventist Theological Seminary, Andrews University, 2003), 307–319.

[96] See Davidson, *Typology in Scripture*, passim, and esp. 421.

[97] For discussion (with bibliography) of typology involving the persons, events, and institutions mentioned in this list, see Richard M. Davidson, "The Eschatological Hermeneutic of Biblical Typology," *TheoRhēma* 6/2 (2011): 5–48.

[98] Note the following examples of other Old Testament types that have been studied in some depth. **Abraham and Isaac:** Jo Ann Davidson, "Eschatology and Genesis 22," *Journal of the Adventist Theological Society* 11/1–2 (2000): 232–247. **Joseph:** Samuel C. Emadi, "Christ, Typology, and the Story of Joseph: A Literary-Canonical Examination of Genesis 37–50" (PhD diss., Southern Baptist Theological Seminary, 2016) and Jan Å. Sigvartsen, *Messiah ben Joseph: A Type in both Jewish and Christian Traditions*, GlossaHouse Studies in Texts and Languages 1 (Wilmore, KY: GlossaHouse, 2018). **Solomon and Shulamit:** Christopher W. Mitchell, *The Song of Songs*, Concordia Commentary (St. Louis, MO: Concordia, 2003), 67–97. **Elijah:** Jonatas Leal, "Indicators of Typology in the Narrative of Elijah: An Investigation into the Predictive Nature of the Typological Use of the Old Testament in the New Testament" (PhD diss., Andrews University [forthcoming]). **Elisha:** Raymond E. Brown, "Jesus and Elisha," *Perspective (Pittsburg)* 12/1–2 (Spring 1971): 84–104; Thomas L. Brodie, "Jesus as the New Elisha: Cracking the Code," *Expository Times* 93/2 (November 1981): 39–42. **Ezekiel:** C. Hassell Bullock, "Ezekiel, Bridge between the Testaments," *Journal of Evangelical Theological Society* 25/1 (March 1982): 23–31. **Cyrus (and the fall of Babylon)**: Louis F. Were, *The Fall of Babylon in Type and Antitype: Why Emphasized in God's Last-day Message?* (Melbourne, Australia: The Author, 1952); **Esther**: Michael Beckett, *Gospel in Esther* (Waynesboro, GA: Paternoster Press, 2002), passim.

study in Exodus typology, set forth in the Old Testament, and proclaimed by New Testament writers as fulfilled in Christ (christologically) and beyond (ecclesiologically and apocalyptically).[99]

Case Study—"Out of Egypt I Called My Son": Matthew 2:15, Quoting Hosea 11:1

Matthew 2:15 represents another instance in which the critical scholars who charge Matthew with unfaithfulness to the Old Testament context[100] have themselves failed to discern the larger context of Hosea 11:1, which unfolds the exodus typology of the Bible writers.[101]

It is true that Hosea 11:1 in its immediate historical context refers to the past historical exodus of ancient Israel from Egypt. The verse reads: "When Israel was a child, I loved him, and out of Egypt I called My son." The next verse describes the historical circumstances of the nation of Israel's turning away from Yahweh to serve the Baals.

However, it is crucial to see not only the immediate context but also the wider context of this verse. C. H. Dodd demonstrates how the New Testament writers often cite a single Old Testament passage as a pointer for the reader to consider the whole larger context of that passage, showing that the larger context of Hosea 11:1—both in the book of Hosea itself and in other contemporary eighth-century prophets—describes a future New Exodus connected with Israel's return from exile and the coming of the Messiah.[102]

In fact, the typological interconnection between ancient Israel's

---

[99] For discussion of the general principles of interpreting biblical typology, including the three phases of the one eschatological fulfillment (inaugurated/Christological, appropriated/ecclesiological, and consummated/apocalyptic), and the mode of fulfillment in each phase, see Davidson, "Biblical Typology," 5–48; idem, "Sanctuary Typology," in *Symposium on Revelation–Book I*, Daniel and Revelation Committee Series, vol. 6, ed. Frank B. Holbrook (Silver Spring, MD: Biblical Research Institute, 1992), 99–130; and idem, *Typology in Scripture,* passim.

[100] See, e.g., S. Marion Smith, "New Testament Writers Use the Old Testament," *Encounter* 26 (1965): 239, who states that in citing Hosea 11:1 Matthew employs "a method that can be rejected outright as an untenable use of Scripture." Cf. Enns, *Inspiration and Incarnation*, 122: "It would take a tremendous amount of mental energy to argue that Matthew is respecting the historical context of Hosea's words, that is, that there actually is something predictive in Hosea 11. In the end such arguments serve only to support one's assumptions rather than challenge them."

[101] For the Old Testament basis and development of Exodus typology, see esp. Friedbert Ninow, *Indicators of Typology within the Old Testament: The Exodus Motif*, Friedensauer Schriftenreihe 4 (Frankfurt am Main: Peter Lang, 2001).

[102] C. H. Dodd, *According to the Scriptures* (London: Collins, 1952), 74–133. Note especially the following passages: Hosea 2:14–15; 12:9, 13; 13:4–5; Isaiah 11:15–16; 35; 40:3–5; 41:17–20; 42:14–16; 43:1–3, 14–21; 48:20–21; 49:3–5, 8–12; 51:9–11; 52:3–6, 11–12; 55:12–13; Amos 9:7–15; Micah 7:8–20. Cf. Jeremiah 23:4–8; 16:14–15; 31:32.

exodus and the Messiah's exodus from Egypt is indicated in the Pentateuch. In the oracles of Balaam in Numbers 23–24, there is an explicit shift from the historical exodus to the messianic exodus. In Numbers 23:22 Balaam proclaims, "God brings *them* out of Egypt; He [God] has strength like a wild ox." In the next oracle, Balaam shifts to the singular, "God brings *him* out of Egypt" (Num 24:8), and in the next and final oracle, referring to the "latter days" (Num 24:14), Balaam indicates the messianic identification of the "Him": "I see Him, but not now; I behold Him, but not near; a Star shall come out of Jacob; a scepter shall rise out of Israel, and batter the brow of Moab, and destroy all the sons of tumult" (Num 24:17).[103]

Thus the Pentateuch and the Latter Prophets (especially Hosea and Isaiah) clearly recognize that Israel's exodus from Egypt was a type of the New Exodus, centering in the Representative Israel, the Messiah. Matthew remains faithful to this larger Old Testament context in his citation of Hosea 11:1. In harmony with the Old Testament predictions, Matthew depicts Jesus as the Representative Israel, recapitulating in His life the experience of ancient Israel, but succeeding where the first Israel failed. The first five chapters of Matthew describe in detail Jesus as the New Israel experiencing a New Exodus.[104] Matthew and the other Synoptic Gospels also depict the death and resurrection of Jesus as a New Exodus.[105]

Thus, far from distorting the original Old Testament context of Hosea 11:1, Matthew "quoted a single verse not as a proof text, but a pointer to his source's larger context. Instead of interrupting the flow of his argument with a lengthy digression, he let the words of Hosea 11:1 introduce that whole context in Hosea."[106] Matthew faithfully captures the

---

[103] For further discussion, see John H. Sailhamer, *The Pentateuch as Narrative: A Biblical-Theological Commentary* (Grand Rapids, MI: Zondervan, 1992), 407–409 and Ninow, *Exodus Motif*, 137–144.

[104] Jesus comes out of Egypt after a death decree (Matt 2:15), and going through His antitypical Red Sea experience in His baptism (Matt 3; cf. 1 Cor 10:1–2). This is followed by His wilderness experience of forty days, paralleling the forty years of ancient Israel in the wilderness. During this time Jesus indicates His own awareness of His role as the New Israel in the New Exodus by consistently meeting the devil's temptations with quotations from Deuteronomy 6–8 (where ancient Israel's temptations in the wilderness are summarized). Finally, Jesus appears on the mount as a new Moses, with His twelve disciples representing the tribes of Israel, and repeats the law as Moses did at the end of the wilderness sojourn. See Davidson, "New Testament Use," 19–21.

[105] Note, e.g., how at the transfiguration the first Moses speaks to the New Moses about His exodus, which He was to accomplish at Jerusalem (Luke 9:31). Jesus' death is His ultimate Red Sea experience. After His resurrection He remains in the wilderness of this earth forty days (like Israel's forty years in the wilderness) and then as the New Joshua enters heavenly Canaan as the pioneer and perfector of our faith. See Estelle, *Echoes of Exodus*, 208–262.

[106] Kaiser, *Uses of the Old Testament*, 52.

wider eschatological, messianic context of this passage as portrayed by Hosea and his prophetic contemporaries.[107]

Promise/Prediction and Fulfillment

The Old Testament contains numerous *predictive* prophecies, estimated to comprise nearly thirty percent of the Old Testament[108]—not to speak of the plethora of Old Testament promises. Inasmuch as apocalyptic (Daniel and Revelation) and classical (conditional) predictive prophecy will be the focus of the next two chapters of this book,[109] here we look particularly at the other major category of promise/prediction—that is, messianic prophecies. Although critical scholars have usually rejected out of hand the promise/prediction of the coming Messiah in the Old Testament, Jesus Himself leads the way in affirming messianic prophecies all through the Old Testament, when He says to the disciples that resurrection evening in the upper room: "These are the words which I spoke to you while I was still with you, that all things must be fulfilled which were written in the Law of Moses and the Prophets and the Psalms concerning Me" (Luke 24:44). Literary studies show how the entire Old Testament is cast in an eschatological, messianic framework.[110] Numerous other studies examine the many specific messianic prophecies in the Bible, revealing how later Old Testament writers understand the core messianic promises/predictions about the Messiah in the Torah, and how the New Testament writers testify concerning the fulfillment of these and other Old Testament prophecies in Jesus.[111]

---

[107] The ecclesiological and apocalyptic dimensions of Exodus typology are set forth by other New Testament writers. See Davidson, "Eschatological Hermeneutic of Biblical Typology," 37–44.

[108] J. Barton Payne, *Encyclopedia of Biblical Prophecy* (Grand Rapids, MI: Baker, 1973), 13, 674–675. According to Payne's count, out of 23,210 verses of the Old Testament, 6,641 (or twenty-eight and one-half percent) contain predictive material.

[109] See also Richard M. Davidson, "Interpreting Old Testament Prophecy," in *Understanding Scripture: An Adventist Approach*, ed. George W. Reid (Silver Spring, MD: Biblical Research Institute, 2005), 183–204 and Jon Paulien, "The Hermeneutics of Biblical Apocalyptic," in *Understanding Scripture: An Adventist Approach*, ed. George W. Reid (Silver Spring, MD: Biblical Research Institute, 2005), 245–270.

[110] See John H. Sailhamer, "The Canonical Approach to the Old Testament: Its Effect on Understanding Prophecy," *Journal of Evangelical Theological Society* 30/3 (September 1987): 307–315; and Richard M. Davidson, "The Eschatological Literary Structure of the Old Testament," in *Creation, Life, and Hope: Essays in Honor of Jacques B. Doukhan*, ed. Jiří Moskala (Berrien Springs, MI: Old Testament Department, Seventh-day Adventist Theological Seminary, Andrews University, 2000), 349–366.

[111] For a review of literature showing the different views with regard to messianic prophecy, and

The author of the present study elsewhere deals with such messianic passages as the quotation of Jeremiah 31:15 in Matthew 2:18 ("Rachel weeping for her children"),[112] New Testament quotations and allusions to Psalm 22 ("The Psalm of the Cross"),[113] the quotation of Psalm 16 in Acts 2:29–33 and 13:31–37 (Old Testament prediction of Christ's resurrection),[114] and the allusion in Matthew 12:2 to Jonah 2 ("the sign of Jonah").[115] Here we look briefly at one case study, the prediction of Isaiah 7:14, that many critical scholars consider to have been misinterpreted by Matthew (Matt 1:23).

Case Study: The Virgin Birth? Matthew 1:23, Quoting Isaiah 7:14

Isaiah 7:14 has been called "the most difficult of all Messianic prophecies"[116] and is perhaps the most studied text in biblical scholarship.[117] The author of the present study elsewhere examines the relevant exegetical issues in this passage, focusing on the question of whether Matthew remains faithful to the Old Testament context of this passage when in Matthew 1:23 he cites it as a prediction of the virgin birth of the Messiah.[118] Here is a brief summary of the evidence: A careful look at the immediate context of Isaiah 7:14 seems to reveal a local dimension to the fulfillment of the prophecy, within the historical setting of the Syro-Ephraimite War of ca. 734 BC, with the birth of Isaiah's

---

upholding the traditional understanding of messianic prophecy, see esp. Rydelnik, *Messianic Hope*, 13–128. Some other helpful studies of the Old Testament messianic prophecies include Gerhard Van Groningen, *Messianic Revelation in the Old Testament* (Grand Rapids, MI: Baker, 1990); James E. Smith, *What the Bible Teaches about the Promised Messiah* (Nashville, TN: Thomas Nelson, 1993); Kaiser, *Messiah in the Old Testament*; Herbert W. Bateman IV, Darrell L. Bock, and Gordon H. Johnston, *Jesus the Messiah: Tracing the Promises, Expectations, and Coming of Israel's King* (Grand Rapids, MI: Kregel, 2012); and Jacques Doukhan, *On the Way to Emmaus: Five Major Messianic Prophecies Explained* (Clarksville, MD: Lederer Books, 2012).

[112] Davidson, "New Testament Use," 21–22.

[113] Ibid., 23–26; cf. Richard M. Davidson, "Psalms 22, 23, and 24: A Messianic Trilogy?" (paper presented at the Evangelical Theological Society annual meeting, San Diego, CA, November 20, 2019), 1–14.

[114] Davidson, "New Testament Use," 26–28.

[115] Ibid., 29–30.

[116] Milton S. Terry, *Biblical Hermeneutics* (New York: Phillips and Hunt, 1883), 331, cited by J. Barton Payne, *Encyclopedia of Biblical Prophecy* (Grand Rapids, MI: Baker, 1973), 291.

[117] For a representation of the immense bibliography, see John D. W. Watts, *Isaiah 1–33*, Word Biblical Commentary 24 (Waco, TX: Word, 1985), 95–103.

[118] See Richard M. Davidson, "The Messianic Hope in Isaiah 7:14 and the Volume of Immanuel (Isa 7–12)," in *"For You Have Strengthened Me": Biblical and Theological Studies in Honor of Gerhard Pfandl in Celebration of His Sixty-Fifth Birthday*, eds. Martin Pröbstle, Gerald A. Klingbeil and Martin G. Klingbeil (St. Peter am Hart: Seminar Schloss Bogenhofen, 2007), 85–96.

son, Maher-Shalal-Hash-Baz. The northern kingdoms of Syria and Israel have banded together to attack their southern neighbor of Judah (Isa 7:1, 4–6). Ahaz, king of Judah, is terrified of the impending invasion, but God sends Isaiah with the comforting word that the northern coalition will not succeed in their plans to overthrow Ahaz (Isa 7:2–3, 7–9). In this situation God gives Ahaz a sign through Isaiah: "Behold, the virgin shall conceive and bear a son, and shall call His name Immanuel" (Isa 7:14).

The succeeding verses give the time frame of the local (partial) fulfillment of this sign: "For before the child shall know to refuse the evil and choose the good, the land that you dread will be forsaken by both her kings" (Isa 7:16). The child would be born in the time of Ahaz, and before it reached the age of accountability, the Syro-Ephraimite coalition would be dissolved. This local interpretation is confirmed in the succeeding chapter. Isaiah goes in to "the prophetess" (his wife, who at the time of the prophecy may have been a virgin), she conceives, and bears a son (Isa 8:3). The link between this son and the prophecy is made in Isaiah 8:4 by a statement clearly parallel with Isaiah 7:16: "for before the child shall have knowledge to cry 'my father' and 'my mother,' the riches of Damascus and the spoil of Samaria will be taken away before the king of Assyria." The time elements implied in Isaiah 7:16 and 8:4 respectively were fulfilled precisely: in 732 BC (within two years of the prophecy of Isaiah 7:14, before the child could say "father" or "mother") Damascus fell, and in 722 BC (before the child was twelve and had reached the age of accountability) Samaria fell. Thus Isaiah 7:14 does seem to have a local dimension of fulfillment.

But there are major hints that the passage also points forward to an ultimate (more complete) antitypical fulfillment in the Messiah: 1) The prophecy and sign of Isaiah 7:14 is addressed not only to Ahaz, but more widely to "you" in the plural, to the "house of David" (Isa 7:13). 2) The Hebrew word *'almah* ("virgin, young woman"), translated in the LXX and Matthew 1:23 as *parthenos* or "virgin," refers to a "young woman of marriageable age, sexually ripe, but unmarried," and therefore (unless she is an immoral woman) a virgin,[119] a description indeed true of Mary, the mother of Jesus, at the time of her conception, but not neatly fitting the circumstances of Isaiah's wife. 3) There are no markers of time in the entire verse;[120] the sign thus could refer to past, present, or future

---

[119] For evidence supporting the translation of *'almah* as "virgin," see esp. Jacques Doukhan, *On the Way to Emmaus*, 81–84. Doukhan, ibid., 71–105, interprets this prophecy as directly messianic and not by way of typology. Although his interpretation is possible, the author of the present study still sees the evidence favoring a typological and not a directly predictive fulfillment.

[120] The verse is literally translated: Behold, an *'almah* [was/is/will be] pregnant, and [was/is/will

(or both), as the time when the virgin/young woman was or would be pregnant, making room for a typological fulfillment.

What is hinted at in the text is made explicit in the larger context of Isaiah 7–12, called the Volume of Immanuel. 4) Although the language used in Isaiah 8:3–4 is so strikingly similar to that of Isaiah 7:14–16 that a local partial fulfillment seems to be implied, when Isaiah's son was born, he was not named "Immanuel" as the prophecy of Isaiah 7:14 predicted. 5) The name "Immanuel" is used later in chapter 8 in a context that seems to move from the local to the cosmic level (see Isa 8:8). 6) In chapter 8 Isaiah and his sons are said to be "signs" in Israel (Isa 8:18) for future events to be brought about by God. 7) These events move from the local level at the end of Isaiah 8 to the eschatological messianic level in Isaiah 9: the land that was in gloom and darkness (Isa 8:22) will become a land where the gloom is removed (Isa 9:1) and "the people who walked in darkness have seen a great light" (Isa 9:2). Most significantly, 8) while Isaiah's son was a sign to Israel, Isaiah predicts that in the messianic age the greater Son, the ultimate fulfillment of Isaiah 7:14, will appear: "For unto us a Child is born, unto us a Son is given, and the government will be upon His shoulder. And His name will be called Wonderful Counselor, Mighty God, Everlasting Father, Prince of Peace" (Isa 9:6). 9) This messianic motif is further expanded in Isaiah 11:1–9, the matching passage in the chiastic structure of Isaiah 7–12.

Finally, in summary, 10) within the wider context of Isaiah 7:14, Isaiah himself, under divine inspiration, indicates that although the prediction will have local and partial fulfillment in the birth of a son in the time of Ahaz, yet this local fulfillment is a type of the ultimate messianic fulfillment in the divine Son, Immanuel. We may diagram the typological relationships in Isaiah's volume of Immanuel as following:

1. Type	Isaiah 7:14 (Immanuel prophecy)
	Isaiah 8:1–4 (local partial fulfillment of Isaiah 7:14 in Maher-Shalal-Hash-Baz)
2. Antitype	Isaiah 9:1–7 (ultimate fulfillment in the Messiah)
	Isaiah 11:1–9 (further description of the Messiah)

Matthew, therefore, far from taking Isaiah 7:14 out of context, recognizes the larger messianic context of Isaiah 7–12, which critical scholarship usually ignores.

---

being] bearing a son. . . and she has called/is calling/will call his name Immanuel [meaning God was/is/will be with us]. See explanation of the grammar in Davidson, "Messianic Hope," 87–88.

The "Big Picture" of Salvation History

Some fifty different proposals have been made by Old Testament and New Testament scholars alike for identifying the theological "center" of Scripture.[121] How does the inner-biblical hermeneutic of the biblical writers relate to the "big picture" of Scripture? The author of the present study offers the following as a case study in the biblical writers' unified understanding of Scripture's "theological center" or "grand metanarrative."

Case Study—Scripture's Theological Center and Individual Biblical Writers

Elsewhere in this study it is argued that a multi-faceted "center" of Scripture emerges out of the "introduction" and "conclusion" of Scripture—that is, Genesis 1–3 and Revelation 20–22.[122] The seven facets or themes that are found in Scripture's bookends and appear to form the "plotline" or grand metanarrative of Scripture are these: 1) creation and the divine design for this planet; 2) the character of the Creator (with implications for theodicy); 3) the rise of the cosmic moral conflict concerning the character of God; 4) the gospel covenant promise centered in the person of the Messianic Seed, Jesus Christ; 5) the substitutionary atonement of the Messiah; 6) the eschatological windup of the moral conflict with the end of the serpent (Satan) and evil; and 7) the sanctuary setting of the moral conflict.[123] The epicenter of this multifaceted metanarrative, and of all inner-biblical interpretation, is Jesus Christ, who fulfills the Old

---

[121] See Richard M. Davidson, "Back to the Beginning: Genesis 1–3 and the Theological Center of Scripture," in *Christ, Salvation, and the Eschaton*, ed. Daniel Heinz, Jiří Moskala, and Peter M. van Bemmelen (Berrien Springs, MI: Old Testament Publications, 2009), 5–10. "Center" is not meant to suggest a grid that leads to a "canon within the canon," but more of an "orientation point" in the light of which the whole coheres together.

[122] Ibid., 5–29. Cf. Richard M. Davidson, "Cosmic Metanarrative for the Coming Millennium," *Journal of the Adventist Theological Society* 11/1–2 (Spring–Autumn 2000): 102–119. The same multi-faceted center also emerges from Scripture's "chronological introduction," the book of Job, which was probably written at the same time as Genesis by Moses.

[123] See Davidson, "Genesis 1–3 and the Theological Center of Scripture," 11–24, for discussion of each facet. See also ibid., 24–26, which shows that Ellen G. White pinpoints just these seven facets as she describes the "grand central theme" of Scripture. See Ellen G. White, *Education* (Mountain View, CA: Pacific Press, 1903), 125–126, 190; Ellen G. White, *The Great Controversy* (Mountain View, CA: Pacific Press, 1911), 299, 423, 678; Ellen G. White, *Gospel Workers* (Washington, DC: Review and Herald, 1915), 315; Ellen G. White, *Patriarchs and Prophets* (Washington, DC: Review and Herald, 1890), 44, 596; Ellen G. White, *Selected Messages* (Washington, DC: Review and Herald, 1958), 1:259, 383; and Ellen G. White, *Testimonies for the Church* (Mountain View, CA: Pacific Press, 1904), 8:77.

Testament types and promises.[124] A growing consensus of scholars now recognize the same basic outline of this "big picture" of Scripture,[125] emphasizing its major "plotline" that moves from creation to fall and then to redemption in Christ and a new creation.[126] Recent studies illustrate how the biblical writers were not only faithful exegetes of biblical passages, but also "thought through Scripture in terms of the big picture."[127] Chou traces this "big picture" in each major era of the Old Testament prophets and in each of the New Testament writers, showing the biblical writers' understanding of God's overarching plan in salvation history, and the continuity and consistency of their inner-biblical hermeneutic.[128] The biblical writers are not only faithful to individual antecedent passages they interpret; they also have a grasp of the "big picture" of Scripture, and faithfully expound on the meaning and significance of individual passages in light of this grand biblical metanarrative.

Conclusion

In their inner-biblical hermeneutic, the biblical writers employ a variety of forms and approaches in their use of Scripture. A survey of the Bible writers' use of Scripture reveals that they are careful, sophisticated, precise exegetes and theologians, faithful expositors of God's Word, even as under inspiration they develop the earlier biblical writers' ideas. In their inner-biblical interpretation, the biblical writers do not take Old Testament Scriptures out of context in their citations, do not read back into the Old Testament what was not originally there. On the contrary, they consistently remain faithful to the Old Testament's intention, and consistently engage in solid exegesis of the Old Testament passages using sound hermeneutical principles. The later biblical writers' interpretation of earlier biblical passages are also consistent with each other, while each provides unique insights that contribute toward a rich theology. The New Testament use of Old Testament passages does not involve "Christological re-interpretation," Hellenistic allegory, rabbinic midrash, Qumran-type *pesher*, or other methods of

---

[124] For a discussion of how Jesus is the very center of inner-biblical interpretation, see Diop, "Innerbiblical Interpretation," 141–145.

[125] See Davidson, "Genesis 1–3 and the Theological Center of Scripture," 28–29, and passim.

[126] See Chou, *Hermeneutics of the Biblical Writers*, 227.

[127] Ibid., 159.

[128] Ibid., 93–105, 130–131, 155–196.

interpretation that distort the original meaning of the Old Testament to which they refer. Rather, the New Testament writers join the Old Testament prophets in remaining faithful to the original passages in their immediate and wider Old Testament contexts. Thus they provide a model for sound contemporary interpretation of Scripture. "The way the prophets and apostles read is the way they wrote and the way we ought to read. They have embedded in the Scriptures the way Scripture should be interpreted. The Bible comes with 'hermeneutic included.' . . . Our hermeneutic then must be one of surrender and obedience."[129]

[129] Ibid., 232.

CHAPTER 9

Understanding Biblical Apocalyptic

Gerhard Pfandl

The Scriptures were written for the purpose of revealing God's will to mankind. Apart from legal, historical, and other types of literature in the Bible,[1] there are two categories of prophetic writings in Scripture: classical and apocalyptic prophecies.

Classical prophecies are primarily found in the writings of the prophets Isaiah, Jeremiah, Ezekiel, and the Minor Prophets. Some classical prophecies are found in the Pentateuch: for example, Jacob's prophecies about his sons' future in Genesis 49, Balaam's prophecies concerning Israel in Numbers 23 and 24, and the blessings and curses in Deuteronomy 28. Such prophecies are also found in the historical books: for example, Samuel's prophecy about what a king in Israel would do in 1 Samuel 8:10–18, and Nathan's prophecy in 2 Samuel 12:10–12 concerning David's future after he committed adultery and murder.

A subsection of classical prophecy is eschatological prophecies. In the Old Testament we find many prophecies about the end of Israel and Judah. Amos in the eighth century BC was the first of the prophets to proclaim that the end (Heb. *qets*) was near (Amos 8:2). He called it "the day of the Lord" (Amos 5:18),[2] a fairly common term appearing about twenty times in the prophetic books (Isa 13:6, 9; 58:13; Jer 46:10; Ezek 13:5; 30:3; etc.). That day would be darkness—disaster—and not light (that is, safety). From the context it seems clear that Amos was correcting an old misunderstanding. Prior to Amos, the Day of the Lord in Israel was seen as a day in which the Lord miraculously intervened to bring victory to

[1] The Bible contains also poetry, songs, wisdom sayings, proverbs, gospels, and letters.

[2] All biblical quotations are from the NKJV, unless otherwise indicated.

His people, like Gideon's victory over the Midianites (Judg 7) or David's defeat of the Philistines (2 Sam 5:17–25). These victories gave them hope for the future conquest of God's enemies (Isa 28:21; Jer 15:19–21).

Amos, however, tells Israel that "the day of the Lord" is the day of God's wrath upon them. The fall of Samaria, the capital of the northern kingdom of Israel, in 722 BC to the Assyrians was indeed a dark day and a radical break in the history of Israel. In fact, it was the end of the kingdom of Israel;[3] tens of thousands of its inhabitants were exiled to Assyria and countries in the east, and people of other nations conquered by the Assyrians were settled in northern Israel (2 Kings 17:24). In time, these people intermarried with the Israelites, left in the country by the Assyrians, and their descendants became the Samaritans (Matt 10:5).

In Judah, the fall of Jerusalem in 586 BC to the Babylonians was also a dark day. Jeremiah called it "the time of Jacob's trouble" (Jer 30:7). It was the end of Judah's monarchy and the end of their national independence.[4] From then on they were ruled in succession by the Babylonians, the Persians, the Greeks, and the Romans—except for about eighty years (142–163 BC) when they gained their independence under the Maccabean kings.[5]

In the New Testament we have eschatological prophecies in the Gospels—Matthew 24, Mark 13, and Luke 21—dealing with events prior to and at the second coming of Jesus. In Paul's letters we find such prophecies in 1 Thessalonians 4:15–17 and 2 Thessalonians 2:1–12. These New Testament prophecies dealing with the end of the world are not called apocalyptic prophecies because they lack the characteristics of apocalyptic prophecies as outlined below.

A Comparison Between Prophetic Genres

In contrast to classical prophecies, which are found throughout Scripture, apocalyptic prophecies are principally found in the books of Daniel and Revelation. While both types have as their author the Holy Spirit (2 Pet 1:21), apocalyptic prophecies are significantly different from classical prophecies. They should not be confused with each other because these differences impact their interpretation.

---

[3] Other prophecies about the fall of the northern kingdom are found in Isaiah 9:8–17, Hosea 7:11–16, and Micah 1:1–7.

[4] Other prophecies concerning the end of Judah are found in Jeremiah 4:5–9; 7:30–34; 9:11; Micah 1:8–16; and Zephaniah 1:4–13

[5] Although the Jews recaptured Jerusalem and rededicated the temple in 165 BC, they had to pay tribute to the Seleucids until ca. 142 BC.

Classical prophecy in the Old Testament is addressed to God's people in Israel and Judah, as well as to the surrounding nations. Repeatedly the prophets were instructed to tell the people, among whom they lived, what God had to say to them. Isaiah in the eighth century BC was told, "Tell My people their transgression, and the house of Jacob their sins" (Isa 58:1). And Jeremiah in the sixth century was instructed, "Now therefore, speak to the men of Judah and to the inhabitants of Jerusalem, saying, 'Thus says the LORD: "Behold, I am fashioning a disaster and devising a plan against you. Return now everyone from his evil way, and make your ways and your doings good."'" (Jer 18:11). Many of the prophets also had specific messages for the nations, like Egypt (Isa 19:1; Jer 43:10–13; Ezek 29:3; Joel 3:19, etc.), Babylon (Isa 13:19; Jer 50:1–3; 51:44), Edom (Isa 34:5; Jer 49:17; Amos 1:11; Oba 1:1, 8), and Moab (Isa 15:1; Jer 48:16; Zeph 2:9).

In the New Testament, the prophetic gift is listed, for example, in 1 Corinthians 12:10 and Ephesians 4:11. The evangelist Philip had four daughters who were prophetesses (Acts 21:8–9). Specific classical prophecies are found in the Gospels: for example, Jesus prophecies about Judas (Matt 26:21–25), Peter (Matt 26:31–34), and His own death and resurrection (Matt 16:21; Mark 8:31; 9:31; Luke 9:22). In the book of Acts, the prophet Agabus warned Paul that he will be bound and delivered to the Gentiles if he insists on going to Jerusalem (Acts 21:10–11). From the examples given, we can see that classical prophecies deal with local events, nations, and situations.

Apocalyptic prophecies, by contrast, do not deal with local problems, but are universal in scope. Daniel's prophecies deal with world history from his time to the end of history.[6] Daniel 2 provides a survey of the world powers that will follow the Babylonian Empire, ending with the stone kingdom that will obliterate all earthly powers and establish God's kingdom that will last forever (Dan 2:44). Daniel 7 covers the same time period but spends seven verses (twenty-five percent of the chapter) dealing with the little horn (the papacy), an important world power not mentioned in chapter 2. The book of Revelation takes up the story in the time of Jesus (Rev 1:1; 12:5) and ends with the second coming, followed by the millennium and the new heaven and new earth (Rev 21–22).

Classical prophecy is conditional in nature[7]—that is, its fulfillment is dependent on the response of the people to whom the prophecy applies.

---

[6] World history in this context refers primarily to the nations which had some contact with Israel. Hence Asian, African, or American nations are not mentioned.

[7] "It should be remembered that the promises and the threatenings of God are alike conditional" (Ellen G. White, *Evangelism* [Washington, DC: Review and Herald, 1970], 695).

This principle is set forth in Jeremiah 18:7–8: "The instant I speak concerning a nation and concerning a kingdom, to pluck up, to pull down, and to destroy *it*, if that nation against whom I have spoken turns from its evil, I will relent of the disaster that I thought to bring upon it." For example, in Deuteronomy 28 God sets before the Israelites the alternatives of blessings for obedience and curses for disobedience. Because of their disobedience, Israel and Judah experienced the curses and had to go into exile. Another typical example is the story of Jonah and the repentance of the Ninevites (Jonah 1-4).

Apocalyptic prophecy is not conditional. It emphasizes the sovereignty of God and His control over history. Sovereignty means that God, as ruler of the universe, is free and can do whatever He wants (Ps 115:3). He is not bound or limited by the wishes of His creatures. He is in control of everything that happens here on Earth, and His will is the final cause of all things, even calamities or evil things, because He allows them: for example, "I form the light and create darkness, I make peace and create calamity [Heb. *ra*ʿ "evil," see KJV]; I, the LORD, do all these things" (Isa 45:7). God's sovereignty is supported by such verses as Isaiah 46:9–11:

> Remember the former things of old, For I *am* God, and *there is* no other; *I am* God, and *there is* none like Me, declaring the end from the beginning, And from ancient times *things* that are not *yet* done, saying, "My counsel shall stand, and I will do all My pleasure," Calling a bird of prey from the east, The man who executes My counsel, from a far country. Indeed I have spoken *it*; I will also bring it to pass. I have purposed *it*; I will also do it.[8]

Time prophecies in classical prophecy generally are given in round numbers of years. The Israelites were to be strangers in a foreign land for four hundred years. (Gen 15:13). They were to be shepherds in the wilderness for forty years (Num 14:33). And the Babylonian captivity was to last seventy years (Jer 25:11–12).

Apocalyptic time prophecies are usually phrased in days, weeks, or months—for example, 2,300 "evenings and mornings" or days (Dan 8:14), three and a half days (Rev 11:9, 11), 1,260 days (Rev 12:6), seventy weeks (Dan 9:24), and forty-two months (Rev 11:2; 13:5)—but they stand symbolically for longer periods of actual time. To interpret these time prophecies historicists have used the year-day principle in

[8] See also Psalm 115:3; Daniel 4:35; and Romans 9:20.

which one day in prophecy is counted as one year in history.[9] This concept rests on a firm biblical and historical foundation and constitutes the backbone of the historicist interpretation of apocalyptic prophecy.[10]

Apocalyptic Prophecy

The term "apocalyptic" from the Greek *apokalypsis* (Rev 1:1) means "an unveiling" or "a revelation." Although the word "apocalyptic" is an adjective, "it has come to function as a noun to describe revelatory literature."[11] The word has a twofold reference; it describes the kind of eschatology that appears in apocalyptic writings and it designates a large body of ancient literature.[12] According to John J. Collins, apocalyptic literature may be defined as a

> genre of revelatory literature with a narrative framework, in which a revelation is mediated by an otherworldly being to a human recipient, disclosing a transcendent reality which is both temporal, insofar as it envisages eschatological salvation, and spatial, insofar as it involves another, supernatural world.[13]

A biblical definition of "apocalyptic" first and foremost affirms that God is in control of the events in heaven and on earth; He overrules and judges the affairs of human beings. Although tracing earthly history, biblical apocalyptic primarily focuses on the time of the end, and, because few events remain to be fulfilled, it reminds the reader that time is running out. Biblical apocalyptic relativizes the power of pagan rulers and provides a meaning to life "that transcends the pain and the agony of this world."[14]

Why did God use symbolic imagery in the biblical apocalyptic books instead of straightforward historical narratives? One reason is that symbols are often "the most convenient or forceful way to portray a

---

[9] See Gerhard Pfandl, "In Defense of the Year-day Principle," *Journal of Adventist Theological Society* 23/1 (2012): 3–17.

[10] See the section "The Use of Numbers" in this chapter.

[11] William Johnsson, "Biblical Apocalyptic," in *Handbook of Seventh-day Adventist Theology*, ed. Raoul Dederen (Hagerstown, MD: Review and Herald, 2000), 785.

[12] See George Eldon Ladd, "Why not Prophetic Apocalyptic," *Journal of Biblical Literature* 76 (1957): 192.

[13] John J. Collins, "The Jewish Apocalypses," *Semeia* 14 (1979): 22.

[14] Johnsson, 800.

message. A picture can replace a thousand words."[15] Secondly, these images contain powerful emotional elements that cannot be expressed in other ways. What the prophet sees is similar to a movie that lets the reader participate in the action. He experiences the supernatural world and sees firsthand what the coming judgment will mean for the world. Through that experience readers "can put their own circumstances into perspective."[16]

We must distinguish between the apocalyptic literature in the Bible (Daniel and Revelation) and the Jewish apocalyptic literature, written largely between 200 BC and AD 100,[17] that was modeled on the book of Daniel. Jewish apocalyptic literature "is essentially a literature of the oppressed who saw no hope for the nation simply in terms of politics or on the plane of human history. The battle they were fighting was on a spiritual level; it was to be understood not in terms of politics or economics, but rather in terms of 'spiritual powers in high places.'"[18] So they looked beyond history to God's intervention that would rectify the injustices done to His people. Well-known works of Jewish apocalyptic literature are: *1 Enoch* (ca. 170 BC), *Testaments of the Twelve Patriarchs* (second century BC), *Apocalypse of Zephaniah* (first century BC), *Sibylline Oracles* (30 BC–AD 150), *Testament of Moses* (first century AD), and *4 Ezra* (ca. AD 100).[19]

The major difference between the biblical and Jewish apocalyptic books is their provenance. Daniel and Revelation were written by the prophets Daniel and John under inspiration and became part of the biblical canon. The Jewish works were written under pseudonyms by unknown Jews who were not inspired. This was recognized by the Jewish sages who excluded all Jewish apocalyptic books from the Old Testament canon.[20]

---

[15] Kenneth A. Strand, "Foundational Principles of Interpretation," in *Symposium on Revelation—Book 1* (Silver Spring, MD: Biblical Research Institute, 1992), 23.

[16] Frederick J. Murphey, "Introduction to Apocalyptic Literature," *The New Interpreter's Bible*, ed. Leander E. Keck, 12 vols. (Nashville, TN: Abingdon Press, 1996), 7:3.

[17] Frederick J. Murphey, "Apocalyptic Literature," *International Standard Bible Encyclopedia*, ed. Geoffrey W. Bromiley, 4 vols. (Grand Rapids, MI: Eerdmans, 1986), 1:151.

[18] D. S. Russell, *The Method and Message of Jewish Apocalyptic* (Philadelphia, PA: Westminster Press, 1964), 17–18.

[19] James Charlesworth, ed., *The Old Testament Pseudepigrapha*, 2 vols. (Garden City NY: Doubleday, 1985), 1: passim.

[20] Some would like to call Daniel a Jewish apocalyptic book, but this is incorrect. All Jewish apocalyptic works were written in the intertestamental and New Testament periods; Daniel was written in the sixth century BC and is a biblical apocalyptic book. See Arthur. J. Ferch,

We must further distinguish between eschatology and apocalyptic. "Eschatology" means the knowledge of the end, or the doctrine concerning the end. It can describe a radical break in the course of history, such as we find in the prophecies concerning Israel and Judah's end; this is sometimes called historical eschatology, or "*Volkseschatologie*" (national eschatology)[21]—*eschaton* being the Greek word for "end." "Apocalyptic," or apocalyptic eschatology, on the other hand, always describes the end of history, the end of the world, when this present age will be followed by God's eternal kingdom.[22]

Characteristics of Apocalyptic Literature

As indicated previously, apocalyptic writings focus primarily on the end of world history and the coming kingdom of God. Other important characteristics of apocalyptic literature are set out below.

Visions and Revelations

Apocalyptic writings use visions as a vehicle of presentation. Daniel's visions in chapters 2 and 7–12, with the exception of Daniel 9, all end with the demise of earthly history and the arrival of the kingdom of God. The book of Revelation, based on John's visions on Patmos, reviews church history from the time of Jesus (Rev 12:5) until the time of the end, and concludes with the second coming of Jesus and the establishment of the new earth (Rev 19:11–21; 21:1–4).

Symbolism and Imagery

Symbols and images were at times used by the classical prophets to declare God's will to the people or to predict the future (Isa 5:1–7; Ezek 17:1–10, 22–24; Zech 1–6). However, in Daniel's visions there is a predominance of symbols and images that were later copied by the Jewish authors of apocalyptic books. Also, the book of Revelation is filled with symbols and imagery, many of which are based on the book

---

Daniel on Solid Ground (Hagerstown, MD: Review and Herald, 1988), 30, William H. Shea, *Daniel 1-7*, The Abundant Life Bible Amplifier (Boise, ID: Pacific Press, 1996), 44.

[21] J. P. M. van der Ploeg, "Eschatology in the Old Testament," in *Witness and Tradition* (Leiden: Brill, 1972), 95; Th. C. Vriezen, "Prophecy and Eschatology," *Vetus Testamentum Supplements* 1 (1953): 224; J. Lindblom, "Gibt es eine Eschatologie bei den alttestamentlichen Propheten?," *Studia Theologica* 6 (1952): 88.

[22] Ladd, "Why not Prophetic Apocalyptic," 193.

of Daniel.[23] Of all the Old Testament books alluded to in Revelation, "Daniel is by far the most used."[24]

Cosmic Dualism

Apocalyptic writings present two opposing personified forces in the universe—God and Satan. However, in contrast to Manichaeism where two opposing principles—light and darkness, God and matter—are eternal,[25] in the book of Revelation, Satan, as a created but fallen angel, is not eternal and clearly inferior to God (Rev 12:7–9; 20:10).

Contrast in Time Periods

There are two distinct and separate ages: the present evil age under the control of Satan (John 14:30), and the good eschatological age that God will establish after His victory over Satan (Dan 2:44; Rev 21:1–5). This new age, the kingdom of God, can only be realized by an incursion of the divine presence into human history. "A radical transformation is necessary, and the new transformed age of the kingdom will be so different from the present age as to constitute a new order of things. Such a transformation cannot be produced by the normal flow of historical events but only by the direct action of God."[26]

Resurrection and Judgment

The biblical apocalyptic writings see the righteous resurrected to a kingdom established on a renewed earth, which the faithful will inherit (Dan 12:2; Rev 20:6). The final judgment in Daniel and Revelation has different phases: 1) a pre-Advent phase (Dan 7:9–14; Rev 14:7) to demonstrate to all beings in the universe that the righteous and the wicked "deserve their destiny because they chose it,"[27] 2) a millennial judgment (Rev 20:4–6) to "determine punishment deserved, according to the works done,"[28] and 3) an executive phase at the end of the

---

[23] Richard Lehmann, "Relationships Between Daniel and Revelation," in *Symposium on Revelation—Book 1*, ed. Frank B. Holbrook, Daniel and Revelation Committee Series 6 (Silver Spring, MD: Biblical Research Institute, 1992), 139–140.

[24] Henry B. Swete, *The Apocalypse of St. John: The Greek Text with Introductions, Notes and Indices*, 2nd ed. (London: Macmillan, 1908; repr. Grand Rapids, MI: Eerdmans, n.d.), CLII.

[25] J. N. Birdsall, "Manichaeism," *The New International Dictionary of the Christian Church*, ed. J. D. Douglas (Exeter: Paternoster, 1978), 624.

[26] Ladd, "Why not Prophetic Apocalyptic," 197.

[27] Norman R. Gulley, *Systematic Theology: The Church and the Last Things* (Berrien Springs, MI: Andrews University Press, 2016), 646.

[28] Gerhard F. Hasel, "Divine Judgment," *Handbook of Seventh-day Adventist Theology*, ed. Raoul

millennium (Rev 20:11–15) that "involves eradication of sin and sinners from the universe so that sin will never rise again."[29]

The Appearance of the Messiah

An important element of the apocalyptic books of Daniel and Revelation is the figure of the Messiah. In Daniel 2 He is symbolized by the stone "cut out of the mountain without hands" (v. 45), in chapter 7 He is the Son of Man (v. 13), in chapter 8 the Prince of the host (v. 11), in chapter 9 Messiah the Prince (v. 25), and, in chapter 12, He is Michael and "the man clothed in linen (vv. 1, 6). In Revelation the Messiah appears in many different images. Two important ones are the Lamb (Rev 5:6; 6:1) and the rider on the white horse on whose thigh is written the name "KING OF KINGS AND LORD OF LORDS" (Rev 19:11–16). The second coming is "the greatest rescue mission of all time, an experience that will be forever unforgettable."[30]

Angelic Interpreters

In apocalyptic writings angels play an important role. In Daniel the angel Gabriel appears and explains to him the visions in chapters 8 and 9 (8:16; 9:21). Although in Revelation the *angelus interpres* is not named, he appears frequently (1:1; 17:1–18; 19:9, 10; 22:1, 6–11). Together with the *angelus interpres*, angels play an important role throughout the book of Revelation, appearing in over fifty verses (Rev 2:1, 8, 12, 18; 3:1, etc.). Additionally, in Revelation the twenty-four elders explain some things in word and song (Rev 4:10–11; 5:8–12; 11:16–18; 19:4).

History of the Interpretation of Apocalyptic Prophecies

Before we look at the principles of how to interpret apocalyptic prophecies, we need to consider the history of the interpretation of Daniel and Revelation, which goes back to the time of Daniel himself. An angel interpreted for Daniel the visions he had received (Dan 7:16; 8:15–16; 9:21–22; 10:10–11; 12:5–9). The Qumran community valued and used the book of Daniel, as indicated by the eight fragments of the book and the nine non-biblical scrolls that were found at Qumran

---

Dederen (Hagerstown, MD: Review and Herald, 2001), 846.

[29] Ibid., 847.

[30] Gulley, 662.

and which deal with the book of Daniel.[31] There is evidence that the Qumran community used some key elements of Daniel in the explanation of their self-understanding.[32]

In the writings of the church fathers we find several commentaries on Daniel,[33] and over time a greater variety of interpretations than for any of the other books in the Bible came into existence. The reason is that images and symbols allow for different interpretations depending on the background and worldview of the interpreter, just as modern art often receives a multitude of interpretations. Over time, several schools of interpretation have come into existence that have for centuries competed for the attention of scholars. These schools of interpretation lead to widely different conclusions as to what the text actually says. For example, interpreters who see the secret rapture in Revelation 4:1 place the rest of the book into the future, while others see it fulfilled in the past or fulfilled throughout history. We will briefly describe the various schools of interpretation that exist today.

The Historicist School

This is the oldest school of interpretation, and until the nineteenth century it was the dominant one. The first historicist interpretation is found in Daniel 2 and 8, where the *angelus interpres* identifies the first three kingdoms as Babylon, Medo-Persia, and Greece (Dan 2:28; 8:20–21). In the New Testament, Jesus refers to "the abomination of desolation" in Daniel 9:27, 11:31; and 12:11 in connection with the future of Jerusalem (Matt 24:15). Historicist interpretations can also be found in the writings of the church fathers, such as Hippolytus[34] and Jerome.[35] It was taught by Joachim of Floris (1130–1202) in the twelfth century[36] and became

---

[31] Only eight other biblical and non-biblical books had more fragments found at Qumran. See Peter W. Flint, "The Daniel Traditions at Qumran," in *The Book of Daniel: Composition and Reception,* ed. John J. Collins and Peter W. Flint (Leiden: Brill, 2002), 329.

[32] John J. Collins, *Daniel,* Hermeneia (Minneapolis, MN: Fortress Press, 1993), 73.

[33] For example, Hippolytus of Rome (ca. 170–236). His Daniel commentary is the oldest surviving Christian commentary on Scripture. Others who wrote on Daniel were Origin (182–254), Polychronius (d. 430), and Jerome (347–420).

[34] For example, he interpreted the four kingdoms in Daniel 2 and 7 as Babylon, Medo-Persia, Greece, and Rome (Hippolytus, *Treatise on Christ and Antichrist* 23–28, in *Ante-Nicene Fathers,* ed. Alexander Roberts and James Donaldson, 10 vols. [Edinburgh, 1885; repr., Peabody, MA: Hendrickson, 1994], 5:209–210).

[35] Like Hippolytus, he also interpreted the four kingdoms in Daniel 2 and 7 as Babylon, Medo-Persia, Greece, and Rome. (*Jerome's Commentary on Daniel,* trans. G. L. Archer, Jr. [Grand Rapids, MI: Baker, 1958], 31–32, 72–75).

[36] Joachim of Floris, *Liber Concordie Novi ac Veteris Testamenti* (Venice: Simon de Luere, 1519), fol. 127.

the standard interpretation of Protestant expositors after the time of the Reformation.

Historicists believe in the divine inspiration of the books of Daniel and Revelation, that the book of Daniel was written by the prophet Daniel in the sixth century BC,[37] and that its main prophecies cover the period from the Babylonian Empire to the second coming of Christ. They believe that the apostle John wrote the book of Revelation and that its prophecies cover the period from John's day to the end of the millennium. They interpret the time prophecies with the year-day principle and generally see the antichrist—portrayed under the symbols of Daniel's little horn, and John's first beast in Revelation 13, as the papacy.[38] Seventh-day Adventists generally use the historicist method in interpreting Daniel and Revelation, because 1) it is used by the angel Gabriel in his explanation of the vision in Daniel 8:20–22, and 2) it is the only method that makes sense when the prophecies are compared with the historical record.

The Historic-Preterist School

The roots of historic Preterism go back to the early centuries of church history. The Jewish historian Josephus (AD 37–100), for example, interpreted the little horn in Daniel 8:9 as the Syrian king Antiochus Epiphanes which became a standard interpretation of this school. Clement of Alexandria (AD 150–215) interpreted the 2,300 days of Daniel 8:14 as six years and four months, "during the half of which Nero held sway,"[39] and the other half his successors. It is not clear how Clement computed the times because Nero alone reigned for about fourteen years (AD 54–68).

---

[37] Albert Barnes, *Daniel*, 2 vols. (1853, repr., Grand Rapids, MI: Baker, 1950), 1:45; Adam Clarke, *The Holy Bible*, 6 vols. (New York: Abingdon, n.d.), 4:562; F. D. Nichol, ed., *The Seventh-day Adventist Bible Commentary*, 7 vols. (Washington DC: Review and Herald, 1953–57), 4:743; and C. Mervyn Maxwell, *God Cares*, 2 vols. (Boise, ID: Pacific Press, 1981), 1:11.

[38] Joseph Tanner, *Daniel and the Revelation* (London: Hodder and Stoughton, 1898), 167; Uriah Smith, *The Prophecies of Daniel and the Revelation*, rev. ed. (Mountain View, CA: Pacific Press, 1944) 520 ; Clarence H. Hewitt, *The Seer of Babylon* (Boston, MA: Advent Christian Herald, 1948), 107; Nichol, *Seventh-day Adventist Bible Commentary*, 4:826; George McCready Price, *The Greatest of the Prophets* (Mountain View, CA: Pacific Press, 1955) 139; Ranko Stefanovic, *Revelation of Jesus Christ*, rev. ed. (Berrien Springs, MI: Andrews University Press, 2009), 419; and Jacques B. Doukhan, *Secrets of Revelation* (Hagerstown, MD: Review and Herald, 2002), 115. Barnes, *Daniel*, 2:326, following Martin Luther, interpreted the first beast in Revelation 13 as political Rome and the second beast as the papacy.

[39] Clement, "Stromata," in *Ante-Nicene Fathers*, 2:334.

Historic Preterism became an important interpretation in the time of the Counter-Reformation. When the Protestant Reformers identified the papacy with the prophesied antichrist in the books of Daniel and Revelation,[40] the Spanish Jesuit Luis de Alcazar (1554–1613) claimed that these prophecies had already been fulfilled in the time of the Roman Empire. Thus, the papacy could not be the antichrist.[41]

Interpreters of the historic-preterist school consider the book of Daniel as a revelation from God, but generally limit the fulfillment of its prophecies to the time period that runs from the time of Daniel in the sixth century BC to the first coming of Christ, following the demise of the fourth kingdom in Daniel 2 and 7—that is, "the empires of the Macedonian Diadochi, and particularly, that of the Seleucidae."[42] Some, like Samuel Lee, identify the fourth kingdom with the Romans.[43] Nevertheless, they all agree that the stone kingdom represents the church, which had its beginning in the time of the Roman Empire.[44]

The book of Revelation is applied to the first century of the Christian era in which the "man of sin" (2 Thess 2:3) appeared in the person of the Roman Emperor Nero and the second coming took place in the destruction of the temple in Jerusalem in AD 70, at which time the Old Testament dispensation came to a close and a new order of things began.[45] Though not visible to the naked eye, except for the judgment on Jerusalem, Jesus came and the resurrection of the righteous took place as predicted in 1 Thessalonians 4:17.[46]

During the twentieth century it seemed that the historic preterist interpretation was disappearing almost completely. However, in recent

---

[40] For example, Martin Luther wrote, "We here are of the conviction that the papacy is the seat of the true and real Antichrist against whose deceit and vileness all is permitted for the salvation of souls. Personally I declare that I owe the Pope no other obedience than that to the Antichrist" (J. G. Walch, ed., *Dr. Martin Luther's Sämmtliche Schriften*, 25 vols. [St. Louis, MO: Concordia, 1881–1910], 15, col 1639, cited in L. E. Froom, *The Prophetic Faith of Our Fathers,* 4 vols. [Washington, DC: Review and Herald, 1950], 2:256).

[41] Norman Geisler, *Systematic Theology*, 4 vols. (Minneapolis, MN: Bethany House, 2005), 4:636. For an extended account of these developments, see Froom, *Prophetic Faith*, 2:484–532.

[42] Otto Zöckler, *The Book of the Prophet Daniel,* Lange's Commentary (New York: Scribner, 1915), 153 and Robert M. Gurney, *God in Control* (Worthing: H. E. Walter, 1980), 33, 45.

[43] Samuel Lee, *An Inquiry into the Nature, Progress, and End of Prophecy,* 3 vols. (Cambridge: University Press, 1849), 2:148 and J. E. Thomson, *Daniel*, Pulpit Commentary (London: Paul Kegan, Trench, Trübner, 1898), 73.

[44] Lee, *Inquiry into the Nature,* 151; Zöckler, *Prophet Daniel*, 78–79; Gurney, *God in Control*, 44–48.

[45] James Stuart Russel, *The Parousia* (London: T. Fisher Unwin, 1887; repr., Bradford, PA: International Preterist Association, 2003), 182, 546.

[46] Ibid., 566.

decades the International Preterist Association has revived this view and is strongly advocating the interpretation that the battle of Armageddon was fought in AD 70 and that Christ returned to this earth at that time.[47]

The Historical-Critical or Modern-Preterist School

The roots of this school of interpretation go back to Porphyry, a philosopher in the third century AD, who taught that the book of Daniel was written by an unknown Jew in the second century BC, and that Daniel's prophecies, therefore, are *vaticinia ex eventu* (Latin for "prophecies written after the event").[48] This view was revived in post-Reformation times, when it was brought out of its obscurity by Hugh Broughton (1549–1612), a fellow of St John's College, Cambridge. It gained prominence in the eighteenth and nineteenth centuries and has today become the dominant force in biblical studies.[49] Historical-critical scholars, who deny the inspiration and authority of Scripture and, therefore, also the existence of true prophecy, see the book of Daniel as a reflection of the political and religious situation of the Jewish people under the Syrian king Antiochus IV Epiphanes, who persecuted the Jews.[50] Not accepting the reality of true prophecies, they believe that the prophecies of the book of Revelation refer to historical events in the time of the Roman Empire during the first century AD. For example, the first beast in Revelation 13 is the Roman Empire and the second beast either paganism[51] or the ministers of the emperor worship.[52]

The Futurist-Dispensational School

One of the defenders of the papacy against the Reformers' identification of the pope with the antichrist was the Spanish Jesuit Francisco

---

[47] Ed Stevens, *What Happened in AD 70?* (Bradford, PA: Kingdom Publications, 1997), 2, 5.

[48] Nichol, *Seventh-day Adventist Bible Commentary*, 4:42.

[49] According to one representative, Daniel's prophecies are "a review of history, in the guise of prophecy" (John J. Collins, *Daniel with an Introduction to Apocalyptic Literature*, Forms of the Old Testament Literature, vol. 20 [1984]: 33).

[50] J. A. Montgomery, *A Critical and Exegetical Commentary on the Book of Daniel*, ICC (Edinburgh: T&T Clark, 1927), 96; Aage Bentzen, *Daniel*, Handbuch zum Alten Testament (Tübingen: J. C. B. Mohr, 1952), 8; Norman Porteous, *Daniel*, (Philadelphia, PA: Westminster, 1965), 13; Collins, *Daniel*, 61; and Carol A. Newsom, *Daniel*, (Louisville, KY: Westminster John Knox, 2014), 11.

[51] Bruce M. Metzger, *Breaking the Code: Understanding the Book of Revelation* (Nashville, TN: Abingdon, 1993), 75; Swete, 162; Isbon T. Beckwith, *The Apocalypse of John* (London: MacMillan, 1919; repr. Eugene, OR: Wipf and Stock, 2001), 633.

[52] Beckwith, 639, 169.

Ribera (1537–1591), who applied most of the prophecies in the books of Daniel and Revelation to the future. He "made Antichrist a future infidel Jew, not a Christian, to reign in Jerusalem, not in Rome. His was the main Roman Catholic counterattack to the Reformation, and became the standard Catholic position."[53]

Futurist-dispensationalist interpreters, like historicists and historic preterists, accept Daniel's authorship of the book in the sixth century BC,[54] but unlike historicists, they generally do not apply the figure of the antichrist to the papacy or another power in the past. Rather, they expect that a personal antichrist will appear in the time of the end and continue in power for seven years and fulfill what is said of the little horn in Daniel and of the beast-antichrist in the book of Revelation.[55]

The Idealist School

Though Origin's (ca. AD 184–253) and Augustine's (AD 354–430) allegorizing method of interpretation may be considered a forerunner, the idealist school is a fairly modern school of interpretation. It does not attempt to find specific historical fulfillments of the prophecies in the books of Daniel and Revelation, but simply takes these prophecies as depicting the spiritual conflict between Christ and Satan in all ages. Fulfillment of the prophecies is, therefore, seen either "as entirely spiritual or as recurrent, finding representative expressions in historical events throughout the age, rather than in one-time, specific fulfillments."[56] Thus the antichrist in the time of John was the Roman Empire as a representative of all anti-Christian governments throughout history.

These major schools of interpretation are not ironclad systems that can in every single instance be neatly separated. At times there is some overlapping, and some interpreters, although primarily following one school, may accept some interpretations from another school as part of their own expositions.

---

[53] Nichol, *Seventh-day Adventist Bible Commentary*, 4:51.

[54] H. C. Leupold, *Exposition of Daniel* (Wartburg Press, 1949; repr., Grand Rapids, MI: Baker 1969), 17; G. Maier, *Der Prophet Daniel*, Wuppertaler Studienbibel (Wuppertal: R. Brockhaus, 1982), 62; John F. Walvoord, *Daniel* (Chicago: Moody, 1971), 11; and Gleason L. Archer, "Daniel," *The Expositor's Bible Commentary*, 12 vols. (Grand Rapids, MI: Zondervan, 1985), 7:6.

[55] In the midst of the seven years, the antichrist will begin to persecute believers. This persecution for three and a half years is called "the great tribulation." See Edward J. Young, *The Prophecy of Daniel* (Grand Rapids, MI: Eerdmans, 1949), 163; Archer, 93–94; Walvoord, *Daniel*, 175-176; and Stephen R. Miller, *Daniel*, NAC (Nashville, TN: Broadman & Holman, 2001), 271. Revelation 4:1 "come up here" represents for futurists and dispensationalists the rapture, and the rest of the book describes events following the rapture.

[56] Steve Gregg, *Revelation: Four Views* (Nashville, TN: Thomas Nelson, 1997), 3.

The Apotelesmatic Principle

Having looked at the various schools of interpretation, we need to consider not another school of interpretation but a method of interpretation that several decades ago created some controversy in the Adventist church. This method is called the apotelesmatic principle; it was one of the issues in the controversy around the teaching of Desmond Ford in the early 1980s.[57] The term "apotelesmatic" was used by Franz Delitzsch in the nineteenth century to explain the fact that in prophecy events are depicted as closely following each other, when in history they are actually separated by long time periods. "All prophecy is complex," he wrote. "That is, it views together what history unrolls, and all prophecy is apotelesmatic, that is, it portrays behind the next epoch-making historical event already the climax at the end."[58] This is similar to what Richard Davidson calls "prophetic telescoping," which means "the prophet frequently jumps from the local, contemporary crisis to the eschatological Day of the Lord (e.g., Joel 2–3), or from one peak of the predictive fulfillment to another, without reference to the valley in between."[59] While this meaning of the term "apotelesmatic" is acceptable, when introduced into Adventism it acquired a different sense with different connotations, as we shall see.

The term "apotelesmatic" was introduced into the Adventist church by George McCready Price, who wrote in his Daniel commentary, "Some scholars have spoken of an apotelesmatic accomplishment of the prophecy, by which is meant that a partial or preliminary fulfillment may take place in one age, then long afterward a much more complete fulfillment."[60] He applied this principle not only to classical but also to apocalyptic prophecy. Thus, he assumed that an apocalyptic prophecy can have a double fulfillment—a position that Desmond Ford extended into multiple fulfillments. However, multiple fulfillments of apocalyptic

---

[57] Desmond Ford was a charismatic preacher and teacher at Avondale College in Australia in the 1960s and 1970s. Following the Glacier View conference in 1980, he lost his job and ministerial license because of his rejection of Ellen G. White's authority in doctrinal matters, his denial of the year-day principle, and his belief that the Adventist sanctuary teaching, specifically the investigative judgment, is not biblical.

[58] F. Delitzsch, "Daniel," *Real-Encyklopädie für protestantische Theologie und Kirche,* ed. J. J. Herzog and G. L. Plitt, zweite Auflage, 18 vols. (Leipzig: J. C. Hinrichs'sche Buchhandlung, 1878), 3:479. See also Carl Friedrich Keil, *Biblischer Commentar über den Propheten Daniel,* Biblischer Commentar über das Alte Testament, part 3, vol. 5 (Leipzig: Dörffling und Franke, 1869), 8.

[59] Richard M. Davidson, "Interpreting Old Testament Prophecy," in *Understanding Scripture: An Adventist Approach*, ed. George W. Reid (Silver Spring, MD: Biblical Research Institute, 2005), 185.

[60] Price, *The Greatest of the Prophets*, 30.

prophecies deny the year-day principle and the historicist method of interpretation by accepting a modified idealistic method of interpretation. Therefore, the Daniel and Revelation Committee of the General Conference, which studied this issue after the Glacier View Conference,[61] concluded that

> apocalyptic prophecies have neither dual nor multiple fulfillments. On the contrary each symbol has but one fulfillment. For example, in the book of Daniel each metal and each beast has only one fulfillment. The ten horns and the one horn in Daniel 7, the one and the four and the one in Daniel 8, have only one fulfillment. Dual, or twofold, fulfillments may be present in some general/classical prophetic predictions where contextual scriptural indications make this clear and the details of the specifications are met in each instance. But apocalyptic prophecy, as found in the books of Daniel and Revelation, has but one fulfillment for each symbol.[62]

Desmond Ford used the apotelesmatic principle in his interpretation of apocalyptic prophecy to affirm that "a prophecy fulfilled, or fulfilled in part, or unfulfilled at the appointed time, may have a later or recurring, or consummated fulfillment."[63] Using this principle, he was able to accept multiple applications of prophetic symbols. Thus the little horn finds a preliminary fulfillment in Antiochus IV Epiphanes (175–164 BC)[64] and later fulfillments in Rome, pagan and papal, as well as in the final antichrist.[65] However, apart from the fact that Antiochus IV persecuted the Jews and desecrated the temple, none of the prophetic details fit the story of Antiochus. For example, 1) the little horn came up among ten horns (Dan 7:8). Antiochus IV did not come up among ten Hellenistic

---

[61] During August 10–15, 1980, a theological conference was held at Glacier View, Colorado, at which more than one hundred theologians and administrators considered proposals of Dr. Desmond Ford on the subject of the sanctuary and the investigative judgment, as well as the role of Ellen G. White in the Seventh-day Adventist Church.

[62] Gerhard F. Hasel, "Fulfillments of Prophecy," *Seventy Weeks, Leviticus, Nature of Prophecy*, Daniel & Revelation Committee Series, ed. Frank B. Holbrook (Silver Spring, MD: Biblical Research Institute, 1986), 290.

[63] Desmond Ford, Glacier View document: "*Daniel 8:14: The Day of Atonement and the Investigative Judgment*," cited in *Ministry*, October 1980, 21. For a critic of Ford's apotelesmatic principle, see Roberto Ouro, "The Apotelesmatic Principle: Origin and Application," *Journal of the Adventist Theological Society* 9/1–2 (1998): 326–342.

[64] Desmond Ford, *Daniel* (Nashville, TN: Southern Publishing Association, 1978), 172.

[65] Ibid., 174.

kings. 2) The little horn became greater than his fellows (Dan 7:20). Antiochus IV Epiphanes was not greater than the other kings in his time. Seleucus I and Antiochus III, the Great, were definitely greater kings than Antiochus IV. 3) According to Daniel 8, the ram (Persia) became great (8:4); the goat (Greece) grew very great (8:8); and the little horn grew exceedingly great (8:9). Antiochus IV was not greater than Medo-Persia or Greece. 4) The little horn comes in the latter days of their kingdom (Dan 8:23). Antiochus IV Epiphanes did not come towards the end of the Seleucid kingdom. He was the eighth king in the Seleucid kingdom and was followed by another twenty kings.

At the Glacier View Conference the apotelesmatic principle was rejected by most of the attendants because "it lacks external control" and "any principle of interpretation that permits any prophecy to mean many things is not a helpful tool."[66] As far as we know, apart from some Adventists,[67] no scholar outside of the church uses the term "apotelesmatic principle" in the interpretation of apocalyptic prophecies,[68] but the idealistic interpretation comes very close to it.[69]

When we compare the various schools of interpretations, we take note of the fact that the specific angelic interpretations in the book of Daniel are along historicist lines (Dan 8:20–21). Jesus Himself used the historicist method in Mark 1:15 when he said, "The time is fulfilled, and the kingdom of God is at hand." He alluded to the seventy-week prophecy in Daniel 9:24–26 that predicted His appearance as the Messiah. Thus, Scripture itself shows that historicism is the method that the angels and Jesus used. It is really the only method that satisfies all the biblical data.

Principles for the Interpretation of Apocalyptic Prophecies

The principles for interpreting classical prophecy are found elsewhere in this book. While there are some parallels, the principles for the

---

[66] "Statement on Desmond Ford Document," *Ministry*, October 1980, 22.

[67] E.g., R. Cottrell, "The Apotelesmatic Principle," Good News Unlimited, http://www.goodnews-unlimited.org/library/exegesisofdaniel/22part6.cfm (accessed July 3, 2018).

[68] B. Ramm, *Protestant Biblical Interpretation* (Boston, MA: Wilde, 1956), 233, speaks of "multiple fulfillments," and L. Berkhof, *Principles of Biblical Interpretation* (Grand Rapids, MI: Baker, 1950), 153, mentions "two or threefold fulfillment." But both refer to general and not apocalyptic prophecy.

[69] While Ford saw specific fulfillments of the little horn (Antiochus Epiphanes, papacy, antichrist at the end of time), the idealist view does not find specific historical fulfillments of the prophecies in Daniel and Revelation, but simply takes these prophecies as depicting the spiritual conflict between Christ and Satan in all ages.

interpretation of classical prophecies cannot simply be applied to apocalyptic prophecy. For example, we have already seen that apocalyptic prophecies, in contrast to classical prophecies, are not conditional and they do not have double or multiple fulfillments.[70] Here are some basic principles for the interpretation of apocalyptic prophecies.

Begin with Prayer

All study of Scripture should begin with a prayer for the Holy Spirit to open our minds to the truths revealed in the passage under study, but it is especially important when we study apocalyptic prophecy, which is largely symbolic. The prophet Daniel led an active prayer life (Dan 6:10). When he had difficulties understanding God's will, he prayed for understanding (Dan 2:17–18; 9:3). We would do well to follow his example.

Remember that Scripture is its Own Interpreter

According to 2 Timothy 3:16, Scripture is inspired by the Holy Spirit and, therefore, trustworthy. A general principle of interpretation is that "scripture interprets scripture, one passage being the key to other passages."[71] For example, the ram and goat in Daniel 8:3, 5 are explained as the kingdoms of Medo-Persia and Greece in Daniel 8:20–21; the many waters on which the great harlot sits in Revelation 17:1 are explained in verse 15 as "peoples, multitudes, nations, and tongues." Bible concordances and dictionaries can be very helpful in this. Nevertheless, every text must be studied in its own context because in the end the immediate context determines the text's meaning. "The search for divine truth must be careful, diligent, and balanced."[72]

Because Scripture was written in Hebrew, Aramaic, and Greek—languages most people do not read—it is recommended to use and compare several translations to ensure that the English text says the same as

---

[70] For other differences, see Jon Paulien, "The Hermeneutics of Biblical Apocalyptic," in *Understanding Scripture,* ed. George W. Reid, (Silver Spring, MD: Biblical Research Institute, 2005), 249. See also Richard M. Davidson and Joel Iparraguirre, "'¿Entiendes lo que lees?': Claves para interpretar las profecías apocalípticas," en *"Porque cerca está el día de YHWH": Estudios en escatología*, ed. Alvaro F. Rodríguez and Roy E. Graf (Lima, Peru: Ediciones Theologika - Universidad Peruana Unión, 2018), 23-58.

[71] Ellen G. White, *Evangelism,* 581. Because the Holy Spirit is the real author of Scripture, a comparison of what He says on a particular topic in different places may help explain a particular text. For example, Daniel 2, 7, and 8 are parallel prophecies; thus Daniel 8:20–21 helps clarify the meaning of the beasts in Daniel 7.

[72] Kenneth Strand, "Foundational Principles of Interpretation," in *Symposium on Revelation—Book 1,* 9.

the original language. It is best to use versions that come as close as possible to the original text.[73]

Pay Attention to the Literary Structure

To understand the messages of Daniel and Revelation, it is important to analyze the books' literary structures. The book of Daniel has historical chapters (Dan 1, 3–6) and apocalyptic chapters (Dan 2, 7–12). The prophetic chapters follow the principle of recapitulation[74]—that is, chapters 2 and 7–12 all cover the same historical period from the time of the ancient kingdoms of Babylon and Medo-Persia to the second advent:

Daniel 2	Babylon to second advent (stone kingdom)
Daniel 7	Babylon to second advent (kingdom given to the saints)
Daniel 8–9	Medo-Persia to second advent (little horn is broken)
Daniel 10–12	Medo-Persia to second advent (the resurrection)

Each vision has its special focus, and later visions enlarge upon and provide further explanations for earlier visions. The book of Daniel clearly shows that the principle of recapitulation is a valid principle of prophetic interpretation, because each vision covers approximately the same historical era but focuses on different aspects of the events depicted.

The book of Revelation, like Daniel, has historical sections (Rev 1–3; 22:6-21), but the rest of the book is apocalyptic. It resembles the book of Daniel in using the same principle of recapitulation or repetition. For example, the seven seals (Rev 6), the seven trumpets (Rev 8–9), and the vision of the cosmic conflict in Revelation 12–14 all describe events beginning in the first century AD and reaching to the final consummation.

Revelation can be divided into two parts: chapters 1–11 and 12–22. Each section begins in the first century and ends with the second coming, but this is not the only way it can be organized. Kenneth Strand discovered that the whole book forms a chiasm[75] with a prologue (Rev 1:1–10a) and

---

[73] For example, use more literal translations like the NASB, ESV, and RSV and compare them with dynamic translations like the NIV and REB. See also Tarsee Lee, "How to Choose a Bible Translation," *Interpreting Scripture*, ed. Gerhard Pfandl (Silver Spring, MD: Biblical Research Institute, 2010), 25–31. See chapter 3 by Clinton Wahlen "Versions, Variants, and the Trustworthiness of Scripture," in the present volume.

[74] For more details, see Ekkehardt Mueller, *When Prophecy Repeats Itself: Recapitulation in Revelation*, BRI Release 14 (Silver Springs, MI: Biblical Research Institute, 2015).

[75] A chiasm is a structure in which the first section corresponds to the last section, the second

an epilogue (Rev 22:6–21). The first part, the historical era, comprises chapters 1–14; the second part, the eschatological judgment era, covers chapters 15–22:5.[76] Others see the chiasm a little differently—for example, reducing the eight visions to seven.[77] At any rate, when interpreting Revelation we must keep in mind whether a passage is part of the historical or eschatological era.

Study the Meaning of Symbols

Daniel and Revelation abound in symbolic language and should be interpreted accordingly. In interpreting symbols, we need to take note of the following: 1) Look for interpretations in the passage itself. For example, in Daniel 8 the ram and the goat in verses 3 and 5 are explained as the kingdoms of Medo-Persia and Greece in verses 20 and 21. In Revelation 1 the "seven stars" in verse 16 are explained in verse 20 as "the angels of the seven churches, and the seven lampstands which you saw are the seven churches." 2) Look for interpretations in other parts of the book or in other books by the same author. 3) With the help of a concordance, study the use of symbols in other parts of Scripture. 4) Sometimes "ancient Near Eastern documents [such as the Jewish apocalyptic books] may throw light on the meaning of symbols, although scriptural use may alter those meanings."[78] 5) Consider the context of the prophecy; what historical fulfillment fits the symbol best?

Take Note of Old Testament Allusions and Types in Revelation

Although the book of Revelation does not formally quote or cite the Old Testament,[79] there are many allusions to Old Testament texts in the book. For example, the seven trumpets harken back to the ten plagues in Exodus: "The first trumpet is especially reminiscent of the hail plague (Exod 9:22 ff.). The second and third recall when Moses turned the waters of Egypt to blood (7:14ff.). . . . The fourth and fifth recall the plague of darkness (10:21ff.)."[80] The first beast in Revelation 13 is a composite of the beasts in Daniel 7. The first angel's message

---

from the beginning with the second from the end, the third from the beginning with the third from the end, etc. It may have a single or a double peak in the middle.

[76] See Kenneth A. Strand, "The Eight Basic Visions," in *Symposium on Revelation—Book 1*, 35–37.

[77] See Stefanovic, *Revelation of Jesus Christ*, 30.

[78] See appendix "Methods of Bible Study," 467, in the present volume.

[79] Jon Paulien, *Decoding Revelation's Trumpets*, Andrews University Seminary Doctoral Dissertation Series, vol. 11 (Berrien Springs, MI: Andrews University Press, 1987), 54 and Wilfred J. Harrington, *Understanding the Apocalypse* (Washington, DC: Corpus Books, 1969), 15.

[80] Paulien, *Decoding Revelation's Trumpets*, 231.

(Rev 14:7) alludes to the creation story in the fourth commandment (Exod 20:11), etc.

Some Old Testament prophecies that were fulfilled in the history of Israel became types of end-time events in the book of Revelation. For example, the Cyrus prophecy in Isaiah 44:28 and 45:1–6 was fulfilled when about 150 years later Cyrus conquered Babylon by diverting the River Euphrates and releasing the Jews from the Babylonian captivity. This event is, in Revelation, a type of what will happen in the time of the end with God's people:

Old Testament	End Time
Literal Israel	Spiritual Israel
Literal captivity	Spiritual captivity
Literal Babylon	Spiritual Babylon
Literal Euphrates	Spiritual Euphrates
The Anointed—Cyrus	The Anointed—Christ

Israel's Old Testament enemies like Babylon, Egypt, Edom, Gog, and Magog, function as types of the end-time enemies of God's people in Revelation. The book is also saturated with sanctuary types. The three sanctuary scenes in Revelation 1:12–20, 4:1–5:14, and 8:2–5 emphasize the three Old Testament festivals—Passover, Feast of Weeks (Pentecost), and the Feast of Trumpets that led up to the Day of Atonement—a theme that dominates in the second half of Revelation. Davidson aptly concludes that "the final book of the New Testament gathers all the major threads of Old Testament sanctuary typology and weaves them into an intricate and beautiful tapestry to form the backdrop for the entire book."[81]

Study the Use of Numbers

Most of the numbers in Daniel and Revelation have symbolic meaning, but not all. In the book of Daniel, for example, the prophecy of "seven times" in 4:16 is not symbolic; it refers to seven literal years. We do not apply the year-day concept to this time period because 1) this is a historical chapter, not a prophetic one, and 2) it is a period of judgment concerning Nebuchadnezzar only. In verse 34 we read, "At the end of the time I, Nebuchadnezzar, lifted my eyes to heaven." This clearly

---

[81] Richard M. Davidson, "Sanctuary Typology," in *Symposium on Revelation—Book 1*, 126.

indicates that the "times" were literal and not prophetic years. The LXX reads "seven years," and most ancient and modern interpreters agree with this translation.

The one thousand years in Revelation 20:3, 7 are also literal and not symbolic because the last three chapters of Revelation contain many literal elements—for example, angels, Satan, Jesus Christ, the resurrection, judgment, second death, lake of fire, new Jerusalem, new heaven and earth, etc. In this context, therefore, it is not necessary to understand the thousand years symbolically in harmony with the general principle that the text's literal meaning should be assumed unless a figure or symbol is clearly being employed.

In the book of Revelation, the number six is a symbol of humanity;[82] it falls short of seven, which is the sacred number. Six is the number of imperfection, the number of a person without God. Hence the "number of the beast . . . is the number of a man: His number *is* 666" (Rev 13:18).[83] Seven is the number of perfection, of completeness.[84] In the book of Revelation we find seven churches (chaps. 2 and 3), seven seals (chaps. 5 and 6), seven trumpets (chaps. 8 and 9), seven last plagues (chaps. 15 and 16), and seven kings (17:10).

As mentioned above, the year-day principle helps to understand the meaning of the symbolic numbers in apocalyptic prophecies. The main points in support of this concept can be summarized as follows:[85]

1) Since the visions in Daniel and Revelation are largely symbolic, with a number of different beasts representing important historical empires (Dan 7:3–7; 8:3–5, 20–21; Rev 13:1, 11), the time periods (e.g., Dan 7:25; 8:14; Rev 12:6, 14; 13:5) should also be seen as symbolic.

2) The fact that the visions in the book of Daniel deal with the rise and fall of known empires in history that existed for hundreds of years indicates that the prophetic time periods must also cover long time periods. For example, the 2,300 evenings and mornings cover

---

[82] Human beings were created on the sixth day and six days were appointed for work.

[83] Seventh-day Adventists have traditionally interpreted the number 666 as a symbol of the papacy. See Smith, *The Prophecies*, 619; Nichol, *Seventh-day Adventist Bible Commentary*, 7:823; Froom, *Prophetic Faith*, 4:1102; and Edwin de Kock, *The Truth About 666* (Edinburg, TX: Edwin de Kock, 2011), 776–790.

[84] God rested on the Sabbath, the seventh day, and the seven-day cycle completes a unit of time—the week. Seven was "a sacred number in virtually all the ancient Semitic cultures" (B. C. Birch, "Number," in *International Standard Bible Encyclopedia*, ed. Geoffrey W. Bromiley (Grand Rapids, MI: Eerdmans), 3:559) and probably part of the memory of the creation week.

[85] See Appendix F in Ford, *Daniel*, 300; and William H. Shea, *Selected Studies on Prophetic Interpretation*, rev. ed., Daniel and Revelation Committee Series (Silver Spring, MD: Biblical Research Institute, 1992), 67–110.

the times of the Medo-Persian and Grecian empires; the 2,300 days, therefore, cannot refer to only six years and about four months. Also, the events depicted in Daniel 9:24–27 could not have happened in seventy literal weeks.

In Revelation 12–14 we have the history of the Christian church from the time of Jesus (12:5) to the second advent (14:14). The time elements of 1,260 days, three and one half times, and forty-two months (12:6, 14; 13:5), all referring to the same time period, only make sense if they represent 1,260 years. There is no three and one-half year time period in church history that would fit the descriptions given in these chapters.

3) The peculiar, distinctive way in which the time periods are expressed indicates that they should not be taken literally. According to the context, the expressions "time, times, and half a time" (Dan 7:25; 12:7; Rev 12:14), "fortytwo months" (Rev 11:2; 13:5), and "one thousand two hundred and sixty days" (Rev 11:3; 12:6) all apply to the same time period, but the natural expression "three years and six months" (as in Luke 4:25; James 5:17) is not used once.

> The Holy Spirit seems, in a manner, to exhaust all the phrases by which the interval could be expressed, excluding always that one form which would be used of course in ordinary writing, and is used invariably in Scripture on other occasions, to denote the literal period. This variation is most significant if we accept the yearday principle, but quite inexplicable on the other view.[86]

4) The prophecies in Daniel 7–8 and 10–12 lead up to the "time of the end" (8:17; 11:35, 40; 12:4, 9), which is followed by the resurrection (12:2) and the setting up of God's everlasting kingdom (7:27). Considering the more than 2,500 years since the sixth century BC, literal time periods of only three and a half to six and a half years are not capable of reaching anywhere near the time of the end. These prophetic time periods, therefore, should be seen as symbolic, standing for long periods of actual time.[87]

5) In Numbers 14:34 and Ezekiel 4:6, God deliberately uses the day-for-a-year concept as a teaching device: "For each day you shall bear your guilt one year" (Num 14:34). And in an acted-out parable the prophet Ezekiel was told to lie 390 days on his left side and forty days

---

[86] Thomas R. Birks, *First Elements of Sacred Prophecy* (London: William E. Painter, 1843), 352.

[87] Shea, *Selected Studies*, 73.

on his right side: "I have laid on you a day for each year" (Ezek 4:6). However, Numbers 14 and Ezekiel 4 are not apocalyptic texts; God, therefore, spells it out—one day stands for one year. In apocalyptic texts this is never stated; it is an underlying principle.

6) The seventy-week time prophecy in Daniel 9:24–27 met its fulfillment at the exact time, if we use a day as symbolic of a year to interpret it. Non-Adventist interpreters, who in other apocalyptic texts do not use the year-day principle, recognize that the seventy weeks are in fact "weeks of years" reaching from the Persian period to the time of Christ.[88] Thus the pragmatic test in Daniel 9 confirms the validity of the year-day concept.

Remember that Apocalyptic Prophecy is Christocentric

Jesus is at the center of most chapters in the book of Daniel:

1. He is the stone in chapter 2.
2. He is the man in the fiery oven in chapter 3.
3. He is the Son of Man in chapter 7.
4. He is the Prince of the host in chapter 8.
5. He is Messiah the Prince in chapter 9.
6. He is Michael in the last vision in chapters 10–12.

In the book of Revelation, Jesus is again the focus of many chapters: the book begins with the statement that it is "the Revelation of Jesus Christ" (Rev 1:1).

1. He is the Son of Man (Rev 1:13).
2. He holds the seven stars in His right hand (Rev 2:1).
3. He is the First and the Last, who was dead, and came to life (Rev 2:8).
4. He has the sharp two-edged sword (Rev 2:12).
5. He is the Son of God, who has eyes like a flame of fire (Rev 2:18).
6. He has the seven Spirits of God and the seven stars (Rev 3:1).
7. He is holy, true, and has the key of David (Rev 3:7).
8. He is the Amen, the Faithful and True Witness (Rev 3:14).
9. He is the Lamb that was slain (Rev 5:6, 11).
10. He is the male Child who was to rule all nations with a rod of iron (Rev 12:5).

---

[88] Kenneth O. Gangel, *Daniel*, Holman Old Testament Commentary (Nashville, TN: Holman Reference, 2001), 266–270; Archer, 114; Sinclair Ferguson, *Mastering the Old Testament: Daniel* (Dallas, TX: Word, 1988), 201–203.

11. He is the Lamb on Mount Zion (Rev 14:1).
12. He is Lord of lords and King of kings (Rev 17:14).
13. He is the rider on the white horse called Faithful and True (Rev 19:11).
14. He is Jesus the root and offspring of David (Rev 22:16).

In the interpretation of apocalyptic prophecy, it is important to determine "where each prophetic outline series passes the time of the cross of Christ, for Old Testament terminology and imagery from that point on would receive a Christological interpretation"[89]—that is, names and geographical terms receive a spiritual and worldwide application. For example, in Daniel 11 is the sequence of the kingdoms as in Daniel 8: Medo-Persia, Greece, and Rome. But from verse 22 on, where the "prince of the covenant" is broken—that is, Jesus is crucified—the fulfillment of prophecy switches to the New Testament and church history. Therefore, the kings of the South and North can no longer refer to the Grecian kings, as they did in the verses prior to verse 22.

Beware of Interpreting Apocalyptic Prophecy with the Newspapers

Adventists have always had a fascination for the interplay between prophecy and current events. In 1878 Uriah Smith, watching the war between Russia and Turkey, predicted that Turkey's end was imminent and that we have reached the preliminary movements of the great battle of Armageddon. The First and Second World Wars were both seen as preludes to Armageddon. The Chinese revolution of 1911 encouraged the idea that Armageddon was to be a war between the nations of the East (the yellow peril) against the West. That Armageddon was a war between the races of East and West dominated Adventist thinking, particularly in Europe, until the middle of the twentieth century. Until the collapse of the Soviet Union, many Christians thought that nation must have a role in prophecy.

In 1991, just before the Gulf War, some Adventists interpreted Daniel 11:40–45 as being fulfilled on the battlefields of Kuwait with George Bush as the king of the North and Saddam Hussein as king of the South. The war was seen as a prelude to Armageddon. And after 9/11 some Adventist ministers saw in the events in New York the beginning of the final events prior to the second advent.

---

[89] Hans K. LaRondelle, "Interpretation of Prophetic and Apocalyptic Eschatology," *Symposium on Biblical Hermeneutics*, ed. Gordon M. Hyde (Washington, DC: Biblical Research Committee, 1974), 231.

More recently, the headlines from the Middle East recording the tensions between the Arabs and the Western powers have led a prominent Adventist theologian to identify the little horn with Islam.[90] Others claim that the king of the South in Daniel 11:25, 40 is Islam.[91]

If there is one thing we should have learned from the past history of failed apocalyptic interpretations, it is this: Don't interpret Scripture by the newspapers! Sensational claims of "prophecy being fulfilled before our very eyes" are usually overtaken by events.

Apocalyptic prophecy generally deals with the larger picture, with trends in history, not with one-day affairs, though one-day affairs may be significant in the overall development. Thus, the symbolic prophecies in Daniel and Revelation must be seen in the larger context of the great controversy between Christ and Satan that has been going on for thousands of years.

The Seventh-day Adventist Church is a movement of prophecy. Our very existence is seen as a fulfillment of Revelation 12:17. Thus more than anyone else, we ought to be careful, consistent, and thorough in our interpretation of apocalyptic prophecy.

Summary

In this chapter we have looked at the characteristics of apocalyptic literature and compared apocalyptic with classical prophecies. Our study of various schools of interpretation has led to the conclusion that the historicist interpretation is the only interpretation that satisfies all the biblical data, and that the apotelesmatic principle is not a valid method of prophetic interpretation. We concluded with eight principles for the interpretation of apocalyptic prophecies.

---

[90] Samuele Bacchiocchi, "Islam and The Papacy in Prophecy," *Endtime Issues*, no. 86, July 6, 2002.

[91] Tim Roosenberg, *Islam and Christianity in Prophecy* (Hagerstown, MD: Review and Herald, 2011), 12. See also Roy Gane, "Methodology for Interpretation of Daniel 11:2-12:3," *Journal of the Adventist Theological Society* 27/1-2 (2016): 294-343. With this article Gane laid the hermeneutical groundwork for the Islam view.

CHAPTER 10

Conditional Prophecies About Israel: Some Hermeneutical Considerations

Elias Brasil de Souza

This chapter[1] addresses the challenge of properly interpreting prophecies about the restoration of Israel in the Old Testament and argues that such prophecies contain conditional elements. They must be understood in light of the New Testament principle according to which the Old Testament promises find their fulfillment in Christ. It must also be stated that this chapter does not deal with the right of the modern state of Israel to exist according to international law. Rather, the purpose of this study is to provide some interpretative guidelines to understand some Old Testament prophecies that may bear on the claim that a theocratic Israel must play a decisive role in the eschatological events.

Indeed, Old Testament promises about the restoration of Israel have raised significant hermeneutical challenges for Christian interpreters throughout the centuries.[2] Among such prophecies are those announcing that God Himself would bring the nations to Jerusalem (cf. Joel 3:1–2; Zeph 3:6–8; cf. Ezek 38:16, 18–23; 39:1–7) to judge and

[1] This chapter is part of the larger study *Salvation and Restoration for Israel: The Interpretation of Conditional Prophecy* (Silver Spring, MD: Biblical Research Institute, 2020), published as a BRI release.

[2] See George Eldon Ladd, *The Blessed Hope* (Grand Rapids, MI: Eerdmans, 1956), 17–34; Charles E. Hill, *Regnum Caelorum: Patterns of Millennial Thought in Early Christianity*, 2nd ed. (Grand Rapids, MI: Eerdmans, 2001); and Timothy P. Weber, "Dispensational and Historic Premillennialism as Popular Millennialist Movements," in *A Case for Historic Premillennialism: An Alternative to "Left Behind" Eschatology*, ed. Craig L. Blomberg and Sung Wook Chung (Grand Rapids, MI: Baker Academic, 2009), 1–22.

destroy the nations there because they rebelled against His authority (Jer 25:31–33; Joel 3:9–17; Isa 34:1–8; 63:1–6; 66:15–18). Israel would "inherit the nations" (Isa 54:3) and the wicked would perish (Zech 14:12–13). Eventually, God would establish His kingdom over all the earth and former enemy nations would come to Jerusalem to worship the Lord (Isa 2; Mic 4; Zech 14:16; Isa 66:23). Interestingly, although such predictions often recognize Israel's failures, they often conclude by depicting a glorious future for the nation (e.g., Isa 2:1–5; Ezek 40–48; Joel 3:1–21; Amos 9:8–15).[3]

Some eschatological systems such as classic premillennialism and dispensational premillennialism, although not in agreement in a number of other areas, in general agree that God has had an eschatological plan for an ethnic and theocratic Israel in which the Old Testament prophecies related to that nation will find fulfillment mainly during the millennium.[4] Then Christ will reign over the world from His seat of power in the Middle East. This literalistic understanding of Old Testament prophecy rests on the presumed unconditionality of God's covenants with Abraham and David. Because God is faithful, it is argued, such promises including the land, Zion (Jerusalem), and the temple must all be fulfilled literally in the theocratic nation located in the Middle East.[5]

To this effect, it is worth noting that several covenants are alluded to or explicitly mentioned in the Bible (Adam, Noah, Abraham, Israel, David, and the New Covenant). They are to be understood as reiterations of the one covenant of redemption.[6] Close examination of such covenants indicates that they contain both unconditional and

---

[3] Francis D. Nichol, ed., *The Seventh-day Adventist Bible Commentary*, vol. 4 of 7 (Washington, DC: Review and Herald, 1978–1980), 30.

[4] For useful overview of some varieties of premillennialism, see Craig A. Blaising, "A Premillennial Response to Robert B. Strimple," in *Three Views on the Millennium and Beyond*, ed. Stan N. Gundry and Darrell L. Block, Zondervan Counterpoints Series (Grand Rapids, MI: Zondervan, 1999), 157–227.

[5] See, e.g., David Rudolph, "Zionism in Pauline Literature: Does Paul Eliminate Particularity for Israel and the Land in His Portrayal of Salvation Available for All the World?," in *The New Christian Zionism: Fresh Perspectives on Israel and the Land*, ed. Gerald R. McDermott (Downers Grove, IL: IVP Academic, 2016), 167–194.

[6] According to Peter J. Gentry and Stephen J. Wellum, *Kingdom Through Covenant: A Biblical-Theological Understanding of the Covenants*, 2nd ed. (Wheaton, IL: Crossway, 2018), 36, "God's one, eternal plan unfolds in history through a plurality of interrelated covenants, starting with Adam and creation and culminating in Christ and the new covenant." See also Gerhard F. Hasel and Michael G. Hasel, *The Promise: God's Everlasting Covenant* (Nampa, ID: Pacific Press, 2002).

conditional elements. Thus, on the one hand, from the perspective of God's sovereignty, the covenant is unconditional and its ultimate purposes for the redemption of the human race will be realized. On the other hand, from the human side, the covenant is conditional because the human party retains the freedom to leave the covenant.[7] That covenant renewals took place in ancient Israel (Deut 5–11; Josh 8:30–35; 24:25; 2 Kgs 22–23; Neh 10:28–36) suggests that the covenant people must periodically decide whether to stay in or out of the covenant.[8]

Thus, to argue that Old Testament prophecies about the theocratic Israel must be fulfilled literally because of the unconditionality of the covenants (especially the Abrahamic one) seems to overlook the conditional aspects of God's covenants.[9] This study does not undertake detailed examination of the covenants, since this would far exceed its intended scope and has been undertaken elsewhere.[10] Rather, the focus of this chapter is on how Jesus and the New Testament writers understood the Old Testament prophecies about the restoration of theocratic Israel—an approach that rests on the Reformation principle that Scripture interprets Scripture.[11] Three main points are discussed in greater detail: 1) the centrality of Jesus in the fulfillment of the Old Testament, 2) the New Testament understanding of the main institutions and concepts related to the covenantal promises of the Old Testament, and 3) an examination of some New Testament passages, which appear to predict the theocratic restoration of national Israel.

---

[7] Some helpful studies on this topic by Seventh-day Adventist scholars are the following: Hans K. LaRondelle, *The Israel of God in Prophecy: Principles of Prophetic Interpretation* (Berrien Springs, MI: Andrews University Press, 1983); Gerhard F. Hasel, "Israel in Bible Prophecy," *Journal of the Adventist Theological Society* 3/1 (1992): 120–148; Richard M. Davidson, "Interpreting Old Testament Prophecy," in *Understanding Scripture: An Adventist Approach*, ed. George W. Reid, Biblical Research Institute Studies 1 (Silver Spring, MD: Biblical Research Institute, 2006), 183–204; and Hans K. LaRondelle and Jon Paulien, *The Bible Jesus Interpreted* (Loma Linda, CA: Jon Paulien, 2014).

[8] Gerald G. O'Collins, "Salvation," in *The Anchor Yale Bible Dictionary*, ed. David Noel Freedman, vol. 5 (New York: Doubleday, 1992), 909–910; and R. J. D. Knauth, "Israel," in *Dictionary of the Old Testament: Historical Books*, ed. Bill T. Arnold and H. G. M. Williamson (Downers Grove, IL: InterVarsity, 2005), 518.

[9] See Bruce K. Waltke, "The Phenomenon of Conditionality Within Unconditional Covenants," in *Israel's Apostasy and Restoration: Essays in Honor of Roland K. Harrison*, ed. Avraham Gileadi (Grand Rapids, MI: Baker, 1988), 123–139; and Jeffrey J. Niehaus, *Biblical Theology*, vol. 2, *The Special Grace Covenants (Old Testament)* (Bellingham, WA: Lexham Press, 2017), 33–35.

[10] See, e.g., Gentry and Wellum.

[11] See Frank M. Hasel, "Presuppositions in the Interpretation of Scripture," in *Understanding Scripture: An Adventist Approach*, ed. George W. Reid, Biblical Research Institute Studies, vol. 1 (Silver Spring, MD: Biblical Research Institute, 2006), 36–37.

Finally, by way of conclusion, some interpretative guidelines are suggested for understanding the Old Testament prophecies about the restoration of theocratic Israel.

Jesus as the Goal of the Old Testament

One of the most foundational hermeneutical assumptions of the New Testament is that the prophetic hope of the Hebrew Scriptures finds fulfillment in Jesus of Nazareth. Jesus Himself claims that the Old Testament Scriptures point to Him (Luke 24:44; John 7:39) and Paul argues that in Jesus all of God's promises are confirmed (2 Cor 1:20). Support for such christological claims are borne not just by isolated passages here and there but by the structure, themes, and flow of the biblical canon. From the opening pages through the last book of the New Testament canon, the conviction emerges that Jesus sums up in His own person and deeds the lofty hopes of Old Testament Israel.

Significantly, the New Testament canon begins with a genealogy, showing Jesus' connections to Abraham and David (Matt 1:1–16). Thus, it becomes clear from the outset that Jesus is the seed of Abraham and thus inherits the promises made to that patriarch. At the same time, the link with David indicates that Jesus came as the promised Son of David, the Seed, the Branch, who arose to claim the throne of Israel as predicted by the Old Testament prophets. The three double sevens of generations may be understood as conveying "a message of completeness and fulfilment."[12] Thus, right at the beginning of the New Testament canon, Jesus emerges as the fulfillment of the covenantal promises made to Abraham and David.

The annunciation to Mary reveals that Jesus is the long-awaited Savior, Immanuel,[13] who epitomizes the covenant (Matt 1:20–23) and will rule Israel forever (Luke 1:32–33), according to God's promise to David (2 Sam 7:12–16). To further emphasize this connection, Luke mentions

---

[12] Chris Wright, "A Christian Approach to Old Testament Prophecy Concerning Israel," in *Jerusalem Past and Present in the Purposes of God*, ed. P. W. L. Walker (Carlisle: Paternoster, 1994), 13. According to another view, the division of the genealogy into three major sections of fourteen elements (Matt 1:17)—fourteen being the numerical value of Hebrew letters for the name David (D=4, W=6, D=4)—may have been intended to stress the link between Jesus and David. See W. D. Davies and Dale C. Allison Jr., *A Critical and Exegetical Commentary on the Gospel According to Saint Matthew*, International Critical Commentary 1 (London: T&T Clark, 2004), 162–163. Cf. R. T. France, *The Gospel of Matthew*, The New International Commentary on the New Testament (Grand Rapids, MI: Eerdmans, 2007), 31.

[13] The covenant means "I will be your God and you shall be my people"—a commitment that found ultimate realization in the incarnation of the Son of God as Immanuel ("God with us").

that Joseph was "of the house of David" (Luke 1:27; 2:4) and refers to Bethlehem, Jesus' birthplace, as "the City of David" (Luke 2:4; 2:11).[14] Later in the temple, Zechariah praises God for having "raised up a horn of salvation for us in the house of His servant David" (Luke 1:69), an allusion to a royal Davidic psalm (Ps 132:17).

The declaration from heaven at Jesus' baptism—"This is My beloved Son, in whom I am well pleased" (Matt 3:17; Mark 1:1; Luke 3:22)—contains significant allusions to the Old Testament. The first half of the verse ("This is My beloved Son") alludes to Psalm 2:7—a royal coronation hymn pointing to the Messiah—and possibly to Genesis 22:2, where God says to Abraham, "Take now your son, your only son Isaac, whom you love." This phrase also occurs at the transfiguration (Matt 17:5; Mark 9:7; Luke 9:35). The second half of the verse ("in whom I am well pleased") connects Jesus with God's affirmation of the suffering servant (Isa 42:1). These two statements "reflect the heavenly Father's understanding of Jesus' dual role: one day a kingly messiah, but for now a Suffering Servant—both appropriate to his unique identity as the divine son."[15]

Consequently, as the rightful heir to the Davidic throne, Jesus stands as the corporate representative of Israel; His life and mission sum up Israel's former experience as He recapitulates the exodus from Egypt and goes through the challenges of the wilderness. Thus, Matthew views Jesus' return from Egypt through a passage that in its Old Testament context refers to Israel during the exodus: "Out of Egypt I called My Son" (Matt 2:15; Hos 11:1; cf. Num 24:8).[16] Israel journeyed through the wilderness for forty years. Likewise, Jesus spent forty days fasting in the wilderness and thereafter He was tempted by the devil (Matt 4:1–3). Using three texts from Deuteronomy (Deut 6:13, 16; 8:3), Jesus defeated the devil. Interestingly, these Deuteronomic passages were instructions God gave to Israel ("God's son") on how to overcome temptation. But unlike Israel, who often failed to resist temptation, Jesus as Israel's representative emerges victorious from His confrontation with the devil.[17]

---

[14] All biblical quotations are from the NKJV, unless otherwise indicated.

[15] Craig L. Blomberg, "Matthew," in *Commentary on the New Testament Use of the Old Testament*, ed. D. A. Carson and Gregory K. Beale (Grand Rapids, MI: Baker Academic, 2007), 14.

[16] See also chapter 8 by Richard M. Davidson, "Inner-Biblical Hermeneutics: The Use of Scripture by Bible Writers," in the present volume.

[17] For an in-depth study of how Jesus recapitulates the history of Israel, see Joel Kennedy, *The Recapitulation of Israel: Use of Israel's History in Matthew 1:1–4:11*, Wissenschaftliche Untersuchungen zum Neuen Testament 2 Reihe, Bd. 57, ed. Jörg Frey (Tübingen: Mohr Siebeck, 2008).

As the gospel narrative unfolds, Jesus calls the first disciples and thus begins to reconstitute the remnant of Israel around His own person (Matt 4:18–19; par. Mark 1:16–20). As Matthew recounts it, Jesus went up to a mountain to deliver His most memorable sermon (Matt 5–7; par. Luke 6). Significantly, the introductory expression saying that Jesus "went up to a mountain" (Matt 5:1) is precisely the same phrase used to state that "Moses went up into the mountain" (Exod 19:3, LXX). Inasmuch as Jesus brings into existence a community of believers constituted as the remnant of Israel,[18] the Sermon on the Mount in a sense recapitulates the covenant between God and Israel at Sinai. In a scene reminiscent of Moses, Jesus pronounces blessings (Matt 5:3–11) and delivers an exposition of the Ten Commandments (Matt 5–7; Luke 6; cf. Exod 20),[19] thus setting the stipulations required by the new covenant relationship.[20] Rather than abrogating the law, Jesus required it to be inscribed in the hearts of His followers (Matt 5:21–48; Jer 31:33).

Interestingly, unlike the old covenant in which the curses are addressed first and then the blessings (Deut 27–28), the curses related to the new covenant—that is, the "woes"—come last (Luke 6), and in Matthew they are addressed to a different audience (Matt 23:13–36). This may imply that "there can be no abrogation of the new covenant and no destruction"[21] of the community that gathers around Jesus. In other words, this is the final and absolute covenant, which encompasses every other covenant and represents God's ultimate stage in the redemption of the human race.

Significantly, shortly before His sacrificial death, Jesus made clear that the "new covenant" would be ratified with His own blood: "For this is My blood of the new covenant, which is shed for many for the remission of sins" (Matt 26:28). Consequently, at the close of His earthly ministry, Jesus once more gathered the renewed Israel around Himself and—in ways reminiscent of Joshua on the brink of the

---

[18] John W. Welch, *The Sermon on the Mount in the Light of the Temple*, Society for Old Testament Study, ed. Margaret Barker (Burlington, VT: Ashgate, 2009), 17. See also Clinton Wahlen, "The Remnant in the Gospels," in *Toward a Theology of the Remnant*, ed. Ángel Manuel Rodríguez, Biblical Research Institute Studies in Adventist Ecclesiology 1 (Silver Spring, MD: Biblical Research Institute, 2009), 61–76.

[19] John M. Frame, *The Doctrine of the Christian Life, A Theology of Lordship* (Phillipsburg, NJ: P&R, 2008), 204; and Carl G. Vaught, *The Sermon on the Mount: A Theological Investigation*, rev. ed. (Waco, TX: Baylor University Press, 2001), 4.

[20] Welch, 67.

[21] Jack R. Lundbom, *Jesus' Sermon on the Mount: Mandating a Better Righteousness* (Minneapolis, MN: Fortress, 2015), 43.

promised land—commanded them to go and conquer the world: "And Jesus came and spoke to them, saying, 'All authority has been given to Me in heaven and on earth. Go therefore and make disciples of all the nations, baptizing them in the name of the Father and of the Son and of the Holy Spirit, teaching them to observe all things that I have comanded you; and lo, I am with you always, even to the end of the age'" (Matt 28:18–20).

A few points call for comment: First, "all authority in heaven and on earth" implicitly identifies Jesus with the rightful Davidic king and the Son of Man, referred to in Daniel 7, who "was given dominion and glory and a kingdom" (Dan 7:14). This does not mean that the prophecy of Daniel 7 finds its fulfillment in the Great Commission. It does mean, though, that the cosmic authority to be given to the Son of Man in Daniel belongs to Jesus. Second, the command for the disciples to reach all nations means that, in Jesus, the ultimate seed of Abraham, "all the nations of the earth shall be blessed" (Gen 22:18). Third, the assurance that "I am with you always" reveals that in Jesus the supreme promise of the covenant is fulfilled. This is God's presence among His people, encapsulated in the messianic title "Immanuel" ("God with us").

From the above overview, it follows that Jesus recapitulated in His own person the trajectory of Old Testament Israel, and through a new covenant gathered around Himself a community of believers to carry on the mission formerly entrusted to theocratic Israel. This implies that Old Testament prophecies related to the future of Israel must be interpreted in light of Jesus and His understanding of the renewed Israel and the new covenant ratified with His blood.

Israel's Geopolitical Institutions

This section explores how the New Testament interprets three interconnected geopolitical institutions—land, city, and temple—that played a crucial role for the existence and identity of God's people in the Old Testament. Because these institutions feature prominently in the prophecies related to Israel, they must receive more careful attention now. Although tightly interrelated and interdependent, for the sake of analysis they are treated separately as follows: First, the theme of land must receive attention since it was a covenantal gift to Israel and thus constituted the foundational infrastructure for the existence of theocratic Israel. Second, Zion/Jerusalem, which, after having been conquered by David, became the capital of the nation and the subject of salvation oracles in the psalms receives attention, will be discussed. Third, the temple as the very locus of God's presence among His people and the organizing center for the life of the people must also be addressed.

Land

The promise of the land stands as one of the most foundational givens of God's relationship with Abraham and his descendants[22] (Gen 12:7; 15:7, 18). According to one count, "'land' is the fourth most frequent noun or substantive in the Old Testament: it occurs 2,504 times. Statistically land is a more dominant theme than covenant."[23] Although in some places the word "land" carries a non-theological meaning, many of its occurrences refer to the land promised to Abraham. Without land it would be virtually impossible for the promises of a great name, a seed, and a great nation to be fully realized. Consequently, "salvation history" and "salvation geography" go hand in hand throughout Scripture.[24] Therefore, it is not surprising that the land features so prominently in the prophetic promises about the future of Israel.

For this reason, the Old and New Testament perceptions of the land must be addressed at this point so that a wholistic biblical understanding of this theme may emerge. As the discussion moves forward, one should avoid certain Western notions that view land ownership in terms of a commercial transaction in which land can be purchased and sold at will, or even taken away from its owners.[25]

First, it should be pointed out, that from a biblical perspective, the land—which ultimately belonged to God (Lev 25:23)—was a gift and Israel would retain the land as long as she remained loyal to the giver.[26] In other words, obedience to the Lord was the condition for Israel to enjoy the blessings and retain possession of the land. Conversely, disobedience would defile the land and cause it to "vomit out" its inhabitants (Lev 18:24–30; 20:22–27). Clearly, the "gift of the land was never intended to be an end in itself, but a means of developing the relationship between God and his people."[27]

---

[22] Norman Habel, *The Land Is Mine: Six Biblical Land Ideologies* (Minneapolis, MN: Fortress, 1993); and Walter Brueggemann, *The Land: Place as Gift, Promise, and Challenge in Biblical Faith*, 2nd ed., Overtures to Biblical Theology (Minneapolis, MN: Fortress, 2003).

[23] E. A. Martens, *God's Design: A Focus on Old Testament Theology*, 2nd ed. (Grand Rapids, MI: Baker Books, 1994), 103–104.

[24] Marlin Jeschke, *Rethinking Holy Land: A Study in Salvation Geography* (Scottdale, PA: Herald Press, 2005), 33.

[25] Ibid., 37.

[26] See Brueggemann, 44–50.

[27] J. G. Millar, "Land," in *New Dictionary of Biblical Theology*, ed. T. Desmond Alexander and

Second, God is the Creator and owner of the whole earth, and He gave one small portion of it to Israel (Exod 19:5). Several laws and regulations given to the Israelites served to remind them that God owned the land and they in turn ought to be loyal to God in order to enjoy and safely dwell in it (Lev 25:23; 27:30–33; Deut 14:22; 26:9–15). Significantly, even the Sabbath commandment was somehow extended to the land in that "the land shall keep a sabbath to the Lord" (Lev 25:2). Hence, land should not be sold permanently because it belonged to God; rather than becoming settled landowners, the Israelites ought to understand themselves as "strangers and sojourners with Me" (Lev 25:23; see 25:8–17).

Third, rest and inheritance are two significant terms associated with the land and occur together in Deuteronomy 12:9, as Moses reminds the Israelites, "As yet you have not come to the rest [*mĕnûḥâ*] and the inheritance [*naḥălâ*] which the Lord your God is giving you." While "rest" indicates peaceful living in the land, "inheritance" (Num 26:53; 36:2; Deut 4:21; Jer 2:7) conveys the gift of the father to the son (e.g., Lev 25:46; Deut 21:15). Thus, in "giving his people his land as *naḥ^alâ*, God reveals that he considers Israel to be his 'son.'"[28]

Fourth, the land promise given to Abraham seems to have envisioned expanding boundaries. According to the promise, Abraham would become a father of many nations, kings, and peoples (Gen 17:4, 16) and his descendants would be as numerous as the stars of heaven (Gen 15:5–7), or as the "dust of the earth" (Gen 28:14) and "sand of the sea" (Gen 32:12), as later reaffirmed to Jacob. Such language, as hyperbolic as it may sound, envisions millions and millions of people. Evidently, such "promises seem to expect a greater number of faithful and obedient descendants than the territory from Dan to Beer Sheba could ever possibly hold."[29] Thus from its inception, the promise gives some indication that in its ultimate realization the promised land would transcend its original Middle Eastern boundaries.

Fifth, given such rich theological contours, it should not be surprising that the land is part and parcel of a number of Old Testament prophecies (e.g., Isa 60; Jer 23:7–8; Joel 3:20–21; Amos 9:14–15). A couple of examples may be taken as representative of many other passages. One case in point is found in Ezekiel 33–48. In this extended section of

---

Brian S. Rosner (Downers Grove, IL: InterVarsity, 2000), 625–626. See also Hans K. LaRondelle, *The Israel of God in Prophecy.*

[28] Millar, 625.

[29] Jeschke, 38.

the book, the prophet envisions the future restoration of the land to the Israelites. Jeremiah proclaimed the restoration of the land and affirmed the reliability of this promise by buying a field in land occupied by enemy armies (Jer 32:1–15).

Upon close reflection it seems evident that the land promise has never been fully realized. Apart from a short period during the reigns of David and Solomon, when the borders were reasonably secure and the nation apparently enjoyed peace, Israel's enjoyment of land was precarious throughout the entire biblical period until the land passed under the sway of Babylon and never again recovered the prosperity enjoyed during the golden age of David and Solomon.

Some Bible-believing Christians, however, argue that because God gave that piece of land to Abraham's descendants, God must bring that promise to realization in a material and literal manner as the promise is usually understood in its Old Testament context. Thus, according to such a view, the modern state of Israel stands as evidence that the promise of the land and many other promises made to Old Testament Israel must apply to the realities of the modern Middle East.[30] Such a claim about the promise of the land, usually bolstered with a string of biblical passages, has a profound impact on the interpretation of Scripture, and thus needs examination from the perspective of the whole biblical canon.

From a biblical perspective, two main complementary explanations may be advanced for such a seemingly limited realization, if not failure, of the promise of the land. On the one hand, the Old Testament makes clear that the promise of the land was conditional upon obedience. By breaking the covenant, theocratic Israel forfeited its covenantal privileges. On the other hand, in spite of the nation's failures, God remains faithful and will bring the covenant promises to fulfillment in unexpected and surprising ways. To understand how this takes place, one must turn to the New Testament and its interconnections with the Old Testament.

At first impression, the silence of the New Testament about the land is deafening. That a theme so frequently addressed in the Old Testament should receive so little, if any, attention seems puzzling.[31] Impressions, however, may deceive, because the land does indeed appear in the New Testament, although in unexpected ways.

First of all, the blessings associated with the land are applied to Jesus. "Come to Me, all you who labor and are heavy laden, and I will give you

---

[30] A collection of essays defending this view may be found in McDermott.

[31] See the extensive study by W. D. Davies, *The Gospel and the Land: Early Christianity and Jewish Territorial Doctrine* (Berkeley, CA: University of California Press, 1974).

rest" (Matt 11:28; cf. Jer 31:23–25).[32] Thus, rest no longer lies in the land but in Jesus, who replaces the yoke of sin with the yoke of discipleship. Jesus also provides a far superior rest (*katapausis*) (Heb 4:8–10) and an eternal salvation (Heb 5:9) compared to that brought about through Joshua in the conquest of the land (Josh 21:44). Also, Jesus takes the metaphor of the vineyard, which in the Old Testament refers to Israel, and applies it to Himself with the qualification that He is the true vine, and that those who abide in Him are the fruitful branches (John 15:1–17). Consequently, the "land and the expected fruitfulness of its people, is [*sic*] now centered in the person of Jesus Christ."[33] In the same vein, Paul takes up the language of "inheritance," which stems from the land promise in the Old Testament, and applies it to salvation in Christ (Gal 3:18). Therefore, God "made us sit together in the heavenly places in Christ Jesus" (Eph 2:5–6). Our ultimate identity lies in our identification with Jesus rather than with a particular land or nation state.

Second, the New Testament expands the land to encompass the whole world. For example, in the third beatitude, Jesus says, "Blessed are the meek, For they shall inherit the earth" (Matt 5:5)—an allusion to Psalm 37:11, which in its original context refers to the promised land.[34] Jesus also commands His disciples to carry the gospel message "to the end of the earth" (Acts 1:8; cf. Rev 14:6), which indicates that His kingdom will eventually occupy the whole world. The land referred to in the fifth commandment, which in its original context referred to Canaan (Exod 20:12; Deut 5:16), becomes the earth in the New Testament: "Honor your father and mother. . . that it may be well with you and you may live long on the earth" (Eph 6:2–3). That such a universal expansion of the promised land was already embedded in the Abrahamic covenant seems evident from Paul's reference to Abraham as "the heir of the world" (Rom 4:13).

Third, another point worthy of note lies in the fact that the New Testament opted for the phrase "kingdom of God/heaven" over the term

---

[32] See Ulrich Luz, *Matthew: A Commentary*, ed. Helmut Koester, Hermeneia: A Critical and Historical Commentary on the Bible (Minneapolis, MN: Augsburg, 2001), 170–172; and George Wesley Buchanan, *The Gospel of Matthew*, ed. Watson E. Mills and George Wesley Buchanan, vol. 1, The Mellen Biblical Commentary (Eugene, OR: Wipf and Stock, 2006), 503–504.

[33] Alistair Donaldson, "The Kingdom of God and the Land: The New Testament Fulfillment of an Old Testament Theme," in *The Gospel and the Land of Promise: Christian Approaches to the Land of the Bible*, ed. Philip Church (Eugene, OR: Pickwick, 2011), 71, Kindle.

[34] Barclay Moon Newman and Philip C. Stine, *A Handbook on the Gospel of Matthew*, UBS Handbook Series (New York: United Bible Societies, 1992), 110.

"land."[35] Interestingly, the exact expression "kingdom of God/heaven" does not occur in the Old Testament, but the idea of God as king occurs in a number of places—not only in the sense that God is the king of Israel (Deut 29:6; Isa 6:1), but that He rules over the nations (Pss 22:28; 29:10; 66:1; 93:1–2; 96:10; 99:1; Dan 7:9–14).[36] So it seems reasonable to propose that because the term "kingdom" (*basileia*) includes not only the concept of rule but also that of territory, the New Testament writers opted for the expression "kingdom of God/heaven" (instead of using the land motif) because it better conveys the global scope of the kingdom announced and embodied by Jesus. Such a kingdom, which grows like a mustard seed (Matt 13:31), is already present and brings salvation here and now (Luke 11:20; 17:21), and yet it is still future (Matt 7:21).[37]

Fourth, the New Testament concludes with the eschatological fulfillment of the land promise: "Now I saw a new heaven and a new earth, for the first heaven and the first earth had passed away. Also, there was no more sea" (Rev 21:1). Here the new covenant is finally consummated, "the return from exile completed,"[38] and God gives back the land to His people—not a stretch of land in the Middle East, but the entire earth—made new.

Zion

After conquering Zion/Jerusalem[39] and making it his capital, David brought the ark to the city and made it into the worship center of the nation (2 Sam 6). By hosting the ark of the covenant, the city "became

---

[35] Donaldson, 58–74.

[36] See Bernard Frank Batto, *In the Beginning: Essays on Creation Motifs in the Ancient Near East and the Bible*, Siphrut: Literature and Theology of the Hebrew Scriptures 9 (Winona Lake, IN: Eisenbrauns, 2013), 114–138; and Daegeuk Nam, "The 'Throne of God' Motif in the Hebrew Bible" (ThD diss., Andrews University, 1989).

[37] George Eldon Ladd, *The Gospel of the Kingdom: Scriptural Studies in the Kingdom of God* (Grand Rapids, MI: Eerdmans, 1959), 13–23.

[38] James M. Hamilton Jr., *Preaching the Word: Revelation—The Spirit Speaks to the Churches*, ed. R. Kent Hughes (Wheaton, IL: Crossway, 2012), 382.

[39] As explained by Leland Ryken et al., *Dictionary of Biblical Imagery* (Downers Grove, IL: InterVarsity, 2000), 980, "Zion is a symbol or metaphor for the historical city of Jerusalem. But behind this metaphor lies a complex cluster of interlocking themes of immense theological significance. In various parts of the Scriptures we find the following concepts associated with the city of Zion: the temple as Yahweh's dwelling place; the covenant people of God, both as the apostate Israel under judgment and the purified remnant who inherit God's blessings; the royal Davidic kingship leading to the idea of the Messiah; the world center from which God's law will be promulgated and to which the Gentile nations of the world will flow; the renewed heavens and earth, where peace and prosperity will reign."

the place where the Sinai covenant (Exod. 19–34) was remembered and cultivated"[40] (Ps 68). And because of its connection with David, Jerusalem also became a chosen city (2 Chr 6:6). With the subsequent construction of the temple by Solomon, Jerusalem became even more significant as the hub of Israel's religious life,[41] the place where the Lord put His name (1 Kgs 11:36; 14:21; 2 Kgs 21:4). Because of the temple, Jerusalem attracted multitudes of pilgrims and worshippers (Pss 120–134). Biblical poets and prophets refer to Jerusalem as the "city of the great King" (Ps 48:2), the mother of nations (Ps 87), and the place where God lives (Isa 4:5; 8:18). A couple of psalms may serve as a sample of many other passages throughout the Old Testament extolling Zion: "Great is the Lord, and greatly to be praised / In the city of our God, / In His holy mountain. / Beautiful in elevation, / The joy of the whole earth, / Is Mount Zion on the sides of the north, / The city of the great King. / God is in her palaces; / He is known as her refuge" (Ps 48:1–3); "The Lord loves the gates of Zion / More than all the dwellings of Jacob. / Glorious things are spoken of you, / O city of God! Selah" (Ps 87:2–3).

With such lofty descriptions, it is not surprising that Jerusalem features so prominently in the eschatology of the Old Testament. Indeed, as announced by the prophets, the restoration of Israel, the rise of the messianic king, and the cutting of a new covenant—to take place after the catastrophic events of the exile—are linked to the rebuilding of Jerusalem. For example, Isaiah prophesies that God will rejoice in Jerusalem and grant unprecedented longevity to its inhabitants (Isa 65:19–20). Ezekiel concludes his book by naming the city "THE LORD IS THERE" (Ezek 48:35). And Zechariah reiterates that the Lord is "zealous for Jerusalem" (Zech 1:13); He will return to Jerusalem (Zech 1:16), defeat the enemies of Jerusalem, and make the city a worship center for the nations (Zech 12–14).

History shows that such prophecies, if taken at face value, remain largely unfulfilled. Although the exiles returned from Babylonia and rebuilt Jerusalem, the epic predictions that the city would become the hub of the world remained far from reality. Therefore, some Bible students argue that since God is a faithful God, who keeps His promises, He will bring these prophecies to fulfillment for national Israel in the Middle East, exactly as the Old Testament prophets predicted.[42] Some

---

[40] P. W. L. Walker, "Jerusalem," in Alexander and Rosner, 589.

[41] Shemaryahu Talmon, "The Signification of Jerusalem in Biblical Thought," in *Literary Motifs and Patterns in the Hebrew Bible: Collected Studies* (Winona Lake, IN: Eisenbrauns, 2013), 291–313.

[42] Craig Blaising, "Biblical Hermeneutics: How are we to Interpret the Relation Between the

believers view the foundation of the modern state of Israel and its subsequent control of all Jerusalem as evidence that God has begun to fulfill His word.[43]

To address this understanding of the biblical prophecies, one should take two factors into consideration. First, the biblical prophecies of the Old Testament given to national and theocratic Israel were set within the bounds of the covenant. This implies that they were conditional upon the nation's loyalty to the covenant. So, the persistent failure of the theocratic nation to abide by the covenant explains why some promises were not realized.[44] A second aspect that must receive attention relates to the interpretation of these prophecies and promises related to Zion by other inspired writers—namely, those of the New Testament.

It should be mentioned that the opening and closing of the New Testament canon reflects the opening and closing of the last book of the Hebrew canon—namely, 1–2 Chronicles. As 1 Chronicles opens with a sequence of genealogies leading up to David, so the New Testament opens with a genealogy that through David leads up to Jesus, the son of David (Matt 1). But even more interesting for the following discussion, just as the Hebrew canon concludes with the decree of Cyrus, allowing the exiles to go up to Jerusalem (2 Chr 36:23), so the New Testament canon (or the whole Bible, for that matter) closes with the New Jerusalem coming down from heaven (Rev 21–22).

Upon closer examination, it becomes apparent that Jerusalem also features significantly in the New Testament and plays a role no less important than it did in the Old Testament. However, Jerusalem emerges with a distinct significance because Jesus redefines old covenant institutions and invests them with new configurations. Interestingly, Jerusalem appears for the first time in the New Testament associated with Herod the Great. According to Matthew, upon hearing the news of the "newborn king of the Jews," "Herod the king . . . was troubled, and all Jerusalem with him" (Matt 2:2–3). Something must have been wrong with Jerusalem because instead of recognizing its legitimate king, the city remained loyal to a tyrant.[45]

Tanak and the New Testament on This Question?," in McDermott, 79–105.

[43] Tuvya Zaretsky, "Israel the People," in *Israel, the Land and the People: An Evangelical Affirmation of God's Promises* (Grand Rapids, MI: Kregel, 1998), 35–59.

[44] Davidson, "Interpreting Old Testament Prophecy," 183–204.

[45] Joel Willitts, "Matthew and Psalms of Solomon's Messianism: A Comparative Study in First-Century Messianology," *Bulletin for Biblical Research* 22/1–4 (2012): 42.

According to the Synoptics, toward the end of His ministry, Jesus undertook a long journey from Galilee to Jerusalem,[46] and the closer He got to the city, the stronger the opposition became. On one particular occasion, Jesus seems to have recognized the theological status of Jerusalem and warned His followers not to swear by Jerusalem, "for it is the city of the great King" (Matt 5:35). Ironically, however, from the larger narrative of the gospels, "the city of the great King" eventually rejected its true king (Zech 9:9; Matt 21:5; Luke 13:34). Clearly, Jerusalem and Jesus had conflicting agendas since Jesus claimed to embody what Jerusalem purported to be—the locus of God's presence and redemptive activity among the chosen nation.

Some of Jesus' most significant messianic activities took place in Jerusalem, such as His triumphal entry into the city (Matt 21:1–11), the temple cleansing (Matt 21:12–17), the lament over Jerusalem (Matt 21:23–23:37), the eschatological discourse (Matt 24:1–25:46), and the Last Supper (Matt 26:17–46). Finally, following the betrayal, arrest, and trial of Jesus (Matt 26:47–27:31), Jerusalem sealed the rejection of its king by nailing Him to a cross. But it should not be forgotten that the resurrection also occurred in Jerusalem (Matt 27:32–28:15), although the biblical text contains little reflection on what these events signify for the city itself. Indeed, the commissioning of the disciples occurred on a mountain in Galilee (Matt 28:16–20). The Gospel of John in turn narrates the ministry of Jesus from a different, though complementary, perspective; it devotes eighty percent of its narrative to events that took place in Jerusalem (compared with thirty percent in Matthew)[47] and mentions at least three visits of Jesus to the city. However, Jerusalem does not perform much better in the Fourth Gospel since, as in the Synoptics, the city "was the center of opposition to Jesus and unbelief in Him."[48]

However, although Jerusalem fell short of its theological vocation and, apparently, had no hope of an eschatological future (Matt 24:15–21; Mark 13:14–19; Luke 21:20), two events associated with Jerusalem bring some theological significance to the city. In reporting about those who rose from the grave after Christ's resurrection, Scripture says that "they went into the holy city and appeared to many" (Matt 27:53).

---

[46] P. W. L. Walker, *Jesus and the Holy City: New Testament Perspectives on Jerusalem* (Grand Rapids, MI: Eerdmans, 1996), 3.

[47] Ibid., 162.

[48] Stephen S. Kim, "The Significance of Jesus' Healing the Blind Man in John 9," *Bibliotheca Sacra* 167 (2010): 312–313. See also Frederick Dale Bruner, *The Gospel of John: A Commentary* (Grand Rapids, MI: Eerdmans, 2012), 307.

Ironically, Jerusalem remained a "holy city" in spite of its "unholy treatment of Jesus."[49] Another event of theological significance for Jerusalem lies in the fact that it was in that city that the Spirit descended upon the disciples and thus empowered the renewed Israel to fulfill the mission which Jesus had commissioned them to do (Luke 24:49; Acts 1:4).

Jerusalem's historical and theological significance stems from the fact that it was the place where Jesus died and resurrected, and from where the gospel spread throughout the world (Rom 15:19). But the New Testament gives no indication that the geographical Jerusalem as a Middle Eastern city will play a prophetic role in the final events. Jesus' command for the disciples to go from Jerusalem and evangelize the world contained no hint that anyone should "ever return in pilgrimage."[50]

Jerusalem is no longer the focus of God's promises. In fact, Acts 4:24–28 applies an Old Testament passage about Gentile nations attacking Jerusalem (Ps 2; cf. Acts 2:34–36) to the Jewish leadership's rejection of and opposition to Jesus.[51] Thus it appears that Zion's role has been taken by Jesus. In fact, no earthly city can "convey or contain the cosmic reconciliation" that God accomplished through Jesus Christ (Rom 8:20–23; Col 1:15–20).[52] Jerusalem has been transcended by the city already anticipated by Abrham, "the city which has foundations, whose builder and maker is God" (Heb 11:10; cf. 12:22).

In the book of Revelation, Zion "points to the establishment of the Messianic kingdom in which his [Messiah's] kingly rule is universalized. Thus, in 14:1–5 the realization of the hope of Jewish expectations that Mount Zion will be the center of the eschatological kingdom is depicted, though the Messiah's reign is inaugurated already with his enthronement in ch. 5."[53] Eventually, Revelation reports a vision of the "great city, the holy Jerusalem, descending out of heaven from God" (Rev 21:10).

To conclude, because Jesus' death and resurrection switched the focus of God's saving work from the earthly Jerusalem to the heavenly one, there is no biblical basis to view the earthly Jerusalem as the privileged

---

[49] Walker, *Jesus and the Holy City*, 49.

[50] Mark Strom, "From Promised Land to Reconciled Cosmos Paul's Translation of 'Worldview,' 'Worldstory,' and 'Worldperson,'" in *The Gospel and the Land of Promise: Christian Approaches to the Land of the Bible*, ed Philip Church (Eugene, OR: Pickwick, 2011), 18, Kindle.

[51] David G. Peterson, *The Acts of the Apostles*, The Pillar New Testament Commentary (Grand Rapids, MI; Eerdmans, 2009), 200.

[52] Strom, 24.

[53] Laszlo Gallusz, *The Throne Motif in the Book of Revelation*, ed. Mark Goodacre, Library of New Testament Studies 487 (New York: Bloomsbury, 2014), 250.

locus of God's end-time events. The present city retains its historical significance given its role in the life of God's old covenant people. But, like Abraham, the followers of Christ should wait for the city that "has foundations."

Temple

Through the tabernacle and later through the temple, the transcendent God (1 Kgs 8:27–30) bestowed His presence on Israel as an expression of His covenant: "I will walk among you and be your God, and you shall be My people" (Lev 26:12). So, from its inauguration under Solomon until its destruction by the Babylonians—which was followed by reconstruction under Zerubbabel and eventual destruction by the Romans—the temple remained the social, political, and religious center of Israel and the Jewish people.[54] As the place of worship, sacrifices, and atonement, the temple played a crucial role in the life of God's people. In the biblical canon, the amount of space devoted to the temple in the books of Psalms and 1–2 Chronicles, for example, provides an instructive example of the profound influence of temple ideas and concepts on the entire Bible.[55]

It must be underscored, however, that the temple had no meaning in itself since its purpose and significance derived from God's presence in it and its relationship with the original temple in heaven. Thus, the temple could not be used as an amulet; indeed, because of Israel's transgression of the covenant, God's presence eventually abandoned the temple (Ezek 1–10), and the magnificent structure erected by Solomon was razed to the ground by the Babylonians.

But even after its destruction, the temple has remained an object of reflection and longing—possibly because it features so prominently in a number of oracles of salvation and prophecies of restoration. For example, Joel speaks of a day when a "fountain shall flow from the house of the Lord and water the Valley of Acacias" (Joel 3:18) and Ezekiel, in turn, gives the most detailed description of the new temple to be erected after the judgment of the exile is over. The temple again would be the locus of sacrifices with a fully operative priestly service (Ezek 44:15–27).

Given this picture, some orthodox groups among Jews and Christians expect the temple to be rebuilt in Jerusalem with the reinstatement of

---

[54] Bruce D. Chilton, "Temple," in *Dictionary of the Later New Testament and Its Developments*, ed. Ralph P. Martin and Peter H. Davids (Downers Grove, IL: InterVarsity, 1997), 1159–1166.

[55] See Dan Lioy, *Axis of Glory: A Biblical and Theological Analysis of the Temple Motif in Scripture*, Studies in Biblical Literature (New York: P. Lang, 2011); Roberto Ouro, "The Sanctuary: The Canonical Key of Old Testament Theology," *Andrews University Seminary Studies* 50/2 (2012): 159–177.

its ritual system.[56] This view stems from a particular understanding of biblical prophecy that must be evaluated in light of the entire Bible. So, attention must now turn to the New Testament to determine how the temple should be understood in its prophetic and typological aspects. A few points are worth mentioning:

In His first encounter with the temple explicitly reported by Luke, Jesus calls it "my father's house (Luke 2:49). Later on, Jesus was brought to the pinnacle of the temple to be tempted (Luke 4:9–12). As one scholar suggests, "Satan apparently has an *entrée* into this holy institution."[57] Subsequently, in a response to His opponents Jesus pronounced a judgment on the temple and this time called it "your house" (Luke 13:35; cf. Matt 23:38). At that point, the temple seemingly had ceased to be God's house. Then, Jesus entered the temple[58] and drove out the vendors and money changers because the "house of prayer" had become a "den of thieves" (Luke 19:46). Finally, upon His death, the veil of the temple "was torn in two" (Matt 27:51; Mark 15:38; Luke 23:45), making the sacrificial system obsolete.[59]

John, the "theologian of a new temple"[60] presents Jesus as the locus of God's presence. In the prologue of his gospel, John says that Jesus "dwelt [*skēnoō*] among us" and "we beheld His glory" (John 1:14). The verb "dwelt" (*skēnoō*)—"to pitch a tent"— and the word "glory" (*doxa*) alludes to God's glory dwelling in the tabernacle/temple (Deut 12:21; 1 Kgs 5:5; 8:16–20, 29). That glory now dwells in Jesus, the ultimate tabernacle/temple. Therefore, worship no longer depends on a holy place but on the person of Jesus (John 4:23–24). By presenting Himself as the source

---

[56] See, e.g., Gershom Gorenberg, *The End of Days: Fundamentalism and the Struggle for the Temple Mount* (Oxford: Oxford University Press, 2002); David Zeidan, "Jerusalem in Jewish Fundamentalism," *Evangelical Quarterly* 78/3 (2006): 225–236; and John W. Schmitt and J. Carl Laney, *Messiah's Coming Temple: Ezekiel's Prophetic Vision of the Future Temple*, 2nd ed. (Grand Rapids, MI: Kregel, 2014).

[57] Walker, *Jesus and the Holy City*, 61.

[58] This should not be understood as if Jesus had entered the actual nave of the temple, which was accessible only to the priests. Rather, Jesus entered one of the external areas of temple building itself, which functioned as an open market for the activities undertaken by the moneychangers and vendors.

[59] According to Daniel M. Doriani, *Matthew*, Reformed Expository Commentary, ed. Richard D. Phillips, Philip Graham Ryken, and Daniel M. Doriani (Phillipsburg, NJ: P&R, 2008), 505, "the phrase 'from top to bottom' [Mark 15:38] means that no man, starting at the bottom, tore the curtain; God himself tore the curtain."

[60] Harold W. Attridge, "The Temple and Jesus the High Priest in the New Testament," in *Jesus and Temple: Textual and Archaeological Explorations*, ed. James H. Charlesworth (Minneapolis, MN: Fortress, 2014), 232.

of living water (e.g., John 7:37–39), Jesus actually claims to be the eschatological temple predicted by the Old Testament prophets (Ezek 47:1–12; Joel 3:18). Admittedly, the distinct and multifaceted portrayals of the temple in the gospels have a number of complexities that cannot be addressed here,[61] but one point stands out clearly: Jesus confronts, judges, and finally takes upon Himself the attributes of the temple.[62]

Also, the picture emerges of the community of believers as a temple. After stating that the community of believers are God's building and mentioning the foundations and construction of such building (1 Cor 3:9–13), Paul says, "Do you not know that you are the temple of God and that the Spirit of God dwells in you? If anyone defiles the temple of God, God will destroy him. For the temple of God is holy, which temple you are" (1 Cor 3:16; cf. 6:17–20). God no longer dwells in a building, but in the community of believers through the Spirit. The equivalent expression "house of God" occurs elsewhere to designate the community of believers as God's dwelling place (1 Tim 3:15; cf. 1 Peter 2:4–10; 4:12–19). However, it must be emphasized that the metaphor for the church as a building conveys the crucial fact that Jews and Gentiles are made into one "whole building, being fitted together" and growing "into a holy temple in the Lord" and a "dwelling place of God in the Spirit" (Eph 2:21–22).

However, the fact that Jesus embodies the temple—something emulated by the community of believers to a certain extent—does not obliterate the vertical typology already anticipated in the Old Testament.[63] In fact, the New Testament shows that because the ritual system of the Israelite sanctuary/temple found its fulfillment in Jesus, the focus of God's redemptive plan shifts from the earthly sanctuary/temple to its heavenly counterpart (Heb 9:11–15).[64] By offering Himself as the final

---

[61] Alan Kerr, *The Temple of Jesus' Body: The Temple Theme in the Gospel of John*, Journal for the Study of the New Testament Supplement Series 220 (New York: Sheffield Academic Press, 2002), 114–115; Paul M. Hoskins, *Jesus as the Fulfillment of the Temple in the Gospel of John* (Eugene, OR: Wipf and Stock, 2007); Welch; YongHan Chung, "The Temple in Matthew's Eschatology: Matthew's Interpretation of the Temple in the Context of First Century Judaism" (PhD diss., Graduate Theological Union, 2011); Lioy; Margaret Barker, *King of the Jews: Temple Theology in John's Gospel* (London: SPCK, 2014).

[62] See Nicholas Perrin, *Jesus the Temple* (Grand Rapids, MI: Baker Academic, 2010), 46.

[63] Richard M. Davidson, *Typology in Scripture: A Study of Hermeneutical Typos Structures* (Berrien Springs, MI: Andrews University Press, 1981).

[64] For a detailed study on Christ's ministry in the heavenly sanctuary, see Ángel M. Rodríguez, "The Sanctuary," in *Handbook of Seventh-Day Adventist Theology*, ed. Raoul Dederen, Commentary Reference Series 12 (Hagerstown, MD: Review and Herald, 2001), 375–417.

sacrifice (Heb 10:10) and becoming a superior high priest (Heb 7:20–28), Jesus opened the way of access to the very throne of God in the heavenly sanctuary, where He intercedes for us (Heb 8:1–2).[65]

As the book of Revelation brings the grand narrative of Scripture to a close, the heavenly sanctuary plays a decisive role in the scenes that introduce the various vision sequences. From a close examination of the literary structure of the book, it becomes clear that the decisive events that take place on earth as the great controversy unfolds are correlated with God's activities in the heavenly sanctuary.[66] Revelation 11:19, for example, reports that John had a vision of the ark of the covenant in the Most Holy Place. This represents a scene of judgment in the heavenly temple with profound repercussions for God's people on earth.

And finally, Revelation 21–22 connects all the lines together and brings the grand biblical narrative to a grand finale. The new earth fulfills God's covenantal promise of land for His people (Rev 21:1) in global terms—not in a piece of real estate in the Middle East. Also, a holy city—the new Jerusalem—comes down from heaven, thus fulfilling in unexpected ways the Old Testament promises and oracles of restoration. Likewise, the promises related to the temple find fulfillment in the new Jerusalem, the tabernacle of God (Rev 21:3a). As the glory of God dwelt in the Most Holy Place of the ancient tabernacle, so God and the Lamb will dwell in the Holy City, which is portrayed as the "temple-city" of the new earth (Rev 21:22).[67] At this point, the essence of the covenant reaches its consummation: "They shall be His people. God Himself will be with them and be their God" (Rev 21:3b).

New Testament Passages Related to Israel

Acts 1:6–7

The text of Acts 1:6–7 has generated some interesting discussions bearing upon the future of Israel: "Therefore, when they had come together, they asked Him, saying, 'Lord, will You at this time restore the kingdom to Israel?' And He said to them, 'It is not for you to know times

[65] For an in-depth study on the vertical typology of Hebrews, see Richard M. Davidson, "Typology in the Book of Hebrews," in *Issues in the Book of Hebrews*, ed. Frank B. Holbrook, Daniel and Revelation Committee Series 4 (Silver Spring, MD: Biblical Research Institute, 1989), 121–186.

[66] Richard M. Davidson, "Sanctuary Typology," in *Symposium on Revelation: Introductory and Exegetical Studies—Book 1*, ed. Frank B. Holbrook, Daniel and Revelation Committee Series 6 (Silver Spring, MD: Biblical Research Institute, 1992), 111–119.

[67] T. Desmond Alexander, *From Eden to the New Jerusalem: Exploring God's Plan for Life on Earth* (Nottingham: InterVarsity, 2008), 20.

or seasons which the Father has put in His own authority'" (Acts 1:6–7). This question seems to imply that shortly before Jesus' ascension, the disciples still expected a kingdom associated with the restoration of national Israel. Moreover, that Jesus cautioned them only in regard to the time of the restoration and did not deny the validity of their question may be an indication that Jesus tacitly agreed to their presumed understanding of the kingdom. At first glance, such understanding of the passage may support a political/national restoration of Israel in fulfillment of the Old Testament kingdom prophecies.[68]

Upon closer examination, however, a more nuanced picture emerges. Admittedly, Jesus did not explicitly address, define, or correct the understanding of the kingdom implied in the question posed by the disciples. However, without explicitly addressing the nature of the kingdom, Jesus explained how to bring the kingdom to realization: "But you shall receive power when the Holy Spirit has come upon you; and you shall be witnesses to Me in Jerusalem, and in all Judea and Samaria, and to the end of the earth" (Acts 1:8). Thus, the restoration of the kingdom may be understood as a process, which starts with the outpouring of the Spirit and continues with the subsequent proclamation of the gospel to the Gentiles. These major steps are part of a process that will lead to the "restoration of all things" (Acts 3:21).

Before considering Acts 1:6–8, one should bear in mind that the early church, as featured in the book of Acts, seems to recapitulate the trajectory of Israel and apparently fulfills some prophecies related to that nation. Thus, the portrait of the church in Acts provides a frame of reference to understand the relationship between the followers of Jesus and Israel and, consequently, the Old Testament prophecies about the future of a national and theocratic Israel.

At the outset, it seems clear that the community of believers gathered around Jesus continued the role and mission of the faithful Israel. In calling themselves the *ekklēsia* (church)—a word often used in the LXX to translate the Hebrew words *qāhāl* and *'ēdâ*, which designate the congregation of Israel[69]—the first followers of Jesus identified their faith with that of Israel. And since they were almost exclusively Jews, their identification with the chosen nation was more than a fictional construct. Indeed, the first followers of Jesus counted

---

[68] See, e.g., Anthony F. Buzzard, "Acts 1:6 and the Eclipse of the Biblical Kingdom," *Evangelical Quarterly* 66/3 (1994): 197–215.

[69] Karl Ludwig Schmidt, "Εκκλησία," in *Theological Dictionary of the New Testament*, ed. Gerhard Kittel, Geoffrey W. Bromiley, and Gerhard Friedrich, vol. 3 (Grand Rapids, MI: Eerdmans, 1964–), 501–535.

themselves to be and were considered by others as a branch of Judaism.[70]

From this perspective some details of the Acts narrative become clearer. First of all, it is significant that Jesus' instructions for the disciples to stay in Jerusalem and the subsequent unfolding of the Acts narrative accord with the prophetic promises of the restoration of Israel. For example, Jesus's command that the disciples stay in Jerusalem to receive the power of the Holy Spirit (Acts 1:8; cf. Luke 24:49) harks back to the promise of the Spirit in Isaiah 32:15, "Until the Spirit is poured upon us from on high"—not to mention the promise of the Spirit reported in Joel 2. So, Israel's restoration by the Spirit promised in the Old Testament comes to fruition in the experience of the first followers of Jesus on Pentecost (Acts 2).

In view of this, it is significant to note that immediately after the ascension, the biblical narrative reports the gathering of the apostles in the upper room followed by the choice of Matthias to be numbered with them (Acts 1:26). Being the first decision of the early Christian community, the theological implications of this episode should not be overlooked. Actually, the number of the twelve apostles is of utmost importance because it connects the leadership of the primitive church with the twelve tribes of Israel.[71] In other words, the twelve apostles represent the leadership of the restored Israel, which inherits the promises made to the chosen nation.[72]

Granting that the early followers of Jesus constituted the remnant of Israel, some aspects of the Acts narrative can make more sense. Apart from the explicit connection with Joel 2, the events of Pentecost can be viewed against a larger backstory. Several Old Testament prophecies link the restoration of Israel with the return of the exiles who have been scattered throughout the world by the Assyrians and the Babylonians. Thus, one of the idyllic prophetic depictions of the future

---

[70] Judith M. Lieu, *Neither Jew Nor Greek? Constructing Early Christianity* (London: T&T Clark, 2002), 1–8.

[71] As Wright, 27, notes, "the number twelve is a stubborn element in the tradition, even though there is some fluidity over the precise names of the disciples: in other words, the intentional symbolism of the embryonic twelve tribes of a restored Israel was clearly remembered. This is strengthened by his reference to them as a 'little flock', which was a term from 'remnant theology' (Luke 12:32; cf. the quotation of Ps. 37:11 in Matt. 5:5), and his saying about their judging the twelve tribes of Israel (Matt. 19:28)."

[72] William Horbury, "The Twelve and the Phylarchs," *New Testament Studies* 32 (1986): 503–527; and Michael E. Fuller, *The Restoration of Israel: Israel's Re-Gathering and the Fate of the Nations in Early Jewish Literature and Luke-Acts*, Beihefte zur Zeitschrift für die neutestamentliche Wissenschaft und die Kunde der älteren Kirche 138, ed. James D. G. Dunn et al. (Berlin: Walter de Gruyter, 2006), 239–245.

Israel shows a multitude of exiles coming back to the homeland (cf. Mic 4:6–7). Since the exiles are described as lame, and are healed upon returning (Isa 35:6; Zeph 3:19), it is not without significance that the first miracle performed by the apostles after Pentecost was the healing of a lame man (Acts 3:8). This is precisely what took place around Pentecost as multitudes of diaspora Jews came to Jerusalem, some of whom were dwelling in the city. Such explicit mention of diaspora Jews dwelling in Jerusalem, witnessing to and being shaped by the outpouring of the Spirit as thousands of them were baptized, indicates that the ingathering of exiles predicted by the Old Testament prophets had begun. In addition, several passages report the advance of the gospel and the growth of the Jewish Christian communities (Acts 4:4; 5:14; 6:1, 7; 9:31, 35, 42; 12:24).[73]

Another point worth considering focuses on the mission of Israel to the Gentiles. Several Old Testament prophecies indicate that the restoration of Israel must be understood within God's larger purpose of bringing Gentiles to conversion.[74] Throughout the Old Testament, a number of prophetic utterances indicate that in the eschatological times Gentiles will flow to Jerusalem to learn from the Lord. Interestingly, from the conversion of Cornelius (Acts 12), the Acts narrative turns to the Gentiles with the missionary journeys of Paul and Barnabas (Acts 13:44–48; cf. Isa 49:6). As the book comes to a close, it becomes evident that more and more Gentile converts are incorporated into the renewed Israel (cf. Acts 26:17–18). In the last chapter, Paul makes an explicit connection between the mission to the Gentiles and the restoration of Israel: "For this reason therefore I have called for you, to see you and speak with you, because for the hope of Israel I am bound with this chain" (Acts 28:20). Clearly, Paul understood his work among Gentiles within the context of the restoration of Israel.[75]

Finally, the restoration of the house of David announced in the Old Testament finds fulfillment in Jesus, who rose from the dead to be enthroned as the final Davidic King (Acts 2:36). However, unlike His royal predecessors, who ruled from Jerusalem, Jesus sat at God's "right hand" (Acts 2:34; cf. Ps 110:1) in heaven thus becoming both "Lord" and "Messiah/Christ." And in heaven Jesus must stay "until the times

---

[73] Richard Bauckham, *The Jewish World Around the New Testament: Collected Essays I*, ed. Jörg Frey, Wissenschaftliche Untersuchungen zum Neuen Testament 233 (Tübingen: Mohr Siebeck, 2008), 365.

[74] Ibid., 367.

[75] Ibid.

of restoration of all things"—that is, the creation of the new heavens and the new earth (Isa 65:17–25; Mic 4:8; 2 Pet 3:7–13).[76]

From the above, it follows that the hope of Israel for a restored kingdom under the rule of a Davidic king began to be fulfilled in Jesus and His Jewish followers, who gathered together to form the nucleus of a renewed Israel. This community of believers under the lordship of Jesus constitutes the true *qāhāl*/*ekklēsia*/church, which inherits the covenantal promises given to God's people in the Old Testament. The renewed Israel, like its Old Testament predecessor under Joshua, undertakes a major work of conquest. But unlike its theocratic counterpart, which aimed at conquering a stretch of land in the Middle East, the restored Israel aims at conquering the world. It knows no borders or limitations, no ethnicity or nationality. It calls everyone everywhere to follow Jesus and join the community of believers.

Romans 11:25–26

Some scholars appeal to Romans 9–11, particularly 11:25–26, as evidence that the Old Testament prophecies about the restoration of Israel must find fulfillment in the establishment of a national/political entity in the Middle East, which during a presumed millennial reign of Jesus Christ on earth will become God's instrument to reach the nations.[77] However, careful examination of the biblical text indicates that rather than a political restoration, the biblical text speaks about the redemption brought about by Jesus. Indeed, the present section of Romans addresses Paul's concern for the salvation of his fellow Jews. Apparently, as the gospel progressed among the Gentiles, the number of Jewish believers may have decreased, and the prospects may have been grim and frustrating given the increasing opposition from his compatriots. Thus, it is from this perspective and context that one should understand the present section of Romans.

To begin with, Paul clarifies that to be an Israelite is not a matter of biological descent from Abraham. Some who claim Abraham as their father are only "children of the flesh." Only the "children of the promise" can be regarded as "the seed" (Rom 9:8). As Paul states elsewhere, "only those who are of faith are sons of Abraham" (Gal 3:7). And this is not an ad hoc argument, because, as Paul argues, Gentiles become sons of Abraham on the basis of the covenant promise that in Abraham all the nations of the earth would be blessed (Gal 3:8; cf. Gen 12:1–3).

---

[76] Bauckham, *The Jewish World Around the New Testament*, 331.

[77] Rudolph, 167–194.

As the argument unfolds, the apostle Paul appeals to the Hebrew Scriptures to assert that Gentiles can become part of the covenant people. Interestingly, statements that in Hosea apply to the restoration of apostate Israel to the covenant become the basis for the incorporation of believing Gentiles into God's people: "I will call them My people, who were not My people" (Rom 9:25–26; cf. Hos 2:23). This idea recurs later as Paul insists that "there is no distinction between Jew and Greek. . . . For 'whoever calls on the name of the Lord shall be saved'" (Rom 10:12–13).

Next, Paul introduces the concept of the remnant, which further reinforces the above argument that the true sons of Abraham are those of faith. In every stage of Israel's checkered history of apostasy and rebellion, God had always preserved a remnant (Rom 9:27–29).[78] Therefore, although the number of ethnic Israelites may be like the sand, "the remnant will be saved" (Rom 9:27; 11:2–5). Clearly, God's people must be defined in terms of faithfulness to God rather than by ethnic or national boundaries.

But although true Israelites continued to exist within national Israel, the apostle was suffering because the vast majority of his own people—who had precedence over the Gentiles in the history of salvation and to whom the gospel was first preached—had rejected God's promised Messiah. For this reason, Paul asks the painful question, "Has God cast away His people?" to which he replies with a resounding "Certainly not!" (Rom 11:1).

One reason for such confidence lies in Paul's own inclusion in the elect: "For I also am an Israelite, of the seed of Abraham, of the tribe of Benjamin" (Rom 11:1). Thus, "that God has not rejected his people is seen not in the latter day restoration of Israel to the land of promise, but in God's call to Paul the Jew to follow Jesus Christ, becoming 'apostle to the Gentiles,' taking the good news of Jesus Christ to the heart of the Roman Empire, and ultimately dying for his faith."[79] By arguing from his experience, once again Paul indicates that the matter under discussion concerns the spiritual salvation of the people of Israel.

Subsequently, the apostle mentions two other reasons for his confidence that his people could still recover: 1) through their failure "salvation has come to the Gentiles," and 2) if their failure meant "riches

---

[78] For an overview of the concept of remnant in the Bible, see Gerhard F. Hasel, "Remnant," in *The International Standard Bible Encyclopedia*, ed. Geoffrey W. Bromiley, vol. 4, rev. ed (Grand Rapids, MI: Eerdmans, 1988), 130–134.

[79] Philip Church, *The Gospel and the Land of Promise: Christian Approaches to the Land of the Bible* (Eugene, OR: Pickwick, 2011), 155, Kindle.

for the Gentiles, how much more their fullness!" (Rom 11:11–12).[80] Apparently, Paul expected his repentant Jewish compatriots to be grafted back again into their own olive tree (Rom 11:23–24), which had already been ingrafted with Gentile believers. With that happening, tremendous benefits would accrue to the world.

This study must now turn to the most crucial passages related to the restoration of Israel in the entire Pauline corpus:[81] "For I do not desire, brethren, that you should be ignorant of this mystery, lest you should be wise in your own opinion, that blindness in part has happened to Israel until the fullness of the Gentiles has come in. And so all Israel will be saved, as it is written: 'The Deliverer will come out of Zion, And He will turn away ungodliness from Jacob; For this is My covenant with them, When I take away their sins'" (Rom 11:25–27).

First, the mystery[82] referred to in the passage may be understood as something that was revealed to Paul through his understanding of the Hebrew Scriptures and the gospel.[83] In the prophetic announcements of salvation Israel usually precedes the Gentiles, who then flow in to join the covenant people. That large numbers of Gentiles accepted the Messiah and thus began to enjoy the blessings of salvation prior to the much-desired massive conversions of Jews may be the mystery referred to in the passage.[84]

Second, the phrase "And so all Israel will be saved" seems to be one of the most controversial and debated statements of Scripture. Three main explanations have been offered for this difficult statement: "all Israel" refers to 1) all Jews throughout human history, 2) all Jews alive during the final stages of earth's history, and 3) the totality of God's

---

[80] Richard N. Longenecker, *The Epistle to the Romans: A Commentary on the Greek Text*, ed. I. Howard Marshall and Donald A. Hagner, New International Greek Testament Commentary (Grand Rapids, MI: Eerdmans, 2016), 886.

[81] James M. Scott, "'And Then All Israel Will Be Saved' (Rom 11:26)," in *Restoration: Old Testament, Jewish, and Christian Perspectives*, ed. James M. Scott, Supplements to the Journal for the Study of Judaism 72 (Leiden: Brill, 2001), 489–527.

[82] "Mystery," as C. E. B. Cranfield, *A Critical and Exegetical Commentary on the Epistle to the Romans*, International Critical Commentary (London: T&T Clark, 2004), 573, explains, "denotes characteristically in the NT not something which must not be disclosed to the uninitiated (which is its connotation in extra-biblical Greek, when used in connection with the mystery cults), but something which could not be known by men except by divine revelation, but which, though once hidden, is now revealed in Christ and is to be proclaimed so that all who have ears to hear may hear it."

[83] Douglas J. Moo, *The Letter to the Romans*, ed. Ned B. Stonehouse et al., 2nd ed., The New International Commentary on the New Testament (Grand Rapids, MI: Eerdmans, 2018), 730–733.

[84] Ibid., 732. See also Cranfield, 573–574.

people constituted by ethnic Jews and Gentile Christians. The first explanation implies a universalism incompatible with other passages of Scripture. The second view may be possible if one focuses on this particular section of Romans only. Since verse 25 refers to ethnic Israel, it would be natural to read "all Israel" in verse 26 as a reference to ethnic Israel. However, if one takes the broad context of chapters 9–11, the third view seems to have stronger exegetical and theological support. In Romans 9:6, 27, Israel is defined in terms of a relationship with God rather than nationality or ethnicity. In addition, the inclusion of Gentiles in the Old Testament covenant promises—which finds confirmation in the book of Acts' portrait of the restored Israel—leads to the conclusion that "all Israel" refers to the totality of God's people constituted by Jews and Gentiles.[85] However, even if one takes the view that "all Israel" refers to ethnic Jews who will accept Christ en masse,[86] there is no indication in the biblical text that such a conversion involves the establishment of a theocratic nation.

Third, Paul brings the argument to a climax with a quote from Isaiah 59:20: "The Redeemer will come to Zion, And to those who turn from transgression in Jacob" (Rom 11:26). Significantly, while the Hebrew text reads "to Zion" and the Septuagint reads "concerning Zion," Paul refers to the Redeemer coming *from* Zion (*ek Siōn*). Through this significant shift, the focus changes from the earthly Zion to the heavenly Zion. As one scholar suggests, Paul "perhaps understood Σιών [Zion] as meaning heaven or the heavenly sanctuary," an idea hintedat elsewhere in the New Testament (Gal 4:26; Heb 12:22; Rev 3:12; 21).[87] Thus, the locus of God's promise is no longer the earthly Zion, but Jesus Christ who comes *to* the heavenly Zion to save Jews and Gentiles alike.[88]

To conclude, although used to postulate a future role for an ethnic and theocratic Israel in the plan of salvation, Romans 11:25–26 seems

---

[85] Clinton Wahlen, "Will All Jews Be Saved?," in *Interpreting Scripture: Bible Questions and Answers*, ed. Gerhard Pfandl, Biblical Research Institute Studies 2 (Silver Spring, MD: Biblical Research Institute, 2010), 351–355.

[86] For this possibility, see Daniel K. Bediako, "The Meaning of 'All Israel Will Be Saved' (Romans 11:26)," *Asia-Africa Journal of Mission & Ministry* 5 (2011): 167, who understands Israel in an ethnic sense but argues "that the salvation Paul envisaged for Israel . . . primarily refers to their acceptance of the gospel of Jesus Christ (cf. v. 14), and thus their participation in the present salvation even in Paul's day." See also Wilson Paroschi, "The Mystery of Israel's Salvation: A Study of Romans 11:26," *Ministry* (May 2011): 21–24.

[87] Cranfield, 578.

[88] Church, 27.

to point in another direction. Significantly, the land, the city of Jerusalem, and other geopolitical features of national Israel are conspicuously absent from Paul's reflection. The passage focuses on the fact that the door of salvation remains open to the Jews and eventually many of them will be grafted into their own olive tree—an event that will result in tremendous blessings for the world. In this way "all Israel" (Jewish and Gentile believers alike) will be saved.

Revelation 7:1–8

The portrayal of the 144,000 from the twelve tribes of Israel—followed by the depiction of a great multitude before the heavenly throne—answers the question "Who is able to stand?," which concludes the previous section of Revelation (6:17).[89] For the purpose of this study, one should note that the term "Israel," along with the detailed enumeration of the twelve tribes, transcends ethnic boundaries—a picture consistent with the eschatological Israel presented elsewhere in the New Testament. The following discussion revisits some of the main arguments to understand eschatological Israel as a multiethnic community of believers in Christ.

In ways reminiscent of Ezekiel 9:6, the 144,000 receive the "seal of the living God" (Rev 7:2) and thus are "protected in the time of universal destruction."[90] Although some claim that this group refers to ethnic Jews who will be sealed for protection from the last plagues,[91] such an interpretation seems inconsistent with the language and imagery of Revelation. In fact, to be consistent with the genre of the book, the 144,000 must be understood as symbolic, and therefore representative of God's end-time covenant people. In support of this interpretation, the following arguments may be advanced:

First, the same group of people are mentioned in Revelation 14:3, as "redeemed from the earth." And significantly, Revelation 5:9 says that those redeemed by the Lamb come from "every tribe and tongue and people and nation." That being so, the 144,000 should be understood as a multiethnic community of believers in Christ.[92]

---

[89] Ranko Stefanovic, *Revelation of Jesus Christ: Commentary on the Book of Revelation*, 2nd ed. (Berrien Springs, MI: Andrews University Press, 2009), 259.

[90] Nichol, 7:783.

[91] Merrill C. Tenney, *Interpreting Revelation* (Grand Rapids, MI: Eerdmans, 1957), 78; and John F. Walvoord, *The Revelation of Jesus Christ: A Commentary* (Chicago, IL: Moody, 1966), 140–141.

[92] G. K. Beale, *The Book of Revelation: A Commentary on the Greek Text*, New International Greek Testament Commentary (Grand Rapids, MI: Eerdmans, 1999), 412–413.

Second, the 144,000 are referred to as "servants" (*douloi*), a term that elsewhere in Revelation "is never used exclusively of Jewish Christians anywhere else in the book, but always refers to believers in general or to all saints."[93] Indeed, this must be a reference to the new covenant community formed by Jews and Gentiles.

Third, the number 144,000, resulting from the square of twelve multiplied by one thousand, conveys the "figurative idea of completeness."[94] The square of twelve comes from the number of the tribes of Israel multiplied by itself or "more likely, the twelve tribes multiplied by the twelve apostles."[95] The fact that both the twelve tribes of Israel and the twelve apostles "form part of the figurative structure of the heavenly city of God, 'the new Jerusalem'"[96] (Rev 21:12–14), lends credence to this suggestion. The combination of the twelve apostles with the twelve tribes makes the 144,000 a designation of the renewed Israel which is constituted by a multiethnic community of believers in Christ. Such language and imagery accord with the broad New Testament way of referring to the covenant community with Israelite imagery and designations (e.g., Rom 2:29; 9:6; 2 Cor 1:20–21; Gal 3:29; 6:16; Eph 1:11, 14; Phil 3:3–8; Titus 2:14; 1 Pet 2:19).[97]

Fourth, several commentators note that the language and imagery of the 144,000 alludes to the census list of Numbers 1.[98] As amply recognized, a census was mostly performed to assess the military strength of the tribes. So, the census recorded in Numbers 1 lists tribe by tribe the number of men, aged twenty years and over, capable of going to war. Revelation 7 in turn not only mentions the number of the sealed ones tribe by tribe but also uses the repeated phrase "of the tribe of" in a clear allusion to the census of Numbers 1:20–45.[99] Moreover, the subsequent observation that the 144,000 "were not defiled with women" (Rev 14:4), which was expected of men preparing

---

[93] Beale, 413.

[94] Ibid., 417.

[95] Ibid.

[96] Ibid.

[97] Ibid., 418.

[98] See, e.g., Richard Bauckham, *The Climax of Prophecy: Studies on the Book of Revelation* (London: T&T Clark, 1993), 210–237; David E. Aune, *Revelation 6–16*, Word Biblical Commentary 52B (Dallas, TX: Word, 1998), 436; Beale, 422; and Craig R. Koester, *Revelation: A New Translation With Introduction and Commentary*, ed. John J. Collins, Anchor Yale Bible 38 A (New Haven, CT: Yale University Press, 2014), 426.

[99] Peter S. Williamson, *Revelation*, ed. Mary Healy, Catholic Commentary on Sacred Scripture (Grand Rapids, MI: Baker Academic, 2015), 139.

for war (Deut 23:9–10; 1 Sam 21:5–6), reinforces the imagery that the 144,000 constitutes "the messianic army of the lion of Judah."[100] Their weapons, however, "are witness and fidelity in the face of death."[101]

Fifth, a final aspect that calls for comment relates to the fact that the tribal list given in Revelation 7 does not match any of the lists of tribes in the Old Testament, as noted in the following table:[102]

Revelation 7	Genesis 49	Numbers 1:5-15	Ezekiel 48
Judah	Reuben	Reuben	Dan
Reuben	Simeon	Simeon	Asher
Gad	Levi	Judah	Naphtali
Asher	Judah	Issachar	Manasseh
Naphtali	Zebulun	Zebulun	Ephraim
Manasseh	Issachar	Ephraim	Reuben
Simeon	Dan	Manasseh	Judah
Levi	Gad	Benjamin	Benjamin
Issachar	Asher	Dan	Simeon
Zebulun	Naphtali	Asher	Issachar
Joseph	Joseph	Gad	Zebulun
Benjamin	Benjamin	Naphtali	Gad

Five major points are worth noticing: 1) Judah, not Reuben (Jacob's firstborn), heads the list, which most likely is due to the fact that the Messiah comes from Judah (Rev 5:4; cf. Gen 49:10; Matt 1:3; 2:6). 2) The tribe of Dan is omitted—and replaced by Manasseh—probably because of its association with idolatry (Judg 18; 1 Kgs 12). 3) Ephraim is also omitted, most likely for the same reason as Dan. As one scholar observes, "Ephraim became for the prophets a symbol of Israel's apostasy and idolatry (Hos 4:17; 8:9–11; 12:1; cf. 2 Chron 30:1, 10). The Psalmist describes Ephraim as 'archers equipped with bows, yet they turned back in the day of battle; they did not keep the

[100] Grant R. Osborne, *Revelation*, Baker Exegetical Commentary on the New Testament (Grand Rapids, MI: Baker Academic, 2002), 315.

[101] C. R. Koester, 426.

[102] Stefanovic, 263.

covenant of God' (Ps. 78:9–10)."[103] 4) Joseph, who is represented by his sons Ephraim and Manasseh in the tribal lists of Numbers 1:5–15 and Ezekiel 48, appears as a tribe in his own right in the list of Revelation 7. 5) The tribe of Levi seems out of place in a military census, and probably for this reason it was excluded from the two Mosaic censuses (Num 1:49; 2:33; 26:1–51; cf. 1 Chr 21:6). However, the inclusion of the tribe of Levi reminds one of the zeal of Phinehas in executing divine vengeance upon the apostate Israelites (Num 25:6–13).[104]

In sum, the language and imagery used to portray the 144,000 show the "completeness of the people of God as the messianic army of Christ."[105] This group constitutes the eschatological Israel, which transcends ethnic and geographical boundaries. This is another instance in which terms and images associated with Old Testament Israel are applied to the eschatological people of God, the renewed Israel, "who follow the Lamb wherever He goes" (Rev 14:4).

Conclusions

The following points emerge as a summary with some suggestive interpretative guidelines:

1) The Old Testament prophetic hope finds its fulfillment in Jesus. As the corporate representative of the nation, Jesus gathered around Himself the remnant of Israel to form the nucleus of a renewed Israel.

2) Although theocratic Israel rejected Jesus, God did not reject the Jewish people. Indeed, hope still exists that many of them will accept Jesus before the consummation of all things.

3) Israel's geopolitical institutions such as the land, city (Zion/Jerusalem), and temple are redefined in the New Testament and expanded.

4) New Testament passages that seem to refer to territorial and ethnic Israel must be interpreted in light of Jesus the Messiah. As the corporate representative of the nation, Jesus sums up Israel and its institutions.

---

[103] Stefanovic, 264.

[104] Bauckham, *Climax of Prophecy*, 222. He notes that "in 1QM, although the priests and Levites do not fight with weapons, they play an essential part in the conduct of war, conducting prayers before, during and after battle, and blowing the trumpets which both direct the troops and call divine attention to the battle. Without them the war could not be a holy war. Consequently, the tribe of Levi is organized on the same military pattern as the other tribes (1QM 4:1–8)" (ibid.).

[105] Grant R. Osborne, *Revelation: Verse by Verse*, Osborne New Testament Commentaries (Bellingham, WA: Lexham Press, 2016), 141.

5) The language and imagery associated with Old Testament Israel are applied to the eschatological Israel, which transcends ethnic and geographic boundaries.

6) The twelve apostles gathered around Jesus constituted the remnant of Israel, from which Jesus formed a renewed Israel. So, the church has not replaced Israel, but was ingrafted into Jesus, the corporate representative of Israel, and together with the Jewish believers constitutes the people of God.

7) Concrete and material aspects of the Old Testament promises to Israel are not obliterated. Distinctive elements of the covenant such as the land, the city, and the temple have been redefined in Jesus. So, when the covenant reaches its consummation, land, city, and temple become even more real and concrete than their typological counterparts.

CHAPTER 11

The Genesis Account as a Test Case for Biblical Hermeneutics

Michael G. Hasel

The creation account in Genesis 1–3 is foundational for the major historical and theological concepts found in Scripture, providing the key philosophical definitions of reality. Foundational biblical concepts include: an absolute beginning and movement through historical time and place (Gen 1:1; John 1:1–4), the nature of God as transcendent Creator (Gen 1:1–2:25), the triune Godhead as expressed in His plurality of creative activity (Gen 1:1–2; 1:26–28; John 1:1–4), the loving character of God and His pursuant nature toward humanity (Gen 1:1–3; Gen 2:9), tution of marriage (Gen 1:26–28; 2:20–25), the institution of the law and the Sabbath (Gen 2:1–3; Exod 20:8–11), the reestablishment of a covenant relationship (Gen 3:9–15), the origin and nature of sin (Gen 3:1–15), the origin and plan of redemption (Gen 3:15), the great controversy (Gen 2:9, 16–17; 3:1–7), and the restoration of God's plan for a perfect creation in the second coming[1]—in short, from a biblical perspective the

[1] On these foundational concepts, see Gerhard F. Hasel, "The Meaning of 'Let Us' in Gen 1:26," *Andrews University Seminary Studies* 13 (1975): 58–66; John T. Baldwin, "Progressive Creationism and Biblical Revelation: Some Theological Implications," *Journal of the Adventist Theological Society* 11 (2000): 174–187; Michael G. Hasel, "In the Beginning," *Adventist Review*, October 25, 2001, 24–27; Norman R. Gulley, "What Happens to Biblical Truth if the SDA Church Accepts Theistic Evolution?," *Journal of the Adventist Theological Society* 15/2 (Autumn 2004): 40–58; Randall W. Younker, "Consequences of Moving Away from a Recent Six-day Creation," *Journal of the Adventist Theological Society* 15/2 (Autumn 2004): 59–70; E. Edward Zinke, "Theistic Evolution: Implications for the Role of Creation in Seventh-day Adventist Theology," in John T. Baldwin, ed., *Creation, Catastrophe and Calvary* (Hagerstown, MD: Review and Herald, 2000), 159–171; Daniel K. Bediako, "Genesis 1:1–2:3 as a Historical Narrative Text Type," *Valley View University Journal of Theology* 1 (2011): 18–35; Richard M. Davidson, "The Genesis Account of Origins," in *The Genesis Creation Account and Its Reverberations in the*

flow of human history originates in creation and ends in re-creation so that protology is the key to eschatology.[2]

However, with the presuppositions of the Enlightenment and the historical-critical method came the impetus for the emerging evolutionary hypothesis of the nineteenth century.[3] Accommodations for the evolutionary hypothesis in biblical studies became increasingly common in the twentieth century, causing a shift in the interpretation of the creation account of Genesis 1–3 from a historical, factual, and literal creation by divine fiat—*creatio ex nihilo*—a few thousand years ago, to a nonliteral interpretation.[4] The first form-critical scholar to suggest that Genesis should not be understood as history but rather as "legend" was Hermann Gunkel, who clearly articulates that "many things reported in Genesis . . . go directly against our better knowledge."[5] What he meant by "our better knowledge" was the naturalistic evolutionary interpretation of scientific data, which should take precedent and inform our biblical exegesis. Evolutionary theory should be taken as the authoritative norm over the Genesis account. Subsequently, different nonliteral genres of interpretation[6] suggested for Genesis include "saga,"[7] "cultic liturgy,"[8]

Old Testament, ed. Gerald A. Klingbeil (Berrien Springs, MI: Andrews University Press, 2015), 59–130; Wayne Grudem, "Theistic Evolution Undermines Twelve Creation Events and Several Crucial Christian Doctrines," in *Theistic Evolution: A Scientific, Philosophical, and Theological Critique*, ed. J. P. Moreland et al. (Wheaton, IL: Crossway, 2017), 783–837; John D. Currid, "Theistic Evolution is Incompatible with the Teachings of the Old Testament," in *Theistic Evolution*; 839–878; and Guy Prentiss Waters, "Theistic Evolution is Incompatible with the Teachings of the New Testament," in *Theistic Evolution*, 879–926.

[2] Michael G. Hasel, "The Relationship between Protology and Eschatology," in *The Cosmic Battle for Planet Earth*, ed. Ron du Preez and Jiří Moskala (Berrien Springs, MI: Seventh-day Adventist Theological Seminary, 2003), 17–32 and Bruce Norman, "The Restoration of the Primordial World of Genesis 1–3 in Revelation 21–22," *Journal of the Adventist Theological Society* 8/1–2 (1997): 161–169.

[3] Todd S. Beall, "Contemporary Hermeneutical Approaches to Genesis 1–11," in *Coming to Grips with Genesis: Biblical Authority and the Age of the Earth*, ed. Terry Mortenson and Thane H. Ury (Green Forest, AR: Master Books, 2008), 131–162.

[4] Concerning the Hebrew term *bārā'* and other exegetical arguments in favor of *creation ex nihilo*, see Paul Copan and William Lane Craig, *Creation out of Nothing: A Biblical, Philosophical, and Scientific Explanation* (Grand Rapids, MI: Baker, 2004).

[5] Hermann Gunkel, *The Legends of Genesis: The Biblical Saga and History* (New York: Schocken, 1964), 1–7.

[6] Steven W. Boyd, "The Genre of Genesis 1:1–2:3: What Means this Text?," in *Coming to Grips*, 163–192.

[7] Jerome Hamer, *Karl Barth* (Westminster, MD: Newman, 1962), 119–122.

[8] S. H. Hooke, *Middle Eastern Mythology* (Baltimore, MD: Penguin Books, 1963), 119–121.

"hymn,"[9] "metaphorical narration,"[10] "doctrine,"[11] "story,"[12] "poetry,"[13] "theology,"[14] "metaphor/parable,"[15] "vision,"[16] "mythology" based on ancient Near East parallels,[17] "liturgy/worship,"[18] and "analogy."[19] This plethora of interpretations in itself raises some serious questions concerning the modern trajectory of form-critical genre studies: 1) There appears to be no major scholarly consensus on the literary genre of the creation account in Genesis, even though it appears certain that the form-critical approach aims to remove Genesis 1 from the category of history. 2) Form-critical approaches that reassign the text to a different genre than history still allow the grammatical interpretation of "days" in Genesis 1 as literal.[20]

Other approaches suggest that the structure of the creation account in Genesis 1 provides merely a literary framework,[21] that the days of

---

[9] Gordon J. Wenham, *Genesis 1–15*, Word Biblical Commentary (Waco, TX: Word Books, 1987), 10.

[10] John H. Stek, "What Says Scripture?," in *Portraits of Creation: Biblical and Scientific Perspectives on the World's Formation*, ed. Howard J. Van Till et al. (Grand Rapids, MI: Eerdmans, 1990), 236.

[11] Gerhard von Rad, *Genesis: A Commentary* (Philadelphia, PA: Westminster, 1972), 65.

[12] J. A. Thompson, "Genesis 1–3. Science? History? Theology," *Theological Review* 3 (1966): 25.

[13] Walter Brueggemann, *Genesis: A Biblical Commentary for Teaching and Preaching* (Atlanta, GA: John Knox, 1982), 26–28 and Bill Arnold, *Encountering the Book of Genesis* (Grand Rapids, MI: Baker, 1998), 23.

[14] Conrad Hyers, *The Meaning of Creation: Genesis and Modern Science* (Atlanta, GA: John Knox, 1984); Bruce R. Reichenbach, "Genesis 1 as a Theological-Political Narrative of Kingdom Establishment," *Bulletin for Biblical Research* 13/1 (2003): 47–69; and Davis Young, *Creation and the Flood: An Alternative to Flood Geology and Theistic Evolution* (Grand Rapids, MI: Baker, 1974), 86–89.

[15] John C. L. Gibson, *Genesis*, Daily Study Bible (Edinburgh: Saint Andrew Press, 1981), 1:55–56.

[16] P. J. Wiseman, *Creation Revealed in Six Days* (London: Marshall, Morgan, and Scott, 1948), 33–34 and Duane Garrett, *Rethinking Genesis: The Sources and Authority of the First Book of the Pentateuch* (Grand Rapids, MI: Baker, 1991), 192–194.

[17] Hermann Gunkel, *Schöpfung und Chaos in Urzeit: Eine religionsgeschichtliche Untersuchung über Gen 1 und Ap Joh 12* (Göttingen: Vandenhoeck & Ruprecht, 1985); Brevard S. Childs, *Myth and Reality in the Old Testament*, Studies in Biblical Theology, 27 (London: SCM, 1962), 31–50; and Peter Enns, *Inspiration and Incarnation* (Grand Rapids, MI: Baker, 2005), 50.

[18] Terence E. Fretheim, "Were the Days of Creation Twenty-Four Hours Long? YES," in *The Genesis Debate: Persistent Questions about Creation and the Flood*, ed. Ronald F. Youngblood (Grand Rapids, MI: Baker, 1990), 26.

[19] C. John Collins, *Genesis 1–4: A Linguistic, Literary, and Theological Commentary* (Phillipsburg, NJ: P&R Publishing, 2006), 124.

[20] Gerhard F. Hasel, "The 'Days' of Creation in Genesis 1: Literal 'Days' or Figurative 'Periods/Epochs' of Time," *Origins* 21/1 (1994): 17.

[21] N. H. Ridderbos, *Is There a Conflict Between Genesis 1 and Natural Science?*, trans. John Vriend (Grand Rapids, MI: Eerdmans, 1957); Meredith G. Kline, "Because It Had Not Rained," *Westminster Theological Journal* 20 (1958): 146–157; Meredith G. Kline, *Genesis. The New Bible Commen-*

creation should be interpreted as (day-age) symbolism,[22] or that the creation narrative depicts a cosmic temple inauguration.[23] What is common to all these nonliteral views is the assumption that the Genesis account of origins is not a straightforward historical account of material creation. Since these ideas are making an increasing impact on evangelical and even Adventist theology,[24] the task in this study is to observe some of the recent trends and discuss important questions and implications of accepting a nonliteral view of the creation account

---

tary: Revised (Downers Grove, IL: InterVarsity, 1970); Henri Blocher, *In the Beginning: The Opening Chapters of Genesis* (Downers Grove, IL: InterVarsity, 1984), 49–59; Lee Irons with Meredith G. Kline, "The Framework View," in *The Genesis Debate: Three Views on the Days of Creation*, ed. David G. Hagopian (Mission Viejo, CA: Crux Press, 2001), 217–256; W. Robert Godfrey, *God's Pattern for Creation* (Phillipsburg, NJ: P&R Publishing, 2003), 52–53; D. F. Payne, *Genesis One Reconsidered* (London: Tyndale, 1964); and Bruce Waltke, *Genesis: A Commentary* (Grand Rapids, MI: Zondervan, 2001), 73–78.

[22] Broad concordists believe the seven days represent longer periods; see Derek Kidner, *Genesis: An Introduction and Commentary*, Tyndale Old Testament Commentaries (Downers Grove, IL: InterVarsity, 1967), 54–58; Hugh Ross and Gleason L. Archer, "The Day-Age View," in *The Genesis Debate: Three Views on the Days of Creation*, ed. David G. Hagopian (Mission Viejo, CA: Crux Press, 2001), 123–163; and Vern S. Poythress, in *Three Views on Creation and Evolution*, ed. James P. Moreland and John Mark Reynolds (Grand Rapids, MI: Zondervan, 1999), 92. The "progressive-creationist" view sees each day to open a new creative period of indeterminate length. See Robert C. Newman and Herman J. Eckelmann, Jr., *Genesis One and the Origin of the Earth* (Downers Grove, IL: InterVarsity, 1977), 64–65; cf. Moreland and Reynolds, *Three Views*, 104. Schroeder tries to harmonize the week into billions of years of "cosmic time." See Gerald L. Schroeder, *Genesis and the Big Bang: The Discovery of Harmony between Modern Science and the Bible* (New York: Bantom, 1990), Gerald L. Schroeder *The Science of God: The Convergence of Scientific and Biblical Wisdom* (New York: Free Press, 1997); and Gerald L. Schroeder, *God According to God: A Physicist Proves We've Been Wrong About God All Along* (New York: Harper One, 2009).

[23] John H. Walton, *The Lost World of Genesis One: Ancient Cosmology and the Origins Debate* (Downers Grove, IL: InterVarsity, 2009); cf. John H. Walton, *Genesis 1 as Ancient Cosmology* (Winona Lake, IN: Eisenbrauns, 2011). For a critique of Walton's views that Genesis only speaks of *functional* origins and not *material* origins, see Richard E. Averbeck, "The Lost World of Adam and Eve: A Review Essay," *Themelios* 40/2 (2015): 226–239, and essays in *Andrews University Seminary Studies* 49/1 (2011).

[24] Ivan T. Blazen, "Theological Concerns of Genesis 1:1–2:3," in *Understanding Genesis: Contemporary Adventist Perspectives*, ed. Brian Bull, Fritz Guy, and Ervin Taylor (Riverside, CA: Adventist Today, 2006), 72, writes, "What we have in Genesis 1 is theological affirmation rather than scientific delineation." Fritz Guy, "The Purpose and Function of Scripture: Preface to a Theology of Creation," in *Understanding Genesis*, 94, maintains that "what Genesis gives us is not scientific cosmology but profound theology (even if it utilizes ancient perceptions of the world)." Larry G. Herr, "Genesis One in Historical-Critical Perspective," *Spectrum* 13/2 (December 1982): 59, 61, states, "Genesis 1 is theological in intent and scientists need not attempt to harmonize the ancient cosmology with the cosmology of modern science" and "the chapter uses the common ancient Near Eastern cosmology in expressing what it takes to be the *theological* (or cosmogonic) truth."

for biblical hermeneutics. In other words, what is at stake in terms of biblical theology when reinterpreting the creation account in Genesis as merely theology, story, or something other than a historical and literal account?

Issues of Biblical Authority, Unity, and Inspiration

Many major Old Testament scholars affirm that the writer of Genesis 1 meant the creation account to be taken literally.[25] James Barr, Regius Professor of Hebrew at the University of Oxford and one of the most important Hebrew scholars, chides evangelicals for their nonliteral interpretation of Genesis while they simultaneously affirm the infallibility of Scripture. He writes, "In fact the only natural exegesis is a literal one, in the sense that this is what the author meant."[26] Gerhard von Rad, the foremost Old Testament scholar of the twentieth century, writes, "What is said here [Gen 1] is intended to hold true entirely and exactly as it stands."[27] "Everything that is said here [in Gen 1] is to be accepted exactly as it is written; nothing is to be interpreted symbolically or metaphorically."[28] Von Rad is even more specific regarding the literal creation week: "The seven days [of creation week] are unquestionably to be understood as actual days and as a unique, unrepeatable lapse of time in the world."[29] If a sequential period of seven, literal and consecutive twenty-four-hour days is what the lexicography, grammar, syntax, terminology and time-boundaries of "evening and morning" demand,[30] then a nonliteral view of the creation account raises serious implications for the authority of Scripture as the inspired Word of God. It assumes that the Bible is not reliable as a source of information about origins and

---

[25] This was the primary theological position taken by theologians through history until the time of the early Reformers. See James R. Mook, "The Church Fathers on Genesis, the Flood and the Age of the Earth," in *Coming to Grips*, 23–52; David W. Hall, "A Brief Overview of the Exegesis of Genesis 1–11: Luther to Lyell," in *Coming to Grips*, 53–78; and James Barr, "Luther and Biblical Chronology," *Bulletin of the John Rylands University Library* 72 (1990): 65.

[26] James Barr, *Fundamentalism*, 2nd ed. (London: SCM Press, 1981), 40.

[27] Gerhard von Rad, *Genesis*, 47.

[28] Gerhard von Rad, "The Biblical Story of Creation," in *God at Work in Israel* (Philadelphia, PA: Fortress, 1984), 99.

[29] Ibid., 65, von Rad does make a distinction between *Historie* and *Heilsgeschichte*, or "salvation history." See chapter 4 by Michael G. Hasel, "History, the Bible, and Hermeneutics," in the present volume; and Frank M. Hasel and Michael G. Hasel, *How to Interpret Scripture* (Nampa, ID: Pacific Press, 2019).

[30] Gerhard F. Hasel, "'Days' of Creation," 21–28.

the beginning of this world and universe. It suggests that the first chapters of Genesis be relegated into categories that contain spiritual and theological meaning but not actual *Historie* based on what actually happened.[31] Is this congruent with the views of the writers of the Old and New Testament? And if it is not congruent, how does this affect the unity of Scripture? What is the impact on the authority of Scripture if modern naturalistic presuppositions and conclusions are accepted as more authoritative than the biblical account and then superimposed upon the creation account?

The biblical writers unanimously reference the people and events of Genesis 1–11 as if they actually occurred the way the Bible describes.[32] Moses, for example, consistently affirms in Exodus a literal seven-day sequence of creation. This includes: 1) the manna falling on six days, but not on the Sabbath (Exod 16:4–6, 21–23); 2) the fourth commandment, which says God created in six days and rested on the seventh as an example for all of creation (Exod 20:9–11); and 3) affirming the Sabbath as a sign, for "in six days the Lord made the heavens and the earth, and on the seventh day he abstained from work and rested (Exod 31:16–17).[33] What would happen to these statements if God did not create in six days? The unity of Scripture would be compromised. Jesus states that "Scripture cannot be broken" (John 10:35)[34] and Paul affirms in 2 Timothy 3:16 that "all Scripture is given by inspiration of God, and is profitable for doctrine, for reproof, for correction, for instruction in righteousness." If only certain parts of Scripture are reliable sources of history and truth, then were the writers of the rest of Scripture, as well as Jesus and Paul, mistaken? Who decides what is historical and what is not?[35] Biblical authority, unity, and the very nature of inspiration would be undermined.

---

[31] See chapter 4 by Michael G. Hasel, "History, the Bible, and Hermeneutics," in the present volume.

[32] Exodus 20:9–11; Psalm 33:6, 9; 89:12; 104; Isaiah 40:28; Matthew 19:4–5; 23:35; 24:37–39; Mark 10:6–9; 13:19; Luke 1:70; 3:34–38; 11:50–51; 17:26–27; John 1:1–3, 10; 8:44; Acts 3:21; 4:25; 14:15; 17:24, 26; Romans 1:20; 5:12, 14–19; 8:20–22; 16:20; 1 Corinthians 6:16; 11:3, 7–9, 12; 15:21, 22, 38–39, 45, 47; 2 Corinthians 4:6; 11:3; Galatians 4:4, 26; Ephesians 3:9; 5:30–31; Colossians 1:16; 3:10; 1 Timothy 2:13–15; Hebrews 1;10; 2:7–8; 4:3–4, 10; 11:4–5, 7; 12:24; James 3:9; 1 Peter 3:20; 2 Peter 2:4–5; 3:4–6; 1 John 3:8, 12; Jude 6, 11, 14–15; Revelation 2:7; 3:14; 4:11; 10:6; 12:1–4, 9, 13–17; 14:7; 17:5, 18; 20:2; 21:1, 4; 22:2–3. See articles in Gerald A. Klingbeil, ed., *The Genesis Creation Account and Its Reverberations in the Old Testament* (Berrien Springs, MI: Andrews University Press, 2015).

[33] Gulley, "Theistic Evolution," 54.

[34] All biblical quotations are from the NKJV, unless otherwise indicated.

[35] See essays in J. K. Hoffmeier and D. R. Magary, eds., *Do Historical Matters Matter to Faith? A Critical Appraisal of Modern and Postmodern Approaches to Scripture* (Wheaton, IL: Crossway, 2012).

The Character of God and Moral Accountability

The relationship between creation and the incarnation of Christ is revealed in the parallel between Genesis 1:1, "In the beginning God created the heavens and the earth," and John 1:1–4, "In the beginning was the Word, and the Word was with God, and the Word was God. He was with God in the beginning." Christ is revealed as the agent of creation. "All things were made through Him, and without Him nothing was made that was made" (John 1:3; cf. Col 1:15–16; Heb 1:1–2). Christ spoke matter into existence at the beginning as "the Spirit of God was hovering over the face of the waters" (Gen 1:2). Psalms 33:9 (ESV) reaffirms, "For he spoke, and it came to be; he commanded, and it stood firm" for "by faith we understand that the universe was formed at God's command, so that what is seen was not made out of what was visible" (Heb 11:3, NIV). God says, "Let us make man in our image" (Gen 1:26). The triune Godhead is found implicitly in Genesis 1 as powerfully working to create an ecosystem for life and to fill that ecosystem with perfect harmony, breathtaking beauty, and diversity. God repeatedly declares this to be "good" and finally "then God saw everything that He had made, and indeed it was very good" (Gen 1:31). The order and perfection of creation reveals the order and perfection of God. It establishes His creative activity as the basis for worship (Exod 20:8–11; Rev 4:11; 14:7).

If God started the process billions of years ago by simply forming matter and allowing it to evolve through the naturalistic processes of evolution, what would this mean for the nature of God? How would we need to reinterpret the character of God? And how would humans respond to such a God? A nonliteral view of creation that allows for a hybrid form of theistic evolution or progressive creation has serious implications.[36]

First, the truth about God would be distorted. He would be robbed of His power to speak fully formed elements and creatures into existence *ex nihilo*. This has implications for Christ's power to change the water into wine, or speak to the paralyzed man at Bethesda, "Rise, take up your

---

[36] Others point out that naturalistic evolution and theistic creation are mutually exclusive ideas that have no common beginning or ending. Evolution presents a process from simple to complex, from partial to complete, or from less perfect to near perfect—in short, progress. Creation presents the opposite trajectory from a perfect world to a broken world, from harmony to disharmony and strife, from love to a world where the thoughts of humanity were "only evil continually" (Gen 6:5)—in short, a digression. One is based on philosophical naturalism that excludes any outside intervention; the other is based on theism that assumes that God interacts in His creation. See Stephen Dilley, "How to Lose a Battleship: Why Methodological Naturalism Sinks Theistic Evolution," in *Theistic Evolution*, 593–631.

bed and walk" (John 5:8), to say to Jairus' daughter, "Little girl, I say to you, arise" (Mark 5:41), or to say "Lazarus, come forth!" (John 11:43). It is by the same power of the word that Jesus demonstrates His creative power to heal and to raise the dead. "To accept His creative power during His life on earth necessitates accepting His creative power in the Genesis record, for both are equally supernatural, and both are given to us through divine revelation."[37]

Second, it would mean that God created matter in the beginning but allowed animals and humans to compete through millions of years of torture and death in a holocaust of survival of the fittest. How is this congruent with a God who warned Adam of the evil of death (Gen 2:17), who notices when a sparrow falls (Matt 10:29), or who came to give life (John 3:16)? The idea that life originates from death is a pagan view of origins.[38] In the Atra-Ḫasis Epic, man is created from the flesh and blood of a slaughtered god mixed with clay, but "no hint of the use of dead deity or any other material of a living one is found in Genesis."[39] The cycle of death and rebirth is so intrinsic to Egyptian ideology that death itself is seen as part of the normal order of creation. On a funerary papyrus of the Twenty-first Dynasty a winged serpent is standing on two pairs of legs with the caption, "Death the great god, who made gods and men."[40] This is "a personification of death as a creator god and an impressive visual idea that death is a necessary feature of the world of creation, that is, of the existence in general."[41] This is the opposite of the God who creates animals and humanity in a perfect world and blesses them (Gen 1:22, 28).

Third, a God who intricately forms the miracle of life so that it can be studied in nature through the complexity of the cell, or the tiny seed that produces a tree, or a bird caring for and feeding her chicks, inspires the desire to worship and invokes an innate sense of moral accountability. Paul spoke to the Athenians "God who made the world and everything in it. . . . now commands all men everywhere to repent, because He has appointed a day on which He will judge the world in righteousness

---

[37] Gulley, "Theistic Evolution," 50.

[38] See Gerhard F. Hasel and Michael G. Hasel, "The Unique Cosmology of Genesis 1 against Ancient Near Eastern and Egyptian Parallels," in *The Genesis Creation Account*, 27–29.

[39] Alan R. Millard, "A New Babylonian 'Genesis' Story," *Tyndale Bulletin* 18 (1967): 3–18.

[40] Papyrus of Henuttawy (BM 10018), Siegfried Schott, *Zum Weltbild der Jenseitsführer des Neuen Reiches,* NWAG 11 (Göttingen: Vandenhoeck & Ruprecht, 1965), 195, pl. 4; and Karol Myśliwiec, *Studien zum Gott Atum*, 2 vols., Hildesheimer Ägyptologische Beiträge 5 (Hildesheim: Gerstenberg, 1978), 1:103.

[41] Eric Hornung, *Conceptions of God in Ancient Egypt* (Ithaca, NY: Cornell University Press, 1982), 81.

by the Man whom He has ordained" (Acts 17:24, 30–31). In Romans 1:20 people are "without excuse," having witnessed the wonders of creation. A nonliteral view of the Genesis account removes this accountability because nature as we know it today would have evolved over millions of years without much or any divine design or providence. "Within the theistic evolution system, the complexity of living things no longer leaves unbelievers 'without excuse' (Rom 1:20)."[42] Naturalistic evolution has a major impact on moral issues in society such as euthanasia, animal and human rights, purpose, and the divine origin of ethics.[43] In the end, humanity is left without a direct, divine origin, removing human dignity and a moral compass.[44]

The Nature of "Adam and Eve" and the Origin of Humanity

The nature of humanity as created by God in His image places all human beings in a unique place at the apex of creation. The triple emphasis in God's creative act (*bārāʾ*) in Genesis 1:27 reinforces the supreme regard humans have in God's special design. Other biblical writers trace the origin of all human beings back to the first two humans, Adam and Eve. The amplification of the creative means in Genesis 2 conveys the personal attention given to this intimate act by God[45] as He carefully fashioned the man out of the dust of the earth and breathed into him the breath of life.[46] God's special creation of Eve is marked by His divine reflection: "It is not good that man should be alone; I will make him a helper

---

[42] Grudem, "Theistic Evolution Undermines," 832.

[43] Stephen Bauer, *Moral Implications of Darwinian Evolution for Human Preference Based on Christian Ethics: A Critical Analysis and Response to the Moral Individualism of James Rachels* (unpublished PhD diss., Andrews University, 2006).

[44] Ibid., 114–120 and James Rachels, *Created from Animals: The Moral Implications of Darwinism* (Oxford: Oxford University Press, 1991), 125.

[45] On the relationship of Genesis 1–2 as complementary and as one of amplification, see Jacques B. Doukhan, *The Genesis Creation Story: Its Literary Structure*, Andrews University Seminary Doctoral Dissertation Series 5 (Berrien Springs, MI: Andrews University Press, 1978); O. T. Allis, *The Five Books of Moses* (Philadelphia, PA: Presbyterian and Reformed, 1943); U. Cassuto, *The Documentary Hypothesis*, trans. I Abrahams (Jerusalem: Magnes, 1961); I. M. Kikawada and A. Quinn, *Before Abraham Was: The Unity of Genesis 1–11* (Nashville, TN: Abingdon, 1985); R. N. Whybray, *The Making of the Pentateuch: A Methodological Study* (Sheffield: Sheffield Academic Press, 1987); Younker, "Genesis 2: A Second Creation Account?," in *Creation, Catastrophe and Calvary*, 69–79; and Currid, "Theistic Evolution," 863–870.

[46] The dust from the ground is the material from which Adam was made and the material to which all humans return; see Vern Polythress, *Did Adam Exist?* (Phillipsburg, NJ: P&R Publishing, 2014), 16.

comparable to him" (Gen 2:18). He built (*banāh*) woman from the rib of Adam and brought her to him (Gen 2:21–22). They were instructed to "be fruitful and multiply; fill the earth and subdue it; have dominion over the fish of the sea, over the birds of the air, and over every living thing that moves on the earth" (Gen 1:28). Humans were created to care for God's creation and fill the planet with families that would honor God and what was created.[47] Adam's historical nature is reaffirmed in Genesis 5:1–5:

> In the day that God created man, He made him in the likeness of God. He created them male and female, and blessed them and called them Mankind in the day they were created. And Adam lived one hundred and thirty years, and begot *a son* in his own likeness, after his image, and named him Seth. After he begot Seth, the days of Adam were eight hundred years; and he had sons and daughters. So all the days that Adam lived were nine hundred and thirty years; and he died.

Not only is the terminology *bārā'* repeated three times here in connection with the creation of Adam, but the text twice refers to "in the day" that God created Him. An evolutionary process is absent here. It also mentions a specific number of years in Adam's life before Eve bore Seth, and a total number of years just like the other antediluvian men in Genesis 5. This assumes a historical existence and a reaffirmation of Genesis 1–2.[48]

The idea of a historical Adam and Eve as humanity's first ancestors is challenged by a nonliteral interpretation of Genesis 1–3 in several ways. First, if God only created matter in the beginning and then left naturalistic evolution to continue the process, then there were thousands of ancestors of the human race. Francis S. Collins states that our species "descended from a common set of founders, approximately 10,000 in number, who lived about 100,000 to 150,000 years ago."[49] Denis Alexander writes, "The

---

[47] Jo Ann Davidson, "Creator, Creation, and Church: Restoring Ecology to Theology," *Andrews University Seminary Studies* 45 (2007): 101–122.

[48] On the chronogenealogies of Genesis 5 and 11, see Gerhard. F. Hasel, "The Genealogies of Genesis 5 and 11 and Their Alleged Babylonian Background," *Andrews University Seminary Studies* 16 (1978): 361–374; Gerhard F. Hasel, "Genesis 5 and 11: Chronogenealogies in the History of Beginnings," *Origins* 7 (1980): 23–37; Gerhard F. Hasel, The Meaning of the Chronogenealogies of Genesis 5 and 11," *Origins* 7 (1980): 53–70.

[49] Francis S. Collins, *The Language of God: A Scientist Presents Evidence for Belief* (New York: Free Press, 2006), 126.

founder population that was the ancestor to all modern humans . . . was only 9,000–12,000 reproductively active people."[50] In other words, the gene pool for our first ancestors was not one man and one woman. This means that Adam and Eve were not really created by God but were born from human parents. This is in direct conflict with Genesis 2, which states that God directly "formed the man from the dust of the ground and breathed into his nostrils the breath of life" (Gen 2:7) and that God "built" Eve from a rib taken from Adam's side (Gen 2:20–25). Luke affirms this in the genealogies when he writes, "Seth, the son of Adam, the son of God" (Luke 3:38). Paul also states explicitly that Adam had no parent when he writes of "the first man Adam" (1 Cor 15:45). "But if Adam had a human father, then he would not be the first man."[51] Likewise, how could Genesis 3:20 refer to Eve as "the mother of all living" when there had been thousands of others living before her?

Second, the order and sequence of creation in which Adam is created first and then later Eve to fully complement the first human parents would no longer be necessary. N. T. Wright suggests that "God chose one pair from the rest of early hominids for a special, strange, demanding vocation. This pair (call them Adam and Eve if you like) were to be representatives of the whole human race."[52] Likewise, John H. Walton suggests that Adam and Eve should be understood as "archetypes" representing Everyman who "embodies all others in the group."[53] Walton states that the Bible "makes no claims" regarding "biological human origins," for Genesis "talks about the *nature of all* people, not the unique *material origins* of Adam and Eve."[54] For Walton, Adam merely had a "visionary experience" when he saw "himself being cut in half and the woman being built from the other half."[55] But nowhere in the text is any terminology used for a visionary experience.

Denis Lamoureux is more explicit: "Adam never existed"[56] and "Holy

---

[50] Denis Alexander, *Creation or Evolution: Do We Have to Choose?*, 2nd ed. (Oxford and Grand Rapids, MI: Monarch, 2014), 265.

[51] Grudem, "Theistic Evolution Undermines," 798–799.

[52] N. T. Wright, "Excursus on Paul's Use of Adam," in *The Lost World of Adam and Eve: Genesis 2–3 and the Human Origins Debate* (Downers Grove, IL: InterVarsity, 2015), 177–178.

[53] John H. Walton, *The Lost World of Adam and Eve: Genesis 2–3 and the Human Origins Debate* (Downers Grove, IL: InterVarsity, 2015), 74.

[54] Ibid., 181.

[55] Ibid., 78–79.

[56] Denis Lamoureux, "No Historical Adam: Evolutionary Creation View," in *Four Views on the Historical Adam*, ed. Matthew Barrett and Ardel B. Caneday (Grand Rapids, MI: Zondervan, 2013), 58.

Scripture makes statements about how God created living organisms that in fact never happened" since "real history in the Bible begins roughly around Genesis 12 with Abraham."[57] Peter Enns argues along a historical-critical process[58] when he writes that Adam is Israel: "Maybe Israel's history happened first, and the Adam story was written to reflect that history. In other words, the Adam story is really an Israel story placed in primeval time. It is not a story of human origins but of Israel's origins."[59] Enns articulates more fully why he takes this position, asserting that "a literal reading of the Genesis creation stories does not fit with what we know of the past. The scientific data do not allow it."[60] After placing Israel and Adam side by side, he concludes that "Adam's story mirrors Israel's story from exodus to exile."[61]

But do these explanations correspond to what Genesis actually says concerning the material creation and origin of Adam and Eve; the order of creation as Paul reaffirms when he writes, "For Adam was formed first, then Eve" (1 Tim 2:13); or what Jesus explicitly states in His confirmation of this special creation?[62] Jesus remarks most succinctly "that He who made them at the beginning, made them male and female" (Matt 19:4). Jesus affirms the Genesis account that the first human parents were made "at the beginning"—not some billions of years after He created matter Jesus affirms that God made them "male and female" and that "what God has joined together, let not man separate" (Matt 19:5–6). Jesus' statement in response to the Pharisees upholds a literal understanding of the Genesis account. To reinterpret Genesis, requires scholars to reinterpret Jesus and Paul. Thus, Enns sets out "to properly address Genesis as ancient literature and Paul as an ancient man,"[63] ultimately placing (with Walton and others) Genesis as ancient premodern literature that requires reinterpretation in the modern world of naturalistic science.

---

[57] Lamoureux, "No Historical Adam," 56, 44.

[58] See the section "The Origin of the Seventh-Day Sabbath" in this chapter.

[59] Peter Enns, "Adam is Israel," *BioLogos,* March 2, 2010, https://biologos.org/articles/adam-is-israel (accessed October 9, 2019).

[60] Enns, *The Evolution of Adam: What the Bible Does and Doesn't Say about Human Origins* (Grand Rapids, MI: Brazos, 2012), 79.

[61] Ibid., 65–66.

[62] In fact, Enns makes no mention of Jesus' important discourse in Matthew 19:3–9 (Mark 10:2–9), emphasizing only the statements of Paul. He also does not mention Revelation 22:1–5, where God will ultimately undo the effects and consequences of sin once and for all; see Norman, "Primordial World."

[63] Enns, *Evolution of Adam*, xvii.

The Origin of the Seventh-Day Sabbath

The seventh-day Sabbath finds its origin at creation.[64] It has been argued that it is the final goal of the creation narrative.[65] What happens to the concept of the Sabbath when a nonliteral view of creation is adopted that reinterprets creation week into a mere framework, or that sees each day representing longer epochs of time encompassing millions of years? How is the Sabbath to be understood in light of the fourth commandment, where God instructs humanity to remember the Sabbath day by pointing back to creation week: "For in six days the Lord made the heavens and the earth, the sea, and all that is in them, and rested on the seventh day. Therefore, the Lord blessed the Sabbath day and hallowed it" (Exod 20:11)? This same phrase is alluded to again in Revelation where humanity at the end time is to "worship Him who made heaven and earth, the sea and springs of water" (Rev 14:7).[66] Does the concept of providing this mutual day of rest and worship for Creator and creature have any meaning if the event itself never took place as described in Genesis? Two interpretations highlight the historical-critical or theistic evolutionary viewpoint of the Sabbath.

The historical-critical approach denies *a priori* the claim of the Mosaic authorship of the Pentateuch and dates the Sabbath passages in Genesis and Exodus to later Israelite tradition or to various schools.[67]

---

[64] Gerhard F. Hasel, "The Origin of the Biblical Sabbath and the Historical-Critical Method: A Methodological Test Case," *Journal of the Adventist Theological Society* 4/1 (1993): 17–46; Gerhard F. Hasel, "The Sabbath in the Pentateuch," in *The Sabbath in Scripture and History*, ed. Kenneth A. Strand (Washington, DC: Review and Herald, 1982); Mathilde Frey, "The Sabbath in the Pentateuch: An Exegetical and Theological Study" (PhD diss., Andrews University, 2011); H. Ross Cole, "The Sabbath and Genesis 2:1–3," *Andrews University Seminary Studies* 41/1 (2003): 5–12; Richard M. Davidson, *A Love Song for the Sabbath* (Hagerstown, MD: Review and Herald, 1988); and Sigve K. Tonstad, *The Lost Meaning of the Seventh Day* (Berrien Springs, MI: Andrews University Press, 2009).

[65] Oswald Loretz, *Schöpfung Mythos: Mensch und Welt nach den Anfangskapiteln der Genesis* (Stuttgart: Katholisches Bibelwerk, 1968), 70: "The goal of the whole creation and of man is God's Sabbath. The creation of the world reaches its completion only through the Sabbath, the seventh day"; see also Gerhard F. Hasel, "The Sabbath in the Pentateuch," 23; and Jiří Moskala, "The Sabbath in the First Creation Account," *Journal of the Adventist Theological Society* 13/1 (2002): 56–58. This is also reflected in Jesus' statement, "The Sabbath was made for man, and not man for the Sabbath" (Mark 2:27).

[66] John T. Baldwin, "Revelation 14:7: An Angel's Worldview," in *Creation, Catastrophe and Calvary*, ed. John T. Baldwin (Hagerstown, MD: Review and Herald, 2000), 19–39.

[67] Both Genesis 1:1–2:3, containing the creation Sabbath, and Exodus 16:22–30, dealing with the Sabbath and manna, are attributed by source critics to the P(riestly) source that is dated either

For Willy Rordorf then, the Jewish Sabbath of Genesis 1–2, Exodus 20, and Deuteronomy 5 "originated after the occupation of Canaan and that the evidence is to be found in documents which date from the early monarchical period," but that "credit for such an invention has not been given to the Israelites."[68] With the dismissal of creation as the origin for the Sabbath, scholars have searched for Sabbath origins outside of Israel, assuming it was borrowed from some other ancient civilization, be it Babylonian, Kenite, Arabic, Ugaritic, or sociological. "In spite of the extensive efforts of more than a century of study into extra-Israelite sabbath origins, it is still shrouded in mystery. No hypothesis . . . commands the respect of a scholarly consensus."[69] Still, historical-critical scholars would not attribute the Sabbath to a divine origin, but rather would limit it to a human invention. This would have some major implications for the Sabbath's authority.

As a proponent of theistic evolution, N. T. Wright argues that "linear time (which was part of God's good creation) continues, but it is now intersected with a new phenomenon, a new kind of time. . . . so time seems now capable of being telescoped together and then pulled apart again. One might call this 'Spirit-time'. . . . All of this is focused on Jesus Christ."[70] For Wright, "now that heaven and earth have come together in Jesus Christ, and now that the new day has dawned, we live (from that point of view) in a perpetual sabbath."[71] The Sabbath—as the seventh day, first day, or any specific day—has ceased to exist and has become part of the Christian "story." The Sabbath is transposed into a

---

to the exilic or post-exilic periods, or later editors and redactors. See Werner Schmidt, *Die Schöpfungsgeschichte der Priesterschrift*, Wissenschaftliche Monographien zum Alten und Neuen Testament, 2nd ed. (Neukirchen-Vluyn: Neukirchner Verlag, 1976), 154–59; Gnana Robinson, *The Origin and Development of the Old Testament Sabbath*, Beiträge zur biblischen Exegese und Theologie (Frankfurt and New York: Peter Lang, 1988), 225–227; and Niels-Erik Andreasen, *The Old Testament Sabbath: A Traditio-Historical Investigation*, SBL Dissertation Series 7 (Missoula, MT: Scholars, 1972), 63–67. Source critics often view the Sabbath commandment in Deuteronomy 5:12–15 as earlier than the Genesis and Exodus references based on their date of the D source or the DtrH. On the date of D and DtrH, see Michael G. Hasel, *Military Practice and Polemic: Israel's Laws of Warfare in Near Eastern Perspective* (Berrien Springs, MI: Andrews University Press, 2005), 2–5, 21–49.

[68] Willy Rordorf, *Sunday: The History of the Day of Rest and Worship in the Earliest Centuries of the Christian Church* (Philadelphia, PA: Westminster, 1968), 18–19.

[69] Gerhard F. Hasel, "Sabbath," in *Anchor Bible Dictionary*, ed. David Noel Freedman (New York: Doubleday, 1992), 5:851.

[70] N. T. Wright, *Scripture and the Authority of God: How to Read the Bible Today* (New York: HarperCollins, 2011), 162–163.

[71] Ibid., 167.

principle of rest that is separated from the specific (historic) day that God designated. This has implications for the eschatological nature of the Sabbath and its relation to last-day events as prophesied in Scripture. The Sabbath loses its special character as a divine test and sign of the Sabbath-keeping remnant living just before Jesus returns (Rev 12:17; 14:12; cf. Ezek 20:12), since it is transformed from a specific time to a "perpetual sabbath" devoid of time altogether. In this way, we see that when literal time, as defined biblically, is removed from creation, so is it also removed from the Sabbath.

The Sabbath's origin at creation as a divine act of God has major implications: 1) Since the Sabbath is rooted in God's design and not man's, only God has the authority to change its time and meaning. 2) Since the Sabbath originated at creation, before Hebrews or Jews existed, it is not to be limited to a particular people, time, or place. It is universal in application. 3) Since the Sabbath was instituted at creation, it is a creation memorial and model established in the creation order. To change this institution is to interfere with God's design, will, and purpose—not that of humanity. 4) To change, remove, alter, or abolish the seventh-day Sabbath would undo what God has ordained. 5) God Himself provides the example of Sabbath observance, having established the rhythm of creating the world in six days and resting on the seventh. 6) God sanctified the Sabbath and "made it holy." Humans do not do this by keeping a day. 7) Just as the Sabbath is linked to the universality of creation, so is the universality of the Sabbath linked to all of humanity.[72] The challenge before us is to acknowledge the seventh day of the week as the biblical day of rest that God instituted at creation and upheld throughout Scripture. We are called to "keep the commands of God [including the fourth commandment] and the faith of Jesus" (Rev 14:12, NKJV) and thus keep the Sabbath in such a way that it gives honor to the Creator God who is also our Savior.

Marriage and the Family

The basis for marriage between a man and a woman finds its divine origin as an institution of creation.[73] The biblical creation

---

[72] Gerhard F. Hasel, "Origin of the Biblical Sabbath," 19–20.

[73] J. Kerby Anderson, *Moral Dilemmas: Biblical Perspectives on Contemporary Ethical Issues*, Swindoll Leadership Library, ed. Charles R. Swindoll (Nashville, TN: Word, 1998), 165, observes, "Foundational to a Christian understanding of sexuality is God's plan in creation found in Genesis 1 and 2." On the divine institution of marriage at creation, see Ron du Preez, "The God-Given Marital Mandate: Monogamous, Heterosexual, Intrafaith," *Journal of the*

account in Genesis tells us that "God was the author of this union."[74] If Sabbath is the final goal of creation, humanity and marriage is the climax.[75] More space is devoted to the creation of humanity than any other aspect of creation in Genesis 1:1–2:3. "In the image of God He created him; male and female He created them" (Gen 1:27). In Genesis 2 this emphasis is enlarged and expanded. Eve is "built" by God of the rib taken from Adam's side. Adam declares, "This is now bone of my bones, and flesh of my flesh; She shall be called Woman, because she was taken out of Man" (Gen 2:23, NASB). Marriage requires that "a man shall leave his father and mother and be joined to his wife, and they shall become one flesh" (Gen 2:24). For what reason is marriage to take place? Woman was taken out of man—his very flesh and bone. The created complementarity of both man and woman is unequivocal biologically so that this one flesh relationship is to take place between a man and a woman.[76] This union is further clarified in the instruction given to the earth's first parents. "Then God blessed them, and God said to them, 'Be fruitful and multiply; fill the earth and subdue it'" (Gen 1:28).

In this way, the foundation of humanity and society on earth is defined in God's creative life-giving work in the beginning. The assurance of humanity's future is based on following His design. The human race is to be perpetuated from each father and mother, also a man and woman. The gift of God's marriage union is His final act in the physical creation. The institution of the Sabbath in time brings this union into communion with the divine agent of creation, Jesus Christ. Our creation in God's image forms the intended identity we have in Jesus Christ, and our acknowledgement of identifying with Him comes

---

Adventist Theological Society 10/1–2 (1999): 23–40; Calvin B. Rock, "Marriage and the Family," in *The Handbook of Seventh-day Adventist Theology*, ed. Raoul Dederan (Hagerstown, MD: Review and Herald, 2000), 725; and Richard M. Davidson, *Flame of Yahweh: A Theology of Sexuality in the Old Testament* (Peabody, MA: Hendrickson, 2007), 15–19.

[74] Geoffrey W. Bromiley, *God and Marriage* (Grand Rapids, MI: Eerdmans, 1980), 3.

[75] Wenham, *Genesis 1–15*, 37, states that the creation of humans in the image of God is "the climax of the six days' work. But it is not its conclusion." Bruce A. Ware, "Male and Female Complementarity and the Image of God," in *Biblical Foundations for Manhood and Womanhood*, ed. Wayne A. Grudem (Wheaton, IL: Crossway, 2002), 72, refers to the creation of man as "the pinnacle of God's creative work," pointing to seven exegetical indicators within the text.

[76] On the biological counterpart-complement concept of pairing between male and female as part of God's design, see Robert A. J. Gagnon, "The Scriptural Case for a Male-Female Prerequisite for Sexual Relations: A Critique of the Arguments of Two Adventist Scholars," in *Homosexuality, Marriage, and the Church: Biblical, Counseling, and Religious Liberty Issues*, ed. Roy E. Gane, Nicholas P. Miller, and H. Peter Swanson (Berrien Springs, MI: Andrews University Press, 2012), 65–70 and Gagnon., *The Bible and Homosexual Practice: Texts and Hermeneutics* (Nashville, TN: Abingdon, 2001), 58–62.

in our worshipping on His seventh-day Sabbath. The loving relationship of the Creator with the family is to be perpetuated from the husband and wife to their children, and on through the generations of history. There is a sacred trust given to the nuclear family as the basis for the rest of culture and society. As their relationship with God and with each other goes, so goes earth's history. Perhaps it is for this reason that the fifth commandment, the seventh commandment, and the tenth commandment address the sanctity of marriage in the honor bestowed to parents and end with the instruction not to covet a neighbor's wife (Exod 20:17).

In the New Testament, the institution of marriage is reaffirmed by Jesus and the apostles. Jesus responds to an inquiry about divorce from the Pharisees by quoting specifically from Genesis 1–2. He says, "Therefore what God has joined together, let not man separate" (Matt 19:6). Jesus affirms Scripture, and Genesis in particular, by stating that the joining together of man and woman came from God and that which God has divinely ordained should not be separated by man.

Paul specifically addresses the foundational nature of Genesis in Romans 1:20–28. Beginning with creation, Paul affirms that all humanity through nature could come to understand the reality of the existence of God. But Paul goes on to state that "they exchanged the truth of God for a lie, and worshipped and served the creature rather than the Creator." This choice to believe in a lie led them to their practice: "For this reason God gave them up to their vile passions," and what follows is the description of same-sex behavior both between two females and between two males (Rom 1:24–26). For Paul, biblically defined sexuality between a man and a woman is "natural" and is intrinsic to the very nature of human beings who are created in the image of God (Gen 1:27). It is the refusal to accept the Creator by exchanging His worship with that of the creature that causes them to be handed over to their lusts. Sexuality then should not be limited merely to behavior and activity; rather it should be understood within a biblically defined concept of created humanity in totality that provides the framework to reinforce moral behavior.

The nonliteral interpretation of the Genesis creation account has consequential implications for the definition of marriage. The unique gift of marriage between a man and a woman has recently witnessed major attempts at deconstruction and redefinition. Many nations of the world have approved same-sex marriages, overturning previous laws that protected the family structure comprising at its center one man and one woman. This is an unprecedented development in many respects and raises new questions about the institution of marriage, the separation of church and state, as well as the sanctity of marriage and the family as defined in Scripture.[77] It raises important questions for Christians. Is marriage a religious institution that is defined by the Bible, a biological necessity for the creation of life, or is it a personal preference that is relegated to the sphere of individual human and civil rights? In short, is marriage a human institution defined by culture and society, or is it a biblical institution defined by God? How Christians have responded to these questions have determined the direction of their churches amidst increased cultural pressure. In 2009 the Evangelical Lutheran Church in America and The Episcopal Church USA both, independently, voted to approve homosexual clergy. Lutherans elected a practicing gay bishop in California (2013), and the Presbyterian Church USA decided to welcome practicing homosexuals as ministers and leaders (2011). In Europe the Scottish Episcopal Church approved same-sex unions in 2017.

What arguments do these churches use to approve same-sex marriage in traditionally Christian countries around the world? Recent books on this subject indicate the key issues in biblical interpretation. These issues involve 1) a redefinition of Genesis 1–2 that emphasizes culture and setting for the stories, 2) a reinterpretation of key passages in Scripture that have historically been seen as prohibiting homosexual behavior, and 3) an application of passages on love and acceptance that take precedence over clearer passages on the subject.

Those who affirm same-sex relationships have reinterpreted Genesis in several ways. Matthew Vines suggests that God needed to provide Adam with a woman because they were the first parents and were required to procreate in order to fill the earth, but implies that this is not a necessity today in our world of overpopulation.[78] He subsequently suggests that Genesis 2 does not emphasize Adam and Eve's differentness, but "their *similarity* as human beings."[79] But while it is true that Adam speaks of Eve as "bone of my bone and flesh of my flesh," this is in comparison with all the different animal species. It then does not follow that sameness and companionship was all that mattered, for they also "became

---

[77] On religious liberty issues, see Alan Reinach, "Wake Up and Smell the Equality: Same-Sex Marriage and Religious Liberty," in *Homosexuality, Marriage, and the Church*, 229–264 and Nancy Pearcey, *Love Thy Body: Answering Hard Questions about Love and Sexuality* (Grand Rapids, MI: Baker, 2018).

[78] Matthew Vines, *God and the Gay Christian* (New York: Convergent, 2014), 45–47; cf. Jay Michaelson, *God vs. Gay: The Religious Case for Equality* (Boston, MA: Beacon, 2012).

[79] Vines, *God and the Gay Christian*, 46.

one flesh." Here, the complementary nature of God's design in making this physically possible becomes a key element.[80] They were the perfect anatomical match for each other. Procreation is an essential purpose for marriage (Gen 1:27) and, even though not all couples are able to have children, the parental role of a husband and wife is also assumed in the fifth commandment.

Others suggest that Genesis is merely descriptive and not prescriptive or proscriptive—that is, it describes what God did, but God did not make marriage between a man and a woman normative or exclude other relationships.[81] But to this we must again appeal to the fifth commandment, which is certainly proscriptive; to the laws in Leviticus; and to Jesus and Paul, who both affirm the creation order as being ordained by God and, therefore, natural. In fact, after God finished the apex of His creation, man and woman, on the sixth day, "God saw everything that He had made, and indeed it was very good" (Gen 1:31). His design was perfect. There was no need in Genesis 1 and 2 for proscriptive statements. It was only after the introduction of sin that such proscriptions were required.

In the end, a nonliteral view of creation or one that minimizes its normative role in Genesis has major implications for the institution of marriage. If naturalistic evolution is true, sex and gender is a historical accident, subject to the flux and flow of history. We could be evolving to dozens of genders, or perhaps to a single gender. The biblical view affirms that both male and female sexes are essential to the identity of humanity, and to understanding the image and nature of God. This, in turn, has significant implications for other doctrines of Scripture, including the unity and harmony of Scripture, the doctrine of humanity, grace, the church, the great controversy, and the character of God.[82]

---

[80] Much more than physical union is implied here. In Genesis 4:1 "Adam knew Eve his wife" and she bore him a son. The term *yāda'*, "to know," can also mean "to experience," to understand," and "to care about" (Rock, "Marriage and the Family," 725; cf. Pearcey, *Love Thy Body*, 138: "The reference to *physical* unity was intended to express joyous unity on all other levels as well – including mind, emotion, and spirit. Scripture offers a stunningly high view of physical union as a union of the whole person across all dimensions.")

[81] John R. Jones, "'In Christ There Is Neither . . .': Toward a Unity of the Body of Christ," in *Christianity and Homosexuality*, ed. David Ferguson, Fritz Guy, and David Larson (Roseville, CA: Adventist Forum, 2008), part 4, 3–42.

[82] Richard M. Davidson, "Homosexuality and the Bible: What is at Stake in the Current Debate," in *Homosexuality, Marriage, and the Church*, 187–208.

The Origin of Sin, Death, and the Plan of Redemption

The world was created in perfect order. This is indicated by the declaration of God six times during the creation narrative that what He created was "good" (Gen 1:4, 10, 12, 18, 21, 25) and the seventh time "God saw all that he had made . . . was very good" (Gen 1:31).[83] There is no indication that death existed before the fall, as indicated by several important parameters.[84] Animals and humans were both given a vegetarian diet, eliminating the need to kill (Gen 1:29–30). God warned Adam and Eve of the tree of the knowledge of good and evil and that the consequences would be death (Gen 2:16–17). This happened *before* the serpent tempted Eve (Gen 3:1–4).[85] When Eve and then Adam ate of the tree of the knowledge of good and evil (Gen 3:6–7), the perfect creation was undone by the entrance of sin.[86] A number of important consequences resulted from their disobedience.[87] Their eyes were opened (Gen 3:7). They recognized that they were naked and were filled with shame, sewing fig leaves to cover themselves (Gen 3:7). They hid from God (Gen 3:8). Adam blamed Eve and Eve blamed the serpent for the fall (Gen 3:12–13). God pronounced a curse that, with the result of sin, would bring pain and suffering (Gen 3:14–19). God drove Adam and Eve from the garden (Gen 3:22–23). Cherubim were placed to

---

[83] Several patterns of seven are found in Genesis 1:1–2:3: 1) the seven consecutive days; 2) God's seven affirmations that what He created was good and then very good; and 2) the repetition of the word *bara'* seven times.

[84] Hans Madueme and Michael Reeves, eds., *Adam, the Fall, and Original Sin: Theological, Biblical, and Scientific Perspectives* (Grand Rapids, MI: Baker Academic, 2014).

[85] For the identification of the serpent in the fall account of Genesis 3, and the fall and role of Satan before humanity's disobedience, see José M. Bertolucci, *The Son of the Morning and the Guardian Cherub in the Context of the Controversy between Good and Evil* (ThD diss., Andrews University, 1985); Norman R. Gulley, *Systematic Theology: Creation, Christ, Salvation* (Berrien Springs, MI: Andrews University Press, 2012), 137–139; Gulley, *Systematic Theology: Prolegomena*, 191–192, 390–453; Walter C. Kaiser, Jr., *The Messiah in the Old Testament* (Grand Rapids, MI: Zondervan, 1995), 38–42; C. F. Keil and F. Delitzsch, "The First Book of Moses (Genesis)," in *Biblical Commentary on the Old Testament* (Peabody, MA: Hendrickson, 2006), 57–59, 62–64; and Kenneth A. Mathews, *Genesis 1–11:26: An Exegetical and Theological Exposition of Holy Scripture*, The New American Commentary (Nashville, TN: Broadman and Holman, 1996), 232–235.

[86] Niels-Erik A. Andreasen, "Death: Origin, Nature, and Final Eradication," in *Handbook of Seventh-day Adventist Theology*, 318–319 and Jacques B. Doukhan, "'When Death Was Not Yet': The Testimony of Biblical Creation," in *Genesis Creation Account*, 329–342.

[87] On several essential consequences to the fall and sin, see Jiří Moskala, "Genesis 3 as a Model for Understanding the Nature of Sin and Salvation," *Journal of the Adventist Theological Society* 27/1–2 (2016): 134–142.

guard the entrance, indicating a separation (Gen 3:24). Cain murdered his brother Abel in the very next chapter (Gen 4:1–8).

The New Testament reaffirms a literal understanding of Adam and the origin of sin and death.[88] Paul attributes the responsibility of sin to Adam and refers to him specifically as "one man": "Sin entered the world through one man, and death through sin, and in this way death came to all men" (Rom 5:12). Adam's act in Genesis 3 sealed the fate of humanity in the transgression of God's command.[89] "Death reigned from Adam to Moses, even over those who had not sinned according to the likeness of the transgression of Adam, who is a type of Him who was to come" (Rom 5:14). Just to make it perfectly clear, Paul reiterates, "As through one man's offense *judgment came* to all men, resulting in condemnation, even so through one Man's righteous act *the free gift came* to all men, resulting in justification of life" (Rom 8:18). Norman Gulley writes,

> It was Adam and not His Creator who brought death to this planet. It was Christ who came to die to put death to death and liberate the fallen race (Rom 4:25). It was the one act of the first Adam that caused this death-condemnation, and the one act of the second Adam's death that provided salvation (Rom 5:18). Christ did not use death to create humans in Eden, He died to save humans at Calvary.[90]

Paul affirms this when he says, "The wages of sin is death, but the gift of God is eternal life through Jesus Christ our Lord" (Rom 6:23). This promise of the Messiah is already given in Genesis 3:15, inaugurating for humanity the plan of salvation.[91] "Actually the major premise of all of Scripture is that death is an abnormal state connected with human moral guilt and not connected with an evolutionary past (Ps 6:5; 30:9; 55:15; Prov 5:5; 7:27; 12:28; Isa 28:15; Jer 21:8; 1 Cor 15:43; Rev 21:8)."[92]

---

[88] On the New Testament analysis of these passages and their direct link to a literal creation of Adam as the first man, see J. P. Versteeg, *Adam in the New Testament: Mere Teaching Model or First Historical Man?*, trans. Richard B. Gaffin, Jr., 2nd ed. (Phillipsburg, NJ: P&R Publishing, 2012) and Guy Prentiss Waters, "Theistic Evolution is Incompatible with the Teachings of the New Testament," in *Theistic Evolution*, 879–926.

[89] John M. Fowler, "Sin," in *Handbook of Seventh-day Adventist Theology*, 241–242.

[90] Gulley, "Theistic Evolution," 48.

[91] Kaiser, *Messiah in the Old Testament*, 38–42; Afolarin O. Ojewole, *The Seed in Genesis 3:15: An Exegetical and Intertextual Study*, Adventist Theological Society Dissertation Series (Berrien Springs, MI: Adventist Theological Society, 2002), 126–134; and Wenham, *Genesis 1–15*, 72–91.

[92] William Edgar, "Adam, History, and Theodicy," in *Adam, the Fall, and Original Sin*, 313.

What, then, are the implications of a nonliteral view of creation that assumes millions of years of naturalistic evolution? An evolutionary perspective would have death present for millions of years prior to the arrival of human beings. Death would be a necessary element of the process to life as thousands of species attempt to be the fittest to survive. The mythical worldview sees death and life as inseparable. In some ideologies, like ancient Egypt, death is where life originates.[93] There is an incessant circle or cycle of death and life,[94] and conflict or violence is a necessary source of life in the mythical idea of continuity.[95] This has serious implications for the biblical view of a transcendent God who created everything perfect and for the origin of sin and its result: death. To separate death as the consequential result of sin, scientists and theologians must reinterpret the first chapters of Genesis and Paul's teachings in light of modern theories of naturalism. Hugh Ross writes,

> There is nothing in Scripture that compels us to conclude that none of these entities [decay, work, physical death, pain, and suffering] existed before Adam's first act of rebellion against God. On the other hand, God's revelation through nature provides overwhelming evidence that all of these aspects did indeed exist a long time period previous to God's creating Adam."[96]

Likewise, Walton argues that death was a part of the non-ordered world before the archetype Everyone, Adam, came to the world.

---

[93] Gerhard. F. Hasel and Michael G. Hasel, "The Unique Cosmology of Genesis 1," 27–29; cf. Rodríguez, "Biblical Creationism and Ancient Near Eastern Evolutionary Ideas," in *The Genesis Creation Account*, 293–328.

[94] John N. Oswalt, *The Bible Among the Myths: Unique Revelation or Just Ancient Literature?* (Grand Rapids, MI: Zondervan, 2009), 61–62.

[95] Ibid., 59; for example, in the Babylonian *Enuma Elish*, Tiamat, the mythical Babylonian monster and goddess of the primeval world ocean, is slain by the creator god Marduk in combat. See George A. Barton, "Tiamat," *Journal of the American Oriental Society* 15 (1893): 1–27; Hermann Gunkel, *Schöpfung und Chaos in Urzeit: Eine religionsgeschichtliche Untersuchung über Gen 1 und Ap Joh 12* (Göttingen: Vandenhoeck & Ruprecht, 1985); Thorkild Jacobsen, "The Battle Between Marduk and Tiamat," *Journal of the American Oriental Society* 88 (1968): 104–108; and Mary K. Wakeman, *God's Battle with the Monster: A Study in Biblical Imagery* (Leiden: Brill, 1973), 16–22. Likewise, in the Atra-Ḫasis Epic, humanity is created from the flesh and blood of a slaughtered god mixed with clay, but "no hint of the use of dead deity or any other material of a living one is found in Genesis" (Gordon H. Johnston, "Genesis 1 and Ancient Egyptian Creation Myths," *Bibliotheca Sacra* 165 [2008]: 187). See Gerhard F. Hasel and Michael G. Hasel, "The Unique Cosmology of Genesis 1," 16–18, 22–23.

[96] Hugh Ross, *Creation and Time* (Colorado Springs, CO: NavPress, 1994), 69.

If death were present before Adam, then what would be the implications for Christ's substitutionary death on the cross, and the plan of redemption? Was Christ's death on the cross truly to pay the legal price for our sin and to eradicate death once and for all? Is His death not the fulfillment of Genesis 3:15, when He becomes the serpent for us though He never sinned (John 3:14–15)? The theological implications of this should not be underestimated.[97] As Richard B. Gaffin, Jr. has titled his book *No Adam, No Gospel*,[98] to remove death as the wages of sin strikes at the heart of the gospel. If death is not related to sin, then the wages of sin is not death, and Christ would have had no reason to die on the cross of Calvary for our sins.[99] To remove a literal creation together with a literal Adam and Eve, made in the image of God, would remove our hope that we might someday be restored to that image by the one who died to pay the ultimate price for our sins.

The Old Creation and the Hope of a New Creation

The advent of Christ is one of the cherished hopes of every believer. In the Old Testament God promises, "Behold, I will create new heavens and a new earth" (Isa 65:17) and it "shall remain before me" (Isa 66:22). The new earth will be a place of peace and life restored, for "the wolf and the lamb shall feed together, and the lion will eat straw like the ox" (Isa 65:25). The very terminology of "heavens and earth" together with the same verb *bārā'*, now as an imperfect and future reality, harkens back to the beginning of Genesis 1–2. Isaiah's statements indicate that the new creation is intimately bound up with the first—one where no violence was present and where animals could live together in harmony without fear, for "there shall be no more curse" (Rev 22:3).

The biblical view of history is linear, moving forward with a purpose and goal in mind.[100] Jesus is affirmed as "Him who is from the beginning"

---

[97] Zinke, "Theistic Evolution," 164–165 and Gregg R. Allison, "Theistic Evolution is Incompatible with Historical Christian Doctrine," in *Theistic Evolution*, 940–941.

[98] Richard B. Gaffin, Jr., *No Adam, No Gospel: Adam and the History of Redemption* (Phillipsburg, NJ: P&R Publishing, 2015).

[99] Marco T. Terreros, *Theistic Evolution and Its Theological Implications* (Medellín: MARTER Editions, 2002); Terreros, "Is all Death the Consequence of Sin? Theological Implications of Alternative Models," *Journal of the Adventist Theological Society* 14/1 (2003): 150–175; and Reinhard Junker, *Leben durch Sterben? Schöpfung, Heilsgeschichte und Evolution*, 2nd ed. (Neuhausen/Stuttgart: Hänssler-Verlag, 2004).

[100] See chapter 4 by Michael G. Hasel, "History, the Bible, and Hermeneutics," in the present volume.

(1 John 2:14), and in Revelation three times as "the Alpha and the Omega" (Rev 1:8; 21:6; 22:13), twice as "the Beginning and the End," (Rev 21:6; 22:13) and "the First and the Last" (Rev 22:13). Christ, who set time in motion for human existence in the beginning will set in place "a new heaven and a new earth, for the first heaven and the first earth had passed away. . . . And God will wipe away every tear from their eyes; there shall be no more death, nor sorrow, nor crying. There shall be no more pain, for the former things have passed away." Once again this new act of creation experienced at the resurrection will be instantaneous at the sound of the voice of Jesus, when "all will be changed in a moment, in the twinkling of an eye, at the last trumpet" (1 Cor 15:51–52). Jesus, speaking of the New Earth, says, "Behold I am making all things new. . . . Write for these things are faithful and true" (Rev 21:5). God promises a new creation that is perfect, just as the first. A place where "there shall be no more death,neither sorrow, nor crying, neither shall there be any more pain; for the former things are passed away" (Rev 21:4, KJV). There will be no more sin (Rev 21:7) and no more curse (Rev 22:3).[101]

But even if a perfect heaven were possible in view of millions of years of naturalistic evolution or progressive creation, what hope would there be for a "new" creation? Would God take another six hundred million years to let it evolve? It is interesting to look again at the views of some of the leading proponents of a nonliteral creation in Genesis. For historical-critics and neo-orthodox theologians like Bultmann, the presuppositions of modernism could not support a literal view of heaven.[102] N. T. Wright, who believes in theistic evolution and does not believe that Adam and Eve were literal people, also does not believe in a literal second coming or a literal heaven. According to Wright, when Paul speaks of the Lord descending in 1 Thessalonians, "he is finding richly metaphorical ways of alluding to three other stories that he is deliberately bringing together . . . the reality to which it refers is this: Jesus will be personally present."[103] Again we see, as with the Sabbath and with a literal Adam and Eve, the writings of the Old Testament and New Testament on the important issue of the second coming and heaven need to be reinterpreted in order to accommodate a naturalistic

---

[101] Roberto Badenas, "New Jerusalem—The Holy City," in *Symposium on Revelation—Book II*, ed. Frank B. Holbrook, Daniel and Revelation Committee Series 7 (Silver Spring, MD: Biblical Research Institute, 1992), 249–256 and Kenneth Mathews, *Revelation Reveals Jesus* (Greeneville, TN: Second Coming Publications, 2012), 2:1081–1132.

[102] Rudolph Bultmann, *Myth and the New Testament* (London: SCM, 1960), 20–21.

[103] N. T. Wright, *Surprised by Hope: Rethinking Heaven, the Resurrection, and the Mission of the Church* (New York: HarperOne, 2008), 132–133.

worldview that limits what the writers themselves affirm as their hope and reality.[104]

For the biblical writers Christ's resurrection, ascension, and His promises were evidence for this hope. Belief in creation gives us the assurance of a new creation that is close at hand. It encourages us to nurture our environment. It gives us the incentive to endure the trials and tribulations of today (2 Cor 4:16–17), and to live pure and upright lives, which give us the joy and certainty of our reward tomorrow (Matt 5:12). It is in this certainty, and as a memorial to the first creation, that we worship every Sabbath. It is this truth that assures us of Christ's soon return. For He has promised, "I go to prepare a place for you. And if I go and prepare a place for you, I will come again and receive you to Myself; that where I am, there you may be also" (John 14:2–3). Jesus was going to heaven and invited His disciples and us to spend eternity with Him, when all will be restored again to what He created in the beginning.

---

[104] Most preterist and idealist interpreters of Revelation argue that the New Jerusalem is not a literal city, but that it represents the people of God. See G. K. Beale, *The Book of Revelation*, The New International Greek Testament Commentary (Grand Rapids, MI: Eerdmans, 1999), 1062; and David E. Aune, *Revelation 17–22*, Word Biblical Commentary (Waco, TX: Word, 1982), 1187. Some argue it represents the victory of God. See J. Massyngberde Ford, *Revelation*, Anchor Bible 38 (Garden City, NY: Doubleday, 1975), 366.

CHAPTER 12

A Survey of Seventh-day Adventist Presuppositions, Perceptions, and Methods of Biblical Interpretation (1845–1910)

Denis Kaiser

Seventh-day Adventists generally perceive themselves as a "People of the Book" who emerged through the direct involvement of God during the latter end of the Second Great Awakening in nineteenth-century North America. One's perception of the early Seventh-day Adventists, their biblical interpretation, and doctrinal beliefs may influence one's perspective on hermeneutical presuppositions, perception of biblical scholarship, and methods of biblical interpretation today. Whereas some may view those early Seventh-day Adventists as a monolithic block whose biblical interpretations are definitive for modern-day believers, others may perceive them as primitive, uneducated Bible students whose views can be simply brushed aside. Some not only discern in the person of Ellen G. White (1827–1915) the direct manifestation of God's guidance of the early Seventh-day Adventist Church, but they also perceive her writings as a final and exhaustive interpretation of Scripture. All those perspectives result from particular views of Adventist history. They also often reflect a too limited view of the hermeneutical presuppositions, perceptions of biblical scholarship, and methods of biblical interpretation that Seventh-day Adventists had during the first sixty some years of their existence. This chapter seeks to present a more nuanced and balanced overview of the presuppositions, perceptions, and methods of Adventist believers from 1845 to 1910, and the impact this had on the interpretation of Scripture.

Presuppositions of Biblical Interpretation

Any attempt to interpret the biblical text is influenced by assumptions about the nature of Scripture. From 1845 to 1910, Seventh-day Adventist writers approached the Bible with particular assumptions about its nature; yet those assumptions did not develop in a vacuum. In agreement with the Protestant Reformers and Pietist thinkers, those Seventh-day Adventist writers believed in the Bible as an inspired revelation from God that was completely clear, reliable, and authoritative. Despite their trust in the end-time manifestation of the biblical gift of prophecy in their midst, they believed in a closed canon that constituted to them the final norm and rule of faith and practice. Their affirmations of the divine inspiration, clarity, reliability, and authority of Scripture will be discussed in the following paragraphs.

The Divine Inspiration of Scripture

From the mid-nineteenth to the early twentieth century, Seventh-day Adventists assumed a priori that Scripture was produced through divine inspiration and was therefore trustworthy. Prior to the 1883 General Conference session, they wrote very little about the nature of divine inspiration.[1]

The decision at that session to correct grammatical imperfections in Ellen G. White's *Testimonies for the Church* revealed the existence of different ideas among Seventh-day Adventists concerning the nature of her inspiration. They all agreed that her inspiration did not differ from that of the Bible writers.[2] Differing views among them on whether such corrections were consistent with her claim to divine inspiration[3] may nevertheless also be indicative of differing Seventh-day Adventist views on the nature of the inspiration of the Bible. Ellen G. White had previously indicated that she was dependent on the Holy Spirit to refresh her memory of the scenes seen in vision before she could clothe them in her own language, not always remembering every detail of the vision.[4] The

---

[1] Alberto R. Timm, "Adventist Views on Inspiration [No. 1]," *Perspective Digest* 13/3 (2008): 24–39, 26–27.

[2] George R. Knight, "The Relationship Between Ellen White's Authority and the Authority of the Bible in Adventism," *Ellen White and Current Issues Symposium* 6 (2010): 35–55, 39; and Merlin D. Burt, "Revelation and Inspiration: Ellen White's Understanding," in *Understanding Ellen White: The Life and Work of the Most Influential Voice in Adventist History*, ed. Merlin D. Burt (Nampa, ID: Pacific Press; Ellen G. White Estate, 2015), 30.

[3] W. C. White to Mary K. White, November 10, 1883.

[4] Ellen G. White, *Spiritual Gifts*, vol. 2 (Battle Creek, MI: James White, 1860), 292–293; and Ellen

delegates resolved to have those grammatical imperfections corrected, explaining, "We believe the light given by God to his servants is by the enlightenment of the mind, thus imparting the thoughts, and not (except in rare cases) the very words on which the ideas should be expressed."[5]

Shortly after the session, George I. Butler wrote a series of ten articles in an attempt to place Adventist beliefs in the nature of divine inspiration on a biblical basis, thereby vindicating the revision of the *Testimonies*.[6] As his suggestion that the Holy Spirit operated in diverse "manners" and "modes" seemed to be in harmony with Ellen G. White's personal testimonial, several ministers recommended the publication of his articles in pamphlet form.[7] Butler's idea of varying degrees, or extents, of divine inspiration[8] seemed nevertheless somewhat speculative, and the thought of some uninspired, albeit true, passages in Scripture[9] was potentially calling for readers to distinguish between inspired and uninspired portions of the biblical canon. In early 1889, Ellen G. White began to take issue with those two latter aspects of Butler's theory and opposed particularly the dissecting of the biblical text.[10] At the same time, the editorial staff of the *Signs of the Times* began to consistently oppose the theory of degrees[11] and advocate verbal inspiration as the

---

G. White, "Questions and Answers," *Review and Herald*, October 8, 1867, 260.

[5] George I. Butler and A. B. Oyen, "General Conference Proceedings," *Review and Herald*, November 27, 1883, 741.

[6] Butler's ten articles on the nature and manner of inspiration were printed in the *Review and Herald* intermittently from January 8 to June 3, 1884.

[7] George I. Butler and Uriah Smith, "General Conference Proceedings," *Review and Herald*, November 25, 1884, 75; and [Uriah Smith], "Notes and Queries," *Review and Herald*, August 11, 1885, 504–505.

[8] George I. Butler, "Inspiration [No. 1]: Its Nature and Manner of Communication," *Review and Herald*, January 8, 1884, 24; and Butler, "Inspiration, No. 9: Is There Any Degree of Imperfection in the Revelation of God to Man?," *Review and Herald*, May 27, 1884, 346.

[9] George I. Butler, "Inspiration, No. 10: Final Conclusions and Reflections," *Review and Herald*, June 3, 1884, 361–362; and Butler, "Inspiration, No. 7: The Books of Solomon, Job, etc.," *Review and Herald*, April 22, 1884, 266.

[10] Ellen G. White, "Sermon by Mrs. Ellen G. White, Delivered in the Seventh-day Adventist Church, Des Moines, Iowa, Sabbath, December 1, 1888, at the State Meeting of the S.D.A. reported by W. E. Cornell," December 1, 1888, Ms 13, 1888; Ellen G. White to R. A. Underwood, January 18, 1889, Lt 22, 1889; and Ellen G. White, "The Discernment of Truth," January 1889, Ms 16, 1889.

[11] See, e.g., E. J. Waggoner, "The Bible the Word of God," *Signs of the Times*, May 6, 1889, 262; E. J. Waggoner, "The Word of the Lord," *Signs of the Times*, April 3, 1893, 339; Louis Gaussen, "Rejected Because Not Understood," *Signs of the Times*, May 20, 1889, 292; *Anonymous*, "All Scripture," *Signs of the Times*, July 7, 1890, 405; and *Anonymous*, "A Growing Danger," *Present Truth*, October 6, 1892, 311. By reprinting Gaussen's and other writers' remarks against the theory of degrees of inspiration, the editors of the *Signs of the Times* indicated their approval of those remarks.

most reliable explanation of inspiration because it seemed to safeguard the very words of Scripture.[12] Through the influence of W. W. Prescott at Battle Creek College, that explanation gained more influence among students and church members in the early 1890s.[13] In her preface to the *Great Controversy* (1888 ed.) and periodical articles, Ellen G. White nevertheless presented an alternative to the theories of degrees of inspiration and the view of verbal inspiration as promoted by some. She suggested that the Bible writers' education, personal study, self-improvement, and spiritual and intellectual endowments all played into their ability to clothe inspired ideas into human language.[14] Her remarks on divine inspiration were more refined and balanced than the statements of any other Seventh-day Adventist writer at the time.

In the early twentieth century, church leaders who had worked closely with Ellen G. White generally advocated that the Holy Spirit operated primarily on the thoughts and ideas of inspired writers. Yet a strong undercurrent of verbal inspiration, which at times gave the impression of divine dictation, continued to exist in the church. Both groups held that divine inspiration had produced a reliable and authoritative account of true historical events that accurately communicates God's character, will, and message.

The Clarity of Scripture

Their belief in the inspiration of Scripture, irrespective of one's conception of the manner of inspiration, led Seventh-day Adventists to affirm the Reformation principle of the clarity of Scripture. They agreed that Scripture clearly reveals the will of God and the plan of salvation. For most Seventh-day Adventists, that clarity did not negate the existence of potentially obscure passages in Scripture.

In 1858, Ellen G. White reasoned that, guided by tradition and preconceived ideas, some "learned men" modified words in the biblical manuscripts; as a result, some plain passages became mystified.

---

[12] See, e.g., J. H. Waggoner, "Theories of Inspiration," *Signs of the Times*, August 3, 1888, 472; E. J. Waggoner, "Letter to the Romans—No. 8," *General Conference Daily Bulletin*, March 16, 1891, 127; M. C. Wilcox, *The Bible: Its Inspiration and Importance*, Bible Students' Library 27 (Oakland, CA: Pacific Press, 1889), 8–14; and Louis Gaussen, "Jesus and the Scriptures," *Signs of the Times*, August 19, 1889, 499.

[13] W. C. White to L. E. Froom, January 8, 1928; W. C. White to Luther Warren, April 13, 1924; and W. C. White to L. E. Froom, January 21, 1929.

[14] Ellen G. White, *The Great Controversy between Christ and Satan* (Battle Creek, MI: Review and Herald, 1888), c, d; and Ellen G. White, "Objections to the Bible," [ca. September 1885–May 1886], Ms 24, 1886.

She nevertheless believed that divine providence had preserved the "perfect harmony" of Scripture because the revelation of God's will and the depiction of His plan of salvation were clearly comprehensible as one part of Scripture explains another.[15] Similarly, other Seventh-day Adventist writers acknowledged the existence of textual variants and difficult passages,[16] and highlighted the need to interpret Scripture with Scripture.[17]

Butler further noted that the Bible "does not tell all we would like to know" because it does not give "a record of all the past or all that will occur," suggesting that it did not offer complete clarity and comprehensiveness.[18] Ellen G. White stressed that God had "conveyed [His testimony] through imperfect expression of human language,"[19] which at times lacks absolute precision because "different meanings are expressed by the same word [and] there is not one word for each distinct idea."[20] A. T. Jones, on the other hand, asserted that divine inspiration produces absolute clarity so that a text always means "exactly what it says."[21] Such a literalistic use of Scripture led Jones to the unwarranted conclusion that human attempts to explain and interpret a biblical passage were not only unnecessary,[22] but also presumptuous.[23] Initially an anomaly, Jones' perspective became more widespread in subsequent years among those who entertained a belief in a form of verbal inspiration that comes close to divine dictation.

In contrast, Ellen G. White saw an inexhaustible depth in Scripture that could not be found through "a surface view of the Scriptures" but only through a prayerful, thoughtful, and patient searching for "the precious jewels of truth" and "the precious golden thread" that was

---

[15] Ellen G. White, *Spiritual Gifts*, vol. 1 (Battle Creek, MI: James White, 1858), 116–117.

[16] See the section on "Textual Criticism" in this chapter.

[17] See, e.g., *Anonymous*, "The Rise and Progress of Adventism," *Review and Herald*, April 24, 1856, 9; and Moses Hull, "A Few Thoughts on 2 Cor. v, 1–4," *Review and Herald*, August 11, 1859, 89.

[18] Butler, "Inspiration, No. 9," 344, 346.

[19] Ellen G. White, *The Great Controversy between Christ and Satan*, [1888 ed.], d.

[20] Ellen G. White, "Objections to the Bible."

[21] A. T. Jones, "The Third Angel's Message—No. 1," *General Conference Daily Bulletin*, January 27, 1893, 9–11; and Jones, "The Third Angel's Message—No. 15," *General Conference Daily Bulletin*, February 23, 1893, 361.

[22] A. T. Jones, "The Gifts: Their Presence and Object," *Home Missionary*, Extra, December 1894, 12; and Jones, "The Sure Interpreter," *Bible Echo*, February 11, 1895, 44.

[23] Jones, "The Third Angel's Message—No. 1," 9–11; Jones, "The Third Angel's Message—No. 15," 361; and Jones, "The Gifts," 12.

"running through the whole [Bible]."[24] In her view, there is an inexhaustible depth in Scripture that continually challenges us to learn more and gain a better and deeper understanding of the Word of God through a careful and deliberate study of the text and context of Scripture.[25] Most Seventh-day Adventist writers therefore desired to know the original meaning of the biblical text and acknowledged the need to interpret biblical passages.

The Reliability of Scripture

Throughout the period of this study, Seventh-day Adventist literature evinces an overall confidence in the trustworthiness of Scripture and does not contain statements intended to question the reliability of supernatural events or historical accounts. Regardless of whether Seventh-day Adventist writers held a word-focused or thought-focused view of inspiration, they all assumed that the Holy Spirit had assisted the biblical writers in the accurate communication of Scripture's message and historical accounts. Not even their recognition of some scribal errors led them to question the reliability of particular passages.[26]

Even Butler stressed that divine inspiration produced "correct," "true," and "reliable" accounts and reasoned that even the supposed "uninspired" passages in Scripture were trustworthy and accurate reports of the writers' wishes and opinions.[27] Despite his pleas to the contrary, the existence of such "uninspired" passages nevertheless called readers to a differentiation between inspired and uninspired parts, leaving no guarantee that the latter were truly accurate. Ellen G. White recognized the potentially destructive ramifications of Butler's ideas for the belief in the reliability of the biblical canon.[28]

---

[24] Ellen G. White, "Objections to the Bible."

[25] Ellen G. White, *The Desire of Ages* (Oakland, CA: Pacific Press, 1898), 78–79, 253–254; Ellen G. White, *Education* (Oakland, CA: Pacific Press, 1903), 188; Ellen G. White, *The Ministry of Healing* (Washington, DC: Review and Herald, 1905), 21–22; and Ellen G. White, "The Holy Spirit an Aid to Bible Study," *Atlantic Union Gleaner*, June 9, 1909, 178. See also Iriann Marie Hausted, "Ellen White's Usage of the Term 'Plain' in the Context of the Interpretation of Scripture," *Ellen White Issues Symposium* 13 (2017): 73–91.

[26] See Denis Kaiser, *Trust and Doubt: Perceptions of Divine Inspiration in Seventh-day Adventist History*, Schriften der Forschung, Historische Theologie 3 (St. Peter am Hart: Seminar Schloss Bogenhofen, 2019).

[27] George I. Butler, "Inspiration, No. 6: How Were the Poetic and Historical Books of the Bible Written?," *Review and Herald*, April 15, 1884, 249; Butler, "Inspiration, No. 7," 266; Butler, "Inspiration, No. 8: In What Sense Are the Scriptures Inspired?," *Review and Herald*, May 6, 1884, 296–297; Butler, "Inspiration, No. 9," 344, 346; and Butler, "Inspiration, No. 10," 361.

[28] Ellen G. White to R. A. Underwood; and Ellen G. White, "The Discernment of Truth."

The Authority of Scripture

All Seventh-day Adventist writers emphasized that Scripture constitutes a perfect and complete revelation that was the church's "rule of faith and practice,"[29] contains "the knowledge necessary for salvation,"[30] and is "the standard of character, the revealer of doctrine, and the test of experience."[31] They stressed that it is authoritative and normative for all Christians throughout the Christian dispensation.[32]

Their belief in the manifestation of the genuine modern-day gift of prophecy in Ellen G. White's experience and ministry raises the question about the relationship between her messages and Scripture. In the view of those Seventh-day Adventist writers, Ellen G. White's non-canonical gift of prophecy did not conflict with the closed canon of the Bible; they simply differed in function.[33] Ellen G. White herself noted, "The Spirit was not given—nor can it ever be bestowed—to supersede the Bible; for the Scriptures explicitly state that the Word of God is the standard by which all teaching and experience must be tested."[34] However, the normative role of Scripture in matters of faith and doctrine was sometimes weakened, beginning in the late 1880s as some key thinkers sought to settle interpretational conflicts by appealing to Ellen G. White's writings—an approach she usually rejected. For example, in 1886, Butler's desire to obtain a letter from Ellen G. White to settle the definition of the law in Galatians met with her reply that God wanted Adventists "to go to the Bible and get the

---

[29] See, e.g., Joseph Bates, *A Vindication of the Seventh-day Sabbath, and the Commandments of God: With a Further History of God's Peculiar People, from 1847 to 1848* (New Bedford, MA: Benjamin Lindsey, 1848), 124; A. T. Jones, "The Principles of Protestantism," *Signs of the Times*, January 29, 1885, 73; and George I. Butler, *Replies to Elder Canright's Attacks on Seventh-day Adventists* (Battle Creek, MI: Review and Herald, 1895), 75.

[30] Ellen G. White, *The Great Controversy between Christ and Satan*, [1888 ed.], d.

[31] Ibid.

[32] See Roy E. Graham, *Ellen G. White: Co-Founder of the Seventh-day Adventist Church*, American University Studies: Series 7, Theology and Religion 12 (New York: Lang, 1985), 45–46; and Zoltán Szalos-Farkas, *The Rise and Development of Seventh-day Adventist Spirituality: The Impact of the Charismatic Guidance of Ellen G. White*, Doctoral Dissertation Series 1 (Cernica: Editura Institutului Teologic Adventist, 2005), 64–65, 71–72, 76–83.

[33] See Richard W. Schwarz and Floyd Greenleaf, *Light Bearers: A History of the Seventh-day Adventist Church*, rev. ed. (Nampa, ID: Pacific Press, 2000), 630; Theodore N. Levterov, *The Development of the Seventh-day Adventist Understanding of Ellen G. White's Prophetic Gift, 1844–1889*, American University Studies: Series 7, Theology and Religion 347 (Frankfurt am Main: Lang, 2015), 133–134; and Knight, "Ellen White's Authority," 39.

[34] Ellen G. White, *The Great Controversy between Christ and Satan*, [1888 ed.], e.

Scripture evidence."[35] Similarly, in 1910, she reproved various leading brethren for employing her writings to support their interpretation of the *tāmîd* ("continual," "daily") in Daniel 8:11–13 and urged them instead to solve the exegetical questions through a mutual, prayerful, and open investigation of the Bible.[36] That approach gained some influence after 1893 among some church members through the influence of A. T. Jones, who, due to his exaggerated views on divine inspiration and the clarity of inspired writings, urged the use of Ellen G. White's writings as an infallible and exhaustive interpreter of Scripture.[37] Those working closely with her cherished her enriching theological and spiritual insights, yet they did not view them as an exhaustive and final word on a given text.[38]

Similar appeals to an extrabiblical authority to settle interpretational conflicts occurred when Butler spoke of the traditional Seventh-day Adventist interpretation of the law in Galatians 3 as an old landmark doctrine, suggesting that it should not be moved.[39] Ellen G. White nevertheless replied that he and others "simply do not know what they are talking about. It never was an old landmark, and it never will become such."[40] As previously mentioned, she saw the solution to the discussion in mutual Bible study rather than an appeal to tradition. She gave the same advice when some Adventists appealed to the traditional Millerite interpretation during the conflict over the *tāmîd* in Daniel 8:11–13.[41]

Seventh-day Adventist writers generally intended to give each biblical text its proper weight and sought to understand it for its own sake. Like other Protestants, they were deeply committed to "theistic common sense . . . because it seemed so intuitive, so instinctive."[42] Following

---

[35] Ellen G. White, "Morning Talk at Minneapolis, Minn.," October 24, 1888, Ms 9, 1888.

[36] For more information on the conflict over the *tāmîd*, see Denis Kaiser, "The Word, the Spirit of Prophecy, and Mutual Love: Lessons from the 'Daily' Controversy for Conflict Resolution," *Ministry*, December 2014, 16–19.

[37] Jones, "The Gifts," 12; Jones, "The Sure Interpreter," 44; Jones, "The Third Angel's Message—No. 1," 9–11; and Jones, "The Third Angel's Message—No. 24," *General Conference Daily Bulletin*, March 26, 1893, 521.

[38] Denis Kaiser, "Ellen White's Role in Biblical Interpretation: A Survey of Early Seventh-day Adventist Perceptions," *Reflections: The BRI Newsletter*, October 2017, 1–6.

[39] See Woodrow W. Whidden, *E. J. Waggoner: From the Physician of Good News to the Agent of Division*, Adventist Pioneer Series (Hagerstown, MD: Review and Herald, 2008), 102.

[40] Ellen G. White, "Peril of Trusting in the Wisdom of Men," 1890, Ms 55, 1890.

[41] Kaiser, "The Word," 16–19.

[42] Mark A. Noll, *America's God: From Jonathan Edwards to Abraham Lincoln* (New York: Oxford University Press, 2002), 113.

William Miller's principles of biblical interpretation, they tried to understand the meaning of biblical terms in light of their "common acceptation"[43] or, in other words, their plain, obvious, and literal meaning.[44] The Seventh-day Adventist antipathy to "hidden mysterious meanings" and spiritualizing interpretations did not, as Don Neufeld notes, "rule out typology, or amplification of literal meanings, that a later inspired writer might bring out. The rule of permitting Scripture to explain Scripture took care of the later."[45] In a few cases, their intuitive acceptance of the commonsense understanding of specific biblical terms nevertheless bypassed the inner-biblical usage of those terms. For example, their commonsense reading of terms such as "only begotten son," "firstborn son," and "Son of God" caused them to neglect how the biblical metanarrative defined those terms in the sense of a spiritual covenant relationship.[46]

These examples simply illustrate that despite the best intentions to maintain Scripture's primary authority, some Seventh-day Adventist writers were sometimes blindsided by their own intuition and sentiments, particularly in times of conflict. Their perception of biblical scholarship and methods of biblical interpretation nevertheless shows a deep commitment to understanding Scripture on its own terms.

---

[43] James White, "Signs of the Times," *Review and Herald*, August 28, 1853, 57; [Uriah Smith], "The Scape-Goat," *Review and Herald*, November 27, 1856, 28; B. F. Snook, "The Holy Sabbath of the Lord: New Testament Evidence," *Review and Herald*, June 12, 1860, 26; and James White, "Our Faith and Hope: Or, Reasons Why We Believe as We Do—No. 9," *Review and Herald*, January 18, 1870, 25.

[44] Sylvester Bliss, *Memoirs of William Miller: Generally Known as a Lecturer on the Prophecies, and the Second Coming of Christ* (Boston, MA: Himes, 1853), 71; and James White, "Revelation XVIII–XXI," *Review and Herald*, March 5, 1857, 141. On Miller's hermeneutics and method of prophetic interpretation, see Jeff Crocombe, "A Feast of Reason: The Roots of William Miller's Biblical Interpretation and Its Influence on the Seventh-day Adventist Church" (PhD diss., University of Queensland, 2011).

[45] Don F. Neufeld, "Biblical Interpretation in the Advent Movement," in *A Symposium on Biblical Hermeneutics*, ed. Gordon M. Hyde (Washington, DC: Biblical Research Committee, of the General Conference of Seventh-day Adventists, 1974), 120.

[46] Jerry Moon, "The Adventist Trinity Debate, Part 1: Historical Overview," *Andrews University Seminary Studies* 41/1 (2003): 113–129; and Denis Kaiser, "¿Los adventistas del séptimo día y los católicos creen en la misma doctrina de la Trinidad?," *Revista Estrategias* 14/1 (2016): 100–107. A brilliant exposition of the use of those words and the Sonship motif in Scripture is found in Ty Gibson, *The Sonship of Christ: Exploring the Covenant Identity of God and Man* (Nampa, ID: Pacific Press, 2018). See also Ty Gibson, *The Heavenly Trio: Exploring the Views of Ellen White and the Adventist Pioneers Regarding the Trinity* (Nampa, ID: Pacific Press, 2020).

Perception and Use of Biblical Scholarship

In the 1850s, there were only a few Seventh-day Adventist ministers, yet the evangelistic field was wide. A system to provide financial support for those engaged in gospel ministry was not developed until 1859, and even when the denomination established Battle Creek College fifteen years later, its education was a long way from an actual formal ministerial training. The lack of a formal ministerial or theological training nevertheless does not betray a glorification of ignorance. Ministers generally knew their Bibles quite well, tried to educate themselves, and read publications of conservative Protestant theologians. A perusal of their perception of the role of the biblical languages, textual criticism, and different approaches to biblical exegesis will illustrate their attitude towards biblical scholarship.

Biblical Languages

Seventh-day Adventist ministers did not consider a knowledge of the biblical languages a necessary requirement for the gospel ministry; yet a number of them found such a knowledge beneficial in their efforts to understand the Bible better and to share their faith with theologically trained ministers of other denominations.

This phenomenon was already visible among Millerite lecturers. William Miller had considered a knowledge of Hebrew or Greek secondary to faith, trust, and confidence in God and His Word for a proper understanding of the Bible. Despite a lack of proficiency in the biblical languages, he felt that God would prevent a humble Bible student "from erring far from the truth."[47] A perusal of Millerite publications nevertheless shows that a number of Millerite writers were proficient in the biblical languages or utilized the insights of those who did.[48] Among the Millerites was, for example, N. N. Whiting, a well-known Baptist Hebrew and Greek scholar.[49]

---

[47] William Miller, "Mr. Miller's Letters—No. 5: The Bible Its Own Interpreter," *Signs of the Times*, May 15, 1840, 26.

[48] See, e.g., William Allen, "On the Designations of Time in Daniel and John: The 1260 Days of Daniel and John, and the 1000 Years of John," *Signs of the Times*, August 15, 1840, 73–74; A. Vallerchamp, "Bible Chronology: Criticism on 1 Kings vi. 1.—The 480 years,—A. M. 5914," *Signs of the Times*, October 15, 1840, 111; George Duffield, "Letter from Rev. Geo. Duffield," *Signs of the Times*, March 1, 1841, 179; and [Josiah Litch], "Review of Dowling's Reply to Miller," *Signs of the Times*, February 1, 1842, 166.

[49] Isaac C. Wellcome, *History of the Second Advent Message and Mission, Doctrine and People* (Boston, MA: Advent Christian Publication Society, 1874), 375; Everett N. Dick, *William Miller and the Advent Crisis, 1831–1844* (Berrien Springs, MI: Andrews University Press, 1994), 88.

Although Seventh-day Adventist writers regularly interpreted biblical terms through the lens of their "common acceptation" and "common sense," it is interesting to observe that they frequently included the meaning of those words in the biblical languages. Don F. Neufeld notes that "Hebrew and Greek terms are frequently quoted, and authorities cited as to meanings of the original terms. Those not versed in the original languages frequently resorted to various translations in order to clarify the meanings of words."[50]

Early Seventh-day Adventists were not able to pride themselves on having formally educated Bible scholars within their ranks. Most of their ministers were primarily self-taught because they had not received many years of formal education; yet a few exceptions existed. Uriah Smith studied at Phillips Exeter Academy from 1848 to 1852, where he learned Latin and Greek.[51] J. N. Andrews may have had some Latin, Greek, or French during his school days, as was typical of the curriculum for secondary schools of the era.[52] Belonging to the next generation of Adventist church leaders, W. W. Prescott had learned Greek and Latin during his years at Dartmouth College in the 1870s.[53] In their study of the Bible, they were therefore able to consult at least the Greek New Testament.

The particular case of Andrews is worth discussing a little more. Pietro Copiz notes that Andrews had taught himself a good working knowledge of Hebrew and Greek, as is evident from the fact that "he was able to use [them] intelligently . . . in dealing with biblical texts" in his *History of the Sabbath and the First Day of the Week*.[54] He further had a good grasp of Latin, which was the key "to the world of scholarship" at that time.[55] His proficiency in Latin is documented by a large number of Latin works in his personal library and by Latin quotations and references in his writings. He owned Bibles in the ancient languages and grammars, lexicons, and readers for most of them,

---

[50] Neufeld, "Biblical Interpretation in the Advent Movement," 119.

[51] Gary Land, *Uriah Smith: Apologist and Biblical Commentator*, Adventist Pioneer Series (Hagerstown, MD: Review and Herald, 2014), 20–21.

[52] Gilbert M. Valentine, *J. N. Andrews: Mission Pioneer, Evangelist, and Thought Leader*, Adventist Pioneer Series (Nampa, ID: Pacific Press, 2019), 47.

[53] Gilbert M. Valentine, *W. W. Prescott: Forgotten Giant of Adventism's Second Generation*, Adventist Pioneer Series (Hagerstown, MD: Review and Herald, 2005), 35.

[54] Pietro E. Copiz, "The Linguist," in *J. N. Andrews, the Man and the Mission*, ed. Harry Leonard (Berrien Springs, MI: Andrews University Press, 1985), 164.

[55] Joseph G. Smoot, "The Measure of the Man: A Tribute to John Nevins Andrews," *Focus* 14/1 (1978): 36.

including a grammar for Samaritan.[56] Andrews initially used even Hebrew words, in Hebrew characters, in *Les Signes des Temps*. Copiz observes that Andrews' articles in *Les Signes des Temps* demonstrate "a good foundation in the original languages of the Bible."[57] In 1875, Andrews engaged competently in a discussion with a Reformed pastor in Prussia, where he was able to utilize his knowledge of the Greek text of the New Testament in his favor.[58]

In later years, Ellen G. White reasoned that not all methods of language acquisition are spiritually profitable.[59] She lamented that a proficiency in Greek and Latin, which was needed for some occupations, but not for many, was often acquired by reading the classics, molding the character of the students by "amusement, dissipation, and vice." She felt that a study of dead languages was secondary to "a training for life's practical duties."[60] She may have had the situation at early Battle Creek College in mind. Thus, in 1875, students enrolled in the five-year classical program took language and reading classes in Latin and Greek for eleven terms and twelve terms respectively. The readings were all taken from classical authors such as Virgil, Thucydides, Homer, Tacitus, etc. Unfortunately, courses on the Bible, religion, or biblical languages were not mandatory.[61]

Textual Criticism

Seventh-day Adventist ministers did not engage in textual criticism, yet their publications testify to their knowledge and use of the writings of other Protestant scholars who did. They did not confuse legitimate textual criticism—the study of textual variants in the extant papyri and manuscripts—with higher biblical criticism, which questioned the historicity of miracles and the reliability of biblical records. Considering Seventh-day Adventist ministers did not receive a formal theological training and many of their members were farmers, it is surprising how often the *Review and Herald* and other Adventist publications quoted and cited the results of textual criticism in support of their doctrinal

---

[56] Copiz, "The Linguist," 164.

[57] Ibid., 165.

[58] J. N. Andrews, "Editorial Correspondence: Labor in Prussia," *Review and Herald*, March 11, 1875, 84. See also Copiz, "The Linguist," 165.

[59] Ellen G. White, *The Ministry of Healing*, 443–444.

[60] Ellen G. White, *The Ministry of Healing*, 443–444.

[61] *Anonymous*, "Programs of Studies, Battle Creek College, 1875," in *School Bells and Gospel Trumpets: A Documentary History of Seventh-day Adventist Education in North America*, ed. Maurice Hodgen (Loma Linda, CA: Adventist Heritage, 1978), 17–18.

positions. A couple examples of the frequent references in Adventist publications to scholarly publications on text-critical matters may suffice as illustrations.

In 1850, Ellen G. White noted she saw in vision that in Daniel 8:11–13, the word "sacrifice" was not present in the original text but had been supplied by translators,[62] a fact that Millerite interpreters had pointed out at least ten years earlier.[63] Eight years later, she added that early on, when there existed only a few copies of the biblical text, some "learned men" changed some words with the aim of making some biblical statements plainer, yet they were guided by their own "established views" and by "tradition," which led in turn to a mystification of that which had been plain before. She was nevertheless convinced that God preserved the "perfect harmony," simplicity, and clarity of Scripture as a whole, with one part explaining another, and with the text in its entirety showing the way of life and the way to life.[64]

Other Seventh-day Adventist writers saw the need to determine the best reading of the biblical text. For example, J. N. Loughborough discussed the position of the comma in relation to the word "today" in Luke 23:43. He highlights that the comma was not part of the original text but was put into the text by the translators. Moving the comma behind the word "today" would change the meaning of the statement and bring it into harmony with the general teaching of Scripture on the subject. He notes,

> We are told that "the Greek Scriptures were originally written in solid blocks of capital letters, without division into sentences, or stops to mark clauses of sentences, and without even division into words." The text was punctuated about the tenth century. Griesbach, in the margin of his MSS, puts the stop after "to-day," so that the text reads the same as punctuated above.[65]

In 1872, J. H. Waggoner published a discussion about the seventh-day Sabbath, which he had with the minister of another denomination. He explained the use of the Greek word *heortē* (festival) in other passages

---

[62] Ellen G. White, "Dear Brethren and Sisters," *Present Truth*, November 1850, 87.

[63] Jerry Moon, "Daily, The," in *The Ellen G. White Encyclopedia*, ed. Denis Fortin and Jerry Moon, 2nd ed. (Hagerstown, MD: Review and Herald, 2013), 751–752.

[64] Ellen G. White, *Spiritual Gifts*, 1:116–117.

[65] J. N. Loughborough, *An Examination of the Scripture Testimony Concerning Man's Present Condition and His Future Reward or Punishment* (Rochester, NY: Advent Review Office, 1855), 103.

and noted that the occurrence of the word in a variant reading of Acts 18:21[66] could be excluded because "the whole clause is either rejected or marked doubtful by Griesbach, Lachmann, Tischendorf, and Sinaitic MS., [and] it is entirely wanting in many MSS."[67]

Sixteen years later, his son, E. J. Waggoner, wrote an article about the textual basis for the doxology in Matthew 6:13. Whereas the Revised Version omitted it because it did "not appear in the most ancient version," Waggoner pointed to remarks in its favor by Dr. Alexander Roberts in his *Companion to the Revised Version of the New Testament* and *The Speaker's Commentary*, edited by Frederic Charles Cook. The latter wrote,

> The principal argument against it rests on its absence from four of the oldest uncial (A B D Z) and five cursive MSS., from the Latin and Coptic versions, and from the citations of the Latin Fathers. On the other hand, it is found, with occasional variations, in the nine uncials and at least 150 cursives, and in the Syriac, Sahdic, Ethiopic, Gothic, and Armenian versions, and is supported by preponderating evidence from the Greek Fathers.[68]

The discussion of such textual-critical matters in periodicals targeting primarily ordinary church members is noteworthy because it shows that the writers, many of them Adventist ministers, teachers, or editors, expected ordinary church members to comprehend and grasp those arguments and discussions. They further deemed the insights of textual-critical research beneficial to determine the best reading of the biblical text.

Biblical Scholarship and Higher Biblical Criticism

In the middle of the nineteenth century, both American Protestants in general and Seventh-day Adventists in particular seemed to lack interest in higher biblical criticism. Seventh-day Adventist ministers knew that higher biblical criticism had originated in Germany and from there

---

[66] This is in reference to the variant reading, "I must by all means keep this feast [εορτην, *heortēn*] that comes in Jerusalem," which in a few later manuscripts precedes the statement, "but I will return to you, if God will." See Acts 18:21 in the KJV, NKJV, and YLT.

[67] J. H. Waggoner and Peter Vogel, *A Written Discussion: By Elder J. H. Waggoner, Seventh-day Adventist, and Elder Peter Vogel, of the Church of Christ Upon the Sabbath* (Quincy, IL: Office of "The Gospel Echo and Christian," 1872), 35.

[68] Quoted in E. J. Waggoner, "The Doxology: The Lord's Prayer," *Signs of the Times*, August 10, 1888, 486.

had spread to other countries, robbing the Bible of its inspiration and undermining faith in its historical reliability.[69] The *Review and Herald* occasionally reprinted critical responses to David Friedrich Strauss' *Das Leben Jesu kritisch bearbeitet* (1835),[70] yet references to other German scholars such as Johann Salomo Semler, Johann Friedrich Eichhorn, and Friedrich D. E. Schleiermacher are almost entirely absent from Seventh-day Adventist publications until the early 1880s.[71] Adventist writers nevertheless quoted and cited American Unitarian scholars who employed critical methods to some extent, such as William Ellery Channing, Andrews Norton, and George R. Noyes, because they maintained, in one way or another, a belief in the divine inspiration of Scripture and offered interpretations that were supportive of Adventist theology.[72] Uriah Smith, editor of the *Review and Herald*, explained the Adventist indifference by pointing to the purpose of the periodical in proclaiming "the truth especially applicable for this time," rather than filling its columns "with infidelity, or German Neology" and then spending time in its refutation.[73]

Adventist writers quoted and reprinted the writings of other Protestant scholars when those provided exegetical, linguistic, and theological explanations supportive of Adventist teachings, even though Adventists did not always agree with the underlying hermeneutical presuppositions of those scholars. For example, they appreciated studies by Moses Stuart[74]

---

[69] *Anonymous*, "The Downward Tendency of Man," *Review and Herald*, February 21, 1854, 35; *Anonymous*, "The World in Miniature," *Review and Herald*, July 28, 1863, 66.

[70] See, e.g., *Anonymous*, "The Devil," *Review and Herald*, May 10, 1860, 195; *Anonymous*, "Christianity and Its Assailants," *Review and Herald*, March 3, 1868, 178; and F. H. Newhall, "The Alleged Discrepancies of Scripture," *Review and Herald*, April 11, 1871, 129; D. M. Canright, "Increase of Skepticism," *Review and Herald*, March 10, 1874, 103; and *Anonymous*, "The Moral World," *Review and Herald*, July 24, 1879, 36.

[71] The mention of Semler and Eichhorn in two reprints seem to be the only two exceptions. See John Cummings, "Various Readings," *Review and Herald*, December 16, 1858, 27; and *Anonymous*, "The Statesman Articles, Article Eight: Patristic Testimony to the First-Day Sabbath," *Review and Herald*, May 20, 1873, 177.

[72] See, e.g., [George R.] Noyes, "Dr. Noyes of Hartford, Ct. …," *Review and Herald*, August 26, 1858, 119; Noyes, "One Spirit in Them," *Review and Herald*, January 16, 1866, 50–51; W. N. Pile, "The Coming Reign of Terror," *Review and Herald*, February 11, 1875, 50; William Ellery Channing, "Gems from Channing," *Review and Herald*, October 9, 1879, 127; and J. B. F., "Learned Men on the Sabbath," *Review and Herald*, May 8, 1856, 30.

[73] [Uriah Smith], "The Review—Its Object," *Review and Herald*, April 10, 1856, 4.

[74] See, e.g., J. H. Waggoner, "The Truth Found: A Short Argument for the Sabbath," *Review and Herald*, January 31, 1856, 142; Uriah Smith, "Mortal or Immortal? Which?: Or, an Inquiry Into the Present Constitution and Future Condition of Man," *Review and Herald*, September 1, 1859, 113; J. N. Andrews, *History of the Sabbath and the First Day of the Week*, 2nd ed. (Battle

and Calvin E. Stowe,[75] who both favored the theory of personal inspiration. They drew from Charles J. Ellicott, a proponent of thought inspiration.[76] They quoted and cited Philip Doddridge,[77] John Pye Smith,[78] and Daniel Wilson[79]—all scholars who advocated some form of the theory of degrees of inspiration. In writing *Thoughts on the Revelation*, Smith made use of the "thoughts" of many other writers.[80] Besides using "freely both the lines of argument and the words of [Millerite writers] Josiah Litch, George Storrs, and others," he also "set forth the views of the best commentators available,"[81] such as Thomas Newton's *Dissertations on the Prophecies* (1746) and Adam Clarke's multivolume commentary *The Holy Bible, Containing the Old and New Testaments* (1836).[82]

Whereas Seventh-day Adventist writers considered sound biblical scholarship a valuable aid in their biblical research, they opposed approaches that undermined faith in the veracity of the biblical text. Ellen G. White noted, concerning the problems of higher biblical criticism,

---

Creek, MI: Steam Press of the Seventh-day Adventist Pub. Assn., 1873), 233, 359–360; and J. N. Loughborough, "The Saints' Inheritance: Purpose of God Concerning the Earth," *Signs of the Times*, July 23, 1874, 38.

[75] See, e.g., Calvin E. Stowe, "Prof. Stowe on the Decalogue," *Review and Herald*, August 2, 1870, 50–51; W. H. Littlejohn, "The Statesman Articles: Article Seven," *Review and Herald*, May 13, 1873, 171; S. B. Whitney, "The Book of Revelation," *Review and Herald*, February 1, 1877, 34; and D. M. Canright, "When Was the Bible Written?," *Signs of the Times*, December 19, 1878, 378.

[76] James White et al., eds., "Religious News and Notes," *Signs of the Times*, November 21, 1878, 351; and *Anonymous*, "The Archaeology of Baptism," *Review and Herald*, May 29, 1879, 170.

[77] See, e.g., J. H. Waggoner, "The Law of God and Baptism," *Review and Herald*, October 24, 1854, 84; Oliver Hoffer, "Explanation," *Review and Herald*, August 25, 1863, 103; J. N. Loughborough, *The Saints' Inheritance: Or, The Earth Made New* (Battle Creek, MI: Steam Press of the Seventh-day Adventist Pub. Assn., 1873), 13; and [Uriah Smith], "To Correspondents: 50. No Man That Sinneth Not," *Review and Herald*, November 6, 1879, 156.

[78] See, e.g., J. N. Loughborough, "Saints' Inheritance," *Review and Herald*, May 26, 1859, 3; [Daniel T.] Taylor, "The Coming Earthquake," *Review and Herald*, November 16, 1869, 162; and Loughborough, "The Saints' Inheritance," July 23, 1874, 38.

[79] James White, "Questions," *Review and Herald*, July 23, 1861, 60; *Anonymous*, "Progress of Skepticism," *Review and Herald*, June 16, 1863, 19; and Daniel Wilson, "Promptness in Charity," *Review and Herald*, August 11, 1868, 127.

[80] James White, "Report from Bro. White," *Review and Herald*, July 16, 1867, 72.

[81] Arthur L. White, "Thoughts on Daniel and Revelation," Ellen G. White Estate Shelf Document, Washington, DC, 1966.

[82] See, e.g., Uriah Smith, *Thoughts, Critical and Practical, on the Book of Daniel* (Battle Creek, MI: Steam Press of the Seventh-day Adventist Pub. Assn., 1873), 336, 343.

> Even Bible study, as too often conducted in the schools, is robbing the world of the priceless treasure of the word of God. The work of "higher criticism," in dissecting, conjecturing, reconstructing, is destroying faith in the Bible as a divine revelation; it is robbing God's word of power to control, uplift, and inspire human lives.[83]

Nevertheless, as no Seventh-day Adventist minister practiced or endorsed critical biblical scholarship, critical scholarship and its theories were not perceived as a direct threat against which they had to defend themselves and their teachings.

Methods of Biblical Interpretation

Seventh-day Adventists saw themselves as "true adherents to the principles of interpretation set forth by W[illia]m Miller."[84] The discovery of the present truths in the post-1844 period, they were convinced, resulted from their consistent application of those principles.[85] Miller's fourteen principles of biblical interpretation were outlined in the Millerite *Signs of the Times* in May 1840.[86] Whereas the first five principles dealt with general principles of Bible study, the other nine principles addressed specifically the study of biblical prophecy. Forty years after the Great Disappointment, Ellen G. White noted that those who "are engaged in proclaiming the third angel's message are searching the Scriptures upon the same plan that Father Miller adopted," followed by a quotation of Miller's general five principles.[87] Those principles may be summarized as follows: A Bible student should study Scripture diligently and prayerfully, with unwavering faith that God will give him understanding. He should bring together all relevant passages, allow each word to "have its proper bearing" or "its proper influence," permit Scripture to be "its own expositor," and formulate an interpretation "without a contradiction." Miller further reasoned that Scripture was the rule of faith only when the Bible student did not rely

---

[83] Ellen G. White, *Education*, 227.

[84] [Uriah Smith], "Is Satan Divided Against Himself?," *Review and Herald*, July 10, 1856, 84.

[85] Ibid. See also O[ren] Hewett, "The Apostasy," *Review and Herald*, November 1, 1853, 135; and William Miller, "To All Who Love the Lord Jesus Christ in Sincerity," *Review and Herald*, April 18, 1854, 98.

[86] Miller, "Mr. Miller's Letters—No. 5," 25–26.

[87] Ellen G. White, "Notes of Travel," *Review and Herald*, November 25, 1884, 738.

for his understanding of Scripture on some teacher, creed, and desire.[88] That point highlights both "the Restorationist imperative to get back to the Bible by bypassing human interpreters" and "the Jacksonian faith in the ability of the common people to understand the Bible without the aid of experts."[89] As Miller had employed a thorough and methodical approach in his comparison of Scripture with Scripture,[90] Seventh-day Adventists frequently affirmed that "the Bible is its own expositor"[91] and "its own interpreter."[92]

Approaches to the Biblical Prophecies

Seventh-day Adventists emerged from the remains of the Millerite movement in the years after the great disappointment. The Millerites had been looking forward to the imminent second coming of Christ, as the fulfillment of the eschatological prophecies of the Bible. That eschatological focus and the hope in the coming of their Savior lived on in the experience of Seventh-day Adventists. They found their identity, message, and mission in the integration of the eschatological passages on the third angel's message, the heavenly sanctuary ministry of Jesus, the seventh-day Sabbath, and the sealing of the 144,000 (Rev 7; 11:19; 12:17; 13; 14:9–12).[93] Therefore, it is not surprising that Seventh-day Adventists wrote largely on those biblical prophecies.

Miller's remaining nine principles of biblical interpretation had particular relevance for the study of the biblical prophecies. As will be seen, those principles imply at least two presuppositions: First, the biblical text exhibits a unity because the same Holy Spirit inspired all Bible writers. Second, since end-time prophecies concern more or less the same period of human history, there may naturally be similarities

---

[88] Miller, "Mr. Miller's Letters—No. 5," 25; and Ellen G. White, "Notes of Travel," 738.

[89] George R. Knight, *A Search for Identity: The Development of Seventh-day Adventist Beliefs*, Adventist Heritage Series (Hagerstown, MD: Review and Herald, 2000), 42.

[90] Ibid., 40.

[91] See, e.g., J. R. Towle, "Letters," *Review and Herald*, June 10, 1852, 24; J. N. Loughborough, "The Two-Horned Beast," *Review and Herald*, March 28, 1854, 79; and F. Gould, "The Bible Rule of Interpretation," *Review and Herald*, November 7, 1865, 183. See also Ellen G. White, *Education*, 190.

[92] See, e.g., Hiram Edson, "The Times of the Gentiles," *Review and Herald*, February 14, 1856, 154; [Uriah Smith], "The Bible," *Review and Herald*, April 29, 1858, 187; and Gould, "The Bible Rule of Interpretation," 182.

[93] Merlin D. Burt, "The Historical Background, Interconnected Development, and Integration of the Doctrines of the Sanctuary, the Sabbath, and Ellen G. White's Role in Sabbatarian Adventism from 1844 to 1849" (PhD diss., Andrews University, 2002); and George R. Knight, *William Miller and the Rise of Adventism* (Nampa, ID: Pacific Press, 2010), 251–290.

between different end-time prophecies. Further, the second presupposition results from Miller's preference for the historicist interpretation of prophecy.[94] Here is a summary of principles six to fourteen: Sixth, in the Bible different visions, figures, and parables often describe the same things, which is why one had to combine them to interpret them properly. Seventh, "visions are always mentioned as such" (2 Cor 12:1). Eighth, figures appear often in prophecy and they "always have a figurative meaning . . . to represent future things, times and events." Here, Miller defined the meaning of such figures as mountains (Dan 2:35, 44), beasts (Dan 7:8, 17), waters (Rev 17:1, 15), a lamp (Ps 119:105), and a day. Ninth, "parables are used as comparisons to illustrate subjects, and must be explained in the same way as figures by the subject and the Bible" (Mark 4:13). Tenth, some figures "have two or more different significations," such as one day is used, for example, for an indefinite period, a year, and a thousand years (Eccl 7:14; Ezek 4:6; 2 Pet 3:8). The year-day principle, as applied to prophetic time periods, finds its basic foundation here. Eleventh, a word should be taken literally "if it makes good sense as it stands and does not violate the laws of nature;" otherwise it should be interpreted figuratively (Rev 12:1–2; 18:3–7). Twelfth, to determine the meaning of a figurative word one was to search in the Bible for a reasonable explanation of it. Thirteenth, only a historical event that met all figures of a given biblical prophecy was to be considered a true fulfillment of that prophecy (Ps 22:5; Isa 45:17–19; 1 Pet 2:6; Rev 17:17; Acts 3:18). Miller considered the fourteenth rule the most important one—a self-sacrificing faith in God's character, His promises, protection of the translation of the biblical text, and His guidance even of those who, trusting in Him, lack a knowledge of the biblical languages.[95]

Miller's principles of biblical interpretation contained two aspects that, if taken independently, could potentially lead in different directions. Thus, some Adventist writers paid more attention to the textual connections (text-oriented approach), whereas others focused more on identifying historical fulfillments of biblical prophecies (history-oriented approach).[96]

---

[94] C. Mervyn Maxwell, "A Brief History of Adventist Hermeneutics," *Journal of the Adventist Theological Society* 4/2 (1993): 209–226, 211.

[95] Miller, "Mr. Miller's Letters—No. 5," 25–26.

[96] Gluder Quispe, *The Apocalypse in Seventh-day Adventist Interpretation* (Lima: Universidad Peruana Unión, 2013), suggests three different emphases to the book of Revelation in Seventh-day Adventist history: first, a biblical-historical emphasis (1862–1944); second, a biblical-theological emphasis (1944–1970); and third, a biblical-exegetical emphasis (1970–present). It should be

The Preference for a Text-Oriented Approach

Miller, James White, and others initially looked for terminological and topical similarities between the different eschatological prophecies in Daniel and the New Testament. They consulted other passages in the Old Testament to clarify the meaning and background of relevant terms used in a given Daniel passage. Only subsequently did they turn to historical events to look for a fulfillment of the prophecy.

An example for that approach is James White's interpretation of Daniel 11. He observed that as the prophecies of Daniel 2, 7, 8, and 10–12 contain numerous terminological similarities, they present parallel accounts covering (almost) the same period of history. Since all those prophecies end with papal Rome, he concluded that despite current political events, Daniel 11:40–45 likewise has to describe the papacy.[97] Previously, James White had published a book on the prophecies of Daniel 2 and 7–9, in which he pointed out the parallels between the chapters (fifty pages). Interestingly, more than fifty percent of the book (an additional sixty-two pages) dealt with the subject of the sanctuary, identifying the sanctuary of Daniel 8:14.[98]

Alberto Timm and Don Neufeld note that a deeper focus on the inner structures of the biblical text gradually moved Seventh-day Adventist writers beyond the initial Millerite understanding of those prophetic passages to a broader understanding of biblical typology, particularly regarding the correlation between the earthly and heavenly sanctuaries and their respective ministries.[99]

The Preference for a History-Oriented Approach

The focus on fulfillments of biblical prophecy in contemporary events and developments also influenced Adventist interpretations of

---

noted that unlike Quispe's book, the present study addresses only the situation until the first decade of the twentieth century. Quispe's argument is based on a selection of a few key Adventist writers, suggesting that the first period was characterized by a historicist approach; the author of the present study perceives different methodological preferences even within the Adventist historicist approach.

[97] James White, "Unfulfilled Prophecy," *Review and Herald*, November 29, 1877, 172; James White, "Where Are We?," *Review and Herald*, October 3, 1878, 116–117; and James White, "Time of the End," *Signs of the Times*, July 22, 1880, 229–230.

[98] James White, *The Prophecy of Daniel: The Four Kingdoms, the Sanctuary, and the 2300 Days* (Battle Creek, MI: Steam Press of the Review and Herald Office, 1859).

[99] Alberto R. Timm, "Historical Background of Adventist Biblical Interpretation," in *Understanding Scripture: An Adventist Approach*, ed. George W. Reid, Biblical Research Institute Studies 1 (Silver Spring, MD: Biblical Research Institute, 2006), 7; and Neufeld, "Biblical Interpretation in the Advent Movement," 120–121.

those prophecies. While matching the details of a biblical prophecy with historical events is a necessary task of the interpreter, the latter may easily open the door to speculation when looking for a historical or contemporary match becomes the driving force in the interpretative process.

In 1859, R. F. Cottrell may likely have had John 16:4 in mind when he wrote, "God is his own interpreter and he is making these prophecies plain."[100] Four years later, he explained that idea more: "God is now interpreting the prophecies of his word by fulfilling them before our eyes. . . . God is his own interpreter, and his interpretation is infallible."[101] There was nevertheless a predicament; whether or not a particular event qualified as a fulfillment of a given prophecy still lay in the eye of the interpreter.

An example for that approach is Uriah Smith's interpretation of Daniel 11:40–45. Like James White and other Adventist writers, he initially perceived the king of the North as the papacy.[102] By 1871, Smith had changed his position and reasoned that Turkey had to be the king of the North.[103] He had lost confidence in the previous position because it seemed "wide of the mark," as the pope was bound to the Vatican and no longer had political power. The contemporary political situation in Turkey and the Middle East seemed to match the biblical text better.[104] James White cautioned against such premature and overly detailed positions on "unfulfilled prophecies," particularly as the biblical text suggested otherwise.[105] He was not opposed to identifying events as historical fulfillments of biblical prophecies, but he stressed that all the particulars of the prophecy had to find a match in the historical event; otherwise, it was better to remain silent on the matter.

A Thematic Approach

The studies of the mid- and late 1840s had led Seventh-day Adventists to a discovery or better understanding of various beliefs such as the seventh-day Sabbath, the heavenly sanctuary, the third angel's message, spiritual gifts, and the sealing of the 144,000. Coupled with previous

---

[100] R. F. Cottrell, "Harmony Between Paganism, Catholicism, and Protestantism," *Review and Herald*, August 11, 1859, 92.

[101] R. F. Cottrell, "God Is His Own Interpreter," *Review and Herald*, August 4, 1863, 78.

[102] Uriah Smith, "Will the Pope Remove the Papal Seat to Jerusalem?," *Review and Herald*, May 13, 1862, 192.

[103] Uriah Smith, "Thoughts on the Book of Daniel: Chapter XI (Continued)," *Review and Herald*, March 21, 1871, 108–109.

[104] Smith, *Thoughts, Critical and Practical, on the Book of Daniel*, 146–147, 330–331, 353.

[105] James White, "Unfulfilled Prophecy," 172.

insights on the second coming of Christ and the state of the dead, they developed an integrated system of doctrinal beliefs that had an eschatological significance.[106] During the first forty-four years of the church's existence, numerous publications dealt with topics such as the law of God;[107] the seventh-day Sabbath;[108] the state of the dead, resurrection, and the destiny of the wicked;[109] and the sanctuary.[110] Applying the principle of the Bible as its own expositor, as a corollary of the principle of the unity of Scripture,[111] Seventh-day Adventists extensively collected biblical passages to support those doctrinal beliefs. The fondness for a pragmatic, debating-style evangelistic ministry to convert other Christians in the 1860s and 1870s necessitated using particular Bible texts as evidence for Seventh-day Adventist distinctives, with a lesser focus on studying entire Bible books to understand their inner structures, depiction of characters, and development of thought.

The discussion over the law in Galatians 3:23–27, previously mentioned, is a case in point. In the early 1850s, Andrews, J. H. Waggoner, and others identified that law as the moral law (Ten Commandments). Yet since that view seemed too close to the prevalent Protestant view that

---

[106] Burt, "Historical Background."

[107] See, e.g., J. H. Waggoner, *The Law of God: An Examination of the Testimony of Both Testaments* (Rochester, NY: Advent Review Office, 1854); R. F. Cottrell, *The Bible Class: Lessons on the Law of God, and the Faith of Jesus* (Rochester, NY: Advent Review Office, 1855); and D. M. Canright, *The Two Laws: As Set Forth in the Scriptures of the Old and New Testaments* (Battle Creek, MI: Steam Press of the Seventh-day Adventist Pub. Assn., 1876).

[108] See, e.g., Joseph Bates, *The Seventh Day Sabbath, A Perpetual Sign: From the Beginning, to the Entering Into the Gates of the Holy City, According to the Commandment*, [1st ed.] (New Bedford, MA: Benjamin Lindsey, 1846); J. H. Waggoner, *The Truth Found: A Short Argument for the Sabbath* (Battle Creek, MI: Steam Press of the Review and Herald Office, 1858); J. N. Andrews, *History of the Sabbath and First Day of the Week: Showing the Bible Record of the Sabbath and the Manner in Which It Has Been Supplanted by the Heathen Festival of the Sun* (Battle Creek, MI: Steam Press of the Review and Herald Office, 1859); and J. W. Morton, *Vindication of the True Sabbath: In Two Parts* (Battle Creek, MI: Steam Press of the Review and Herald Office, 1860).

[109] See, e.g., D. P. Hall, *Man Not Immortal: The Only Shield Against the Seductions of Modern Spiritualism* (Rochester, NY: Advent Review Office, 1854); J. N. Andrews, *The Wicked Dead: Are They Now Being Punished?* (Battle Creek, MI: Seventh-day Adventist Pub. Assn., 1865); D. M. Canright, *History of the Doctrine of the Immortality of the Soul* (Battle Creek, MI: Steam Press of the Seventh-day Adventist Pub. Assn., 1871); and Uriah Smith, *Man's Nature and Destiny: Or, The State of the Dead, the Reward of the Righteous, and the End of the Wicked* (Oakland, CA: Pacific Press, 1884).

[110] Uriah Smith, *The Sanctuary and the Twenty-Three Hundred Days of Daniel VIII, 14* (Battle Creek, MI: Steam Press of the Seventh-day Adventist Pub. Assn., 1877); and J. N. Andrews, *The Sanctuary and Twenty-Three Hundred Days* (Battle Creek, MI: Steam Press of the Seventh-day Adventist Pub. Assn., 1872).

[111] [James White], "The Sabbath," *Review and Herald*, April 7, 1851, 62.

this text taught the abolishment of the commandments, Seventh-day Adventists came to argue that it actually talked about the abolishment of the ceremonial law.[112] When E. J. Waggoner advocated his father's view on Galatians 3 in the 1880s, Protestants pressed for the legislation and enforcement of Sunday laws on local, state, and national levels.[113] George I. Butler's hostile reaction to E. J. Waggoner's view was spurred more by its potential ramifications—Seventh-day Adventists might conclude the Ten Commandments are no longer relevant—than by actual textual and intertextual concerns. Failing to question whether or not the Galatians text had anything to do with the abolishment of a law, Butler reasoned that since the Ten Commandments had not been abolished, the text had to refer to the ceremonial law.[114] In later years, Ellen G. White reasoned that the law in Galatians was twofold, suggesting that both perspectives, Butler's and Waggoner's, were therefore one-sided and actually parts of a larger and more comprehensive understanding of the passage.[115] This example illustrates how practical concerns at times narrowed the possible meanings of a given text rather than unfolded the deeper biblical meaning against the backdrop of the immediate and wider context of Scripture.

The potential of linking various theological beliefs to a central motif was also recognized by several Adventist writers. Ellen G. White referred to the sanctuary as "the key which unlocked the mystery of the disappointment," "open[ing] to view a complete system of truth."[116] Andrews, Smith, and others explicitly linked the sanctuary to numerous other beliefs, yet did not move beyond that basic connection to produce a full-fledged systematic theology that had "the sanctuary as its integrating principle."[117] Ellen G. White also employed the Great

---

[112] J. N. Andrews, "Discourse with Brother Carver," *Review and Herald*, September 16, 1851, 29; J. N. Andrews, *Thoughts on the Sabbath, and the Perpetuity of the Law of God* (Paris, ME: James White, 1851), 22, 25; and Waggoner, *The Law of God*, 74, 80–81, 98, 108. Cf. Stephen Pierce, "Answer to Bro. Merriam's Question Respecting the Law of Gal. III, in Review No. 3, Vol. X," *Review and Herald*, October 8, 1857, 180–181.

[113] Whidden, *E. J. Waggoner*, 92–94.

[114] George I. Butler, *The Law in the Book of Galatians: Is It the Moral Law, or Does It Refer to That System Peculiarly Jewish?* (Battle Creek, MI: Review and Herald, 1886).

[115] Ellen G. White, *Selected Messages*, 2 vols. (Washington, DC: Review and Herald, 1958), 1:233.

[116] Ellen G. White, *The Great Controversy between Christ and Satan: From the Destruction of Jerusalem to the End of the Controversy*, The Spirit of Prophecy, vol. 4 (Battle Creek, MI: Steam Press of the Seventh-day Adventist Pub. Assn., 1884), 268.

[117] Alberto R. Timm, "The Seventh-day Adventist Doctrine of the Sanctuary (1844–2007): A Brief Historical Overview," in *"For You I Have Strengthened Me": Biblical and Theological Studies in Honor of Gerhard Pfandl in Celebration of His Sixty-Fifth Birthday*, ed. Martin Pröbstle

Controversy motif as a major theme in her writings and a structuring element of her theology.[118] She added that "the sacrifice of Christ as an atonement for sin is the great truth around which all other truths cluster,"[119] a remark that complements the previous perspective because she perceived the great controversy as a conflict over God's character of unselfish, other-centered love.[120] The love of God was ultimately revealed through Christ's life and death. Therefore, she added, "In order to be rightly understood and appreciated, every truth in the Word of God, from Genesis to Revelation, must be studied in the light which streams from the cross of Calvary, and in connection with the wondrous, central truth of the Saviour's atonement."[121]

A Text-Oriented Approach

Besides thematic and prophecy-focused approaches to Scripture, Seventh-day Adventist literature also contains evidence of a text-focused approach towards biblical passages that intends to pay attention to the inner structures of biblical passages.

Thus, the 1858 "Great Controversy Vision" seemed to prompt Ellen G. White to be mindful of the broad biblical narrative of the conflict between good and evil, the character of God, and the plan of redemption. Later, she stressed how every biblical passage was to be viewed in light of Scripture's "grand central theme, of God's original purpose for the world, of the rise of the great controversy, and of the work of redemption."[122] She expounded on that grand narrative in three sets of books—*Spiritual Gifts*, volumes 1, 3, and 4 (1858, 1864); *Spirit of Prophecy*, four volumes (1870–1884); and the five books of the Conflict of the Ages series (1888–1917)[123]—that may be considered a spiritual commentary on

---

(St. Peter am Hart: Seminar Schloss Bogenhofen, 2007), 335–337.

[118] Joseph J. Battistone, *The Great Controversy Theme in the Writings of Ellen G. White* (Berrien Springs, MI: Andrews University, 1975); Herbert E. Douglass, "Great Controversy Theme," in Fortin and Moon, 850–853.

[119] Ellen G. White, Diary entry for July 30, 1901, Ms 70, 1901.

[120] Ellen G. White, *Patriarchs and Prophets* (Oakland, CA: Pacific Press, 1890), 33, 338.

[121] Ellen G. White, Ms 70, 1901.

[122] Ellen G. White, *Education*, 190. See also Richard M. Davidson, "Bible, Interpretation of," in Fortin and Moon, 652.

[123] See Ellen G. White, *Patriarchs and Prophets*; Ellen G. White, *Prophets and Kings* (Mountain View, CA: Pacific Press, 1917); Ellen G. White, *The Desire of Ages*; Ellen G. White, *The Acts of the Apostles* (Mountain View, CA: Pacific Press, 1911); and Ellen G. White, *The Great Controversy* (1888 ed.); and Ellen G. White, *The Great Controversy* (Mountain View, CA: Pacific Press, 1911). One might add Ellen G. White, *Thoughts from the Mount of Blessings* (Oakland, CA: Pacific Press,

that narrative. She stressed the need to allow each word to have its proper meaning in light of its immediate and broader context.[124] She employed the same approach in multiple article series in the *Review and Herald*, *Signs of the Times*, and other periodicals. In her comments on the biblical narratives, she employed Scripture in at least four different ways, using it exegetically, theologically, typologically, and parenthetically.[125] As she believed that "the Bible was given for practical purposes,"[126] she was more interested in its practical-spiritual application to the life of the believer than in debating the minutiae of exegetical particularities.

Another Adventist writer who was fond of publishing commentaries on the biblical books was E. J. Waggoner, yet his commentaries consistently focused on the gospel motif in those books. Thus, he wrote commentary series, in article and book form, on Galatians, Isaiah, Romans, Hebrews, and John.[127]

The history of the Sabbath School lesson topics provides an interesting indicator of tendencies in the denomination's approach to Scripture. From 1852 to 1862 only twenty-two percent of the time was spent in successive study of a Bible book, yet in the following sixteen years, engagement with longer biblical passages decreased even more as Sabbath Schools focused merely on the first fifty-two lessons, dealing with the commandments of God and the faith of Jesus (Rev 14:12). After 1886, the church nevertheless gave more attention to the study of Bible books. Thus, from

---

1896), and Ellen G. White, *Christ's Object Lessons* (Battle Creek, MI: Review and Herald, 1900).

[124] Ellen G. White, *The Great Controversy between Christ and Satan*, [1888 ed.], 521; Ellen G. White, *The Desire of Ages*, 719; and Ellen G. White, *Education*, 189. See Davidson, "Bible, Interpretation of," 652.

[125] Jon Paulien, "The Interpreter's Use of the Writings of Ellen G. White," in *Symposium on Revelation: Introductory and Exegetical Studies*, ed. Frank B. Holbrook, Daniel and Revelation Committee Series 6 (Silver Spring, MD: Biblical Research Institute, 1992), 163–174; Gerhard Pfandl, "Ellen G. White and Hermeneutics," in Reid, 309–328; and Frank M. Hasel, "Ellen G. White's Use of Scripture," in *The Gift of Prophecy in Scripture and History*, ed. Alberto R. Timm and Dwain N. Esmond (Silver Spring, MD: Review and Herald, 2015), 297–315.

[126] Ellen G. White, *Selected Messages*, 1:20. See also Ellen G. White, "Objections to the Bible."

[127] E. J. Waggoner, *The Gospel in the Book of Galatians: A Review* (Oakland, CA: n.p., 1888). During his European years (1892–1903), he wrote a number of articles and editorials on Isaiah in the *Present Truth*; see E. J. Waggoner, *Treasures in Isaiah: Good News in "The Gospel Prophet"* (Brushton, NY: Teach Services, 2004). From October 1895 to September 1896, a weekly series of articles on the Epistles to the Romans appeared in the *Signs of the Times*; see E. J. Waggoner, *Waggoner on Romans: The Gospel in Paul's Great Letter* (Paris, OH: Glad Tidings Publishers, [1990s?]). At the 1897 General Conference Session, he presented a series of studies on the book of Hebrews; see E. J. Waggoner, *Studies in the Book of Hebrews* (Brushton, NY: Teach Services, 1998). From December 1898 to June 1899, the *Present Truth* published a series of articles on the Gospel of John; see E. J. Waggoner, *Waggoner on the Gospel of John* (Brushton, NY: Teach Services, 2004).

1886 to 1889, church members spent almost fifty percent of the time studying a biblical book.[128] Starting October 27, 1888, church members studied the Epistle of 2 Peter passage by passage.[129] The model of studying an entire biblical book passage by passage was frequently repeated for the next half century, with some striking differences to the lessons on biblical books in the late twentieth and early twenty-first centuries. Whereas small Bible books such as James, Philippians, 1 Peter, 1 John, and Daniel (1891, 1893, and 1895) were studied for one quarter, larger books were studied progressively for several quarters in a row. For example, church members spent two quarters each in Mark, Acts, Galatians, and Genesis (1891, 1892, 1898, 1900); three quarters in Hebrews (1889–1890); one entire year each in Luke, John, and Acts (1894, 1896–1898); and more than five quarters on the life of Christ (1899–1900).[130] Studying a biblical book progressively over an extended period permitted a more in-depth exposure to the line of thought and inner structures of those books.

Summary and Conclusion

This chapter described Seventh-day Adventist presuppositions about the nature of Scripture, perceptions and use of biblical scholarship, and methods of biblical interpretations from 1845 to 1910. It was shown that Seventh-day Adventists were deeply committed to Scripture. Their confidence in its clarity, reliability, and authority resulted from their firm belief in the divine inspiration of the Bible writers. Notwithstanding the views particular Seventh-day Adventist writers held on divine inspiration, all of them perceived the biblical text as a reliable account of past events, God's will, and His message of salvation. They regarded the Bible as the ultimate and normative authority in matters of faith and practice.

By the mid-1890s, different understandings of divine inspiration nevertheless led to different perspectives on the need and legitimacy of biblical interpretation and the role of Ellen G. White's writings in biblical interpretation. Whereas the influence of A. T. Jones led some to the unfortunate and unwarranted idea that no interpretation

---

[128] Daniel Ulvoczky, "A History of the Adult Sabbath School Lesson: Development in the 19th Century" (term paper, Andrews University, 2015), 10, 15, 21.

[129] *Sabbath School Lessons on the Third Angel's Message and the Second Epistle of Peter: July to December 1888* (Oakland, CA: International Sabbath School Association, 1888), 19–32.

[130] Office of Archives, Statistics, and Research, "Adult Sabbath School Lesson Topics," https://www.adventistarchives.org/sabbathschoollessons (accessed October 7, 2019).

whatsoever is needed because the meaning of the Bible was taken literalistically just as it reads, and while he elevated Ellen G. White's writings as the final, exhaustive interpreter of Scripture, most Seventh-day Adventist ministers seemed to see the need for an interpretation of the biblical text. Ellen G. White also supported the need to carefully interpret Scripture.[131] Rather than elevating her own writings as the interpretative key to Scripture, she repeatedly pointed back to the Bible as the authoritative norm to interpret itself and refused to use her writings as a shortcut to serious Bible study.[132] Hence, many of the early Seventh-day Adventists appreciated the careful text-critical, linguistical, exegetical, and theological research of other Protestant scholars as long as the latter did not undermine faith in the historicity of the biblical account and the veracity of the biblical message. While knowledge of the biblical languages was not a requirement for ministerial workers, some of the early Seventh-day Adventist ministers had a proficiency in those languages and employed them for more substantive explanations of Seventh-day Adventist theology. Their appreciation of Miller's fourteen principles of biblical interpretation is reflected in their thematic studies in support of Seventh-day Adventist theological distinctives as well as in the text-oriented and history-oriented approaches to biblical prophecies. The writings of various Seventh-day Adventist writers indicate that in their use of those approaches, they had different preferences and affinities. They all desired to employ clear biblical passages to interpret passages that were more difficult to understand, yet in the heat of inner-denominational theological discussions, some ministers tended to appeal to Adventist tradition or to define biblical terms through the lens of common sense rather than their biblical usage. Despite such shortcomings of some, the writings of the early Seventh-day Adventists are largely characterized by the aspiration to follow the advice that Miller gave to a young minister in 1832: "You must preach *Bible*[,] you must prove all things by *Bible*[,] you must talk *Bible*, you must exhort *Bible*, you must pray *Bible*, and love *Bible*, and do all in your power to make others love *Bible* too."[133]

---

[131] See Pfandl, "Ellen G. White and Hermeneutics," 309–328.

[132] See chapter 13 by John C. Peckham, "The Prophetic Gift and *Sola Scriptura*," in the present volume.

[133] William Miller to Truman Hendryx, March 26, 1832, quoted in Knight, *A Search for Identity*, 39.

CHAPTER 13

The Prophetic Gift and *Sola Scriptura*

John C. Peckham

How does the principle of *sola Scriptura* relate to the prophetic gift, particularly as exhibited in the writings of Ellen G. White? Although the concept is rooted much earlier in Christianity, the phrase *sola Scriptura* is a Latin phrase stemming from the Protestant Reformation, often translated as "Scripture alone" or "by Scripture alone." However, there are various understandings of what this phrase means in practice. How should the *sola Scriptura* principle be understood and function relative to other factors that affect understanding and practice? Does recognition of prophetic writings outside of Scripture undermine the *sola Scriptura* principle? How does the authority of Scripture relate to the authority of other prophetic communications such as the prophetic writings of Ellen G. White?

This chapter will address these questions by outlining a constructive understanding of *sola Scriptura*, with special focus on how such an understanding is compatible with recognizing noncanonical prophets. This will be undertaken in three parts. First, this chapter will outline a constructive understanding of the *sola Scriptura* principle as closely related to the authority of the biblical canon as "canonical," avoiding isolationism on the one hand and creedalism and other forms of communitarianism on the other. Second, this chapter will address Ellen G. White's testimony regarding the unequaled authority of Scripture and its relation to her prophetic writings. Finally, the chapter will briefly take stock of how we might answer the questions raised above, in light of the material considered throughout the chapter.

What is the *Sola Scriptura* Principle?

For the purposes of this chapter, the *sola Scriptura* principle is defined as follows: the *sola Scriptura* principle maintains that Scripture possesses unique, infallible, and unequaled authority (subordinate only to God himself) in all matters of faith and practice. In order to better understand this principle, and how it relates to the recognition and use of noncanonical prophetic writings, it is crucial to understand what *sola Scriptura* affirms and what *sola Scriptura* denies.

What the *Sola Scriptura* Principle Affirms

If we never, strictly speaking, encounter Scripture *alone*, in a way free from the influence of all other factors, what sense does it make to affirm the phrase *sola Scriptura*? In order to address this question, we need to more clearly understand the ways in which Scripture stands alone and the ways in which it does not function alone. Understanding this will shed light on how the *sola Scriptura* principle is compatible with recognizing noncanonical prophets.[1]

While Scripture does not function in isolation and we never read it free from the influence of other factors, Scripture is rightly understood as "alone" in the following three ways:

1. Scripture is the unequaled, uniquely normative source of divine revelation, divinely commissioned to function as the rule of faith and practice.
2. Scripture is the fully trustworthy and uniquely sufficient rule of faith and practice.
3. Scripture is the final norm of faith and practice that is normative for all others.

In other words, Scripture alone is the uniquely normative, divinely commissioned, trustworthy and theologically sufficient, and interpretatively normative rule of faith and practice. Here, normative authority means an authority that functions as the "norm" or "standard" or "rule" of faith and practice over and against other factors.

This study refers to this conception as canonical *sola Scriptura* in order to differentiate it from other conceptions of what *sola Scriptura*

---

[1] Put differently, as will be seen later, one of the reasons some people intuitively think the *sola Scriptura* principle is incompatible with the recognition and use of noncanonical prophetic writings is because they misunderstand what the *sola Scriptura* principle means and how it functions in the first place.

means.[2] This understanding of *sola Scriptura* is bound up with recognition of the sixty-six books of the biblical canon as a unified corpus that God has commissioned to function as the rule of faith and practice (further discussed below).[3] As such, to say Scripture is "canonical" is to say that Scripture rules, it rules as a whole, and it rules because it has been commissioned to have ruling authority by the Ruler Himself. That is, Scripture is "canonical" in that it is the divinely commissioned rule of faith and practice.

There are three integral principles that are corollaries of canonical *sola Scriptura*. These are: *tota Scriptura*, *analogia Scriptura*, and spiritual things are Spiritually discerned.

First, *tota Scriptura* affirms that *all* of Scripture (as a unified collection) functions as the infallible source, sufficient basis, and final norm of theological interpretation (2 Tim 3:16). Accordingly, we should not emphasize parts of Scripture while neglecting or downplaying others. The whole canon of Scripture must be allowed to function as the rule of our faith and practice. Second, the analogy of Scripture (*analogia Scriptura*) approaches Scripture as a unified and internally consistent collection of writings such that each text should be understood in light of the entire biblical canon (Isa 8:20; Luke 24:27, 44–45). Scripture,

---

[2] The author of the present study makes a more extensive case regarding this understanding of *sola Scriptura* in John C. Peckham, *Canonical Theology: The Biblical Canon, Sola Scriptura, and Theological Method* (Grand Rapids, MI: Eerdmans, 2016).

[3] For a discussion of the nature and proper recognition of the biblical canon as a divinely commissioned corpus, see Peckham, *Canonical Theology*, especially chapters 1–3. In this regard, to explain in more detail, "the history of canon reception is complicated and messy indeed and, while there appears to have been considerable agreement among the earliest post-apostolic Christians regarding a number of books (e.g., the gospels, some corpus of Paul's letters, and others), the extant evidence appears to be insufficient to settle debates regarding when the canon was *functionally* 'closed'" (Peckham, *Canonical Theology*, 67). As such, conclusions regarding dating canon recognition must remain tentative. However, in the view of the author of the present study, "the extant evidence suggests that, very early, Christians viewed some group of NT books as 'Scripture' and thus as functionally 'canonical'" (ibid.). As Michael Kruger, *The Question of Canon* (Downers Grove, IL: IVP Academic, 2013), 31, puts it, early Christians were "able to say which books are (and are not) Scripture," which does not appear to be "materially different than saying which books are in (or not in) a [functional] canon." Accordingly, Kruger departs from the oft-repeated claim that before the fourth century, Christians possessed a "boundless, living mass of heterogeneous" texts as at best "obscurant, and at worst misleading" (ibid., 33). In his view, "early Christians did possess an authoritative corpus of books long before the fourth century, even if the edges were not entirely solidified" (ibid., 36). Kruger lays out a detailed and convincing case for this view based on the historical evidence in his book *Canon Revisited: Establishing the Origin and Authority of the New Testament Books* (Wheaton, IL: Crossway, 2012). However, even when early Christians recognized some books as functionally canonical, that did not mean they considered only those canonical books to be good for reading; other books were also endorsed as good for reading, but not "canonical."

then, should be allowed to provide its own norm of interpretation. This is related to the often-misunderstood saying, "Scripture interprets itself," which does not mean that Scripture requires no interpretation. Every reading of Scripture (or of anything else) is already an interpretation. Further, it is very obvious that Scripture can be interpreted variously, given that so many people arrive at differing interpretations. Jesus Himself highlights that Scripture can be interpreted in various ways when He asks, "What is written in the Law? How does it read to you?" (Luke 10:26).[4] While Scripture can be interpreted variously, however, not all interpretations are valid. Interpreters of Scripture should always seek and engage the broader teachings of Scripture to help understand any part of Scripture and every interpretation should be continually subjected back to the rule of Scripture itself. Third, "spiritual things are spiritually discerned" (see, e.g., 1 Cor 2:11–14) teaches that the Holy Spirit should be continually sought for guidance and illumination. With this basic understanding of what canonical *sola Scriptura* affirms in mind, we are now in a position to move on to what canonical *sola Scriptura* denies.

What the *Sola Scriptura* Principle Denies

While the canonical *sola Scriptura* principle affirms the unequaled, uniquely normative authority of Scripture, it is crucial to understand four things this principle does not affirm.

First, canonical *sola Scriptura* does not claim that Scripture is the only source of knowledge or even the only source of revelation. The Bible itself affirms there is a partial revelation about God that can be seen through nature, typically called "general revelation" (Ps 19:1–4; Rom 1:18–23), and references special revelation that is not included in the canon (e.g., special revelation to the oral prophets, the content of which is often unrecorded).

Second, the canonical *sola Scriptura* principle does not affirm that all theological doctrine or church practice requires direct biblical statements. Every doctrine should be grounded in Scripture and every practice should be governed by biblical principles, but one must also pay attention to what may be demonstrably inferred from what Scripture says and recognize that Scripture does not directly address every issue.[5]

Third, the canonical *sola Scriptura* principle does not affirm that

---

[4] All biblical quotations are from the NASB, unless otherwise indicated.

[5] For example, Scripture does not directly address smoking and yet the Adventist position on health and healthful living is grounded in Scripture.

Scripture excludes reason and/or requires no interpretation, or that one's private interpretation of Scripture is the correct understanding of Scripture. As such, canonical *sola Scriptura* does not exclude the proper use of one's faculty of reason (e.g., Acts 17:2; 18:4), without which we could not even read Scripture, but maintains that Scripture, which is infallible, should not be subjected to being judged or ruled by human reason or experience, which are fallible (1 Cor 3:19–20; cf. Prov 28:26; Jer 17:9; Rom 1:21; 3:11; 1 Tim 6:20) and should themselves be subjected to divine revelation.

Fourth, the canonical *sola Scriptura* principle does not affirm that interpretive communities and traditions should be dismissed and/or ignored. In this and other ways, canonical *sola Scriptura* avoids isolationism and the private interpretation of Scripture; that is, it avoids isolationist approaches, which understand *sola Scriptura* to mean that Scripture can and should be interpreted privately by each individual, apart from the influence of any community, traditions, or other factor.[6] In reality, no one reads Scripture in a way that is entirely free from influence by factors outside the Bible. Every person reads Scripture from some perspective. There is no neutral perspective from which we can approach Scripture. We each bring with us a framework of previous understandings that affect our interpretation of the Bible, whether we intend to or not. As such, although the influences of known presuppositions can be mitigated and corrected, we cannot arrive at an interpretation that is free from all presuppositions. Indeed, the expectation that one could read Scripture in isolation from all other factors makes one more susceptible to the danger of unintentionally allowing such factors to unduly affect one's reading. Attempting to read in isolation also cuts off helpful resources, such as commentaries and the insights of others around us, and thus leaves the reader with blind spots that could be exposed by reading within community and across communities.

In contrast, canonical *sola Scriptura* includes the recognition that the very way we read and understand Scripture is always affected by a host of factors, many of which have been passed down to us from our families and religious communities. Some of what is passed down to us is very good; some may need to be critiqued, reformed, or even rejected. According to canonical *sola Scriptura*, all traditions—and every other factor we consider—should be intentionally and carefully held up for scrutiny by the unequaled, final, and uniquely normative standard of Scripture.

---

[6] Peckham, *Canonical Theology*, 12, refers to this as "reductionist *sola Scriptura*."

As such, canonical *sola Scriptura* also avoids creedalism and other forms of communitarianism.[7] While there is a very important and helpful role played by community, communitarian approaches go beyond the appropriate role for community by maintaining that Scripture is to be interpreted according to some community-determined, normative standard outside the Bible, whether that be the community or community leadership itself or some past tradition (e.g., the ecumenical creeds).[8]

However, the adoption of any normative standard outside of the Bible undermines the unique ruling authority of the canon of Scripture.[9] This is not only true with regard to what "sources" one grants authority to relative to faith and practice. It also relates to whether one adopts anything outside of Scripture as normative with regard to the interpretation of Scripture. This is because normative authority to interpret means that the meaning of anything can be controlled by the designated normative interpreter. For example, if a teacher gives his students a class syllabus, but claims the teacher is the only one who has the right to interpret it, then the syllabus has no functional authority at all. The teacher could claim it means whatever the teacher wants it to mean, regardless of what it actually states. Similarly, whether intentionally or not, the adoption of any normative arbiter of interpretation from outside of Scripture, inevitably undermines the *functional* canonical authority of Scripture.

In order for the Bible to actually function as the uniquely normative rule of all faith and practice, the interpretation of the Bible cannot be ruled by anything else, whether that be a creed, a group of people, or any person's private interpretation. Every aspect of faith and practice should be tested by Scripture, while Scripture itself should never be subordinated to any external standard.

Sola Scriptura and Canonicity

As its label suggests, the canonical *sola Scriptura* principle depends on the *canonical* nature and authority of Scripture. Accordingly, in order

---

[7] To be very clear, criticisms of "communitarian" approaches are not intended to criticize *community* or undermine the very important and positive role that community should play. The problem is not community, but the investing of normative authority in anything other than that which God has appointed to function with such authority.

[8] For a further discussion and analysis of communitarian approaches, including many that are increasingly popular among Protestants, see Peckham, *Canonical Theology*, chapter 4.

[9] This is one reason Adventists hold the stance that the Bible is our "only creed," as stated in the preamble to the 28 Fundamental Beliefs.

to understand how *sola Scriptura* relates to the prophetic gift outside of Scripture, it is necessary to understand the nature and authority of the canon—that is, what the canon of Scripture is and how it is authoritative in virtue of what it is.

Alongside a basic understanding of the nature and authority of the canon of Scripture, it is crucial to answer the question of whether the *sola Scriptura* principle itself has canonical authority. In other words, is *sola Scriptura* itself a biblical principle? Understanding this will, in turn, help us understand how *sola Scriptura* and the authority of Scripture relates to the authority of other prophetic communications.

The *Sola Scriptura* Principle as a Canonical Principle

Although the phrase *sola Scriptura* does not appear in Scripture, the principle itself follows from biblical teachings. Put simply, if it follows from biblical teachings that Scripture possesses unique authority over all other factors such as reason, experience, tradition, and extra-biblical prophetic messages, then the canonical *sola Scriptura* principle follows from biblical teachings.[10]

That Scripture claims normative authority relative to faith and practice is seen in many texts, including 2 Timothy 3:16: "All Scripture is inspired by God and profitable for teaching, for reproof, for correction, for training in righteousness" (2 Pet 1:20–21; 1 Thess 2:13).[11] Scripture further includes claims of Scripture's trustworthiness in statements such as "The Scripture cannot be broken" (John 10:35). Additionally, canonical prophets and apostles claim their messages are from God Himself and serve a particular covenantal purpose, thus holding divinely commissioned *ruling* authority.[12]

Scripture further includes claims of normative authority over tradition, reason, and experience. While humans need to make careful use of reason and experience, Scripture warns against the human capacity for self-deception (see Jer 17:9) and repeatedly attests to the

---

[10] For a more detailed discussion, see Peckham, *Canonical Theology*, chapter 6.

[11] Some take Paul's statement here as a reference to only the Old Testament Scriptures, but a strong case can be made that New Testament authors used the term *Scripture* as a technical term to refer to a particular kind of revealed and inspired writing, which extended beyond the Old Testament, inclusive of apostolic writings (see the apparent reference to the very words of Luke 10:7 as "Scriptures" in 1 Timothy 5:18. See also the reference to a collection of Paul's letters as "Scriptures" in 2 Peter 3:15–16). In the view of the author of the present study, although the New Testament Scriptures were still in process of coming to be when 2 Timothy 3:16 was written, Paul's affirmation of existing Scripture in this instance lends itself to an application to all "Scripture" that can be correctly identified as such, even while parts of the canon were yet to be written.

[12] See the section "The Canon as a Covenant Witness Document" in this chapter.

fallibility of both human reason and experience, especially in light of the fall (see, e.g., Ps 14:1–3; Rom 1:21; 3:11). As such, Proverbs 28:26 warns, "He who trusts in his own heart is a fool" (see, further, Job 11:7; Prov 4:12; Isa 55:8–9; Rom 11:3; 1 Cor 2:16). 1 Corinthians 3:19–20 adds, "The wisdom of this world is foolishness before God" and "the Lord knows the reasonings of the wise, that they are useless" (see also 1 Cor 2:1–16; 1 Tim 6:20). Accordingly, human reason and experience should be subjected to and tested by the standard of God's Word (Matt 24:24–26; cf. 2 Cor 11:3–4; Gal 1:8).[13]

Further, Jesus explicitly subordinates tradition to the "word of God" and the "commandment of God," sharply criticizing those who "invalidated the word of God" and transgressed "the commandment of God for the sake of your tradition" (Matt 15:6, 3; cf. Mark 7:5–13; Col 2:8). Here, Jesus challenges not only tradition, but also the interpretive authority of religious leaders.[14] Accordingly, Peter rejects the high priest's orders to stop teaching in Jesus' name, answering, "We must obey God rather than men" (Acts 5:29). Further, Paul teaches that the apostolic testimony itself is not merely "the word of men" but it is in truth, "the word of God" (1 Thess 2:13). If the New Testament Scripture is the written record of the first-century apostolic testimony, then it is "the word of God," which we recognize by faith, and should be treated as such. These and other biblical texts do not indicate that all tradition is to be rejected (2 Thess 3:6), but they do suggest that Scripture, being the Word of God, is authoritative over a given community's traditions.

Even the New Testament apostles expected their testimony to be tested by existing Scripture. According to Acts 17:11, 13, the Bereans confirmed "the word of God" that was "proclaimed by Paul" by "examining the Scriptures daily *to see* whether these things were so." This put in practice the principle stated in 1 John 4:1, "Test the spirits to see whether they are from God." In the Old Testament, this standard for testing is set in Isaiah 8:20, "To the law and to the testimony! If they do not speak according to this word, it is because they have no dawn." The principle that all is to be tested by the final authority of *existing* Scripture was repeatedly endorsed and implemented by Jesus and others, including in statements such as those that begin with the words "it is written" (Matt 4:4–10; Acts 23:5; Rom 3:4, 10).[15]

---

[13] See also Romans 1:21; 2 Corinthians 3:14–15; 4:4; Romans 1:26–27; Galatians 5:24; 1 Timothy 3:2–4.

[14] This is not to say that religious leaders have no authority, but that even the interpretations of religious leaders must be subjected to the uniquely normative standard of Scripture.

[15] Note, also, that Paul exhorts the Corinthians "not to exceed what is written" (1 Cor 4:6; cf. 14:37).

In this regard, Paul urges, "Even if we, or an angel from heaven, should preach to you a gospel contrary to what we have preached to you, he is to be accursed!" (Gal 1:8; cf. 2 Cor 11:2–4). Likewise, John exhorts, "If anyone comes to you and does not bring this teaching, do not receive him into *your* house, and do not give him a greeting" (2 John 10; cf. Rev 22:18). It seems that following these instructions today would require employing Scripture as the standard of true doctrine (that is, the rule of faith). This is just what canonical *sola Scriptura* advocates, which entails that noncanonical prophetic writings must be tested by and subject to the biblical canon, a subject to which we now turn.

The Canon as a Covenant Witness Document

As noted earlier, canonical *sola Scriptura* is bound up with recognition of the sixty-six books of the biblical canon, approached as a unified corpus that God has commissioned to function as the rule of faith and practice. In this view, the books of the biblical canon possess intrinsic, ruling authority by virtue of being writings that God has appointed to be the rule of faith and practice.[16] Further, in this view, the canon as a whole is a covenant witness document such that the writings in it are the writings of *covenantal* prophets and apostles (or close associates of apostles).[17]

Covenantal prophets and apostles include those recipients of revelation and inspiration commissioned by God to witness to and communicate God's covenantal revelation that pointed to Christ (the Old Testament) and God's covenantal revelation that testified to the Christ event—the incarnation, ministry, death, and resurrection of Christ (the New Testament).[18]

---

[16] For more on these and other claims regarding the sixty-six-book canon of Scripture, see Peckham, *Canonical Theology*, chaps. 2–3. To say that the writings of Scripture are divinely commissioned or appointed, however, should not be taken to mean that God chose or dictated the very words of Scripture. As the author of the present study understands it, God revealed and inspired Scripture in such a way that (in most cases) the writers of Scripture wrote in their own words (according to their own background, personality, location, and literary style), communicating what God had revealed to them in various ways and doing so under the indeterministic guidance of inspiration.

[17] To say the canon of Scripture is a covenant witness document is to say that the Old Testament canonical writings might be seen as depositing the written text of the covenantal relationship between God and His people and the New Testament might be seen as containing the Christ-commissioned canonical documentation of the new covenant. See, further, Andreas J. Köstenberger and Michael J. Kruger, *The Heresy of Orthodoxy* (Wheaton, IL: Crossway, 2010), 109–115; Peckham, *Canonical Theology*, 22–28; cf. Kevin Vanhoozer's view of the "canon" as "a divinely initiated covenant document" in *The Drama of Doctrine: A Canonical-Linguistic Approach to Christian Theology* (Louisville, KY: Westminster John Knox, 2005), 134.

[18] "Covenantal revelation" is used to mean revelation given in the context of and as a recording witness to the old and new covenants.

Covenantal prophets and apostles are intrinsically canonical (that is, they possess unique *ruling* authority) because they have been commissioned by God (the Ruler) to receive and transmit the divinely revealed and inspired rule of faith and practice.

Put differently, the biblical canon consists of the covenant witness leading up to the Christ event and the covenant witness to the Christ event (Heb 1:1–2). As such, the Old Testament is effectively ratified by Christ (evidenced in the way Christ and his apostles relate to, speak of, and use the Old Testament Scriptures) and the New Testament is commissioned by Christ.[19] In particular, the New Testament is commissioned as the unrepeatable, first-generation witness to the incarnate Christ, the supreme and sufficient revelation of God, manifested historically and publicly in a manner attested to not by merely a few recipients, but by a veritable cloud of witnesses (1 Cor 15:3–15).[20] As such, via Christ's first advent, the Old Testament and New Testament have been *publicly* ratified and commissioned by the Ruler Himself (Luke 24:44–49; Acts 1:8; 10:39–43; 22:14–15) in a way that no further prophetic messages could be (prior to Christ's second advent).

Accordingly, the New Testament is the testimony of the first-hand apostolic witness to the incarnate and risen Christ, Himself the ultimate revelation of God who promised the apostles that the Holy Spirit "will teach you all things, and bring to your remembrance all that I said

---

[19] On the New Testament attestation of the Old Testament, see, e.g., Luke 24:27, 44–45; 2 Timothy 3:16; 2 Peter 1:20–21; cf. John 1:45; 5:39; Acts 10:43; 1 Peter 1:20–12. Further, Matthew writes, "All this has taken place to fulfill the Scriptures of the prophets" (Matt 26:56; cf. 1:22; 2:15–17, 23; Luke 1:70; 24:27, 44–45; Acts 1:16; 3:18). Likewise, Paul speaks of God establishing believers both "according to my gospel and the preaching of Jesus Christ" and "by the Scriptures of the prophets, according to the commandment of the eternal God" (Rom 16:25–26; cf. 1:2; 3:2; 15:4). Accordingly, Paul contends that he serves "the God of our fathers, believing everything that is in accordance with the Law and that is written in the Prophets" (Acts 24:14; cf. 23:5; John 1:45; 2 Cor 4:2). Elsewhere, Paul "for three Sabbaths reasoned with them from the Scriptures'" and "demonstrate[ed] by the Scriptures that Jesus was the Christ" (Acts 17:2; 18:28; cf. 1 Cor 15:3). This and other New Testament evidence suggests the "canonical" authority of some recognized corpus of OT Scripture.

[20] Importantly, Jesus Himself commissioned the apostles to record, proclaim, witness to, and disseminate His acts, teachings, and commands, and make disciples of all nations (cf. Matt 28:19–20; Acts 1:8). Jesus "appointed twelve" to "be with Him" and to "send them out to preach, and to have authority" (Mark 3:14–15). When sending them, Christ declares they will bear "testimony" to "governors and kings" and "to the Gentiles," but says, "It is not you who speak, but *it is* the Spirit of your father who speaks in you" such that those who do not "receive you, nor heed your words" will face judgment (Matt 10:18, 20, 14–15; cf. John 14:26). In John 20:21, Jesus declares to the apostles, "As the Father has sent Me, I also send you" (cf. John 17:8, 18). Further, Jesus tells them, "The one who listens to you listens to me, and the one who rejects you rejects me," suggesting their commission as Christ's authoritative ambassadors (Luke 10:16).

to you" (John 14:26) and "guide you into all truth" (John 16:13; cf. 8:31; Jude 3; Acts 1:8). These promises not only attest to the truth of the apostolic testimony; they also testify to the full sufficiency of the truth revealed to the apostles.

Once the Ruler has come in Christ, there cannot be any further revelation that is not subject to the *ruling* (that is, canonical) authority of the Old Testament prophets and first-generation apostolic testimony that Christ ratified and commissioned via His first advent. As such, the biblical canon is closed historically. It is the result of God's action of revelation and inspiration to covenantal prophets and apostles, producing a covenant witness leading up to Christ (the Old Testament) and testimony to the unrepeatable first-century Christ event (the New Testament). In other words, once God has come in the flesh, any future claim to the prophetic gift must be tested by the rule that has been ratified and/or commissioned by the risen Christ and witnessed to by the cloud of witnesses in the apostolic age. This brings us to the question of how the canonical (ruling) authority of the Bible relates to the authority of noncanonical prophets.

The Canon of Scripture and Noncanonical Prophets

Scripture itself attests to genuine noncanonical prophetic messages, which possess authority by virtue of being divinely revealed and inspired. For instance, Enoch prophesied (cf. Jude 14), but the Bible records very little about Enoch and the content of his prophetic message. Similarly, Huldah is identified as a prophet, but did not write any canonical books, and only one of Huldah's prophetic messages is recorded in Scripture (2 Kgs 22:14–20; 2 Chr 34:22–28).[21] The Old Testament also refers to "the chronicles of Nathan the prophet" and "the chronicles of Gad the seer" (1 Chr 29:29), the "prophecy of Ahijah," and "the visions of Iddo the seer" (2 Chr 9:29), but no writings included in the biblical canon are attributed to these prophets.[22] In New Testament times, the gospels record only a few statements from John the Baptist's extensive prophetic preaching (Matt 3).

Further, Paul writes of claimed prophetic utterances that were subject to apostolic authority (cf. 1 Cor 14:37) and of some prophesying whose messages were to be tested in the churches according to the principle "the spirits of prophets are subject to prophets" (1 Cor 14:32; cf. 14:29–33; 11:4–5; 1 John 4:1–2; 1 Thess 5:19–22). This attests that there could have

---

[21] Numerous other prophets appear in Scripture who did not write any books of the biblical canon, including Noah, Deborah, Miriam, Elijah, Elisha, and John the Baptist.

[22] According to some traditions, however, Nathan and Gad contributed to 1–2 Samuel, particularly relative to those sections after the death of Samuel, recorded in 1 Samuel 25.

been prophetic messages in New Testament times that were not of the same *functional* authority as the apostolic testimony, but subject to it. Scripture further indicates that prophetic messages would be given long after New Testament times (see, e.g., Rev 11:3; 6; 12:17; 19:10; cf. Joel 2:28–30; Acts 2:17–20), and Adventists believe that Ellen G. White's prophetic gift is an example of this.

In Old Testament times and onward, any claim to the prophetic gift was to be tested by previously attested covenantal revelation (cf. Isa 8:20). The unique, "ruling" prophetic authority of Moses was miraculously attested by God Himself before Israel (see, e.g., Num 12:2–15; cf. John 5:45–47) and Moses was commissioned to record divinely authoritative teachings, prescribed as a covenantal rule (Deut 4:2) to be passed down to future generations (Deut 4:1–2; 6; 29:29; 31:10–13). Those who came after Moses were subject to the standard of the prophetic messages of Moses (Deut 4:1–6). Later prophets were to be tested by earlier, divinely attested prophets (Isa 8:20).

Once Jesus came, He provided the ultimate witness to and attestation of the Old Testament Scriptures—both in the way that He spoke of and utilized them (Luke 24:27) and by the fact that He came to fulfill them (Matt 5:17–18; cf. John 5:38–39, 45–47; Acts 10:43).[23] As such, the apostolic testimony was to be tested by the Old Testament Scriptures (Acts 17:11–13) and claims of other prophetic messages were to be tested (see 1 Thess 5:19–22; 1 John 4:1–2) and were subject to what Jon Paulien calls the "unique authority of the apostle[s]," an authority derived from their "nearness to the Christ event."[24]

---

[23] See, e.g., how Christ repeatedly refers to and uses Old Testament Scripture as authoritative (e.g., Matt 4:4–10; Matt 5:17–19; 7:12; 11:13–14; 12:3–6, 39–42; 15:4–6; 19:4–9; 21:42–44; 22:29–32, 37–40, 43–45; 24:9–21; 26:31–32, 54–56; Mark 1:44; 7:6; 10:3; 12:26; Luke 8:21; 11:28; 16:16–17; 24:27, 44–45; John 2:22; 5:39; 10:34–35; 17:12, 17). See also the way the rest of the New Testament testifies to Old Testament writings as authoritative Scripture (e.g., Acts 17:2; 18:28; Rom 1:2; 4:3; 9:17; 10:11; 11:2; 1 Cor 15:3–4; Gal 3:8; 2 Tim 3:16; 2 Pet 1:20–21).

[24] Jon Paulien, "The Gift of Prophecy in Scripture," in *Understanding Ellen White*, ed. Merlin Burt (Nampa, ID: Pacific Press, 2015), 16, writes, "As a result [of their divinely appointed role], the apostle is to be obeyed just as much as the word of the Lord Himself (1 Thess. 2:13). This is true not only of the apostle's personal presence, but in the apostle's absence his written word substitutes for his presence (1 Cor. 5:3,4; Col. 2:5; 2 Cor. 13:10; Eph. 3:4). It is to be obeyed without question (1 Cor. 7:6,10, 25, 40; 9:14; 14:37, 38; 1 Thess. 4:11; 2 Thess 3:4, 6, 10, 14). The unique authority of the apostle is due to his or her nearness to the Christ event" as an inspired witness thereof. Similarly, Michael Kruger, *The Question of Canon* (Downers Grove, IL: IVP Academic, 2013), 153, writes, "Given the authoritative role of the apostles in early Christianity, and the manner in which they were commissioned to speak for Christ, an apostolic writing would bear the highest possible authority. Indeed, it would bear Christ's authority."

Thus, Paul writes, "If anyone thinks he is a prophet, let him recognize that the things that I write to you are the Lord's commandment. But if anyone does not recognize this, he is not recognized" (1 Cor 14:37–38; cf. Luke 10:16; Rev 1:3). Paulien infers from this that "any noncanonical prophet in the New Testament era was subject to the authority of the New Testament, which was written by the apostles."[25] If so, it follows that any noncanonical prophet would be subject to the authority of the New Testament and to the authority of the Old Testament that preceded it and to which the New Testament itself attests.

Yet, if noncanonical prophetic messages are just as divinely revealed and inspired as canonical writings and thus possess divinely granted authority, what is the difference between the authority of the biblical canon and the authority of noncanonical prophetic messages? While some mistakenly assume that the authority of any genuine prophet would be equivalent to the authority of any other, God sometimes distinguishes between the functional authority of recipients of prophetic messages—as He did when Moses was challenged by Aaron and Miriam (Num 12:1–8)and as can be seen regarding the authority of an apostle over those prophesying in 1 Corinthians 14:37.

Accordingly, the relative authority of prophetic messages corresponds to the relative functional authority that is granted by God. As such, if the biblical canon is correctly recognized to be the divinely commissioned rule of faith and practice, it follows that the functional authority (that is, the authority God grants for some function or functions) of noncanonical prophetic messages would be subordinate to the ruling, "canonical" authority of Scripture. The difference between the authority of canonical prophets/apostles and noncanonical prophets is that the former hold uniquely normative ruling authority by virtue of the divine commission of their messages to function as the rule of faith and practice (as covenantal witnesses). In Paulien's words, while "[t]here are no degrees of inspiration," the apostles were "used as the standard to judge between those who exercised the true gift of prophecy and those who did not." As such, the apostles "functioned as an epistemological standard, and the NT would likewise do so after they were gone."[26]

In this regard, there is a significant historical—and thus functional—difference between canonical prophets/apostles and any later prophet. Noncanonical prophets are removed from the covenantal revelation and historical context in which that revelation was received,

---

[25] Paulien, "Gift of Prophecy," 19.

[26] Paulien, "Gift of Prophecy," 22–23.

publicly attested, and commissioned. Now that Jesus has come as the supreme and sufficient revelation of God, any prophet has to be tested by the covenantal revelation that the Ruler (Jesus) has historically and publicly ratified and commissioned to function as the rule until He returns—the Old Testament and New Testament. No later prophetic revelation could meet this epistemological standard of being a revealed and inspired testimony to a public covenantal event with a cloud of witnesses, and no later revelation is needed beyond the supreme and sufficient revelation of God via the Christ event.

Put differently, any prophet after the Christ event can only be properly recognized insofar as they recognize Christ (1 John 4:2). The one who properly recognizes Christ ought also to recognize the ruling authority of the Scriptures of the covenantal prophets that Christ Himself recognized (the Old Testament Scriptures, cf. Luke 24:44–45) and of those apostles whom Christ commissioned as the uniquely authoritative historical witnesses (see Luke 10:16; 24:44–49; Acts 1:8, 22; 2:32; 3:15; 5:29–32; 10:39–43; 13:31; 22:14–15; 26:16; 1 Cor 15:15) to the Christ event, who delivered not merely the "word of men," but truly "the word of God" (1 Thess 2:13), resulting in the New Testament. Hence, any noncanonical prophecy is subject to that covenantal revelation that Christ Himself attested and commissioned—the canon of Scripture.

Here, the distinction between magisterial and ministerial authority is crucial. The "canonical" or ruling authority that Scripture holds by virtue of being commissioned to hold such authority by the Ruler Himself is often spoken of as *magisterial authority*, which is normative over other ingredients of theological understanding but is itself not normed by other earthly authorities. Other factors might have a ministerial—or servant—authority, but such factors are themselves to be tested and ruled by Scripture. As such, genuine noncanonical prophets have a special kind of ministerial authority, but such authority is always to be tested by and subject to the magisterial ruling authority of the biblical canon.

Ellen G. White and the *sola Scriptura* Principle

We now shift to a consideration of how Ellen G. White relates her own prophetic gift to Scripture.[27] This study first focuses on Ellen

[27] In the writing of this section of the chapter, the author of the present study is deeply indebted to the excellent work on the relationship of Ellen G. White and Scripture that appears in many other sources, including Merlin Burt, "Ellen G. White and *Sola Scriptura*" (paper presented at the Seventh-day Adventist Church and Presbyterian Church USA Conversation, Louisville,

G. White's affirmation of *sola Scriptura*. Then it considers some ways Ellen G. White's writings and ministry shed light on the relationship between her writings and Scripture.

Ellen G. White on *sola Scriptura*

Ellen G. White speaks to the *sola Scriptura* principle in numerous instances, only a few of which will be highlighted here. For example, she writes, "There is need of a return to the great Protestant principle—the Bible, and the Bible only, as the rule of faith and duty."[28] Elsewhere she writes, "God will have a people upon the earth to maintain the Bible, and the Bible only, as the standard of all doctrines and basis of all reforms."[29] Again, of the founders of the Adventist church, she writes, "[We] took the position that the Bible, and the Bible only, was to be our guide; and we are never to depart from this position."[30] Here and elsewhere she strongly affirms the *sola Scriptura* principle.

Indeed, she repeatedly affirms the Bible as the *only* rule or standard of faith and practice. For instance, she writes: "The Bible and the Bible alone, is our rule of faith."[31] Again she affirms Scripture is to be "the only rule of faith and doctrine."[32] That this affirmation rules out creedalism

---

KY, August 23, 2007). https://adventistbiblicalresearch.org/sites/default/files/pdf/Burt%2C%20Ellen%20White%20%26%20Sola%20Scriptura.pdf (accessed January 2, 2018); Frank M. Hasel, "Ellen G. White's Use of Scripture," in *The Gift of Prophecy in Scripture and History*, ed. Alberto R. Timm and Dwain N. Esmond (Silver Spring, MD: Review and Herald, 2015), 297–315; Alberto R. Timm, "Sola Scriptura and Ellen G. White: Historical Reflections," in *The Gift of Prophecy in Scripture and History,* 285–296; Alberto R. Timm, "The Authority of Ellen White's Writings," in *Understanding Ellen White*, ed. Merlin Burt (Nampa, ID: Pacific Press, 2015), 55–65; R. Clifford Jones, "Ellen White and Scripture," in *Understanding Ellen White*, 45–54; George Knight, "Bible, Ellen G. White's Relationship," in *The Ellen G. White Encyclopedia,* ed. Denis Fortin and Jerry Moon (Hagerstown, MD: Review and Herald, 2013), 647–649; Denis Kaiser, "Ellen G. White's Role in Biblical Interpretation: A Survey of Early Seventh-day Adventist Perceptions," in *Reflections: The BRI Newsletter* 60 (2017): 1–6; Denis Fortin, "Ellen White and the Development of Seventh-day Adventist Doctrines," in *Understanding Ellen White*, 107–117; and Remwil R. Tornalejo, "*Sola Scriptura:* A Comparison of Luther and the Adventist Understanding," in *Here We Stand: Luther, the Reformation, and Seventh-day Adventism,* ed. Michael W. Campbell and Nikolaus Satelmajer (Nampa, ID: Pacific Press, 2017), 26–34.

[28] Ellen G. White, *The Great Controversy* (Mountain View, CA: Pacific Press, 1950), 204.

[29] Ibid., 595.

[30] Ellen G. White, Letter 105, 1903, in *Counsels to Writers and Editors* (Nashville, TN: Southern Publishing, 1946), 145.

[31] Ellen G. White, *Counsels on Sabbath School Work* (Washington, DC: Review and Herald, 1938), 84. Cf. Ellen G. White, *Gospel Workers* (Washington, DC: Review and Herald, 1948), 249.

[32] Ellen G. White, "The Value of Bible Study," *Review and Herald*, July 17, 1888. This is in keeping with what James White wrote in the first publication of Sabbatarian Adventists: "The Bible is a perfect and complete revelation. It is our only rule of faith and practice. . . . True visions are

is clear when she writes further, "The Bible, and the Bible alone, is to be our creed, the sole bond of union."[33] Accordingly she writes, "I recommend to you, dear reader, the Word of God as the rule of your faith and practice. By that Word we are to be judged."[34]

Ellen G. White also repeatedly affirms the "unerring truthfulness"[35] and trustworthiness of Scripture, sometimes referring to Scripture as an "unerring standard"[36] and "an unerring counselor, and infallible guide."[37] As she puts it, "the Holy Scriptures are to be accepted as an authoritative, infallible revelation of His will. They are the standard of character, the revealer of doctrines, and the test of experience."[38] Ellen G. White also directly affirms the sufficiency of Scripture, writing, "The Bible contains all the principles that men need to understand in order to be fitted either for this life or for the life to come."[39] Elsewhere she writes, "The truth of God is found in His word. Those who feel that they must seek elsewhere for present truth need to be converted anew."[40]

She further affirms the sufficiency of Scripture relative to interpretation, emphasizing that "the Bible is its own expositor."[41] She does not mean by this that Scripture requires no interpretation. Indeed, she notes that apart from the guidance of the Holy Spirit, we are "continually

---

given to lead us to God, and his written word; but those that are given for a new rule of faith and practice, separate from the Bible, cannot be from God, and should be rejected" (James White, *A Word to the Little Flock* [Gorham, ME: 1847], 13). Many other early Adventists also clearly made this distinction between the uniquely normative authority of Scripture and the value of noncanonical prophetic revelations, including those of Ellen G. White. For more on this, see Theodore N. Levterov, *Accepting Ellen White: Early Seventh-day Adventists and the Gift of Prophecy Dilemma* (Nampa, ID: Pacific Press, 2017).

[33] Ellen G. White, *Selected Messages* (Washington, DC: Review and Herald, 1958), 1:416. Indeed, as Merlin Burt, "Ellen White and Sola Scriptura," 6, notes, "in all, Ellen G. White's published writings contain the phrase 'Bible and the Bible only' forty-five times and 'Bible and the Bible alone' forty-seven times."

[34] Ellen G. White, *Early Writings* (Washington, DC: Review and Herald, 1945), 78.

[35] Ellen G. White, "The Importance of Bible Study," *Youth's Instructor*, May 7, 1884.

[36] Ellen G. White, *The Ministry of Healing* (Mountain View, CA; Pacific Press, 1942), 462.

[37] Ellen G. White, *Fundamentals of Christian Education* (Nashville, TN: Southern Publishing, 1923), 100. Frank M. Hasel, "Ellen G. White's Use of Scripture," 314–315, notes, "While she is aware that in transmission and the process of copying the Bible some mistakes were made, it is remarkable that she never saw it as her task to pinpoint these mistakes or elaborate on any deficiencies or so-called biblical errors."

[38] Ellen G. White, *The Great Controversy*, vii.

[39] Ellen G. White, *Education* (Nashville, TN: Southern Publishing Association, 1923), 123.

[40] Ellen G. White, *Testimonies, for the Church* (Mountain View, CA: Pacific Press, 1948), 8:192.

[41] Ellen G. White, *Education*, 190.

liable to wrest the Scriptures or to misinterpret them."[42] Rather, she affirms that Scripture itself is to provide the context and standard of biblical interpretation, ruling out the adoption of any normative interpreter of Scripture (or standard of interpretation) outside of the Bible itself. Accordingly, she repeatedly issues strong warnings against investing normative authority in tradition. For example, writing of some who "claim the authority of tradition and of the Fathers," she warns that "in so doing they ignore the very principle which separates them from Rome—that the Bible, and the Bible alone, is the religion of Protestants."[43]

Yet, she leaves no room for the isolationist view that Scripture is the only valid source of knowledge or that one should only read Scripture. She affirms "revelations" in God's second book of nature, while emphasizing that such "revelations" are "partial and imperfect."[44] Further, she often uses non-inspired sources and, as Remwil R. Tornalejo puts it, "allowed for the fact that other biblical tools and resources can be helpful as an aid to study the Bible."[45]

Ellen G. White further warns against being overconfident in our interpretations, writing,

> There is no excuse for any one in taking the position that there is no more truth to be revealed, and that all our expositions of Scripture are without an error. The fact that certain doctrines have been held as truth for many years by our people, is not a proof that our ideas are infallible. Age will not make error into truth, and truth can afford to be fair. No true doctrine will lose anything by close investigation.[46]

Similarly, she warns not to think "our ideas, because long cherished," are "Bible doctrines and on every point infallible," such that we are "measuring everyone by the rule of our interpretation of Bible truth. This is our danger, and this would be the greatest evil that could ever come to us as a people."[47]

---

[42] Ellen G. White, *Testimonies*, 5:704.

[43] Ellen G. White, *The Great Controversy*, 448. Ellen G. White here is not rejecting all writings of the past, but criticizing a particular elevation of the authority of tradition that would undermine the uniquely normative authority of Scripture.

[44] Ellen G. White, *Education*, 16.

[45] Tornalejo, "Sola Scriptura," 31.

[46] Ellen G. White, *Counsels to Writers and Editors*, 35.

[47] Ellen G. White, *The Ellen G. White 1888 Materials* (Washington, DC: Ellen G. White Estate, 1987), 830.

Instead, she urges, "Make the Bible its own expositor, bringing together all that is said concerning a given subject at different times and under varied circumstances."[48] In this regard, she adds, "The word of God, as a whole, is a perfect chain, one portion linking into and explaining another."[49] She further explains, "The Bible is its own expositor. Scripture is to be compared with scripture. The student should learn to view the word as a whole and to see the relation of its parts. He should gain a knowledge of its grand central theme—of God's original purpose for the world, of the rise of the great controversy, and of the work of redemption."[50] In these and many other statements, Ellen G. White affirms that Scripture is to be interpreted with Scripture (*analogia Scriptura*) and *all* of Scripture is to be carefully examined (*tota Scriptura*).[51]

Alongside these principles, Ellen G. White also consistently affirms the principle that spiritual things are spiritually discerned. For instance, she writes, "A true knowledge of the Bible can be gained only through the aid of the Spirit by whom the word was given."[52] Accordingly, she counsels readers to "compare scripture with scripture" and "lay yourselves and your opinions on the altar of God, put away your preconceived ideas, and let the Spirit of heaven guide into all truth."[53] Yet, far from advocating a passive reading of Scripture, as if asking for the Spirit's direction will guarantee a perfect understanding, she notes, "The most valuable teaching of the Bible is not to be gained by occasional or disconnected study." Rather, many of Scripture's "treasures lie far beneath the surface and can be obtained only by diligent research and continuous effort."[54]

Her own words best sum up her position on *sola Scriptura*:

> God will have a people upon the earth to maintain the Bible, and the Bible only, as the standard of all doctrines, and the basis of

---

[48] Ellen G. White, *Counsels on Sabbath School Work* (Hagerstown, MD: Review and Herald, 1966), 42-43.

[49] Ellen G. White, *Early Writings*, 221.

[50] Ellen G. White, *Education*, 190. Ellen G. White, *Testimonies*, 4:499, writes, "The Bible is its own interpreter, one passage explaining another. By comparing scriptures referring to the same subjects, you will see harmony and beauty of which you have never dreamed."

[51] Frank M. Hasel, "Ellen G. White's use of Scripture," 303, notes in this regard that "Ellen G. White refers to virtually every chapter of each biblical book."

[52] Ellen G. White, *Education*, 189.

[53] Ellen G. White, *Selected Messages*, 1:412.

[54] Ellen G. White, *Education*, 123.

> all reforms. The opinions of learned men, the deductions of science, the creeds or decisions of ecclesiastical councils, as numerous and discordant as are the churches which they represent, the voice of the majority—not one nor all of these should be regarded as evidence for or against any point of religious faith. Before accepting any doctrine or precept, we should demand a plain "Thus saith the Lord" in its support.[55]

Ellen G. White on the Relation between Scripture and Her Writings

Ellen G. White both reserves unique authority for the biblical canon and affirms the gift of prophecy outside the Bible. She writes:

> During the ages while the Scriptures of both the Old and New Testament were being given, the Holy Spirit did not cease to communicate light to individual minds, apart from the revelations to be embodied in the Sacred Canon. The Bible itself relates how, through the Holy Spirit, men received warning, reproof, counsel, and instruction, in matters in no way relating to the giving of the Scriptures. And mention is made of prophets in different ages, of whose utterances nothing is recorded. In like manner, after the close of the canon of the Scripture, the Holy Spirit was still to continue to work, to enlighten, warn, and comfort the children of God.[56]

Yet, she clearly distinguishes between her writings and the Bible and affirms the ultimate authority of the Bible. She writes, "Our position and faith is in the Bible. . . . And never do we want any soul to bring in the Testimonies ahead of the Bible."[57] Elsewhere she insists that her writings are not "an addition to the word of God," as some "make it appear."[58] She emphasizes, in this regard, that "the Spirit was not given—nor can it ever be bestowed—to supersede the Bible; for the Scriptures explicitly state that the Word of God is the standard by which *all* teaching and experience must be tested."[59] Again, she explains, "God has, in that Word, promised to give visions in the 'last days'" but this is "not for a new rule of faith, but for the comfort of His people, and

---

[55] Ellen G. White, *The Great Controversy*, 595.

[56] Ibid., viii.

[57] Ellen G. White, *Evangelism* (Washington, DC: Review and Herald, 1970), 256.

[58] Ellen G. White, *Testimonies*, 4:246.

[59] Ellen G. White, *The Great Controversy*, vii.

to correct those who err from Bible truth."[60]As she puts it, her writings were given as a "lesser light to lead men and women to the greater light [the Bible]."[61] Accordingly, she writes, "The Lord desires you to study your Bibles. He has not given any additional light to take the place of His Word."[62] She thus instructs,

> In public labor do not make prominent, and quote that which Sister White has written, as authority to sustain your positions. . . . Bring your evidences, clear and plain, from the Word of God. A "Thus saith the Lord is the strongest testimony you can possibly present to the people. Let none be educated to look to Sister White, but to the mighty God, who gives instruction to Sister White.[63]

Indeed, she taught that her writings would not have been needed if the Bible had been carefully studied, again attesting to the sufficiency of Scripture. She writes: "If you had made God's word your study, with a desire to reach the Bible standard and attain to Christian perfection, you would not have needed the Testimonies. . . . The written testimonies are not to give new light, but to impress vividly upon the heart the truths of inspiration already revealed."[64]

Ellen G. White also did not believe her writings should be used as the basis of doctrine. She consistently pointed people to the Bible itself and, as has been "historically demonstrated" in numerous studies on this matter, "Ellen White's writings were not the source of any Seventh-day Adventist doctrine."[65] A number of cases highlight that the function of Ellen G. White's prophetic gift was not as the basis of doctrine or as a

---

[60] Ellen G. White, *Early Writings*, 78.

[61] Ellen G. White, *Evangelism*, 257. As Tim Poirier understands it, this "greater light-lesser light" analogy communicates that "just as the moon derives its light from the sun and reflects only what that source emits, so her messages are seen as deriving their authority from scripture, serving only to mirror the principles presented therein" (Tim Poirier, "Contemporary Prophecy and Scripture: The Relationship of Ellen G. White's Writings to the Bible in the Seventh-day Adventist Church, 1845–1915" [research paper, Wesley Theological Seminary, March 1986], quoted in Burt, "Ellen G. White and *Sola Scriptura*," 7).

[62] Ellen G. White, *Selected Messages*, 3:29.

[63] Ibid., 3:29–30.

[64] Ellen G. White, *Testimonies*, 2:605.

[65] Burt, "Ellen G. White and *Sola Scriptura*, 9. Alberto R. Timm, "The Authority of Ellen White's Writings," 60, adds, "all Seventh-day Adventist doctrines were derived from and grounded on the Scriptures."

final and *normative* interpreter of Scripture.[66]

One such case is the question of the time the Sabbath begins each week. At a conference in 1855, J. N. Andrews argued from Scripture that Sabbath is from sunset to sunset. A few days after the conference, in vision Ellen G. White asked an angel when the Sabbath begins and the angel replied, "Take the word of God, read it, understand, and ye cannot err. Read carefully, and ye shall there find *what* even is, and *when* it is."[67] She and the others came to accept the biblical study of J. N. Andrews, resolving the issue from Scripture. As Denis Kaiser explains this event, God "did not use Ellen White's visions to supersede Scripture but He used them to point Adventists to the Bible."[68]

The deeply divisive controversy over the law in Galatians, which came to a head at the 1888 General Conference Session, provides another striking example. Regarding this controversy, Ellen G. White insisted that the disputants should not try to prove their case from her writings, but should "go to the Bible and get the Scripture evidence."[69] General Conference President G. I. Butler and Uriah Smith pleaded with Ellen G. White to settle the matter and referenced a testimony Ellen G. White had previously given to J. H. Waggoner that they thought would settle the issue. Ellen G. White, however, wrote to Butler: "I have no knowledge of taking any position on the matter [of the law in Galatians]. I had not with me the light that God had given me on this subject, and which had been written, and I dared not make any rash statement in relation to it till I could see what I had written upon it."[70] Later, she would write about this, "Why was it that I lost the manuscript and for two years could not find it? God has a purpose in this. He wants us to go to the Bible and get the Scripture evidence."[71] It was in this context that she wrote to Butler and Smith, "We want Bible evidence for every point we advance."[72] Also, in this context, she wrote, "My cry has been,

---

[66] For more on this, see Fortin, "Ellen White and the Development of Seventh-day Adventist Doctrines."

[67] Ellen G. White, *Testimonies*, 1:116.

[68] Kaiser, "Ellen G. White's Role in Biblical Interpretation," 2.

[69] Ellen G. White, *The Ellen G. White 1888 Materials*, 153.

[70] Ellen G. White, *Manuscript Releases* (Silver Spring, MD: Ellen G. White Estate, 1990), 9:217–218. Cf. Ellen G. White, *The Ellen G. White 1888 Materials*, 32.

[71] Ellen G. White, *The Ellen G. White 1888 Materials*, 153.

[72] Ibid., 36. Just prior to this, in the same letter to Butler and Smith, she wrote, "If we have any point that is not fully, clearly defined, and [that] can bear the test of criticism, don't be afraid or too proud to yield it" (ibid., 35). Later in the same letter, she writes, "Let none feel that we know all the truth the Bible proclaims" (ibid., 36).

Investigate the Scriptures for yourselves, and know for yourselves what saith the Lord. No man is to be authority for us."[73]

Thirteen years later, in an address to church leaders the night before the 1901 General Conference session began, Ellen G. White stated,

> I do not ask you to take my words. Lay Sister White to one side. Do not quote my works again as long as you live until you can obey the Bible. . . . I exalt the precious word [of Scripture] before you today. Do not repeat what I have said, saying, "Sister White said this," and, "Sister White said that." Find out what the Lord God of Israel says, and then do what He commands.[74]

As Frank M. Hasel puts it, in both word and deed, Ellen G. White "valued the authority of the Bible above any other authority, including her own prophetic ministry."[75] She continually directed people back to the Bible in order to settle doctrinal disputes and consistently called Adventist believers to "a diligent study of the Scriptures, and a most critical examination of the positions we hold. God would have all the bearings and positions of truth thoroughly and perseveringly searched, with prayer and fasting."[76]

Notably, Ellen G. White even exhorts readers to judge her prophetic writings by the Scriptures. She writes, "If the Testimonies speak not according to this word of God, reject them."[77] Note that this advice can only be followed if Ellen G. White's writings are not employed as a normative interpreter of Scripture. Ellen G. White's writings possess a ministerial kind of prophetic authority and may serve as an aid in understanding the Bible, but they are not to be taken as a normative standard in addition to the Bible or as a normative interpreter of the Bible. To employ Ellen G. White's writings as such would contradict the *sola Scriptura* principle and would also contradict what Ellen G. White herself counsels with regard to her own writings. In this regard, Frank M. Hasel explains, Ellen G. White did not advocate herself "as the authoritative source for the interpretation of Scripture. Rather, she time and again affirms the great Protestant principle: 'The Bible is its own

---

[73] Ellen G. White, *The Ellen G. White 1888 Materials*, 188.

[74] Ellen G. White, *Manuscript Releases* (1990), 5:141. See also Burt, "Ellen G. White and *Sola Scriptura*," 13.

[75] Hasel, "Ellen G. White's Use of Scripture," 298.

[76] Ellen G. White, *Testimonies*, 5:708.

[77] Ibid., 5:691.

expositor.' . . . She did not assume the role of being the authoritative interpreter of Scripture but encouraged others to be diligent students of Scripture themselves."[78]

For example, in the midst of the 1888 controversy, some interpreted a passage from Ellen G. White's book *Sketches from the Life of Paul* as conclusive evidence that the law in Galatians referred only to the ceremonial law.[79] However, Ellen G. White insisted, "I cannot take my position on either side until I have studied the question."[80] After such study, Ellen G. White's conclusion on the law in Galatians differed from those who had appealed to her writings as settling the issue in their favor.

Similarly, in the context of a considerable dispute over the meaning of "the daily" in Daniel 8:11–13, some leaders believed statements in Ellen G. White's *Early Writings* clearly endorsed their view. Ellen G. White, however, "repeatedly urged individuals involved in the dispute to stop using her writings" to attempt to settle this dispute.[81] She wrote, "I cannot consent that any of my writings shall be taken as settling this matter. . . . I now ask that my ministering brethren shall not make use of my writings in their arguments regarding this question."[82] Her son, W. C. White, "concluded that God desired to have this matter settled through 'a thorough study . . . of the Bible and history' rather than 'by a revelation.'"[83]

Cases like these highlight some problems with attempts to use Ellen G. White's writings as a normative interpreter of Scripture. For one, Ellen G. White's own writings also need to be interpreted and have been—and continue to be—variously interpreted. Moreover, Ellen G. White herself rejected attempts to use her writings this way and those who have tried to use her writings thusly have often come to incorrect conclusions. In this regard, Denis Kaiser explains, attempts to deduce the "final meaning of a text . . . from the commentary of an inspired writer" fails to account for numerous realities.[84] For one, Ellen G. White's use of or commentary regarding a given biblical passage does not

---

[78] Hasel, "Ellen G. White's Use of Scripture," 302.

[79] See George R. Knight, *A User-Friendly Guide to the 1888 Message* (Hagerstown, MD: Review and Herald, 1998), 60.

[80] Ellen G. White, *The Ellen G. White 1888 Materials*, 153.

[81] Kaiser, "Ellen G. White's Role in Biblical Interpretation," 3.

[82] Ellen G. White, *Selected Messages*, 1:164.

[83] Kaiser, "Ellen G. White's Role in Biblical Interpretation," 3, quoting in part from W. C. White to P. T. Magan, July 31, 1910, W. C. White Correspondence File, Ellen G. White Estate.

[84] Kaiser, "Ellen G. White's Role in Biblical Interpretation," 4.

exhaust "the depth of its meaning."[85] Further, "Ellen White occasionally applied biblical principles to particular circumstances without intending to establish a universal rule for all and every situation" and she sometimes "used one particular passage in different ways at different points in her life."[86]

Beyond these problems, it is inappropriate to use Ellen G. White's writings as a final and normative interpreter of Scripture because doing so would shift normative authority to her writings as their final interpreter, displacing the normative authority of Scripture to function as, in Ellen G. White's words, "its own expositor."[87] As George R. Knight explains, "Ellen White never viewed herself as the final divine commentary on the Bible. Never did she take the position that 'you must let *me* tell you what the Bible really means.'"[88] While her spiritual insights can be a great blessing and illuminate Scripture, "it is absolutely crucial that we study her writings in the light flowing out of the Bible rather than to study the Bible in the light of her writings."[89] Kaiser notes further, "We may value the beneficial insights and spiritual truths brought out in [Ellen G. White's] comments on Scripture without limiting the meaning of Scripture and the discovery of biblical truth by making her the final word and thus functionally a part of the canon."[90]

Taking Stock

Now, we are in a position to revisit some questions introduced at the outset of this chapter: Does recognition of prophetic writings outside of Scripture undermine the *sola Scriptura* principle? How does the authority of Scripture relate to the authority of other prophetic communications, such as the prophetic writings of Ellen G. White?

First, it will be helpful to see a brief summary of some basic tenets that might be distilled from the preceding material. In the discussion of the *sola Scriptura* principle, we saw that:

1) The (canonical) *sola Scriptura* principle affirms the uniquely normative authority of Scripture as the rule of faith and practice, including relative to interpretation, but it does not exclude other

---

[85] Kaiser, "Ellen White's Role in Biblical Interpretation," 4.

[86] Ibid.

[87] Ellen G. White, *Education*, 190.

[88] George R. Knight, "How to Read Ellen White's Writings," in *Understanding Ellen White*, ed. Merlin Burt (Nampa, ID: Pacific Press, 2015), 68.

[89] Ibid.

[90] Kaiser, "Ellen G. White's Role in Biblical Interpretation," 4.

authoritative prophetic revelation. To briefly unpack this premise, we saw that Scripture is *alone* with respect to being a source that is: 1) infallible and divinely commissioned to function as the rule of faith and practice, 2) theologically sufficient by itself, and 3) normative relative to theological interpretation, by itself. This entails not only that Scripture is the source of doctrine and unique standard of practice, but also that there can be no final and normative interpreter of Scripture from outside the Bible, since the adoption of any such interpretive arbiter would undermine the functional ruling authority of Scripture. Further, the uniquely normative authority of Scripture refers to the totality of Scripture (*tota Scriptura*), which is to be interpreted by the analogy of Scripture (*analogia Scriptura*) and guided by the Holy Spirit (spiritual things are spiritually discerned). Yet, there are other sources of knowledge and revelation, including noncanonical prophets, which are themselves to be tested by the uniquely normative rule of Scripture. This brings us to a second premise:

2) The uniquely normative authority of Scripture (*sola Scriptura*) depends on the canonical nature of Scripture; the canon is closed historically/organically by God's redemptive actions (especially the Christ event) and this understanding of *sola Scriptura* is itself a "canonical" principle.

To briefly unpack this second premise, we saw that Scripture possesses uniquely normative authority by virtue of the nature and authority of the canon as the divinely commissioned *rule* of faith and practice. The canon is a covenant witness document, commissioned by the Ruler to function as the rule of faith and practice. It thus contains covenantal revelation given via covenantal prophets and apostles, culminating with the testimony to the unrepeatable first-century Christ event. The biblical canon is thus closed historically/organically by God's redemptive action relative to the Christ event, in virtue of which the canon is uniquely normative over noncanonical prophetic messages. This *sola Scriptura* principle follows from the Bible's teachings relative to the authority of covenantal prophets and apostles. This undergirds a third premise:

3) Noncanonical prophets may be correctly recognized as authoritative, but they are to be tested by and subordinate to the uniquely normative authority of the canon of Scripture.

To briefly unpack this third premise, there are other prophets outside the canon of Scripture, commissioned by God and thus authoritative. However, any claims to prophecy are to be tested by previous covenantal revelation. Now that Christ has come, all other claims are to be tested by the rule that Christ has ratified and commissioned (the

Old Testament and New Testament). The Ruler has come and the rule He prescribes is to rule until the Ruler returns. The recognition of noncanonical prophets is itself endorsed by the canon of Scripture and is consistent with the *sola Scriptura* principle because *sola Scriptura* does not exclude other sources of authoritative revelation but subjects other sources to the uniquely normative (canonical) rule of Scripture. As such, noncanonical prophets may possess a special kind of ministerial (servant) authority, but the biblical canon alone is to function with magisterial (ruling) authority, including relative to the interpretation of Scripture, by virtue of being commissioned to rule by the Ruler Himself.

Given this view of canonical *sola Scriptura*, it is perfectly consistent to recognize Ellen G. White's prophetic gift and hold that her noncanonical prophetic authority is a ministerial authority that is not on par with the uniquely normative magisterial authority of the canon of Scripture. If Scripture is rightly identified as holding uniquely normative "canonical" authority, it follows that no extra-biblical manifestation of the prophetic gift—no prophetic writing outside of Scripture—can hold ruling authority over—or on par with—Scripture. This is not a matter of degrees of revelation or degrees of inspiration, but a matter of differing functional authority (magisterial versus ministerial authority). The relative authority of prophetic messages is grounded in the functional authority for which God grants them. One need posit no deficiency in the prophetic gift of noncanonical prophets in order to recognize that such prophetic gifts are given for a different function than that of the unique "canonical" function of the biblical canon.

As a covenant witness document closed via the Christ event, the biblical canon provides a unique function as a historically open (that is, available to all) marker and standard by which any later claims to prophetic authority are to be perpetually tested until the Ruler returns. This provides a very helpful standard to avoid the mistaken acceptance of false prophets who might spring up in later ages, historically distant and thus disconnected from the string of covenantal revelation (in a vacuum, as such) and who might be mistakenly granted canonical authority, whereupon (if their writings were consistently taken as possessing "canonical" or ruling authority) it would be impossible to ever recognize them as "false." This view is consistent with what Ellen G. White herself affirms about the unique ruling authority of Scripture (*sola Scriptura*) and about the relation of her own writings to Scripture.

From the brief survey of Ellen G. White's statements on these matters, we can distill the following significant points (without claiming to be exhaustive).

1) Scripture is to be our only rule of faith and practice—the unequaled standard by which positions are to be judged.

2) Scripture is sufficient and should be understood by comparing Scripture with Scripture, taking Scripture as a whole.

3) The biblical canon is to be distinguished from noncanonical prophetic messages, including the writings of Ellen G. White herself. She insists her writings are not an addition to the Bible, but a lesser light to the greater light.

4) Ellen G. White further insists that her writings are not the source of doctrine and should not be employed as a final and normative interpreter of Scripture—instead, "we want Bible evidence for every point we advance"—and she urges that even her writings should be rejected if they conflict with Scripture.

Even apart from the arguments relative to canonical *sola Scriptura*, it follows from Ellen G. White's writings that Scripture possesses uniquely normative authority (*sola Scriptura*) and that her prophetic writings are themselves to be tested by Scripture (cf. 1 John 4), which she repeatedly calls the *only* rule of faith and practice.

Of course, if Scripture is the *only* rule of faith and practice, Ellen G. White's own writings cannot also be a rule of faith and practice. As such, to employ her writings as a rule, either using them as a basis of doctrine or as a final normative interpreter of Scripture, is inconsistent with her very writings and her own practice and prescriptions. Anyone who believes in Ellen G. White's prophetic gift should understand and apply her writings in a way that is consistent with how she understood her prophetic gift and instructed that her writings be used—insisting, as she did, for "Bible evidence for every point we advance."[91] As such, those who deeply respect and appreciate the ministerial authority of Ellen G. White's prophetic gift should reserve normative "ruling" authority for the canon of Scripture, as she herself did and instructed others to do. To do otherwise is, ironically, to implicitly deny her ministerial authority as a prophet.

If Scripture is rightly identified as the only rule of faith and practice, then (other than the Ruler Himself) nothing else can hold such ruling authority. As prophetic, Ellen G. White's writings are authoritative, but as noncanonical their authority is a ministerial authority that is functionally subordinate to that of the biblical canon—the only rule of faith and practice.[92] In all this, recognition of noncanonical prophets and their

---

[91] Ellen G. White, *Manuscript Releases*, 16:285.

[92] As Burt, "Ellen G. White and *Sola Scriptura*," 11, puts it, in this regard "neither early Adventists

ministerial authority is affirmed by the teachings of Scripture itself and is perfectly consistent with the canonical *sola Scriptura* principle.

nor Ellen White herself saw her prophetic experience as incompatible with" the "principle" of *sola Scriptura*. "Rather they saw her visions as a *fulfillment of biblical predictions* and *subject to biblical authority*."

CHAPTER 14

Recent Trends in Methods of Biblical Interpretation

Frank M. Hasel

"The most terrible fight is not when there is one opinion against another, the most terrible fight is when two men say the same thing—and fight about the interpretation, and this interpretation involves a difference of quality."—Søren Kierkegaard[1]

With the rise of the modern world[2] and in the wake of the Enlightenment, a shift of seismic proportions occurred that had significant implications for the interpretation of the Bible. A new understanding of history and modern presuppositions generated an entire arsenal of new historical-critical methods[3] with far-reaching consequences and radical

---

[1] Søren Kierkegaard, *The Journals*, as quoted in *A Kierkegaard Anthology*, ed. Robert Bretall (New York: Modern Library, 1946), 434.

[2] Cf. the monumental study on the change in biblical interpretation that took place in the rise of the modern world by Henning Graf Reventlow, *The Authority of the Bible and the Rise of the Modern World* (Philadelphia, PA: Fortress, 1985), and his landmark four-volume study: Reventlow, *History of Biblical Interpretation, Volume 1: From the Old Testament to Origen*, ed. Susan Ackerman and Tom Thatcher, trans. Leo G. Perdue, Resources for Biblical Study 50 (Atlanta, GA: Society of Biblical Literature, 2009); Reventlow, *History of Biblical Interpretation, Volume 2: From Late Antiquity to the End of the Middle Ages*, ed. Susan Ackerman and Tom Thatcher, trans. James O. Duke, Resources for Biblical Study 61 (Atlanta, GA: Society of Biblical Literature, 2009); Reventlow, *History of Biblical Interpretation, Volume 3: Renaissance, Reformation, Humanism*, ed. Susan Ackerman and Tom Thatcher, trans. James O. Duke, Resources for Biblical Study 62 (Atlanta, GA: Society of Biblical Literature, 2010); and Reventlow, *History of Biblical Interpretation, Volume 4: From the Enlightenment to the Twentieth Century*, ed. Susan Ackerman and Tom Thatcher, trans. Leo G. Perdue, Resources for Biblical Study 63 (Atlanta, GA: Society of Biblical Literature, 2010). See also Michael Legaspi, *The Death of Scripture and the Rise of Biblical Studies* (Oxford: Oxford University Press, 2010).

[3] Sometimes it is said that there is no single historical-critical method (singular), but only

results for the interpretation of Scripture. We will begin with a short historical overview of historical-critical scholarship, its presuppositions, and some of the implications for the interpretation of Scripture. Some more recent approaches, which can be seen as reactions to and even criticisms of the prevailing historical-critical approach that dominated biblical scholarship for the majority of the twentieth century, can only adequately be understood with a good knowledge of this historical background and the basic principles that govern modern critical scholarship. We will then turn to some important new approaches in the area of biblical interpretation. Within the limits of this chapter we are not able to deal with all new methods of biblical interpretation that have come up in the last fifty years or so. However, we will focus on some approaches that seem to be of greater affinity to Seventh-day Adventist hermeneutics because they focus on the canonical text of Scripture and value the literary nature of the Bible. We will also briefly address some postmodern and reader response approaches and we will deal with a gospel-centered approach to hermeneutics.[4]

---

historical-critical methods (plural) of biblical scholarship, because the historical-critical approach has generated a plethora of methods that have been used and accepted in scholarship. While there are numerous methods that have grown out of the assumptions of historical-critical scholarship, there is an overarching framework of presuppositions that are foundational to the different approaches.

[4] For helpful overviews of different hermeneutical approaches, see Horst Klaus Berg, *Ein Wort wie Feuer: Wege lebendiger Bibelauslegung* (Munich: Kösel Verlag, 1991); Heinz-Werner Neudorfer and Ekkhard J. Schnabel, eds., *Das Studium des Neuen Testaments, Band 1: Eine Einführung in die Methoden der Exegese* (Wuppertal: R. Brockhaus Verlag, 1999); Neudorfer and Schnabel, eds., *Das Studium des Neuen Testaments, Band 2: Spezialprobleme* (Wuppertal: R. Brockhaus Verlag, 2000); A. K. M. Adam, ed., *Handbook of Postmodern Biblical Interpretation* (St. Louis, MO: Chalice, 2000); Joel M. LeMon and Kent Harold Richards, eds., *Method Matters: Essays on the Interpretation of the Hebrew Bible in Honor of David L. Petersen* (Atlanta, GA: Society of Biblical Literature, 2009); Anthony C. Thiselton, *Hermeneutics: An Introduction* (Grand Rapids, MI: Eerdmans, 2009); Joel B. Green, ed. *Hearing the New Testament: Strategies for Interpretation*, 2nd ed. (Grand Rapids, MI: Eerdmans, 2010); Stanley E. Porter and Jason C. Robinson, *Hermeneutics: An Introduction to Interpretive Theory* (Grand Rapids, MI; Eerdmans, 2011); Douglas Mangum and Douglas Estes, eds., *Literary Approaches to the Bible*, Lexham Methods Series 4 (Bellingham, WA: Lexham, 2016); Douglas Mangum and Amy Balogh, eds., *Social & Historical Approaches to the Bible*, Lexham Methods Series 3 (Bellingham, WA: Lexham, 2016); William W. Klein, Craig L. Blomberg, and Robert L. Hubbard Jr., *Introduction to Biblical Interpretation*, 3rd ed. (Grand Rapids, MI: Zondervan, 2017), esp. 99–116; Michael J. Gorman, ed., *Scripture and Its Interpretation: A Global, Ecumenical Introduction to the Bible* (Grand Rapids, MI: Baker Academic, 2017); Raymond E. Brown and Sandra M. Schneiders, "Hermeneutics," in *The New Jerome Biblical Commentary*, ed. Raymond E. Brown, Joseph A Fitzmyer, and Roland E. Murphy (Englewood Cliffs, NJ: Prentice Hall, 1990), 1146–1165; and Ian Provan, *The Reformation and the Right Reading of Scripture* (Waco, TX: Baylor University Press, 2017), esp. 455–648. See also the helpful overview in Steven L. McKenzie, ed., *The Oxford Encyclopedia of Biblical Interpretation*, 2 vols. (Oxford:

The Genesis of Modern Historical-Critical Scholarship

Historical-critical scholarship, as it is taught at almost all leading universities around the world,[5] is a child of modern times. We can understand it adequately only if we take into consideration the historical developments that gave rise to this new way of thinking. The modern world emerged over a longer period of time from the fifteenth to nineteenth centuries. Since the fifteenth century, people and nations in Europe not only gained greater worldwide influence but a process of modernization began to significantly change the living conditions and the thinking of people. This change is closely connected to at least two major factors: 1) many

---

Oxford University Press, 2013); John Barton, ed., *The Cambridge Companion to Biblical Interpretation* (Cambridge: Cambridge University Press, 2006); J. W. Rogerson and Judith M. Lieu, eds., *The Oxford Handbook of Biblical Studies* (Oxford: Oxford University Press, 2008); and several chapters in John Riches, ed., *The New Cambridge History of The Bible: From 1750 to the Present* (Cambridge: Cambridge University Press, 2015) that provide a historical overview and document the shift in scholarly methods and new concerns in the twenty-first century.

[5] Manfred Oeming points out that the modern historical-critical method of biblical interpretation, which has differentiated itself into a whole set of methodological steps, is the highlight of theological science. Despite the fact that the historical-critical method has come under some serious criticism in recent years, Oeming affirms that the historical-critical method "represents the scientific standard, which every student has to learn at University. Scientific is downright synonymous with historical-critical" (Manfred Oeming, *Biblische Hermeneutik: Eine Einführung* [Darmstadt: Wissenschaftliche Buchgesellschaft, 1998], 31, Frank M. Hasel's translation). While Oeming acknowledges that the historical-critical method finds itself in a deep crisis (45), he nevertheless maintains that it has foundational significance for biblical interpretation and "is indispensable and absolutely essential" (46, Frank M. Hasel's translation). Similarly, John Barton, "Historical-Critical Approaches," in Barton, *Cambridge Companion*, 9, states that historical criticism, while it has come under a cloud, "is still practiced, however, by a large number of scholars even in the English-speaking world, and by many more in areas where German is the main language of scholarship." This perspective is shared by John J. Collins, *The Bible After Babel: Historical Criticism in a Postmodern Age* (Grand Rapids, MI: Eerdmans, 2005), 4, who writes, "'Historical criticism' is the label usually applied to what might be termed 'mainline' biblical scholarship over the last two centuries or so." More recently, New Testament scholar Ulrich Wilckens, *Theologie des Neuen Testaments, Band III: Historische Kritik der historisch-kritischen Exegese, Von der Aufklärung bis zur Gegenwart* (Göttingen: Vandenhoeck & Ruprecht, 2017), 1, confirms that "the historical-critical method of biblical exegesis currently is the undisputed part of academic theology that is taken for granted in all of theological studies, in fact, in Protestant faculties as much as in [Roman] catholic faculties" (Frank M. Hasel's translation). See also Klaus Berger, *Die Bibelfälscher: Wie wir um die Wahrheit betrogen wurden* (Munich: Pattloch, 2013), who claims that the historical-critical scholarship of the last two hundred years has left the church in a desolate state (9, 345). From a Roman Catholic perspective, see Joseph A. Fitzmyer, S.J., *The Interpretation of Scripture: In Defense of the Historical-Critical Method* (Mahwah, NJ: Paulist Press, 2008), 59–73; and Johannes Paul II, "Die Interpretation der Bibel in der Kirche," Verlautbarungen des Apostolischen Stuhls 115, Päpstliche Bibelkommission, April 23, 1993, http://www.vatican.va/roman_curia/congregations/cfaith/pcb_documents/rc_con_cfaith_doc_19930415_interpretazione_ge.html (accessed June 23, 2020).

momentous discoveries and inventions[6] that emerged in rapid succession and 2) economic, intellectual, and sociopolitical changes of great magnitude.[7] All these revolutions led to an acceleration of historical change[8] and eventually brought about a different relationship to one's historical consciousness that led to the emergence of a new thinking. The recognition of the historical character and change of human existence anchored an awareness of historical conditioning and relativity that became typical of the historical-critical thinking of modernity. Furthermore, this period is characterized by a modern understanding of science where tradition progressively lost its dominant role of explaining the present within various fields of inquiry. In the place of tradition, two new authorities emerged: experience and reason. Empirical and experimental methods quickly gained the upper hand in the natural sciences and helped to explain the reality around us. Verifiable methods became more and more important in modern science. The historical-critical methodology that emerged in this context "presupposed a naturalistic worldview that explained everything in terms of natural laws and excluded the possibility of supernatural intervention."[9] Consequently, scholars influenced by this thinking treated the Bible as any other literature and not as God's special revelation.[10]

---

[6] With regard to discoveries and inventions, one could mention the mechanical watch, the printing of books with mechanical letters (Gutenberg), spectacles or glasses, the compass, gunpowder, guns, cannons, the telescope and microscope, blood circulation in the human body, steam engines, railroads, motors and factories, X-rays, electricity, photography, the telephone, etc. During this time, new continents were discovered (North and South America, Australia) and a new way of seeing the world emerged. Provan, 360, speaks about an "Information Explosion" that took place.

[7] It has been pointed out that "radical advances in human science created popular confidence in the scientific method, which in turn produced a revolutionary and more scientific method for studying history. Also, in the nineteenth century, *developmentalism*—the idea that evolving historical progress underlies everything—became widespread as the dialectical philosophy of G. W. F. Hegel, which shaped the social philosophy of Karl Marx, and the evolutionary theory of Charles Darwin attest" (Klein, Blomberg, and Hubbard, 99). Cf. Siegfried Zimmer, *Schadet die Bibelwissenschaft dem Glauben? Klärung eines Konflikts* (Göttingen: Vandenhoeck & Ruprecht, 2007), 132–133, for a list of some of those significant changes.

[8] While there has always been historical change, there undoubtedly took place an acceleration of change that still affects us today.

[9] Klein, Blomberg, and Hubbard, 99.

[10] "Among the labels we might use to characterize modern biblical interpretation, *autonomy* may be the most apt description. Biblical interpreters must operate autonomously, or independently—independent of the interpreter's own faith (or lack of faith), independent of the church's theology, and independent of the church's (or any other) authority and influence. Biblical interpreters should go wherever the text leads them. As for the biblical materials, they must be read without consideration for how they have been read by previous interpreters, without reference to their

A religious-political factor also helped pave the way for human reason to gain a new universal significance next to experience. A horrendous thirty-year religious war (1618–1648) between Protestants and Catholics left central Europe devastated and in ruins. It was one of the most destructive conflicts in human history.[11] The Thirty-Year War left entire regions devastated, resulting in some eight million fatalities not only from military engagement, but also from violence, famine, and the plague. Catholics and Protestants, who both claimed supremacy and sovereignty in the interpretation of Scripture, demonstrated to a whole generation how inhumane they could be.[12] This traumatic experience helped pave the way to abandon any recourse to ecclesiastical tradition or external authority (be that the church or the Bible).[13] Instead, a new common denominator in all human beings was sought that would guarantee an objective criterion and norm for what is right, which would help overcome tyrannical structures, privileges, and traditions and lead the way to equality and equal human rights. The German philosopher Immanuel Kant (1724–1804) called his own age "an age of criticism" where "religion through its sanctity and law-giving through its majesty, may seek to exempt themselves from it. But they then awaken just suspicion, and cannot claim the sincere respect which reason accords only to that which has been able to sustain the test of free and open examination."[14] Thus, Kant's famous definition of Enlightenment became the dominant paradigm of modern thinking:

> Enlightenment is man's emergence from his self-imposed immaturity. Immaturity is the inability to use one's understanding without guidance from another. This immaturity is self-imposed when its cause lies not in lack of understanding, but in lack of resolve and courage to use it without guidance from another.

---

location within the biblical canon, and indeed, quite apart from their status as Scripture. This approach reflects the values of the eighteenth-century **Enlightenment** and its aftermath" (Joel B. Green, "Modern and Postmodern Methods of Biblical Interpretation," in Gorman, 188, emphasis in the original).

[11] Peter H. Wilson, *Europe's Tragedy: A New History of the Thirty Years War* (London: Penguin, 2010), 787.

[12] This fact has recently been pointed out by Wilckens, 359.

[13] James C. Livingston, *Modern Christian Thought: From the Enlightenment to Vatican II* (New York: Macmillan, 1971), 3, points out that "the ideal of the Enlightenment is the duty of not entertaining any belief that is not warranted by rational evidence, which means by the assent of autonomous reason rather than biblical or ecclesiastical authority."

[14] Immanuel Kant, *Critique of Pure Reason*, trans. Norman Kemp Smith (London: Macmillan, 1929), A xii.

> *Sapere Aude*! ["Dare to know!"] "Have courage to use your own understanding!"—that is the motto of the enlightenment.[15]

The explanatory power and the amazing reliability and predictability of physical, chemical, biological, and mechanical processes made it possible for the empirical-rational approach to reality to become so successful. It became the prevailing approach to explain natural phenomena in the Western world. Through its success and the ensuing economic power, this naturalistic and materialistic mindset quickly spread around the globe. Its pervasive influence is still with us. It has brought up powerful and very influential alternative explanations for the origin of life on this earth. The evolutionary hypothesis of Darwin and his intellectual successors has become the dominant[16] model of explanation that tells us where we come from and how life began and evolved. Evolutionary premises have not only shaped biology but also geology, the social sciences, and even theology and ethics.

The endeavor to use your own reasoning powers as an autonomous agent[17] without guidance or control from another external authority resulted in what has become known as the "historical-critical method."

The Historical-Critical Method

The historical-critical approach to biblical interpretation builds on influences stemming from the Age of Enlightenment and rationalism.[18]

---

[15] Immanuel Kant, "What Is Enlightenment?," The Literary Link, http://theliterarylink.com/kant.html (accessed August 10, 2020). Immanuel Kant sets forth human reason as the decisive norm for biblical interpretation much more forcefully in his 1798 publication "Der Streit der Fakultäten" (*Kant's gesammelte Schriften* Band VII, [Berlin: Druck und Verlag Georg Reimer, 1917], 36–75), where he pleads that revelation is only acceptable where it is in harmony with reason. The rare publication can be found online at Gallica, https://gallica.bnf.fr/ark:/12148/bpt6k25542w/f46.image (accessed August 10, 2020).

[16] The evolutionary model is so dominant and all-powerful that it often does not tolerate any alternative explanation of the origin of life in the public square.

[17] Robert Grant, *The Bible in the Church: A Short History of Interpretation* (New York: Macmillan, 1960), 105–108.

[18] Alvin Plantinga, "Two (or More) Kinds of Scripture Scholarship," in "*Behind the Text*": *History and Biblical Interpretation*, ed. Craig Bartholomew et al. (Grand Rapids, MI: Zondervan, 2003), 27. See also Edgar Krentz, *The Historical-Critical Method* (Philadelphia, PA: Fortress, 1975), 16–30. Gerald A. Klingbeil, "Historical Criticism," in *Dictionary of the Old Testament: Pentateuch*, ed. T. Desmond Alexander and David W. Baker (Downers Grove, IL: InterVarsity Press, 2003), 401, points out that "*Historical criticism* is a generic term describing differing methods of approaching an ancient text, all of which share common philosophical and methodological presuppositions developed during the period of enlightenment in the seventeenth century onward." Similarly,

Thus, historical criticism "introduced into biblical interpretation a new method based on a secular understanding of history"[19] that "embodies substantial discontinuities with the Reformers, and the Christian tradition generally, on issues such as the meaning of the literal sense, the place of tradition in interpretation, the goal of reading Scripture, and the role of the Holy Spirit in understanding."[20] Everything had to be explained within the immanent, closed nexus of naturalistic history. Historical criticism functions with a number of presuppositions that determine its principles and result in various methods of interpretation. Its classic expression was formulated by Ernst Troeltsch (1865–1923), who contrasted the new "scientific" method with the dogmatic method that was practiced widely until the twentieth century.[21] In contrast to a supernatural explanation of Scripture through divine inspiration, the Bible was now interpreted as any other book on the basis of three foundational principles: 1) the principle of criticism, 2) the principle of analogy, and 3) the principle of correlation.[22]

The Principle of Criticism

The first principle of the historical-critical approach mentioned by Troeltsch is the principle of criticism. This principle of criticism is not

---

Craig G. Bartholomew, *Introducing Biblical Hermeneutics: A Comprehensive Framework for Hearing God in Scripture* (Grand Rapids, MI: Baker, 2015)), 11, states that these methods have regularly been "applied to the Bible with the in-built assumption that God can neither act nor speak" in Scripture or anywhere else.

[19] Krentz, 1; see also 24.

[20] Richard N. Soulen and R. Kendall Soulen, "Historical Criticism," in *Handbook of Biblical Criticism*, 3rd ed. (Louisville, KY: Westminster, 2001), 79.

[21] On the lasting influence of Ernst Troeltsch on modern and even postmodern theology, Roy Harrisville states, "His [Troeltsch's] definition of the task and method of criticism, but above all his conclusions and his guarantee, spawn of eclecticism, would live to outlive their assailants into the end of the twentieth century. There are signs everywhere that it may be Troeltsch, the romantic historicist, who speaks for religion in the years to come" (Roy A. Harrisville and Walter Sundberg, *The Bible in Modern Culture: Theology and Historical-Critical Method from Spinoza to Käsemann* [Grand Rapids, MI: Eerdmans, 1995], 179). See also Paul Wells, "The Lasting Significance of Ernst Troeltsch's Critical Moment," *Westminster Theological Journal* 72/2 (2010): 199–217.

[22] Cf. Ernst Troeltsch, "Über historische und dogmatische Methode in der Theologie," in *Gesammelte Schriften*, vol. 2 (Aalen: Scientia Verlag, 1962), 729–753; see also Ernst Troeltsch, "Historiography," in *Encyclopaedia of Religion and Ethics*, ed. James Hastings, John A. Selbie, and Louis H. Gray, vol. 6 (Edinburgh: T&T Clark, 1908–1926), 716–723. Soulen and Soulen, "Historical-Critical Method [The]," in *Handbook of Biblical Criticism*, 78, point out that "the historical-critical method rests on presuppositions whose validity cannot be demonstrated by historical investigation alone and that are finally philosophical and theological in character."

just the exercise of critical discernment[23] in the sense of evaluating and analyzing the biblical text. It is not a neutral approach in the analysis and interpretation of Scripture. The principle of criticism has a definite and decisively negative connotation, as it criticizes the Bible unfavorably.[24] This negative character was clearly perceived by Troeltsch himself,[25] and others have perceptively observed the negative result of this kind of criticism in subsequent history.[26] This critical method is not neutral, but has inherent presuppositions that call into question the sacred and authoritative status of Scripture.[27] It works on several assumptions that are foundational to historical criticism. The criticism of the written text is founded not just on careful textual, grammatical, or lexical evidence, but on rational principles where supernatural revelation is categorically excluded as an explanation. According to Collins, "one of the assumptions of historical criticism is that texts are human products."[28] The principle of criticism includes the idea that the text is approached from a strong rational and naturalistic perspective, where the possibility of miracles and divine intervention in history is rejected from the outset. This exclusion of God in the critical inquiry of the Bible is often called

---

[23] Contra Amy Balogh and Douglas Mangum, "Introducing Biblical Criticism," in Mangum and Balogh, *Social and Historical Approaches to the Bible*, 4–7; and Fitzmyer, 69.

[24] According to Gerhard Ebeling, "The Significance of the Historical Critical Method for Church and Theology in Protestantism," in *Word and Faith* [London and Philadelphia: 1963], 42–43, as quoted in Klaus Scholder, *The Birth of Modern Critical Theology: Origins and Problems of Biblical Criticism in the Seventeenth Century* (London: SCM Press, 1990), 2, "historical criticism is more than 'lively historical interest' . . . it is not concerned with the greatest possible refinement of the philological methods, but with subjecting the tradition to critical examination on the basis of new principles of thought." What does this criticism inevitably entail? According to Ebeling, "it [this critical method] is—not just, say, where it oversteps its legitimate limits, but by its very nature—bound up with criticism of content" (Ebeling, 42, as quoted in Scholder, 2). Thus, criticism inevitably and by its very nature leads to a criticism of the content of the Bible.

[25] Troeltsch, "Ueber historische und dogmatische Methode in der Theologie," 731–732. According to Troeltsch, this criticism corrodes and disintegrates a thousand times the traditional biblical message and changes it, making it only probable but never certain (731). According to Troeltsch, this affects everything (734) and relativizes everything (737).

[26] See more recently Berger and Wilckens, among many others.

[27] Contra Balogh and Mangum, "Introducing Biblical Criticism," 4–7; and Fitzmyer, 69, who claims that the method is per se neutral and contra Christopher M. Hays, "Toward a Faithful Criticism," in *Evangelical Faith and the Challenge of Historical Criticism*, ed. Christopher M. Hays and Christopher B. Ansberry (Grand Rapids, MI: Baker Academic, 2013), 1–23, who calls for "faithful criticism" and "critical faith" (23).

[28] Collins, 6.

"metaphysical naturalism."[29] "For the sake of scientific endeavor and responsible historical inquiry, the world must be *regarded* as if it were a closed system of natural causes."[30] According to Troeltsch, this affects the entire relationship to all transmission and tradition and results in the relativity of all knowledge. It makes all of our conclusions tentative. We no longer can state biblical things with certainty—only with a greater or lesser degree of probability.[31] Therefore, all our conclusions will always be open to revision.[32] The principle of historical criticism not only means that scholarship is an ongoing process, but that "its results are always provisional and never final."[33] This is very different from a general openness to learn new things. It means, as has been observed, that

> absolute certainty is never available. . . . This element of uncertainty in biblical scholarship has always been especially unsettling for church authorities and for traditional theologians, more so even than heretical conclusions, because it implies that anything we believe may be subject to revision in light of new evidence and undercuts any idea of unchangeable revealed truth.[34]

Furthermore, the principle of criticism means that when something is not documented or proven externally, the Bible is not given the benefit of the doubt, but the reliability and trustworthiness of Scripture is questioned instead. It is on the basis of the principle of analogy that the degree of probability of a biblical statement is critically determined. This leads us to the second foundational principle of historical criticism: the principle of analogy.

---

[29] Murray Ray, "Theological Interpretation and Historical Criticism," in *A Manifesto for Theological Interpretation*, ed. Craig G. Bartholomew and Heath A. Thomas (Grands Rapids, MI: Baker Academic, 2016), 97. Klein, Blomberg, and Hubbard, 99, point out that "the historical-critical method presupposed a naturalistic worldview that explained everything in terms of natural laws and excluded the possibility of supernatural intervention."

[30] Ray, 98.

[31] "The principle of *criticism* affirms that judgments about the past are not to be classified simply as true or false but are to be seen as claiming only a greater or lesser degree of probability" (Edgar V. McKnight, *Post-Modern Use of the Bible: The Emergence of Reader-Oriented Criticism* [Nashville, TN: Abingdon, 1988], 47, emphasis original).

[32] Troeltsch, "Ueber historische und dogmatische Methode in der Theologie," 731; and similarly Van A. Harvey, *The Historian and the Believer* (New York: Macmillan, 1966), 14.

[33] Collins, 6.

[34] Ibid.

The Principle of Analogy

The principle of analogy refers to "the fundamental homogeneity of all historical events."[35] The past is known through human experiences in the present, which are not radically dissimilar to the experiences of past persons.[36] Thus, the present becomes the key to our knowledge of the past. Based on the identity of all historical happenings in human experience, the principle of analogy virtually gains the power of omnipotence.[37] According to Troeltsch, this principle of analogy is all-pervasive. It cannot be restricted to a single aspect of theology, but rather affects the entire methodology and way of thinking. It is like a small piece of leaven (yeast) that quickly permeates the entire dough.[38] If you give it your finger you will have to give your whole hand.[39] When the present human experience serves as the key to what could have taken place in the past, any supernatural explanation and involvement is excluded categorically and the singularity of certain supernatural events in history becomes obliterated.[40] Furthermore, since basically any event beyond

---

[35] Troeltsch, "Ueber historische und dogmatische Methode in der Theologie," 732.

[36] V. A. Harvey, *The Historian and the Believer*, 14.

[37] Troeltsch, "Ueber historische und dogmatische Methode in der Theologie," 732. Gerhard F. Hasel, *Biblical Interpretation Today* (Washington, DC: Biblical Research Institute, 1985), 76, points out that "Troeltsch and his followers replace the omnipotence of God in His words and acts with the omnipotence of the modern historian who interprets the past by means of an omnipotent principle of analogy."

[38] Eta Linnemann, a reputable former historical-critical scholar who later had a conversion experience and renounced the atheistic presuppositions of the historical-critical method, stated that "one can no more be a *little* historical-critical than a *little* pregnant (Eta Linnemann, *Historical Criticism of the Bible: Methodology or Ideology?* [Grand Rapids, MI: Baker, 1990], 123). For a balanced evaluation of Eta Linnemann and her contribution to theology, including some Adventist reactions to her, see Robert W. Yarbrough, "Eta Linnemann: Friend or Foe of Scholarship?," *Master's Seminary Journal* 8/2 (1997): 161–189.

[39] Troeltsch, "Ueber historische und dogmatische Methode in der Theologie," 734.

[40] Even in Evangelical and Adventist scholarship, the impact of Troeltsch's methods are far more pervasive than is often admitted. It has been said that "even in evangelical scholarship, notions of continuous history, critical analysis, and the matrix of the present as we know it leads to the relativization of the specific content of the Bible. If the central events of incarnation and resurrection are excepted from the process, this approach is applied to large tracts of Bible history, and to questions about its content and authorship" (Wells, 213–214). For some Evangelical examples, see Peter Enns, *Inspiration and Incarnation: Evangelicals and the Problem of the Old Testament* (Grand Rapids, MI: Baker Academic, 2005); Kenton L. Sparks, *God's Word in Human Words: An Evangelical Appropriation of Critical Biblical Scholarship* (Grand Rapids, MI: Baker Academic, 2008); John H. Walton and D. Brent Sandy, *The Lost World of Scripture: Ancient Literary Culture and Biblical Authority* (Downers Grove, IL: InterVarsity, 2013); and Hays and Ansberry, *Evangelical Faith*; for an Adventist example, see Jerry Gladson, *Out of Adventism: A Theologian's Journey* (Eugene, OR: Wipf and Stock, 2017).

our own culture and experience would be excluded, such an approach becomes very ethnocentric. No wonder that even Troeltsch himself points out that such an approach has something devilish about it.[41]

The Principle of Correlation

The third principle of historical criticism is the principle of correlation. It states "that the phenomena of man's historical life are so related and interdependent that no radical change can take place at any one point in the historical nexus without affecting a change in all that immediately surrounds it."[42] This means that any historical event or text has to be understood and explained solely in terms of its immanent-historical context. No explanation of a supernatural intervention as a principle of historical explanation can be used.[43] Instead, the whole historical process is a closed unit, which means that everything that is stated in Scripture is conditioned by human forces and has to be explained by this-worldly (i.e., immanent) factors. Thus, there cannot be any supernatural miracles[44] and no event can be regarded as a final revelation or as absolute since every manifestation of truth is relative and historically conditioned. The concomitant antisupernaturalism of the principle of correlation presupposes that the origin and content of the Bible has to be explained on purely innerhistorical grounds, where the Bible becomes a document of the past—that is, a thoroughly human product—and needs to be treated like any other document. It can be understood only in its immediate historical and cultural context.

Various Interpretive Methods of Historical Criticism

When these principles of historical criticism were applied to the interpretation of Scripture, a variety of different methods evolved, attempting to explain the transmission of the biblical text, its development,

---

[41] Troeltsch, "Ueber historische und dogmatische Methode in der Theologie," 734. More recently, other theologians have seen similar challenges in this method. Cf. Oeming; Berger; and Wilckens.

[42] Troeltsch, "Ueber historische und dogmatische Methode in der Theologie," 733.

[43] According to V. A. Harvey, *The Historian and the Believer*, 29–30, for Troeltsch this meant "(1) that no critical historian could make use of supernatural intervention as a principle of historical explanation because this shattered the continuity of the causal nexus, and (2) that no event could be regarded as a final revelation of the absolute spirit, since every manifestation of truth and value was relative and historically conditioned."

[44] Cf. the helpful analysis in Gerhard F. Hasel, *Biblical Interpretation Today*, 73–75.

and origins,[45] and thereby its meaning. These methods included source criticism,[46] form criticism,[47] redaction criticism,[48] and variations of other criticisms that sometimes may be at odds with each other.[49] "What these methods have in common is a general agreement that texts should be interpreted in their historical contexts, in light of the literary and cultural conventions of their time."[50] It is positive to acknowledge that biblical texts have a historical context that needs to be taken into consideration when we want to understand it properly. However, by denying the divine inspiration of the biblical books and by questioning whether the biblical writers traditionally associated with the writing of various books of Scripture actually wrote them, the Bible became a product that is historically conditioned by purely immanent cause and effect relations. Instead of divinely inspired writers, the composition of the biblical material had to be explained through long processes of transmission, composition, and redaction before the final biblical text

---

[45] Richard E. Burnett, "Historical Criticism," in *Dictionary for Theological Interpretation of the Bible*, ed. Kevin J. Vanhoozer (Grand Rapids, MI: Baker Academic, 2005), 290.

[46] Source criticism is the oldest of modern critical methods. It is concerned with discovering the sources an author has used in producing his work. Source criticism goes *behind* a writer of a given text to an earlier stage of writing. See C. M. Tuckett, "Source Criticism," in *A Dictionary of Biblical Interpretation*, ed. R. J. Coggins and J. C. Houlden (Philadelphia, PA: Trinity Press, 1990), 646–648. See also Soulen and Soulen, "Source Criticism," in *Handbook of Biblical Criticism*, 178; Johannes P. Floss, "Form, Source, and Redaction Criticism," in Rogerson and Lieu, 603–607; and Paul L. Redditt, "Source Criticism," in Vanhoozer, *Dictionary for Theological Interpretation of the Bible*, 761–763.

[47] Form criticism analyzes the oral tradition underlying the written biblical material and is concerned with the classification of typical structures of oral tradition history and their relation to social settings in life (German: *Sitz-im-Leben*). See John Muddiman, "Form Criticism," in Coggins and Houlden, 240–243. On form criticism or *Formgeschichte*, see Edgar V. McKnight, *What Is Form Criticism?* (Philadelphia, PA: Fortress, 1989); Gene M. Tucker, *Form Criticism of the Old Testament* (Philadelphia, PA: Fortress, 1985); Klaus Koch, *Was ist Formgeschichte: Neue Wege der Bibelexegese* (Neukirchen-Vluyn: Neukirchener Verlag, 1974); and Floss, 591–603.

[48] "Redaction Criticism (fr[om] [the] Ger[man] Redaktionsgeschichte) is a method of biblical criticism that seeks to lay bare the historical and theological perspectives of a biblical writer by analyzing the editorial (redactional) and compositional techniques and interpretations employed in shaping and framing the written and/or oral traditions at hand" (Soulen and Soulen, "Redaction Criticism," in *Handbook of Biblical Criticism*, 158). See also Norman Perrin, *What Is Redaction Criticism* (Philadelphia, PA: Fortress, 1984); C. M. Tuckett, "Redaction Criticism," in Coggins and Houlden, 580–582; and Floss, 608–611.

[49] So James Barr, *History and Ideology in the Old Testament* (Oxford: Oxford University Press, 2000), 32–58; and more recently Collins, 4. See also Steven L. McKenzie and Stephen R. Haynes, eds., *To Each Its Own Meaning: An Introduction to Biblical Criticism and Their Application* (Louisville, KY: Westminster John Knox, 1993), esp. 11–99; and Linnemann, 130–141.

[50] Collins, 4. "Historical criticism seeks to answer a basic question: to what historical circumstances does this text refer, and out of what historical circumstances did it emerge?" (Burnett, 290).

emerged. Consequently, the Bible was rendered historically relative and not universally binding. This historical reconstruction of the origin of Scripture led to a disunity of the Bible. Instead of seeing a unity in the biblical material, based on the divine inspiration of Scripture, these methods try to delineate the different and often conflicting sources that brought about the biblical text and attempt to reconstruct the history *behind* the biblical text in order to explain its genesis and meaning. Thus, it has been observed that historical critics tend to "focus on what lies *behind* the text rather than the text itself."[51] Because historical criticism assumes the autonomy of the interpreter, it is not constrained by any external authority and does not work within the bounds of church traditions. It is therefore no surprise that some of its findings were critical of some dogmas of the church and led to a new evaluation of the biblical meanings. While the historical-critical interpretation of the biblical material often questioned traditional interpretations and even undermined the certainty of the biblical message, it nevertheless assumed a definite meaning and historical intent of the text. This was positive and was possible because an "assumption for biblical criticism is that texts have an inherent and objective meaning that can be discerned."[52] This distinguishes historical-critical approaches from postmodern approaches that are more reader oriented in which there is no definite meaning of the text apart from the reader who "constructs" it.

The fact that *within* historical criticism many of its "assured results" have been challenged could be seen as an indication that the method has been significantly discredited. But we should heed the words of J. W. Rogerson, who points out, "It must be stressed that these questionings of the old scholarly conclusions do not amount to a rejection of the historical criticism. *They are refinements that presuppose it.*"[53] Thus, the principles of historical criticism continue to be alive in much of current

---

[51] Burnett, 291. This "atomistic occupation with individual parts of the biblical witness, especially the various historical-psychological circumstances from which it arose, contributed to confusion over what the biblical witness as a whole is about: it's actual content, subject matter, and theme" (ibid.). Wolfhart Pannenberg, "The Crisis of the Scripture Principle," in *Basic Questions in Theology*, vol. 1 (Philadelphia, PA: Fortress, 1983), 7, points out that contrary to Martin Luther, "the person and history of Jesus is no longer to be found in the texts themselves but must be discovered behind them. Thus, the question arose for theology as to which is now to be considered theologically normative, the biblical texts themselves or the history to discovered behind them."

[52] Balogh and Mangum, "Introducing Biblical Criticism," 3.

[53] J. W. Rogerson, "Historical Criticism and the Authority of the Bible," in Rogerson and Lieu, 843, emphasis added. Similarly, Oeming, 46, maintains that despite its deficits, the historical-critical method will remain decisive for biblical scholarship and is indispensable and irreplaceable.

biblical scholarship.[54] The question is whether the principles of historical criticism can be modified and used moderately when combined with faith.

Modified Historical Criticism

Since the emergence of the historical-critical method as the leading method of biblical interpretation, there have been several attempts to modify the method to make it more palatable, especially for Evangelical scholars who also work from a faith perspective. Several factors can contribute to a desire to use a modified use of the historical-critical method. The widespread use of this method in academic settings around the world and the fact that it has become the accepted scholarly method and academic standard in most universities makes it attractive for some who want to use it at least to some degree—and even more so when one wants to participate in the scholarly discussion and be accepted in the scholarly community. On the other hand, the devasting consequences of the historical-critical method and mindset on the spiritual lives of countless students and practitioners made it clear that, without some modification, the critical method has rather disastrous effects on the Christian faith. Among other things, it calls into question the status of the Bible as a sacred and authoritative source for theology. Thus, it is understandable that some theologians have suggested a modified use of the historical-critical method that is more moderate in its critical conclusions and even claims to be open to faith, while using the same historical-critical methods of investigation. Those who propose such a modification usually maintain that the historical-critical method is a neutral method that is indispensable because the Bible deals with history. If the historical method is used correctly, they claim, it is a tool that can be a blessing. However, when used incorrectly it can be a curse.[55] Especially among Evangelical scholars, who accept the idea

---

[54] An illustration of this fact for Old Testament scholarship can be seen in Gerald A. Klingbeil, "Of Pillars and Foundations: Seven Thesis Statements Concering the Hermeneutics of the Pentateuch," *DavarLogos* 18/2 (2019): 1-30.

[55] So recently Balogh and Mangum, "Introducing Biblical Criticism," 1–20; Hays, "Towards a Faithful Criticism," 1–23; Christopher B. Ansberry and Christopher M. Hays, "Faithful Criticism and a Critical Faith," in Hays and Ansberry, *Evangelical Faith*, 204–222; David Crump, *Encountering Jesus, Encountering Scripture: Reading the Bible Critically in Faith* (Grand Rapids, MI: Eerdmans, 2013); Roy A. Harrisville, *Pandora's Box Opened: An Examination and Defense of Historical-Critical Method and Its Master Practitioners* (Grand Rapids, MI: Eerdmans, 2014); Sparks; Enns, *Inspiration and Incarnation*; Balogh and Mangum, "Introducing Biblical Criticism"; and Zimmer. From a Roman Catholic perspective, similarly Fitzmyer; and Christian Smith,

of divine inspiration, an intense debate has gone on for decades about whether historical-critical methods are appropriate for Evangelical Christian scholars.[56] Some Evangelical scholars have begun to use the

---

The Bible Made Impossible: Why Biblicism Is Not a Truly Evangelical Reading of Scripture (Grand Rapids, MI: Brazos Press, 2011). For a helpful overview of the significant current discussion, see D. A. Carson, "The Many Facets of the Current Debate," in *The Enduring Authority of the Christian Scriptures*, ed. D. A. Carson (Grand Rapids, MI: Eerdmans, 2016), 3–40.

[56] This issue came to the forefront of Evangelical scholarship in the 1970s and 1980s when many articles appeared in the *Journal of the Evangelical Theological Society*, arguing for or against the adoption of historical-critical methods. Some exemplary references shall suffice to illustrate this debate. See Alan F. Johnson, "The Historical-Critical Method: Egyptian Gold or Pagan Precipice?," *Journal of the Evangelical Theological Society* 26 (1983): 3–15. Another survey of the debate can be found in Grant R. Osborne, "Round Four: The Redaction Debate Continues," *Journal of the Evangelical Theological Society* 28 (1985): 399–410. See also Robert L. Thomas, "Historical Criticism and the Evangelical: Another View," *Journal of the Evangelical Theological Society* 43 (2000): 97–111; and Robert W. Yarbrough, "Should Evangelicals Embrace Historical Criticism? The Hays-Ansberry Proposal," *Themelios* 39/1 (2014): 37–52. There are prominent Evangelical scholars who criticize the use of the historical-critical method because of its antisupernatural and anti-Bible presuppositions; see Norman L. Geisler, *Systematic Theology*, vol. 1, *Introduction, Bible* (Minneapolis, MN: Bethany, 2002), 315–349; Geisler, "Beware of Philosophy: A Warning to Biblical Scholars," *Journal of the Evangelical Theological Society* 42/1 (1999): 3–19; Noel Weeks, *The Sufficiency of Scripture* (Carlisle, PA: Banner of Truth Trust, 1988); Gerhard Maier, *Biblical Hermeneutics* (Wheaton, IL: Crossway Books, 1994); Gregory K. Beale, *The Erosion of Inerrancy in Evangelicalism: Responding to New Challenges to Biblical Authority* (Wheaton, IL: Crossway, 2008); and the contributions in Carson, *Enduring Authority*; or the earlier classic treatments in J. I. Packer, *"Fundamentalism" and the Word of God* (1958; Grand Rapids, MI: Eerdmans, 1990); Edward J. Young, *Thy Word Is Truth* (1957; Grand Rapids, MI: Eerdmans, 1984); and Gresham J. Machen, *Christianity and Liberalism* (1923; Grand Rapids, MI: Eerdmans 2009), to name but some. There are others who claim that biblical criticism is useful, such as Millard J. Erickson, *Christian Theology*, 2nd ed. (Grand Rapids, MI: Baker Academic, 1998), 114; and more recently Balogh and Mangum, "Introducing Biblical Criticism" and others. A similar debate has surfaced in Adventist circles where a number of Adventist scholars have suggested using the historical-critical method or a modified version of it for Adventist biblical interpretation. A helpful historical overview of this development with regards to the issue of inspiration can be found in Alberto R. Timm, "A History of Seventh-day Adventist Views on Biblical and Prophetic Inspiration (1844-2000)," *Journal of the Adventist Theological Society* 10/1–2 (1999): 486–541. See also the discussion in Robert K. McIver, "The Historical-Critical Method: The Adventist Debate," *Ministry*, March 1996, 15-16; and Roy Gane, "An Approach to the Historical-Critical Method," *Ministry*, March 1999, 5–9, who seem to favor a modified use of it, and other articles in the same issue. Larry G. Herr, "Genesis One in Historical-Critical Perspective," *Spectrum*, December 1982, 51, states that "the historical-critical method of Bible study, used properly, can be a valid and powerful tool for Seventh-day Adventists." John C. Brunt, "A Parable of Jesus as a Clue to Biblical Interpretation," *Spectrum*, December 1982, 42, claims in a sweeping statement, "Indeed, virtually all Adventist exegates [sic] of Scripture do use historical-critical methodology, even if they are not willing to use the term. The historical-critical method deserves a place in the armamentarium of Adventists who are serious about understanding their Bibles." That such a sweeping statement is a gross overstatement and reflects

historical-critical method moderately. Because they still uphold some typical Evangelical convictions, not all of their critical investigations have had the same drastic conclusions and negative effects that are part and parcel of the intellectual presuppositions and philosophical assumptions of historical criticism.[57] The crucial question remains, however, as to whether such a moderate use, which tries to be open to the idea of transcendence and faith, can really be harmonized with the worldview out of which the critical method arose and whether a modified use is consistent with its critical assumptions.[58] The decisive question has been: "is

---

perhaps more the wishful thinking of the author than the actual reality among Adventist scholars is seen in the official statement of the Seventh-day Adventist Church, "Methods of Bible Study," (voted by the General Conference Committee in Annual Council, Rio de Janeiro, October 12, 1986) https://www.adventistbiblicalresearch.org/materials/bible-interpretation-hermeneutics/methods-bible-study (accessed August 12, 2020), and also the appendix in this volume, 463-473, which specifically rejects historical-critical methodology and even a modified use of it, and by countless respected Adventists who have decisively rejected any use of historical-critical methods. See discussions in the *Journal of the Adventist Theological Society*, and here exemplarily: Richard M. Davidson, "The Authority of Scripture: A Personal Pilgrimage," *Journal of the Adventist Theological Society* 1/1 (1990): 41; and Richard M. Davidson, "Biblical Interpretation," in *Handbook of Seventh-day Adventist Theology*, ed., Raul Dederen (Hagerstown, MD: Review and Herald, 2000), 58–104.

[57] Yet even with a moderate use of the historical-critical method, several key biblical teachings were inevitably called into question. See the discussion in Hays and Ansberry, *Evangelical Faith*, which specifically deals with the historicity of Adam and the fall, the fact or fiction of the exodus, problems with prophecy and the canon, as well as the historical Jesus and the Pauline authorship of the epistles. See also the critical interaction with critical scholarship among Evangelicals in Vern Sheridan Poythress, *Inerrancy and Worldview: Answering Modern Challenges to the Bible* (Wheaton, IL Crossway, 2012); Poythress, *Inerrancy and the Gospels: A God-Centered Approach to the Challenge of Harmonization* (Wheaton, IL: Crossway, 2012); Beale; and D. A. Carson, "The Many Facets of the Current Discussion," 3–40.

[58] Reventlow, *Authority of the Bible*, 2, observes that the historical-critical method as typically employed "cannot be detached from a quite specific understanding of the world and of reality." Similarly Scholder, 2–3. Scholder makes clear that what he is "concerned with here is not a series of individual critical observations. It is an intellectual process which ended with the dethroning of the Bible as the authoritative source of all human knowledge and understanding" (ibid., 7–8).

What complicates the matter is that a moderate or modified historical-critical stance is often difficult to discern and even more difficult to figure out because several of those who practice it have made some positive contributions to the church and scholarship. This is aptly pointed out by Helge Stadelmann, *Evangelikales Schriftverständnis: Die Bibel verstehen – der Bibel vertrauen* (Hammerbrücke: Jota, 2005), 73–91, esp. 75, with several illustrations from well-known Evangelical scholars. Stadelmann points out, however, that when foundational biblical teachings are affected, the problem becomes more obvious. In other areas radical-critical theologians often succeed in concealing their efforts so skillfully that ordinary church members often do not realize what is happening (ibid., 74). Similarly, Ángel M. Rodríguez, "The Use of the Modified Version of the Historical-Critical Approach by Adventist Scholars," in *Understanding Scripture: An Adventist Approach*, ed. George W. Reid (Silver Spring, MD: Biblical Research Institute, 2005), 341, states, "One of the problems we face in our task is that those who argue for the modified

it possible to use the historical-critical method without being influenced by its critical presuppositions?"[59] To this we add the following questions: Will a modified use of the historical-critical method also lead one to criticizing the content of Scripture? Will it result in content criticism (*Sachkritik*) of the Bible?

There is one scholar who has prominently tried to modify the historical-critical method, perhaps more than anyone else in Protestant scholarship, Peter Stuhlmacher at the University of Tübingen. In his book *Vom Verstehen des Neuen Testaments: Eine Hermeneutik*[60] he promoted a detailed hermeneutic of consent with the biblical text. In addition to the three principles delineated by Troeltsch ("criticism," "analogy," and "correlation"),[61] Stuhlmacher suggested a fourth principle that he called a "hermeneutic of consent" or of sympathetic understanding (*Einverständnis*),[62] in which a certain "openness to an encounter with the truth of God coming to us from out of transcendence" is added.[63] Through the power of this fourth principle, we may regain something that is without analogy and cannot be found in historical investigation alone. Thus, Stuhlmacher did not allow the historical-critical approach to carry the full critical weight in biblical study.[64] Rather than limiting the meaning and significance of the biblical text to those

---

system have not stated clearly the modifications they are making to the historical-critical method." While Rodriguez acknowledges that some who use a modified version of the historical-critical method mean it well and "are not attempting to destroy the church and/or its message. That commitment should be acknowledged" (343); however, we have to realize that even good intentions do not always lead to proper and correct conclusions and sometimes even end up criticizing some of the content of the Bible.

[59] Rodriguez, 341. It has been pointed out that "once history is thought to be an autonomous realm with its own set of methods for establishing intelligibility or meaning, then scholars must not only figure out which pieces of information will count as evidence; they must also develop ways of ordering and interpreting the evidence" (Gorman, 209).

[60] Peter Stuhlmacher, *Vom Verstehen des Neuen Testaments: Eine Hermeneutik* (Göttingen: Vandenhoeck & Ruprecht, 1986).

[61] Peter Stuhlmacher, *Historical Criticism and Theological Interpretation of Scripture* (Philadelphia: PA: Fortress, 1977), 44–46.

[62] Such a hermeneutic of sympathetic understanding "seeks first and foremost to read the Scriptures within the historical and theological context in which they were written, with empathy, before submitting them to an external criticism concerning their content (*Sachkritik*)" (Scott Hafemann, "The 'Righteousness of God': An Introduction to the Theological and Historical Foundation of Peter Stuhlmacher's Biblical Theology of the New Testament," in *How to Do Biblical Theology*, ed. Dikran Y. Hadidian, Princeton Theological Monograph Series 38 (Eugene, OR: Pickwick, 1995), xxxii.

[63] Stuhlmacher, *Historical Criticism*, 89.

[64] E. V. McKnight, *Post-Modern Use of the Bible*, 83.

meanings that historical criticism could recover, Stuhlmacher tried to place the interpretation of the text in the total canonical context of the Bible and developed an interpretation of the biblical text that "is undertaken in light of the history of the interpretation and influence of the text and of the mature dogma resulting from the ecclesiastical interpretation of Scripture."[65] Stuhlmacher did not think it an option to abandon all historical-critical investigation of Scripture, but sought to temper it with an openness to transcendence and a careful listening to the reception of the text. While it is commendable to see that there is a certain openness to transcendence, even a modified critical method still remains critical, as Stuhlmacher himself clearly admits. According to him, "content criticism (Sachkritik) of the biblical texts is a nonnegotiable element of all theological interpretation."[66]

Stuhlmacher's proposal has triggered significant objections. It has been pointed out that "for those trained in the rigorous application of historical criticism, the modified historical approach [of Stuhlmacher] was not satisfying. . . . The reformulation of the historical method was in effect a repudiation of the method as accepted and practiced by New Testament historians."[67] It therefore comes as no surprise that Stuhlmacher later abandoned his fourth principle of consent, due to the criticism received from his colleagues at the University of Tübingen, and returned back to the classical three principles elucidated by Troeltsch. In his monumental two-volume work on the biblical theology of the New Testament,[68] Stuhlmacher acknowledges that he carefully listened to the arguments and objections of his critics and reconsidered his approach.[69] The conclusion from these considerations are remarkable: according to Stuhlmacher, in order to correctly understand the texts of the Bible in their own language,

> we currently have only one scientifically approved and tested method available, the *historical-critical method*, which is used in all historical sciences. In practice it consists of an entire ensemble

---

[65] Stuhlmacher, *Vom Verstehen*, 241–242, as quoted in English in E. V. McKnight, *Post-Modern Use of the Bible*, 84.

[66] Stuhlmacher, *Vom Verstehen*, 247, Frank M. Hasel's translation. Maier, 302, points out that that theological content criticism of Scripture by its very nature distinguishes between time-conditioned statements and what is abidingly valid and sacrifices part of what the Bible contains.

[67] E. V. McKnight, *Post-Modern Use of the Bible*, 86–87.

[68] Peter Stuhlmacher, *Biblische Theologie des Neuen Testaments*, vol. 1, *Grundlegung von Jesus zu Paulus* (Göttingen: Vandenhoeck & Ruprecht, 1992).

[69] Ibid., 1:x.

> of individual methods, which are embedded in a general procedure that follow specific basic principles. Ernst Troeltsch has called it "criticism", "analogy" and "correlation."[70]

Thus, Stuhlmacher himself recognizes that a modified use of the historical-critical method is not consistent with its presuppositions and will not work.

With regard to a moderate use of historical criticism, Gerhard Maier raises the following concern: "The question arises whether a movement so deeply stamped by history as historical criticism can really be overcome by a 'moderate' revision."[71] Indeed, as we have seen with Stuhlmacher and Linnemann,[72] the historical-critical method is not neutral and cannot be separated from its philosophical presuppositions. The one who starts working on its premises inevitably will engage in some form of content criticism of Scripture. Furthermore, while the inspiration of Scripture is being pondered by some who engage in moderate criticism, it has been pointed out that "moderate criticism, however, does not go beyond personal inspiration," which makes "the content of biblical statements . . . quite decidedly subordinate to content criticism (Sachkritik)."[73]

---

[70] Stuhlmacher, *Biblische Theologie des Neuen Testaments*, 1:10, Frank M. Hasel's translation. The original quote by Stuhlmacher reads: "Um dieses Interpretationsziel zu erreichen, steht uns z.Z. nur ein einziges wissenschaftlich bewährtes Verfahren zur Verfügung, die von allen historischen Wissenschaften angewandte *historisch-kritische Methode*. In der Praxis besteht sie aus einem ganzen Ensemble von Einzelmethoden, die in ein Gesamtverfahren eingebettet sind, das bestimmten Grundsätzen folgt. Ernst Troeltsch hat sie 'Kritik', 'Analogie' und 'Korrelation' genannt."

[71] Maier, 370.

[72] Eta Linnemann, a former devout practitioner of historical criticism who has turned away from historical-critical theology, states, "And whoever gets involved in historical-critical theology will end up in a similar situation. One can no more be a *little* historical-critical than a *little* pregnant" (Linnemann, 123).

[73] Maier, 371. This can also be seen in the Adventist context, with Alden Thompson, *Inspiration: Hard Questions, Honest Answers* (Hagerstown, MD: Review and Herald, 1991), 144–145, favoring a model of personal inspiration where the text of Scripture is not inspired and hence subject to "error," "mistake," "contradiction," and "differences." This leads Thompson to criticize the content of Scripture when it comes to the number of people in the exodus; the global nature of the flood; the historical reliability of statements in Samuel, Chronicles and Kings; and the trustworthiness of New Testament writers quoting the Old Testament, where "one inspired writer cannot be the final interpreter of another" (205). He also postulates a law pyramid (115) where some laws are more important than others, which leads to a consequential ethic. For a theological response to Alden Thompson's views that affect the interpretation of Scripture, see the discussion in Frank Holbrook and Leo Van Dolson, eds., *Issues in Revelation and Inspiration* (Berrien Springs, MI: Adventist Theological Society, 1992). Alden Thompson republished his book in 2016 (Alden Thompson, *Inspiration: Hard Questions, Honest Answers* [Gonzales, FL: Energion, 2016]). He added a bridge chapter for non-Adventist readers to make the book more appealing to non-

This means that insofar as moderate criticism "exercises content criticism, it cannot dispense with a second authority alongside Scripture."[74] It also has implications for the unity of Scripture, for wherever "content criticism is regarded as necessary, the unity of Scripture is lost."[75] Without the unity of Scripture, the Bible can no longer be the theological norm that distinguishes truth from error, and one can no longer compare Scripture with Scripture. The Bible has effectively lost its ability to interpret itself.

These significant problems with the historical-critical method, even when used only moderately, have led the Seventh-day Adventist Church to officially state unambiguously that even a modified use of the historical-critical method is unacceptable for Seventh-day Adventist scholars.

> In recent decades the most prominent method in biblical studies has been known as the historical-critical method. Scholars who use this method, as classically formulated, operate on the basis of presuppositions which, prior to studying the biblical text, reject the reliability of accounts of miracles and other supernatural events narrated in the Bible. *Even a modified use of this method that retains the principle of criticism which subordinates the Bible to human reason is unacceptable to Adventists.*[76]

While some Adventist scholars have proposed using the historical-critical method, or using it moderately, "the question is whether in *practice* it is possible to fully separate presuppositions from methodology."[77] Ángel Manuel Rodríguez, ater carefully examining various Adventist approaches where a moderate use of the historical-critical approach had been adopted, comes to the conclusion that "the modifications they introduced are minimal and consist mainly of the recognition

---

Adventists, he slightly changed the title of one chapter to avoid a fragmenting impression on the minds of some readers, and he added seven section dividers with a selection of his wife's art and photos. While he acknowledges that dialogue took place between the authors of the Adventist Theological Society publication and himself and says, "I understand their positions much better now" (iv), the republished book unfortunately shows no sign that the robust criticism offered by others has led to a substantial change of his position. This is also evident in his chapter "Bible Study," in *The Future of Adventism: Theology, Society, Experience*, ed. Gary Chartier (Ann Arbor, MI: Griffin and Lash, 2015), 281–299.

[74] Maier, 372.

[75] Ibid.

[76] "Methods of Bible Study," as quoted in the appendix 463, emphasis added.

[77] Rodriguez, 341.

that God is still active in the production of the final form of the text."[78] However, when this modified use "is applied to key Adventist doctrinal issues, the result becomes damaging to Adventist doctrines and to the biblical understanding of the nature of inspiration and authority of the Scriptures."[79] Some repercussions of such a moderate view for the interpretation of Scripture are that "the Bible is not always historically reliable, making it necessary to reconstruct the history of Israel."[80] Furthermore, there is a strong tendency to consider the Bible to be culturally conditioned; sometimes even miracles are rejected by some Adventists who practice this approach.[81] Rodríguez aptly points out that while some Evangelical scholars who claim to have a high view of Scripture have been using a modified version of the historical-critical method, this is much more difficult for Adventists because of the centrality of Scripture in our theology and thinking. Since we do not accept any creeds as normative for our theology, our doctrinal statements are more immediately affected by any modification of our hermeneutics.[82] The moment we submit the Bible to the norm of human reason and start to criticize the content of Scripture (Sachkritik), we have started a trajectory that depends only on how deeply and extensively we are willing to apply this criticism to Scripture.[83]

Consequences of Historical Criticism

Historical criticism has become the dominant approach in the academic study of the Bible.[84] It is the academic standard practiced in most universities and is still practiced by a large number of English-speaking scholars as well as German scholars.[85] For many Christians, belief in the inspiration of Scripture "entailed a belief in its historical accuracy."[86] This belief was thoroughly shaken by historical criticism and led to a widespread conviction in many mainline churches that

---

[78] Rodriguez, 349.

[79] Ibid.

[80] Ibid.

[81] Ibid.

[82] Ibid.

[83] Stadelmann, 74.

[84] See the overview in Harrisville and Sundberg.

[85] So John Barton, "Historical-Critical Approaches," 9.

[86] So Collins, 6.

biblical texts did not necessarily always report historical events[87] and that the Bible cannot be trusted when it comes to its historical statements. Critically dissecting Scripture and reconstructing layers of its composition behind the canonical biblical text has alienated the biblical text from most readers. The text in this relativistic and humanly conditioned form has lost its transforming power.[88] The interpretation of the Bible has become a dry academic exercise that often even is detrimental to one's spirituality.[89] As has been pointed out, "the brutal fact is that for a disturbing number of students and preachers, critical analysis fosters a tendency to treat the Bible as an atomized reality, divided into a series of seemingly endless, discrete texts reflecting the points of view of particular authors, but not the sweep and grandeur of God's word."[90] Such an approach has not only led to a "secularization of Christianity,"[91] but also has had far-reaching consequences for many theological truths of Scripture.[92] From a historical-critical point of view, there cannot be a supernatural creation of this world, there is no literal Adam as a historical person,[93] there is no fall, there are no miracles—thus, there is no virgin birth, nor bodily resurrection—and there is no predictive prophecy. There is no regeneration, no answer to prayers, there is a different understanding of salvation and judgment, and there is no supernatural second coming of Jesus Christ in power and glory.[94] In

---

[87] So Collins, 7.

[88] Cf. the discussion in Frank M. Hasel, "Reflections on the Authority and Trustworthiness of Scripture," in Holbrook and Dolson, 201–220.

[89] So Berger, 53.

[90] Harrisville and Sundberg, 10.

[91] So Berger, 53–54.

[92] This has implications for the historicity of Adam and the fall, whether the exodus and other Old Testament events are fact or fiction, if there can be real predictive prophecy, what we can know about the historical Jesus, whether Paul was the author of all the epistles that are attributed to him, and much more. Cf. the discussion in Hays and Ansberry, *Evangelical Faith.*

[93] There is a lively debate on the historicity of Adam even in Evangelical circles that subscribe to the inerrancy of Scripture. See Peter Enns, *The Evolution of Adam: What the Bible Does and Doesn't Say About the Human Origins Debate* (Downers Grove, IL: InterVarsity, 2015); and Hans Madueme and Michael Reeves, eds., *Adam, the Fall, and Original Sin: Theological, Biblical, and Scientific Perspectives* (Grand Rapids, MI: Baker Academic, 2014), esp. 3–81; and Wayne Grudem, "Biblical and Theological Introduction: The Incompatibility of Theistic Evolution with the Biblical Account of Creation and with Important Biblical Doctrines," in *Theistic Evolution: A Scientific, Philosophical, and Theological Critique*, ed. J. P. Moreland et al. (Wheaton, IL: Crossway, 2017), 69–80.

[94] As can be seen even from this brief listing, this is not a minor and peripheral issue. It affects the central features of the biblical-Christian faith. This is pointed out by Nigel M. de S. Cameron, *The Evangelical/Liberal Debate* (Leicester: Religious and Theological Studies Fellowship, 1984), 8.

short, from protology to eschatology we find the biblical message affected by historical criticism. The results of critical scholarship "made the Bible a strange, unused, and even silent book."[95] The historical-critical and hypothetical reconstruction of pre-stages behind the biblical text has effectively robbed the existing text of its transforming spiritual power, making the Bible a dry and lifeless book with no inherent authority. It has distanced the text from the reader and has produced results that are threatening or hostile to the Christian faith or that have become so technical as to be totally irrelevant to the needs of the church. This plight has triggered a wide variety of alternative hermeneutical approaches. There is now a plurality of methods *en vogue* in interpretation[96] and "the proliferation in this century of new, distinctive approaches to Bible interpretation is nothing short of stunning."[97] Newer approaches provide "an exciting but also bewildering array of methods"[98] that frame different questions and offer new ways of looking at the biblical text. Within the limits of this chapter it is impossible to deal with all recent methodologies and their various nuances.[99] Instead we will look more

[95] Krentz, 3; cf. James Smart, *The Strange Silence of the Bible in the Church* (Philadelphia, PA: Westminster, 1970), 15–31. Alister McGrath, "Reclaiming our Roots and Vision: Scripture and the Stability of the Christian Church," in *Reclaiming the Bible for the Church*, ed. Carl E. Braaten and Robert W. Jenson (Grand Rapids, MI: Eerdmans, 1995), 69, calls it the "Babylonian Captivity of Scripture" where Scripture is held in bondage to critical scholarship and where "Scripture has thus become subservient to the needs and requirements of a fragmented academic community, in which originality and innovation are valued and 'faithfulness to tradition' is regarded as derivative, tedious and tantamount to some form of intellectual fascism." Similarly, Robert W. Yarbrough, "The Last and Next Christendom: Implications for Interpreting the Bible," *Themelios* 29/1 (2003): 37, writes that "it is time to escape our Babylonia captivity to scholarly trends that too facilely reject the core of the Christian message."

[96] Cf. Anthony Thiselton, "The Future of Biblical Interpretation and Responsible Plurality in Hermeneutics," in *The Future of Biblical Interpretation: Responsible Plurality in Biblical Hermeneutics*, ed. Stanley E. Porter and Matthew R. Malcom (Downers Grove, IL: InterVarsity, 2013), 11. Also Gerd Theißen, *Polyphones Verstehen: Entwürfe zur Bibelhermeneutik* (Berlin: LIT Verlag, 2015), 197–209.

[97] Klein, Blomberg, and Hubbard, 112.

[98] James L. Resseguie, *Narrative Criticism of the New Testament: An Introduction* (Grand Rapids, MI: Baker Academic, 2005), 17.

[99] For a concise overview of some of the most important new approaches, see the literature in footnote 4. Some of these new approaches, like feminist criticism and liberation theology, are critical of the often male, Western, and white privileged interest of the practitioners of historical criticism and point to the practical needs of the poor, marginalized, and oppressed. While offering different interpretations, it has been observed that feminist theology and liberation theology "are structurally very similar" because both "hold that one can understand the Bible aright only if one begins from a position of self-identification with the oppressed (women and/or the poor) and interprets texts in the light of that commitment" (John Barton, "Biblical Criticism and

closely at those approaches that give priority to the final form of the canonical text and where the existing canonical literary structures of the biblical text receive greater attention. In addition, we will examine some aspects of postmodern reader-response approaches, where the meaning is controlled not so much by the existing text anymore, but rather by the modern reader. Furthermore, we will briefly look at recent christological hermeneutical approaches that seem to have gained new impetus in some quarters.

Canonical Criticism

Canonical criticism has its roots in the school of biblical theology. Its most well-known representatives are Brevard Childs[100] and James Sanders.[101] The term "canonical criticism"[102] is used more by Sanders, whereas Childs prefers to speak about a "canonical approach." These terms are used rather ambiguously with reference to a variety of recent interpretive approaches that share an appreciation of the canonical accepted texts as the locus of meaning and seek to unfold the meaning of texts within their canonical context.[103]

Interpretation 1: Old Testament," in *The Blackwell Encyclopedia of Modern Christian Thought*, ed. Alister E. McGrath [Oxford: Blackwell, 1993], 39). This similarly holds true of other approaches like gender criticism. J. W. Rogerson, 844, points out that despite their severe criticism of certain biases in much of historical-critical scholarship, "in many cases, however, liberation theology and feminist criticism did not abandon historical criticism but used it to investigate those areas of concern that traditionally had been overlooked." Thus, "to the extent that these approaches utilized the methods of historical criticism, they can be regarded as having broadened historical criticism rather than refuted it" (ibid.).

[100] Brevard S. Childs, *Old Testament Theology in Canonical Context* (Philadelphia, PA: Fortress, 1986); Childs, *Introduction to the Old Testament as Scripture* (Philadelphia, PA: Fortress, 1979); Childs, *Biblical Theology of the Old and New Testaments: Theological Reflection of the Christian Bible* (Minneapolis, MN: Fortress, 1993); and Childs, *Biblical Theology in Crisis* (Philadelphia, PA: Westminster, 1970).

[101] James A. Sanders, *Canon and Community: A Guide to Canonical Criticism* (Philadelphia, PA: Fortress, 1984); and Sanders, *Torah and Canon* (Philadelphia, PA: Fortress, 1972).

[102] On canonical criticism, see Kent D. Clarke, "Canonical Criticism: An Integrated Reading of Biblical Texts for the Community of Faith," in *Approaches to New Testament Study*, ed. Stanley E. Porter and David Tombs, Journal for the Study of the New Testament Supplement Series 120 (Sheffield: Sheffield Academic Press, 1995), 170–221; Frank M. Hasel, "Canonical Criticism," in *The Encyclopedia of Christian Civilization*, ed. George Thomas Kurian, vol. 1 (Oxford: Wiley-Blackwell, 2011), 368–369; Corrine L. Carvalho, "Canonical Criticism," in McKenzie, 1:69.

[103] This makes the canonical approach "attractive to those who want to avoid historical methods that appear to question the authenticity of the Bible" (Carvalho, 70).

Canonical approaches raise important questions about the form and function of Scripture as well as how to appropriately interpret the Bible. While not ignoring the developments and insights of modern critical methods of studying the Bible,[104] they aim to understand the canon of Scripture as the normative context for reading the Bible.[105] In contrast to source criticism, which seeks to determine the sources and traditions behind a text, or form criticism, which seeks to identify the various forms within a text and traces the development of the oral, preliterary state and life situations ("Sitz-im-Leben") in which they arise, or redaction criticism, which analyzes the editorial and compositional techniques that shape the assumed written and oral traditions, canonical criticism focuses on the unity of the text as accepted by believing communities. It is not so much concerned with phases of the text's prehistory, but rather takes the canonically accepted text as the starting point for all exegesis and theology.[106] By affirming the final form of the canon as authoritative, canonical criticism places a valid emphasis on more text-centered approaches in the interpretation of Scripture. Biblical texts are read as a unified whole because they are the sacred Scriptures of the church and as such bear coherent witness to God. Rather than aiming to recover the author's original intention when writing a text or reconstructing the ancient historical and social background of its authors, canonical criticism aims to recover the role this text has played in the life of the church and tries to recover the reasons why the church admitted that text into the canon.

---

[104] Carvalho, 70, states of Childs' canonical approach that "he allows that secular interpretations of biblical texts have a kind of internal legitimacy and often have a role to play in a text's interpretation." Dale A. Brueggemann, "Brevard Childs' Canon Criticism: An Example of Post-Critical Naiveté," *Journal of the Evangelical Theological Society* 32/3 (1989): 312, points out that "for all his expressions of dissatisfaction with critical methods, Childs does not call for an anti-critical approach; rather, he calls for a post-critical approach. He wants to hold on to all his critical tools and their yield while yet turning to a unified text to discover present-day meaning." Similarly, Christopher Seitz, "Canonical Approach," in Vanhoozer, *Dictionary for Theological Interpretation of the Bible*, 100, points out that "a canonical approach does believe that the depth dimension uncovered by historical tools is a reality that must be dealt with constructively and with great theological sensitivity."

[105] "Canonical reading sees the choices offered by such a historical approach, and yet reckons that the final form is itself a statement, fully competent to judge and constrain the prehistory reconstructed by such methods" (Seitz, 100).

[106] For James Sanders, in contrast to Childs, the canonical text is the end product of various redactions and reformulations of earlier traditions and he stresses the role of the community in the creation of that formal element of canon. Thus, for Sanders the canon does, in fact, contain conflicting or self-correcting points of view. See Sanders, *Canon and Community*.

While valuing the canonical text in its final form is important, canonical criticism, as the name implies, is not a revival of a precritical hermeneutic and is not devoid of critical elements. It has been recognized that Childs sets his canonical interpretation of the Bible alongside more traditional critical methods and practices these interpretive methods alongside each other.[107] Representatives of canonical criticism often rely on the results of modern historical criticism to state how different prebiblical traditions conjoin in the shaping of biblical books in Scripture. But rather than aiming at the implications of those critical reconstructions of the biblical text, canonical criticism insists that a biblical theology must be built on the final form of the biblical text, not on some reconstructed earlier form. Thus, it focuses on and is interested in the question of how this elusive and even contradictory text of Scripture lived in the life of the community of faith to which it belonged. It assumes that as a result of the process of canonization, the hermeneutics necessary to interpret biblical texts should be sought from within the text itself. It thus aims to be both critical and confessional. This union between criticism and believing community is an unresolved crux in canonical criticism.[108] Furthermore, the canonical approach

---

[107] Maier, 325. This is admitted by Childs himself, who makes it quite clear that his position is not merely a moderated conservative viewpoint, which—if stripped of some minor liberal influences—would be quite acceptable as an orthodox approach to Old Testament interpretation. Brevard S. Childs, "Response to Reviewers of *Introduction to the Old Testament as Scripture*," *Journal for the Study of the Old Testament* 16 (1980): 58, states, "Actually the dynamics of a canonical approach to the Old Testament is sharply at odds with the Fundamentalist position. The role assigned to the history of tradition, the function of the community as tradents of the tradition, and the time-conditionality of the canonical witness, all move in a direction which is antithetical to conservatism." Childs credits the modern critical approach, however, to disregard the canonical shape of the biblical text. "The usual critical method of biblical exegesis is, first, to seek to restore an original historical setting by stripping away those very elements which constitute the canonical shape. Little wonder that once the biblical text has been securely anchored in the historical past by 'decanonizing' it, the interpreter has difficulty applying it to the modern religious context" (Brevard S. Childs, *Introduction to the Old Testament as Scripture* [Philadelphia, PA: Fortress, 1979], 79). For James A. Sanders, "Hermeneutics" in *The Interpreter's Dictionary of the Bible*, Supplementary Volume, ed. Keith Crim (Nashville, TN: Abingdon, 1976), 403–404, "the canon includes the process whereby early authoritative traditions encountered ancient cultural challenges, were rendered adaptable to those challenges, and thus themselves were formed and re-formed according to the needs of the believing communities. . . . That process itself is as canonical as the traditions which emerged out of it."

[108] Seitz, 101, observes that "canonical reading is therefore not an exact science, but a theological decision about what the proper parameters for interpretation are: the final-form presentation and the arrangement and sequencing that it exhibits, over against the simple history of the text's development as this is critically reconstructed." According to Kent D. Clarke, "it will once more be the work of future scholars to determine whether canonical criticism should act on par

> insists that it is the texts *per se* that are canonical. The texts are not simply windows through which one views a historical event that is then canonical. While some texts do have a relationship to historical events, a canonical approach shifts the focus from the factuality of the text to its role as a witness.[109]

This is an important distinction that indicates why canonical criticism is problematic for a Seventh-day Adventist hermeneutic. While a canonical approach is attractive for Adventists because it focuses on the objective reality of the canonical text, rather than on a critically reconstructed history behind the text, we are also interested in the factuality and truth of the historical events that the Bible recounts. While focusing on the canonical shape of the biblical text is commendable, the historical factuality and truthfulness of what the biblical text states is important too. To use the words of the apostle Paul: "If there is not resurrection of the dead, not even Christ has been raised; and if Christ has not been raised, then our preaching is vain, your faith also is vain" (1 Cor 15:13–14, NASB). Biblical faith affirms the historical factuality and truth of what the Bible reports. Otherwise our faith would be deficient and even be in vain.

Appealing to the canonical form of biblical texts does not mean that canonical criticism has adequately solved the question as to which texts are to be considered canonical.[110] Furthermore, it uses a definition of canon that includes not only the final literary stage in the Bible's composition, but also its form during the development process itself. Thus, canonical-critical approaches grant a new role to the believing

---

with historical criticism, or whether historical criticism should be subordinated to canonical criticism" (220). In the words of James Sanders, a leading proponent of canonical criticism, this tension is evident, and "canonical criticism may perhaps be the corrective to what happened because of the Enlightenment, when the Bible was taken from the church lectern into the scholar's study. The movement of canonical criticism is that of the scholar's being openly willing to be a servant of the believing communities. Not those believing communities who are so frightened of Enlightenment study. . . . They have not taken the necessary prior steps; they have not demonstrated the depth of faith necessary to be 'honest to God'. They live by the fear that the faith will disappear if they allow honesty. . . . On the other hand, it is for those faithful who have discerned the hand of God in the Enlightenment just as the ancient biblical authors discerned the hand of God in the international Wisdom they learned from others. It may help those faithful to discern the immense power for truth the Bible conveys" (Sanders, *Canon and Community*, xvi).

[109] Carvalho, 70.

[110] An unresolved issue is whether there could be a Jewish biblical theology or why Roman Catholic, Orthodox, and Protestant communities each have distinct canons (cf. Carvalho, 71; and D. A. Brueggemann, 317).

community in the act of interpretation. The normative authority of the canonical text is not necessarily inherent in the text itself. Neither does the normative character reside with the content of the text. Instead its authority is conferred by the believing community of the time under investigation.[111] Sanders, who affirms that canonical criticism rests squarely on all the conclusions of biblical higher criticism during the past two hundred years,[112] makes clear that inspiration does not reside in the author but in the community.[113] This means that "the canon becomes more a heuristic model for opening up truth than an actual vehicle of truth. The Bible is no longer the Word of God and does not contain the words of God. Rather, it speaks with the authority of God when we read it as if it were the Word of God."[114]

This raises a number of questions with regard to biblical interpretation. Does such an understanding of the nature of Scripture do justice to the biblical understanding of inspiration? The Bible does not speak about an inspired community, but speaks of inspired individuals speaking to the community (Heb 1:1).[115] Furthermore, can a text be adequately understood based on its role in the life of the believing community alone? What is the role of the church in the process of interpretation? Should not the historical context also play a significant role for understanding the biblical text adequately? Why do the intentions of the canonizing community enjoy a preferential place for interpreting the Bible rather than those of the original inspired writers? And what is the function of more recent interpreters in the process of understanding the biblical text in the life of the church today?

Canonical criticism has opened the door to an approach that reflects a more biblical theology, where all of Scripture in its final, canonical form is taken into consideration to uncover a comprehensive theology of the Bible. Rather than focusing on critical reconstructions of the biblical text that lead to disparate theologies within the Bible, a unified view of

---

[111] D. A. Brueggemann, 321, perceptively raises the question: if we are willing to give the believing community "that much authority, why not follow their exegesis too—allegory and all? This is the key issue. If authority is in the process and the process is human, then the methodology of the process has the same authority as its product. If the canon that resulted from hermeneutical moves in the early Church has authority, then the hermeneutical moves have authority."

[112] Sanders, *Canon and Community*, 37.

[113] Ibid., 19, 40. See also Childs, *Old Testament Theology in Canonical Context*, 26. On this see also the discussion in John N. Oswalt, "Canonical Criticism: A Review From a Conservative," *Journal of the Evangelical Theological Society* 30/3 (1987): 317–325, esp. 322.

[114] D. A. Brueggemann, 326.

[115] Oswalt, 322.

the biblical text brings the canonical text of Scripture back into focus. This is positive. However, the role that canonical criticism assigns to the history of tradition as well as to the function of the community as tradents of the traditions, and the time conditionality of the canonical witness, all move in a direction antithetical to an understanding of Scripture as the object of divine inspiration. We know God both because of what He did in history as well as what He faithfully commissioned to be written down of those actions in Scripture. Both cannot be separated.[116] It has been pointed out that "to say that we should look upon what the Bible tells us about its origins with the greatest skepticism and yet accept what it tells us about God with childlike faith demands a compartmentalization of thought that is fallacious."[117] To interpret a passage solely by reference to its literary context without being convinced about the truthfulness of its historical reference ignores the contextual nature of Scripture. The Bible teaches us its truth in the context of human experiences and conveys that truth in a connected form of thought. This means that "if we interpret the statements of the Bible apart from the experiences through which they were mediated and apart from the literary context in which they now appear we must inevitably misinterpret them."[118]

As such, canonical criticism is a response from within a more liberal, rather than a more conservative, approach to Scripture. This leads us to some other approaches that also focus on the biblical text, albeit more from a literary perspective.

Literary Approaches: Literary Criticism, Rhetorical Criticism, Narrative Criticism

Dissatisfaction with the dominance of the historical-critical method led to the emergence of new literary approaches in biblical scholarship.[119] While the historical-critical methodology has largely left

---

[116] Oswalt, 321.

[117] Ibid., 320.

[118] Ibid., 321–322. Speaking as an Evangelical scholar, Oswalt, 322, points out that "if we evangelicals have for too long ignored the wholeness of Biblical books in our preoccupations with proof-texts and promises and with proving the historical statements correct, let us not now veer into the opposite ditch with an unhealthy dismissal of historical context. It is true that it is the present text that holds authority over us, but it would be dangerous, as I think I see some of us doing, to abandon the attempt to understand that text's meaning in its first historical setting. Between them, literary and historical contexts provide the channel for us to determine the meaning of any passage for our own lives. To destroy one bank of any channel is to move from river to swamp."

[119] Paul R. House, *Beyond Form Criticism: Essays in Old Testament Literary Criticism* (Winona

us with a fragmented biblical text, in which the history behind the biblical text became more important than the canonical text itself, new literary approaches focus on the literary qualities of the biblical text. Literary approaches such as the new literary criticism,[120] narrative criticism,[121] and rhetorical criticism,[122] as diverse and different as they are, all have in common that they focus on the literary features of the Bible. They "begin with the assumption that the Bible is literature and proceed using tools, strategies, and methodologies of literary analysis."[123] Rather than tracing back historical developments behind the final form of the canonically accepted text,[124] this new hermeneutical approach focuses on the literary structures of the biblical text and has given rise to an investigation of the literary qualities of the biblical text. In 1968 James Muilenburg, in his presidential address to the Society of Biblical Literature, called on biblical studies to embrace new critical approaches. After praising the accomplishments of form criticism, Muilenburg urged biblical scholars to go "beyond" form criticism to take up questions

---

Lake, IN: Eisenbrauns, 1992), 3, states, "Besides the influence of interdisciplinary trends, literary criticism arose at least in part because of impasses in older ways of explaining Scripture. Many thinkers concluded that historical criticism, the standard means of biblical analyses, had almost run its course. . . . These methodologies obscure the unity of large and small texts alike. . . . An overemphasis on historical criticism subsumed textual issues." This focus on the text and its rhetorical features led to the emergence of a wide range of different approaches. Within the limits of this chapter it difficult to do justice to all details and aspects. What complicates matters even more is the fact that different definitions have made the term "literary criticism one of the most potential ambiguous terms in the field of biblical studies" (so Soulen and Soulen, "Literary Criticism," in *Handbook of Biblical Criticism*, 105). There are nevertheless some common points that we will focus on for the purpose of this chapter.

[120] On the history and meaning of the term "literary criticism" and especially in the sense of composition criticism, see John Barton, "Reflections on Literary Criticism," in LeMon and Richards, 523–540.

[121] On narrative criticism, see Patricia K. Tull, "Narrative Criticism and Narrative Hermeneutics," in McKenzie, 2:37–46; Robert C. Tannenhill, "Narrative Criticism," in Coggins and Houlden, 488–489; and M. A. Powell, "Narrative Criticism," in *Dictionary of Biblical Interpretation*, ed. John H. Hayes, vol. 2 (Nashville, TN: Abingdon Press, 1999), 201–204.

[122] On rhetorical criticism, see David A. deSilva, "Rhetorical Criticism," in McKenzie, 2:273–283; J. I. H. McDonald, "Rhetorical Criticism," in Coggins and Houlden, 599–600; and W. Randolph Tate, "Rhetorical Criticism," in *Interpreting the Bible: A Handbook of Terms and Methods* (Peabody, MA: Hendrickson, 2006), 322–324.

[123] Rhiannon Graybill, "Literary Criticism, Literary Theory, and the Bible," in McKenzie, 1:515. Similarly, Leland Ryken, "Literary Criticism," in Vanhoozer, *Dictionary for Theological Interpretation of the Bible*, 457.

[124] Historical-critical biblical interpreters tried to explain the historical milieu of passages through a reconstruction of the ancient world from which the text presumably emerged, including their assumed written and oral precursors.

of aesthetics, style, and literary technique that focus on the text of Scripture.[125] Muilenburg's method became known as "rhetorical criticism" and was an important step toward literary criticism.[126] Another important voice was Robert Alter, who stressed the "composite artistry"[127] of the final form of the text. Alter's work brings into biblical studies the methods and interests current in secular literary criticism.[128] Literary critics did not abandon historical-critical methods completely.[129] Rather, "under Alter, the redactor [of the biblical text], long familiar from source criticism, becomes an artist"[130] who skillfully arranges the text in its finished form. Alter's book *The Art of Biblical Narrative* became an immediate and lasting success.[131] In narrative criticism, the "what" of the text (its content) and the "how" of the text (its rhetoric and structure) are analyzed as a complete tapestry and organic whole. The form of the biblical text defines the meaning that is communicated through it. Thus, the literary analysis of the text itself and not the external circumstances that have given rise to the text become more important, because the form and content of the text are inseparable.

A close reading and a painstaking analysis of form, rhythm, structure, genre, and narrative can draw one's attention to the artistry, beauty, and craftmanship of the biblical text. Seventh-day Adventists do take seriously the literary, rhetorical, and narrative dimensions of the biblical text in its final canonical form. To focus on the biblical text this way is something positive. Such aspects are worthy of attention and can be profitably investigated insofar as they help us understand Scripture, and as long as we approach them with the proper presuppositions and submit to the truth claims of the biblical text.

---

[125] James Muilenburg, "Form Criticism and Beyond," *Journal of Biblical Literature* 88/1 (March 1968): 1–18.

[126] The journal *Semeia*, published by the Society of Biblical Literature from 1974 to 2002, served as an early forum for literary approaches to the Bible, covering narrative approaches (*Semeia* 9, 15, 26, 46, 63), reader-response criticism (*Semeia* 31, 48), textuality (*Semeia* 40, 50, 65), genre (*Semeia* 43), intertextuality (*Semeia* 69, 70), semiotics (*Semeia* 81), poststructuralism (*Semeia* 50, 54), and the ethics of reading (*Semeia* 77).

[127] Robert Alter, *The Art of Biblical Narrative*, 2nd ed. (1981; New York: Basic Books 2011), 131ff.

[128] Barton, "Reflections on Literary Criticism," 526.

[129] So Resseguie, 19, 23.

[130] Graybill, 518.

[131] See also Robert Alter, *The Art of Biblical Poetry* (New York: Basic Books, 1985). Another important work on biblical narrative is Meir Sternberg, *The Poetics of Biblical Narrative: Ideological Literature and the Drama of Reading* (Bloomington, IN: Indiana University Press, 1987).

However, there are also a number of aspects that deserve critical attention from a Seventh-day Adventist perspective. It is true that biblical stories have captivated readers of the Bible from earliest times, particularly because these stories were understood to tell us something about people and events that actually happened. But the issue that deserves critical attention is the relationship between the persuasive biblical text to the historical reality about which it might talk. Many literary and rhetorical critics retain their skepticism about the ability of the persuasive biblical text to provide us with reliable access to what actually took place. George Kennedy, for instance, sums up the merits of rhetorical criticism when he writes,

> Rhetoric cannot describe the historical Jesus or identify Matthew or John; they are probably irretrievably lost to scholarship. But it does study a verbal reality, our text of the Bible, rather than the oral sources standing behind the text, the hypothetical stages of its composition, or the impersonal workings of social forces, and at its best it can reveal the power of those texts as unitary messages.[132]

In other words, rhetorical criticism studies the "verbal reality" of the biblical text, but cannot say anything regarding *historical* reality. Others point out that "proponents of narrative hermeneutics assert that narrative meaning differs fundamentally from propositional truth."[133] Hans Frei and the movement sometimes referred to as the "Yale School"[134] (where Frei taught), argue that both conservative and liberal approaches to the Bible attempt to locate meaning in the historical event, not in the text. Instead Frei looks to the text, *as a text*, and to the literary narrative itself, as the locus of meaning.[135] In his important study on biblical narrative, Hans Frei points out that attempts to distill abstract, universal human truths from biblical narratives or to use these narratives to reconstruct historical events actually "eclipse" narrative meaning itself.[136] For decades biblical critics and conservative scholars equated literary meaning with authorial intent, assuming

---

[132] George A. Kennedy, *New Testament Interpretation Through Rhetorical Criticism* (Chapel Hill, NC: University of North Carolina Press, 1984), 158–159.

[133] Tull, 2:37.

[134] David Lauber, "Yale School," in Vanhoozer, *Dictionary for Theological Interpretation of the Bible*, (Grand Rapids, MI: Baker Academic, 2005), 859–861.

[135] Because of his distance to the liberal position, this approach is sometimes called "postliberalism."

[136] Hans Frei, *The Eclipse of Biblical Narrative: A Study of Eighteenth and Nineteenth Century Hermeneutics* (New Haven, CT: Yale University Press, 1974), 280.

that information about writers' biographies, social circumstances, and cultural context shed light on the meaning of the text. But in newer literary approaches the literary work has its own integrity and meaning quite apart from what the author intended or the historical setting in which it originated. This shift eventually paved the way for giving a greater role to the reader for the discernment of the text's meaning, as we will see in the discussion on reader-response criticism in the present study.

We have to keep in mind that "contemporary narrative criticism arose only in the past four decades, particularly as it became clearer that the biblical storytellers were not simply recording historical events as eyewitnesses, nor merely copying down oral epics, but rather crafting stories with sophistication and skill."[137] Thus, close literary reading of the biblical text is pursued by literary critics "without undue reference to authors and historical settings"[138] because the interpretive goal is "clarifying not the world behind the text but the world created by the text."[139] Biblical stories may still function as records of significant history, but in much of literary criticism they function only poetically to fire our imagination, provoke repentance, inspire worship, etc., and thus shape the way readers understand themselves and their present circumstances.[140] In other words, "narrative criticism is not interested in questioning the accuracy of such [biblical] reports or in determining what historical occurrences might have inspired the tales."[141] It is the world of the text that is created by the text that determines its meaning, not its historical reference point. "'Events' are simply the incidents or happenings that occur within a story."[142] Thus, literature aims to get

---

[137] Tull, 2:38–39.

[138] Ibid., 2:39.

[139] Ibid., 2:39. Graybill, 519–520, states that "the literary approach has likewise been criticized for refusing to historicize the text or to acknowledge the significance of its cultural contexts, although more recent work does much to address these criticisms." See also David F. Ford, "Narrative Theology," in Coggins and Houlden, 490.

[140] Powell, 2:201–202.

[141] Ibid., 2:203.

[142] Ibid. Powell illustrates this when he writes, "When God declares that Jesus is the 'Beloved Son' (Luke 3:22) or when the narrator of Luke's Gospel says that Jesus is 'full of the Holy Spirit' (Luke 4:1), readers are not expected to wonder whether these things are really so" (Powell, 2:204). The decisive thing is the effects that biblical literature is expected to have on the implied reader. By analyzing the biblical narratives through literary tools, narrative critics unwittingly set the stage for the reappraisal of biblical stories as oral events that led to the new approach of performance criticism. For a helpful overview of this approach, see Kelly R. Iverson, "Performance Criticism," in McKenzie, 2:97–105; and Bernhard Oestreich, *Performance Criticism of*

the reader to share an experience, rather than letting the reader primarily grasp ideas, which means that the text "enacts rather than states propositionally."[143]

Seventh-day Adventist interpreters are interested in a close reading of the literary work of the biblical text in its final form. In a sense, narrative criticism "was in many respects a response to traditional historical-critical approaches and attempted to bring renewed focus on the final form of the biblical texts, arguing that the scriptural narratives were creative and unified stories."[144] In this sense narrative criticism has performed a valuable service in rediscovering some features of the biblical text and its narrative. It locates the meaning of the text within the text. This comports well with Seventh-day Adventist hermeneutics, which also focuses on the final form of the text taken as a unity. But it has been pointed out that "there is simply no reason to believe, in principle, that a persuasive text cannot also be a trustworthy text, whether concerning the past or anything else."[145] This is a serious pitfall connected with this approach. Even rhetorical art can communicate reality. "Therefore any thoroughgoing suspicion of art or rhetoric vis-à-vis truth and virtue is unjustified."[146] Another concern has to do with the relationship between methods of literary hermeneutics that were developed for the interpretation of secular literature and their application to the interpretation of the Bible. According to two experts in the field,

> this is a question that has been raised from the advent of the development of biblically focused literary hermeneutics. Such a question involves more than simply querying the appropriate literary practices and techniques for study of the Bible. It probes issues of possible philosophical and literary difference between secular and religious texts, especially with regard to such fundamental concepts as referentiality, historicity, transcendence, and truth claims.[147]

---

the Pauline Letters (Eugene, OR: Cascade, 2016), 7–97.

[143] Ryken, 457. It is here that newer approach of performance criticism comes into play. Here the dynamic of the performance of the biblical text within an oral/aural milieu receives attention. It seeks to investigate "how orality and performance shaped the composition, presentation, transmission, and reception of the biblical traditions" (Iverson, 2:97–105).

[144] R. S. Sugirtharajah, "Performance Criticism," in McKenzie, 2:97.

[145] Provan, 512.

[146] Ibid., 513.

[147] Porter and Robinson, 291–292.

These are valid questions that deserve careful further reflection. Within the limits of this chapter, we want to point out that we have to be mindful that in focusing on story or stories many interpreters using a narrative critical approach have actually separated the biblical narrative from real history[148] and have not given enough attention to the historicity of the text or the events of the narrative.[149] Narrative critics often assume that when they study the Bible as literature, the biblical texts must be viewed as fiction.[150] With regard to the New Testament material, it has been pointed out that in much of narrative criticism the biblical narrative is abstracted "from historiographical intention" and thus

> it has tended to assimilate the gospel texts to purely fictional narratives which are not constrained by a direct external referent. It assumes that history and narrative must go their separate ways: for those with historical interests, various historical-critical strategies are available, while for those with a more literary orientation, ahistorical literary-critical analysis is a fruitful possibility.[151]

This is equally done in Old Testament scholarship. A textbook for students by David M. Gunn and Danna Nolan Fewell deals with narrative criticism in the Old Testament.[152] Written to help students understand alternative approaches in biblical interpretation, the authors differentiate two alternatives: 1) an exegesis that seeks objective truth through the traditional way of anchoring truth in history, and 2) a rhetorical-critical approach. They prefer the latter:

> the "serious" human views self and society as objective realities in a world of ostensible, essential truths and values—the "common

---

[148] While it is possible to convey truth in stories that are fictional, the decisive question is how theology should be concerned with historical facts and whether the Bible reports historical reality and how it is related to it. See Ford, 490.

[149] Stephen J. Nichols and Eric T. Brandt, *Ancient Word, Changing Worlds: The Doctrine of Scripture in a Modern Age* (Wheaton, IL: Crossway, 2009), 122.

[150] So Klein, Blomberg, and Hubbard, 125. See also D. A. Robertson, *The Old Testament and the Literary Critic* (Philadelphia, PA: Fortress, 1977); D. A. Templeton, *The New Testament as True Fiction* (Sheffield: Sheffield Academic Press, 1999); and Wayne C. Booth, *The Rhetoric of Fiction*, 2nd ed. (Chicago, IL: University of Chicago Press, 1983).

[151] Francis Watson, *Text and Truth: Redefining Biblical Theology* (Grand Rapids, MI: Eerdmans, 1997), 34. While this does not necessarily seem to result from the nature of the method itself, it is often associated with this approach. See Klein, Blomberg, and Hubbard, 125–126.

[152] David M. Gunn and Danna Nolan Fewell, *Narrative in the Hebrew Bible* (Oxford: Oxford University Press, 1993).

> sense" view. Truth is an eternal object which needs to be discovered. Reason and science, reemphasized by the Enlightenment, are the prescribed tools of revelation [*sic*]. The "rhetorical" human fashions the world through language, manipulating reality rather than discovering it, since reality is that which is construed as reality rather than some objective essence.[153]

Such a separation of history and biblical text is unacceptable for a Seventh-day Adventist hermeneutic and does not do justice to the biblical material itself. It ignores the fact that the biblical text is historically constituted and that history plays an important role in our understanding of the biblical text.[154] Furthermore, some proponents of narrative hermeneutics depreciate the religious value of the biblical text in favor of its aesthetics.[155] It has been asserted that "narratives function differently from propositional truth claims" and that "many components and customs discernable in biblical storytelling correspond to those of modern fiction."[156] Hence for many literary critics, "narrative meaning differs fundamentally from propositional truth statements"[157] and the stories as recorded in the Bible are often seen as artistic literary creations that do not necessarily report "factual" history.

In the conviction of Christian believers throughout the centuries, however, the reliability of the historical facts as recorded in the Bible gives credibility to biblical faith because they believe that God acts in history and puts His Word to the test in the historical fulfillment of prophecy. "The Bible has both facts (propositions) and stories."[158] As J. Gresham Machen puts it pointedly: "No facts, no good news; no good news, no hope. The Bible is quite useless unless it is a record of facts."[159] This shift from "history" to "story" is "indicative of a broader shift in theological and philosophical discourse away from the quest

---

[153] Gunn and Fewell, 10.

[154] See the discussion in chapter 3 by Michael G. Hasel, "History, the Bible, and Hermeneutics," in the present volume.

[155] This is seen by Klein, Blomberg, and Hubbard, 126, although they see this as an abuse that can be divorced from the method itself.

[156] Tull, 2:41.

[157] Ibid., 2:37.

[158] Nichols and Brandt, 123.

[159] J. Gresham Machen, *The Christian Faith in a Modern World* (New York: Macmillan, 1936), 57, as quoted in Nichols and Brandt, 123. Machen then expresses what this record of facts can do for us: "It will probe very deep into your life. It will reveal the dark secrets of your sin. But then it will bring you good tidings of salvation as no word of man can do" (ibid.).

for secure foundations."[160] To such a postmodern approach we will now briefly turn.

Postmodern Reader-Response Approaches

As in virtually every other field of study, the specter of postmodernism[161] has affected the world of biblical interpretation as well.[162] According to Princeton theologian Diogenes Allen, this postmodern shift is a massive intellectual revolution "that is perhaps as great as that which marked off the modern world from the Middle Ages."[163] Whereas literary critical approaches focused their attention on the text itself rather than on historical questions, postmodern approaches go a step further. The horizon of the quest for meaning here shifts from the close analysis of

---

[160] So Collins, 137.

[161] The term "postmodern" is difficult to define because there is no single definition of it. "Commonly speaking, however, postmodern refers to a style of thought that is suspicious of modern rationalist accounts of truth, reason, and objectivity; that distrusts single explanatory frameworks or Metanarratives; that sees the world and personal identities as diverse, dispersed indeterminate, and ungrounded; and that celebrates (or is resigned to) an approach to life and thought that is playful, eclectic, pluralistic, and subversive of traditional boundaries" (Soulen and Soulen, "Postmodern Biblical Interpretation," in *Handbook of Biblical Criticism*, 140). A similar description is offered by Klein, Blomberg, and Hubbard, 126, who describe "postmodernism" as a broad term that is used in different ways by various authors but it usually involves a cluster of such convictions and values as: 1) an ideological pluralism in which no one religion or worldview contains absolute truth; 2) the impossibility of objectivity in interpretation and the treasuring of value-laden approaches; 3) the importance of human communities in shaping ourselves and our interpretive perspectives; 4) a rejection of the negative modernist evaluation of religion and spirituality; 5) an emphasis on the esthetic, the symbolic, and ancient tradition; 6) the formative role of narrative in understanding our own life pilgrimages and those of others, along with the rejection of the existence of any overarching metanarrative that can give meaning to all individual stories; and 7) language as determinative of thought and meaning.

For an important introduction to postmodernism from a representative of postmodern thought, see Jean-François Lyotard, *The Postmodern Condition: A Report of Knowledge* (Minneapolis, MN: University of Minneapolis Press, 1984). For a readable introduction to postmodern thought, see David Harvey, *The Condition of Postmodernity: An Inquiry into the Origins of Cultural Change* (Oxford: Basil Blackwell, 1992); C. Butler, *Postmodernism: A Very Short Introduction* (Oxford: Oxford University Press, 2003); and Hans Joachim Türk, *Postmoderne* (Mainz: Matthias Grünewald-Verlag, 1990). For an Evangelical Christian perspective, see Gene Edward Veith Jr., *Postmodern Times: A Christian Guide to Contemporary Thought and Culture* (Wheaton, IL: Crossway, 1994); David S. Dockery, ed., *The Challenge of Postmodernism: An Evangelical Engagement*, 2nd ed. (Grand Rapids: Baker, 2001); and Stanley J. Grenz, *A Primer on Postmodernism* (Grand Rapids, MI: Eerdmans, 1996).

[162] Barry Harvey, "Anti-Postmodernism," in Adam, *Postmodern Biblical Interpretation*, 1.

[163] Diogenes Allen, *Christian Belief in a Postmodern World* (Louisville, KY: Westminster, 1989), 2.

the biblical text to the recipient and reader of the text.[164] The implication of this new interpretive situation "constitutes something of an emergency"[165] for biblical interpretation. Dissatisfaction with a focus on the author (as in historical criticism) or a focus on the text (as in various forms of literary criticism) eventually shifted the focus to the reader.[166] In postmodern approaches we find a move beyond and away from methods and conclusions where meaning is fixed and where meaning resides in the text to a position where the meaning is largely or wholly the product of individual readers or the interpretative community.[167] Thus, the radically new feature of postmodern interpretation is that the reader is positioned *before* the text.[168] The reader replaces the emphasis of the text itself.

It is claimed that once a text is written the historical author has no control over its meaning.[169] Since a text has unrealized potential and requires a reader[170] to actualize this potential meaning, the reader assumes an active role in the process of interpretation—not only shaping, but also creating meaning.[171] Reading the text becomes a dynamic and transactional process between the text and the reader that is open-ended and quite unpredictable. The reader, already possessing preconceptions and preunderstandings, encounters the text, is affected by the text, and creates a world in response to the text, and then returns to encounter the text again. In each subsequent encounter the reader further transforms the meaning he or she creates, by organizing and reorganizing the reading of the text. Such a reading never quite arrives at the ultimate

---

[164] See the informed discussion and overview in Herbert H. Klement, "Postmoderne Exegese und der theologische Wahrheitsanspruch," in *Theologische Wahrheit und die Postmoderne*, ed. Herbert H. Klement (Wuppertal: R. Brockhaus Verlag, 2000), 46–71.

[165] Walter Brueggemann, *Texts Under Negotiation: The Bible and Postmodern Imagination* (Minneapolis, MN: Fortress, 1993), 1.

[166] Kathy Reiko Maxwell, "Reader-Response Criticism," in McKenzie, 2:198.

[167] Klein, Blomberg, and Hubbard, 127.

[168] Cf. W. Randolph Tate, "Postmodern Interpretation," in McKenzie, 2:132–140.

[169] Maxwell, 2:198.

[170] Within reader-response criticism there is a plurality of responses that depend on views taken of language, self, world, text and meaning, and the relationship of all. Within the limits of this chapter we cannot deal with all aspects and understandings of different readers. For a concise overview of different varieties, see Edgar V. McKnight, "Reader-Response Criticism," in Hayes, 2:372–373.

[171] David Alan Black and David S. Dockery, *Interpreting the New Testament: Essays on Method and Issues* (Nashville, TN: Broadman and Holman, 2001), 159.

meaning of a text.[172] Because the reader necessarily reads subjectively, the meaning cannot be objective, but the meaning of a text is multivalent and the reader can never arrive at the ultimate meaning of a text.[173]

According to Wolfgang Iser, a leading proponent of this new approach, the reader is the primary source, even the creator, of the meaning of a text. Iser writes, "It is in the reader that the text comes to life."[174] Thus, "the interpretation we do in a contemporary context will be seen as the translation or recording of aspects of meaning uncovered in an experience of the reader into some sort of language and conceptuality shared by some community of contemporaries."[175] Other more radical postmodern critics such as Stanley Fish[176] complete the shift to the reader. His now-well-known question "Is there a text in this class?" emphasizes the plurality of meaning in a text.[177] Richard Rorty stresses truth in community,[178] where truth is a product of the group, rather than a matter of objective facts or absolutes. Consequently, things are true only within the group and the idea of truth is limited to its function within groups (truths in the plural), rather than functioning as true for all people in all times and places.[179]

Recognizing the reader's context and showing an awareness for the fact that we are all situated in a certain context is an important aspect of the interpretative process.[180] The postmodern mindset at work in reader-response criticism, however, goes beyond such an awareness and poses some significant problems for Seventh-day Adventist

---

[172] Maxwell, 2:200–201.

[173] According to E. V. McKnight, *Post-Modern Use of the Bible*, 241, "the meaning of a text is inexhaustible because no context can provide all the keys to all of its possibilities."

[174] Wolfgang Iser, *The Act of Reading: A Theory of Aesthetic Response* (Baltimore, MD: John Hopkins University Press, 1978), 19. Iser identified the reader as the "co-creator" of the text, but according to Maxwell, 2:198, he "maintained that neither the text nor the reader contained meaning. Instead, the meaning of a text was found in the ever-changing gap between text and reader."

[175] E. V. McKnight, *Post-Modern Use of the Bible*, 267.

[176] Stanley Fish, *Is There a Text in the Class? The Authority of Interpretive Communities* (Cambridge, MA: Harvard University Press, 1980).

[177] Fish delights in showing that even texts that seem to communicate the most clearly objective and recoverable meaning can be understood in quite different ways.

[178] Richard Rorty, *Objectivity, Relativism, and Truth: Philosophical Papers* (Cambridge: Cambridge University Press, 1991).

[179] Nichols and Brandt, 124.

[180] See Frank M. Hasel, "Presuppositions in the Interpretation of Scripture," in Reid, 27–46, and the discussion in chapter 1 by Kwabena Donkor, "Presuppositions in Hermeneutics," in the present volume.

hermeneutics.[181] Its main weakness lies in its relativism.[182] Through the focus on the reader, the text has lost its ability to be the final and decisive norm for theology. If the meaning is created by the reader and is not defined and decided by the biblical text alone, then the Bible "offers no place for us to stand, no reference point beyond our experience."[183]

According to this postmodern approach, since all interpretation occurs within a variety of contexts from which the interpreter cannot escape, objective knowledge and a definite meaning are not inscribed within a text and can never be achieved. The meaning of a text can differ from reader to reader and from "performance" to "performance" as different readers perform the text in different circumstances and contexts.[184] The meaning of a piece of writing lies neither in the author's intentions nor within the words of the text itself, but in the interplay between the text and the reader.[185] In other words, meaning is inextricably bound to the interpretive context and is linked to the activities of the reader.[186] Since there are multiple readers, "the meaning of a text is inexhaustible because no context can provide all the keys to all of its possibilities."[187] As such, from a phenomenological perspective, there are no objective texts and no definite meanings.

Since it is assumed by postmodern critics that every person who reads a text does so under the pressure of an ideology (political, theological, economic, etc.), we have a multitude of different readings of Scripture, including feminist, liberation, postcolonial, lesbian, gay, bisexual, transgender, queer criticism, psychoanalytic criticism, ideological criticism, reader-response criticism, receptions criticism, rhetorical criticism, etc.[188] Thus,

---

[181] For a Seventh-day Adventist response to postmodernism, see Norman R. Gulley, *Systematic Theology*, vol. 1, *Prolegomena* (Berrien Springs, MI: Andrews University Press, 2003), 455–517.

[182] So Klein, Blomberg, and Hubbard, 130.

[183] Nichols and Brandt, 125.

[184] Soulen and Soulen, "Reader-Response Criticism," in *Handbook of Biblical Criticism*, 157.

[185] John Barton, "Reading and Interpreting the Bible," in *Harper's Bible Commentary*, ed. James Luther Mays (San Francisco, CA: Harper and Row, 1988), 11.

[186] Tate, 138.

[187] E. V. McKnight, *Post-Modern Use of the Bible*, 241.

[188] E. V. McKnight, "Literary Criticism," in *Dictionary of Jesus and the Gospels*, ed. Joel B. Green and Scot McKnight (Downers Grove, IL: InterVarsity, 1992), 476, points out that "the nature and role of the reader varies in the different forms of reader-response criticism, but in all forms there is a movement away from the view of interpretation as the determination by an autonomous reader of *the* meaning of an autonomous text. In one form (reader-reception criticism) an attempt is made to situate a literary work within the cultural context of its production and

> postmodernists may deliberately read the Bible against the grain of the dominant scholarship in order to articulate an alternative vision of biblical meaning that better coheres with the interests of women, the wider global community, and readers whose dissident understanding of Scripture has been suppressed in the name of cultural homogeneity.[189]

In this open-ended way of reading the biblical text, the biblical text has lost its ability to determine its own meaning and there is even a certain similarity to the allegorical interpretations of the past.[190] This raises a number of questions: "do our various responses to literary works produce the same (or similar) readings?; can literary texts genuinely enjoy as many meanings as readers are able to create?; are some readings essentially more valid and justifiable than others?"[191] These questions deserve close attention. Is it possible that various readers can produce the same or a similar meaning and thus arrive at theological unity? In light of the multiple and pluralistic readings that are possible, how do we justify some readings over others as being more valid and justifiable?[192] Furthermore, radical reader-response criticism cannot really explain "how texts transform readers, generating interpretations and behavior that cut against the grain of their preunderstandings, presuppositions, and social conditioning."[193]

Since the external reader becomes the locus of understanding, the crucial question is how meaning is created. The decisive question is

---

then explore the shifting relations between this context and the changing contexts of historical readers. Another form (aesthetic-response criticism) emphasizes the process by which a reader actualizes a text. A text is marked by gaps which the reader must complete and blanks which the reader must fill in. Psychological approaches to the reader emphasize the stages of development of individual readers or the role played by the "psychological set" of readers."

[189] A. K. M. Adam, "Postmodern Biblical Interpretation," in *The New Interpreter's Dictionary of the Bible*, ed. Katharine Doob Sakenfeld (Nashville, TN: Abingdon, 2006–2009), 572.

[190] Michael Cahill, "Reader-Response Criticism and the Allegorizing Reader," *Theological Studies* 57/1 (1996): 89–96. Similarly Anthony C. Thiselton, *Hermeneutics: An Introduction* (Grand Rapids, MI: Eerdmans, 2009), 314-316.

[191] Todd Davis and Kenneth Womack, *Formalist Criticism and Reader-Response Theory* (New York: Palgrave, 2002), 51.

[192] Heinzpeter Hempelmann points out this difficulty in Rorty's thinking and approach and raises the question of why a reading of Adolf Hitler should be preferred to that of Mother Theresa if both are legitimate readings. See Heinzpeter Hempelmann, "Selbstbeschneidung der Vernunft? Postmoderne Rationalitätskritik als Chance und Herausforderung für christliche Theologie," in Klement, *Theologische Wahrheit und die Postmoderne*, 92–93.

[193] Klein, Blomberg, and Hubbard, 131.

about who determines the meaning of a text.[194] It has been aptly pointed out that "neither authors nor texts can control a reader's interpretation. It does not follow, however, that the author's intention is inaccessible or that the text means anything its readers take it to mean."[195] If we see the biblical text as a communication between the author and us, then we will have to search for a meaning that is author-intended.[196] It has been pointed out that

> if you read the Bible merely as great literature, merely for its aesthetic value, or merely for its suggestive moral guidance, not as communication from God, then you can interpret the text in any way you choose. Your main interpretive question will be: *What does this text mean to me?* If, however, you believe that the Bible is God's revelatory word to you and that the Scriptures function as communication from God to you, you should interpret the Bible by looking for the meaning that God, the author, intended. Your interpretive question should be: *What is the meaning God intended in this text?*[197]

Given the postmodernist critique of language as something that is time conditioned and ideologically encumbered, the Bible for postmodern interpreters is no propositional revelation and our view of Scripture must be reevaluated accordingly. Ultimately, within a postmodern framework, community takes precedence over doctrinal propositions.[198] We should remember, however, that in Scripture we find

---

[194] Actually, the issue is much more complex than what we have delineated in this brief discussion, and there are numerous scholars from a wide range of philosophical positions who dismiss the author's authority over meaning in texts. Some claim that each culture and community determines its own meaning apart from the author. Others maintain that language is incapable of objectively describing reality; thus, there is no real meaning at all in any text. For further reading on this subject, cf. Kevin Vanhoozer, *Is There a Meaning in This Text?: The Bible, the Reader, and the Morality of Literary Knowledge* (Grand Rapids, MI: Zondervan, 1998).

[195] Ibid., 282. While God accomplishes what He intends in communicating to us through the Bible, this does not mean that readers always respond to His message as He desires.

[196] Scott J. Duvall and J. Daniel Hays, *Grasping God's Word: A Hands-On Approach to Reading, Interpreting, and Applying the Bible*, 3rd ed. (Grand Rapids, MI: Zondervan, 2012), 194.

[197] Ibid., 194.

[198] Douglas Groothuis, "The Postmodernist Challenge to Theology," *Themelios* 25/1 (1999): 4, points out that "along these lines, some claim that theology should be primarily narratival in nature and not systematic or abstract. Telling the Christian story should replace stipulating Christian doctrine."

> a wealth of literary forms—poetry, history, wisdom literature, prophecy, and more—but every form consists of propositional content. In other words, Scripture is informative and correct on every matter it addresses. It discloses knowledge about the nature of God, humanity, salvation, ethics, history, and things to come. This revelation came through a variety of cultures and individuals, but it is no less propositional for that.[199]

In postmodern thinking the discovery and explication of factual information about the history of the people in the Bible and their religious convictions or the discovery and display of dogmatic truth is not intended.[200] In fact, the postmodern mindset is fundamentally suspicious of any modern rationalist accounts of truth, reason, and objectivity.[201] There is a deep-seated distrust of any single explanatory framework or metanarrative. In postmodern thinking biblical truth is not one and undivided, the same for all men everywhere at all times. Instead truth is socially constructed, contingent, and inseparable from the peculiar needs and preferences of certain people in a certain time and place. At the end of day, "truth is simply what we, as individuals and as communities, make it to be—and nothing more. Truth dissolves into a host of disconnected 'truths', all equal to each other but unrelated to one another: there is no overall, rational scheme of things."[202] This notion has many implications for biblical interpretation and leaves no value, custom, belief, or eternal verity totally untouched.[203] The biblical text is seen as diverse, dispersed, indeterminate, and pluralistic. "The great interpretive reality is that there is no court of appeal behind these many different readings. . . . The postmodern

---

[199] Groothuis, 5.

[200] E. V. McKnight, *Post-Modern Use of the Bible*, 263.

[201] Douglas Groothuis, "The Biblical View of Truth Challenges Postmodernist Truth Decay," *Themelios* 26/1 (2000): 13, points out that "for these postmodern thinkers, the very idea of truth has decayed and disintegrated."

[202] Ibid., 13. Groothuis points out one significant difference this perspective brings with it: "It is one kind of problem to believe an untruth, to take as fact something that in reality is a falsehood, yet still believe that truth exists and can be known. If one believes, for instance, that Jesus never claimed to be God Incarnate, historical evidence can be marshalled to refute this claim. However, it is another kind of problem too if one believes that truth itself is merely a matter of personal belief and social custom, so that the truth about Jesus depends on who you take him to be; in this case, no amount of evidence or argument about particular matters of fact will change one's belief" (ibid., 15).

[203] Walter Truett Anderson, *The Future of the Self: Exploring the Post-Identity Society* (New York: Tarcher, 1997), 27.

situation is signified precisely by the disappearance of any common, universal assumption at the outset of reading."[204]

By contrast, Seventh-day Adventists believe that the Bible functions as a communication from God to human beings and that it originates from God's revelation in it and inspiration of it. "One could further argue, theologically, that all humans—created in God's image—share common interpretive conventions and hence are part of a single interpretive community that requires meaning to transcend the perceptions of individual readers or interpretive communities."[205] Biblically speaking, God's purpose is to communicate His will to us. And this communication has a specific propositional content. The limitless possibilities of postmodern approaches, in contrast, have a touch of randomness and arbitrariness. But a Bible that can mean anything really means nothing.[206] While we do not conflate our interpretations with the meaning of the biblical text, the text of Scripture stands in judgment over our interpretation and we are subject to the words of Scripture. Therefore, for Seventh-day Adventists, the biblical text itself constitutes the most appropriate context for interpretation if the reader attends to the biblical text on its canonical level. The meaning of the text is what the author intended to communicate when he wrote the text. The text follows the conventions of language—syntax, grammar, word meaning, and so on. And meaning is tied to the context, not determined solely by grammar and dictionary definition.[207] How the reader should respond to the meaning of a text is called "application."[208] The biblical "meaning" on the other hand,

> is something we can validate. It is tied to the text and the intent of the author, not to the reader. Therefore, the *meaning* of the text is the same for all Christians. It is not subjective and does

---

[204] Walter Brueggemann, *Theology of the Old Testament* (Minneapolis, MN: Fortress Press, 1997), 61–62.

[205] Klein, Blomberg, and Hubbard, 130.

[206] So Collins, 16, quoting Robert Morgan. Biblical authority is a useless notion unless we know how to determine what the Bible means.

[207] Duval and Hays, 197.

[208] "Thus, it would be incorrect for us to ask in a Bible study, 'What does this passage *mean* to you?' The correct question sequence is 'What does this passage *mean*? How should you *apply* this meaning to your life?'" (Duvall and Hays, 195). Others point out that "in some cases, what pass for competing *interpretations* should probably be viewed as alternative *applications*. As we will argue, original meaning remains fixed, even as contemporary significance varies" (Klein, Blomberg, and Hubbard, 131).

> not change from reader to reader. *Application*, on the other hand, reflects the impact of the text on the reader's life. It is much more subjective, and it reflects the specific life situation of the reader. The *application* of the meaning will vary from Christian to Christian, but it will still have some boundaries influenced by the author's meaning.[209]

With these brief but important observations we will now turn to another approach to biblical interpretation that takes the propositional aspect of Scripture more seriously and suggests interpreting Scripture from a christological perspective.

Christological Hermeneutical Approaches

Recently a number of theologians have proposed a christological approach in biblical hermeneutics, where Jesus Christ, the gospel, the message of justification by faith, or some other central theme of Scripture becomes a key for interpreting the Bible.[210] This approach seems attractive for several reasons. Jesus is central for our salvation and faith. Therefore, Jesus should be central for our understanding of Scripture as well. Such an approach seems to be commanded by Scripture itself and practiced by the gospel writers and apostles who

---

[209] Duvall and Hays, 195–196.

[210] See Stanley J. Grenz, *Renewing the Center: Evangelical Theology in a Post-Theological Era* (Grand Rapids, MI: Baker Academic, 2000); Graeme Goldsworthy, *Gospel-Centered Hermeneutics: Foundations and Principles of Evangelical Biblical Interpretation* (Downers Grove, IL: InterVarsity, 2006); Zimmer; Christian Smith, *The Bible Made Impossible*, 93-126; Graeme Goldsworthy, *Christ-Centered Biblical Theology: Hermeneutical Foundations and Principles* (Downers Grove, IL: InterVarsity, 2012); and Michael Williams, *How to Read the Bible Through the Jesus Lens: A Guide to Christ-Focused Reading of Scripture* (Grand Rapids, MI: Zondervan, 2012). For some Adventist representatives of this perspective, see Rolf J. Pöhler, "Die Rechtfertigung durch den Glauben als hermeneutisches Prinzip: Christologische Schriftauslegung und adventistische Theologie," *Spes Christiana* 11 (2000): 46–60; Rolf J. Pöhler, "Does Adventist Theology Have, or Need, a Unifying Center?," in *Christ, Salvation, and the Eschaton: Essays in Honor of Hans K. LaRondelle*, ed. Daniel Heinz, Jiří Moskala, and Peter M. van Bemmelen (Berrien Springs, MI: Adventist Theological Seminary, 2009), 205–220; and Charles Scriven, "Shall We Slumber Through a Hermeneutics Problem?," *Spectrum*, September 4, 2019, https://spectrummagazine.org/views/2019/shall-we-slumber-through-hermeneutics-problem (accessed August 11, 2020). For a critical interaction with christological hermeneutics, see Frank M. Hasel, "Presuppositions in the Interpretation of Scripture," 27–46, esp. 40–43; Frank M. Hasel, "Christ-Centered Hermeneutics: Prospects and Challenges for Adventist Biblical Interpretation," *Ministry* (December 2012): 6–9; and Frank M. Hasel, "Gospel Centered Hermeneutics: Prospects and Challenges for Adventist Biblical Interpretation," *TheoRhēma* 6/2 (2011): 49–88. The presentation in this chapter closely follows these discussions in *TheoRhēma* and *Ministry*.

present Jesus as the explanation of the Old Testament (cf. Luke 24:27, 44–45; John 5:39–40; Rom 10:4; 2 Cor 1:20; 2 Cor 3:14–16; Gal 3:24; Col 1:25–2:3). After all, it is Jesus who unites both Old and New Testaments. Does not Jesus have priority over the Bible because He is *the* revelation of God?[211] Furthermore, a Christ-centered hermeneutic can dispel charges of being sectarian by having Christ firmly established as the interpretative key for the understanding of Scripture.[212] This hermeneutical approach does not follow postmodern thinking or other modern trends, but is significantly influenced by Martin Luther, who left a lasting legacy with this approach.

Martin Luther and His Christological Hermeneutics

It was Martin Luther, who, while affirming the authority of Scripture and heralding the *sola Scriptura* principle, also proposed another hermeneutical principle that can be termed the "christological principle." This christological principle has been instrumental in bringing about a subtle, yet significant shift in the understanding of theological authority and the hermeneutics of the Bible. While affirming the divine authority of Scripture and the priority of the Bible over church tradition, Luther's theological authority was closely connected to his understanding of the gospel. For Luther it was Christ and the gospel of justification by faith alone, to which Scripture attests, that constituted the theological *center* of Scripture and thus its final authority.[213] For Luther the *content* of Scripture is Christ, and from this fact, he seems to repeatedly judge its authority. All Scripture revolves around Christ as its authentic center. This "christological concentration" can be seen as the decisive element in Luther's interpretation and use of Scripture.[214] That is, Luther did not actually contend "for the primacy of Scripture in the strict sense, but for the primacy of the gospel to which Scripture attests

---

[211] So Zimmer.

[212] It seems as if Norman Gulley favored a christological arrangement of biblical faith for this very reason (see Norman R. Gulley, "Toward a Christ-Centered Expression of Faith," *Ministry*, [March 1997]: 24–27).

[213] Here Luther's famous preface to the epistle of James comes to mind, where he claims that what does not point to Christ or draws out Christ is not apostolic, even if Peter or Paul were to teach it. On the other hand, what "drives home" Christ is apostolic, even if it were to come from Judas, Annas, Pilate, or Herod. See *LW* 35, 396; *WADB* 7, 385.

[214] Cf. Frank M. Hasel, *Scripture in the Theologies of W. Pannenberg and D. G. Bloesch: An Investigation and Assessment of its Origin, Nature and Use*, European University Studies, Series XXIII Theology 555 (Frankfurt am Main: Peter Lang, 1996), 44–46.

and hence for the primacy of Scripture as the attestation to the gospel."[215] Luther valued the Bible "because it is the cradle that holds Christ. For this reason, the gospel of justification by grace through faith served as Luther's hermeneutical key to Scripture."[216] If Scripture does not refer to Christ, it must not be held to be true Scripture.[217] Luther's understanding of the gospel became the basis for determining the relative authority of the various canonical writings.[218] If Scripture is queen, Christ is king—even over Scripture![219] This means that if a passage of Scripture seems to be in conflict with Luther's Christ-centered interpretation, his interpretation becomes "gospel-centered criticism of Scripture."[220] Christ and Scripture can be set over against each other because Luther ultimately *ranked* the personal Word (Christ), the spoken Word (Gospel), and the written Word (Scripture). Such ranking leads to a canon within the canon, which compromises the strength of the Scripture principle, where Scripture is the sole source of its own exposition. For "if Scripture is interpreted either by a doctrinal center or by a tradition it is no longer Scripture that is interpreting itself—rather

---

[215] Grenz, *Renewing the Center*, 57–58.

[216] Ibid, 58.

[217] Cf. *WA* 18, 607; *LW* 34:112 (*Theses Concerning Faith and Law*).

[218] Here the danger of a "canon within the canon" becomes very real. It is a well-known fact that Luther called the book of James "an epistle of straw"—meaning an empty, useless, worthless epistle—because he could not find Christ and the gospel of justification by faith alone in the book of James and its emphasis on the importance of works. Cf. Martin Luther, "Preface to the New Testament," in *Martin Luther's Basic Theological Writings*, ed. Timothy Lull (Philadelphia, PA: Fortress, 1989), 117. In the German Luther Bible, Luther moved the book of James towards the end of the canon, where it occupies a different place than in English Bible translations.

[219] In his 1535 *Lectures on Galatians*, while replying to opponents who adduce biblical passages stressing works and merits, Luther stresses the following point: "You are stressing the servant, that is Scripture—and not all of it at that or even its most powerful part, but only a few passages concerning works. I leave this servant to you. I for my part stress the Lord, who is the King of Scripture" (*LW* 26, 295; *WA* 40, I, 459, 14–16). In the same year, Luther again underscored Scripture's servant status relative to Christ when he wrote, "Briefly, Christ is Lord, not the servant, the Lord of the Sabbath, of law, and of all things. The Scriptures must be understood in favour of Christ, not against him. For that reason they must either refer to him or must not be held to be true Scriptures. . . . Therefore, if the adversaries press the Scriptures against Christ, we urge Christ against the Scriptures. We have the Lord, they have the servants; we have the Head, they the feet or members, over which the head necessarily dominates and takes precedence. If one of them had to be parted with, Christ or the law, the law would have to be let go, not Christ. For if we have Christ, we can easily establish laws and we shall judge all things rightly. Indeed, we would make new decalogues, as Paul does in all the epistles, and Peter, but above all Christ in the gospel" (*LW* 34, 112, 40–53).

[220] Paul Althaus, *The Theology of Martin Luther*, trans. Robert C. Schultz (Philadelphia, PA: Fortress, 1966), 81.

it is we who are interpreting Scripture by means of a doctrine or tradition, to which Scripture is in practice, being subjected."[221] Thus, it is not surprising that Luther's christological method "sharpened into a tool of theological criticism"[222] where ultimately the interpreter becomes the judge and stands above Scripture. The irony of this theological criticism is that it is done in the name of Jesus Christ and the gospel.

The Relationship Between Christ and the Bible

Ultimately the issue in any gospel-centered hermeneutic boils down to the issue of the proper relationship between Christ and the Bible. Christ Himself showed the disciples how Scripture pointed to Him (Luke 24:25–27). Scripture testifies about Christ (John 5:39). But the decisive question is this: how are we to understand the relationship between Christ and Scripture? It appears that God uses words and the medium of speech to lead us to an encounter with the person of Christ. The living and speaking God of Scripture has chosen to reveal Himself through the Word. God has seen it fit to commit His spoken Word through the biblical authors to the medium of writing, thus generating the Bible, the written Word of God. Without Scripture we would not know much about Jesus.[223] The Word-incarnate (Jesus Christ) cannot be separated from the Word-inscripturated (Holy Scripture). Jesus Himself turned to Scripture to make Himself known. When He met the disciples on the way to Emmaus, He began "with Moses and all the Prophets" and explained to them "what was said in all the Scriptures concerning himself" (Luke 24:27, NIV). Later that night Jesus again pointed to Scripture when He made it clear to the disciples that everything written about Him "in the Law of Moses, the Prophets and the Psalms" (Luke 24:44, NIV) must be fulfilled. "Then he opened their minds so they could understand the Scriptures" (Luke 24:45, NIV). Without Scripture providing a reliable account of Jesus' ministry and death, the gospel of Christ would not be known to us and would be of little use.

Jesus Himself repeatedly referred to Scripture as the authoritative norm for faith and practice. He asked the lawyer, "What is written in the Law? How do you read it?" (Luke 10:26, NIV). When the lawyer cited

---

[221] Brian Gaybba, *The Tradition: An Ecumenical Breakthrough?* (Rome: Herder, 1971), 221.

[222] Werner Georg Kümmel, *The New Testament: The History of the Investigation of Its Problems*, trans. S. McLean Gilmour and Howard C. Kee (Nashville, TN: Abingdon, 1972), 24.

[223] On the few extrabiblical references to Jesus, see F. F. Bruce, *Jesus and Christian Origins Outside the New Testament* (London: Hodder and Stoughton, 1974); and Gerd Theissen and Annette Merz, *Der historische Jesus* (Göttingen: Vandenhoeck & Ruprecht, 1996), 35–124.

Deuteronomy 6:5 and Leviticus 19:18, Jesus commended him for having answered correctly (Luke 10:28). In similar fashion Jesus made the same point: "Have you never read in the Scriptures?" (Matt 21:42, NIV); "Haven't you read" (NIV; Matt 12:3, 5; 19:4; 22:31; Mark 12:10, 26; Luke 6:3); "Let the reader understand" (Matt 24:15; Mark 13:14).

Whether Jesus spoke to scribes or to common people, He always assumed the full authority of all of Scripture. For Jesus, Scripture is the sole authoritative source whereby we can discriminate between right and wrong. He Himself abided by Scripture. Jesus quoted the Scriptures and referred to Scripture, rather than to His personal word, to refute the devil during the temptations (Matt 4:4, 7, 10). Speaking about the proper faith response to Him as Messiah, He said, "Whoever believes in me, *as the Scripture has said,* streams of living water will flow from within him" (John 7:38, NIV, emphasis added). Scripture authenticates Jesus as the Christ. When Scripture is not the context for our understanding of Jesus Christ, Jesus becomes the pretext for judging Scripture! Never do we find Jesus criticizing parts of Scripture. Neither do we find the apostles doing so. Not once do they insinuate that parts of Scripture are not trustworthy or lack divine authority. Jesus does not abrogate the law and the prophets; He upholds them. He also affirms the historicity of Old Testament figures such as Adam and Moses and events such as creation.

Symphonic Theological Perspectives or Monophonic Theological Center?

We have to carefully distinguish between a central theme in Scripture and a theological center that functions as a hermeneutical key whereby other portions and statements of Scripture are relegated to a secondary or inferior status. A theological center that functions as a hermeneutical key leads to a canon within the canon that does not do justice to the fullness, richness, breadth, and scope of divine truth as we find it in all of Scripture. A monophonic center ultimately leads to a criticism of the content of Scripture. To postulate a "gospel hermeneutic," whereby Jesus Christ functions as the hermeneutical key for the interpretation of Scripture, is reductionistic. The biblical material is too rich and multifaceted to limit it to one theme or center. Rather than a monophonic center, the Bible presents us with a more encompassing "symphonic" theological perspective.[224]

---

[224] Cf. Vern Sheridan Poythress, *Symphonic Theology: The Validity of Multiple Perspectives in*

To the perennial question of what the central element of Scripture is, we respond by posing another question: "where does one find the central point of a symphony or a play? Of course, there are central themes, but no single point can be taken as the center, unless it be the unity of the whole."[225] We need to allow Scripture in its entirety (*tota Scriptura*), in all its multifaceted voices and genres, to reveal the richness and depth of God's wisdom to us. Only such a symphonic reading of the Bible will be able to do justice to the multiplex phenomena of Scripture under the unifying guidance of the one Holy Spirit.

Ellen G. White and Christological Hermeneutics

This leads us to the question of whether Ellen G. White advocated a christological hermeneutic. A close reading of Ellen G. White's writings reveals that she acknowledges central themes[226] in Scripture, such as the plan of redemption:

> The central theme of the Bible, the theme about which every other in the whole book clusters, is the redemption plan, the restoration in the human soul of the image of God. From the first intimation of hope in the sentence pronounced in Eden to that last glorious promise of the Revelation, "They shall see His face; and His name shall be in their foreheads" (Revelation 22:4), the burden of every book and every passage of the Bible is the unfolding of this wondrous theme,—man's uplifting,—the power of God, "which giveth us the victory through our Lord Jesus Christ." 1 Corinthians 15:57.[227]

Similarly, she writes:

> The sacrifice of Christ as an atonement for sin is the great truth around which all other truths cluster. In order to be rightly understood and appreciated, every truth in the Word of God, from Genesis to Revelation, must be studied in the light that

---

Theology (Grand Rapids, MI: Zondervan, 1987). See also Alberto R. Timm, "Understanding Inspiration: The Symphonic and Wholistic Nature of Scripture" *Ministry*, August 1999, 12–15.

[225] William Dyrness, *Themes in Old Testament Theology* (Downers Grove, IL: InterVarsity, 1979), 19.

[226] Richard M. Davidson, "Back to the Beginning: Genesis 1–3 and the Theological Center of Scripture," in Heinz, Moskala, and van Bemmelen, 5–29.

[227] Ellen G. White, *Education* (Mountain View, CA: Pacific Press, 1952), 125.

> streams from the cross of Calvary. I present before you the great, grand monument of mercy and regeneration, salvation and redemption—the Son of God uplifted on the cross. This is to be the foundation of every discourse given by our ministers.[228]

A careful reading of her writings reveals, however, that Ellen G. White never uses these central themes as a hermeneutical key whereby she criticizes Scripture and relegates some parts of the Bible to being more inspired than others. Notice how she mentions a great central theme and in one breath also affirms that all Scripture is inspired, and that Scripture should be compared with Scripture:

> The Bible is its own expositor. Scripture is to be compared with scripture. The student should learn to view the word as a whole, and to see the relation of its parts. He should gain a knowledge of its grand central theme, of God's original purpose for the world, of the rise of the great controversy, and of the work of redemption. . . . Every part of the Bible is given by inspiration of God and is profitable. The Old Testament no less than the New should receive attention. As we study the Old Testament we shall find living springs bubbling up where the careless reader discerns only a desert.[229]

Ellen G. White does not mean to separate Christ from the Scriptures.[230] When she writes, "The sacrifice of Christ as an atonement for sin is the great truth around which all other truths cluster,"[231] she is not proposing a theological center that would function as a tool for theological criticism, or a canon within the canon, whereby important statements of Scripture can be distinguished from allegedly less important passages or even wrong teachings. Rather, "*every truth in the Word of God, from Genesis to Revelation*, is to be studied in the light that streams from the cross of Calvary."[232] And even where she describes

---

[228] Ellen G. White, *Gospel Workers* (Washington, DC: Review and Herald, 1948), 315.

[229] Ellen G. White, *Education*, 190–191.

[230] "Her emphasis on the fact that Christ is the Author and culmination of divine revelation does not lead Ellen White to deny or downplay the crucial role of the Holy Scriptures as a revelation from God" (Peter van Bemmelen, "Revelation and Inspiration," in Dederen, 55).

[231] Ellen G. White, *Evangelism* (Washington, DC: Review and Herald, 1946), 190.

[232] Ibid., emphasis added.

"Christ as the living center"[233] who unites the biblical doctrines, she at once affirms that "the truth for this time is *broad in its outlines*, far reaching, *embracing many doctrines*."[234] While Christ certainly is central to her religious thought,[235] Ellen G. White never ceases to emphasize that *all* of Scripture is to be followed and that no part of Scripture is to be neglected. In this sense she can affirm the centrality of certain biblical themes without denigrating other parts of Scripture as unimportant. According to her, no man has the right to judge Scripture by selecting those passages that are deemed more important than others. She writes, "Do not let any living man come to you and begin to dissect God's Word, telling what is revelation, what is inspiration and what is not, without a rebuke. . . . We want no one to say, 'This I will reject, and this will I receive,' but *we want to have implicit faith in the Bible as a whole and as it is*."[236] To use Ellen G. White in support of a christological hermeneutic, where Christ or the gospel functions as a hermeneutical key, is to misuse her and distort her numerous clear statements to the contrary.

The Living Word of God Through the Written Word of God

God has arranged for the Holy Spirit to lead us to the Living Word (Jesus Christ) through the written Word (Holy Scripture). This is how God in His wisdom has chosen to make His revelation universally available. Scripture is central to our faith and to our devotion to God because there is no witness to Jesus Christ other than the written Word of God. We have no other Christ than the one the biblical writers present to us. Submitting to Jesus Christ, the living Lord, entails our faithful

---

[233] Ellen G. White to A. T. Jones, March 15, 1894, Lt 103, 1894.

[234] Ibid., emphasis added.

[235] Cf. her statement that "of all professing Christians, Seventh-day Adventists should be foremost in uplifting Christ before the world" (Ellen G. White, *Evangelism*, 188). See also Peter van Bemmelen, "'The Matchless Charms of Christ': Theological Significance of this Phrase in Ellen White's Writings," in Heinz, Moskala, and van Bemmelen, 231–240.

[236] Ellen G. White, *SDA Bible Commentary*, vol. 7, *Phil.–Rev. (EGW Comments)* (Washington, DC: Review and Herald, 1957), 919, emphasis added. Similarly, Ellen G. White, *Christ's Object Lessons* (Washington DC: Review and Herald, 1900), 39, writes, "Many professed ministers of the gospel do not accept the whole Bible as the inspired word. One wise man rejects one portion; another questions another part. They set up their judgement as superior to the word; and the Scripture which they do teach, rests upon their own authority. Its divine authenticity is destroyed"; see also Ellen G. White, *Selected Messages*, vol. 1 (Washington, DC: Review and Herald, 1958), 17, 42, 245; and Ellen G. White, *Testimonies for the Church*, 9 vols. (Mountain View, CA: Pacific Press, 1855–1909), 5:700–701, 8:319.

submission to the written Word of God. This is what Jesus did. Individually, as well as corporately, we stand under the authority of Scripture because Jesus rules us by Scripture. We do not worship paper and ink nor idolize a book, but simply acknowledge that the Bible is the source that tells us all about Jesus Christ. Through Holy Scripture we have learned to know and love Him (1 Pet 1:8). This is not bibliolatry, but Christianity in its most authentic form. The Spirit of Christ who dwells in Christians never leads them to doubt, criticize, go beyond, or fall short of Bible teaching. The Holy Spirit never draws us away from the written Word, any more than from the living Word. Instead, He keeps us in constant, conscious, and willing submission to both together. *Sola Scriptura* without Christ is empty, but Christ without Scripture—whose son is He? Without Scripture we would not know that Jesus is the Messiah and He could not be our Savior. Thus, our loyalty to the Bible is part of our loyalty to Christ. What is needed is not our human criticism of Scripture—not even in the name of Christ!—but the critical examination of ourselves, the church, and all other areas by Scripture, for which the biblical text alone is divinely fitted.

Concluding Thoughts

Modern historical-critical scholarship has focused on the historical reconstruction of the biblical material *behind* the biblical text. It has tried to recover the meaning of the biblical text in the reconstruction of the historical context in light of the analogy of current events and the correlation of immanent cause and relations. This has fragmented the biblical material into multiple and conflicting sources and has distanced the text from the modern reader. Attempts to use a modified historical-critical method that is amplified with faith or a hermeneutic of consent remain unsatisfactory, because the historical-critical principles are incompatible with faith. Even a modified version of historical criticism leads to the criticism of the content of Scripture. Whenever our hermeneutics leads us to criticize the content of Scripture (content criticism or *Sachkritik*), Scripture no longer serves as the final authority in theology. Methodological criticism and doubt are not the appropriate responses to faith and do not do justice to the character of Scripture as a divinely inspired book.

Canonical approaches have tried to recover an interpretation where the final canonical text of Scripture is read in the life of the church. While the focus on the canonical text of Scripture is something that resonates with our Adventist approach to hermeneutics, "canonical criticism" does not fully abandon historical critical investigations. This is an unresolved incongruency. Furthermore, canonical approaches have shifted the attention from the factuality of the biblical text to its role as a witness, which seems to downplay the historical character of the biblical material itself. It also raises important questions about the role of the community in interpretation.

Newer literary approaches have focused on the final canonical text of Scripture and have uncovered literary features that were largely lost in historical-critical research. While literary approaches that respect the canonical form of the biblical text have the potential to uncover a helpful understanding of the biblical message and have shown many intratextual connections among different parts of the canonical text, many literary approaches focus exclusively on the literary shape of the text, without dealing with the historical dimension of it. By focusing on the biblical "story," the historicity of biblical persons and events is often bracketed and neglected. This is a significant deficiency that should not be overlooked because it raises important questions about the historical truth and factuality of the biblical account as well as the importance of historical reliability for the truthfulness of the Bible and its propositional character.

Postmodern approaches to biblical interpretation focus on the reader rather than the text. Here the danger is that the text no longer has a definite meaning. Rather, the text gains a life of its own through the reader. This leads to multiple meanings where the text can be appropriated very differently by different readers and audiences. Here the text of Scripture loses its determinative role for theology and the reader becomes the key for interpretation. The Bible can no longer function authoritatively and loses its ability to be a decisive and final norm for theological questions because its propositional character is not acknowledged. Seventh-day Adventist hermeneutics cannot follow postmodern approaches, where the authority of the text shifts to the reader and thus to the community of interpretation. In light of the relativistic character of postmodern approaches, we do well to remind ourselves that "ordinary people do not and cannot live as if human conversation were ultimately relativistic and self-defeating."[237]

In christological hermeneutics, Jesus Christ is elevated as a hermeneutical key over Scripture. As attractive as it sounds, it ultimately also leads to content criticism, where the content of the Bible is criticized—even in the name of Christ. This leads to a critical dissection of

[237] Klein, Blomberg, and Hubbard, 134.

Scripture and ultimately to a canon within the canon. Perhaps one of the most subtle forms of biblical criticism is performed in the very name of Jesus Christ, where in christological hermeneutics Jesus is used as a hermeneutical key to determine which passages of Scripture are acceptable and which passages are not. Such content criticism of Scripture ultimately robs Scripture of its authority and theological unity so that Scripture can no longer serve as God's inspired norm to be followed. Such an approach does not do justice to the way Jesus Christ Himself and the apostles dealt with Scripture. For them, Scripture—all of Scripture—was authoritative and given for our instruction (John 5:46–47; 7:38; Rom 15:4).

When we carefully look at these different approaches to biblical interpretation, we realize that we are here not just dealing with equally legitimate alternatives, but a difference of quality, making this issue so significant and contentious. This calls for a spirit of fair-mindedness,[238] prudence, and discernment. This is needed because in some of the previously discussed approaches there are some aspects that on the surface look attractive and even similar to what Seventh-day Adventists espouse for our biblical-historical hermeneutics.[239] The biblical-historical method affirmed by Seventh-day Adventists is informed by biblical presuppositions and thus is broader in its scope than a historical-critical approach that systematically excludes the supernatural dimension that Scripture attests. This biblical-historical approach does not start with methodological criticism which operates within the narrow bounds of human analogy and immanent factors of correlation. Instead it is grounded in God's supernatural revelation that is accepted in faith and sustained by a love for God's Word. Seventh-day Adventists do not use methodologies that arise from a philosophical mindset that works on a closed worldview where any supernatural dimension is categorically excluded or regarded as unlikely. Therefore, we should be careful not to use approaches that work on premises that exclude the supernatural dimension or negate the historical veracity of the biblical events that are testified in Scripture. This calls for a deliberate approach in biblical hermeneutics that does not just copy other approaches in biblical interpretation that are *en vogue* right now, but develops a methodology that is truly biblical and historical in nature.

---

[238] On the blessings of fair-mindedness, see Philip E. Dow, *Virtuous Minds: Intellectual Character Development* (Downers Grove, IL: InterVarsity, 2013), 46–54.

[239] On the use of the term "biblical-historical," see Maier, 375–409. For a Seventh-day Adventist perspective, see Richard M. Davidson, "Biblical Interpretation," in Dederen, 58–104, who calls for a "historical-biblical" method (94–95).

As Seventh-day Adventists, we are grateful for all hermeneutical approaches that value and respect the biblical text in its canonical form and where the text of Scripture retains its authority over the reader. For Seventh-day Adventists, the text of Scripture is the carrier of its meaning. Meaning is determined by what the author fixed in the words of Scripture. However, when the meaning of the text is no longer decisive and no longer a property of the biblical text, Scripture loses its authority and power to reform and correct our thinking and our acting. When the reader becomes the creator of meaning and everything is subjected to the constraints of methods that work purely on immanent accounts, God's voice is no longer perceptible in Scripture. The Bible is not just given to satisfy intellectual curiosity or for the analysis of its meaning from a critical distance. The biblical message is given to us by God who desires that we embrace it joyfully and practice faithfully what we have discovered. The Bible seeks our obedient response and is given to change and transform our lives. For this to happen, the text of Scripture needs to have a definite meaning that can be discovered and discerned by the reader. Where the text loses this quality, it morphs into a chimera of cacophonous voices. It loses its power to guide, lead, correct, and equip (2 Tim 3:16–17). When the meaning no longer resides in the text but is instead created in front of the text by the reader, the Bible forfeits its authority for theology, faith, and practice. The shifting sands of our situatedness do not provide the stability and power to transform our lives. When the biblical text loses its historical credibility, it becomes an expression of human fantasy and no longer provides hope. Biblical hope is grounded not in wishful thinking, but in the faithful promises of God that are established and confirmed through His mighty acts in history. This is why biblical hope is connected with responsibility and why the credibility of the biblical account and even the trustworthiness of God can be tested by the historical fulfillment of His words (Isa 41:22, 26; 44:7).

Any method that is used as a tool of biblical criticism in which the content of Scripture is criticized—even when done in the name of Christ—should be avoided by Seventh-day Adventists. This also applies to methods where the historical reality of biblical events are ignored or set aside, or where the propositional nature of God's revelation and divine inspiration is denied. When we "use" Christ without adhering to all of Scripture, we do not follow Christ at all but misuse His name. Even though some of the text-oriented modern approaches might seem to come closer to what Seventh-day Adventists have promoted as sound hermeneutical procedures,[240] we have to recognize that they often still do not accept divine revelation and inspiration as foundational to Scripture and thus do not regard the biblical stories as anchored in real history. This eventually will have far-reaching consequences for our theology and faith. The perceptive words of Romano Guardini deserve attention: "The destructions of an avalanche do not begin with the rubble in the valley, but where in the lofty heights the little particles get loose."[241] These subtle beginnings of criticism, where human reason is elevated above Scripture, should carefully be avoided. When methods are adopted that give interpretative priority to the reader rather than to the biblical text, the authority of Scripture is eliminated and the Bible ceases to be the final norm for our theology. When the reader determines the meaning of the Bible, the content of the Bible is affected because it is constantly changing. This is not a debate over minor theological questions or peripheral issues (*adiaphora*). Our hermeneutic ultimately affects the central features of our faith and the very nature of who we are as Bible-believing Christians. We are not saved by our hermeneutics; we are saved through faith in Jesus Christ alone! However, we cannot know what the Bible tells us about Jesus Christ and His salvation when our hermeneutic is deficient or when we create the biblical meaning ourselves. Thus, the issue of biblical interpretation is a watershed for theology. It significantly shapes the outcome of our theology, message, and mission.[242] Therefore, the great question is that of biblical hermeneutics. Everything else follows in its wake.

This means that as Adventist scholars, theologians, pastors, and members, we need to be cognizant of new hermeneutical approaches and know the principles on which they are founded so that we can understand their strengths as well as their deficiencies. Biblical hermeneutics need to be practiced with discernment and in harmony with the biblical principles that acknowledge the divine inspiration of Scripture and affirm the full canonical text of the Bible as the ultimate source for its meaning and the final authority for all theological questions. For God delights in "him who is humble and contrite of spirit, and who trembles at My word" (Isa 66:2, NASB) and speaks "My word in truth" (Jer 23:28, NASB) .

---

[240] See the appendix "Methods of Bible Study," in the present volume.

[241] Romao Guardini (1885–1965) in *Frankfurter Hefte* (1948/4), 351, Frank M. Hasel's translation.

[242] Frank M. Hasel and Michael G. Hasel, *How to Interpret Scripture* (Nampa, ID: Pacific Press, 2019), 8.

Appendix: Methods of Bible Study[1]

Bible Study: Presuppositions, Principles, and Methods

1. Preamble

This statement is addressed to all members of the Seventh-day Adventist Church with the purpose of providing guidelines on how to study the Bible, both the trained biblical scholar and others.

Seventh-day Adventists recognize and appreciate the contributions of those biblical scholars throughout history who have developed useful and reliable methods of Bible study consistent with the claims and teachings of Scripture. Adventists are committed to the acceptance of biblical truth and are willing to follow it, using all methods of interpretation consistent with what Scripture says of itself. These are outlined in the presuppositions detailed below.

In recent decades the most prominent method in biblical studies has been known as the historical-critical method. Scholars who use this method, as classically formulated, operate on the basis of presuppositions which, prior to studying the biblical text, reject the reliability of accounts of miracles and other supernatural events narrated in the Bible. Even a modified use of this method that retains the principle of criticism which subordinates the Bible to human reason is unacceptable to Adventists.

The historical-critical method minimizes the need for faith in God and obedience to His commandments. In addition, because such a method de-emphasizes the divine element in the Bible as an inspired book (including its resultant unity) and depreciates or misunderstands apocalyptic prophecy and the eschatological portions of the Bible, we urge Adventist Bible students to avoid relying on the use

---

[1] The document can be found in Rajmund Dabrowski, ed., *Statements, Guidelines and other Documents of the Seventh-day Adventist Church* (Silver Spring, MD: Review and Herald Publishing Association, 2005), 209-218; and online at https://www.adventist.org/articles/methods-of-bible-study/ (accessed: 06-29-2020)

of the presuppositions and the resultant deductions associated with the historical-critical method.

In contrast with the historical-critical method and presuppositions, we believe it to be helpful to set forth the principles of Bible study that are consistent with the teachings of the Scriptures themselves, that preserve their unity, and are based upon the premise that the Bible is the Word of God. Such an approach will lead us into a satisfying and rewarding experience with God.

2. Presuppositions Arising From the Claims of Scripture

1. Origin

1. The Bible is the Word of God and is the primary and authoritative means by which He reveals Himself to human beings.

2. The Holy Spirit inspired the Bible writers with thoughts, ideas, and objective information; in turn they expressed these in their own words. Therefore the Scriptures are an indivisible union of human and divine elements, neither of which should be emphasized to the neglect of the other (2Peter 1:21; cf. *The Great Controversy*, v, vi).

3. All Scripture is inspired by God and came through the work of the Holy Spirit. However, it did not come in a continuous chain of unbroken revelations. As the Holy Spirit communicated truth to the Bible writer, each wrote as he was moved by the Holy Spirit, emphasizing the aspect of the truth which he was led to stress. For this reason the student of the Bible will gain a rounded comprehension on any subject by recognizing that the Bible is its own best interpreter and when studied as a whole it depicts a consistent, harmonious truth (2Tim. 3:16; Heb. 1:1, 2; cf. *Selected Messages*, Book 1, 19, 20; *The Great Controversy*, v, vi).

4. Although it was given to those who lived in an ancient Near Eastern/Mediterranean context, the Bible transcends its cultural backgrounds to serve as God's Word for all cultural, racial, and situational contexts in all ages.

2. Authority

1. The sixty-six books of the Old and New Testaments are the clear, infallible revelation of God's will and His salvation. The Bible is the Word of God, and it alone is the standard by which

all teaching and experience must be tested (2Tim. 3:15, 17; Ps. 119:105; Prov. 30:5, 6; Isa. 8:20; John 17:17; 2Thess. 3:14; Heb. 4:12).

2. Scripture is an authentic, reliable record of history and God's acts in history. It provides the normative theological interpretation of those acts. The supernatural acts revealed in Scripture are historically true. For example, chapters 1-11 of Genesis are a factual account of historical events.

3. The Bible is not like other books. It is an indivisible blend of the divine and the human. Its record of many details of secular history is integral to its overall purpose to convey salvation history. While at times there may be parallel procedures employed by Bible students to determine historical data, the usual techniques of historical research, based as they are on human presuppositions and focused on the human element, are inadequate for interpreting the Scriptures, which are a blend of the divine and human. Only a method that fully recognizes the indivisible nature of the Scriptures can avoid a distortion of its message.

4. Human reason is subject to the Bible, not equal to or above it. Presuppositions regarding the Scriptures must be in harmony with the claims of the Scriptures and subject to correction by them (1Cor. 2:1-6). God intends that human reason be used to its fullest extent, but within the context and under the authority of His Word rather than independent of it.

5. The revelation of God in all nature, when properly understood, is in harmony with the written Word, and is to be interpreted in the light of Scripture.

3. Principles for Approaching the Interpretation of Scripture

1. The Spirit enables the believer to accept, understand, and apply the Bible to one's own life as he seeks divine power to render obedience to all scriptural requirements and to appropriate personally all Bible promises. Only those following the light already received can hope to receive further illumination of the Spirit (John 16:13, 14; 1Cor. 2:10-14).

2. Scripture cannot be correctly interpreted without the aid of the Holy Spirit, for it is the Spirit who enables the believer to understand and apply Scripture. Therefore, any study of the Word should commence with a request for the Spirit's guidance and illumination.

3. Those who come to the study of the Word must do so with faith, in the humble spirit of a learner who seeks to hear what the Bible is saying. They must be willing to submit all presuppositions, opinions, and the conclusions of reason to the judgment and correction of the Word itself. With this attitude the Bible student may come directly to the Word, and with careful study may come to an understanding of the essentials of salvation apart from any human explanations, however helpful. The biblical message becomes meaningful to such a person.

4. The investigation of Scripture must be characterized by a sincere desire to discover and obey God's will and word rather than to seek support or evidence for preconceived ideas.

4. Methods of Bible Study

1. Select a Bible version for study that is faithful to the meaning contained in languages in which the Bible originally was written, giving preference to translations done by a broad group of scholars and published by a general publisher above translations sponsored by a particular denomination or narrowly focused group.

   Exercise care not to build major doctrinal points on one Bible translation or version. Trained biblical scholars will use the Greek and Hebrew texts, enabling them to examine variant readings of ancient Bible manuscripts as well.

2. Choose a definite plan of study, avoiding haphazard and aimless approaches. Study plans such as the following are suggested:

   1. Book-by-book analysis of the message
   2. Verse-by-verse method
   3. Study that seeks a biblical solution to a specific life problem, biblical satisfaction for a specific need, or a biblical answer to a specific question

4. Topical study (faith, love, second coming, and others)
5. Word study
6. Biographical study

3. Seek to grasp the simple, most obvious meaning of the biblical passage being studied.

4. Seek to discover the underlying major themes of Scripture as found in individual texts, passages, and books. Two basic, related themes run throughout Scripture: (1)The person and work of Jesus Christ; and (2)the great controversy perspective involving the authority of God's Word, the fall of man, the first and second advents of Christ, the exoneration of God and His law, and the restoration of the divine plan for the universe. These themes are to be drawn from the totality of Scripture and not imposed on it.

5. Recognize that the Bible is its own interpreter and that the meaning of words, texts, and passages is best determined by diligently comparing scripture with scripture.

6. Study the context of the passage under consideration by relating it to the sentences and paragraphs immediately preceding and following it. Try to relate the ideas of the passage to the line of thought of the entire Bible book.

7. As far as possible ascertain the historical circumstances in which the passage was written by the biblical writers under the guidance of the Holy Spirit.

8. Determine the literary type the author is using. Some biblical material is composed of parables, proverbs, allegories, psalms, and apocalyptic prophecies. Since many biblical writers presented much of their material as poetry, it is helpful to use a version of the Bible that presents this material in poetic style, for passages employing imagery are not to be interpreted in the same manner as prose.

9. Recognize that a given biblical text may not conform in every detail to present-day literary categories. Be cautious not to force these categories in interpreting the meaning of the biblical text. It is a human tendency to find what one is looking for, even when the author did not intend such.

10. Take note of grammar and sentence construction in order to discover the author's meaning. Study the key words of the passage by comparing their use in other parts of the Bible by means of a concordance and with the help of biblical lexicons and dictionaries.

11. In connection with the study of the biblical text, explore the historical and cultural factors. Archaeology, anthropology, and history may contribute to understanding the meaning of the text.

12. Seventh-day Adventists believe that God inspired Ellen G. White. Therefore, her expositions on any given Bible passage offer an inspired guide to the meaning of texts without exhausting their meaning or preempting the task of exegesis (for example, see *Evangelism*, 256; *The Great Controversy*, 193, 595;Testimonies, vol. 5, pp. 665, 682, 707-708; *Counsels to Writers and Editors*, 33-35).

13. After studying as outlined above, turn to various commentaries and secondary helps such as scholarly works to see how others have dealt with the passage. Then carefully evaluate the different viewpoints expressed from the standpoint of Scripture as a whole.

14. In interpreting prophecy keep in mind that:

    1. The Bible claims God's power to predict the future (Isa 46:10).
    2. Prophecy has a moral purpose. It was not written merely to satisfy curiosity about the future. Some of the purposes of prophecy are to strengthen faith (John 14:29) and to promote holy living and readiness for the Advent (Matt 24:44; Rev 22:7, 10, 11).
    3. The focus of much prophecy is on Christ (both His first and second advents), the church, and the end-time.
    4. The norms for interpreting prophecy are found within the Bible itself: The Bible notes time prophecies and their historical fulfillments; the New Testament cites specific fulfillments of Old Testament prophecies about the Messiah; and the Old Testament itself presents individuals and events as types of the Messiah.
    5. In the New Testament application of Old Testament prophecies, some literal names become spiritual: for example, Israel represents the church, Babylon apostate religion, etc.
    6. There are two general types of prophetic writings: non-

apocalyptic prophecy as found in Isaiah and Jeremiah, and apocalyptic prophecy as found in Daniel and the Revelation. These differing types have different characteristics:

a. Nonapocalyptic prophecy addresses God's people; apocalyptic is more universal in scope.
b. Nonapocalyptic prophecy often is conditional in nature, setting forth to God's people the alternatives of blessing for obedience and curses for disobedience; apocalyptic emphasizes the sovereignty of God and His control over history.
c. Nonapocalyptic prophecy often leaps from the local crisis to the end-time day of the Lord; apocalyptic prophecy presents the course of history from the time of the prophet to the end of the world.
d. Time prophecies in nonapocalyptic prophecy generally are long, for example, 400 years of Israel's servitude (Gen. 15:13) and 70 years of Babylonian captivity (Jer. 25:12). Time prophecies in apocalyptic prophecy generally are phrased in short terms, for example, 10 days (Rev. 2:10)or 42 months (Rev. 13:5). Apocalyptic time periods stand symbolically for longer periods of actual time.

7. Apocalyptic prophecy is highly symbolic and should be interpreted accordingly. In interpreting symbols, the following methods may be used:

   a. Look for interpretations (explicit or implicit) within the passage itself (for example, Dan. 8:20, 21; Rev. 1:20).
   b. Look for interpretations elsewhere in the book or in other writings by the same author.
   c. Using a concordance, study the use of symbols in other parts of Scripture.
   d. A study of ancient Near Eastern documents may throw light on the meaning of symbols, although scriptural use may alter those meanings.

8. The literary structure of a book often is an aid to interpreting it. The parallel nature of Daniel's prophecies is an example.

15. Parallel accounts in Scripture sometimes present differences in detail and emphasis (for example, cf. Matt 21:33, 34; Mark 12:1-11;

and Luke 20:9-18; or 2Kings 18-20 with 2Chron. 32). When studying such passages, first examine them carefully to be sure that the parallels actually are referring to the same historical event. For example, many of Jesus' parables may have been given on different occasions to different audiences and with different wording.

In cases where there appear to be differences in parallel accounts, one should recognize that the total message of the Bible is the synthesis of all of its parts. Each book or writer communicates that which the Spirit has led him to write. Each makes his own special contribution to the richness, diversity, and variety of Scripture (*The Great Controversy* , v, vi). The reader must allow each Bible writer to emerge and be heard while at the same time recognizing the basic unity of the divine self-disclosure.

When parallel passages seem to indicate discrepancy or contradiction, look for the underlying harmony. Keep in mind that dissimilarities may be due to minor errors of copyists (*Selected Messages*, Book 1, p. 16), or may be the result of differing emphases and choice of materials of various authors who wrote under the inspiration and guidance of the Holy Spirit for different audiences under different circumstances (*Selected Messages*, Book 1, pp. 21, 22; *The Great Controversy*, vi).

It may prove impossible to reconcile minor dissimilarities in detail which may be irrelevant to the main and clear message of the passage. In some cases judgment may have to be suspended until more information and better evidence are available to resolve a seeming discrepancy.

16. The Scriptures were written for the practical purpose of revealing the will of God to the human family. However, in order not to misconstrue certain kinds of statements, it is important to recognize that they were addressed to peoples of Eastern cultures and expressed in their thought patterns.

    Expressions such as "the Lord hardened the heart of Pharaoh" (Ex. 9:12) or "an evil spirit from God..." (1Sam 16:15), the imprecatory psalms, or the "three days and three nights" of Jonah as compared with Christ's death (Matt. 12:40), commonly are misunderstood because they are interpreted today from a different viewpoint.

A background knowledge of Near Eastern culture is indispensable for understanding such expressions. For example, Hebrew culture attributed responsibility to an individual for acts he did not commit but that he allowed to happen. Therefore the inspired writers of the Scriptures commonly credit God with doing actively that which in Western thought we would say He permits or does not prevent from happening, for example, the hardening of Pharaoh's heart.

Another aspect of Scripture that troubles the modern mind is the divine command to Israel to engage in war and execute entire nations. Israel originally was organized as a theocracy, a civil government through which God ruled directly (Gen. 18:25). Such a theocratic state was unique. It no longer exists and cannot be regarded as a direct model for Christian practice.

The Scriptures record that God accepted persons whose experiences and statements were not in harmony with the spiritual principles of the Bible as a whole. For example, we may cite incidents relating to the use of alcohol, polygamy, divorce, and slavery. Although condemnation of such deeply ingrained social customs is not explicit, God did not necessarily endorse or approve all that He permitted and bore with in the lives of the patriarchs and in Israel. Jesus made this clear in His statement with regard to divorce (Matt 19:4-6, 8).

The spirit of the Scriptures is one of restoration. God works patiently to elevate fallen humanity from the depths of sin to the divine ideal. Consequently, we must not accept as models the actions of sinful men as recorded in the Bible.

The Scriptures represent the unfolding of God's revelation to man. Jesus' Sermon on the Mount, for example, enlarges and expands certain Old Testament concepts. Christ Himself is the ultimate revelation of God's character to humanity (Heb. 1:1-3).

While there is an overarching unity in the Bible from Genesis to Revelation, and while all Scripture is equally inspired, God chose to reveal Himself to and through human individuals and to meet them where they were in terms of spiritual and intellectual endowments. God Himself does not change, but He progressively unfolded His revelation to men as they were able to grasp it

(John 16:12; *The SDA Bible Commentary*, vol .7, p. 945; *Selected Messages*, Book 1, p. 21). Every experience or statement of Scripture is a divinely inspired record, but not every statement or experience is necessarily normative for Christian behavior today. Both the spirit and the letter of Scripture must be understood (1Cor. 10:6-13; *The Desire of Ages*, 150; *Testimonies*, vol. 4, pp. 10-12).

17. As the final goal, make application of the text. Ask such questions as, "What is the message and purpose God intends to convey through Scripture?" "What meaning does this text have for me?" "How does it apply to my situation and circumstances today?" In doing so, recognize that although many biblical passages had local significance, nonetheless they contain timeless principles applicable to every age and culture.

5. Conclusion

In the "Introduction" to *The Great Controversy* Ellen G. White wrote:

> The Bible, with its God-given truths expressed in the language of men, presents a union of the divine and the human. Such a union existed in the nature of Christ, who was the Son of God and the Son of man. Thus it is true of the Bible, as it was of Christ, that "the Word was made flesh, and dwelt among us." John 1:14. (p. vi).

As it is impossible for those who do not accept Christ's divinity to understand the purpose of His incarnation, it is also impossible for those who see the Bible merely as a human book to understand its message, however careful and rigorous their methods.

Even Christian scholars who accept the divine-human nature of Scripture, but whose methodological approaches cause them to dwell largely on its human aspects, risk emptying the biblical message of its power by relegating it to the background while concentrating on the medium. They forget that medium and message are inseparable and that the medium without the message is as an empty shell that cannot address the vital spiritual needs of humankind.

A committed Christian will use only those methods that are able to do full justice to the dual, inseparable nature of Scripture, enhance his ability to understand and apply its message, and strengthen faith.

This statement was approved and voted by the General Conference of Seventh-day Adventists Executive Committee at the Annual Council Session in Rio de Janeiro, Brazil, October 12, 1986

Scripture Index

Index of Non-Biblical Books

APOCRYPHA OR
APOCRYPHAL BOOKS

DEAD SEA SCROLLS
AND RELATED TEXTS